Twentieth Century Limited

A History of Recent America

Houghton Mifflin Company

Boston

Dallas   *Geneva, Illinois*   *Hopewell, New Jersey*

Palo Alto   *London*

Twentieth Century Limited

A History of Recent America

Complete Edition

David W. Noble

University of Minnesota

David A. Horowitz

Portland State University

Peter N. Carroll

103299

Art Credits

Dedication

To Maggie Kuhn and the Gray Panthers, whose struggle for the rights and dignity of older Americans is helping to create a vision of the future in which the young can free themselves from traditions of self-interest and competition and come to celebrate traditions of community and cooperation.

Contents

Preface

The history of the United States in the twentieth century is usually told from the perspective of the government in Washington, D.C. Such a focus leads most history books to stress the role of the nation's political leaders — the politicians and Cabinet members who wield power in Congress, enact legislation, and shape foreign policy. Yet these political leaders constitute a limited segment of American society. For the most part, national politicians have been white males with Anglo-Protestant cultural roots, and often they have been relatively wealthy.

A historical perspective that focuses on Washington politicians, therefore, tends to ignore the existence of social groups that have not participated in — or have been denied access to — political power: racial and ethnic minorities, women, and poor people in general. To correct this imbalance, *Twentieth Century Limited* not only examines the history of the political leaders, but also explores the historical role of non-leadership groups. Many of these political outsiders shared the attitudes and values of the leadership groups. But many did not. This book attempts to explain the differences as well as similarities among various social groups.

In presenting a pluralistic history of the United States, we emphasize the relationships among the nation's leaders and the other social groups, thereby trying to avoid the "tunnel-vision" view that treats minority cultures as exclusive entities. We examine the areas of society in which dominant groups have dramatically influenced the lives of minority Americans. But we are also aware of aspects of minority culture that have been resistant to the influence of the leadership groups. Moreover, we take into account those aspects of society that reflect the influence of cultural minorities on the dominant groups.

By examining the pluralistic history of the American people, we emphasize the importance of human choice in shaping major historical patterns. Many textbooks explain such broad issues as urbanization, industrialization, and overseas expansion as the result of mysterious, impersonal forces. By contrast, we try to explain how specific decisions have created the structure and texture of American society.

This book traces the rise of a corporate bureaucratic culture that supplanted an earlier, more individualistic society based on small businesses and farms. This transformation of American society also involved a broader acceptance of "liberal-rational" values that promised progress, efficiency, and order. As a result, Americans of the twentieth century have placed great confidence in the ability of educated experts to solve social, economic, and political problems. Increasingly, Americans have looked to professionals who frequently have had government backing and have seemed to offer unlimited vistas of prosperity and expansion.

In recent years, however, Americans have become increasingly aware of the limits of corporate society. The failures of American foreign policy since World War Two, the crisis of energy resources, the threat of ecological disaster, the decline of voter participation, the increasing difficulty of social mobility, and the growing disparity of personal wealth — all reinforce a sense of limits. These problems sometimes appear to be new. But *Twentieth Century Limited,* as its title implies, demonstrates that the crises of the sixties, seventies, and eighties have historical roots that both are obvious and offer the possibility of resolution.

Besides the textual material, this book includes in each chapter a biographical sketch of a significant though often ignored American whose life illuminates a specific historical issue and a list of additional reading for students who wish to embark on further research. We have also written seven special sections, or spotlights, that feature a particularly significant or controversial issue. These essays are designed to spark student debate and curiosity.

David W. Noble
David A. Horowitz
Peter N. Carroll

Acknowledgments

In preparing this book, we have benefited from a variety of institutional aids, colleagues, friends, and family.

David Noble acknowledges the invaluable assistance of Lois Noble in editing and typing the manuscript.

David Horowitz appreciates the financial and clerical assistance provided by the department of history, the college of social science, and the office of graduate studies and research at Portland State University. Gerry Foote and Joni Ueland provided valuable assistance in assembling research materials. Dorothy Childester did a superb performance under the pressure of typing deadlines. The author is also grateful to Michael Horowitz for galley proofreading and generous moral support, and to Charlene Lowry Horowitz, whose patience and understanding enabled him to survive the completion of this task.

Peter Carroll extends thanks to Lorraine Whittemore of the San Francisco State faculty manuscript service. Leo Ribuffo added wit, criticism, and sturdy advice, though not necessarily in that order. Jeannette Ferrary shared fully in this enterprise, smoothing the rough points, intensifying the satisfactions.

All three authors wish to thank the following reviewers, who contributed to the development of the manuscript: Allen F. Davis, Temple University; J. Carroll Moody, Northern Illinois University; and Robert C. Twombly, City University of New York.

Chapter 1

THE CRISIS OF THE 1890s

Frederick Jackson Turner was a young historian in 1893 when he traveled from the University of Wisconsin to Chicago to present a scholarly paper called "The Significance of the Frontier in American History." The historians who gathered to hear Turner's address had chosen Chicago as the site of their annual meeting because that city was simultaneously hosting the Columbian Exposition, a world's fair held to celebrate four centuries of European settlement in the New World. The central theme of the fair was the great material progress made by the American people since Columbus's ships first touched land in the Western Hemisphere.

Turner's message contrasted sharply with the optimism of his surroundings. "American democracy," he declared, "was born of no theor-

ist's dream, it came stark and strong and full of life out of the American forest and it gained new strength each time it touched a new frontier." But, Turner announced, "The free lands are gone." Calling attention to the statistics of the 1890 census, which showed there was no longer a western frontier, Turner suggested that the United States was approaching a period of crisis. "The material forces that gave vitality to Western democracy are passing away," he stated. After experiencing centuries of democracy, a period in which Europeans could become Americans by exchanging the rigid class system of the Old World for equality and freedom in the New, the United States was undergoing a revolutionary decline documented by "the familiar facts of the massing of population in the cities and the contemporaneous increase of urban power, of the massing of capital and production in fewer and vastly greater industrial units."

THE DECLINE OF
RURAL AMERICA

In speaking of the "massing of population in the cities," Turner appealed to statistics that showed the 1880s as the ten years of most rapid urban expansion in American history up to that time (and since). Chicago had been chosen as the site of the world's fair because it was the most rapidly growing major city in the United States. Leaping from a population of 200,000 in 1870 to 500,000 in 1880, it had doubled to one million inhabitants in 1890. Major eastern cities such as Boston, New York, and Philadelphia continued to grow rapidly as they had since the early nineteenth century. But now the greatest growth was in midwestern cities — Chicago, Milwaukee, Kansas City, Denver, Minneapolis, and St. Paul — which more than doubled their size in the 1880s. If these trends of urbanization continued, Turner suggested, the United States would cease to be a country of farms and small towns. Many Americans, like Turner, were frightened by such a future. In 1789, when more than 90 percent of the people made their living in agriculture, the founding fathers had insisted that only a society of small farmers, owning their own land, could make wise political decisions.

Many nineteenth-century Americans shared the belief that representative government depended on an independent, property-owning population. The closing of the frontier implied that the era of democracy was approaching an end. Turner's talk attracted attention at the time because it expressed the thoughts of so many Americans who feared the loss of the simpler and more equal society of 1789.

This sense of crisis was particularly acute in the South, which, unlike the Northeast, had remained a region of farmers and had not undergone significant urbanization or industrialization. The Civil War had brought the destruction of the large cotton plantations that had sustained the antebellum South. These had been replaced by small farms run by free blacks and whites. Black farmers usually became sharecroppers, with each family farming a part of the former plantation. They gave part of their crop to the white landowner for rent and another part of the crop to white storekeepers who supplied them with seed, fertilizer, tools, clothes, and food on credit. The many white farmers who became producers of cotton after the breakup of the plantations also turned to storekeepers for credit. This credit system forced both black and white farmers to concentrate their energies on a cash crop rather than on diversified farming. They had little time even to grow their own food. The interest they paid on the credit was a heavy burden because the storekeepers had borrowed money from local bankers, who had borrowed from large state bankers, who in turn had borrowed from bankers in New York. At the end of this chain, farmers often paid from 20 to 40 percent interest on their debts.

To try to meet these payments, individual farmers attempted to produce a larger cash crop. Much of America's cotton, however, was sold overseas, and the expansion of American production was matched by the emergence of new growing areas such as Egypt. As world production increased faster than demand, the price of cotton fell steadily from 15¢ a pound in 1870 to 6¢ a pound in 1890. But interest rates and the cost of farm machinery and fertilizer did not fall, and the burden of debt became more intense for most farmers. The South, which was 90 percent rural, felt these economic pressures more than other regions. Southern farmers became desperate as the price of cotton fell below the cost of production by 1893. Black farmers faced the loss of any hope that they could save enough money to escape tenancy by purchasing their farms, and more white farmers lost their lands and were forced into tenancy.

While the southern farm economy experienced a crisis after the Civil War, a small minority of upper-middle-class businessmen and lawyers proposed the creation of a "New South," which might imitate northern patterns of industrialization and urbanization. Proponents of the New South usually controlled the dominant Democratic parties of the South. In state politics they supported programs that promised low taxes for northern industry that would come South. Such tactics left the tax burden on the farmers. In the 1870s and 1880s, white and black farmers in Virginia had formed a successful political coalition to challenge the elite that dominated that state's politics. This statewide political rebellion represented the first of many political protest movements by farmers throughout the agricultural states.

Though these political protests began at the state level, they had a profound influence on the national party system by the end of the decade. From the farmers' perspective, the government in Washington remained in the hands of politicians who supported the interests of northern industry and ignored the position of southern farmers. Northern factory owners, for example, had persuaded Congress to pass protective tariffs that raised the cost of imported iron and steel above that of iron and steel manufactured in the United States. Such policies enabled American industry to compete with European products on the domestic market. But farmers were outraged that they had to sell their crops on an unprotected world market while they were forced to buy machinery and supplies on a protected national market.

The farmers also resented government policy that limited the amount of money in circulation to the quantity of gold and silver in the national treasury. This conservative economic policy reflected the political strength of the large bankers of the Northeast. But the currency supply was not growing as fast as the economy. The resulting shortage of money kept interest rates high, as industrialists and farmers, trying to expand, bid against each other for money to borrow. Yet because of this policy of currency deflation, prices remained stable except where artificially raised by tariffs.

POPULISM

Some farmers had turned to a Greenback party from 1876 to 1884 in the hope of increasing inflation. But although there were farmers who turned to protest politics in the 1880s to fight the problem of money, tariffs, and taxes, the first massive effort of southern cotton farmers to escape their economic hardships was nonpolitical. A Farmers Alliance, begun in Texas by Charles W. Macune, spread rapidly throughout the cotton states. Organized at a grassroots level into forty thousand suballiances, this movement developed thousands of local newspapers and mobilized thousands of speakers who tried to educate the farmers on the need to develop farmer-owned cooperatives. Such businesses would enable farmers to purchase supplies and to market crops without becoming indebted at high interest rates to storekeepers. A parallel Colored Alliance for black farmers, which claimed a million members, was also organized.

By 1890, however, white and black leaders of the alliance realized that this people's effort to create a cooperative and decentralized economy could not succeed without using the power of the national government. The centralized control of the money supply, which rested in the hands of northeastern and foreign bankers, made it difficult for alliance cooperatives to obtain enough capital to construct an effective

alternative purchasing and marketing structure to that of the storekeepers. Alliance leaders, therefore, decided to press the national government to establish a subtreasury plan under which the government would build warehouses throughout the farm areas of the country. Farmers could then choose to store their crops safely rather than put them on the market when prices were low. Later, when the market improved, they could sell at a more favorable price. Meanwhile, the government would accept these crops as collateral for loans to the farmers. This credit not only would free farmers from high interest rates but also would

These Kansas farmers, like many others throughout the West and South, participated in a major effort at adult education in order to understand the national crisis of the late nineteenth century and to find solutions to it. The Populist party developed out of these grass roots meetings. (Kansas State Historical Society, Topeka)

serve to increase the money supply and thus stimulate the inflation of agricultural prices that the farmers wanted.

Since neither of the two major parties, the Republicans and Democrats, accepted the subtreasury plan or even seemed to be aware of a general crisis among farmers, alliance leaders proceeded to build the Populist party. Southern leaders were joined in this effort by a Northern Farmers Alliance, which was especially strong in the wheat-growing areas of the Great Plains —Kansas, Nebraska, western Minnesota, and the Dakotas. This vast area had been settled by whites only since the Civil War. Like the South, but unlike the Midwest that stretched from Ohio to Minnesota, this region had seen little urbanization or diversified farming. Farmers of the Great Plains borrowed money to raise a wheat crop, which, like cotton, depended on an overseas market. These wheat farmers, like cotton growers, suffered from declining prices ($1.50 a bushel in 1870 to .60 a bushel in 1890), high interest rates, and high costs for machinery and supplies, whose prices were protected by the tariff. While 1,750,000 new farms were developed in the West between 1890 and 1910, this expansion could not keep up with the rapid growth and population. In rich agricultural states such as Illinois and Iowa, more than 20 percent of the farmers were forced into tenancy by the 1890s.

When the new Populist party drafted its platform at Omaha in 1892, it advocated not only the subtreasury plan but also government ownership of railroads and the telegraph, a federal income tax, and the direct election of senators.

Farmers' interest in railroads reflected the great expansion of transportation networks after the Civil War. In the South, the laying of 113,000 miles of track opened new land for cotton cultivation because farmers could now get their crops to market. The expansion of wheat growing into the Great Plains also depended on the construction of railroads extending from eastern and southern seaports, from which much of the wheat was shipped abroad. The farmers discovered, however, that the railroads operated to a large extent outside a competitive situation. Usually only one railroad ran through a town to which farmers brought their crops for shipment. Knowing that the farmers had no choice but to ship on their line, railroad companies felt free to charge very high rates or to keep unpredictable schedules.

To protest these conditions, midwestern farmers had created a farmers' organization, the Patrons of Husbandry (better known as the Grange) in the 1870s. The grangers successfully pressured state legislatures to create commissions to regulate the prices and schedules of the railroads and grain elevators. The United States Supreme Court upheld these granger laws in the case *Munn v. Illinois* in 1877. But in 1886 the Court ruled in the *Wabash* case that states could not regulate railroads that did business across state lines; according to the Court, only the national Congress could regulate interstate commerce. Partly in response to reform pressure from the East and South as well as the Midwest, and partly in response to the desire of the railroads themselves to control competition, Congress created the Interstate Commerce Commission (ICC) in 1887 to establish reasonable rates in interstate traffic and to stop unfair practices such as the payment of rebates to large shippers.

By 1892, however, the Populists, headed by their presidential candidate, James B. Weaver, a former Greenback party leader, wanted government ownership of the railroads and the telegraph because they doubted the ability of

Mary Elizabeth Lease

1853-1933

The most important woman political leader in 1892 was Mary Elizabeth Lease. She gave a speech seconding the nomination of James B. Weaver as the Populist Party presidential candidate at the party's Omaha convention that year. She was invited to join his campaign because of her reputation as one of the most effective political speakers in the country.

In 1892 and for decades to come, it would be impossible for a woman to play such a major role in the established Republican and Democratic parties. Only the developing societies of the Great Plains and Rocky Mountain states provided opportunities for women to be important political leaders.

Lease was born in Pennsylvania to immigrant parents who fled the 1840s famine in Ireland. Still loyal to Catholicism, she went west to Kansas to teach in a parochial school. There, she married a Protestant farmer, quickly had four children, and eventually turned away from her unhappy marriage to gain training as a lawyer.

At the end of the 1880s, she began to speak for the Farmer's Alliance to support its effort to create a major reform movement among farmers. Tall, thin, dressed in black, she warned her listeners that they were living in sin as long as they allowed evil men to gain control of the nation. Connecting evangelical Protestantism with the principles of Jacksonian democracy, she insisted that the Americans of 1830 had been good citizens and good Christians because they were independent and equal. Then no one was exploited and no one was an exploiter. But now big corporations and big banks were ushering in class divisions and threatening to destroy America's Protestant democracy.

After 1892, she came to doubt the ability of the Populists to save any kind of good society.

In her bitterness, she dropped her analysis of the ways in which corporations and large banks, under the control of wealthy Anglo-Protestants, were distorting the system, and shifted the blame for all the problems of the 1890s onto an international conspiracy of Jews. Some ex-Populists, including a number of women leaders in Kansas and other western states, turned to the left and became socialists. But others turned to the right and searched for scapegoats. This was especially true in the South, where Tom Watson, after 1896, became bitterly antiblack.

In her book, The Problem of Civilization Solved *(1895), Lease advocated the conquest of the world by the white race as the way of solving all the economic problems caused by the end of the frontier in Europe as well as America. She enthusiastically supported American imperialism in 1898. She declared that it is "as natural for us to take the Philippines as it was for our forefathers to take the thirteen colonies." Ironically, cut off from the reform movements that gave her an opportunity to express her talents and energy, she spent the rest of her life in obscurity.*

state and national regulatory commissions to serve the interests of the general public. Populists realized that judges on state courts and on the Supreme Court usually ruled in favor of large companies and against the regulatory commissions. From 1887 to 1897, the ICC lost 90 percent of the cases it brought to court; moreover, in 1896 the Supreme Court ruled in the Maximum Freight case that even though the ICC could deny unjust rates, it could not establish just ones.

The Populists also questioned the willingness of the judiciary to deal fairly with the problem of corporate monopolies. The concentration of investment capital by huge corporations alarmed many Americans. In response to these fears, Congress passed the Sherman Antitrust Act in 1890 to stop "conspiracy in restraint of trade" and to encourage business competition. The presidents of the 1890s — Harrison, Cleveland, and McKinley — however, showed little interest in using this law to slow the development of large corporations. And when a suit was brought against the sugar trust in 1895, the Supreme Court declared in the case *United States* v. *E. C. Knight Company* that the control of 98 percent of all United States sugar production by this single company was not a conspiratorial restraint of trade, since only one company was involved. The court also argued that manufacturing was not the same as trade and that the Sherman Act did not apply to manufacturing.

Besides feeling that the judiciary frustrated the will of the people, Populists believed that the election of United States senators by state legislatures, as established in the Constitution, also led to undemocratic results. As they perceived the rich growing richer, they saw wealthy industrialists buying the votes of legislators and winning election to the Senate which, for the Populists, had become a million-aires' club. Populists therefore demanded a constitutional amendment providing for the direct election of senators. Furthermore, they believed that the introduction of an income tax would stop the amassing of huge fortunes that made political manipulation possible. When the Populist platform voiced its concern that the nation was threatened by "two great classes — tramps and millionaires," a situation suggesting that the United States was "rapidly degenerating into European conditions," the party looked to the implementation of its four platform points to halt that deterioration. The Populists promised "to restore the government of the Republic to the hands of 'the plain people' with which it originated." The party also insisted that its purposes were "identical with the purposes of the National Constitution."

BLACKS AND THE
CASTE SYSTEM

The political conflict of the 1890s between farmers and industrialists was complicated by the presence of blacks as voting citizens. Despite Populist rhetoric, the Constitution of the 1890s already differed greatly from the original document drafted by the founding fathers. The passage of the Thirteenth, Fourteenth, and Fifteenth Amendments during the Civil War and Reconstruction radically altered the patterns of 1789 by admitting blacks into citizenship. The Thirteenth Amendment abolished slavery. The Fourteenth Amendment created national citizenship for black men, a provision that allowed blacks access to the federal courts and assured them rights of geographic mobility.

The Fifteenth Amendment eliminated race as a criterion for preventing men from voting. Thus by 1870 blacks were brought into politics in the North as well as the South.

These constitutional changes, however, did not alter the caste attitudes of most northern and southern whites. The founding fathers believed that all white men who owned property were sufficiently rational and independent to vote in a responsible way. These standards excluded women and blacks from the right to vote because both groups remained dependent on the will of white men; neither women nor blacks could be trusted to exercise an independent choice.

Such caste attitudes extended beyond legal restrictions on blacks and defined them as an unclean and inferior race that must be socially segregated. Under the code of this white racism, no white woman could be sexually available to any black man, but all black women were sexually available to any white man. Moreover, no black man could be aggressive or violent toward any white man. Denying the potential of rational responsibility to adult black men, white racism defined adult black males as boys totally dependent on white men. Adult black men, like white boys, were supposed to show nothing but respect toward their white superiors.

To preserve the traditional caste system after the passage of the Civil War–Reconstruction amendments, whites created an informal pattern of first- and second-class citizenship. Under this double standard, black men would not disrupt the political system because they would accept the necessity of white leadership. Such patterns perpetuated procedures established during the Civil War whereby blacks had served in the citizen army, but always under the command of white officers. It was not until the Korean War in 1950 that blacks were permitted to give orders to whites in the armed services.

Black participation in southern politics was also limited by the overwhelming power of a single political party, the Democrats, in which whites monopolized leadership positions. Yet 90 percent of the black population of the United States lived in the South at the end of the nineteenth century. Although only 10 percent of the national population, they constituted about half the population of South Carolina, Louisiana, and Mississippi and more than 40 percent of the population of Alabama and Georgia. Blacks continued to be concentrated in the best agricultural counties, where they had been brought as slaves; they comprised 80 to 90 percent of the population in these "black belt" counties. Often, as in Mississippi, the dominant white Democrats allowed blacks to hold minor county political positions and to elect a small number of black men to the state legislature.

The emergence of populism, however, threatened to upset the political and racial status quo. A new group of white political leaders now asked blacks to reject the leadership of white Democrats and instead follow the Populists. Although most white Populists continued to support the social segregation of the caste system, they were prepared to challenge aspects of white racism by stressing the economic solidarity of poor white and black farmers.

Tom Watson, a leading Populist of Georgia, argued that America's democratic society of productive farmers would be destroyed by parasitical aristocrats if white and black farmers did not cooperate. In his words, "The People's Party says to these two men, 'You are kept apart that you may be separately fleeced of your earn-

ings. You are made to hate each other because upon that hatred is rested the keystone of the arch of financial despotism which enslaves you both. You are deceived and blinded that you may not see how the race antagonism perpetuates a monetary system which beggars both.'" Speaking strongly against the lynch law, Watson included a black on the executive committee of the Georgia Populist party. This young black minister, H. S. Doyle, gave sixty-three speeches in the Populist campaign of 1892 and was protected by white farmers from theats of violence that came from some New South Democratic leaders.

But New South Democrats in Virginia and Mississippi had already found a formula to defeat this majority of white and black farmers and to open the South to urbanization and industrialization. Recognizing the potential power of white and black farmers, New South Democratic leaders moved to break the farmer coalition on racial lines. The first step in implementing this racial split was the use of a mythic history of Reconstruction. Though blacks had generally accepted the political leadership of whites and had engaged in little violence against whites, New South Democrats appealed to an underlying white racism against blacks by asserting that Reconstruction had been a time of violence in which blacks raped, murdered, and pillaged with impunity. To restore order and preserve the honor of white women, the Democratic leaders urged all white men to close ranks in the Democratic party.

In emphasizing the importance of preserving the purity of the Anglo-Saxon race, Democratic leaders warned that the Populist party was dangerously dividing whites along economic lines and giving blacks the balance of power whereby they could determine which group of whites would hold office. From this position of power, the Democrats argued, blacks would renew the orgy of rape, murder, and arson of Reconstruction. To avoid this recurrence, all whites must reject class politics and live by the spiritual principles of racial purity within the Democratic party. Furthermore, to provide future security all blacks must be excluded from politics. This philosophy was implemented in Virginia in the 1890s.

In Mississippi, the white elites used similar tactics to stop the development of a white-black Populist coalition before it could become established. A constitutional convention called in 1890 established new restrictions on voting. The Fifteenth Amendment had barred only restrictions that applied to race. The passage of literacy qualifications and poll tax requirements evaded the Fifteenth Amendment; but these restrictions were especially prejudicial toward blacks, since most descendants of slaves lacked sufficient property and education. Indeed, Mississippi politicians insisted that the only purpose of the convention was to disenfranchise blacks; the purpose of the disenfranchisement, they claimed, was to avoid a repetition of the black atrocities of Reconstruction. But underlying these motives was a desire to destroy the power of the black-white farmer coalitions. It was no accident, therefore, that many lower-income whites also were disenfranchised by the new voting standards. The immediate impact of the constitutional changes in Mississippi was to reduce black voting from 40,000 to 1,500 and white voting from 85,000 to 40,000. By 1910 every southern state established similar constitutional restrictions on voting.

By exaggerating the race issue, Democratic politicians succeeded in obscuring the important economic divisions of the region. No one was more adept at this strategy than Pitchfork

Ben Tillman of South Carolina. Tillman captured control of his state's Democratic party in 1890 by attacking the New South leaders as not being sufficiently antiblack. These leaders, according to Tillman, betrayed racial democracy because they did not demand segregation of streetcars, railroads, and other public facilities. Tillman developed the theory that if there was one people, there should be only one party and one leader to represent that racially unified people. During the 1890s he preached the necessity of violence to keep the will of the people vigorous and healthy. For example, he advocated lynching blacks suspected of rape. After the collapse of populism in 1896, many southern states supported similar lower-middle-class demagogues who preached the triumph of racial democracy and the replacement of political elites with spokesmen of the common man. Although leaders such as Tillman or James K. Vardaman of Mississippi asked for economic reforms that would help poor whites at both the state and national level, they insisted that the first priority of politics was to preserve white supremacy. In this way, these leaders encouraged poor whites to forget their inability to defeat northern corporations or to eliminate the great gap between rich and poor in their own states.

In North Carolina, where a coalition of white and black farmers held power until 1898, Thomas Dixon wrote a series of novels to justify the disenfranchisement of blacks and the substitution of racial politics for class conflict. These novels, especially *The Leopard's Spots* (1902) and *The Clansman* (1905), were immensely popular in the North, where they helped to win white approval for the antiblack crusade, the disenfranchisement of blacks, and the establishment of Jim Crow segregation. The purpose of Dixon's novels was to persuade southern and northern whites that adult black men were not boys or Sambos. A sexless and nonviolent Sambo, lazy, irresponsible, childish in his appetites for food, music, and sex, could not be viewed as a dangerous figure. Dixon argued that beneath the Sambo mask was a cunning and powerful animal capable of lusting after white women and of creating an orgy of rape, murder, and arson if white men were divided. The proliferation of such racial stereotypes effectively undermined an alliance of poor whites and blacks and enabled an upper-middle-class elite dedicated to the New South to maintain power.

LABOR AND INDUSTRY

Though many northerners shared the racial attitudes of southern leaders, the political divisions caused by the Civil War continued to influence party alignments. Most northern farmers felt a deep emotional loyalty to the Republican party because it had saved the union. This commitment was intensified by the identification of the Republican party with Protestant cultural values. In contrast, most northern farmers viewed the Democratic party as the party of secession. Moreover, since pre–Civil War Catholic immigrants had tended to join the Democratic party, northern Protestants saw the Democrats as protectors of an alien, even un-American, culture.

These sectional and cultural divisions also prevented industrial workers from creating a united front. Though the post–Civil War period saw the emergence of huge factories owned by a few men, in which workers neither owned the means of production nor shared in industrial decision making, factory workers

failed to create a unifying class consciousness. Instead, the workers emphasized their cultural differences from each other.

The inability to overcome these differences partly reflected fundamental economic changes in the late nineteenth century. Until the Civil War, most industrial workers were employed in small shops. Like farmers, they believed that the uniqueness of America was its classless society in which workers and shop owners shared a basic economic and social equality. Most workers also hoped to save enough money to open their own shops, since only a small amount of capital was needed to obtain a farm or start a factory. After the Civil War, however, the growth of large corporations altered the economic and social vision of American workers. As corporations accumulated vast amounts of capital, the sense of social and economic equality between owner and worker disappeared. Moreover, the average worker could no longer expect to accumulate sufficient capital to open a factory that would be competitive with the large and more efficient plants.

By 1870, therefore, many workers feared the "massing of capital" that Frederick Jackson Turner later described. Hundreds of thousands joined the National Labor Union, whose leaders argued that the new large-scale factories must be owned by the workers, or else a propertyless and powerless wage-earning class, similar to the European proletariat, would develop in America. But the National Labor Union collapsed during the depression of 1873, when mass unemployment enabled employers to hire new workers to replace union members. In the 1880s another mass labor movement, the Knights of Labor, attempted to unify all productive Americans, skilled or unskilled, white or black. Although the Knights advocated such immediate reforms as the eight-hour day, the

Federal troops were used to break the strike of railroad workers in 1894. Troops also had been used against strikes in the 1870s and 1880s. (Library of Congress 23805/262/10546W)

union's leader, Terrence V. Powderly, emphasized the larger goal of creating a cooperative movement as an alternative to "wage slavery." These aspirations, together with a series of successful strikes, enabled the Knights to increase membership from 40,000 in 1880 to 800,000 in 1886. For many of these workers, the labor movement offered an alternative to a corporation-dominated society.

This aggressive labor activity, as well as the radicalism of a growing number of anarchists, encountered the stiff resistance of economic, political, and cultural leaders. During the 1870s, large railroads and industrial corporations relied on local police and state and federal troops to break strikes. Now at the end of the 1880s, the urban middle class called for the renewed use of police power to suppress the dangers of radicalism. In 1886 Chicago police disbanded radical mass meetings, but not before a bomb exploded in Haymarket Square, killing several police officers. In the aftermath, most middle-class newspapers and magazines joined the leading ministers and professors in blaming anarchists for the violence. These cultural leaders also supported a judicial decision that found a group of Chicago anarchists guilty, despite flimsy and contradictory evidence. John Peter Altgeld, who sympathized with labor, was elected governor of Illinois in 1892 and pardoned the men who had not yet been executed.

The isolation of the labor movement was further demonstrated by middle-class support of "union busting" in the 1890s. As economic conditions deteriorated, culminating in the depression of 1893, employers became more aggressive in repressing labor. In 1892 Henry Clay Frick, Andrew Carnegie's partner, ordered a 20 percent pay cut for workers at the Homestead, Pennsylvania, steel plant. When workers called a protest strike, Frick fired them and hired a small army of Pinkerton detectives to guard the new strike-breaking workers. The old workers engaged in a battle with these private police, in which nine strikers and seven Pinkertons were killed. The state governor then

In the Homestead strike of 1892, management deployed a small army of Pinkerton detectives against the strikers. The workers fought back but were finally defeated, in part because of their ethnic diversity. (THE GRANGER COLLECTION, New York)

ordered troops to disarm the strikers. Frick discharged all union workers, cut wages 50 percent, ended employee grievance committees, and required a twelve-hour work day. Steel workers would not be able to unionize again until the end of the 1930s.

As the depression persisted, workers who made Pullman sleeping cars also suffered wage cuts even though they were expected to pay existing rents for their company-owned houses. In 1894 the Pullman workers, joined by the American Railway Union, went on strike. The railroad companies, however, won an injunction against the union from the courts on the grounds that strike activities violated the Sherman Antitrust Act by restraining trade. United States Attorney General Richard Olney ordered federal troops to Chicago to suppress the strike. Twenty strikers were killed in the resulting conflict, and union leader Eugene V. Debs was sent to jail.

The bloody Homestead and Pullman strikes weakened organized labor throughout the country. By 1896 union membership had declined to less than 200,000 from the high of 800,000 in the 1880s. Most of these surviving union men had made their peace with industrial society. As members of the American Federation of Labor (AFL), they supported leaders such as Samuel Gompers, who had abandoned the dream of the Knights of Labor to create a classless producers' democracy. The AFL also decided that it was impossible to organize unskilled workers. Instead, the AFL hoped that the unions of skilled craft workers might survive both the depression and the hostility of corporate leaders and the urban middle class if they accepted the new industrial order in which union members formed a permanent wage-earning class.

Populist leaders had hoped to bring labor into a coalition with farmers on the basis of a shared identity as producers. They believed that farmers and industrial workers faced a common threat from a new elite that gained its wealth by manipulating the economy. The great issue that divided many farmers and workers, however, was inflation. Though urban workers had gained real wage increases since the Civil War, most workers still could not easily support their families. Only by taking in boarders or having their wives and children work could they pay for basic necessities. They were desperately opposed, therefore, to any rise in food prices. But most agricultural workers supported inflationary policies, particularly increased food prices. Moreover, unlike industrial workers, most farmers owned their own farms and means of production. Even the Populists who wanted consumer and producer cooperatives envisioned these institutions as operating on top of what essentially was a system of small, independent businesses. These economic differences between farmers and industrial workers were intensified by the political events of the 1890s.

A NEW PARTY SYSTEM

Grover Cleveland, the Democratic presidential candidate of 1892, won the most decisive victory for his party since the Civil War. The overwhelming rejection of the incumbent Republican, Benjamin Harrison, may have reflected a growing discontent with the power of the large corporations and the link that many voters saw between the corporations and the Republican party. In office, however, Cleveland soon infuriated many loyal Democrats, especially southern farmers.

Cleveland's problems resulted from a major

economic collapse that began in 1893. As businesses and banks failed, people responded in panic and brought their bank notes (paper money) to be redeemed in precious metal (gold or silver). Though it was legal for the treasury to demand the acceptance of silver, Cleveland insisted that the government should maintain a gold standard and ordered that only gold be used in exchange for paper money. By preventing the circulation of silver, Cleveland's policy reduced the total monetary supply and caused further deflation. Increasing the money supply would have increased available capital and might have stimulated economic growth. But Cleveland's choice instead intensified business cutbacks. Meanwhile, the government also had to buy gold to meet public demand for hard metal. Large New York bankers like J. P. Morgan made huge profits in the transactions as they negotiated to import gold from Europe. Many Americans saw a conspiracy between the Cleveland administration and the multimillionaire bankers that allowed them to obtain huge profits at the expense of the average taxpayer.

Populists felt a further sense of betrayal by the passage of the Wilson-Gorman tariff. Cleveland had campaigned in 1892 against the high McKinley tariff passed by the Republicans in 1890. But the new tariff presented by the Democrats retained the same high levels of protection. Many Democrats shared with the Populists this sense of betrayal and were willing to blame the Cleveland administration for the depression of 1893. Most of these angry Democrats, however, continued to distrust the Populists. When they deserted Cleveland in 1894, therefore, they voted for Republican candidates. The result was the most dramatic reversal of party membership in the history of the House of Representatives, as the Republicans suddenly won an overwhelming majority of 132.

The Populists, unlike the Republicans, did not benefit much from this desertion of Democrats. But Populist strength did increase in the South, where there was no effective Republican party. In the West, four states won by the Populists in 1892 were taken by Republicans in 1894. Western Populists, therefore, were more willing than those in the South to consider fusion with Democrats between 1894 and 1896. These westerners had lost hope that the Populist party could replace the Democratic party as one of the two major national parties.

The electoral disaster of 1894 persuaded many Democratic leaders to take control of the party from Cleveland in 1896. Democrats like Ben Tillman and William Jennings Bryan of Nebraska expected to win over many Populist farmers if they shifted the Democratic party away from support of the gold standard. Democratic advocacy of the purchase of unlimited amounts of silver at one-sixteenth of the current price of gold by the Treasury would increase the amount of money in circulation and meet the Populists' demand for inflation. In 1896 these "silver Democrats" gained control of the Democratic convention and nominated Bryan for the presidency. In his acceptance speech, the Democratic Bryan adopted the vocabulary of the Populists. The candidate spoke of two Americans — oppressed producers and an oppressive, parasitical plutocracy — and he promised to restore the America of Jefferson and Jackson. "We have petitioned," Bryan preached, "and our petitions have been scorned; we have begged, and they have mocked when our calamity came. We beg no longer; we entreat no more; we petition no more. We defy them!" And, he concluded, "Having behind us the producing masses of the nation, we will answer their demand for a gold standard by saying to them: "You shall not press down upon the brow of labor this crown of thorns, you shall not crucify mankind upon a cross of gold."

Bryan's definition of "producing masses," however, embraced farmers and small businessmen who owned their own means of production. He did not recognize the growing class of industrial wage earners or tenant farmers. He did not accept the Populist emphasis on the subtreasury plan and on cooperatives. Increased coinage of silver, inflation, lower interest rates, and a lower tariff were enough, for Bryan, to take America out of the hands of the large corporations and restore it to independent farmers and small businessmen.

Urban workers who had deserted the Democratic party of President Cleveland were not attracted to Bryan's platform. Increasingly the cities were becoming centers of Catholic immigration. Bryan's appeal to restore the independent farmer and his private property offered little to the propertyless Catholic workers. Worse still, in the eyes of urban Catholics, was Bryan's identification of the Democratic party with the Protestant heritage of the farmers in the South and West. Until 1896 Catholic immigrants had looked to the Democratic party to protect their culture from the efforts of the Republican party to impose Protestant values on it. In the states of the Northeast, where most of the Catholic immigrants settled, it was the Republicans who demanded conformity to the dominant Anglo-Protestant society. Such conformity meant that immigrants would have to give up their languages and learn English in the public schools. These institutions also would teach immigrant children the Protestant work ethic and a Protestant understanding of the Bible. As Catholics moved from the East into the Midwest, it was Republicans in those states who tried to stop the creation of a parochial school system where immigrant children

might be protected from the pressures of the public schools for Anglo conformity. Democrats, however, had worked in the legislatures of the eastern and midwestern states to block these Republican efforts.

In 1896 these Catholics listened in dismay as Bryan declared that the Democratic party represented the evangelical Protestant farmers and small businessmen of the South and West and that the party would restore the virtues of the evangelical culture of the early nineteenth century. The Republican candidate, William McKinley, exploited this confusion by suggesting that the Republican party would be tolerant of Catholic culture. McKinley also persuaded many urban workers that precisely because Republicans were associated with big business, they could end the depression. With extremely high unemployment, with a Democratic party concerned about farmers rather than workers, with no effective Labor or Socialist party, many workers felt they had no choice but to vote Republican and hope for the restoration of prosperity and employment. Almost every major city in the East and Midwest and on the Pacific Coast offered Republican majorities, unlike 1892 when Cleveland had carried most cities.

Although the Republicans in 1896 solidified the position they had gained in 1894, their victory in 1896 seemed to be one of expediency more than political principle. The America of the founding fathers — a republic of many small farmers, craftsmen, and businessmen who were independent owners of their means of production — no longer seemed possible. But the new urban middle class that controlled the Republican party rejected the alternative ideal of cooperative industrial and agricultural democracy put forward by the Knights of Labor and the Populist party. And this Protestant middle class did not have a vision of a pluralistic society in which the cultures of Catholics, Jews, American Indians, and Afro-Americans would be accepted as equal in worth to Anglo-American culture. President McKinley took office in March 1897, therefore, without a clear vision of a new America to replace the lost world of 1789. And he represented a Republican party that was successful as much from the confusions and weaknesses of its opponents as from its own strengths. Yet Republicans had demonstrated considerable skill in persuading upper-income groups to channel their wealth into the Republican organization.

The Republican campaign of 1896 had been managed by the wealthy Ohio industrialist Mark Hanna. To broaden Republican appeal, Hanna took advantage of the new mass-circulation newspapers and magazines and other techniques of communication for the campaign. He systematically organized the big-business community to provide funds for the party treasury. And he produced the best publicized, best financed, and best organized presidential campaign in American history. The Republicans spent $2 million, four times as much as the Democrats. Hundreds of speakers were sent across the country. Two hundred and twenty million pamphlets, many in the languages of the new immigrants, were distributed, and marches of a hundred thousand people were organized in New York and Chicago. Parades on a more modest scale were held in smaller cities and towns. Though the major premise of this campaign was the restoration of prosperity, Republican campaign literature also focused on the un-American qualities of Bryan and the

MAP 1.1   THE ELECTION OF 1896

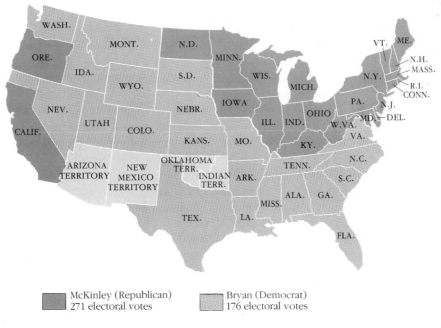

McKinley (Republican)
271 electoral votes

Bryan (Democrat)
176 electoral votes

philosophy of populism. Republicans succeeded in linking Bryan to populism because many Populists had indeed supported fusion of the two parties. By linking their own platform to the Democrats, Populists hoped for an easy victory of their principles in 1896.

However, some southern Populists, led by Tom Watson, bitterly opposed fusion. For Watson, joining with Democrats meant the end of the experiment of white and black farmers working together. And the end of populism in the South, he believed, meant the triumph of one-party politics, in which the New South Democrats would remain in control. Watson also wanted to continue to emphasize the broad range of Populist reforms. He disliked, therefore, Bryan's emphasis on the silver issue.

The Watson forces failed to control the Populist convention of 1896. The party instead voted to back Bryan as its presidential candidate. As a compromise, the Populists nominated Watson as the vice presidential candidate rather than the regular candidate of the Democratic party. Amid this confusion, the Populists ceased to be an effective political party. Watson's fears for the South were fulfilled as more southern states disenfranchised all blacks as well as large numbers of poor whites. And, as Watson warned, the South remained under control of the minority of upper-middle-class men dedicated to the creation of a new urban-industrial South.

Major Republican newspapers in 1896 claimed that Populists and now the Democrats had committed themselves to radical and un-American ideas from Europe. *The Philadelphia Press* insisted that the Democratic platform "rests upon the four cornerstones of organized repudiation, deliberate confiscation, chartered communism, and enthroned anarchy," and the *New York Tribune* added that the Democratic platform was "the hysterical declaration of a reckless and lawless crusade of sectional animosity and class antagonism. No wild-eyed and rattle-brained horde of the red flag ever proclaimed a fiercer defiance of law, precedent, order, and government." Republicans accused Bryan's supporters of being un-American radicals because the Democrats advocated government regulation of the money supply, which violated the "natural laws" of the capitalist marketplace. According to these laws, government should not interfere in the economy but should allow the laws of supply and demand and free competition to operate. Ironically, however, the Populists and Democrats accused the Republicans of similar violations. Bryan's supporters charged that the development of large corporations violated the same natural laws of the marketplace. Pointing out that there was no free competition when one or several large corporations dominated an area of production such as oil or steel, they condemned the artificial manipulation of prices and wages.

PROTESTANTISM AND THE NEW EMPIRE

President McKinley took office with the country still bitterly divided about the solution to the economic crisis. By 1900, however, when McKinley won re-election with a larger majority, much of the bitterness seemed to be gone. One major factor in creating this era of good feelings during his first administration was a return of prosperity through higher farm prices and a reduction of unemployment. But another major factor in creating a political consensus was the way in which a war with Spain provided an area of common identity for the white Protestant majority.

The founding fathers had defined the Revo-

American Catholic leaders such as Cardinal Gibbons worked hard to show that they supported the Spanish-American War with the same intensity as did most Protestant ministers, and that they were not loyal to Catholic Spain. (Library of Congress 18909/10908)

lution of 1776 as completing the rejection of medieval Catholic tradition that had begun in Europe during the Reformation. The most important American historians of the nineteenth century — George Bancroft, William Prescott, John Motley, and Francis Parkman — described the United States as God's chosen nation in which the progressive forces of Protestantism had reached final and perfect culmination. For these historians, who served as political philoso-

phers and secular theologians for the national culture, it had been the destiny of the Reformation to free the individual from the tyranny of medieval monarchies, which in turn were rooted in the tyranny of the church of Rome. They described the Roman Catholic church as the anti-Christ that taught people to reject God: this "Holy Mother Church, linked in sordid wedlock to governments and thrones, numbered among her servants a host of worldly and the proud, whose service of God was but the service of themselves."

For these historians the victory of "English Protestantism and popular liberty" was predestined by God. After the defeat of the Spanish Armada in 1588 and the removal of France from North America in 1763, medieval Catholicism had lost its power to profane the virgin land of the Western Hemisphere. The United States, as heir of the Protestant Reformation, was the fulfillment of God's plan to create a Protestant citadel in the New World. Such logic also explained how revolutions in Spanish America in the early nineteenth century had eliminated Spain from the Western Hemisphere, with the exception of its control of the islands of Puerto Rico and Cuba.

By the 1890s the Cubans too were revolting against Spain, against what American Protestants saw as a last corrupting vestige of Spanish medievalism within the purity of the Western Hemisphere. Such perceptions prepared Americans to believe newspaper stories that chronicled the atrocities committed by Spanish troops as they attempted to suppress the rebellion. And many Americans supported journalists, ministers, and educational leaders who demanded that the United States drive Spain from its American possessions. Such a way, they predicted, would lead to an easy victory, since decadent Spain lacked the strength to resist the Protestant republic.

Protestant agitation for a war against Spain may have emerged from Protestant fears of increasing Catholic immigration to the United States. In the 1880s major Protestant theologians such as Josiah Strong had been horrified to realize that the rapidly growing cities were filled with Catholic immigrants. For Strong, Protestantism was a frontier religion that was in danger of dying with the closing of the agricultural frontier. It must regain its vigor by

going overseas. According to preachers and polemicists like Strong, the American Anglo-Saxon Protestant must find an overseas frontier and Christianize the inferior colored races. Revitalized by overseas expansion, Protestantism could then meet the challenge of Catholicism at home. Strong's extremely popular writings were echoed by politicians like Republican Senator Albert Beveridge of Indiana, who declared, "God has not been preparing the English-speaking peoples for a thousand years for nothing but idle self-contemplation. No! He has made us the master organizers of the world that we may administer government among savages and servile peoples." Henry Watterson, a nationally renowned Democratic editor from Kentucky, agreed that "We [must] escape the menace and peril of socialism and agrarianism, as England escaped them, by a policy of colonization and conquest."

THE CORPORATION AND THE NEW EMPIRE

Popular enthusiasm for a war against Spain coincided with a new foreign policy, one that was shared by the Republican and Democratic administrations of the 1890s. The Democrat, Cleveland, was more reluctant than the Republican, McKinley, to acquire overseas bases. But like his Republican predecessor, Harrison, and his successor, McKinley, Cleveland believed in the necessity of American economic expansion abroad. The consensus on foreign policy in this decade contrasted with the political confusion and conflict on domestic issues. Such continuity in foreign policy reflected the fact that few Americans were strongly concerned with international relations. The average citizen remained primarily interested in local affairs. But the leaders of the large corporations, who usually could reach agreement on the national economy, were especially interested in developing a foreign policy that protected American business. Indeed, the United States's international relations increasingly reflected the needs and aspirations of the business elite.

One of the primary concerns of American corporation leaders was to locate adequate markets for the ever-increasing production of American manufacturers. Iron and steel firms that produced three million tons in 1870 were producing thirty million tons in 1900. Starting well below English iron and steel production in 1870, they had far surpassed English output by 1900. This growth rate was also must faster than that of Germany. Such production led to

a remarkable jump in the value of American exports, from $450,000 in 1870 to $1.5 billion in 1900. While agricultural products such as wheat and cotton continued to be the most important export items, the proportion of manufactured exports increased from 15 percent to 32 percent of the total goods sold outside the United States during the decade of the nineties. This burgeoning output led corporation leaders to seek government assistance in encouraging and protecting economic expansion.

Many farmers and small businessmen also were interested in foreign trade, but these groups could not influence government officials in the same way that executives of large corporations could. For example, although there were 669 iron and steel firms in 1900, five or

FIGURE I.I   IRON AND STEEL PRODUCTION, 1870–1900

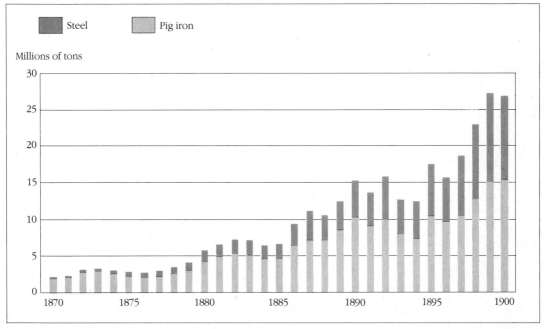

six of the major steelmakers could control the prices charged in the national market. The executives of these giant firms could easily reach agreement on the tariff levels they desired and could support lobbyists in Congress to communicate such information to the legislature. In contrast, there was no possibility for the ten million farmers to reach agreement on the prices they would sell their crops on the world market. Unlike the steelmakers, who often made agreements on limiting or expanding production, each of these millions of farmers felt he was in competition with every other farmer. Each felt the need to produce as much as possible to support his family. And each often found that by increasing production, the farmers had forced down the prices they received.

The power of the steel executives to influence the national government was increased by their ability to control their employees as well as the capital invested in their firms. These steel executives had directed 78,000 workers in 1870 but had 272,000 employees under them in the 1890s. (Employment in manufacturing, mining, and construction had grown from three million in 1870 to nine million in 1900, a jump from 20 to 30 percent of the work force.) The capital controlled by the steel executives increased from $121 million in 1870 to $590 million in 1900. Such wealth and power enabled a corporate elite to influence policy making on all levels of government.

The emergence of large-scale corporations after the Civil War reflected the importance of capital accumulation and business efficiency. It is possible that the Civil War served to stimulate the growth of corporations. A major problem in moving from small-scale to larger business was to find efficient forms of organization to facilitate the flow of orders from the top to the bottom with the expectation that they would be carried out effectively. During the war years, some businessmen became familiar for the first time with the complex table of organization that had been created to give order to the huge Union army.

The first large corporations were railroad companies, and many corporation officers had been officers in the Civil War. These men easily understood the corporate table of organization. At the top was the president and the board of directors. They commanded six major divisions: engine repairs, cars, bridges, telegraph, printing, and service. Within these divisions were hierarchies for the local agents, train crews, and foremen. Workers wore uniforms that symbolized their equivalency to privates, sergeants, lieutenants, or captains. Each railroad worker was expected to carry a watch so that schedules could be precise and coordinated. These private bureaucracies grew so rapidly that in 1890 an eastern railroad with headquarters in Boston had three times as many employees as the Massachusetts state government and a budget six times as large. Like generals then, corporation executives had tremendous power because they could expect obedience from thousands of men. They commanded the energy of these men and also the physical resources mobilized by that company. Andrew Carnegie in 1890 commanded a system that had iron mines in Minnesota, a fleet to carry the ore to Pennsylvania, railroads that transferred the ore from Great Lakes ports to smelting plants, and factories that turned out such finished products as barbed wire from the raw steel.

By 1890 these corporate executives were bringing their concepts of systematic growth to the State Department. Throughout the nineteenth century many secretaries of state had been interested in promoting American trade abroad, but they had viewed this interest as a particular opportunity at a particular time. Beginning with Secretary of State James G. Blaine in 1889, however, there was a new sense that the State Department must formulate a consistent and continuous policy to make opportunities for the expansion of overseas trade. Instead of reacting to an opportunity that might appear in a specific Asian or Latin American country, the State Department believed in the establishment of a coherent Asian policy that was coordinated with an equally well-developed policy for Latin America.

This change of outlook assumed a new centralization of decision making. In the past, American ambassadors who lived abroad might inform the secretary of state of an opportunity to which the State Department might react. Now, however, initiative was to start with the secretary of state in Washington and flow down the table of organization. Under this scheme, foreign ambassadors had the responsibility to create opportunities to implement a previously established foreign policy.

Secretary of State Blaine had called a Pan-American conference in 1890 to stimulate trade with Latin America. Secretary of the Navy Benjamin Tracy had established a new Naval War College to train officers to prepare the navy to serve this new foreign policy. This decision implied that the navy had rejected its traditional role of coastal defense and was prepared to compete in Asia and Africa as well as Latin America. Top State Department officials and navy officers believed that the growth of American industrial production had now made the United States a great world power. To compete effectively with other world powers required a powerful navy. Captain Alfred Mahan of the Naval War College was the great theoretician for the use of the navy to support the systematic expansion of overseas trade. In his well-received book of 1890, *The Influence of Seapower on History,* Mahan argued that America's future greatness depended on overseas raw material and markets. A strong navy was necessary to guarantee these materials and markets. The efficient operation of this navy also depended on a canal through Central America so the fleet could quickly shift from the Atlantic to the Pacific. Mahan also advocated that the United States acquire colonies throughout the world to serve as coaling stations for the fleet.

THE UNITED STATES IN THE WORLD ARENA

The Democratic Cleveland administration shared the assumptions of its Republican predecessors that the United States was now a great power. Not only did Cleveland's secretary of state, Richard Olney, assume that he should attempt to expand foreign trade, but he also believed that the United States should replace England as the most influential power in Latin America. After most of the South American countries had declared independence from Spain in the early nineteenth century, the United States had warned Europe not to attempt to push these countries back into colonial status. This Monroe Doctrine of 1823 had been enforced by the English fleet, for England also wanted an independent Latin America that would be open to world trade. Now in the 1890s, the United States felt sufficiently powerful to restrain European influence in Latin America while replacing England as the major trading nation in that area. When a boundary dispute broke out between Venezuela and the

After taking the Philippine Islands from Spain in the Spanish-American War, the American government resorted to large military force to suppress the efforts of Filipino patriots to wrest independence from the United States. (Brown Brothers)

English colony British Guiana in 1894, the Cleveland administration informed England that it would arbitrate the dispute and would expect England to accept the decision reached by the United States.

Although it had resisted acquiring the Hawaiian Islands, the Cleveland administration expressed this new sense of American power when a rebellion erupted in Cuba against Spanish rule in 1895. The United States told Spain that it planned to play a major role in the negotiations between Spain and the rebels. In 1896 the Republican platform called for Cuban in-

dependence, the building of a strong navy, acquisition of the Hawaiian Islands, and the purchase of the Virgin Islands in the Caribbean from Denmark. President McKinley, therefore, continued the policy of the Cleveland administration to pressure Spain, finally giving Spain an ultimatum to allow American mediation of the conflict in Cuba. When the Spanish government refused, McKinley asked Congress to declare war on Spain in April 1898.

The tiny American army of twenty-eight thousand was enlarged by volunteers and

MAP 1.2   THE AMERICAN EMPIRE IN THE PACIFIC, 1900

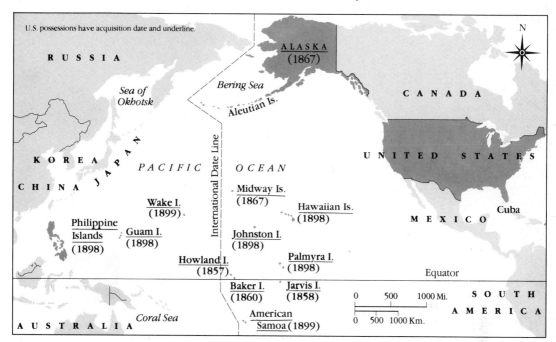

smashed Spanish forces in Cuba in less than two months. The American fleet easily destroyed Spanish naval forces in Cuba, and a squadron of American ships sailed into the Philippine Islands to destroy the Spanish fleet in Manilla Bay. As early as 1895, naval officers had planned an attack on this Spanish colony. Their thinking reflected the importance of the Philippines as a naval base to support American commercial expansion in China. The acquisition of the Philippines completed a chain of naval bases stretching from California to China. Hawaii had been annexed in 1898, and the island of Guam, also taken in 1898, filled the large stretch of ocean from Hawaii to the Philippines.

In declaring war against Spain, Congress had promised in the Teller Amendment that the purpose of the war was to make Cuba in-

dependent and not to absorb it as an American colony. Naval strategists, however, wanted to strengthen American control in the Caribbean to protect any canal that might be built through Central America. The United States therefore demanded the Caribbean island of Puerto Rico from Spain as part of the peace settlement. Although Cuba was not directly incorporated into the American empire, the McKinley administration forced the Cubans to include the Platt Amendment in their constitution of 1900. This constitutional provision gave the United States the right to send troops into Cuba at any time to regulate Cuban politics. Cuba also granted the United States a permanent naval base.

The acquisition of the Philippines catapulted the United States to great-power status in East Asia. The McKinley administration then moved to develop a foreign policy that would support a large market in China for American textiles, oil, lumber, and steel. Faced with the possibility that Japan, Germany, France, and Russia might carve China into colonies from which American trade would be barred, Secretary of State John Hay issued Open Door notes in 1899 and 1900. These diplomatic letters announced the United States's commitment to keep China an independent nation. Hay hoped this position would be successful because it was supported by England and because the interests of the other nations might balance each other off.

McKinley won an overwhelming vote of confidence in his re-election in 1900. Besides restoring domestic prosperity, he had presided over a remarkable territorial expansion of the

The United States government, like those in Europe, linked nationalism with military sacrifice by burying its dead from the Spanish-American War in Arlington National Cemetery at Washington, D. C. (THE GRANGER COLLECTION, New York)

United States. But the American victory had been less than complete. In the Philippines, the United States encountered stiff opposition from a Filipino guerrilla movement, led by Emilio Aguinaldo, that demanded national independence. In defending the new acquisitions, therefore, the McKinley administration adopted the same antiguerrilla tactics that Spain had applied to Cuba. Peasants were placed in concentration camps and their villages and crops burned so they could not support the independence fighters. Torture was used to break the morale of rebel leaders. This guerrilla war would drag on for more than a decade. But its ultimate irony was apparent by 1900: the United States had become an imperial power with thousands of troops stationed in conquered territories, the Philippines, Puerto Rico, and Cuba.

The fears of the historian Frederick Jackson Turner, that the end of the western frontier would force the United States to become more like the nations of Europe, seemed to be fulfilled. The commitment of the national government to the development of overseas trade was leading the United States into military and colonial competition with the expansionist nations of the world. This realization prompted a short-lived debate in 1898 and 1899 over annexation of the Philippines. Several prominent Americans, including Bryan, former Presidents Cleveland and Harrison, Andrew Carnegie, Samuel Gompers, and writers such as Mark Twain and William D. Howells spoke against annexation because they feared that an imperial America would lose its republican institutions. Leagues were formed in many cities to oppose territorial expansion. Although some of the participants saw colonialism as a violation of American principles of self-determination, the leagues argued that commercial expansion did not require annexation of territory. This objection, however, was stifled by "imperialists" in the McKinley camp who answered that the Open Door to the Far East could be tapped only through control of strategic naval bases and that territorial possession of islands such as the Philippines would assure the security of such bases.

By 1900, therefore, the United States not only shared the patterns of rapid urbanization and industrialization that characterized England and Germany, but had joined European nations as an international economic and military power. Young leaders such as Theodore Roosevelt disagreed with Turner's pessimism over the nation's future. For them, the overseas frontier and the urban-industrial frontiers at home were making possible a society they called a "new" democracy. Meanwhile, other Americans had greater difficulty in making the adjustment to urban industrialism and the great concentrations of wealth and power that it spawned. From the hopes and concerns of both groups sprang the Progressive movement, the most important expression of American culture between 1900 and 1913.

SUGGESTED READINGS

The sense of crisis in the 1880s and 1890s is described by Richard Hofstadter, *The Age of Reform* (1955), by Frederic Jaher, *Doubters and Dissenters* (1964), and David W. Noble, *The Progressive Mind* (1970).

The development of the corporation, which was a major factor in threatening the traditional American identity as a nation of small businessmen, is analyzed in Ralph and Muriel Hidy, *Pioneering in Big Business* (1955), Alfred Chandler, *Strategy and Structure* (1961), and Robert Wiebe, *The Search for Order* (1967). *Main Currents in Modern American History* (1976) by Gabriel Kolko is an excellent recent survey of American economic history that begins with the formation of the corporation. Another fine analysis of the ways in which corporations were able to rapidly consolidate their power is *America By Design: Science Technology, and the Rise of Corporate Capitalism* (1977) by David F. Noble.

Hofstadter's unsympathetic analysis of Populism has been challenged by Norman Pollack, *The Populist Response to Industrial America* (1962), James Youngdale, *Populism: A Psychohistorical Perspective* (1975), and Lawrence Goodwyn, *Democratic Promise: The Populist Movement in America* (1976). Goodwyn's book is especially useful in providing a sense of the vitality of rural society as farmers created new organizations to give new expression to the tradition of a producers' democracy.

There are no recent books that provide the same high level of description and analysis of the ways in which the National Labor Union and the Knights of Labor also fought to preserve a producers' democracy. A useful study of this conflict in the labor movement, however, between parties and individuals who rejected the corporation and the concentration of ownership and those who accepted the wage system is Gerald Grob, *Workers and Utopia* (1961). *Samuel Gompers* (1963) by Bernard Mandel is a biography of the leading spokesman for the acceptance of the status of a permanent wage-earning class by the labor movement.

C. Vann Woodward pioneered the study of the connections between the crisis of the 1890s and racism in southern politics in *The Strange Career of Jim Crow* (1954). Since then, the power and depth of white racism in the na-

tional culture has been described by George Fredrickson, *The Black Image in the White Mind* (1971). Sheldon Hackney, *Populism to Progressivism in Alabama* (1969), provides a case study of the breakdown of the attempt at an economic politics that questioned the caste system. J. Morgan Kousser, *The Shaping of Southern Politics: Suffrage Restriction and the Establishment of the One-Party South, 1880–1910* (1974), uses quantitative analysis to argue the dominant role of higher-income whites in disenfranchising blacks.

Robert F. Durden, *The Climax of Populism: The Election of 1896* (1965), relates the third party to national politics. Useful overviews of politics in the late nineteenth century can be found in John A. Garraty, *The New Commonwealth* (1968), and Paul W. Glad, *McKinley, Bryan, and the People* (1964). *Money and American Society* (1968) by Walter T. K. Nugent analyzes the major conflicts over inflation and deflation, gold, silver, and greenbacks.

Specialized studies on midwestern politics that emphasize the influence of religious and other cultural issues in party allegiance are R. T. Jensen, *The Winning of the Midwest* (1971), and Paul Kleppner, *The Cross of Culture: A Social Analysis of Midwestern Politics* (1970). Both studies reflect recent developments in quantitative historical research.

Henry May, *Protestant Churches and Industrial America* (1963), and Paul A. Carter, *The Spiritual Crisis of the Gilded Age* (1971), describe the confusions in the major Protestant denominations by the 1880s. Walter LaFeber, *The New Empire* (1963), relates those confusions to the enthusiasm of those denominations for overseas missionary activity. An older study, A. K. Weinberg, *Manifest Destiny* (1935), is still useful in analyzing the interrelationship of the Protestant traditions of mission and national expansion. LaFeber's major concern, however, is with the crisis of American capitalism. His analysis show's the influence of William A. Williams, who reestablished the economic interpretation of American imperialism with *The Tragedy of American Diplomacy* (1959). Harold and Margaret Sprout, *The Rise of American Naval Power* (1939), is still the best book on this key element in the expansion of the 1890s. David Healy, *U.S. Expansionism: The Imperialist Urge in the 1890s* (1970), provides a good overview. R. L. Beisner, *Twelve Against Empire: The Anti-Imperialists* (1968) looks at some cultural leaders who opposed military expansion. Rubin F. Weston, *Racism in U. S. Imperialism* (1972), explores the irony that white racism may have checked the urge to take overseas colonies with nonwhite populations.

Chapter 2

In 1880 most Americans built the patterns of their lives around the rhythms of rural and small-town culture. By 1920, however, the rhythm of the city, with its offices and factories, its movie houses and dance halls, influenced the patterns of life for people in the towns and on the farms. This rapid transition from a village to an urban-industrial society caused great stress within the dominant Anglo-Protestant culture. To qualify for careers in the emerging corporations, for example, middle-class boys were forced to spend more time in school. At the same time, a wave of immigrants from southern and eastern Europe arrived in the cities and found jobs as unskilled laborers in the factories and mines. To assimilate the children of the immigrants into the discipline of industrial society and to encourage respect for the existing political and social order, Amer-

ican leaders created a system of compulsory education. As an expression of the dominant Anglo-Protestant culture, the new school system succeeded in disciplining both the new immigrants and the children of the middle classes. But the leadership groups were less successful in keeping harmony between men and women of the middle class. The first decades of the twentieth century were marked, therefore, by an identity crisis for the males and females within Anglo-Protestant culture.

CITY VERSUS COUNTRY

Throughout the nineteenth century, the number of people living in cities increased far faster than the population of the countryside. But at

31

In 1900, almost 90 percent of blacks lived in the South, the vast majority working as sharecroppers or farm laborers. Between 1900 and 1920, however, they began to move into northern cities that were already crowded with European immigrants. (Amistad Research Center)

least until 1880, most of the millions of immigrants from Europe came across the sea hoping to establish themselves as farmers. As the last of the American Indian lands on the Great Plains were appropriated by white settlers, however, this dream faded. By 1890 most second or third sons of farmers who owned their own land could look forward only to becoming tenants or hired people on someone else's land if they wanted to remain in rural America. As

tenancy rates increased in the Midwest during the decades before World War One, almost two million Americans fled from this region to the prairie provinces of Canada with expectations of becoming landholding farmers on this last major agricultural frontier in North America.

But most of the sons and daughters of farmers who could not look forward to remaining on their parents' lands or marrying a neighboring farmer were moving into towns and cities. In this urban frontier, they expected to find jobs. Between 1860 and 1910 the proportion of Americans living in towns and cities increased from 25 to 40 percent. As a result of migration from the American countryside and almost thirty million immigrants from Europe, the number of large cities with populations of more than 100,000 grew from 9 to 50, the number of medium-size cities with populations of 25,000 to 100,000 grew from 26 to 178, and the number of small cities with populations from 10,000 to 25,000 grew from 58 to 369.

Even though it was not until 1920 that half the American people lived in towns and cities, most Americans had the feeling by 1890 that the future was controlled by the city. "The city is the nerve center of our civilization," wrote Josiah Strong in his widely read book *Our Country* (1885). The rapid growth of American cities, he remarked, "is full of significance."

Throughout the nineteenth century, the leaders of American society were generally Anglo-American Protestants, descendants of British immigrants who came to America in the colonial period. These leaders traditionally praised the independent farmer, or yeoman, as a model of honesty and wisdom. But by the 1880s and 1890s, the mass media, which included city newspapers, national magazines, popular plays, and the entertainment of vaudeville, began to portray farmers as "hayseeds." The hayseed was not a figure to be respected but rather one to be laughed at. He had none of the wisdom of the yeoman. Instead he was distinctly behind the times. He did not understand that there was a new America in which he lagged behind the progress of the cities and of industry. In sum, the hayseed was narrow and intolerant as well as old-fashioned.

Until the 1880s, rural Americans could define the city dweller as a "city slicker." In contrast to the honesty and integrity of the yeoman, the city slicker was a dishonest trickster. When the city slicker went to the country, the real America, and tried to trick the yeoman, the wise farmer always allowed the city slicker to make a fool of himself by letting him develop his dishonest scheme, which the yeoman saw through from the beginning. But by 1890 the hayseed now confronted a city dweller who was "up-to-date," who was so busy making progress that he had no time for tricks and who smiled at the refusal of the hayseed to accept new technology, new lifestyles, new clothes, new haircuts. It was an exceptional man who did not have a beard and long hair in 1880, but it was an exceptional man who had a beard and hair over the ears in 1910. In the cartoons of 1910, hayseeds have beards and lack the short urban haircut.

Although farmers throughout the nineteenth century produced crops to be sold in the marketplace and used the money received from these crops to buy manufactured goods, farm families made most of their own clothes and provided most of their own food. As farm machinery became more important in the planting and harvesting of crops by the 1880s and 1890s, however, farmers took the opportunity to produce more cash crops and less food for themselves. Farm wives became more involved in the money economy and purchased more of their clothes and other household goods. To be up-to-date, they became consumers rather than producers. Like the city dwellers, they could buy the latest fashions by ordering from Sears Roebuck or Montgomery Ward catalogues and they could keep in touch with the latest ideas through the rapidly expanding post office system.

By the 1890s, for the first time, a large part of the American population was crowded into industrial towns and cities and could continue no longer the traditional rural forms of rest and recreation. Street cars, however, enabled people to escape from the cities on Sundays to parks, lakes, or the sea shore. (The Whaling Museum, New Bedford, Mass.)

THE SHAPE OF STREETCAR CITIES

Yet the urban style of separating production from consumption was itself a new way of city life. In 1850 the largest cities in the United States were limited to a radius of about two miles from the center. A person could walk this distance in going to work or to shop. Actually, in these "walking" cities most people lived near the small manufacturing shops where they worked or lived above the stores they owned. Since almost all city enterprises in 1850 operated on a small scale, there was a mixture of dwellings and business throughout the entire city. By the 1860s and 1870s, well-to-do and poor people also lived next to each other.

In the streetcar city new technologies made possible the expansion of the city beyond the walking limits. Passenger cars, drawn by horses on tracks, could carry people longer distances to shop or work. By the 1880s the transformation of these streetcars into electric trolleys pushed out the boundaries of big cities such as Boston, Philadelphia, and New York to eight or ten miles from the center. Chicago, the largest of the many big cities growing in the Midwest, called its center the "Loop" because streetcars converged at that point and then turned to go back to the boundaries of the city. The largest cities such as New York, Chicago, Philadelphia, and Boston also developed subways and elevated trains to move the huge numbers of people coming into the central city to work. By 1920 it was clear that the largest of the streetcar cities, New York with six million people and Chicago with three million people, reflected new patterns of urban life that sharply separated where one worked from where one lived and segregated the residential areas of the rich from those of the poor.

The large cities flourished as centers of railroad networks. Manufactured goods from the cities spread throughout the country on railroads, and food — vegetables from Florida, wheat from Kansas, pork from Iowa — moved into the cities on the railroads. Large factories employing many blue-collar workers, and large corporation offices, banks, and insurance companies employing many white-collar employees, concentrated near the centers of the cities where the railroad and streetcar lines transported both large quantities of goods and large numbers of people.

When hundreds or even thousands of people worked for a firm doing business on a national scale, it became impossible for everyone to live close to work. Meanwhile, other technological breakthroughs also changed the nature of urban life. The development of electrical eleva-

tors, for example, encouraged the construction of skyscraper office buildings. And when many office towers were crowded into the central business area, a huge inflow of people moved into the city center every morning and formed an outflow every afternoon.

The geography of the streetcar city that emerged in the 1880s involved a center dominated by the office buildings of the large corporations. The first ring outside this center consisted of manufacturing plants served by the railroads. The next ring comprised old housing where both the poor and the wealthy had lived before the era of urban expansion. Now only the poor lived there. Beyond this ring of the very poor came what urban historians call the "zone of emergence." Nearly half the city dwellers between 1880 and 1914, according to recent estimates, could afford to move out of the slums. Thus private building contractors erected apartments, duplexes, and small single-family houses on a mass scale for the lower-middle-class people who could afford to escape the central-city slums. This housing, though built by private enterprise, tended to express only a few architectural forms. The next ring consisted of middle-class houses that were larger and had more variety than those in the zone of emergence.

Small clusters of stores, schools, churches, and offices of doctors, dentists, and lawyers developed in these residential rings where major streetcar lines crossed. But these rings were largely segregated from the major areas of industrial production and office buildings. It was expected that women would spend their lives with their children in this residential segregation. Daughters, when they became wives, would remain here. Sons, when they married, would establish their families here and travel each morning, five days a week, into the urban center to work in the world of men and return every evening on the streetcar to home and the world of women and children. Upper-middle-class people tended to live outside the city limits in more exclusive suburbs, and the men went to work on commuter trains. Some of the very rich (in the 1880s, 70 percent of the national wealth was held by less than 10 percent of the population) had luxury apartments on the edge of the commercial centers. They also owned large estates about fifty miles from the

A group of artists, the ash-can school, ceased painting the rural landscape or upper-class portrait and created instead vivid pictures of lower-class life in the growing cities. Here Bellows finds vitality and dignity in the midst of the terrible overcrowding. (Cliff Dwellers, 1913. George Wesley Bellows/American 1882–1925. Oil on canvas, 39½″ x 41½″. Los Angeles County Museum of Art: Los Angeles County Fund)

city centers and summer homes near seashores, lakefronts, or mountains. The upper middle class, trying to imitate the upper class, built or rented more modest summer cottages.

Although the rich gained their wealth from the corporations that had headquarters in the cities and although the career opportunities for upper-middle-class and middle-class men were found in the expanding cities, the flight of these leadership groups from the central city to the suburbs or country estates reflected not only a desire for clean air and space but also a nostalgia for America's rural past. Even in the zone of emergence for the lower middle class between the inner-city poor and the well-to-do in the suburbs, there was an almost desperate desire to have a small lawn. Only that half of the people who were very poor had to live without grass.

The urban pattern that emerged in the 1880s and 1890s prevailed until the end of the 1970s. The American city served as a frontier in which poor rural people from Europe and America came to live in the slums that surrounded the manufacturing and commercial urban core. As they found economic opportunities in the city and escaped from poverty, they moved outward to find better housing and a more pleasant environment for their children. If men became very successful, they could then move their families into a rural environment and commute to their urban careers every morning.

Well-to-do Americans justified this economic pattern by developing a "trickle-down" theory of housing. According to this theory, the incoming poor would take over the worst housing left behind by the previous generation of poor; it assumed that the earlier generation had become successful enough to move out to the next ring. Reflecting this theory, the construction industry concentrated on building houses on the expanding suburban frontier for those who had become wealthy enough to afford new housing. This theory, of course, did not expect anyone to remain poor for more than one generation. And it did not consider the likelihood that slum housing would deteriorate over time.

Although the very rich and the upper middle class allowed this pattern of deteriorating housing for the urban poor to develop in the new streetcar cities, a pattern that has meant worsening conditions in the central cities even now, they did take some pride in the cities that they controlled economically and socially. They built ample central-city parks and zoos, founded large libraries and art and natural history museums, and supported opera houses and concert halls for the symphonies that by 1900 were established in every major American city. Huge department stores were located in the central city, and to these shopping places housewives made special trips from the suburbs.

POPULAR CULTURE IN THE CITY

Although many public facilities were open to the poor, urban institutions reflected the cultural values of the wealthy. The opera and symphonies, for example, not only were expensive, but they also demanded a special set of musical values. Fewer lower-income people even went to free public institutions such as libraries. Instead, poorer people supported other cultural institutions. They attended large baseball parks that became the homes of professional teams. In addition, big amusement parks, usually built on the edge of a lake or the seashore, attracted middle- and lower-income groups.

The culture of the big cities soon spread throughout the nation. As baseball became professionalized, a hierarchy of leagues was established. The lowest league level was in the smaller cities. If a player was successful, he moved to a higher league in the medium-size cities. And if he continued to be successful, perhaps a star, he moved to the big leagues whose teams were in the largest cities of the East and Midwest. The same pattern held for vaudeville acts, which began in small towns and hoped to make it into the "big time," playing the theaters with the most prestige in New York and Chicago. Vaudeville, moreover, was dominated by booking agencies that operated in big cities and sent out acts to play in theaters on a national circuit.

Watching a country boy become a baseball star or a poor immigrant become a vaudeville star might reassure poorer audiences that the urban frontier did allow for upward mobility. If middle-aged men in these audiences had not themselves become stars, they could hope that their sons would do better. Most of the stars in baseball in 1900 came from a rural Protestant background. Vaudeville, in contrast, provided a special opportunity for the children of Irish and Jewish immigrants. Comedians from these ethnic backgrounds discovered that audiences enjoyed hearing them tell jokes about themselves.

Blacks, who were barred from the chain of baseball leagues leading to the major leagues, could sometimes find a place in vaudeville by also directing humor against themselves. In the 1850s white men had blackened their faces and had satirized blacks in minstrel shows. By the 1890s black entertainers put greasepaint on their faces and did new versions of the songs, dances, and humor of the minstrel shows, hu-

Vaudeville began as entertainment for the lower class in the great urban centers of the late nineteenth century. Since immigrants formed a major part of the city population, much of the humor was ethnic, often conveyed in dialect. (Historical Pictures Service, Inc.)

mor that usually made the blacks appear as fools.

By World War One, the movie industry, which had begun in New York and New Jersey, moved to Hollywood, California, because the favorable climate allowed outdoor filming. Movies by this time were challenging vaudeville as the most popular form of urban entertainment. They also reflected the values of urban America. When movies began to be shown throughout rural and small-town America, the film industry could define the styles and morality of the countryside as young people dreamed of imitating the stars on the screen. As early as 1903, for example, a series of movies —*The Corset Model, The Pajama Girl, The Physical Culture Girl,* and *At the Dressmaker's*— showed young women in their underwear. These violations of the modesty expected of respectable women in the nineteenth century were an indication of the new sexual morality that would become dominant in the 1920s.

Dance halls provided another new form of urban entertainment for the middle and lower middle class. Between 1890 and 1914 a whole new style of fast dancing developed among young people. Much of the music for this dancing, beginning with ragtime, was strongly influenced by African rhythms. Patterns of African music had survived slavery and had been transmitted through Afro-American culture, much of it in oral tradition. By the 1890s various fusions of African rhythm with European melody and harmony had emerged. Almost all American popular music from ragtime in the 1890s to rock in the 1960s has expressed this Afro-American influence.

Despite the influence of black music, however, white society continued to define everything black as worthless and to uphold racial caste attitudes. Just before World War One, a black boxer, Jack Johnson, was driven from the country because he had violated the caste pattern that prohibited blacks from showing violence to white men, even in a professional ring. Johnson had further flaunted the caste patterns by openly establishing sexual relationships with white women. Johnson's problems revealed the social limitations placed on blacks even in the world of entertainment.

CASTE AND CLASS IN THE CITY

White Americans supported the caste system so fervently in the years between 1880 and 1920 that they laid the foundations for the urban crisis of the 1960s and 1970s. Small numbers of blacks had lived near poor whites of the northern cities throughout the nineteenth century. A few of these blacks had attained middle-class status by providing services for wealthy whites who lived nearby. As the streetcar cities expanded, however, the wealthy distanced themselves from the poor, and the remaining whites began to pressure blacks to leave the mixed neighborhoods and move into all-black areas. By 1900, as thousands of blacks began to migrate from the rural South to such northern cities as Baltimore, Washington, Philadelphia, and New York, they found themselves forced into rigidly defined ghettos in the central slums.

The experience of black migrants to the city, therefore, was totally different from that of the white Jewish and Catholic immigrants from rural Europe. Russian Jews or Italian Catholics tended to settle in neighborhoods with other Russian or Italian immigrants. The white ethnic ghettos were voluntary and not forced like those of the blacks. Because they were voluntary, they did not have the same high percentage of a single population group. Ethnic settlements, despite cultural clustering, remained open to members of other cultural groups.

Not only were the ghettos of the white immigrants a mixture of ethnic groups but their members were free to move out of the central-city slums to better housing in the zone of emergence once they had achieved some economic success. Such mobility was unavailable to blacks. As the New York and Chicago ghettos grew to thirty or forty thousand by 1910, a new kind of black middle class appeared. The small number of black businessmen and professionals provided services to poor urban blacks rather than to wealthy whites. And they had to live within the boundaries of the ghetto, regardless of education or income. This black middle class remained small because the average black remained poor. Every white immigrant group experienced some upward economic mobility between 1890 and 1914. The average black did not.

In Boston, black families were slightly more stable than those of the Irish immigrants, with fathers and mothers present in more than 80 percent of black homes. Blacks also had more education than the incoming Irish. Yet blacks

This black woman and her grandchildren were evicted from their urban shack so that the ground could be cleared for a larger building. Throughout the twentieth century, urban renewal has frequently worked to the disadvantage of the poor because most new housing has been built for middle and upper-income families. (The Whaling Museum, New Bedford, Mass.)

did not keep pace with Irish economic gains. In 1890, 8 percent of the blacks had white-collar jobs, 11 percent were skilled blue-collar workers, and 81 percent were unskilled manual workers. By 1910, 10 percent of the blacks had white-collar jobs, while the skilled workers had declined to 8 percent, and unskilled workers had increased slightly to 82 percent. In contrast to these figures, 32 percent of the sons of Irish immigrants born in the United States had white-collar jobs in 1890, while 34 percent were skilled, and 34 percent were unskilled workers. By 1910, 45 percent of the Irish-American sons were white-collar workers. The proportion of skilled blue-collar workers had dropped to 21 percent, and the number of unskilled remained steady at 34 percent.

There were sharp differences in the rates of upward economic mobility among the different immigrant groups throughout urban America in the 1880–1920 period. Catholic peasants from Poland or Italy had little experience with craft or industrial skills or with small business. In contrast to immigrants from Germany or England, who more often had such skills, Poles and other Slavs and Italians began working at the bottom of American industry. Many of their children tended to remain in industrial jobs. German and English immigrants, however, began with higher-level jobs, and their sons quickly climbed higher. Irish immigrants also were unskilled peasants and they too did not move upward as fast as the more skilled immigrants from Scandinavia, Germany, and England. But they did experience greater mobility than the Poles, Slavs, and Italians because they spoke English and because, unlike the other groups, they intended to stay in the United States rather than return to the "old country."

Massive migration from Ireland had begun in the 1840s when famine killed one-third of the total population of the English-controlled island. By 1890 almost half the survivors had come to America. Fleeing starvation, Irish immigrants had little desire to return to their homes. Their commitment to America differed from the attitude of the millions of Catholics coming from southern and eastern Europe between 1890 and 1920.

Although southern and eastern Europeans were pushed toward the United States by exploding populations that created land and job shortages in their native regions, it was the hope of many that by earning sufficient money in the United States, they could return home and buy land. During the generation from 1890 to World War One, almost 50 percent of Italian and Slavic immigrants returned to Europe. Some then came back to the United States a second time. A few made the trip between the continents several times. Because of this expectation, young men came and left their young women behind. Women represented only one-third of the Catholic immigrants from southern and eastern Europe.

Most of these immigrants found work in heavy industry, where they constituted 60 to 80 percent of the work force. But their wages were not adequate to support a family. Men who were not married or whose wives had remained in Europe boarded with other immigrant families. By sharing housing and food under conditions of intense crowding, most were able to save money to send to relatives in Europe.

Expecting to go home and therefore willing to work for low wages, live in poor housing, and endure a work week of seven twelve-hour days in the steel mills, the Slavic and Italian workers had little interest in developing a sense of worker solidarity as part of an American labor movement. Moreover, factory owners did

Unmarried lower-class women around 1900 often worked in factories such as this one in Minneapolis. Married women of that class were more apt to do piece work at home. (Minnesota Historical Society)

not encourage these workers to develop industrial skills. Instead, businesses invested in machinery that did not require skilled operatives. While craft workers remained important in German and English factories, American management preferred the assembly line, where a worker would repeat one simple action over and over again.

In European industrial countries such as Germany, England, and the Scandinavian nations, a strong sense of labor unity developed by 1900. Labor unions became influential in bargaining with management about working conditions and possessed significant political force in Socialist Labor parties. The American industrial work force, however, became unionized more slowly and did not obtain significant political power until the foundation of the Committee for Industrial Organization (CIO) in 1935. The major cause of this later development was the immigrant nature of American industrial labor. Not only did many of these workers intend to leave America, but also their cultural differences interfered with the efforts of union organizers who attempted to solidify the working class. In a large steel mill, there might be fifteen different languages or dialects spoken. Some local unions, which were established before 1914, might have members who were all Czech, Italian, Polish, or German. These local unions served more as social clubs, which eased the loneliness of living in a strange land, than as centers of economic and political bargaining.

In 1910 workers whose parents had been born in America were twice as likely to belong to unions as those whose parents were immigrants. Native-born Americans, who had industrial skills and union backgrounds, found it difficult to establish a sense of solidarity with immigrant workers not only for cultural reasons but for economic ones as well. As the factories filled with new immigrants, native-born workers won promotion to the ranks of foremen. Here they could identify with management rather than with the workers they bossed. Unlike the southern and eastern European newcomers, many English and German immigrants came to America with industrial and labor-union backgrounds. But like the Yankee workers, these experienced industrial workers remained culturally separated from the Slavs and Italians and could obtain some upward mobility on their own. It was the English and German workers who were most likely to get the few skilled jobs that remained in the fac-

tories, to become foremen, or to move into the lower ranks of management. Moreover, the sons of Yankee or immigrant workers from northern Europe could hope to build on the success of their fathers and have an even better chance of rising into the lower or middle ranks of white-collar jobs.

These deep divisions within the American industrial work force retarded the development of industrial unions. Without such mass unions, there was little possibility for the emergence of strong Socialist Labor parties that existed in Scandinavia, Germany, and England. Workers in American factories were forced to work longer hours than workers in Europe, their jobs were duller and more repetitive, and they were pressured to work at a more intense and rapid pace. This demand for speed, the long work days, and the lack of adequate safety precautions caused the accident rate to be three times higher in American than in European factories. In 1908, for example, there were thirty thousand fatal and two million nonfatal accidents.

The ability of upper-class Anglo-Protestants to dominate the process of industrialization reflected their wealth, social organization, and historical advantages. Workers, in contrast, were ethnically divided; they were newcomers to America, and many did not intend to stay. These disadvantages were accentuated by the highly unstable and transient residential patterns of lower-income whites in the cities during the forty years after 1880.

It was in these decades that Catholic and Jewish immigrants became the majorities in most northern and midwestern cities. Forty percent of the five million people in New York, the nation's largest city in 1910, were foreign born and 38 percent were the children of immigrants. The same pattern prevailed in Chicago, the second largest city: 36 percent of its two million people were foreign born and 42 percent were the children of immigrants. In Cleveland, a city of 600,000, the proportion was 35 percent foreign born and 40 percent second generation. Recent statistical studies of a number of cities have revealed, however, that during each decade until 1920, huge numbers of people were moving from city to city looking for jobs. By 1890, 60 percent of the people who lived in Omaha in 1880 had left the city; 50 percent left San Francisco during those same years. But these cities were growing in size because more people were moving in than out. Boston grew from 363,000 to 448,000 between 1880 and 1890, as 138,000 families left the city and 153,000 families moved in.

ANGLO-PROTESTANTS, JEWS, AND CATHOLICS

In this vast flux of rootless people, upper-income Anglo-Protestants were the stable group. Their stability enabled them to retain social, economic, and partial political control of the eastern and midwestern cities, even though they constituted a minority of the total population. Once Jewish immigrants had established neighborhoods, however, they moved less within the city or from city to city than other immigrant groups. The first major Jewish immigration had come from Germany in the 1840s and 1850s; in the 1880s there were nearly 200,000 Jews in the United States, most of them German in origin. Better educated and more affluent than many other immigrants, these German Jews were successful in establishing themselves in the expanding cities.

Many also turned away from their religious heritage and joined Congregational and Unitarian churches.

Most upper-class and upper-middle-class Anglo-Protestants rebuffed the attempts of German Jews to integrate with their culture. Feeling threatened, perhaps, by Jewish education or wealth, or motivated by plain prejudice, the American leadership class moved to keep Jewish Americans out of their elite business and educational institutions. Successful Jewish businessmen were barred from the downtown clubs where corporate executives met for lunch to discuss business. Already in the 1880s, wealthy Jews also were excluded from well-to-do residential neighborhoods or from membership in the country clubs where suburbanites socialized. The children of wealthy Jews were excluded from private schools that provided precollege training for the children of Protestant elites, and only a very small quota was admitted to the Ivy League colleges where private-school graduates continued their elite education.

Between 1890 and 1914 the small number of German Jews were joined by more than two million Jews from Poland and Russia. Unlike the Italian and Slavic Catholic peasants who hoped to return to Europe, these Jews were fleeing political persecution and, like the Irish, intended to stay in America. Their migration, therefore, included as many women as men. On the average, they were poorer than the German Jews and they had experienced rigid segregation in their native countries. But they had some success as small merchants and they possessed a deep commitment to scholarship. With a strong tradition of family solidarity in the face of outside hostility, they quickly established themselves as small merchants and manufacturers in eastern and midwestern cities. Indeed, more than half of all Jewish immigrants settled in New York City alone. German and eastern European Jews experienced more upward economic mobility than any other immigrant group and by 1914 were sending a higher proportion of their children to college than the others.

Jews attained economic success even though they were excluded from positions in the major corporations and banks controlled by the Anglo-Protestant elite. Barred from practicing corporation law, Jewish lawyers specialized in criminal and real estate cases. Jewish businessmen also participated significantly in the development of new entertainment enterprises such as vaudeville, the movies, and popular music.

Many of the east European Jews were committed to religious tradition, and their presence in America revitalized the temple as a center of Jewish life. Part of this religious commitment was a belief that God would make it pos-

The rigid anti-Semitism of Anglo-Protestant elites kept Jewish businessmen and lawyers out of many established areas of business at the turn of the century. Some of the business skills of Jews, therefore, were directed into the rapidly developing popular culture of the cities such as vaudeville, popular music, and movies. Here is an early moving picture theater in the Jewish section of New York City. (Brown Brothers)

sible for Jews to return to Israel someday. This religious tradition of Zionism, which most German Jews had rejected in the 1870s and 1880s, was reinforced by a new political tradition of Zionism that was strong among Jews from Slavic countries. Having experienced persecution as a result of political anti-Semitism, some Polish and Russian Jews believed that a Jewish national state in Palestine was necessary as a refuge from anti-Semitism. By 1914 the east European immigrants had won the support of some of the German Jews such as Louis Brandeis to either religious or political Zionism and asked President Wilson, during World War One, to work for the establishment of a Jewish homeland in Palestine. One group of American Jews in 1917, therefore, was in the paradoxical situation of urging Zionism to protect European Jews while insisting that the United States was their promised land. For them, religious freedom in America eliminated the need to seek refuge in Israel. The strength of American Judaism could be seen in the emergence of Yiddish newspapers and a vital Yiddish theater in New York. Jews also established their own hospitals and cemeteries.

Catholic leaders also worked to preserve Catholic culture in the general community. In the 1880s these leaders perceived the public schools as being dominated by Protestants and so they resolved to build a separate Catholic school system, which would reach from kindergarten to universities and be located in every major city. Most of the American bishops came from Irish backgrounds, and they insisted that all education in the schools be done in English, denying German, Polish, and Italian Catholics their own languages. Irish-American domination also existed in the Southwest, where Irish-American priests and bishops showed little respect for the culture of the Spanish-speaking

Americans in Texas, New Mexico, Arizona, and California.

In addition to a parochial school system, Catholics established fraternal organizations, hospitals and cemeteries, and a widespread network of book stores where special books, magazines, and even games were sold, to strengthen a sense of Catholic cultural identity. Since the Catholic hierarchy expected the literature to be in English, most of the writers had an Irish-American background, and the movement failed to engage many of the lowest-income Catholics who did not speak English. Italian immigrants felt especially hostile to church leadership and did not attend Mass with the regularity of the Irish immigrants.

NATIVE AMERICANS AND CHICANOS

One of the strongest patterns in American history has been the intensity with which Anglo-Protestants have segregated blacks and have attempted to integrate Native Americans in the culture of white society. The census of 1890, which suggested the end of the geographic frontier and thereby created a crisis for Anglo-Protestants, also revealed a crisis for the Indian tribes of the Great Plains and Rocky Mountain regions. Within a single generation, railroads had penetrated this vast area. Moreover, white hunters and the army had greatly depleted the buffalo and other game animals on which the Indians depended for food. By 1890 all the tribes had suffered military defeat and were restricted on reservations, where they were fed by the government. Their homes and much of their way of life destroyed, many Native Americans looked to prophets such as Wovoka who promised miraculous salvation from white power. Wovoka's prophecy was that God would soon cover the world with a new layer of earth. This would bury all white people while Indians were elevated by a dance revealed to Wovoka. This Ghost Dance was carried from Nevada, where Wovoka lived, as far away as the Dakotas.

White reservation officials believed that the dance was dangerous and arrested the Sioux chiefs. When one of the chiefs, Sitting Bull, was killed by reservation police, his band sought refuge with another chief, Big Foot. The Seventh Cavalry caught the Indians at Wounded Knee Creek in South Dakota, and Big Foot surrendered in December 1890. While the troops were disarming the braves, however, a shot was fired. Soldiers opened fire, killing

When the Sioux were first placed on reservations, their camps still expressed their communal way of life that was based on following the buffalo herds. Gradually, in the twentieth century, the circle of tepees gave way to shacks and dugouts scattered across the reservation. (Library of Congress 26039/262/19725)

Quanah Parker

1852-1911

The most important leader in spreading the peyote cult among the Native Americans of the Great Plains was a Comanche chief named Quanah (Eagle). His white mother had been taken in a raid by his tribe against the first invasion of Anglos into the Texas plains country. Only five at the time, she quickly forgot English and became an adult member of the tribal community. When her husband, the Chief Nokoni, was killed by whites, her Anglo family, the Parkers, persuaded her to join them. She took her daughter, Prairie Flower, but left her son, Quanah, with the tribe to fulfill his destiny to become a chief.

The Parkers, however, returned to persuade Quanah to join them after his mother and sister had died of illness. Quanah learned ranching from his Anglo relatives, but he had a premonition that he would die, as his mother and sister had, if he did not return to his tribe. He became critically ill, and the Parkers, in desperation, sought help from a Mexican woman, a curandera, who had ancient medical skills and used herbs and prayers. In curing Quanah, she introduced him to the spiritual as well as medical powers of the Aztec sacramental substance, the fruit of a cactus, peyote.

Quanah returned to the Comanche and served as a spiritual guide for them in developing religious rituals of communion that focused on the sacramental use of peyote to alter the consciousness of those who ate it and help them reach higher levels of spirituality. Quanah also served as a guide to friends from other tribes, the Kiowa, Cheyenne, Arapaho, Sac and Fox, Shawnee, and Kickapoo, who lived with the Comanche in western Oklahoma.

The major patterns of the ceremonies brought together some of the rituals Quanah had learned from the curandera with influences from the rituals of the Plains tribes as well as the Christianity to which they had been exposed. This fusion added to the religious power of the peyote cult. In the 1880s, under the shock of military defeat by the whites and imprisonment on the reservations, the Native Americans of the Plains had turned to religious prophets such as Wovoka who promised that God would soon destroy all whites.

By 1900, however, that prophecy had failed, and the tribes now gained strength from prophets like Quanah who gave them a way of developing a new Native American culture that was strong enough to incorporate some white ways and still define its own future. Quanah died in 1911 before the official development of the Native American church, which spread the sacramental use of peyote to all of the North American tribes, crossing into Canada. But he had provided an example of successful fusion of red and white culture even in his family lifestyle. He had become a successful rancher, but his ranch was built from the land allotments of his extended family, which included eight wives. And as he resisted efforts of the state and national governments to ban the use of peyote, he resisted the efforts of those governments to destroy the extended family.

300 of the 350 Sioux men, women, and children. Black Elk, a young survivor of the massacre, later interpreted this event as the end of the Native American way of life. He wrote: "I did not know then how much was ended. When I look back now from this high hill of my old age, I can still see the butchered women and children lying heaped and scattered all along the crooked gulch as plain as when I saw them with eyes still young. And I can see that something else died there...a people's dream died there...the nation's hoop is broken and scattered. There is no center any longer, and the sacred tree is dead." But Black Elk was mistaken. Despite great pressure by white society since 1890, Native Americans have not relinquished their unique cultures and have preserved an independent identity.

The most important strategy used by the government to destroy the communal lifestyle of the Indians was to force them, through the Dawes Act of 1887, to accept the white value of private property. Reservation land was divided into 160-acre units, which were alloted to adult males. The United States government expected these men to become independent farmers. Under this program Native Americans lost sixty million acres in the 1890s. The government soon discovered that many Indians could not succeed economically because their land was not sufficiently fertile. Others were cheated out of their land by white men. The government believed that under this system of individual land ownership, the reservation would disappear. But the economic failure of the allotment system forced the government to increase the number of employees in the Bureau of Indian Affairs (BIA), which supervised the reservations. These BIA officials were needed to handle the economic affairs of "restricted" Indians, those who could not support themselves and whose land was held "in trust" by the government.

White government officials on the reservations possessed dictatorial power, which they used to destroy the authority of the tribal chiefs. No effective local government by the Indians was allowed. The Creeks, Cherokees, Choctaws, Chickasaws, and Seminoles, who had been driven out of the Southeast in the 1830s and promised a permanent home in Oklahoma, now were told in the 1890s that they could not continue the sophisticated political and educational systems they had developed during the nineteenth century.

Given the dictatorial power of the government agents, the sole politics on the reservation consisted of personal rivalry among those Indians currying favor with the officials. All Indian groups tended to split into "mixed bloods," who wanted to cooperate with whites, and "full bloods," who were determined to retain their traditions. Whites also expected that the education of Native American children in church-related private schools and public schools on the reservations would quickly teach the children white values. But many of the children, removed from the tribes and sent to boarding schools, rejected their teachers and "returned to the blanket."

To eliminate tribal customs, the government encouraged white churches to establish missions on the reservations. Although many Indians became members of these churches, they seemed to graft Christianity onto their own traditions. Many Native Americans, however, went beyond introducing their ways into white churches and developed their own church. A religious ceremony based on the cactus fruit peyote, which altered the consciousness of its users, emerged among Oklahoma Indians around 1900 and soon spread to most of the Plains tribes. In this religious ceremony the object of worship, the Great Spirit, often was identified with Jesus, and crucifixes usually were present. The religion promised hope for its members and helped many to overcome the alcoholism that permeated reservation life. The white churches joined the government in trying to stop the development of what came to be called the Native American church. But its wide success, accomplished by the time of World War One, indicated that in spite of great pressure Indians were capable of cultural creativity on their own terms.

The Native American church had little influence on the Pueblo in New Mexico and the Navaho in Arizona. These two tribal groups were unique in escaping the individual allotment of communal land and the destruction of tribal government. Moreover, the Pueblo, having been influenced by Spanish culture for four hundred years, had incorporated some aspects of Catholicism in their tribal religion.

Most of the population of Mexico had Indian ancestry and, while the Catholicism of Mexico incorporated few specific tribal ceremonies, it had been strongly influenced by Native American tradition. After the Mexican War of 1846 the United States had claimed the Southwest, and it appeared that Anglo-Protestant culture might completely overwhelm the Spanish-American heritage in this region. But in New Mexico, which did not become a state until 1912, a resistant cultural group of sixty thousand Nuevo Mexicanos thwarted Anglo dominance. Underground groups such as La Mano Negra and Las Corras Blancas used violence to try to stop the transfer of land by the territorial government from the Nuevo Mexicanos to Anglo-controlled mining and ranching interests. Congress appointed a Court of Private Lands Claims in 1891 to determine the legal title of lands that the Spanish-Americans argued belonged to them since the sixteenth and seventeenth centuries. By World War One, this court had upheld Anglo claims in 80 percent of the cases, and Nuevo Mexicano land-holding was sharply reduced. Yet this community still had enough strength in 1912 to force the state constitution to recognize the legal equality of the Spanish and English languages and to authorize the training of teachers in both languages. Once New Mexico was in the union, however, the dominant Anglos disregarded these provisions and the public schools taught only English.

Soon after 1900, the national government initiated dam-building projects throughout the Southwest, making available more than a million acres of good agricultural land. Anglo commercial interests saw the possibility of using some of this land in Texas and Arizona for cotton and other acreage in Texas and Southern California for vegetables that could be shipped on newly developed refrigerator cars to northern cities. Anglos, wanting cheap labor to cultivate these crops, eagerly attracted workers from across the border in Mexico.

Surplus Mexican labor was available in the 1900–1920 period because of high birthrates in that country during the 1880s. At the same time, Anglo commercial interests had built a network of railroads that extended from Mexico into the United States for carrying minerals and ore. The railroads also served as highways for Mexican immigrants traveling north.

These social and economic changes in Mexico stimulated violent political revolution between 1910 and 1920. During this decade a million Mexicans died and many others sought refuge across the border in the United States. A number of refugees were middle class and some were revolutionary leaders. They estab-

lished strong cultural centers with vigorous newspapers in such cities as San Antonio, Texas, and Los Angeles. This great influx was responsible for the rapid increase in the number of permanent Mexican immigrants in the United States, which jumped from 100,000 in 1900 to 500,000 by 1920. The major population flow in the Southwest was no longer dominated by the Anglos.

Most of the Mexican-Americans (Chicanos) had become a permanent, migrant, agricultural labor force that traveled across the country cultivating and picking crops as they ripened. The workers were paid the lowest possible wages by Anglo landowners; they lived in shacks and their children worked with them in the fields. To keep wages low, Anglo agricultural corporations persuaded Congress in 1917 to waive immigration restrictions on agricultural labor. As a result, if the Chicanos organized strikes for better pay and living conditions, their employers could always import new workers from Mexico to displace the strikers. Socially the Anglos in the Southwest defined the Chicanos as a dirty and inferior race comparable to blacks. Without property, speaking Spanish, and constantly moving, the Chicanos were not able to develop significant political power until the 1960s.

A NEW ADOLESCENCE

Even though it dominated the development of the urban-industrial frontier, the Anglo-Protestant middle class was undergoing great internal stress. Before corporations became the major institutions of American economic growth, middle-class status usually meant being a small businessman. This class tended to see the development of "character" as the key to success. It was strength of character that enabled young men to leave home and become independent. By 1900, however, most of the opportunities for young men to enter the middle class lay in developing careers in the expanding corporations. Jobs in the professions, for example, increased from 230,000 in 1870 to 1,150,000 in 1910, and those in trade, finance, and real estate from 800,000 to 2,800,000 in the same period. The key to a successful career, then, was not so much character as it was education.

Before the Civil War it seemed possible for a young man of sixteen who had great strength of character to leave home and with hard work, rather than inherited wealth, to establish a business of his own. The formation of U.S. Steel as the first billion-dollar corporation in 1901, however, reflected the huge sums necessary to finance the factories that produced for the national market. As factory production increased and new machinery could be operated by unskilled workers, many teenaged boys took jobs in the factories. They found, however, that they were in dead-end jobs. Any increase in wages for this unskilled labor peaked by the time the average worker was twenty-five.

If the sons of the middle class were to escape these dead-end jobs, it seemed clear that they would have to stay in school longer. This pressure led to a significant increase in the number of students going to high school and then to college. The new emphasis on education for a career changed the nature of college education. Earlier in the nineteenth century, colleges, like families, tried to develop character in the students. In the new situation, however, a college freshman was expected to be a high school or private school graduate, and he came to college at the age of eighteen to prepare for a career. The emphasis on formal education meant it

was no longer possible for a young man to become a lawyer, doctor, engineer, or college professor by working directly as an apprentice under established professionals in these fields. Now in order to become certified as a lawyer, one went to law school; or as a doctor, to medical school; or as an engineer, to engineering school; or as a college teacher, to graduate school. Between the Civil War and 1900, professional associations were organized in all these fields to ensure that standards were upheld in the training of new members and that established members did not betray their professional standards.

As young men spent more time in formal training, psychologists noticed a significant change in the stages of life. Reflecting this insight, psychologist G. Stanley Hall invented the concept of adolescence to justify the lengthening dependence of young middle-class men on their fathers. The parents of these young men, who were no longer encouraged to leave home at sixteen but who were to be supported until graduation from college at twenty-two, were informed by Hall and other theorists that their sons were incapable of emotional maturity until their early twenties. Thought to be psychologically immature for several years after they reached sexual maturity, these older "boys" were to be protected from the stress of sexual as well as economic decisions until they came of age. The consequent fear of youthful sexuality on the part of middle-class parents caused them to become obsessed with masturbation. Indeed, a best-selling book, *Natural History and Hygiene* (1900), by Dr. J. H. Kellogg provided anxious fathers and mothers with thirty-nine signs they should look for in their sons in order to tell if they were practicing this form of self-destruction.

Many other books were written to guide

young men in the new urban environment. The authors cautioned them to avoid the temptations of drink and fallen women. Young men were advised to marry women of character like their mothers. Such women would help their careers and provide a home that protected their husbands from the evils that abounded in the city. But these self-help books, often written by doctors, also revealed a fear of all women.

In the mid-nineteenth century, middle-class culture had developed a "cult of true womanhood" that defined respectable women as incapable of expressing sexual pleasure. Women, therefore, were supposed to be more spiritual than men. But contradicting this idea of female spirituality was the belief that women were controlled by their bodies and not by their minds. This concept justified the exclusion of women from politics because, it was claimed, they could not think as rationally as men could. Men, therefore, were put in the impossible situation of viewing their mothers and their wives as sexless but, at the same time, as being completely defined by sex. In the eyes of a man, a woman could quickly change, then, from an individual of angelic spirituality into a creature of frightening bodily appetites.

Many doctors in the late nineteenth century believed that "Woman was what she is in health, in character, in her charms, alike in body, mind, and soul because of her womb alone," and after menopause she was "degraded to the level of a being who has no further duty to perform in this world." Young men were warned not to allow their wives to become interested in sexual pleasure because such a woman would become "a drag on the energy, spirit, and resolution of her partner." Young married men, according to this view, needed all their energy to pursue their careers and could not afford to "spend" any in unnecessary sexual activities.

This growing fear of women's sexuality in the late nineteenth century contributed to the development by male doctors of operations to remove the hood above the clitoris, the clitoris itself, or the ovaries. These extreme and infrequent operations, according to the doctors, made women "tractable, orderly, industrious, and cleanly." Male doctors further established control of female sexuality when they persuaded middle-class women to forego childbirth at home with the help of midwives. By 1900 most middle-class women delivered their babies in the scientific environment of the hospitals with the help of doctors who had professional training. But working-class women continued to have their babies at home. Perhaps one reason that doctors were concerned with controlling the sexuality of middle-class women was that increasing numbers of these women were choosing to limit the size of their families. In that sense, the middle-class woman was asserting independent control of her body.

The desire by upper-middle-class men to control bodily activities also influenced the development of team sports. The shift from baseball, which focused on the individual, to football, with its emphasis on team work, reflected the commitment of the upper middle class to a corporate economy. In 1850 individual enterprise was viewed as the key to the growth of the marketplace, and baseball, the national game at the time of the Civil War, did indeed remain popular with the lower middle class in 1900. Baseball, like the economy of small businessmen of the Civil War era, assumed that each individual on the team, as both a hitter and fielder, could demonstrate his individual skills; record keeping distinguished one athlete's prowess from another's. But members of the upper middle class, who were pioneering the development of the corporation, began to introduce football as a major college sport for their sons in the 1880s and 1890s.

Although under the new definition of adolescence young men were not supposed to make independent judgments until they were college graduates, they were encouraged by their elders to develop very aggressive characteristics while they were in school. This aggression, however, was channeled into team cooperation rather than individual competition. And the football team was like the corporation or army regiment, which could defeat the enemy by the strong discipline of its members. It concentrated energy in a disciplined group whose success depended on all members of the team moving together at the same time. Obedience to the coach and quarterback was essential. The football stadium thus served as a training ground for the talents necessary for corporate success.

The new definition of adolescence, as worked out by the middle class, proposed that boys were instinctively violent. Until they matured, boys were like early primitive man who also was instinctively violent. This predisposition toward violence was to be encouraged, provided it was controlled by adult men. The private schools of the upper middle class developed patterns of military discipline for the boys who boarded at such schools. Similarly the Boy Scouts of America, which emerged soon after 1900, encouraged the sons of the urban middle class to learn the skills of primitive man in the fields and forests outside the city. But such activities were strictly supervised by the military discipline of an adult scoutmaster, and boys were expected to wear uniforms that displayed the badges of rank.

All the major middle-class magazines in the

1890s viewed men of power as national heroes. These ideal men would have "steel blue eyes," a "prominent chin showing [an] aggressive spirit," and "jaws wired with steel." They would have the "shoulders of a Hercules," an "intense animal vitality," and "tremendous, even gigantic, physical endurance." An easterner with an Ivy League background, Owen Wister, wrote the first successful cowboy novel, *The Virginian* (1906), which celebrated such a hero. Adolescents also were encouraged to identify with the simple and violent hero of the Tarzan stories, written by Edgar Rice Burroughs.

The new pattern of delaying economic and sexual maturity for young men was extended to the lower middle class when attendance in public high schools was made compulsory after 1900. By 1917 thirty-eight states had enacted laws demanding that young people remain in school until they were sixteen. Disciplined and competitive sports, played in uniforms under the direction of adults, which first developed in the private schools and eastern universities, became the most prestigious activity for high school boys.

A NEW IDENTITY FOR WOMEN

The problems of achieving adult status for young middle-class men were shared by the young women of the same class. In the nineteenth century it was expected that middle-class women, unlike those of the lower classes, would stay at home and not go out to earn money. The pressures on middle-class married women were pointedly identified in this Philadelphia newspaper statement: "A woman is nobody. A wife is everything. The ladies of Philadelphia therefore are resolved to maintain their right as wives, virgins, and mothers, and not as women." In contrast, half of the black wives were employed as servants and, in the South, in agriculture as well. Almost every young black woman worked before marriage, as did most of the newly arrived immigrant women. Many of these female immigrants from southern and eastern Europe worked in factories. Where resistance to work outside the home was an especially strong tradition, as among Italians, the women worked at home making such goods as cigars, hats, and artificial flowers.

In the first decades of the twentieth century, more women took jobs before marriage. The rapid expansion of public schools, hospitals, and libraries created many special "women's" jobs as teachers, nurses, and librarians. But in 1900 only 10 percent of employment opportunities for women were of such vaguely professional character. Thirty-six percent of all female employment was in domestic services, 24 percent in manufacturing, and 15 percent in agriculture; 8 percent was in sales, and 4 percent in secretarial work. By 1920, however, the expanding paperwork of the corporations and government agencies caused stenography to provide 17 percent of all jobs for women.

An indication of the increasing confusion about the role of women in middle-class society was the decision to send girls to college. Unlike their brothers, college-bound girls were not to be trained for careers. Instead they were expected to marry after graduation and spend their lives, like their less-educated mothers, as nurturers of husbands and children. Although college-educated young women were supposed to revert to a dependent status as adults, the campus years away from home provided the

first break in the chain of the nineteenth-century middle-class pattern of young women staying at home with their mothers until they moved into the homes of their husbands.

In contrast to the college experience of young men, which was designed deliberately to delay their independence and prolong their childishness, this further stage of education for women probably increased their chances of developing a sense of personality independent of their parents. The new adolescence for teenage males stressed their dependence on adult leadership. College years meant a special youth culture of organized sports, recreational activities, fraternities, social events, and student government. These "playful" activities were a forced substitute that kept young men from direct participation in social and economic "realities." For women, life at home was supposed to shield them from those "realities."

Many young women felt a great sense of liberation on going off to college, and they developed a sense of self-worth in making friendships with other women. This lifestyle and the opportunity for friendships with other women prevailed at the most prestigious women's colleges such as Vassar and Mount Holyoke and proved so attractive that more than half the graduates from these schools, in the generation before World War One, chose not to marry. Barred from most of the professional careers held by men from their social group, many of these upper-middle-class women devoted their energies to reform as volunteer social workers.

Charlotte Perkins Gilman, in her book *Women and Economics* (1898), grappled with the basic problem of middle-class women — namely, that they could be either married and dependent or single and independent (although without many economic opportunities). Gilman had become so depressed in the first years of her marriage that she was unable to fulfill her responsibilities as a wife and mother, and she left her husband and child. Speaking from her experience, she wrote: "The more absolutely woman is segregated to sex functions only, cut off from all economic use and made wholly dependent on the sex relations as a means of livelihood, the more pathological does her motherhood become." Gilman advocated that all married women hold jobs outside the home. This lifestyle would be possible if such household duties as cooking and child raising were collectivized. Some women and men could choose as their profession to be cooks for groups of families or to work in nurseries caring for the children of women who worked in industry or education.

The use of maids by Anglo-Protestant middle-class women reached its peak around 1890 and then declined. Middle-class women filled part of their leisure time by joining clubs such as this one in New York City, where they often listened to lectures or concerts. (Brown Brothers)

Gilman, however, like many of the feminist leaders of 1900, felt uneasy about sexual pleasure, fearing that sexuality perpetuated female dependence on men. But within the middle class, there were signs that inhibitions on female sexuality were breaking down. By 1900 the practice of chaperoning single women began to decline, and more respectable young women were "petting" with young men in the new separate youth culture. Even the commitment to premarital virginity was weakening.

By 1900 it was possible to imagine independence for a woman as a form of personal happiness. Kate O'Flaherty Chopin, in her novel *The Awakening* (1899), explored the life of a woman, Edna Pontellier, who decides that her relationship to her husband and children was one of duty, not of love. Deciding to sacrifice herself no longer, she sought personal fulfillment in a love affair with a younger man. Chopin realized that the social pressures against this kind of choice were so great that the novel would have to end in the tragedy of Edna's suicide.

Another novel, Sinclair Lewis's *Main Street* (1920), presents perhaps the only woman in American literature before World War Two not to be totally crushed by her rebellion. Carol Kennicott, a college graduate just before World War One, feels suffocated in a marriage that denies her any independence. Having lived in the youth culture of young women who manage to escape direct male domination, and having held a job in the city, she is unable to accept the myth of true womanhood in the small town where her husband has his medical practice. She is defeated, however, when she tries to develop a lifestyle as a "liberated" woman. She leaves her husband, taking her child with her when she goes to a distant city to find a job. Eventually she returns to her hus-

band, but with newly won strength to resist the social pressures that define a married woman as childlike, merely a cipher without her husband.

Chopin and Lewis accurately portrayed in their novels the overwhelming odds against women who challenged the established social order that defined a woman's life as dependent on that of men. Even the partial liberation of the middle-class women who went to college put them in a new position of dependence on men. Just as male doctors were working to take childbirth and health care out of the home and the control of women and put them into the hands of professionals, so too did college-educated women insist that the rearing of children must be based on scientific principles, not on traditions passed down from generations of mothers to their daughters. College education for young middle-class women, therefore, broke the apprenticeship relation of daughters to their mothers and encouraged them to look for expert advice as an alternative foundation for their roles as housewives and mothers.

This expert advice came from male members of the medical and academic professions. The experts advised college-educated women to reject the undisciplined and "womanly" traditions of their mothers and to be more like professional men in providing disciplined and objective training for their children. Dr. L. Emmett Hold, whose *Care and Feeding of Children* was one of the most influential of the child-care books from 1894 to 1920, told women to feed and hold their children according to a strict schedule. He warned them not to break the schedule to pick up babies when they cried; nor should they give them pacifiers. John B. Watson, a leading psychologist, argued that "no one today knows enough to raise a child." He agreed with Holt, however, that scientific principles could replace useless tradition. He also agreed with Holt that such scientific principles were opposed to maternal affection. "Never hug and kiss them," he insisted, "never let them sit on your lap." For Watson it was absolutely necessary for the proper discipline of that child that it be toilet trained as early as possible. Breaking away from their mothers, therefore, college-educated women by 1920 accepted a new type of dependence — the advice of medical and academic experts who were men.

SUGGESTED READINGS

The decline of rural America is discussed in Henry Nash Smith, *Virgin Land: The American West as Symbol and Myth* (1950), Richard Hofstadter, *The Age of Reform* (1955), and Robert Wiebe, *The Search for Order* (1968). Howard Chudacoff, *The Evolution of American Urban Society* (1975), provides an excellent overview of the process of urbanization. Sam Bass Warner, *Street-Car Suburbs* (1971), describes the emergence of the ring pattern of the twentieth-century city. He also discusses the economic and social pressures that made for the standardization of most city and suburban housing.

Urban entertainment is the subject of Orrin Klapp, *The Collective Search for Identity* (1969), Michael Novak, *The Joy of Sports* (1976), David Voight, *America Through Baseball* (1976), Gregory P. Stone, *Games, Sports, and Power* (1972), Roy Huss and Norman Silverstein, *The Film Experience* (1968), and Albert McLean, Jr., *American Vaudeville as Ritual* (1965).

Stephan Thernstrom, *The Other Bostonians* (1973), uses masses of statistical evidence to find the different patterns of upward economic mobility experienced by Anglo-Protestants, the various European immigrants, and blacks between 1880 and 1920. Anglo-Protestant fear of the new immigration is described by John Higham, *Strangers in the Land: Patterns of American Nativism* (1955), and Barbara Solomon, *Ancestors and Immigrants* (1956). The special fear of Jewish immigrants, expressed by the white Protestant elite, is the subject of *The Protestant Establishment: Aristocracy and Caste in America* (1964) by E. Digby Baltzell.

Oscar Handlin's *The Uprooted* (1951) gives the major outlines of European migration to America, and Milton Gordon, *Assimilation in American Life* (1964), discusses the survival of ethnic identity. Moses Rischin, *The Promised City: New York's Jews, 1870–1914* (1970), and Irving Howe, *World of Our Fathers* (1976), offer rich descriptions of the Jewish community. Paul Messbarger, *Fiction with a Parochial Purpose: Social Use of American Catholic Literature, 1884–1900* (1970), provides an interesting insight into the Catholic community dominated by Irish-Americans.

Walter T. Hagan, *American Indians* (1961), is a useful overview. Dee Brown, *Bury My Heart at Wounded Knee* (1971), and Ralph Andrist, *The Long Death* (1964), give a sense of the tragedy experienced by western Native Americans in the generation after the Civil War. H. Craig Miner, *The Corporation and the Indian, 1865–1907* (1976), describes the loss of Indian lands. Hazel Hertzberg, *The Search for an American Indian Identity* (1971), is a study of the resurgence of Native American self-confidence. Excellent overviews of Chicano society and history are provided by Joan W. Moore and Alfredo Cuellar, *Mexican Americans* (1970), and Leo Grebler, Joan W. Moore, and Ralph C. Guzman, *The Mexican-*

American People (1970). The first thorough studies of the developing black ghetto are Gilbert Osofsky, *Harlem: Making of a Ghetto* (1966), and Allan Spear, *Black Chicago: The Making of a Negro Ghetto* (1967).

William O'Neill, *Everyone Was Brave: The Rise and Fall of Feminism in America* (1967), Peter Filene, *Him Herself: Sex Roles in Modern America* (1974), and William Chafe, *Women and Equality* (1977), are perceptive discussions of the crisis of male and female roles by 1900. Joseph Kett, *Rites of Passage* (1977), is an excellent description of the patterns of the new adolescence developing in the late nineteenth century and the stress it placed on the middle-class family. Burton J. Bledstein, *The Culture of Professionalism: The Middle Class and the Development of Higher Education in America* (1976), emphasizes the relationship of careers to this new adolescence.

Chapter 3

SOCIAL REFORM IN THE PROGRESSIVE ERA

The reform movement known as progressivism was built around the idea of a new democracy, created as an alternative to the old democracy of many small and independent producers. As industrial production became concentrated in a small number of large corporations, an emerging new middle class of urban business executives and professional men began to envision a democracy of consumers. Through legislative reform and the creation of appropriate political and social institutions, the new democracy attempted to construct a rational response to the needs of urban industrialism. Its goal was the attainment of order and harmony in a society torn apart by the chaotic conditions of late-nineteenth-century capitalism.

WOMEN REFORMERS AND PROSTITUTION

Even though women could not vote in most states and were thereby barred from activity in the political parties, middle-class women were attracted to the idea of a new democracy. From about 1850 on, women of the middle class began having fewer children. Enjoying greater life expectancy after child rearing, they began to seek out activities beyond the home. But since economic pressures did not force them to earn part of the family income, these women entered the world of men still encumbered by the Cult of True Womanhood, a mid-nineteenth-century role pattern that stressed female purity and isolated middle-class women from economic productivity outside the home. Such women compared the purity of the domestic fireside to the corrupt environment of the marketplace in which their husbands worked. Leaving the segregation of the home in the late nineteenth century, middle-class women hoped to purify both men and the marketplace.

A major concern of these women after the Civil War was the abolition of prostitution. The family in the home was supposed to live by the principle of shared love, and no family member was meant to exploit others selfishly. At home, men were guided by the pure, nonsexual love of their wives. But outside the home environment, men behaved selfishly and became prisoners of sexual lust. Once in the marketplace, they sexually exploited the helpless young women who were slaves in houses of prostitution.

For women reformers, joined by many male Protestant ministers, a major crusade of the 1870s and 1880s, therefore, was to end the double standard. Middle-class men were to be saved from the ethical code that allowed them to be promiscuous. Abolishing prostitution would not only liberate the female slaves, but also free their male customers to be as monogamous and as disinterested in sex as their wives. Two of the first American women physicians, Elizabeth Blackwell and Caroline Wilson, were leaders in this crusade for social purity, as was Antoinette Blackwell, the first woman ordained as a Protestant minister. The purity crusade also won the support of established leaders for women's rights such as Susan B. Anthony and Frances Willard, president of the Women's Christian Temperance Union (WCTU).

From its experience with millions of soldiers during the Civil War, the American Medical Association (AMA) advocated government regulation and medical inspection of prostitutes. But women reformers formed Moral Education societies to lobby against the regulation bills being considered by a number of state legislatures and Congress. By 1885, when these women called a National Conference for Moral Education, they had forced the AMA to withdraw its support of regulation, and their campaign had defeated all legislative attempts to establish government regulation of prostitution.

In crusading against prostitution, these middle-class Anglo-Protestant women were challenging one of the major tenets of nineteenth-century Protestantism — the idea that the individual always was responsible for his or her actions regardless of environmental circumstances. But for women like the Blackwells, there was a close relationship between sin and social environment. They clearly realized that urban growth depended on the migration of young people from the American and European countryside. Girls from rural backgrounds easily became lost and bewildered in this chaotic urban environment. Wicked men just as easily misled them with false promises; suddenly they found themselves as white slaves in houses of prostitution, trapped until an early death provided their only escape.

Women of the Anglo-Protestant elite maintained close contact with activists in England such as Josephine Butler and Florence Nightingale, who had fought against regulation in a similar English environment of rapidly growing cities. These reformers had established a White Cross Society in the Church of England to give sex education to lower-class girls and to provide them with safe housing as they arrived in the city. The Protestant Episcopal Church, the sister organization in America of the Church of England, emulated the White Cross Society,

These middle-class women in Minneapolis were characteristic of the efforts of Anglo-Protestant women during the Progressive Era to teach social responsibility to the lower class. Later, professional social workers would take over many of these reform activities. (Minnesota Historical Society and Norton & Paul, Minneapolis)

while the interdenominational WCTU created a White Shield Society for the same purpose. Traveler's Aid societies also were established in railroad stations and ports in both England and the United States to provide safety for rural immigrants to the city.

Purity crusaders further attempted to protect young women in the unstable urban environ-ment by persuading states to pass laws that raised the age of sexual consent. In some states a girl of seven could legally consent to sexual relations with a man. This standard made con-victions for sexual exploitation or rape of young women almost impossible. Persistent lobbying to raise the age, however, succeeded in a num-ber of states by 1900. Most of the new laws set the age of consent at fourteen or sixteen. But in the Broderick Act of 1899, Congress set the age of consent at twenty-one for the District of Columbia and the territories. Application by all states of the higher age standard was the goal of the social purity movement.

Committed to the idea that the individual was strongly influenced by the social environment, purity crusaders wanted teenage prostitutes placed in reformatories instead of jails. Imprisonment, they believed, might permanently corrupt young women through exposure to hardened criminals. Instead, the reformers were confident that young fallen women could be redeemed when placed in a healthy environment. A related reform was to have young prostitutes cared for by police matrons rather than by policemen, who might sexually abuse the girls. Women activists of the 1890s were successful in getting a number of states to institute reformatories and assign police matrons to young offenders.

WOMEN AND SOCIAL REFORM

By the 1890s a number of highly visible and important men such as Lyman Abbott, a Protestant theologican and editor of the magazine *Outlook,* were drawn to the purity crusade. Abbott's commitment reflected a more general conversion of many men and women in the Protestant churches to a larger movement known as the Social Gospel. The theology of the Social Gospel embraced the purity movement's insistence on the relationship between sin and social environment, emphasizing that many individuals could be redeemed from sinfulness if their environment were improved.

Although the Social Gospel antagonized southern Methodists and Baptists, who clung to nineteenth-century doctrines of complete individual responsibility, it provided the purity crusade with a forceful ally.

Women reformers believed that the ideal of the nineteenth-century home provided the foundation for a philosophy of social responsibility and control. One of the signs of social irresponsibility that most bothered the purity crusaders was the "continental" Sunday given over to picnics, dancing, and beer drinking. The Cult of True Womanhood had defined religion as the near-monopoly of women, since women were considered purer and more spiritual than men. Sunday at the home of the Victorian middle-class woman was a day of spirituality and culture. Respectable families went to church and then to lectures, concerts, or museums.

To end the continental Sunday and restore the "puritan" Sabbath, women reformers urged the prohibition of the sale of liquor. The Women's Christian Temperance Union, founded in 1874 expressly to lobby for prohibition legislation, which they hoped would open the door to other reforms to help women and children, won wide support among women in the late nineteenth century. Prohibition activists reasoned that America could not become temperate until the purity of the home became universal. As Dr. Will K. Kellogg, founder of a cereal empire and a convert to the purity crusade, wrote, "The exorbitant demands of the sexual appetite encountered among civilized people are not the result of a normal instinct, but are due to the incitements of an abnormally stimulating diet, including alcohol, the seduction of prurient literature and so-called art, and the temptations of impure associations."

Women purity crusaders pressed their cause

on many fronts. Accepting leadership from Josiah Leeds in Philadelphia and Anthony Comstock in New York, women activists worked for censorship of books, newspapers, magazines, and theater in the attempt to create a wholesome and nonsexual environment. Under this pressure, states also began to legislate against abortions. Until the passage of such laws, states had worked within the inherited English common law, which had permitted abortions well into pregnancy. The purity crusade also managed to ban birth control literature from circulation and to prohibit the sale of devices for birth control. After a National Purity Congress in 1895, activists pressed editors of large newspapers toward self-censorship of unsavory material. Three years later, both the International League of Press Clubs and the American Newspaper Publishers Association came out in favor of a pure press free from suggestive sexuality.

The purity crusade further persuaded states to pass laws forcing drugstores to stop selling heroin and morphine across the counter. The momentum of the crusade soon accelerated from the local to the national level. Congress passed the Harrison Narcotic Act in 1914, which required federal registration of all drug producers, a record of all sales, a tax on receipts, and a doctor's prescription for drugs. The success of the purity crusade was demonstrated by the establishment of vice commissions to suppress prostitution in every major city by 1900. Congress also passed the Mann Act of 1910, which made it a federal crime to transport a woman across state lines for immoral purposes.

In their concern to make all society as pure as the mid-nineteenth-century home was supposed to be, women reformers attempted to es-

tablish wholesome guidance for the children of poor and immigrant families. The League for the Protection of the Family (1896) advocated compulsory education as a means of getting poor children into classrooms, where middle-class women could create such an environment as teachers. The Mothers Congress of 1896 became the forerunner of the national Parents-Teachers Association. As the purity crusade became organized into a number of national institutions by the 1890s, women leaders felt impelled to make reform a profession. Their aspirations toward professionalism paralleled the emphasis on professionalism by the men of the new middle class. Anna Gorlin Spencer, a Unitarian minister, left the pulpit to participate in the professional education of social workers at the New York School of Social Work. Women leaders also pushed for the establishment of a Teachers College at Columbia University in New York to serve as a professional model for teachers colleges throughout the nation.

WOMEN AND THE VOTE

The movement to win the vote for women gained a new identity and strength from the purity crusade in the 1890s. Middle-class women had become active in reform during the 1840s when some of them supported the abolitionist movement. The philosophy of the abolitionists was based on the natural law doctrines of the Declaration of Independence. In crusading for the liberty of blacks, women of the white Protestant elite discovered that they, themselves, had little liberty. They were bitterly disappointed that the Fourteenth Amendment in 1867 specifically included only black males as

Margaret Sanger

1883-1966

Many middle-class women dramatically changed their views on family size, birth control, and their own sexuality during the Progressive era. The woman who most forcefully symbolized this revolution was birth control crusader Margaret Sanger. Her briefly published magazine, the Woman Rebel, *described women in 1912 as enslaved "by the machine, by wage slavery, by bourgeois morality, by customs, laws, and superstitions."*

Sanger was brought before the courts several times between 1912 and 1917 for breaking laws that forbade public discussion of birth control methods. But by 1920 she had the support of most middle-class women leaders for her crusade to make knowledge of birth control techniques available to all women. And she had disassociated this crusade from the general concern for human liberation that had been her position in 1912.

Sanger was one of eleven children born to a lower-income family in the factory town of Corning, New York. She hated her father for killing her mother at an early age with all these children. But she loved him for breaking with his Catholic faith and for encouraging her to be independent. Without the financial support to become a doctor, Sanger went into nursing as a career because "the thought of marriage was akin to suicide." After graduation, however, she married a man from a higher economic and social background. For a decade Sanger lived a suburban life with her three children. Then she and her husband decided to move to Greenwich Village and lead a liberated lifestyle. Her magazine, the Woman Rebel, *expressed the hopes of many middle-class male and female radicals that a peaceful revolution was about to take place that would free all individuals to fulfill their own identities.*

Sanger preached birth control for middle-class women so they could be free to develop a rich sex life apart from child bearing. She misread the writings of Sigmund Freud to mean that the father of psychiatry wanted women to escape from the repression of their capacity for bodily pleasure. Sanger found support for this misreading from the Swedish feminist Ellen Key. She visited the English psychologist and authority on sex Havelock Ellis and inspected birth control clinics in Holland in 1914 and 1915 while avoiding arrest for her attempts to bring birth control information to lower-income women in New York.

Between 1917 and 1920, however, Sanger abandoned her war against repressive institutions and became the head of national organizations dedicated to the spread of birth control information. Working with women from the traditional elites, she emphasized that birth control must be taught to the poor to stop the growing population of the "unfit foreigners" from southern and eastern Europe. With this change in attitude, Sanger won increasing support from men of the American-born Protestant elite.

citizens and therefore constitutionally excluded women from citizenship for the first time.

From 1869 to 1890 two major middle-class women's organizations worked to win full citizenship for women. Elizabeth Cady Stanton headed the National Woman's Suffrage Association and Lucy Stone headed the American Woman's Suffrage Association. Stone wanted to focus on the single issue of winning the vote and did not sympathize with Stanton's wide social criticisms. In 1890, however, the two organizations merged as the National American Woman's Suffrage Association (NAWSA). Stanton and Susan B. Anthony now were willing to restrain their general criticisms of the male establishment and to focus on winning the vote. Only the new western states of Wyoming, Colorado, Idaho, and Utah, entering the Union in the 1890s, included women as voters. There were no hopeful signs that women's suffrage would win in any of the older states. Indeed, it was not until 1910 that the next state, Washington, enfranchised women. Illinois, in 1913, was the first state east of the Mississippi to accept women as voters.

There is strong evidence that winning the vote for women was not a popular reform among either middle-class women or men until World War One. Membership in NAWSA increased from only 13,000 in 1893 to 45,000 in 1907 and to 100,000 in 1915. Then it exploded to two million in 1917. The appeal of universal principles of justice embodied in the Declaration of Independence was not effective in any state that had a well-established governmental structure.

National enfranchisement of women, enacted by the Nineteenth Amendment in 1920, may have come about because middle-class women associated themselves with other reforms that were more popular with middle-class

By 1890, middle-class women were intensifying their campaign to win the vote. This poster of one of the major women leaders, Frances Willard, dramatizes the outrage respectable women felt at being barred from citizenship, as were convicts, idiots, Indians, and insane people. (Sophia Smith Collection/Smith College)

danger," Carrie Chapman declared in 1894. "There is but one way to avert the danger — cut off the vote of the slums and give it to women." For Catt, the vote for women would double the political strength of Anglo-Protestants throughout the country without doubling the immigrant and black vote. Ninety percent of all blacks lived in the South, and since black men were now effectively disenfranchised in that region, there was no real chance for black women to enter into politics. In the North, suffragists recognized that a much higher percentage of middle-class people voted than of the lower class. By 1903, NAWSA also favored a national literacy test for voting that would disqualify many immigrants, male and female. These views made it possible for a delegate at the 1903 convention to declare that NAWSA "has always recognized the usefulness of woman suffrage as a counterbalance to the foreign vote, and as a means of legally preserving white supremacy in the South."

PROHIBITION AND NATIONAL REFORM

The movement for women's suffrage was greatly benefited by women's endorsement of prohibition. Protestant men more readily supported prohibition legislation than they did women's rights, but they recognized the potential political strength of like-minded women.

Prohibition was the most powerful symbol for reform during the progressive period because it created a sense of a united Anglo-Protestant culture. Protestant fundamentalists and Social Gospel advocates were deeply suspicious of each other but agreed on the importance of prohibition. This common interest pro-

men. Many of these reforms denied the universal principles of the Declaration of Independence and were designed to restrict rather than expand rights exercised by all citizens. By 1900 the new leaders of NAWSA, Carrie Chapman Catt and Anna Howard Shaw, were asking that women get the vote so they could help men of the white Protestant elite protect the purity of the nation from immigrants and blacks. "This government is menaced with great vided a bond between the Northeast and Midwest, where the Social Gospel was strongest, and the South and West, where fundamentalism was strongest. Within the South, deep antagonisms between lower-middle-class farmers and upper-middle-class whites who looked toward urban industrialism were bridged by the shared commitment to prohibition. On this issue, academic agnostics in the social sciences and universities found themselves in agreement with both Social Gospel and fundamentalist ministers. Businessmen and professors also discovered a mutual concern in prohibition. And Protestant men were forcefully reminded by Protestant women that it was the women who had pioneered the prohibition issue in the 1880s and 1890s.

Middle-class reformers in the cities also saw prohibition as a tool in the crusade to clean up urban politics. Urban professionals frequently complained that city elections were controlled by "the dangerous classes who are readily dominated by the saloon." Indeed, saloons served as centers for the political machines created by big-city bosses. Drinking places also functioned as social centers where new immigrants could gather to speak their ethnic languages and reinforce their sense of ethnic culture. And unions and radical political groups readily used such places as natural meeting halls.

The men of the new middle class who wanted to recapture control of the city in the 1890s could easily see the value of the Anti-Saloon League, which was founded in 1895. If the government banned saloons, the power of the political machine would collapse. Since Protestant elite reformers hoped to introduce the rationality and efficiency of the corporation to city government, they thought it necessary to undermine ethnic culture, which they saw as irrational and inefficient. For example, the

number of church holidays brought over from Europe conflicted with the ideal of a standardized work week. A strong sense of ethnic identity also might lead workers to question the authority of American-born leaders. The ideal of a corporate team working cooperatively left no more room for independent unions or radical politics than it did for ethnic diversity.

Medical authorities also supported the prohibition movement. Frequently quoted in the muckracing journals of the Progressive era, scientists pointed out that "every function of the normal human body is injured by the use of alcohol — even the moderate use; and that the injury is both serious and permanent." By 1917 the American Medical Association endorsed national prohibition. Its president, Dr. Charles Mayo, declared that the medical profession believed alcohol to be "detrimental to the human economy."

A major impetus for prohibition, however, came from industrialists. Industry increasingly felt pressure from progressive reformers to provide safer working conditions for employees, since the rate of factory and mine accidents was much higher in the United States than in other industrial countries. Progressives argued that unsafe working conditions violated principles of rationality and efficiency, and that accidents forced unnecessary suffering on workers and their families. U.S. Steel established the first major industrial safety program in 1908. As the states began to implement workmen's compensation laws in 1911, it became a matter of economic interest for businessmen to reduce the rate of accidents.

Major corporations stressed that temperance was essential to industrial safety. The National Safety Council, formed by leading industrialists in 1912, declared that "the drinking of alcoholic stimulants is productive of a heavy percentage of accidents and of disease affecting the safety and efficiency of working men." Business leaders distributed Anti-Saloon League pamphlets to their workers. Impressed by the success of local prohibition in a number of cities, manufacturers and large-scale employers shifted from temperance to support for national prohibition. Businessmen claimed to discover that prohibition "has been accompanied by an increase in bank deposits. It is invariably beneficial to employers of labor and in cities where it has been in force for more than a year, there is but little discontent with the dry regime among the masses."

In the South, prohibition won support from a coalition of urban reformers and Protestant fundamentalists. The reformers, led by Episcopalian minister Edgar Gardner Murphy and Presbyterian spokesman Alexander McKelvey, were concerned with crime among blacks and lynchings by white vigilantes. McKelvey argued that blacks were "a child race in the south, and if drunkenness caused three-fourths of the crime ascribed to it, whiskey must be taken out of the Negro's hands." But reformers blamed the availability of liquor for the political irrationality and social instability that bred lynchings. One prohibitionist asserted that "two-thirds of the mobs, lynchings, and burning at the stake are the result of whiskey drunk by bad black and bad white men." McKelvey pleaded that prohibition would not only control blacks but would discipline whites, since its enactment signified "the deliberate determination of the stronger race to forego its own personal liberty for the protection of the weaker race."

Most white southerners, however, supported prohibition out of a fundamentalist commitment to purity. Using thousands of southern Methodist and Baptist churches as a base, the Anti-Saloon League built a powerful southern coalition of local organizations committed to voting counties or cities dry. By 1907 two-thirds of the counties in the South had exercised this local option. In the next two years, Georgia, Mississippi, North Carolina, Tennessee, and Alabama adopted state prohibition. Fourteen more states across the nation enacted prohibition between 1914 and 1916, while the Webb-Kenyon Act of 1913 permitted dry states to interfere with the transportation of liquor across their own state lines.

When marchers in a huge parade in Washington, D.C., demanded a constitutional amendment to make the entire country dry in 1913, lower-middle-class whites in the South were convinced that fundamentalist values were about to prevail nationally. Equating fundamentalism with the American way, southern Baptists and Methodists were threatened by the infusion of Catholics and Jews into the nation's mainstream. And they were angry at the development of liberalism among northern Protestants, which effectively divided the ranks of Protestants in the face of these alien religions. But the growth of prohibitionist sentiment after 1900, climaxing in congressional acceptance of the Eighteenth Amendment in 1917, seemed to indicate that history was now moving against the modernist heresy and the Old World faiths of Catholicism and Judaism.

LIBERAL PROTESTANISM AND REFORM

While religious fundamentalists were confident that the United States was about to be redeemed in 1917 by returning to an earlier time of purity, theologians of liberal Protestantism believed that Americans had evolved to a new, higher level of spirituality. Until the 1880s almost all Protestants in Europe and America had accepted the Bible as the literal revelation of the word of God. By 1850, however, European scholars believed they had evidence that the Bible was written over a period of several thousand years. This revisionist view of the Bible made it easier for some Protestants to accept the idea of evolution when it was given persuasive expression by the Englishman Charles Darwin in the 1860s and 1870s. These liberal or modernist Protestants gave up the literal interpretation of the Bible and moved toward interpreting it symbolically. For instance, they believed that God had not actually created the world in seven days; rather the word "day" symbolized millions of years. For converts to liberal Protestantism, God revealed himself through time, and physical evolution was an expression of that continuing revelation. Part of the new revelation was the goodness of cities and industry.

Liberal Protestants delivered the hopeful message that the urban-industrial environment did not mark the loss of Christian democracy but rather created the opportunity for more democracy. Walter Rauschenbusch, a Baptist minister who had a congregation in New York City before he became a professor at Rochester Theological Seminary, emerged as the most important spokesman for liberal Protestantism and the Social Gospel. In his first book, *Christianity and the Social Crisis* (1907), Rauschenbusch argued that industrialism had brought humanity to a new era in history that gave added urgency to the age-old choice between the Kingdom of God on Earth and the triumph of evil. He reassured his readers that industrialism, by increasing international communications and transportation, was creating a world-wide community or family. Rauschenbusch and other spokesmen for the Social Gospel held up the nineteenth-century family as the alternative model to laissez faire capitalism. But at the same time that he mustered evidence from historians, economists, and sociologists to prove that the world was becoming more cooperative, Rauschenbusch insisted that the birth of the new era could be assured only through a Christian spiritual revival.

Inspired by the broad reform energies of his generation, Rauschenbusch believed by 1912 that spiritual regeneration was occurring in the hearts of the majority of Americans. The "social awakening of our nation," he proclaimed, "has set in like an equinoctical gale." In the progressive movement, he saw "religious energy rising from the depth of that infinite spiritual life in which we all live and move and have our being." Rauschenbusch shared the progressive faith in a coming millenium, and for this theologian of the Social Gospel, the Christian virtues of family, cooperation, love, and equality had become established in the churches, schools, and politics and were about to win over the economy.

PROFESSORS AND REFORM

John Dewey, the most famous philosopher of education in the Progressive period, also looked to industrialism to usher in a new worldwide cooperative community. Dewey shared Rauschenbusch's faith that industrialism could destroy undemocratic societies and liberate individuals. For Dewey, however, the schools would play a central role in hastening the transition from the old overcompetitive order. Schools would "see that each individual gets an opportunity to escape from the limitations of the social group in which he was born," Dewey wrote, "and to come into living contact with a broader environment." Dewey supported the emphasis that social reformers placed on compulsory schooling in the Progressive era. He argued that "the intermingling in the school of youth of different races, differing religions, and unlike customs creates for all a new and broader environment. Common subject matter accustoms all to a unity of outlook upon a broader horizon than is visible to the members of any group while it is isolated." The foremost advocate of "progressive" education, which stressed learning by doing instead of memorization, Dewey hoped to create a neighborly and flexible school environment in which children could experiment. Youngsters trained in experimental and democratic values could then reconstruct society as they grew into adulthood.

For men such as Rauschenbusch and Dewey, industrialism had replaced the frontier as the dynamic force in American life. When the historian Frederick Jackson Turner pointed out in the 1890s that the United States was becoming more like Europe as it urbanized and industrialized, he warned of the loss of the nation's frontier heritage of liberty. But progressive historians such as Charles Beard insisted that urbanization and industrialism meant the beginning of liberty and a new democracy.

As a young man, Beard went to England to see for himself the impact of mass production on the nation in which industrialism had first developed. Beard returned with good reports, which were included in *The Industrial Revolution* (1901). If Americans were appalled by the "chaos and anarchy" resulting from the mechanization of production between 1865 and 1900, Beard argued, they should look to England, where industrialism was maturing. There they would see the inevitable growth of a new harmonious order of industrial democracy. "Within the last 100 years," Beard wrote, "the world has witnessed a silent revolution in English politics, which has resulted in the vesting of power in the hands of the people." For Beard, industrialism represented inevitable evolutionary progress, and he was confident that a steadily modernizing America would usher in economic democracy. Economic cooperation in the corporation, he proclaimed, pointed "to higher forms of industrial methods in which the people, instead of a few capitalists, will reap the benefits."

Through his writings on the Constitution and the founding fathers, Beard became the most influential historian of the progressive movement. Progressive reformers often expressed frustration over the system of checks and balances written into the heart of the Constitution. Beard's study of 1912, *The Supreme Court and the Constitution,* attempted to justify Theodore Roosevelt's attack on the Court for blocking social reforms. Beard emphasized that the founding fathers had given power to the Court deliberately to hinder the development of democracy. "Judicial control was a new and radical departure," Beard wrote, "which did not spring from Anglo-Saxon ideas but from the practical necessity of creating a foil for the rights of property against belligerent democracy." Beard's most famous book, *An Economic Interpretation of the Constitution* (1913), attempted to demythologize the creation of the Constitution by demonstrating the selfish economic motives of the founding fathers.

As war broke out in Europe in August 1914, American professors viewed Germany with fascination. Many had received their academic training in Germany and had brought home the seminar method of graduate school teaching. They appreciated German leadership in medicine and the use of research laboratories to improve industrial production. Others admired German innovations in urban government and social legislation. But in *German Philosophy and Politics* (1915), John Dewey found Germany to be an industrial nation that still maintained vestiges of feudalism through its Junker aristocracy. Dewey predicted conflict between Germany and the United States, since the Germans were preserving medievalism and Americans were trying to establish an international industrial democracy. The educational philosopher urged American participation in a war against German leaders in 1917. Such a just war, he argued, would use force, not violence, to free people from artificial patterns and exploitation so they could live in productive harmony with natural patterns such as industrialization and democracy.

Although Thorstein Veblen, an economist who influenced academic progressives and socialists, became a bitter opponent of American involvement in World War One, his analysis of industrialism led him to share Dewey's views on the German aristocracy. Veblen reasoned that industrialism erased national differences among workers. "The discipline of the machine," he argued, "inculcates in the habits of life and thought of the workman regularity of sequence and mechanical precision." In *Imperial Germany and the Industrial Revolution* (1914), Veblen described a Germany with an industrial population that worked by the same rational, efficient, and democratic principles as did English and American workers. But German workers awaited liberation from the Prussian masters who had begun the war in 1914. Veblen believed that the Junker aristocracy,

desperate to preserve feudal privileges and medieval values, had precipitated war to halt the spread of industrialism. With his faith in mechanization, Veblen joined those academic progressives, Social Gospel ministers, and women reformers who believed that industrialism was creating a common experience for mankind. Such shared experience would be the foundation for a new national culture in the United States that erased ethnic distinctions and emphasized democracy, neighborliness, and cooperation. And the common experience of industrialism would tie the people of the world so closely together that conflict among nations eventually would be eradicated.

BUSINESS AND EDUCATIONAL REFORM

Like Dewey and the academic progressives, business leaders desired a common culture nurtured through the schools. But corporate leaders supported compulsory high schools because they linked education to the needs of a corporate economy. One of these needs was the development of a sense of clock time. Work in factories and offices was expected to start exactly at 8 A.M., with lunch at noon and dismissal promptly at 5 or 6 P.M. Schools consequently placed great emphasis on rigid industrial time by beginning and ending classes with a bell and by harshly punishing tardiness. Compulsory education also made truancy from school a juvenile crime.

While many businessmen shared Dewey's dislike of nineteenth-century individualism, their notion of teamwork differed vastly from Dewey's concept of democratic cooperation. Each school day began with a common pledge of allegiance to the flag. The first grade moved up to the second grade as a group, while the eighth and twelfth grades graduated together as a group. In high school each class moved from one room to another room, from subject to subject, as a group. Discipline was of great importance in teaching children to sit quietly during each class in preparation for the long periods of concentration expected in the industrial work force. Collective discipline demanded that each class move simultaneously through the halls at the end of the hour with minimal talking and wandering. Children learned not to violate the laws of large institutions. As William Bagley, the author of *Classroom Management* (1907), which had thirty printings, put it, "The mechanical routine of the classroom is slowly transforming the child from a little savage into a creature of law and order, fit for the life of a civilized society."

Contrasting with Dewey's hope for a neighborly classroom, the teamwork expected by bus-

Most northern and midwestern cities had Americanization classes for the immigrants who made up almost half the population of urban America. Here some of the children of immigrants are taught the English language and learn the history that began with English colonies in the New World. (Brown Brothers)

iness leaders met the needs of the hierarchical corporation, which separated employees from management. Students were sorted out in a hierarchy, with some receiving the grade of A, some B, C, D, or F, for failure. Teachers impressed on students that it was individual initiative that earned these grades, and there was little time for a teacher with a large class to be concerned with reasons why some students were not doing well. Substantial recent statistical analysis has indicated that family background, rather than inherited biological qualities, is the most important factor in both academic and economic success. But the children of the poor were taught to believe there was a parallel between the schoolroom, where each individual could choose to be an A or an F student, and the outside world, where each could choose to be rich or poor. They were led to believe, therefore, that family background could be ignored in determining one's place on the economic pyramid, where a few were rich and many were poor.

Bagley's book was a response to criticism from businessmen that educational methods were "unscientific, crude, and wasteful." The answer to these criticisms, according to Bagley, was to make school systems as similar to corporations as possible. "A board of education is only a board of directors, the tax payers, the stockholders. The superintendent is a sales manager; the teachers, salesmen. It is proper to say that the schools are like factories turning out graduates, which, in turn, become employees of the business houses and may be considered the raw material of business."

School superintendents, at the head of the school system, were to receive professional training as business managers of large organizations. They were not trained in the specific content of an academic area or educational philosophy. Education, for them, was a "problem of economy: it seeks to determine in what manner the working unit of the school plant may be made to return the largest dividend upon the material investment of time, energy, and money." Under this system, standardized tests assumed key importance as a way of determining whether teachers were efficient in preparing their students, since the tests compared student work in different classrooms and schools. As in the corporation, authority flowed downward from the superintendent, and there was little participation by teachers or students in making educational decisions. Dewey's hopes for an educational system that might blur class divisions, therefore, were defeated by school reforms that molded young people to the patterns of corporate culture.

THE SETTLEMENT HOUSE AND REFORM

The frustrations that Dewey encountered in the public schools were shared by the group of women reformers active in the settlement house movement. The movement had begun among a small group of young upper-class Englishmen in the early 1880s. Inspired by religious spokesmen of the Social Gospel, Oxford and Cambridge University students established Toynbee Hall in London to experiment with living among the poor. Suddenly sensitive to poverty and social injustice, they hoped to bring a richer cultural environment to the poor and to learn from what they believed to be the less materialistic and acquisitive values of the working class.

Because the English tradition of male social service was virtually nonexistent in America, young middle-class women seeking alternatives to marriage could assume leadership in introducing the settlement house to the United States. A small number of young men, however, did participate in the settlement house movement and often accepted leadership from women. Envisioning a democratic society in which a true melting pot of Anglo-Protestant and ethnic cultures would come into being, leaders such as Jane Addams, Lillian Wald, and Florence Kelley helped to create more than four hundred settlement houses by 1910. These young women saw themselves as the vanguard of reform, saving the city from the evils that Addams listed as "insanitary housing, poisonous sewage, contaminated water, infant mortality, the spread of contagion, adulterated food, impure milk, smoke-laden air, ill-ventilated factories, dangerous occupations, juvenile crimes, unwholesome crowding, prostitution, and drunkenness." The young men and women of the settlement house movement hoped to establish a sense of community among slum dwellers that was based on the virtues of the middle-class home. Most settlement houses had day nurseries, playgrounds, kindergartens, and bath facilities. Classes in housekeeping and cooking were offered, as well as instruction in music and art. Some provided rooms for working girls to live in.

The optimism of the middle-class reformers about the settlement houses reflected their belief that industrial prosperity had made poverty unacceptable. Fiction writers of this period such as Hamlin Garland, who described rural poverty in his *Main-Travelled Roads* (1891), and Stephen Crane, who described the way in which urban poverty drove an innocent girl to prostitution and suicide in his novel *Maggie: A Girl of the Streets* (1892), had a great impact on middle-class readers who were conscious of the new wealth being created by industrialism. And in 1912 a Federal Commission on Industrial Relations concluded that there was no physical need for poverty in the twentieth century.

The women leaders of the settlement houses accepted the soundness of an economic system that could produce so much wealth. Consequently they focused their energies on correcting abuses within the system. The two problems that attracted most concern were those of child labor and the working conditions of women. Settlement house leaders like Kelley, Wald, and Addams joined with southern progressives like the Rev. Edgar Gardner Murphy to form a National Child Labor Committee. The committee lobbied with the state and national governments to prohibit children under fourteen from working in factories, to keep those under sixteen out of mines, and to protect child laborers from night work and work shifts of more than eight hours a day. (The number of children under sixteen working in southern textile mills had increased 130 percent during the 1890s.) The reformers won partial victories in a number of states, and in 1916 Congress passed the Keating-Owen child labor law based on these recommended standards. In 1918, however, the Supreme Court struck down such restrictions as unconstitutional.

Increased concern for children during the Progressive era materialized in the formation of a Children's Bureau in the Department of Commerce and Labor in 1912. Another major initiative by settlement house workers resulted in the government's providing aid for dependent children. By 1914 twenty states had programs that paid mothers' pensions to widows or abandoned wives to help support their children.

These pensions ranged from $2 to $15 a month for the first child and a smaller amount for other children in the family.

Florence Kelley, educated as a lawyer, was instrumental through the National Consumers League in persuading states to pass legislation providing for maximum hours and minimum wages for women. Kelley argued that under-

paying and overworking women encouraged prostitution and the breakdown of the family. The National Consumers League marshaled the research of Josephine Goldmark and others as statistical evidence of the conditions under which women worked. Indeed, it was this research that Louis Brandeis used in his arguments before the Supreme Court in 1908 in

Young Anglo-Protestant women were leaders in establishing settlement houses in the central cities. Here they tried to give the new immigrants, especially the children and women, a glimpse of middle-class life and to encourage them to change their life styles. (Brown Brothers)

defense of an Oregon law limiting the hours that women could work. Paul Kellogg, a leader in the developing field of social work, also headed a multivolume study of urban and industrial life in Pittsburgh, which included a volume by Elizabeth Beardsley Butler on working women. Butler's statistics indicated how poorly women were paid. She attributed this underpayment to the industrialists' practice of employing primarily girls who were members of families, since, as one employer admitted, "We don't pay the girls a living wage in this trade." Butler's findings were confirmed on the national level by the multivolume *Report on the Condition of Woman and Child Wage Earners* (1910–1913), published by the United States Bureau of Labor. Lobbyists for the reform of minimum wages soon organized into the Women's Trade Union League, which became the major voice for the movement. But women reformers did not have as much success with minimum wage reform as they had with setting maximum hours.

Concerned about the environment of women, leaders of the settlement houses worked to improve the conditions of slum housing. By 1900 a number of cities and states had instituted building and sanitary codes establishing minimum standards for ventilation and toilet facilities for new buildings. The New York Tenement House Law of 1901 also ordered the inspection of older housing. This New York law became the model that most large cities adopted by 1910.

The initial optimism felt by women reformers about the soundness of the private enterprise system, however, inevitably was called into question by the trickle-down pattern of housing that resulted from such a system. Private industry was not constructing much good housing for the poor, since there was little incentive to

do so. City and state inspectors could not condemn unsanitary and unsafe older housing for the poor because there was no alternative shelter for lower-income people. And reformers, because they accepted the soundness of the system, could not commit themselves to the kind of government-built housing emerging in European cities.

THE FAILURE OF SOCIAL SECURITY

The slow pace of housing reform in the United States reflected the fact that Americans lagged significantly behind the industrial nations of Europe in social legislation. Industrial workers in both Europe and America faced frequent interruptions of income from unemployment caused by periodic depressions or ongoing technological change, which made jobs obsolete. Moreover, workers could lose income through disabling job accidents or illness, or their families could become impoverished if breadwinners died of illness or became too old to work. To end these insecurities, Germany, England, and the Scandinavian countries moved rapidly to implement insurance to compensate for industrial accidents, unemployment, sickness, and old age.

In the United States, however, the weakness of both labor unions and Socialist political parties helped to delay such changes. Furthermore, the United States lacked the strong tradition of upper-class paternalism that existed in England and Germany. Not faced by a major threat from the small Socialist party headed by Eugene Debs or by the limited sense of aristocratic paternalism represented by Theodore Roosevelt, the American middle class resolutely preserved as much as it could of the nineteenth-century tradition of voluntarism. For the middle class, compulsory insurance robbed individuals of their initiative. Most people, they believed, were naturally lazy and needed the fear of falling dependent on others to keep themselves industrious and efficient. Furthermore, private charity was thought sufficient to sustain workers during recessions or illness, while personal savings and family care could tend to the aged.

Many lower-income ethnics and blacks tried to soften this harsh system by contributing to fraternal organizations in order to provide for their funerals. By 1910 a few of the larger corporations had established benefit funds for their employees as a form of welfare capitalism. At that time about 150,000 workers, only a very small part of the labor force, were eligible for death benefits of $50 to $100 and could receive $5 a week for thirteen weeks of temporary disability. However, Samuel Gompers of the American Federation of Labor (AFL) remained opposed to all forms of compulsory social insurance. Perhaps because labor had so little political power in America in contrast to Germany and England, Gompers did not want to be indebted to a government completely dominated by business. Gompers argued that if workers received adequate wages, unions could run their own social security system. In 1910 most unions paid their members death and disability benefits that were similar to those paid by the large corporations. But again, only a small percentage of the labor force was enrolled as union members.

Women reformers were most concerned with the issue of workman's compensation because of their interest in protecting the family. They were joined in this cause by the group of male economists and political scientists who formed the American Association for Labor Legislation (AALL) in 1906. Both political and business leaders were in sympathy with compulsory insurance for temporary or permanent disability resulting from industrial accidents. Employers realized that the compensation program substituted predictable costs for the insurance premiums that companies once paid to cover liability suits. Insurance companies approved of the compensation laws enacted in forty states between 1909 and 1920 because the states worked through the private insurance companies rather than handling the insurance through their own agencies. Most of the policies guaranteed half pay for a maximum of eight years for permanent job-related disability.

When the AALL brought up unemployment, health, and old age insurance, however, the defenders of the tradition of middle-class voluntarism argued that it was destructive of individual initiative to give help to people who were not working. But obviously, the unemployed were not working, the retired were not working, and health problems that developed in home had nothing to do with work.

Sponsors of these reforms pointed to statistics indicating that the sickness and death rates of American workers were higher than those of workers in England and Germany. They had little difficulty in demonstrating that only meager medical aid was available to the poor and that often major illness could reduce a family from middle-class respectability to poverty. And they invoked arguments of the German and English paternalists that social insurance made for a more productive work force, a significant consideration in a wartime situation. Alerted by the battle over workman's compensation, however, the American Medical Association and the insurance companies banded to-

This girl, working in a cotton mill in South Carolina in 1908, was typical of the large number of children employed in factories at the beginning of the twentieth century. Efforts by Progressive reformers to end child labor were defeated by the courts. (Photo by Lewis W. Hine, Jr. National Child Labor Committee/WPA)

gether to lobby against comprehensive social insurance in both the state and national governments. Theodore Roosevelt's Progressive party of 1912 came out in favor of unemployment and health insurance, and these items were discussed in several state legislatures before 1917. But social security reform failed offstage during World War One when it was associated with the German enemy. Identifying Americanism with entrepreneural capitalism

during the war, the head of the Prudential Life Insurance Company spoke out against old age pensions. Social insurance, he argued, would erode the "fear of old age dependency," which was the "most powerful incentive which makes for character and growth in a democracy."

The power of business groups, then, effectively blocked significant housing reform and unemployment, old age, and health insurance. It was not until the loss of business prestige after the economic crash in 1929 that old age and unemployment insurance were pushed through in 1935, and Congress continued to debate national health insurance in 1980.

WHITE PROGRESSIVES AND
THE BLACK COMMUNITY

The inability of academic and women reformers to initiate change without the support of the business community was duplicated by the problems of the National Association for the Advancement of Colored People (NAACP). Many settlement workers, who were able to overcome their prejudices toward Jews and Catholics and could visualize these ethnic groups making a contribution to a new pluralistic America, did not overcome their prejudice toward blacks. Almost all settlement houses were segregated and most, such as Jane Addams's Hull House, dealt only with whites. In 1910 there were only ten that catered to the needs of blacks.

Settlement workers often explained this practice as a reflection of the fact that neighborhoods were segregated in the cities and the settlement was a neighborhood organization. But they also explained that the presence of blacks tended to keep whites from coming to a settlement. The majority of the whites who did work in all-black settlements took a condescending attitude toward their neighbors. For a Philadelphia reformer, "Our settlement has its unique problem for it deals not with a race that is intellectually hungry, but with a race at the sensation stage of its evolution and the treatment demanded is different." Boston white reformers in 1910 decided it was best to encourage blacks to remain in the South because the blacks they were helping in Boston were "low and coarse, revealing much more of the animal qualities than the spiritual."

There were, however, a few white reformers who were concerned with the growing black ghettos in northern cities. Susan Wharton of the Philadelphia College settlement raised money to finance a project by the black scholar, W. E. B. DuBois, that was published as *The Philadelphia Negro: A Social Study* (1907). Another settlement worker, Mary White Ovington, made her own study of black conditions in New York, "Half a Man," and John Daniels described the black ghetto in Boston in his book *In Freedom's Birthplace*. These sympathetic whites found that the job and housing situation was worse for blacks than for the new white immigrants. Frances Kellor, a member of a New York settlement, recognized the great pressures on young black girls from the rural South to enter into prostitution when they arrived in northern cities and she helped found the National League for the Protection of Negro Women.

This small group of sympathetic white reformers did not place these conditions in national perspective until 1908 when, in the attempt to drive all blacks out of town, a white mob killed a number of blacks in Springfield, Illinois, the home of Abraham Lincoln. William English Walling, a well-to-do white southerner who had become a settlement house worker in the North, subsequently wrote a magazine article in the *Independent* that warned that the antiblack crusade was spreading out of the South and that white liberals must fight to keep the North from surrendering to race hatred. Walling, Mary White Ovington, and Henry Moskowitz, another New York settlement house worker, met and decided with the help of friends like Florence Kelley and Lillian Wald to call for a national conference in 1909 that would organize resistance to the antiblack crusade. They also invited a number of black leaders such as W. E. B. DuBois and William Monroe Trotter to attend.

The National Association for the Advancement of Colored People (NAACP) was established in 1910 as the result of the conference. It pledged to fight racial segregation, to work for equal educational opportunities for blacks and whites, to regain the vote for blacks, and to see that the Fourteenth and Fifteenth Amendments were enforced. Walling and White were afraid that the NAACP would appear too radical to win support from moderates and invited Oswald Garrison Willard, the editor of the *New York Post* and the *Nation,* to become a leader of the organization. All the officials of the new organization were white with the exception of W. E. DuBois, who became the editor of the NAACP's magazine, the *Crisis.* The major strategy of the NAACP was to bring suits in the courts to emphasize that the antiblack crusade violated the Fourteenth and Fifteenth Amendments. NAACP attorneys won a significant victory in 1915 when the Supreme Court ruled that grandfather clauses, which denied the vote to descendants of slaves, were unconstitutional. The Court also ruled in 1917 that laws passed by a number of southern cities to force residential segregation were unconstitutional. But the NAACP did not address the social problems of unemployment or underemployment for blacks in the cities and the terrible overcrowding in the ghettos.

The limitations of the NAACP partly reflected disagreements within the black community. Both Trotter and DuBois were born and raised in Massachusetts and both graduated from Harvard. Trotter went on to be a successful businessman and newspaper editor, while DuBois earned a Ph.D. at Harvard, did further study in Germany, and became a professor at Atlanta University, an all-black school. By 1900 both were attacking Brooker T. Washington, who had emerged during the 1890s as the most important spokesman for the black community. Trotter and DuBois were angry that Washington seemed to be urging blacks to passively accept disenfranchisement and segregation of public accommodations. A 1905 meeting of black leaders at Niagara, Canada, in which they had participated, had called on American blacks to regain the vote, civil rights, and educational opportunities. This Niagara movement had its roots in a National Afro-American League, established in 1890 under the leadership of the militant black editor T. Thomas Fortune. Fortune and other black leaders were aware of the growing antiblack crusade and wanted to organize to resist its development. Handicapped by lack of funds, the league collapsed but was replaced by the National Afro-American Council in 1898, which had the same goals. But by 1902 the council had been taken over by Booker T. Washington, who drove militant leaders such as DuBois and Ida Wells-Barnett out of office. The broader issue of social reform or individual self-help also divided DuBois and Washington. DuBois, a scholar in the new discipline of sociology, argued, as did white social reformers, that the individual's environment must be changed if the individual was to have a better life. Washington, however, agreed with conservative white businessmen that individuals could pull themselves up by their own bootstraps regardless of their social and economic environments.

Cut off from the small black middle class of businessmen, ministers, teachers, lawyers, and doctors who seemed to solidly back Washington, DuBois and Trotter were not enthusiastic about appealing to the mass of black people who were without property or education. DuBois talked of leadership by the "Talented Tenth" and said he "could not slap people on the back and make friends of strangers." Trotter said that he wanted to be part of a reform movement with "dignified" people of the "very best class." It is not surprising that DuBois turned to the well-educated white professionals who offered him financial support for his fight to regain political and civil rights for blacks in 1909.

While Trotter and DuBois sought the leaders for a national black awakening, black middle-class women in northern cities, such as Mary Church Terrell and Ida Wells-Barnett, encouraged others of their class to organize to help low-income blacks. They were joined by black men like William Lewis Bulkley, who founded the Commission for Improving the Industrial Condition of the Negro in New York. Bulkley organized day care centers for working mothers and night schools where working men and women could learn to read and write. These efforts led to the creation of the National Urban League (1911), which helped migrating blacks from the South find jobs in northern cities. But white racism frustrated the efforts of this organization, and employment prospects for northern blacks remained bleak.

This failure caused a number of black intellectuals such as the journalist John E. Bruce to give up on white America. A founder of the Negro Society for Historical Research in 1911, Bruce advocated that blacks cut themselves off from white American history, which came from Europe, and find their roots in Afro-American history, which linked them with Africa. Bruce, like many black leaders, rejected both Washington and DuBois because of their dependence on the white community. After 1914 he threw his support behind Marcus Garvey, who preached black nationalism to the masses in the northern ghettos.

SOUTHERN PROGRESSIVES AND THE BLACK COMMUNITY

Progressive reformers in the North failed to successfully challenge white racism and the exclusion of blacks from the mainstream of the nation's life. Their experience underscored the difficulty that all white reformers had in understanding the structures of power in the new urban-industrial society and in building movements that could challenge that power. In the South, however, the issue of race relations took on an entirely different tone. There, white progressives of the new middle class felt certain that there could be no new democracy in their region until all blacks were disenfranchised and socially segregated.

For the urban progressives of the southern middle class, blacks constituted the leading impediment to a true union of North and South. At the turn of the twentieth century, 90 percent of the nation's blacks still lived in the South. If the new South was to join the nation, whose politics was basically white, politics in the South had to be for white men only. Southern progressives also believed that black voting made the region's politics irrational by introducing the emotional issue of race into political discourse. They reasoned that southerners could achieve a higher level of politics once blacks were removed from political activity. Segregation of public facilities and accommodations, furthermore, would alleviate anxieties over possible social integration between the races.

In North Carolina, Josiah William Bailey, a leader of progressive politics, traced the beginning of progress in his state to the defeat of the black and white political coalition that had ruled in the 1890s. "Consider what a train of blessings has followed upon the victories of 1898 and 1900," he wrote. "Since White Supremacy was established, North Carolina is a new state." For the Reverend Edgar Gardner Murphy, who was active in national reform movements with settlement house leaders such as Jane Addams and Florence Kelley, "the conscious unity of race has become the broader ground of a new democracy."

When blacks were disenfranchised by most southern states in the 1890s, however, the race issue did not disappear from southern politics. Many lower-income whites could not accept their defeat in national politics in 1896 by northern Republicans or in their own states by the small middle-class group trying to build the new urban-industrial South. In Mississippi, where the first constitutional convention had disenfranchised blacks in 1890, James K. Vardaman used the primary to win the gubernatorial nomination of the Democratic party in 1903 by asking poor whites to join him in an antiblack crusade. Vardaman campaigned across the state in a white suit and hat, in a white wagon drawn by white oxen, to persuade the voters to overthrow the middle-class elite because they had not stripped blacks of every aspect of citizenship, including access to public schools. Vardaman's method of joining poor

white resentment against middle-class whites to resentment against blacks was so successful that one of his lieutenants, Theodore ("the man") Bilbo, could still use it to win the governorship in 1916, shouting to his audiences that "We are the lowbrows," "We are the red necks."

In the decade after 1900, Cole Blease in South Carolina and Tom Heflin in Alabama used the same kind of demagoguery to win political office. Hoke Smith, a middle-class progressive, came to power in Georgia in 1908 by joining forces with poor white populists. Smith demanded that blacks be taken out of politics by the passage of laws establishing poll taxes and literacy tests for voting. Blacks, of course, had already been taken out of Georgia politics because the state had adopted the primary method of nominating candidates. The Supreme Court accepted explicit racial discrimination in primaries until 1944. Since the Democratic party was the only effective political group in the South up to that time, exclusion from primaries meant nonparticipation in the region's only meaningful elections.

As the antiblack crusade seemed to reach a climax by 1910, Tom Watson of Georgia found that he could excite white southerners with fears of Catholics and Jews. Watson had become disillusioned with politics after the collapse of populism. When he returned to Georgia politics in 1904, Watson blamed the collapse of southern populism on the presence of blacks in politics. After inciting whites to violence against blacks in 1906 and 1908, his publications, *Watson's Jeffersonian Magazine* and *Watson's Jeffersonian Weekly,* began to print stories about "The Roman Catholic Hierarchy, the Deadliest Menace to Our Liberties" and "The Sinister Portent of Negro Priests." Soon Watson was calling for the lynching of Leo Frank, the Jewish superintendent of a factory in Atlanta. When a young worker, Mary Thayer, was murdered, Frank was accused. For Watson, Frank must be guilty because of his physical appearance: "those bulging satyr eyes ...the protruding fearfully sensual lips; and also his animal jaw." He must be guilty because he was a Jew who had a "ravenous appetite for the forbidden fruit — a lustful eagerness enhanced by the racial novelty of the girl of the uncircumcized." And, wrote Watson, he would not be convicted in a court because of the "gigantic conspiracy of Big Money.... Frank belonged to the Jewish aristocracy, and it was determined by the rich Jews that no aristocrat of their race should die for the death of a working-class gentile."

Watson's call for Frank's lynching was promptly fulfilled by a group of unmasked men who went unpunished. To symbolize the commitment of the white South to racial democracy, he also asked for the re-creation of the Ku Klux Klan of the 1870s. Watson's dream was soon fulfilled when a new Klan was founded outside Atlanta in 1915.

The antiblack crusade in the South produced a crisis for the region's black leadership. The burdens of black survival fell upon Booker T. Washington. Washington was born into slavery in Virginia at the end of the 1850s and went to school at Hampton Institute, established by New England religious philanthropists after the Civil War. Here he was taught the virtues of thrift, hard work, and self-reliance. In the 1880s Washington traveled to Alabama to start a similar school with only a small amount of financial aid. Obtaining funds from white northern philanthropists and having the students construct their own buildings, he built a major college at Tuskegee. Washington's educational program was designed to break down the slave heritage of dependency on white

Lynching was common in the South in the 1880s, with almost as many whites as blacks as victims. By the 1890s, however, blacks had become the scapegoats for the general economic and social problems in the South and thus they were increasingly the most frequent victims. (Historical Pictures Service, Inc.)

leadership and to teach the black to be personally self-reliant and self-disciplined. In order to promote economic independence, Tuskegee Institute also emphasized skills in agriculture and trade.

Washington leaped into national prominence with a speech at the Atlanta Exposition in 1895. Here white leaders of the New South were celebrating the modest economic growth that had taken place and were projecting a future of major industrial transformation. In his speech Washington declared that it had been a mistake for blacks to have been given so much political power during Reconstruction because political power must rest on social and economic achievement. It followed, then, that blacks would not now ask for political equality but would first work to establish themselves as a productive economic force in the South and would achieve good habits of social discipline and character before becoming concerned with political rights.

Washington was aware that the constitutional conventions called in Mississippi and South Carolina to disenfranchise blacks were being discussed favorably in all southern states. He knew that the rate of lynchings was increasing and that they were taking on the more rigidly ceremonial form of burning blacks in front of large public gatherings of white men, women, and children. Washington understood the momentum toward completely ending the black's status as even a second-class citizen. In a South dominated by a white population that was increasingly using the black as a scapegoat for its frustrations, Washington saw the need to save as much of the status of citizenship for blacks as possible.

To keep from handicapping the economic progress of the white South, Washington argued, the black needed education to become a more efficient and productive worker. Education was the crucial point for Washington. All would not be lost if blacks temporarily were pushed out of politics; all would not be lost if they temporarily were pushed into segregated public facilities. All would be lost, however, if they were barred from education and the right to hold property. But the logic of the antiblack

crusade, when pushed to its extreme, demanded that blacks lose every right of citizenship, including education and the holding of property.

Washington fought this logic by emphasizing the natural docility of the black and by insisting that southern blacks would gratefully accept a restricted and qualified second-class citizenship. Blacks were, he declared, "the most patient, faithful, law-abiding, and unresentful people that the world had seen." Washington also stressed the economic benefits of the second-class citizenship for the white South, which needed a trained, docile labor force if economic growth was to take place. Desperately Washington appealed to the white southern capitalists and asserted that "in all things that are purely social, we can be as separate as the five fingers, yet one as the hand in all things essential to mutual progress."

Washington and the others fought against the spread of disenfranchisement to other southern states like Alabama, Louisiana, Georgia, and Maryland through the use of lawyers who received payment from anonymous sources. They also fought against the further spread of Jim Crow laws in public transportation.

By 1900 Washington and most southern black leaders hoped that education would remain available to blacks. But although black schools survived, a great gap emerged in southern expenditures for white and black children during the Progressive era. The spending ratio in 1890 was $2 for whites to $1 for blacks. By 1914 the ratio had become $10 for a white child in contrast to $1 for a black child. The major cause for these diverging costs was the increased outlays for newly established public high schools and colleges for whites. High schools and colleges for blacks, however, were financed mainly by private donations and were vulnerable to legal destruction by southern state government. By fawning before the white man and pretending to be incapable of producing significant change in race relations, educated black leaders managed to save black education in the South.

Southern blacks also managed to retain the citizenship right of geographic mobility, theoretically guaranteed by the Fourteenth Amendment. Slowly the black population moved within the South toward the Southwest and into the towns and cities. And there was another slow migration to the North, which accelerated dramatically during World War One. In southern cities the loss of direct control over blacks on the plantation seemed to find a substitute in segregation laws and practices. Whites made no systematic effort to suppress the development of black leadership in the ghetto, nor did the legal system prevent the emergence of black teachers, ministers, lawyers, doctors, bankers, or businessmen. But the economic situation created by the antiblack crusade worked against Washington's hopes for black self-help. Under slavery, blacks had comprised most of the South's skilled craft workers and continued to have their skills employed by whites in the 1870s and 1880s. By the 1890s, however, whites were refusing to hire black craft workers or blacks providing services such as barbers. Economic depression in agriculture also made it difficult for blacks to establish themselves as independent farmers.

The antiblack crusade in the South had repercussions in national politics as well. When Theodore Roosevelt became president in 1901, he invited Booker T. Washington to lunch at the White House. Roosevelt, who approved of Washington's minimization of black political involvement, consulted with Washington on the distribution of minor federal jobs to black

Republicans in the southern states. But the president reacted to sharp criticism from southern whites about his hospitality and never asked Washington back. Roosevelt demonstrated his intense commitment to the caste system in 1906 when he dismissed three companies of black soldiers for participating in a riot in Brownsville, Texas, in which a white man was killed. The president reacted so strongly to the notion that black men must not show violence toward whites that he ordered dishonorable discharges for the blacks without holding an investigation of the situation.

President William Howard Taft gave his approval to the disenfranchisement of southern blacks and directed patronage to white-supremacist Republicans from the South who supported the president's drive for re-election in 1912. But southern racial attitudes were most visible in the administration of Democrat Woodrow Wilson, a Virginia reformer. Advised by southern progressives in his cabinet, Wilson officially segregated the federal civil service, established separate dining and toilet facilities for whites and blacks in federal offices, and stormed out of a presidential meeting with northern black leaders.

Despite the inhospitable national and regional racial climate, Washington and other black spokesmen such as DuBois did manage to blunt the extreme logic of the antiblack crusade and preserved some aspects of citizenship for blacks. These remaining areas of citizenship, such as education, provided the foundation in the 1950s for the black revolution that sought to restore political rights and destroy segregation.

SUGGESTED READINGS

Donald J. Pivar, *Purity Crusade: Sexual Morality and Social Control, 1868–1900* (1973) provides an excellent overview of the role of middle-class women in initiating the movement for the control of prostitution and in spreading the spirit of reform into other areas. Paul S. Boyer, *Purity in Print: The Vice Society Movement and Book Censorship in America* (1968), describes one of these areas. Sidney Ditzion, *Marriage, Morals, and Sex in America* (1953), David Kennedy, *Birth Control in America: The Career of Margaret Sanger* (1970), and G. Barker-Benfield, *The Horrors of the Half-Known Life* (1976), discuss the major attitudes toward sexuality held by middle-class women and men.

The importance of prohibition in the Progressive era is the subject of Joseph Garfield, *Symbolic Crusade* (1963), Andrew Sinclair, *Era of Excess* (1962), and James Timberlake, *Prohibition and the Progressive Movement* (1963). Its special role in the South is discussed by Jack T. Kirby, *Darkness at the Dawning: Race and Reform in the Progressive South* (1972). The vitality of evangelical Protestantism in both the city and the country is described by William McLaughlin, *Modern Revivalism* (1959), and C. H. Hopkins, *The Rise of the Social Gospel in American Protestantism, 1865–1915* (1940), describes the emergence of liberal Protestantism.

Sidney Fine, *Laissez-Faire and the General Welfare State* (1957), James Weinstein, *The Corporate Ideal in the Liberal State, 1900–1918* (1968), Jean B. Quandt, *From the Small Town to the Great Community* (1970), R. Jackson Wilson, *In Quest of Community* (1968), and Jack Tager, *The Intellectual as Reformer: Brand Whitlock and the Progressive*

Movement (1968), are good studies of the reform impulse to overcome the fragmentation of the urban environment.

The special role of women in this effort is the subject of Robert Bremner, *From the Depths: The Discovery of Poverty in the United States* (1956), Roy Lubove, *The Professional Altruist: The Emergence of Social Work as a Career* (1965), and two books by Allen F. Davis, *Spearheads of Reform: The Social Settlements and the Progressive Movement* (1967) and *American Heroine: Life and Legacy of Jane Addams* (1973). Winning the vote for women is described by Eleanor Flexner, *Century of Struggle* (1959), and Aileen Kraditor, *The Ideas of the Woman Suffrage Movement, 1890–1920* (1965).

Roy Lubove has pioneered in analyzing middle-class resistance to social welfare in the early twentieth-century. He clarifies the attitudes and groups that limited significant reform in slum housing and in establishing unemployment insurance, old age pensions, and health insurance in his books, *The Progressives and the Slums* (1962) and *The Struggle for Social Security* (1968). Philip Taft, *The AFL in the Time of Gompers* (1957), and David Brady, *The Steelworkers* (1960), point to the weakness of and contradictions among labor leaders in dealing with the issues of social security.

August Meier, *Negro Thought in America, 1880–1915* (1963), C. F. Kellogg, *NAACP* (1970), June Sochen, *The Unbridgeable Gap: Blacks and Their Quest for the American Dream, 1900–1930* (1937), and Robert L. Allen, *Reluctant Reformers: Racism and Social Reform Movements in the United States* (1974), capture the frustrations of black leaders and the difficult relationships between black and white reformers.

Chapter 4

PROGRESSIVE POLITICS, 1890–1916

Both the Democratic and Republican parties successfully resisted the attempts of farmers and workers to use national politics to preserve a "producers" democracy in the 1880s and 1890s. But while the national parties prevented such reform, another kind of political activity emerged in cities. By the 1890s many of the new middle class had become active in developing reform politics in cities throughout the nation. Called "progressivism," this political activity promised to alter the existing pattern of party politics.

CITY BOSSES AND ETHNIC POWER

Middle-class reform in the cities had its roots in the shift of political power that occurred in late-nineteenth-century industrial centers in the East and Middle West. As northern cities filled with immigrants and doubled their population almost every ten years following the Civil War, Anglo-Protestant elites lost confidence in their ability to provide political order and turned away from city politics. Instead, they fulfilled political ambitions in state or national politics, or channeled their energies in the development of large-scale corporations that operated regionally or nationally. Establishment leaders who wanted a continued influence in municipal affairs engaged in humanitarian causes and raised funds for hospitals and schools.

As streetcar cities began to take on the new patterns of specialized and spatially divided districts and neighborhoods, existing forms of municipal government proved a handicap to providing order. Most city governments imitated

WHAT'S TO BE DONE ABOUT IT?

THESE CONGESTED CITIES.   THESE BROAD PRAIRIES OF THE WEST.

This cartoon illustrates the bewilderment that many Americans felt at the rapid growth of major cities having a dense population. And they did not understand the pressures of mechanization which were beginning to push farmers off the land. (Historical Pictures Service, Inc.)

the checks and balances of the national government, with two legislative councils elected from local districts and a major elected at large. Such government organization led to inefficiency, which was aggravated by the dependence of cities on state legislatures. When cities needed new powers to deal with expansion, legislatures usually gave them only one new specific power at a time. Philadelphia, for example, was governed by thirty separate municipal boards in the 1880s.

Besides problems of leadership and archaic political structure, huge new industrial cities intensified economic insecurity and personal alienation. During periods of economic crisis such as those of 1873 and 1893, farmers usually could feed themselves. But unemployed urban workers could neither buy nor grow food. Farm families typically cared for sick or elderly members. But this kind of family support was difficult among low-income urban dwellers. Urban charities developed by establishment elites in the late eighteenth and early nineteenth century were designed for cities with small and homogeneous populations and had served workers who were employed in small shops where owners often had a sense of personal responsibility for their employees. This kind of charity could not cope with the large and ethnically divided populations of the late-nineteenth century. Nor could it cope with workers who were employed in large shops or factories where little personal relationship existed between employer and employee.

Anglo-Protestant leaders who deserted urban politics were replaced by the city "bosses" of the 1870s and 1880s. Most of these men came from modest or low-income backgrounds. The new urban leaders developed political "machines" that provided extralegal ways to bypass constitutional checks and balances impeding response to social and economic problems. Many of the first bosses were immigrants from Ireland or second-generation Irish-Americans. The Irish had an advantage over all other immigrant groups in developing leadership because they spoke English. Irish-Americans also transferred their political experience from Ireland, where they had struggled for political survival in a country dominated by Englishmen and had created an underground government of their own. Irish political leaders, like military leaders, demanded absolute obedience and loyalty to a hierarchical political party. Since one expected to use violence and other illegal activity against an English establishment, Irish political activity often was secret.

Ethnic political bosses acted as political brokers in the large cities of the late nineteenth century. As expanding streetcar cities fragmented into different neighborhoods separated by class, ethnic, or caste distinctions, city bosses attempted to reconcile conflicting social and economic interests. For example, wealthy businessmen eagerly competed for the privilege to build public transportation and to provide natural gas, electricity, or telephone service for the city. Once the municipal government had granted a private corporation the franchise to provide such a service, that corporation then had a monopoly, since there was only one streetcar, gas, electric, or telephone company. With high profits guaranteed by such a monopolistic position, businessmen were willing to pay city bosses large amounts of money to grant them franchises.

To stay in power, bosses had to be able to deliver franchises and contracts to Anglo-Protestant businessmen. But to maintain political power, the bosses also had to provide for the needs of the lower-income ethnic voters who composed the majority of the electorate. The boss's political machine served as a ladder of upward mobility. Since the leadership of the corporations was predominantly Anglo-Protestant, ambitious and talented ethnics found city politics one of the few avenues open to the development of leadership skills. Success in the political machine also meant upward economic mobility, since higher political positions brought a larger share of the graft that came from selling franchises and contracts and from other sources of corruption.

City bosses served their constituents by forcing businessmen to use ethnically owned small construction companies on large building projects. Through this practice Irish-American and later Italian-American contractors became millionaires in cities such as Boston, New York, Philadelphia, Chicago, San Francisco, and St. Paul, while bosses received "kickback" payments from favored contractors. In the unstable economy of the late nineteenth century, marked by periods of large-scale unemployment in the cities, political machines could reach down to lower-income ethnic voters and promise them jobs on city construction projects.

Urban political machines also provided jobs in city services, particularly the modern police and fire departments created after the Civil War. The popular-culture figure of the "Irish cop," still found in movies, television, radio, cartoons, and the comics, has accurate historical roots. Low-income ethnics felt lucky to escape from the threat of job layoffs in the private economy and win job security as city employees. Since the national government did not begin to provide pensions for the elderly until the passage of the Social Security Act in 1935, and most private corporations had no effective pension plans until after World War Two, city employees were the privileged minority of low- and medium-income workers who had pensions for their old age. In turn, policemen, firemen, teachers, city clerks, and janitors were reminded that they owed their jobs to the boss, and they demonstrated appropriate loyalty on election day.

The ability of the boss to provide a network of personal relationships in the fragmenting streetcar city came from the nature of the machine itself. A city boss actually was the coordinator of a group of neighborhood bosses, each representing the ethnic constituency of his own district. Neighborhood bosses got much of their graft by protecting gambling and prostitution operations and by allowing saloons to stay open after hours or on Sundays. When there was a crisis of illness or unemployment in a family,

it was the responsibility of the neighborhood boss to provide food and fuel. City bosses demonstrated their concern for the voters by building parks and playgrounds. New York's Tammany Hall provided food baskets on holidays and organized summer picnics and trips to the amusement park for children. Since both capitalist and prevailing Protestant theory insisted on absolute self-reliance for the individual and opposed government provision of unemployment or medical insurance, the bosses delivered these services at an unofficial and unauthorized level. The recipients of such assistance often were Catholic and Jewish immigrants whose cultural traditions made charity and group support for the individual an acceptable practice or even a religious responsibility. Although Italian and Slavic neighborhood bosses had difficulties with the English language and lacked the political experience of the Irish, they constantly tried to limit the power of the Irish city bosses and increase their own authority. This internal political friction between Catholic immigrant groups was paralleled by the resentment expressed by Italian, Polish, and German Catholics to the domination of the hierarchy of the Catholic church in America by the Irish.

THE PROFESSSIONAL CLASS AND URBAN REFORM

By the early 1890s young professionals in the new middle class of the cities began an attack on corrupt rule by undemocratic bosses. Strongly critical of their fathers' abandonment of the cities to the machines, the new generation of Protestant elite urbanites promised to apply organizational and managerial skills to defeat the bosses and create a "new democracy." In New York, reform outrage at machine corruption propelled Theodore Roosevelt to the presidency of the City Board of Police Commissioners in 1895. By the late 1890s and early 1900s, reform mayors included Seth Low of New York City, Joseph W. Folk of St. Louis, James D. Phelan of San Francisco, and Mark Fagan of Jersey City.

Middle-class professionals argued that the emphasis of farmers and workers on a producers' democracy divided society into warring factions. Instead they suggested that all people in the new urban-industrial America were no longer producers, but should be viewed as consumers. To say that only producers were responsible citizens denied the rights of white-collar workers, who were the fastest growing segment of the labor force. The new middle class proposed a democracy of consumers that would include all citizens and establish universal standards to protect the rights of all. While Anglo-Protestant professionals were a small minority of the total urban population, they nevertheless accepted the responsibility to govern as spokesmen for the new democracy until the urban majority could be liberated from ethnic or class loyalties. Establishment professionals, who did not see themselves as an ethnic or a class group, hoped to instill the commitment to impersonal and universal standards that they defined as professionalism.

Outraged at the personal nature of the city machines and the party loyalty of low-income voters, middle-class reformers began to push for nonpartisan city elections. Cities, like corporations, they argued, should be run by experts in administration. The reformers criticized the emotional attachments of voters to political parties, insisting that the professional skills of candidates were more important than party labels.

If people had to vote for a list of candidates with no party identity, reformers contended, voters would be forced to learn each candidate's professional qualifications for administering city services. To further disassociate city elections from party politics, reformers worked to move elections from November to the spring and to odd years, so they would not coincide with state and national elections.

While urban reformers were only partially successful in establishing these changes in some cities, they were completely successful in having the printing of ballots taken out of the hands of political parties. Instead of requesting Democratic or Republic ballots, voters now received ballots that included the candidates of both parties. One could now cast a "secret" ballot. Voting also moved from saloons, which were centers of political activity for the bosses, to public schools and libraries. To make it more difficult for the bosses to steal elections, the reformers established rules for registration in advance of voting. To register, a person had to be a resident of a precinct for a certain period of time. Since lower-income people were moving constantly from city to city or from neighborhood to neighborhood, these residency requirements made it impossible for large numbers of the poor to qualify. City bosses, however, often ordered registrars to ignore such requirements and continued to bend rules to win elections. Despite electoral reform, bosses such as New York's Charles Francis Murphy and Cincinnati's George H. Cox held municipal power during the years of Progressive ferment.

White Protestant reformers also pushed for civil service standards that required candidates for city jobs to compete with each other in passing exams that tested their qualifications to be firemen, policemen, or clerks. Under this system, officials of the government bureaucracy, rather than city bosses, would decide who should obtain municipal jobs. Like twentieth-century I.Q. tests, civil service examinations incorporated the standards and values of the white Protestant middle class and therefore put Americans from different ethnic or class backgrounds at a disadvantage. If young people wanted to get ahead, they had to learn white Protestant middle-class standards and values in the public schools or be taught in parochial schools that surrendered ethnic values and taught the values of the nation's majority.

Another tactic that establishment reformers used to depersonalize politics was to replace election of city council members by specific neighborhoods with a system by which they would be elected at large. The reformers argued that citywide elections brought men into government who represented the entire city rather than special ethnic or class groups. With its emphasis on universal citizenship and the common interest of all consumers, this approach reflected the concept of a new democracy advocated by the professional middle class. But at-large elections combined with nonpartisan elections to dampen the interest of voters. Loss of voter interest and difficulties in meeting the new residency and registration requirements reduced the level of voter participation in urban elections about 20 percent during the period 1890–1917. In order to guarantee that the White Protestant middle class, rather than ethnic lower-income groups, controlled the policies of the public schools, reformers also moved to have city school boards elected at large.

A major irony of urban political reform was that much of the electoral success of the new middle class was itself based on personal relationships. Professionals and businessmen came together in organizations such as the local chamber of commerce or municipal research bureau, where they established informal social networks that served as the foundation for middle-class political strategy.

Once in power, the reformers established commissions to regulate the rates charged by the utility and transportation monopolies. Experts determined a fair rate of profit to protect the consumer from unreasonable charges. Reform administrations also promised to hold down city spending and therefore hold down taxes.

Since the reformers undermined the informal welfare system provided by the bosses, they frequently were opposed by lower-income voters. Thus reformers were never able to keep control of city government for very long. In New York City, for instance, the Tammany Hall organization recaptured the city in 1901 with the political slogan "To Hell with Reform."

Some reform mayors, however, were concerned with social welfare and were popular with lower-income voters. In Detroit, Hazen S. Pingree took office to end boss rule. But he did not crusade against the saloons or prostitution. While Pingree was concerned with regulating the rates of the street railways and public utilities, he also provided parks, schools, and a lower tax burden for the poor. During the depression of 1893, the Detroit mayor established relief for the poor and created public works jobs for the unemployed. Samuel M. Jones and Thomas L. Johnson, mayors of the Ohio cities of Toledo and Cleveland, showed similar sympathies for the poor. Jones and Johnson believed in private enterprise, but they emulated the Populists by advocating government ownership of monopoly transportation and utility companies. By 1915 two-thirds of the nation's municipal waterworks were owned and operated by city governments. But although cities such as Toledo, Cleveland, Milwaukee, San

Francisco, and Schenectady assumed public ownership of gas, electric, and public transportation, the new middle class preferred the use of regulatory commissions to control monopolies. As Socialist political parties became major factors in a number of cities between 1900 and 1912, establishment professionals became even more hostile toward the advocates of "municipal socialism."

CITY BOSSES AND NATIONAL REFORM

Since the informal welfare system of the city bosses helped to minimize the suffering of the unemployed and the poor, machine politics worked against the development of a strong Socialist movement among urban lower-income groups. Furthermore, the boss system encouraged the preservation of ethnic identities, thereby discouraging the growth of a cross-cultural American working class. Within the politics of the urban machine, people were encouraged to think of themselves as Irish-American, Polish-American, Italian-American or German-American workers rather than as American workers who had a common class interest.

The state and national reformers who created the Progressive movement after 1900 were more open to the use of government regulations to help lower-income groups than were the urban reformers of the 1890s. Perhaps the new middle class had more confidence when it became aware of its wider political power. As they began to work for housing and health reform in the cities, for government pensions for widows, for compensation for workers injured on the job, for limitations on child labor and on the hours for working women, and for

safety standards in factories, progressive reformers soon encountered support from city bosses. Urban machines such as New York's Tammany Hall also supported the Sixteenth Amendment to the Constitution, which legalized a federal income tax. Since machine leaders favored a more just tax system that could reach the wealth of the very rich (in 1900, 19 percent of the people controlled 50 percent of the nation's wealth), they welcomed an income tax that could tax the rich.

Bosses in New York, Boston, and elsewhere also supported the Seventeenth Amendment, which shifted the election of United States senators from the state legislatures to the voters in general elections. By 1900 most state legislatures had a heavy overrepresentation of rural and small-town people. As the cities grew rapidly throughout the nineteenth century, rural-dominated state legislatures refused to reapportion representation in the legislatures to reflect the new urban population. (Substantive legislation reapportionment awaited a 1962 Supreme Court decision). A constitutional amendment taking the election of United States senators out of the hands of the rural-controlled legislatures was seen, therefore, as a victory for the city populations.

The alliance between the urban bosses and social reformers led to changes in labor law. Two members of Tammany Hall, Alfred E. Smith (the presidential candidate of the Democratic party in 1928) and Robert F. Wagner (the most important leader and sponsor of social security legislation in the United States Senate in 1935), headed a Factory Investigation Committee in 1911. This committee was authorized to investigate working and safety conditions in New York factories after 145 young women were killed in a fire at the Triangle Shirtwaist Company. It recommended

The 1911 fire at the Triangle Shirtwaist factory in New York City, which killed many young women workers called attention to safety conditions in American factories being much worse than those in European countries. In response to the tragedy, the state of New York did pass regulatory legislation. (Brown Brothers)

changes in the working conditions in factories, and many of the recommendations were put into law by the New York State legislature. City bosses, therefore, provided leadership for an "urban liberalism," an important part of the progressive wings of both the Republican and Democratic parties.

THE NEW MIDDLE CLASS AND A NEW DEMOCRACY

Between 1896 and 1900, members of the new middle class were no longer faced with the threat that Populists might establish a successful coalition of farmers and industrial workers committed to a producers' democracy. The American Federation of Labor (AFL), which, under the leadership of Samuel Gompers, accepted the existing capitalist system and the permanence of a wage-earning class, was the nation's only effective organization by 1900. Furthermore, farmers who had survived the depression of the 1890s increasingly were turning to agricultural organizations that emphasized specific material gains much as the AFL did.

Although the dream of a producers' democracy had faded by 1900, a new coalition emerged to combat the antisocial excesses of the large corporations. Leaders of the AFL accepted the world of large corporations but wanted state governments and especially the national government to give labor unions the same kind of legal standing received by corporations. Even midwestern farmers who had opposed populism continued to be angry at the way railroads used their monopoly position against the economic interests of rural America. And they continued to be angry at the high costs forced on them by the tariffs demanded by the large industrial corporations and by the extensive control of the money supply by New York bankers.

The progressive coalition found a common theme in the control of the large corporation. But the idea of control meant different things to different groups. Small businessmen and many farmers wanted to stop the growth of corporations and perhaps even restore the nineteenth-century marketplace of small competitors. The professionals of the new middle class, however, accepted the continued growth of the large corporation. Middle-class reformers called for government regulations to force the corporations to be more rational and efficient in their

economic policies and more responsible in their social policies. They were joined in this approach by some AFL unions and leaders of large corporations interested in stabilizing the national economy. Men like the Ohio industrialist Mark Hanna and George Perkins, a top executive of U. S. Steel, had decided that the large corporation could not survive the price competition of the free marketplace. A large corporation with perhaps hundreds of thousands of employees had huge fixed costs. Thus it was very important for corporation executives to be able to predict earnings for several years ahead. Sharp fluctuations in prices would make such prediction impossible. Business leaders like Hanna and Perkins, therefore, welcomed government regulations that would limit price competition.

One of the first political leaders able to bring most of these groups together in an effective reform coalition was Robert LaFollette of Wisconsin. LaFollette was an ambitious farm boy who had gone to the University of Wisconsin to become a lawyer. During the 1880s he had established a successful law practice and began to work his way up in the state Republican party organization. LaFollette saw no significant weaknesses in the free enterprise system and strongly defended the establishment against critical farmers and workers. He emphasized that any individual who worked could become a financial success. Unsuccessful farmers and workers had nothing to blame, according to LaFollette, but their own lack of character and moral strength. He did not question the way in which a small group of lumber and railroad millionaires controlled the Republican party and the state. LaFollette was rewarded for this loyalty and sent, as a young man, to the United States House of Representatives.

But in 1890 LaFollette and most Republicans were swept out of office in Wisconsin because the Republicans in the state legislature had passed a law demanding compulsory education for all children in the English language. Wisconsin had a huge immigrant population of Germans, Scandinavians, and Poles. These groups, both Lutherans and Catholics, supported parochial schools where teaching was in the immigrant languages. The angry immigrants voted solidly for the Democrats in 1890, but the depression of 1893 began to restore Republican strength in 1894 and 1896.

When LaFollette was ready to return to Republican politics in 1898, however, he no longer saw farmers, workers, and the poor as the major threat to the free enterprise system. Now, like the Populists and Knights of Labor of the 1880s, he pointed to the railroads, the large industrial corporations, and the large New York banks as the major source of the nation's problems. But as LaFollette campaigned to capture the Republican party of Wisconsin from boss rule, he presented himself as a hero of a new democracy based on a "new" citizenship. A good citizen, according to LaFollette, was one who was concerned with public interest and not with a particular economic group. Populists and the Knights of Labor spoke for such economic groups, rather than for the whole community, because they identified democracy with the kind of work people did.

Politicians of the Wisconsin Democratic party, who represented the ethnic concerns of Germans, Norwegians, or Poles, also spoke for a selfish group instead of supporting the public interest. For LaFollette, the selfish motives of big business could be driven from control of the Republican party in Wisconsin and from its control of the state and national economy only when average people gave up their divisive job and ethnic identities to become good citizens who shared a common identity as consumers and taxpayers. LaFollette therefore called for a great moral and political crusade of the "people" against the "interests."

Winning control of the Republican party and then the governorship of Wisconsin in 1900, LaFollette used his position of leadership to continue to educate voters. He called for primaries that would place the nomination of party candidates in the hands of the people and take that power out of the hands of bosses who had operated behind closed doors in "smoke-filled rooms" at party conventions. He accepted the idea of William U'Ren of Oregon that the people should have the right to initiate legislation directly through petitions or to recall public officials without waiting for the next election. He called for greater control of utilities and railroads and for tax reform that would force the railroads and large corporations to pay their fair share. He was able to raise state taxes on railroads from $1.9 million to $3.4 million a year.

LaFollette emphasized the importance of newspapers in the investigation of boss power. He urged newspaper editors to become crusaders for reform to help create both an informed and involved public. To mobilize public opinion to demand a change in the political system, LaFollette also encouraged his followers to hold mass meetings, to engage in petition campaigns, to establish reform leagues, and to educate themselves through lectures on specific economic and social issues. In Iowa and Indiana, Republican insurgents Albert B. Cummins and Albert J. Beveridge emulated LaFollette by riding reform waves to the governor's chair, while Charles Evans Hughes and Hiram Johnson accomplished the same feat in New York and California.

A NATIONAL
PROGRESSIVE MOVEMENT

Defending the system against farmers and workers, middle-class Americans before 1896 had been hostile to those writers who pointed to major social and economic problems. Powerful books such as *Progress and Poverty* (1879) by Henry George, *How the Other Half Lives* (1890) by Jacob Riis, and *Wealth Against Commonwealth* (1894) by Henry Demarest Lloyd had described and analyzed such problems without receiving general approval from middle-class readers. By 1900, however, the new middle class wanted to be informed about social and economic problems because it was confident that it could solve them on its own terms. Replacing the small-circulation magazines (less than 100,000) of the old middle class such as *Harpers* and the *Atlantic* was a group of magazines that appealed to the new middle class. Magazines like *McClure's* (750,-000 circulation) and *Collier's* (1 million circulation) featured "muckracking" articles that described boss control of city and state governments and of the United States Senate, as well as corruption in industries such as oil, railroads, insurance, and Wall Street banking. The writers of these articles, such as Lincoln Steffens, Ida Tarbell, Ray Stannard Baker, and David Graham Phillips, became nationally famous as muckraking journalists. They had some influence on progressive political leaders and thus had an impact on reform legislation. By carry-

ing stories on urban reform movements in cities like San Francisco, Denver, New Orleans, St. Louis, Minneapolis, Cleveland, and New York, or on reform governors in Oregon, California, Missouri, Wisconsin, Georgia, or Pennsylvania, the muckraking magazines helped to create a sense of a national reform movement that was making "progress" toward the achievement of a new democracy.

When LaFollette went to the United States Senate in 1905, he hoped to build a progressive movement among Republican senators that would overthrow the leadership of the party's conservatives. LaFollette's first chance to participate in the making of reform legislation came quickly in 1906 when the Senate made a major effort to give the Interstate Commerce Commission (ICC) strong powers to set rates charged by the railroads. LaFollette affirmed that "the welfare of all the people as consumers should be the supreme consideration of the Government." He was disappointed that President Theodore Roosevelt did not provide more vigorous leadership, but he accepted the legislation that passed Congress, the Hepburn Act, as a step in the right direction.

LaFollette rapidly became a major figure in the Senate because he represented growing discontent among midwestern Republicans with the tariff policy of the national party. After McKinley's second defeat of Bryan in 1900, the Democratic party no longer seemed to offer a viable alternative to the high-tariff tradition of the Republican party. The lack of reform vigor among Democrats was demonstrated by the ability of conservative Democrats to capture the national convention from Bryan in 1904 and nominate the New York judge Alton B. Parker as the party's presidential candidate.

During the 1904 campaign, Parker dropped

Bryan's attack on the Republicans as the party of privilege and monopoly power. The only major issue Parker used against his opponent, Theodore Roosevelt, was that of the president's unstable personality and his centralization of national power. Roosevelt, the Republican vice presidential candidate in 1900, had succeeded to the presidency after McKinley had been assassinated in September 1901.

Given the weakness of the Democratic party as a vehicle of reform, conflict intensified between progressives and conservatives within the Republican party after 1901. Republican progressives from the Midwest, especially from Wisconsin, Minnesota, and Iowa, began to talk of lowering the tariff. Governor Albert B. Cummins offered the "Iowa Idea" that tariff duties should be suspended for an industry that had fallen under the monopolistic control of one or two large corporations. President McKinley had felt these midwestern pressures and was planning for reciprocity treaties that would reduce the tariff on imports from those foreign nations lowering their own barriers against American goods.

When Roosevelt took over the presidency, he decided that the tariff issue might shatter party unity and worked successfully to keep the tariff from being considered by Congress throughout both his terms. But the increasing frustration of midwestern Republicans finally exploded in 1909 against his handpicked successor, William Howard Taft, and the Republican party became badly divided by 1912.

ROOSEVELT AND CORPORATE PROGRESSIVISM

LaFollette's ambition to become the most important national leader of Republican progressivism was frustrated by Theodore Roosevelt's ability to gain and hold that identity. Roosevelt, like LaFollette, had become active in Republican politics in the 1880s. Unlike LaFollette, however, he was born into a very old and wealthy New York family. By the 1880s Roosevelt reacted against the lack of vigor among the gentlemen of his father's generation. As a student at Harvard, he had become concerned with the need for the United States to continue its tradition of frontier expansion. He became an admirer of Admiral Alfred T. Mahan's views on the importance of naval power for overseas expansion. Roosevelt also wrote a multivolume history, *The Winning of the West*. By the 1890s Roosevelt was an advocate of the preservation of wilderness areas to remind Americans of their tradition of frontier exploration. He also encouraged the conservation of natural resources, in part because he wanted a guaranteed source of coal, oil, and timber for the expanding armed forces, especially during periods of national mobilization for total war.

Associating himself with both the vigor of the expanding officer corps of the navy and army and the vigor of the expanding professionalism of the new middle class, Roosevelt rejected his father's contempt for politics and accepted the discipline of the Republican party. He served in the New York state legislature at the age of twenty-two, and became a civil service commissioner and then police commissioner of New York City. Roosevelt continued his party activity at the national level when he became assistant secretary of the navy in McKinley's first administration. But he resigned this position to lead a volunteer regiment into battle in Cuba during the Spanish-American War. Roosevelt built this regiment around a group of cowboys from his Dakota ranch, where

American leaders of the 1890s resolved that the United States should become a great world power with an overseas frontier. A Panama canal was viewed as critical to such a policy. And Theodore Roosevelt, here inspecting the construction, took great pride in his role in acquiring the canal zone. (Brown Brothers)

he had spent a great deal of time in the 1880s. The newspapers chose to dramatize his "rough-riders" in battle, and Roosevelt returned a war hero. He became governor of New York in 1898 and was elected as McKinley's vice president in 1900. When the assassination of McKinley brought Roosevelt to the presidency, he was distrusted by the conservative Republicans who dominated Congress and by the Republicans, like Senator Mark Hanna of Ohio,

who wanted to develop corporate progressivism within the Republican party. During the early 1890s Roosevelt had enjoyed the thought of having radical farmers and workers shot down in the streets. "I like to see a mob handled by regulars," Roosevelt declared, "not overscrupulous about bloodshed." But by 1900 he shared the concern of LaFollette and other middle-class reformers with making the new industrial corporations act in a socially responsible way.

Frederick Winslow Taylor

1856-1915

The most important spokesman for the importance of engineering in the development of corporate capitalism was Frederick Winslow Taylor. Like Theodore Roosevelt, he was born into an old established eastern family. And like Roosevelt, he was distressed by the decadence and lack of vigor of his father's generation. Taylor, Roosevelt, and other young members of the new middle class were determined to restore order and stability to America. They believed that the older generation of Anglo-Protestants had lost control of society and were incapable of establishing discipline for the new immigrants in the cities and factories.

The optimism of the young men of the new middle class was based on qualities to be found in new professionals. Unlike their fathers, who were undisciplined amateurs, these young men admired professionals as men of order, efficiency, and rationality. Until the late nineteenth century, lawyers, doctors, professionals, and engineers gained their training through apprenticeships with older men. Now in the new universities, professionals were being trained according to national standards.

As an engineer, Taylor was concerned with making the production of both machines and men more rational and efficient. "The disciplinary relations," Taylor wrote, "within the manufacturing organization must be definite and strict." Developing machines that could cut steel more quickly, Taylor also kept records of the time it took workers to accomplish a task and the motions they made during the process. These "time and motion" studies formed the basis of "scientific management."

In 1906, Taylor became president of the professional organization, the American Society of Mechanical Engineers. More and more engineers were taking management positions in corporations and they pictured Taylor as a hero of *their program to cut costs by improving both machines and the work habits of men in the factories. Engineers, not businessmen, according to Taylor should run the corporations. "The shop (indeed, the whole works) should be managed by the planning department," he argued, and a group of his followers started an organization, The New Machine, to replace politicians with engineers.*

When Taylor died in 1915, his memory was honored by the Taylor Society, by which engineers voiced commitment to the goal of making the American economy and society still more rational and efficient. By World War One, individuals most concerned with scientific management instituted widespread psychological testing that was to help them determine where workers could be best fitted into the industrial process to increase plant production.

Since the muckrakers were not able to create a sense of a national reform movement out of many city and state reforms until Roosevelt's second term, the president moved very cautiously before his election in 1904. Nelson Aldrich, a millionaire from Rhode Island whose daughter had married a Rockefeller, was the Republican leader in the Senate. Aldrich opposed legislation to limit or regulate the corporations and dismissed any talk of a new democracy with the statement that "most people don't know what they want." "Uncle Joe" Cannon from Illinois, Speaker of the House of Representatives, rigidly dominated House Republicans. A spokesman for small-town businessmen who were overrepresented in state legislatures throughout the country, Cannon had declared, "I am God-damned tired of listening to all the babble for reform." But Roosevelt was willing to work with these men and wrote to a friend in 1902 that "My experience for the last year and a half has made me feel respect and regard for Aldrich, who together with men like Joe Cannon, are the most powerful factors in Congress."

Despite his caution in dealing with these Republican conservatives in Congress, Roosevelt had begun to make a reputation as a progressive before 1904. He planned to use the presidency as a "bully pulpit" to call for a higher moral tone throughout American society. "One of the chief things I have tried to preach to the American politician and the American businessman," Roosevelt said, "is not to grasp at money." Many middle-class men were longing for a strong figure who would end the moral confusion of the 1890s and felt they had found him in Roosevelt. William Allen White, an editor of a small-town newspaper in Emporia, Kansas, who became accepted as a national spokesman for small-town support of progressivism, was one of these men. Roosevelt, White wrote, "has inspired more men to right-eousness in public life than a millionaire could call forth with all the millions of Wall Street."

During his first administration, Roosevelt was able to engage in two major actions that ex-pressed his attitudes toward corporations. "Our aim is not to do away with corporations," he told Congress in 1902. "On the contrary, these big aggregations are the inevitable develop-ment of modern industrialism, and the effort to destroy them would be futile." For Roosevelt, the friends of corporate property "must realize that the surest way to provoke an explosion of wrong and injustice is to be short-sighted, nar-row-minded, greedy, and arrogant." When fi-nanciers who represented J. P. Morgan and John D. Rockefeller created the Northern Se-curities Company in 1901, Roosevelt was out-raged. Voters were afraid of railroad monopolies and of the power of Wall Street. Now these two combined to bring all the railroads serving the western half of the country into a single company and end whatever competition ex-isted between the major railroads. For Roose-velt, this constituted the kind of corporate arro-gance and insensitivity to public opinion that might lead to the resurgence of agrarian and worker radicalism. The president ordered his attorney general, Philander Knox, to use the Sherman Antitrust Act to break up the com-pany. The government suit was successful in 1904.

After winning the *Northern Securities* case, Roosevelt personally asked the chief executives of U.S. Steel and the International Harvester Company to cooperate with the newly created Bureau of Corporations. These "gentlemen's agreements" provided that the bureau quietly would investigate corporate procedures and

make recommendations for more responsible business practices in the future. Roosevelt had persuaded Congress in 1903 to establish a De-partment of Commerce and Labor. The Bureau of Corporations was within this new depart-ment, and Roosevelt planned to use it to regu-late large corporations rather than use the Sher-man Antitrust Act to dissolve them. To teach corporate leaders to accept government regula-tion, however, the president held out the threat of the Sherman Antitrust Act. When Standard Oil executives refused to cooperate with the Bureau of Corporations, Roosevelt ordered them sued under the Sherman Act, and the Supreme Court broke Standard Oil into several smaller companies in 1906.

In order to preserve stability in the work-place and discourage a strong socialist move-ment, Roosevelt urged corporate leaders to accept labor unions that worked within the capitalist system. The president's position was similar to that of Mark Hanna's influential Na-tional Civic Federation, an organization that frowned upon corporate price competition and sought harmony between labor and manage-ment. To win the support of organized labor, Hanna had invited Samuel Gompers, head of the AFL, to serve as an NCF vice president.

Roosevelt's concern for stable labor relations led to his public support of the United Mine Workers during a 1902 strike in hard coal. UMW president John Mitchell, a member of NCF, had called the strike to win union recog-nition and a 10 percent pay raise. But compe-titive mine owners tried to smash the union movement with strikebreakers and private secu-rity forces. George Baer, the spokesman of the owners, adamantly refused negotiations with Mitchell and declared that "God in His infinite wisdom had given control of the property interests of this country to good men" who would do what was right for their workers. The owners continued to refuse bargaining with Mitchell, even when Roosevelt called them to a conference in Washington. Faced with a fuel shortage in the cities and the kind of arrogant language that might inspire workers to revolution, Roosevelt threatened to declare a national emergency and use the army to seize the mines. This warning frightened the owners into accepting arbitration from a presidential commission that included a union representative.

ROOSEVELT, THE ELECTION OF 1904, AND PRESIDENTIAL ACTIVISM

Roosevelt's "corporate progressivism" appeared to align the Republican party with workers and consumers. To enlarge upon McKinley's appeal to urban ethnic groups, Roosevelt had appointed several Catholics and Jews to positions in the federal government. Personally popular with many Americans, Roosevelt won the first presidential landslide of the twentieth century, defeating the Democrat Parker in 1904 by 7.6 million votes (56 percent) to 5.1 million votes (38 percent). But the percentage of eligible voters who participated in the election dropped from over 71 percent in 1900 to less than 65 percent. Part of the decline occurred because reform-minded Democrats stayed home. Parker received 1.3 million fewer votes than Bryan had in 1900. But Socialist voters increased from nearly 100,000 in 1900 to 400,000.

More confident after this victory, Roosevelt increased his activism during the second term, enlarging the federal bureaucracy as well as the power of the presidency. The number of government employees doubled from 200,000 to 400,000 between 1900 and 1916. Roosevelt's most consistent use of executive power during his first administration had come in the area of natural resources. Conservation was the most important subject in his first address in 1901. Emphasizing the efficient use of vital natural resources more than the preservation of virgin wilderness, Roosevelt planned to withdraw most of the forest lands owned by the national government from unplanned economic exploitation by private interests. But western congressmen opposed the scheme because it threatened to slow the rate of economic growth. To reconcile these politicians to his policy, Roosevelt promised that the national government would build dams and irrigation systems throughout the West. According to Roosevelt's plans, this program, embodied in the New Lands Reclamation Act of 1902, would open millions of acres of desert land to farming.

Roosevelt also transferred the public forest lands from the Department of the Interior to the Department of Agriculture, where the Forestry Bureau was headed by his friend Gifford Pinchot. Pinchot, like Roosevelt, came from an established eastern family. He had gone to Germany to study, attracted by German leadership in developing conservation policies that would sustain yields from their forests for generations to come. Pinchot and Roosevelt were determined to apply these techniques of scientific management to American forests. Both believed that planning by government experts for the multiple use of forests by lumbermen, cattle ranchers, and vacationers pointed in the direction of corporate progressivism. The free enterprise system needed overall planning and control by government professionals who could take the problems of the entire national economy into account in a way that private interests could not. Roosevelt also persuaded Congress to pass the Antiquities Act in 1906, which allowed presidents to protect wilderness areas from economic development until Congress could incorporate them into the national park system.

Roosevelt's conservation policies pleased those progressives who advocated a consumers' democracy. The president built on this identification with consumers by providing leadership for three pieces of reform legislation in 1906 — the Hepburn Act, the Pure Food and Drug Act, and the Meat Inspection Act.

The Hepburn Act increased the size and jurisdiction of the Interstate Commerce Commission and provided the agency with greater authority to set transportation rates. Under its provisions, federal courts could demand that railroad rates represent "reasonable" margins of profit. The law met the progressive coalition's demand for rate control over the railroads, long regarded as the major symbol of monopoly control in the national economy. But many railroad executives also supported government regulation that provided greater economic stability and left them free from inconsistent regulations by the states. A number of railroad leaders therefore approved of the Elkins Act of 1903, which forbade rebates from railroads to large shippers, and rallied to support the popular Hepburn bill three years later.

Regulatory legislation concerning food, drugs, and meat came in the midst of a public uproar over unsanitary and unsafe conditions in those industries. The Pure Food and Drug Act prohibited the production and sale of adulterated goods and outlawed false labeling of food and and drug items. The Meat Inspection Act established federal inspection to ensure that

packers met sanitary standards set by the government. Muckraking articles in major magazines and Upton Sinclair's novel *The Jungle* (1906), which described the filth, including rats, that regularly went into meat products intensified the public discontent that encouraged Congress and the president to act. But leadership for passage of the consumer bills came from government bureaucrats such as Harvey Wiley, a chemist for the Department of Agriculture, and business groups such as the National Board of Trade. Large meatpacking and drug companies accepted the new legislation because it set standards of production that they could meet more easily than their small competitors. One of the largest meat companies, Swift, advocated passage in newspaper advertisement that read "It is a wise law." High standards also promised to discourage foreign competitors by creating a better reputation for American products in overseas markets.

Roosevelt understood the growing enthusiasm in both political parties for reform within the capitalist system. Despite attacks by midwestern progressives like LaFollette, who charged that the president ignored tariff and banking reforms and compromised too easily with conservative congressional leaders, Roosevelt continued to use the presidency to explain the need for change. He tried to persuade the American people to give up their ideal of the nineteenth-century marketplace dominated by small farmers and independent businessmen. He urged them instead to accept large corporations and labor unions and to support a national bureaucracy that could regulate the activities of both. By 1908 Roosevelt's desire to check both irresponsible profiteering and the threat from a growing Socialist party brought him to espouse the need for income and inheritance taxes to keep the rich from monopolizing national wealth. The president also criticized the courts for hostility toward labor unions, state workmen's compensation laws, and state regulation of working conditions for women.

TAFT AND THE PROGRESSIVE MOVEMENT

Roosevelt's inability to share leadership prevented him from supporting a vigorous successor like LaFollette to carry out the changes that the president wanted in the Republican party. Instead, Roosevelt chose William Howard Taft to be the Republican presidential candidate in 1908. Taft was a lawyer and government bureaucrat who had been governor general of the Philippines and had served as Roosevelt's secretary of war. The Republican candidate promised voters to continue Roosevelt's reform programs and administer them with efficiency; but Taft did not appear to be the kind of leader who would initiate his own reforms. Nevertheless, Roosevelt campaigned vigorously for him, and Taft prevailed easily over Bryan, who had regained control of the Democratic party. Taft won over 7.6 million votes and Bryan 6.4 million, but Bryan brought many reform-minded Democrats back to the polls, amassing over 1.3 million more votes than Parker had in 1904. As the percentage of voter participation returned to 68 percent, the Democrats finally checked the steady growth of Republican strength in the United States Senate. There had been forty-three Republicans and thirty-nine Democrats in the Senate of 1894. By 1906 the ratio was sixty-one Republicans to thirty Democrats. This division remained static

in 1908, while the Democrats gained eight seats in the House of Representatives, cutting the Republican majority to 219–172.

Despite popular support for political reform, Taft did not share Roosevelt's eagerness to carry the struggle further. "We are not in favor of the rule of all the people as an end desirable in itself," the new president declared. "The lesson must be learned that there is only a limited zone within which legislation and governments can accomplish good." Taft believed that Americans should avoid "a constant contemplation of the suffering and misfortune of the world."

But while the president feared Roosevelt's increasing demands for inheritance and income taxes and labor reform, Taft was not afraid to force the tariff issue that his predecessor had avoided. Calling Congress into special session in 1909, the president requested a moderate reduction from the high levels of the Dingley Tariff of 1897. But Taft infuriated midwestern Republican progressives when he accepted the Payne-Aldrich Tariff, which raised rates and threatened overseas crop sales. For men like LaFollette, the president had betrayed progressivism by supporting the conservatism of Senator Aldrich. Progressives found further evidence of this betrayal when Taft dismissed Gifford Pinchot, Roosevelt's director of national forests. The president's conservatism was opposed to both strong executive power and to leadership by administrative specialists. Instead, Taft entrusted decisions to the legislature, the courts, and the marketplace. Accordingly, the Pinchot firing was prompted by congressional suspicion of Roosevelt's conservation policies and the president's belief that Pinchot's administrative planning violated the operation of the free marketplace. Taft also replaced

Roosevelt's conservation-minded secretary of the interior, James R. Garfield, with Richard Ballinger, who argued that free enterprise should develop the resources on national lands.

While progressive Republicans charged that the Taft administration was permitting a conspiracy of big businessmen to gain control of land that Roosevelt had withdrawn from economic development, the president began to believe that progressives were conspiring to wrest control of the Republican party from him. When progressive Republicans, led by George Norris of Nebraska, organized to break the power of House Speaker Cannon, Taft refused to support them. Once the progressives defeated Cannon, the break between progressive Republicans and the president was complete.

As the 1910 congressional elections neared, Taft seemed to be leading the Republican party in a reactionary direction. Aided by strong support from the growing American Federation of Labor, the Democrats won control of the House of Representatives for the first time since 1892 and captured ten Republican seats in the Senate. As conservative Republicans met defeat in several states in the East, Midwest, and West, Democratic progressives captured national attention. In New Jersey, Woodrow Wilson won the governorship on a reform platform, while Montana progressive Thomas T. Walsh captured a Democratic Senate seat from a conservative Republican.

As lines between progressives and conservatives hardened in 1910, Roosevelt returned from a lengthy trip in Africa to make his first full identification with the progressive emphasis on the new democracy. He attracted national publicity with a speech at Osawatomie, Kansas, which called for reform legislation in the spirit of a "New Nationalism." The former president stressed the need for national political leaders to establish regulatory policies that would direct the actions of capitalists, workers, and farmers, away from selfish concerns toward a unified national interest. "Our country," Roosevelt declared, "means nothing unless it means the triumph of a real democracy, the triumph of popular government." Taft had vetoed the admission of the Arizona territory as a state because its constitution included the recall of judges. For the president, this represented the "possible tyranny of a popular majority" and threatened the "independence of the judiciary." But Roosevelt now accepted recall of judges because their decisions barred "the path to industrial, economic, and social reform" and hampered the expansion of government power.

Taft believed by 1911 that Roosevelt had become dangerously radical and that it was the president's responsibility to keep Roosevelt or LaFollette from capturing the following year's Republican nomination. Accordingly, Taft began to work through conservative Republican leaders to line up delegates to support him at the national convention. He was particularly successful in winning support from delegates of the southern states, where the progressive movement was monopolized by the Democratic party.

Unlike Roosevelt, Taft hoped to preserve the nineteenth-century marketplace of small producers. As a result, the president initiated twice as many antitrust suits in four years as Roosevelt had in eight. In order to embarrass Roosevelt, Taft began proceedings against U.S. Steel. During a sharp financial panic in 1907, Roosevelt had prevailed upon J. P. Morgan, the most powerful banker on Wall Street, to release money into the economy to halt the financial decline. Morgan had agreed, but won the president's promise to avoid antitrust action against U.S. Steel, in which Morgan had large financial interests. Roosevelt felt that such an agreement was proper, since U.S. Steel earlier had agreed to supervision by the Bureau of Corporations.

Taft's suit not only reversed the assurance of his predecessor, but made Roosevelt appear to be a tool of Wall Street rather than a progressive. Eastern progressives easily convinced an angry Roosevelt to oppose Taft at the 1912 convention, creating a bitter split within the Republican party. Reformers such as LaFollette were aware that the Democrats were increasing their strength by identifying more strongly with progressivism. But Taft and other conservative Republicans opposed progressive demands such as the enactment of constitutional amendments to permit a federal income tax and direct election of United States senators. Republican progressives reasoned that opposition to popular reform programs could compound the Democratic party victories of 1910 with further Republican losses in 1912.

While reform-minded Republicans opposed the renomination of Taft, eastern progressives differed sharply with progressives from the Midwest and West. Reformers such as Albert Beveridge of Indiana, Albert Cummins and Jonathan Doliver of Iowa, Moses Clapp of Minnesota, Joseph Bristow of Kansas, and William Borah of Idaho joined LaFollette's battle against the "money trust" of eastern finance and industry. In his campaign to win the Republican presidential nomination, LaFollette emphasized competition as the way to protect consumers from monopoly control by the large corporations. But LaFollette's effort failed to appeal to "corporate" progressives such as U.S. Steel's George Perkins and generated little enthusiasm in the industrial East. In contrast, Roosevelt spoke of limited competition in a stable environment that would allow large corporations to

engage in long-range planning. Impressed by Roosevelt's emphasis on government regulation of competition and aware of his national popularity, midwestern and western progressives joined eastern reformers in abandoning LaFollette and supporting the Roosevelt nomination.

Roosevelt easily defeated Taft in the minority of states that now used primaries to select delegates to the national convention, humiliating the president in his home state of Ohio. But conservative Republicans named the delegates in the majority of states where regular party machinery rather than primaries made the decision, and Taft won a first-ballot nomination. Although Roosevelt had preached loyalty to the Republican party all his life, he now agreed to become the presidential candidate of insurgent Republicans who formed the Progressive party as a third force in American politics. LaFollette, however, refused to support Roosevelt.

Although Roosevelt out-polled Taft in the 1912 presidential election, the split in Republican ranks enabled the Democrats to capture the White House and Senate and to consolidate their control of the House. Woodrow Wilson, a progressive Democrat, won 6.3 million votes; Roosevelt, 4.1 million; Taft, 3.5 million; and Eugene Debs, the candidate of the Socialist party, received nearly 1 million. In the electoral college, however, Wilson won an impressive 435 votes, while Roosevelt tallied 88 and Taft a mere 8.

WILSON AND CORPORATE PROGRESSIVISM

Roosevelt's New Nationalism stressed the need to provide a stable environment in which cor-

MAP 4.1   THE ELECTION OF 1912

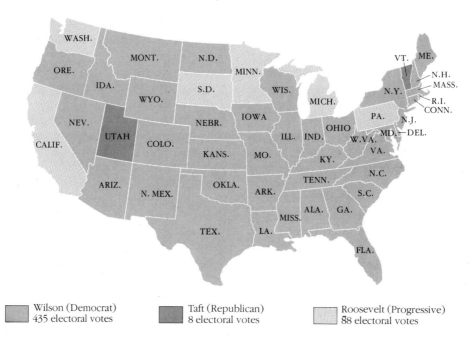

Wilson (Democrat)
435 electoral votes

Taft (Republican)
8 electoral votes

Roosevelt (Progressive)
88 electoral votes

porations could plan and grow. The Progressive party platform marked a departure in political rhetoric with its admission that "the corporation is an essential part of modern business. The concentration of modern business is both inevitable and necessary for national and international business efficiency." Wilson, in contrast, spoke of a "New Freedom" that would restore competition for small businessmen and farmers. "If America is not to have freedom of enterprise," the Democratic candidate declared, "then she can have freedom of no sort whatever."

Like Roosevelt, however, Wilson represented a mixed constituency. Part of the president's support came from southern agrarians such as

Mississippi's Senator James K. Vardaman, who wished to restrain the growth of corporations and make them responsive to the average voter. But Wilson, a Virginian, also was part of a whole generation of young middle-class southerners who wanted their region to overcome its provincialism. These urban progressives wanted the South to give up its emphasis on agrarianism as well as evangelical Protestantism and to share in the national patterns of urbanization and industrialization. They urged white middle-class southerners to forget the past that separated them from the rest of the nation and to commit themselves to a future in which they would share in the national leadership.

When Wilson became president, he surrounded himself with southern progressives such as Postmaster General Albert Burleson from Texas, Secretary of the Treasury William Gibbs McAdoo from Georgia, and Secretary of the Navy Josephus Daniels from North Carolina. Congressman Carter Glass, a leader of progressive reform in Virginia, also advised the White House in the Wilson years. Progressives such as Daniels and Glass, spokesmen for the new South of cities and factories, advocated leadership by government experts who would impose efficiency, rationality, and responsibility on the large corporations.

Despite these differences, both southern agrarians and progressives joined other Americans in supporting Wilson's proposals for regulation of the corporations through government commissions and backed the president's legislative remedies for the problems of consumers as well. Wilson enthusiastically endorsed the Underwood Tariff of 1913, which provided the first significant reduction in import duties since the pre–Civil War years. Consumers and farmers rejoiced that prices on many manufactured goods would be lowered, while industrialists approved of the reduced costs for imported raw materials. Proponents of the lower tariff also hoped both to stimulate foreign sales by erasing trade barriers and to promote American industrial efficiency through worldwide competition. Ratification of the Sixteenth Amendment in 1913 enabled Congress to pass an income tax bill that provided the treasury with money to replace lost tariff revenues. The Wilson administration also passed the Clayton Antitrust Act in 1914, which attempted to block loopholes in the Sherman Act by barring interlocking directorates, price fixing, and stock ownership in competing firms.

While the Clayton Act fulfilled the New Freedom promise to discipline monopolistic corporations, the law also demonstrated Wilson's commitment to corporate progressivism. Supported by the National Civic Federation and the Chamber of Commerce, the Clayton Act sought to avoid the "destructive competition" that prevented intelligent corporate planning. To the relief of corporations operating upon uncertain guidelines, the legislation clarified the limits of corporate competition by specifying "unfair practices." The Wilson administration hoped to administer the Clayton Act through the Federal Trade Commission, which Congress created to replace the Bureau of Corporations in 1914. Taft had believed that the courts should implement antitrust regulations. But the Federal Trade Commission followed Roosevelt's preference for a regulatory commission that could handle changing business circumstances. Both the Clayton Act and the FTC established predictable ground rules for corporate competition, so that antitrust policy would not be left to arbitrary officials or court decisions in each presidential administration.

While Wilson managed to please both corporate and anticorporate progressives with an innovative antitrust policy, he accomplished the same feat in regard to banking. Following the financial panic of 1907, Wall Street bankers had encouraged Congress to study ways in which the government could stabilize the nation's banking system. The conservative Republican Senator Nelson Aldrich led that task as head of the newly created National Monetary Commission. Meanwhile, the continuing hostility of farmers and small businessmen to the concentration of financial power in New York led to the establishment of the Pujo Committee in the House, which investigated Wall Street amid great publicity and sought to disperse the power of eastern bankers. Both inquiries played a role in Congress's creation of the Federal Reserve system in 1913.

Although the decentralizing forces thought they had prevailed, the Federal Reserve supported the needs of large bankers. Under the system, twelve Federal Reserve banks represented twelve regions of the country. These banks were owned by private bankers. All private banks that wanted to operate nationally were required to invest part of their capital in the Federal Reserve bank in their district. In addition to these national banks, any statewide bank could invest in the Federal Reserve bank as well. A Federal Reserve Board, appointed by the president, decided on the rate of interest to be paid by the regional Federal Reserve bank to investor banks. If the board wanted to encourage expansion, it lowered the interest rate, making it easier to borrow money; to curb inflation, it raised interest rates. The Federal Reserve system also provided reserves to cover local financial crises and established the nation's first coordinated check clearance.

Despite Wilson's plea for competition in the New Freedom, the president appeared to agree with Roosevelt's insistence that the trend toward big business was inevitable. "Nobody can fail to see that modern business is going to be done by corporations," Wilson declared, emphasizing that "the old time of individual competition is gone by." Repeatedly the president stressed that "I am not one of those who think that competition can be established by law against the drift of a worldwide economic tendency." For Wilson the future was one in which "we will do business on a. great and successful scale, by means of corporations." The president's selection of regulatory commissioners reflected these beliefs. Eastern financiers continued to dominate banking policy through presidential appointments to the Federal Reserve Board. Creation of the Federal Reserve actually reversed the gains that smaller state banks had made in competition with larger national banks since 1900. Wilson also appointed corporate executives to the Federal Trade Commission, which continued to rely on the private rulings for businessmen that had characterized Roosevelt's Bureau of Corporations.

The greatest irony of the Progressive period was that the leaders of the growing Socialist party agreed with Roosevelt and Wilson that the growth of corporations was caused by impersonal economic forces and was therefore inevitable. Eugene Debs was converted to socialism when the federal government had put him in jail for leading a strike of railroad workers in 1894. Debs's conversion enabled him to see that it was impossible for farmers and workers to stop the inevitable concentration of the means of production in fewer hands. But Debs did not agree with men like Daniel DeLeon, the head of the Socialist Labor party, that violent revolution would be necessary to overthrow corporate capitalism after it had impoverished all the workers. For Debs and most American Socialists, it was possible for the productive people to become a majority political party. When Socialists had become the dominant political power by working within the constitutional process, they could socialize the large industrial corporations. Socialists believed that the more concentrated the economic system, the easier the Socialist takeover would be.

With Debs its major leader, the Socialist party increased its voter support from below 100,000 in 1900 to 400,000 in 1904 and to nearly one million in 1912. It had strength among Jewish workers in New York and German workers in Milwaukee, Slavic and Italian immigrants in Chicago, and iron miners in Minnesota. Socialism also appealed to many Anglo-Protestant farmers in east Texas, northern Louisiana, Arkansas, Oklahoma, and the Great Plains states. More than one thousand Socialists held political offices in city and state governments by 1912, while five daily Socialist newspapers were published in English and eight dailies in other languages. Of the two hundred Socialist weeklies that reached 500,000 subscribers, the most popular was the *Appeal to Reason,* published in Kansas. A number of intellectuals and artists also became Socialists during the Wilson administration. An Intercollegiate Socialist Society flourished with chapters in sixty colleges, while socialism had sufficient appeal among some Protestant ministers to enable them to form a Christian Socialist Fellowship.

Socialists such as Debs, however, did not consider the possibility that the growth of corporations was aided by the extension of government power. Socialists and anticorporate progressives like LaFollette saw the development of government commissions at the city, state, and national level as the triumph of the people over the selfish interests of big business. But they were not aware of the extent to which corporate progressives wanted regulatory commissions to minimize competition because corporations hoped to flourish better without the instability of price competition. Socialists and LaFollette progressives also saw the growth of executive power for mayors, governors, and presidents as a victory for the people, reasoning that narrow business interests often controlled the courts and the legislatures. But they failed to see that strong executives could surround themselves with nonelected experts and bureaucrats who could set policies without the

advice and participation of the average voter. Nor did they anticipate the interrelationships between the growing bureaucracies of the large private corporations and the new government regulatory agencies.

Like Roosevelt, Wilson hoped to reverse the appeal of socialism by presenting himself as the spokesman of all the American people. Wilson's first act as president was to speak to a special session of Congress called to consider the administration's legislative program, the first presidential appearance before Congress since 1800. The president shared Roosevelt's belief that reforms in the interests of workers, farmers, and consumers could protect corporate capitalism from revolution. The Clayton Act, for example, specifically exempted labor unions and agricultural organizations from antitrust prosecution and restricted the use of court injunctions against union activities. Pressed to rally reform and labor support during the election year of 1916, Wilson worked successfully for more legislation helpful to workers. Congress provided workmen's compensation for federal employees, passed the Adamson Act to establish an eight-hour day for railroad workers, and barred goods made by children under sixteen in the Keating-Owen Labor Act. Such labor legislation kept Samuel Gompers and other leaders of the American Federation of Labor loyal to the president during both the election campaign and the controversies surrounding American entry into World War One.

Wilson also won the support of farm organizations with his support in 1916 of federally funded land banks. The president adamantly had opposed government financing of rural credits as an unfair extension of assistance to special interests. But his conversion to the farm crusade for low-interest loans marked a new involvement of the federal bureaucracy in the national marketplace. The administration also supported legislation that provided government matching funds to states for the placing of agricultural specialists in every rural county in the nation. While the agricultural extension service benefited some small farmers, its introduction of new farming techniques proved most helpful to large farmers who could afford to adopt innovative methods. The Wilson administration further involved government agencies in social programs with the Smith-Hughes Act of 1917, which brought federal funds into the states to support vocational education.

Wilson's program for regulation of labor, agriculture, and corporations by government experts found its most explicit expression in the appointment of Louis Brandeis to the Supreme Court. Brandeis was the first Jew to sit on the Court, and there was great controversy over his appointment. Although Roosevelt and Wilson held firm to the caste system separating whites and blacks, both were willing to modify the caste system separating Anglo-Protestants from Jews and Catholics. Progressive commitment to professionalism was so strong that leaders such as Roosevelt and Wilson could visualize a white aristocracy of talent, rather than one of inherited family position, characterizing government bureaucracies.

Corporate progressives were impressed by Brandeis because he persuaded the Supreme Court in *Muller* v. *Oregon* (1908) to uphold the constitutionality of an Oregon law setting maximum working hours for women. Earlier in *Lochner* v. *New York* (1905), the Court had held that it was unconstitutional for a state to set maximum hours. Brandeis, therefore, had argued against legal precedent based on nineteenth-century principles of a free marketplace

and emphasized the existence of a new and modern twentieth-century industrial environment. His legal brief cited current economic practices, the sociological implications for the family of excessive work loads for women, and health statistics that pointed to the social costs of illness from overwork. Brandeis became a major adviser to Wilson in 1913 because the president liked his emphasis on the way government experts could keep large corporations from becoming inefficient in their business practices.

By 1917, therefore, the Wilson administration had laid the foundation of the modern state. Based on Roosevelt's New Nationalism, the economy would be managed by government experts and corporate executives who adhered to the logic of rational efficiency and noncompetitive planning. Federal laws and agencies would encourage social stability by providing assistance to workers, farmers, and consumers and by granting elements of power to the organizations that represented them. Wilson was the key ideological and political leader of the progressive movement that moved to acclimate the American people to a corporate society espousing liberal ideals. He accomplished this by enlarging the power of the federal government and the presidency. In doing so, Wilson also laid the foundation for a state in which the president could use government agencies to enforce his special vision of national unity and minimize any significant dissent. These economic and political changes played a major role in the nation's response to involvement in World War One.

SUGGESTED READINGS

Two good collections of essays are Blaine A. Brownell and Warren E. Stickle, eds., *Bosses and Reformers: Urban Politics in America, 1880–1920* (1973), and Bruce M. Stave, ed., *Urban Bosses, Machines, and Progressive Reformers* (1972). A fine study by a political scientist is Theodore F. Lowi, *At the Pleasure of the Mayor: Patronage and Power in New York City* (1964), and Chicago is analyzed in two books, Joel A. Tarr, *A Study in Boss Politics: William Lorimer of Chicago* (1971), and Harold F. Gosnell, *Machine Politics, the Chicago Model* (1973). The reaction of Anglo-Protestant elites is the subject of Arthur Mann, *Yankee Reformers in an Urban Age* (1954), and John G. Sproat, *The Best Men: Liberal Reformers in the Gilded Age* (1968). Zane L. Miller, *Boss Cox's Cincinnati: Urban Politics in the Progressive Era* (1968), analyzes the complex relationship of reformers and bosses, as does Melvin G. Holli, *Reform in Detroit: Hazen S. Pingree and Urban Politics* (1969). Robert D. Cross, *The Emergence of Liberal Catholicism in America* (1959), and John D. Buenker, *Urban Liberalism and Progressive Reform* (1973), discuss the role of the new immigrants in state and national reform, as does Irwin Yellowitz, *Labor and the Progressive Movement in New York State* (1965).

Political scientist Walter Burnham presents a brilliant analysis of the revolutionary change in politics at the end of the 1890s in his book, *Critical Elections and the Mainstream of American Politics* (1972). Whereas Burnham is critical of this change, David P. Thelen defends it in his two books, *The New Citizenship: Origins of Progressivism in Wisconsin, 1885–1900* (1972) and *Robert M. LaFollette* (1976). Ga-briel Kolko, *The Triumph of Conservatism* (1963), provided the first major description of corporate progressivism. Useful biographies of three different kinds of middle-class political leaders are Alpheus T. Mason, *Brandeis* (1946), Richard Leopold, *Elihu Root* (1954), and John Braeman, *Albert J. Beveridge* (1971). Good biographies of Roosevelt as a progressive reformer are John Morton Blum, *The Republican Roosevelt* (1954), George E. Mowry, *The Era of Theodore Roosevelt* (1958), and William H. Harbough, *Power and Responsibility: The Life and Times of Theodore Roosevelt* (1961). John A. Garraty, *Right Hand Man: The Life of George W. Perkins* (1960), illuminates Roosevelt's ties with large corporations such as U. S. Steel.

Charles Forcey, *The Cross Roads of Liberalism* (1961), and David W. Noble, *The Progressive Mind* (1970), examine the influence on Roosevelt of political theorists such as Herbert Croly. David M. Chalmers, *The Social and Political Ideas of the Muckrakers* (1964), demonstrates the role of these writers in helping to shape progressivism. The attitudes of the Supreme Court that frustrated Roosevelt are described in Robert McCloskey, *The Modern Supreme Court* (1972), and Loren P. Beth, *The Development of the American Constitution, 1877–1917* (1971).

The conflict of philosophies between Taft and Roosevelt is clarified in Samuel P. Hays, *Conservation and the Gospel of Efficiency* (1959), and Donald E. Anderson, *William Howard Taft* (1973). Arthur S. Link, *Woodrow Wilson and the Progressive Era* (1954), is the standard work by Wilson's major biographer.

The most important studies of socialism and radicalism for this period are Roy Ginger, *The*

Bending Cross: A Biography of Eugene Victor Debs (1949), David Shannon, *The Socialist Party in America* (1955), James Weinstein, *The Decline of Socialism in America* (1967), Melvin Dubofsky, *We Shall Be All: A History of the Industrial Workers of the World* (1969), and John P. Diggins, *The American Left in the Twentieth Century* (1973).

Spotlight: The Anthracite Coal Strike of 1902

In May 1902, leaders of the United Mine Workers called out on strike their members in the anthracite coal fields of Pennsylvania and Ohio. The miners wanted a pay raise, shorter hours, and recognition of their union, but their demands were rejected by the mine owners. As the strike dragged on through the summer and into the fall, however, it became much more than a simple conflict of interest between the owners of the mines and the men who worked in them. A generation earlier, most Americans had lived on farms or in small towns. Their energy needs for heating were met by local supplies of wood. Most of the energy to drive their machines came from horses. But the huge new factories of 1900 depended on energy from coal, either through direct burning to turn steam engines or indirectly from electrical motors powered by coal-burning generating plants. And the populations of the rapidly expanding cities also depended on coal for heat in winter. A severe shortage of coal in the winter of 1902 could have caused a national crisis comparable to one that would result from a severe shortage of oil and natural gas today.

As the coal mines became crucial to the industrial economy between 1870 and 1900, the owners used private detectives to infiltrate the ranks of workers so that union organizers could be identified and fired. When worker attempts to establish independent bargaining groups survived this kind of harassment, management expected cooperation from local police and the state militia to smash union organizations. As a last resort, the mine owners anticipated support from the federal government and the use of federal troops. Now, in 1902, they requested a federal court to issue an injunction against the strike. They also asked President Roosevelt to have the attorney general bring a suit against the strikers under the Sherman Antitrust Act and to send troops into the coal fields to force the workers into an immediate return to the mines.

Roosevelt had applauded President Cleveland in 1894 when he used federal troops to break up the railroad workers' strike. He also approved of the federal arrest, prosecution, and imprisonment of Eugene Debs and the leaders of the American Railway Union. But by 1901, when McKinley's assassination brought him to the presidency, Roosevelt had changed his mind about the relationship of property owners to their employees. He no longer believed in ruthless repression of the work force. Roosevelt now warned that continuation of this repressive policy by the owners of property and by government would result in the development of a strong Socialist movement in the United States. Workers, seeing the establishment as their enemy, might accept the socialist theory of the inevitability of class warfare and work for the revolutionary overthrow of capitalism. Roosevelt was aware that Debs had been radicalized after his imprisonment in 1894 and had begun to build a Socialist party in 1900. "The growth of the Socialist party in this country," Roosevelt warned "is far more ominous than any populist movement in times past."

Roosevelt as president, therefore, was in agreement with the leadership of the National Civic Federation (NCF), which had been founded in 1900. These leaders represented the thinking that was emerging among the men who managed the new giant corporations. For them, the 1880s and 1890s had been characterized by chaotic competition among companies, a destructive tendency for the entire business community. NCF leaders hoped to avoid price competition among the large corporations in order to end cycles of boom and bust. They also believed that corporate managers should promote accord with their workers to ensure internal stability. The NCF proclaimed as its goal, therefore, the restoration of the "normal sense of social solidarity which is the foundation stone of democracy." Its leadership pledged to end the conflict between capital and labor that had caused their relationship to "become strained almost to the breaking point." It was the duty of the NCF to "bring into closer and more harmonious relations these two apparently antagonistic forces," even by accepting conservative trade unions when necessary.

The most important founder of the NCF was Senator Mark Hanna of Ohio, a millionaire owner of coal mines and steel mills. Hanna had used his organizational skills and contacts with the business community to raise much more money for McKinley's presidential campaign in 1896 and 1900 than had been thought possible. Hanna hoped to use his influence with McKinley to lead the Republican party away from its commitment to individualistic capitalism and toward Hanna's vision of corporate capitalism. He saw the NCF as the focal point where successful businessmen, influential corporation lawyers, newspaper publishers, and college presidents who were loyal to the Republican party could work out the philosophy of corporate capitalism and spread its doctrines throughout the party. Labor leaders Samuel Gompers and John Mitchell were active in the NCF. Mitchell declared he was "glad to be a part of this peace movement" because he believed unions could exist only if the large corporations were willing to tolerate them. And he knew that the business and political leaders of the NCF were willing to tolerate them because they hoped they would "stand as a strong bulwark against the great wave of socialism."

By the end of the summer of 1902, Mitchell asked the national government to arbitrate the issues of wages and hours. He surrendered on the issue of union recognition because he knew that although the members of the NCF and President Roosevelt were solidly in favor of better working conditions and wages for labor, they were not solidly in favor of union organization. George Perkins, for example, who was a partner of the J. P. Morgan banking house and who was on the board of directors of U.S. Steel, was an active leader of the NCF. But Perkins shared the antiunion paternalism of Elbert Gary, the chairman of U.S. Steel. Corporate leaders could avoid unions, according to Gary, if "you make certain that the men in your employ are treated as well, if not a little better, than other men who are working for people who deal and contract with unions...and so far as you can, cultivate a feeling of friendship."

Roosevelt was eager to provide arbitration. He had resented being placed in the unimportant position of vice president. Now that fate had brought him to the presidency, he was determined to become the national leader of the Republican party and ensure his nomination as the Republican presidential candidate in 1904. Hanna, as Roosevelt saw it, was his only serious rival for the nomination. As a convert to Hanna's notions of corporate capitalism and corporate progressivism, Roosevelt nevertheless believed that the presidency provided a much stronger platform for teaching those concepts to the American people than did the NCF. Like Hanna, Roosevelt wanted to "subordinate the interests of the individual to the interests of the community." But more than most leaders of the NCF, Roosevelt was sure that the government rather than the large corporation could lead the individual toward social responsibility. "The sphere of the State's action may be vastly increased," Roosevelt declared, "without in any way diminishing the happiness of either the many or the few."

Roosevelt disagreed, therefore, with Perkins that corporate executives could represent all the different economic groups in the country. Perkins believed that

119

"the officers of the great corporations instinctively lose sight of the interest of any one individual and work for what is the broadest, most enduring interest of the many." For Perkins, these corporate officers standing on "commanding heights" were "no longer controlled by the mere business view" but were able to act "the part of the statesman." Roosevelt, however, was sure that only the president was capable of that kind of statesmanship. And his experience with corporate leaders in the anthracite strike crisis confirmed this view.

Hanna, as a leader of the NCF, wanted the mine owners to deal with a "safe" labor leader like Mitchell. But he also wanted a settlement to help ensure his re-election to the United States Senate from Ohio. Since J. P. Morgan provided capital to many of the owners, Hanna asked Perkins to have Morgan put pressure on them. "There are several important places where U.S. Steel could do me lots of good," Hanna pleaded. "I am bleeding at every pore already and can't bear the burden."

Morgan, however, was afraid that he did not have enough influence with the owners to force them into arbitration and refused Hanna's request for help. But in the fall of 1902, Roosevelt called the mine owners and Mitchell to the White House to discuss arbitration. At first the owners withstood Roosevelt's pressure to arbitrate. Many believed that labor had no right to share in decisions of wages and hours. Property owners, they argued, must be completely free to control their property as they saw fit. For one of them, George F. Baer, "The rights of laboring men will be protected and cared for, not by the labor agitator, but by the Christian men to whom God in His infinite wisdom has given control of the property interests of the country."

The owners angered Roosevelt because he felt they looked only at their immediate economic interests rather than considering the future of the entire capitalist system. They did not understand the need to keep men like Mitchell loyal to that system. Instead, Roosevelt reported, they "used insolent and abusive language about Mitchell" and "in at least two cases assumed an attitude toward me which was one of insolence."

Roosevelt in turn informed the owners that if they refused arbitration, he would seize the mines and have the government run them. Roosevelt expressed his vision of the great power that presidents in the twentieth century should exercise when he declared, "I do not know whether I would have any precedents [for taking the mines], but in my judgment it would have been imperative to act, precedent or no precedent." "A great exertion of federal authority," he concluded, "was the only feasible means of meeting the challenge of the times."

The owners now agreed to the creation of an Anthracite Coal Strike Commission to arbitrate the issues, but only if no representative from organized labor was included. Mitchell had always wanted arbitration but he insisted that labor should be represented. Roosevelt broke this impasse when he appointed an "eminent sociologist" to serve on the commission along with an army engineer, a mining engineer, a federal judge, and a businessman. The "sociologist" was E. E. Clark, head of a railroad union and therefore acceptable to Mitchell as a representative of labor. He was also acceptable to the mine owners since he was not called a union representative.

The miners returned to work in the fall when the commission began to deliberate. In March of 1903, the commission awarded the workers a 10 percent pay increase and shorter hours, but it warned the workers to remember their dependence on management. "The union must not undertake to accuse, or to interfere with, the management of the business of the employer." And the commission report also warned the union that it could not control nonunion workers. "All men are free to work upon what terms, and at what time, and for whom it may please them to do so," the commissioners declared. They added, "The right to remain at work where others have ceased to work, or to engage anew in work which others have abandoned, is part of the personal liberty of a citizen." These statements represented Roosevelt's own labor philosophy. He accepted unions but only in an open shop, where workers were not under pressure to belong to the union.

Roosevelt had accomplished many of his goals in his handling of the coal strike. He had saved the nation from an energy crisis. He had established a more active role for the government in the economy. He had strengthened the presidency. He had taught corporation leaders such as Morgan and Perkins that the president could reconcile conflicts of interest better than they could. And he had forced Hanna, as chairman of the Republican National Committee, to acknowledge that it was Roosevelt, not Hanna, who headed the party and would be the party's presidential candidate in 1904. He also had indicated to "safe" labor leaders like Mitchell that their loyalty to corporate capitalism would be rewarded. And he had won the political support of most of that minority of skilled workers who were members of labor unions. Looking forward to 1904, Roosevelt was sure that he could build a strong majority by adding the votes of "farmers and small businessmen" to those of "upper-class mechanics." With this constituency, he did win a landslide victory in 1904.

But Roosevelt discovered that his commitment to corporate capitalism and corporate progressivism was severely limited by the refusal of most capitalists to accept his philosophy. Like the NCF, Roosevelt declared, "Our enemies are the socialists among the labor people and the anarchists among the capitalists." The irony, however, was that during his years as president, the capitalist "anarchists" were more successful in organizing than were the corporate capitalists of the NCF. The National Association of Manufacturers (NAM) was founded in the 1890s to promote overseas trade. By 1902, however, the NAM was taken over by businessmen who wanted to destroy all unions. Working through the organization of the NAM, they began to develop a national movement to break unions in every part of the country. For the NAM, all unions "had exactly the same end and aim as socialism." In 1903 David Parry, the president of the NAM, denounced Roosevelt's arbitration of the coal strike. "We do not want any more national arbitration tribunals to haggle with labor trusts," Parry declared, "as to the terms upon which they will consent to allow industry to proceed in this country."

The NAM successfully used the courts to harass unions, although the NCF tried to contain their antiunion campaign. When Samuel Gompers was brought to court because the American Federation of Labor had supported the Metal Polishers Union in its strike against Buck's Stove and Range Company, he was defended by Alton B. Parker. Parker, who had been the presidential candidate of the Democratic party in 1904, was a Wall Street lawyer, active in the NCF. Some of his fees were paid by Andrew Carnegie, the largest contributor to the NCF.

From 1902 to 1912, therefore, Roosevelt was angered and frustrated by these capitalist "anarchists" and the support they found for their antilabor policies in both the state and federal courts. Furthermore, the Socialist party grew in size as Debs warned labor that the NCF wanted "to take it by the hand and lead it into harmless channels." But as long as the NAM seemed to have more support among capitalists, there seemed little danger that the NCF could "chloroform the labor movement into a more submissive mood."

It is not surprising, then, that Roosevelt hoped for another presidential term in 1912 to breathe new life into that philosophy of corporate progressivism that he seemed to have so successfully expressed at the beginning of his presidency in 1902, when he resolved the anthracite coal strike.

Chapter 5

PROGRESSIVE FOREIGN POLICY AND WORLD WAR ONE

In the century after the Declaration of Independence, most American leaders believed that the United States was steadily distancing itself from the culture of Europe. One of the main characteristics of American "exceptionalism," these leaders felt, was the absence of Old World power politics in the Western Hemisphere. In contrast to the United States, the nations of Europe supported large armies and navies, joined entangling alliances, and fought wars for overseas empires.

In the last two decades of the nineteenth century, however, American leaders seemed to be following Old World patterns of power politics. During this period the United States began to build a large modern navy and fought a successful war for overseas empire against Spain in 1898. This type of power politics per-

sisted after 1900. Besides expanding the army and navy, the administrations of Roosevelt, Taft, and Wilson acted vigorously to increase American trade in Europe, Asia, Africa, and South America. They also established an unofficial alliance with England and urged military leaders to develop plans for possible war against Germany and Japan.

AMERICAN "EXCEPTIONALISM" AND WORLD WAR ONE

But when the United States entered World War One in April 1917 as an ally of England and France against Germany, President Wilson continued to believe that America was remaining distinct from the European balance-of-power system. Indeed, Wilson and his advisers were confident that World War One would end international power politics; it was "the war to end all wars." American leaders thought that the entire world was standing on the threshold of a new economic order that would eliminate traditional power rivalries. In this vision of the future, the world would become an open marketplace where individual businessmen could trade freely — that is, without any restrictions from national governments. American leaders hoped that the United States, where many states shared a single national market, would become the model for a new world in which a number of nations would share a common international market.

These aspirations were the basis of the Open Door policy developed by the McKinley administration in 1899. In keeping the potentially vast China market open to the trade of all nations, American leaders saw China as a model for the rest of the world. These leaders desired to break up the empires that England, France, Germany, and other European nations had constructed in Asia and Africa, precisely because these empires blocked the free flow of world trade.

Thus the political leaders of the United States in 1917, especially President Wilson, seem to have been blinded by their faith in American exceptionalism to the ways in which they themselves had used power politics to expand American markets overseas. Overlooking their own involvement in the exercise of international power, they underestimated the commitment of European imperialism. Consequently, Americans felt disappointment and bitter frustration when the peace settlement of 1919 failed to eliminate international power politics.

Another unexpected and frightening result of World War One for American leaders was the creation of a revolutionary Marxist government in Russia in 1917. This government, under the leadership of Nicolai Lenin, offered an alternative vision of international peace to that put forward by Wilson. This alternative world view derived from Karl Marx, a German exile who spent most of his working life in England and who developed a thorough, systematic, and complex criticism of capitalism in the mid-nineteenth century. Marx argued that the capitalist emphasis on individual enterprise could never achieve social justice. Industrialism, Marx predicted, would spread throughout the world, creating an international working class. Driven by intensifying social and economic injustice in every nation, this class would engage in revolutions to overthrow the capitalist ruling class. According to Marx, the international solidarity of the working class would eliminate the kinds of national competition that caused wars.

Marxist ideas became popular with many industrial workers of Western Europe, who formed strong Labor parties. But no powerful Socialist Labor parties emerged in the United States. Sectional, racial, and ethnic divisions undermined the development of a sense of worker solidarity. Unlike German and English capitalists who found themselves on the defensive against the theories of international socialism, American capitalists were free to develop a theory of international capitalism based on the tradition of American exceptionalism.

Many American business and political leaders, supported by social scientists and historians, recognized that industrialism was destroying American isolation and pushing the United States into world affairs. But in this view, and contrary to the ideas of Marx, industrialism would be the basis of international capitalism, not international socialism. Their confidence partly reflected the weakness of socialism within the United States, which led American businessmen to exaggerate their strength abroad. The rivalry between England and Germany, in which each nation neutralized the strength of the other, also fostered an impression that American power was greater than it really was and encouraged American leaders to overestimate their influence during World War One.

When American leaders in the 1890s resolved that the United States should begin to assume a role as a world power, dramatic changes were transforming the pattern of international relations. First, to set the scene, there had been no major wars in Europe since 1814, and during this century of relative peace, England emerged as the major power. By 1890, however, Germany had surpassed England in industrial production and population and was endeavoring to acquire an overseas empire in Africa and Asia. France and Russia also were trying to expand their empires. In Asia, Japanese leaders had decided to industrialize their nation and to seek overseas markets and sources of raw materials. Threatened by these developments, English political leaders began to reconsider their policy of isolation and no entangling alliances with countries on the European continent. To check the growing military and naval power of Germany, England slowly moved toward an alliance with France and France's ally, Russia.

To add American power to the coalition against Germany, England also sought better relations with the United States. To this end the English government supported the United States during the Spanish-American War. Moreover, England ingratiated itself with American leaders by voluntarily withdrawing from Latin America. This action smoothed the way for United States domination of the Western Hemisphere. Prior to 1900, England and the United States had agreed to share in the building and control of any canal through Central America. In the Hay-Pauncefote Treaty of 1901, however, England withdrew its claims and backed the United States as the sole builder and fortifier of such a canal. England also endorsed the American Open Door position in China.

Predominantly Anglo-Protestant American leaders responded warmly to English overtures toward friendship. These leaders had reacted to the large Slavic and Italian immigration in the 1890s by emphasizing that the true American heritage was Anglo-Saxon. American and English cultural leaders agreed that the two Anglo-Saxon nations should cooperate if the traditions of Anglo-American liberty were to be exported to the rest of the world. American leaders recognized the decline of English power and, therefore, feared dynamic Germany as the greatest threat to the expansion of American trade in Asia and Latin America. By the end of the 1890s, officers at the Naval War College were drafting war games against Germany; at the same time, German naval officers were seriously considering the possibility of war against the United States.

THEODORE ROOSEVELT AND AMERICAN EXPANSION

When Theodore Roosevelt became president in 1901, he decided to move quickly to take advantage of the new monopoly of American power in Latin America. His resolution partly reflected a new attitude toward foreign policy

MAP 5.1   THE AMERICAN EMPIRE IN THE CARIBBEAN

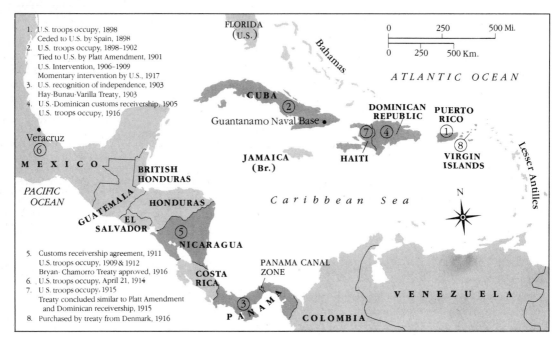

1. U.S. troops occupy, 1898
   Ceded to U.S. by Spain, 1898
2. U.S. troops occupy, 1898–1902
   Tied to U.S. by Platt Amendment, 1901
   U.S. Intervention, 1906–1909
   Momentary intervention by U.S., 1917
3. U.S. recognition of independence, 1903
   Hay-Bunau-Varilla Treaty, 1903
4. U.S.-Dominican customs receivership, 1905
   U.S. troops occupy, 1916

5. Customs receivership agreement, 1911
   U.S. troops occupy, 1909 & 1912
   Bryan- Chamorro Treaty approved, 1916
6. U.S. troops occupy, April 21, 1914
7. U.S. troops occupy, 1915
   Treaty concluded similar to Platt Amendment
   and Dominican receivership, 1915
8. Purchased by treaty from Denmark, 1916

Used by permission of Charles Scribner's Sons from History of American Foreign Policy *by Alexander De Conde.*
Copyright © 1963 Charles Scribner's Sons.

among American political leaders. This outlook involved a willingness to take some decisive action and then, after the event, create public opinion to support that action. For example, McKinley had claimed the Philippines as an American colony at a time when most Americans did not even know where the Philippines were. But Roosevelt possessed a much greater personal commitment than McKinley did to presidential leadership, both in domestic and foreign policy. As a proponent of traditional warrior virtues, Roosevelt realized that he could exercise considerable initiative in foreign policy because of the constitutional power given the president in foreign affairs, especially the control of the armed forces.

Roosevelt's decisiveness had a major impact on the construction of the Panama Canal. Faced with two alternatives for a canal, one through Nicaragua, the other through Panama, then a province of Colombia, Roosevelt signed a pact with Colombia (Hay-Herran treaty) in 1903 for the rights to build a canal through Panama. The Colombian senate, however, rejected the treaty on the grounds that the purchase price — the immediate payment of $10 million and annual payments of $250,000 — for a canal zone were insufficient. At the same time, Philippe Bunau-Varilla, a representative of a French company that had failed in an earlier attempt to build a canal but that stood to gain from any canal built through Panama, was working in New York with a Wall Street lawyer, William Cromwell, to hire people in Panama to incite a revolution of independence from Colombia. Roosevelt, impatient with delays caused by "little brown people," was eager to send part of the American fleet to support the revolution. He ordered American ships to Panama to prevent Colombian troops from landing there and justified his action by invoking an 1846 treaty with Colombia in which the United States had promised to help Colombia kept Panama open to the free flow of trade. Immediately recognizing the independence of Panama, Roosevelt signed a treaty with Bunau-Varilla, still in the United States, as the official diplomatic representative of the new nation. This treaty gave Panama the same financial terms originally offered Colombia.

Boasting "I took the Canal Zone," Roosevelt then issued the Roosevelt Corollary to the Monroe Doctrine in 1904. He declared that the United States had the responsibility to intervene in any Latin American country if its government was incapable of preserving stability. Acting on this intent, he sent the navy to take control of Santo Domingo in 1905 to establish stable finances. After he forced the government of Santo Domingo to sign a treaty permitting American control over its economy, the United States Senate rejected the treaty. Roosevelt then announced that he would implement the treaty anyway, under his presidential power to make "executive agreements."

Just as Roosevelt overestimated American power in Latin America because he did not realize how much it depended on English support, he overestimated American power in Asia because his belief in Anglo-Saxon racial superiority prevented him from taking the Japanese seriously. The Japanese had defeated China in war in 1895, and Russia, in 1904. To demonstrate that the United States was a great power in the Pacific, Roosevelt arranged for Russia and Japan to sign their peace treaty in Portsmouth, New Hampshire. At this point Roosevelt supported the Japanese because he believed that the Russians were a greater threat to the American Open Door policy in China. Through the peace treaty, Japan took direct control of Korea and indirect control of much of the northern Chinese province of Manchuria. Roosevelt, however, then began to worry about Japanese expansion in China. He was also concerned about the flow of Japanese immigrants into California, where anti-Japanese violence had occurred and the state legislature talked of barring any more Japanese. Roosevelt persuaded the Japanese government voluntarily to restrict the number of people coming to America and then tried to overawe the Japanese by sending the fleet on a visit to Tokyo. In the end, though, Roosevelt had to offer concessions to the Japanese in the Root-Takahira treaty of 1908. He accepted Japanese restrictions on the Open Door in Manchuria in return for Japan's promise to respect the policy in the rest of China.

Diplomatic leaders in Roosevelt's administration believed that they were forging a systematic foreign policy designed to remove barriers to trade throughout the world. But these same leaders fully expected that American business and industry would prove more efficient than its English, German, or Japanese competitors, and that American businessmen would dominate the world market. Clearly the United States was pursuing a policy of national interest in Asia and Latin America, whatever its

This sign reflects the intense hostility toward Japanese immigrants that characterized white Californians in the early twentieth century. President Theodore Roosevelt persuaded the California legislature to limit its discriminatory legislation against Japanese settlers by striking a bargain with the Japanese government to restrict the number of emigrants to America. (UPI Photos)

affirmations of internationalism. At the same time, the United States was obviously engaged in a balance-of-power diplomacy.

These contradictions surfaced in Theodore Roosevelt's relationships with Europe in 1905. Despite the strong American tradition of isolation from European politics, Roosevelt believed that his leadership could prevent a war between Germany and France as both competed to expand their empires in North Africa. He therefore proposed a conference of European powers to meet in Algeciras, Spain, to mediate the conflict. With American delegates present, the meeting rejected the German position. This conference thus strengthened the informal alliance between the United States and England and France. German suspicions of the United States, of course, were intensified. Meanwhile,

128

the American delegates managed to persuade both France and Germany to admit American businessmen into the African territory under dispute.

LATIN AMERICA AND ASIA IN THE TAFT AND WILSON ADMINISTRATIONS

Despite the expansion of American foreign policy under President Roosevelt, most American voters continued to ignore foreign affairs and generally assumed that the United States remained isolated from the rest of the world. Most Americans also showed little awareness that their leaders were systematically reshaping the armed services along the patterns of the great European powers, especially Germany. The navy had grown rapidly in the late nineteenth century, and the Naval War College had been established in order to devise a world strategy. But President Roosevelt pushed for much greater expansion of the navy. The American Navy League, founded in 1903, attempted to educate the American people and to lobby with Congress for a bigger navy. And the same politicians and businessmen who worked for a large navy also advocated a strong army to serve as an instrument for big-power diplomacy. Elihu Root, a Wall Street lawyer, as both secretary of war after 1899 and secretary of state after 1905, was the most important proponent of a powerful army for balance-of-power world politics. He established an Army War College and a general staff to plan worldwide strategy. This general staff under the aggressive leadership of General Leonard A. Wood was modeled directly on the German general staff.

Root was unable to win congressional support for an army as large as he wanted. But through his persuasion Congress passed the Dick Act in 1903, which placed state militias under the control of the national government for the first time. This act established the National Guard and allowed regular army officers to work and teach in local communities throughout the country. In Root's view this National Guard could swiftly and efficiently supplement the force of the regular army in times of crisis.

The expansion of the armed services reflected a growing awareness within the federal government of the importance of foreign policy. Similarly, the civilian bureaucracy, which also increased greatly in size in this period, became more aware of international relations. Both the departments of Agriculture and Commerce, for example, sent government officials abroad to seek markets for American farm products and manufactured goods.

The strength of the government's commitment to economic expansion could be seen in the administration of William Howard Taft, Roosevelt's successor in the White House. Though Taft lacked Roosevelt's dynamic leadership, he continued his predecessor's policies of encouraging American business expansion in foreign countries. American corporate investment overseas had increased from $1 billion in 1900 to $3 billion in 1910. Taft's notion of "Dollar Diplomacy" endeavored to protect and accelerate such investments. He ordered marines into Nicaragua to maintain a regime that was friendly to American investors and he kept troops there even after the Senate refused to accept a negotiated treaty. Congress, however, did not always criticize such aggressive foreign policies. In 1912 it passed the Lodge Corollary to the Monroe Doctrine, denying Japanese companies the right to buy property in Mexico.

Taft and his secretary of state, Philander C. Knox, a Wall Street lawyer, moved to limit Japanese influence in Manchuria by trying to arrange for American bankers to lend China funds for the repurchase of Chinese railroads owned by Japan. The Taft administration also forced European nations to allow American bankers to join an international group planning to build railroads in China. The Japanese, however, successfully blocked these plans.

When Woodrow Wilson became president in 1913, he inherited a twenty-year-old foreign policy based on the willingness of the executive branch to take aggressive action to expand American economic interests abroad. At first, however, Wilson and his secretary of state, William Jennings Bryan, repudiated the Republican policy of Dollar Diplomacy. Though Bryan had supported war to liberate Cuba in 1898, he subsequently opposed the retention of the Philippines. Like Republican politicians, Bryan desired the expansion of American trade abroad, especially the sale of agricultural products, but he thought such commerce could be accomplished without acquiring colonies or using military force. Like many of the anti-imperialists of 1900, Bryan believed that an imperial American could not preserve the liberties of its citizens at home. And like some of the anti-imperialists, he feared the annexation of colonies whose "colored" populations might corrupt the purity of the white race. As secretary of state, he was surprised to learn that the totally black population of the Caribbean nation Haiti spoke French. "Dear me," Bryan said, "think of it! Niggers speaking French."

Soon, however, Wilson and Bryan were using the armed forces to intervene in Central America and the Caribbean even more often than had Roosevelt and Taft. Woodrow Wilson had been one of the first Ph.D.s to gradu-ate from Johns Hopkins University and, until 1910 when he entered politics, he had participated in the reconstruction of American university life as a teacher, scholar, and college president. He shared the enthusiasm of the new university professors who felt that they were leaders of a new society at home and abroad. Franklin H. Giddings, one of the first influential sociologists, had written in his book *Democracy and Empire* (1900) that "it must be our great objective to improve our institutions until we can bring blessings to lower peoples and set them on the road to rapid progress. Such a civilization we have a right to enforce on the earth. We have a right to work for the enlightenment of all peoples and to give our aid to lift them into local self-government." Wilson, the professor as president, agreed. "When properly directed," he insisted, "there is no people not fitted for self-government."

With more complicated motives than his predecessors, therefore, Wilson was impelled to intervene in Nicaragua, Cuba, Santo Domingo, and Haiti. In Haiti, Wilson sent the marines to pressure the Haitian government to sign a treaty (in effect until 1934) that assured United States control of the country's finances, public works, army, and foreign relations. The Senate approved this treaty in 1916 without a dissenting vote. Wilson also accepted the strategic outlook that, since the 1890s, has been central to the American concept of becoming a world power. He informed Denmark that the United States would have to consider forcibly seizing the Virgin Islands unless that country agreed to sell its Caribbean possessions to the United States. Denmark acquiesced and in 1916 sold the islands to the United States for $25 million.

Wilson's grandest ambition for forcing progress in Latin America focused on Mexico. Democratic forces had created a revolution there in

1911, but General Victoriano Huerta had led a successful counterrevolution in 1913. Wilson refused to recognize Huerta's government on the grounds that it lacked popular support. Yet Mexico was a much larger country than any other Caribbean or Central American nation, and it was much more difficult for Wilson to intimidate leaders in Mexico than those in smaller countries such as Nicaragua or Haiti. Still, Wilson gave Huerta an ultimatum to relinquish control of Mexico, and he asked European countries not to recognize Huerta. He also informed them that the United States would allow no shipments of arms to be sent to Huerta. But Wilson did allow guns to be sent to General Venustiana Carranza, whose forces were trying to overthrow Huerta. In April 1914, Wilson ordered the American fleet to seize the Mexican port of Veracruz to stop supplies from reaching Huerta. Carranza's revolutionary army then captured Mexico City but could not stop chaotic fighting throughout the country.

With the fall of Huerta, Wilson threw his support behind General Francisco Villa, who seemed stronger than Carranza. But Carranza fought back and isolated Villa in the mountains of northern Mexico. Wilson then switched his support back to Carranza and recognized his government in October 1915. In desperation, Villa tried to sink Mexico back into chaos by luring American troops across the border. To provoke Wilson, he burned the town of Columbus, New Mexico, killing nineteen Americans. General John J. Pershing marched American troops three hundred miles south into Mexico in pursuit of Villa. President Carranza, however, did not welcome this massive invasion of his country, even against his enemy Villa, and demanded that Wilson withdraw the troops. Wilson refused, and, making the first use of the Dick Act of 1903, mobilized the National

Guard and drafted a war message. But Carranza avoided a direct confrontation with Pershing's army. He instead accepted mediation that led to Mexican and American negotiations. Finally in February 1917, Wilson withdrew the troops.

Although Wilson's initial goal — "teach the Mexicans to elect good men" — seemed to have been frustrated, the president still believed in the importance of teaching other peoples "to elect good men." In attempting to extend his lesson to Asia, however, Wilson again failed to overcome the limits on American power. Despite Wilson's efforts, the Japanese increased their industrial and naval strength in China. And they were able to do in Asia what the United States had done in Latin America — take advantage of the bitter divisions of the European powers.

When war erupted in Europe in 1914, Japan immediately joined England and France against Germany. During the war, Japan, like the United States, did not suffer huge population losses or the disruption of its economy. Japan's primary motive in participating in the war was the chance to seize the extensive island empire Germany controlled throughout the Pacific Ocean. These islands later served as bases for Japanese military and naval activity during World War Two. Japan also seized German-held leases on the Shantung Peninsula of China. With no effective European power left in China, Japan issued Twenty-One Demands to the Chinese government in 1915. This order would have reduced China to a Japanese protectorate, but Wilson's strong protest managed to restrain the Japanese government.

Wilson's defense of Chinese independence reflected a continued commitment to the Open Door policy. Though early in his administration he had hesitated to support American business in Manchuria, Wilson moved after 1915 to check Japan's expansion by encouraging American bankers to invest in China. Yet American influence in Asia remained weak. In the Lansing-Ishii agreement of 1917, the Japanese reaffirmed their respect for the Open Door policy, but the United States simultaneously recognized that Japan had special interests in China because it was geographically closer to China than to any other country.

Wilson's belief in the inferiority of "colored" peoples of the world, such as the Japanese, had led him in 1913 to accept a law passed by the California legislature barring Japanese from owning land in that state. Wilson's racial attitudes were similar to those of the governor of California, who stated, "We have prevented the Japanese from driving the root of their civilization deep into California soil." But in 1917 Wilson found himself forced to acknowledge and respect Japanese power. One reason he was afraid to see World War One drag on and on until both Germany and England were exhausted was that such a disaster might lead to the collapse of "white" civilization and allow "yellow" people to achieve a dominant world status.

WILSON AND NEUTRALITY

When the war broke out in Europe, Wilson declared it "a war with which we have nothing to do, whose causes cannot touch us." He asked the American people to be "neutral in fact as well as in name." Wilson's neutrality contrasted with the stance of Theodore Roosevelt and many other upper-middle-class Anglo-Protestant leaders in the Republican party who called for immediate entry into the war on the

side of the Allies, England and France, against the Central Powers, Germany and Austria-Hungary. Wilson's opposition was not based on antipathy to war as an instrument of foreign policy. "There are times in the history of nations when they must take up the instruments of bloodshed in order to vindicate spiritual conceptions," he had written, "and when men take up arms to set other men free, there is something sacred and holy in the warfare. I will not cry peace as long as there is sin in the world."

Wilson shared Roosevelt's sympathy for England. But he wanted to avoid the fighting so that the United States could control the peace. Wilson saw the war as a revolutionary opportunity to end European empires and open the whole world to free trade. He believed the war had been caused by the competition of European empires. Unlike American expansion overseas, which, in Wilson's eyes, was peaceful because it depended on the economic competition of individual businessmen, the Europeans depended on political and military power to expand. Thus competition involved nations, not individuals, and became military rather than economic. The result was World War One.

Wilson hoped that the terrible costs of the war would teach all European nations the necessity of ending imperial competition. Instead of expanding an area of trade by extending imperial boundaries, the European powers, Wilson felt, should accept the American position of free trade. When the time was right, Wilson expected the United States to provide leadership for a peace settlement based on an international Open Door. "We are the mediating nation of the world," he declared. "We are compounded of all the nations of the world. We are, therefore, able to understand all nations." It would be futile for the United States to enter the war to destroy the German and Austro-Hungarian empires while saving the English, French, and Russian empires.

But while he waited for the opportunity to initiate a new international community, Wilson's pro-English and anti-German attitudes curtailed his freedom of action. Both England and Germany established naval blockades that violated international law. Worse, for Wilson, was that these blockades violated the very principles of free trade that he believed to be essential for the future world community. England not only blockaded German ports but restricted trade to Holland and the Scandinavian countries because goods could be sent from those countries to Germany. The German fleet had not yet reached parity with England's and did not dare challenge the English fleet on the open sea. German naval strength turned, therefore, to a new weapon, the submarine, to stop supplies from reaching England.

Wilson protested the actions of the English navy through 1916. But many members of the State Department, among them Secretary Robert Lansing, were so pro-English that they privately informed English leaders that the United States would not go to war to end their illegal blockade. Wilson, on the other hand, was so anti-German that he refused to tolerate their submarine warfare. Submarines were vulnerable to gunfire and they could attack armed merchant ships only by surprise. Many of these ships, carrying munitions and other war supplies to England or France, also carried passengers. When they were sunk by torpedoes, many lives were lost. England, which controlled and censored communications coming from Europe to America, exploited this advantage by painting a picture of the German army as totally barbaric and engaged in the ruthless rape and murder of civilian populations. Now

these German "Huns," as described by British propaganda, were murdering civilians on the high seas.

Major American newspapers, most of whose editors were Anglo-Americans, readily accepted the English description of the Germans. Just twenty years before — in the period from 1895 to 1898 — they had described the Spanish as representatives of the medieval past who required purging if progress was to continue. Now in the period from 1914 to 1917, they portrayed the German leaders as representatives of the Dark Ages — an enemy that had to be destroyed in the name of progress. Backed by the major newspapers and magazines owned by the Anglo-Protestant upper middle class, Wilson sent stronger and stronger notes of protest to Germany. When Wilson's warnings seemed to threaten war, Bryan resigned as secretary of state, believing it was not a neutral policy for the United States to tolerate England's violation of international law while refusing to compromise with Germany.

In 1915 the English ship *Lusitania,* carrying munitions, was sunk by a submarine and 1,198 passengers died; 198 of them were Americans. Many congressmen wished to support the proposed McLemore Resolution, warning Americans not to travel to a Europe at war. Wilson, however, refused to accept this limitation on the right of Americans to travel anywhere in the world. In June 1916 he delivered an ultimatum to Germany to stop sinking merchant and passenger ships. Wilson warned that the United States would seriously consider war if German policy did not change. Although Germany bowed to Wilson's wishes, the president was concerned that the logic of his decisions now limited his options. "Any little German lieutenant can put us into the war," he confessed, "at any time by some calculated outrage." The president feared that American entry into the war against Germany would undermine his ability to pressure England and France into relinquishing their empires.

These fears were fulfilled when Germany renewed its submarine warfare in February 1917. By that time German leaders were desperate. After two years of war, they had been unable to defeat England and France. Bowing to American pressure on submarine warfare, they had watched as the American economy became increasingly integrated with the economies of England and France. The English blockade halted most American commerce with Germany, but American trade with the Allies increased from $825 million in 1914 to $3.2 billion in 1916. Not only were the Allies dependent on American supplies, but they relied on American loans to buy those supplies. In contrast to $300 million lent to Germany, American bankers provided loans of $2.5 billion to England and France before the United States officially entered the war. For German strategists then, victory hinged on cutting the link between the American and Allied economies. The German general staff believed that total submarine warfare could starve England and break the morale of the Allied armies before American military forces could reach Europe. They also were willing to take the gamble at this time because Russia had collapsed as a military factor and German troops could be moved from the eastern to the western front.

Wilson's pro-English attitudes were partly responsible for his willingness to allow the American economy to become integrated with that of the Allies, even though such integration limited his ability to pressure the Allies to open their empires to free trade. But Wilson, like many American leaders, did not separate his commitment to the abstract principle of free trade from his defense of American national interest. He had been a graduate student at Johns Hopkins when Frederick Jackson Turner was developing his ideas about the end of the American agricultural frontier. Wilson agreed with Turner that "the days of glad expansion are gone" and that "our life grows tense and difficult." He also shared Turner's belief that overseas expansion was necessary to replace the lost frontier. "Our industries have expanded to such a point that they will burst their packets," Wilson warned, "if they cannot find a free outlet to the markets of the world."

Wilson might have tried to force England to end its illegal blockade by threatening an embargo on goods necessary for their war effort. But he made no such threat both because of his pro-English attitude and because he feared that stopping overseas trade would cause a serious economic depression for the United States. Recognizing the importance of foreign trade as a stimulant to the domestic economy, Wilson permitted the Federal Reserve banks to guarantee loans to the Allies in 1915 so England and France could increase their purchases of American food and manufactured goods. Similar motives later led Wilson to overlook his professed commitment to competition. In 1918 he endorsed the Webb-Pomerene Act, which permitted American corporations to join together in price fixing and other monopolistic practices when they engaged in overseas trade. Wilson also supported the Edge Act of 1919, which allowed bankers to cooperate to control overseas investments.

Wilson, who spoke about ending the use of military power in foreign affairs, had also taken a contradictory position in 1915 by urging the United States to increase the size of its army and navy. In 1914 he had opposed preparedness, but he began to change over to the views of men like Theodore Roosevelt. The president claimed that such mobilization would encourage belligerent countries to respect American rights. But he faced so much opposition in Congress to his preparedness campaign that he toured the nation exhorting the people to support his program. The president's appeal succeeded. In June 1916, Congress passed the National Defense Act, strengthening the army. Two months later Congress passed a Naval Appropriations Bill, which once more greatly expanded the size of the navy. While advocating preparedness, Wilson sent his close friend Colonel Edward House to England and Germany in 1915 and again in 1916 to encourage those nations to accept American mediation of the war. But House informed English leaders that Wilson was sympathetic to them and would not allow Germany to gain a military victory. German leaders also showed little interest in mediation. By the summer of 1916, Wilson prepared for his re-election campaign without any sign that the warring nations would accept his efforts to make peace.

In seeking re-election, Wilson had to confront a reunited Republican party. Theodore Roosevelt, whose feud with Taft had enabled Wilson to win in 1912, refused to lend further leadership to the Progressive party and endorsed the Republican candidate, Charles Evan Hughes. Wilson hoped to win re-election by attracting some of the progressive Republicans who had left the party in 1912 to follow Theodore Roosevelt. To obtain the support of the progressives who shared Roosevelt's criticisms of the way in which the judicial system blocked reform legislation, Wilson appointed Louis D. Brandeis to the Supreme Court. Wilson also backed several legislative acts that were similar to those proposed by Roosevelt in 1912. They included the Keating-Owen Child Labor Act, which barred goods made by children under sixteen from interstate commerce; the Adamson Act, which established an eight-hour day for

railroad workers; and a Workmen's Compensation Act for federal employees.

Such legislation not only pleased upper-middle-class progressives but also appealed to the part of the labor movement that had been loyal to the Republican party. To win farm votes, Wilson supported a Farm Loan Act. But Wilson won the most enthusiastic support in 1916 because of his continued position of neutrality. The strongest spokesmen for war in November 1916 were Republican leaders such as Roosevelt and Henry Cabot Lodge. In contrast, the campaign slogan of the Democrats was "He kept us out of war." The evidence is that the average voter in both the Republican and Democratic parties wanted to continue a policy of isolation. Wilson won a narrow victory of 9.1 to 8.5 million, holding the southern and western states while the Republicans carried most of the northeastern and midwestern states.

After his re-election in November, Wilson renewed his efforts to define the war as a revolution that would create a new world order. In January 1917, just before the Germans announced that they would begin unrestricted submarine warfare, the president unveiled his vision of a just peace in a major speech. He called for "a peace without victory," a peace that would depend not on military strength, with some nations more powerful than others, but on a world marketplace guaranteed by freedom of the seas. In such a world of competition by individual businessmen, there would be no need for large navies or armies. Wilson also hinted at his commitment to a league of nations to enforce this new world community.

Then in February 1917, Wilson had to confront the German challenge to his 1916 ultimatum. What now would happen to "peace without victory"? On February 3 an American ship, *Housatonic,* was sunk by a submarine, leading Wilson to break diplomatic relations with Ger-

MAP 5.2   THE ELECTION OF 1916

Wilson (Democrat)
277 electoral votes

Hughes (Republican)
254 electoral votes

many. On February 24 the United States intercepted a message, known as the "Zimmerman telegram," in which Germany had offered Mexico a treaty. This document discussed restoring Texas, New Mexico, and Arizona to Mexico in return for Mexican military aid against the United States. On February 26 Wilson asked Congress to arm American merchant ships sailing to England.

WILSON AND THE PEACE MOVEMENT

As Wilson adopted a militant stance toward Germany, progressive Republican senators from the Midwest, like Robert LaFollette of Wisconsin and George Norris of Nebraska, led a filibuster to block the president's request for armaments. Though upper-middle-class Anglo-Protestants, mostly Republicans from the Northeast, had advocated the expansion of the armed services and even called for peacetime conscription, a smaller group from this same social class and geographic area had endeavored to foster a peace movement throughout the early twentieth century. Particularly active were the American Society for International Law, the American Society for the Judicial Settlement of International Disputes, the New York Peace Society, and the American Peace Society. The book publisher Edward Ginn had given his fortune to establish the World Peace Foundation,

Women, much more than men, protested against what they saw as the drift of the United States toward participation in World War One. These members of the Woman's Peace Party in 1916 object to a law by the New York state legislature establishing military training in high schools. (Brown Brothers)

and Andrew Carnegie had funded the Carnegie Endowment for International Peace. Concern for this peace movement was particularly strong among middle-class women of the Progressive era, one of whom was Jane Addams.

Peace organizations had hoped that the civilized world was moving away from war when the great powers met in Holland for the First Hague Conference in 1899 and the Second Hague Conference in 1907 to discuss disarmaments and when a Permanent Court of International Arbitration was established. During the Roosevelt, Taft, and Wilson administra-

tions, arbitration treaties were signed between the United States and all major countries except Germany. The signatory nations pledged to wait a specific period of time if a conflict developed between them and the United States before considering the settlement of the issue by war. During this "cooling off" period, arbitration might reach a peaceful settlement.

Although the peace groups had been disappointed when Wilson urged armed preparedness in 1915, most of them backed the president against his Republican opponent in the election of 1916. Some even supported Wilson once the war began because he promised that this would be the war to end all wars. Furthermore, the president's peace plans included a League of Nations, a favorite solution of peace groups such as the League to Enforce Peace.

The midwestern and western progressive Republicans who stood against the war in 1917, however, were not part of this peace movement. Rather they represented the anticorporate wing of the progressive movement. Midwesterners such as LaFollette and Norris resented the domination of the State Department by officials who largely came out of the eastern universities and whose policies of overseas expansion seemed geared to the needs of corporate finance and industry. By 1917 anticorporate progressives began to see the Navy League and the National Security League as creating a kind of "military-industrial complex" in which large corporations came to depend on government contracts for armaments to provide them with large profits.

The Midwest and West were more opposed to the war than the Northeast and South because Anglo-American culture did not have deep roots in these more recently settled regions. Given the lack of enthusiasm toward the war on the part of lower-income groups in the country, however, another reason for isolationism in the Midwest and West was the greater participation of the average citizen in politics there than in other regions. In the South, blacks and many lower-income whites had been driven out of politics between 1890 and 1914. In the Northeast, many of the millions of new immigrants from southern and eastern Europe either had chosen not to enter politics or had been discouraged from trying by the Anglo-Protestant urban elites. The Anglo-American upper middle class, which provided bipartisan wartime leadership, therefore had much more

influence in the East and South than in the Midwest and West, where more of the immigrants and lower-income Anglo-Americans remained in the political process.

When Wilson asked Congress to declare war on April 2, 1917, however, much of this criticism was muted because the Zimmerman telegram and the sinking of American ships seemed to define the struggle as a defense against German aggression. Many Americans, including congressmen, reluctantly decided that they had no choice but to fight to defend their country. Senator William Borah, a progressive Republican from Idaho, typified these sentiments when he proclaimed: "I join no crusade; I seek no alliances. I make war alone for my country and its honor." In this vein Wilson could expect great loyalty for such a war, but less commitment to his vision of remaking the world.

Nevertheless, the transformation of the nineteenth-century college to the twentieth-century university helped to provide Wilson with a generation of upper-middle-class young men schooled in military discipline and collective loyalty. Between 1912 and 1917, many university presidents supported the Plattsburg system, advocated by General Leonard Wood, which provided that college students spend part of every summer learning to be soldiers. Educators also supported the Wilson administration's call for conscription into the armed forces, and established Reserve Officer Training Corps (ROTC) programs on their campuses. ROTC permitted students to take military training during the entire school year.

While universities encouraged military training by 1917, they associated the kind of professionalism demanded in course study with a militant personality. Traditional "hazing" of underclassmen emphasized this tendency. Freshmen had to prove their worth by demonstrating self-discipline in accepting humiliation from upperclassmen. But at the end of their first year, male students could throw away the special hats, usually beanies, that had identified them as freshmen and no longer had to obey blindly the humiliating commands of elders. Since they had proved themselves as men, surviving freshmen were permitted to act like men by engaging in a pitched battle in June, often fought with bamboo canes, against the sophomores. The next September, now sophomores themselves, they took on the responsibility of hazing the freshmen and testing their dedication to the system. When General Wood concluded that conscription would "nationalize" American "individualism" and create a healthy sense of social responsibility, it was this elite group of college students who best understood him.

With American entry in the war in April 1917, the heavily pro-English college presidents and faculties moved swiftly and efficiently to suppress all criticism of the war. The American Association of University Professors (AAUP), formed in 1915 to protect academic freedom, declared that professors ought not to be critical during the crisis of the war. The few professors who dared openly to oppose the war because they were pacifists, socialists, or simply did not believe that Germany should be blamed for starting the war, were fired from their jobs and then often blacklisted. The historian Charles Beard, for example, lost his job at Columbia University for advocating the toleration of pacifist professors.

Wilson established a Committee on Public Information (CPI), run by the progressive journalist George Creel, to stimulate public support for the war. The CPI created a vast amount of patriotic propaganda by putting anti-German posters in every public place. The CPI recruited seventy-five thousand speakers who gave four-minute talks on the reasons for the war before millions of people who formed the audiences for vaudeville shows or movies. J. Franklin Jameson, the editor of the *American Historical Review,* and other leaders of the American Historical Association created a National Board for Historical Service, which mobilized historians throughout the country to write historical pamphlets explaining the causes of the war. They also produced texts for high schools that demonstrated the evils of the Central Powers and the virtues of the Allies. Jameson placed his organization at the service of the CPI, and some leaders of the profession, such as Guy Stanton Ford of the University of Minnesota, worked directly for the CPI.

The enthusiastic desire of most college presidents and faculty members to serve the national government found its climax in October 1918 when the 516 most important colleges and universities throughout the country voluntarily turned themselves into military schools with the purpose of training their 140,000 students as officers for the army. Private colleges and state universities that accepted this role of providing training for the Students' Army Training Corps now had their budgets supported by the national government. Such aid saved many of them from financial difficulties caused by declining enrollments and the loss of private donations funneled into the war effort. College administrators and professors enthusiastically supported the wartime leadership of President Wilson, a former history professor and university president himself. To a large extent, the overwhelmingly Anglo-Protestant elite of higher education also approved of the corporate progressivism expressed in Wilson's legislative program.

WILSON, THE ECONOMY, AND
CIVIL LIBERTIES

The war presented the new universities an unprecedented opportunity to fulfill their sense of service to the nation and to provide that leadership by an educated elite that they believed necessary for the continued progress of the United States. At the same time, corporate progressives in the business community and national politics also saw opportunities to implement concepts of national planning in the wartime emergency.

American political and military leaders reckoned that the whole society had to be mobilized as quickly and efficiently as possible. Once the United States entered the war, these leaders learned that the German submarine campaign was sinking 900,000 tons of shipping each month and was cutting off England's food supplies. They also discovered that, with the military collapse of Russia and the transfer of most German troops to the western front, the Allied armies were on the defensive. By the fall of 1917, actions by the American navy against the German submarines had cut the loss of cargo ships to 300,000 tons a month. This figure was soon reduced to 200,000 tons, and the flow of supplies to England was assured. An army of one million Americans reached the western front by the spring of 1918, and when it grew to two million by the fall of 1918, Germany was on the brink of military defeat. Surrender came in November.

This rapid mobilization of the armed forces was facilitated by the mobilization of the economy. For two years, 1917 and 1918, corporate progressives from the academic, political, and business communities had the chance to create the kind of economy they had advocated since 1900, a rationalized economy without the unpredictable element of price competition. These reformers had urged political leaders to help the managers of the great private corporations reach agreement on prices and production quotas. They had encouraged the government and corporation leaders to take a paternalistic attitude toward labor and supported the growth of labor unions that accepted the leadership of upper-middle-class politicians and businessmen. In return for this loyalty, labor was to be given adequate pay, shorter hours, and better working conditions.

These goals were implemented during World War One. The War Industries Board (WIB), headed by Bernard Baruch from Wall Street, decided production goals for corporations in war industries and controlled the flow of raw materials so that war production would have top priority. Most government contracts went to the largest corporations without competitive bidding. This guaranteed large profits to the corporations who cooperated with the WIB.

Herbert Hoover, another millionaire, was appointed head of the Food Administration. He paid farmers huge amounts of money to increase land under cultivation. Large crops of wheat fed the Allies and larger crops of cotton provided cloth for the war. For a brief while, farmers enjoyed unprecedented prosperity as their incomes jumped 30 percent. Unlike World War Two, food was not rationed, but Hoover encouraged Americans to have meatless days and to cut back on the use of wheat and sugar.

A Fuel Administration assured first priority for coal to factories in war production; and nonessential industry and private dwellings had to do without fuel if there was a shortage. A Railroad Administration created a national system out of the several private companies. Railroad executives worked directly for the government and received a profitable rental for their lines.

The War Labor Board (WLB) supported the formation of unions and collective bargaining. Union membership, which had hardly grown since 1905, now jumped from 2.5 million to 5 million. The stimulus of the war to industrial and agricultural production doubled the gross national product from $40 billion to $80 billion a year, and the average wage of workers jumped from $600 to $1,400 between 1916 and 1920. The WLB successfully encouraged corporations to move toward the eight-hour day, while a U.S. Employment Service helped find jobs for those who wanted to get into war production. This dramatic shift away from the traditional emphasis on individual self-sufficiency in the competitive marketplace continued with the Military and Naval Insurance Act of 1917, which helped retrain disabled veterans so they could re-enter the work force. The government also assumed responsibility for building public housing for some of the war workers in shipyards and munitions plants.

Corporate progressives envisioned a society without internal conflict or dissent. From 1900 on, the docile American Federation of Labor represented the main alternative to a Socialist Labor movement. Samuel Gompers and other AFL leaders supported Wilson when he first advocated preparedness in 1915. For Gompers, increased military spending was an obvious way out of the economic slump of 1913–1914. Predictably Gompers pledged the support of the AFL to Wilson's war effort in 1917. Such patriotism, the union leader believed, could lead to the end of unemployment and to an increase of union membership, higher wages, shorter hours, and perhaps a voice in shaping other government policies.

Contrasting with the AFL's support of the war, the majority of the Socialist party, under the leadership of Eugene Debs, stood firmly behind total opposition. For Debs and many other American Socialists, the war served only the interests of a capitalist elite and was being fought for the economic interests of that class. Through conscription, the elite forced the common people to fight its battles, and Debs bitterly criticized the drafting of American workers. A number of Socialist leaders, however, broke from the party and supported Wilson, sharing the president's view that international peace and democracy depended on the defeat of German militarism.

Perhaps because Socialist Labor movements were so strong in England, France, and Germany, Socialist leaders could more easily identify with government policies in those countries. These European Socialists supported the war efforts of their nations. In the United States, however, labor had developed little political influence by 1914. American Socialists were still struggling to establish an effective political party that could influence economic and social policies. Standing so far from the center of national politics, most American Socialists would not accept the war, thus leaving themselves open to being defined as un-American.

In order to counteract wartime dissent, the Wilson administration asked Congress to pass the Espionage Act of 1917, which made it a crime to aid the enemy or to discourage military service. The president also authorized the postmaster general to keep treasonable newspapers and magazines out of the mails. A Sedition Act made it a crime to "utter, print, write or publish any disloyal, profane, scurrilous, or abusive language" about the armed forces or the government. This legislation justified the imprisonment of Debs and other Socialist leaders such as Rose Pastor Stokes for criticizing the war.

These Norwegian-American singers in Minnesota represent one of the many ethnic cultures that remained vital until World War One. The war brought great pressures for recent immigrant families to become Americanized and to give up the languages, customs, and holidays that did not fit into the Anglo-American tradition. (Minnesota Historical Society)

Socialist newspapers and magazines such as the *Masses* and the *Appeal to Reason* were banned from the mails. In Oklahoma, the state with the highest proportion of its population enrolled in the Socialist party, a "Green Corn" rebellion of farmers protesting American entry into the war was smashed by the presence of government troops.

Declared a party of treason by the governments, its leaders in jail, and its newspapers and magazines prohibited from circulation, the American Socialist movement was further splintered when a number of its intellectuals, including William English Walling and W. J.

Ghent, rejected the party's war position and supported the president. More complications came when Lenin and the Bolsheviks took control of the Russian Revolution, and American Socialists were forced to decide whether to support this Communist movement. Many of the party's immigrant federations began to move toward the establishment of an American Communist party, whereas most Anglo-Protestant Socialists decided to keep their separate identity as the Socialist party.

Much of the domestic repressiveness caused by the war, however, came from vigilante groups such as the Home Defense League and the Knights of Liberty. Many middle-class An-glo-Protestants in the East and Midwest felt they were outnumbered by millions of German-Americans, Irish-Americans, and Scandinavian-Americans, as well as by the newest immigrants from eastern and southern Europe who were not enthusiastic supporters of the war. Exerting the pressure of their patriotic organizations, these middle-class Americans attempted to force support for the war, including the purchase of wartime "liberty" bonds. One of these patriotic groups, the American Protective League, gained government status in that its 250,000 members were issued cards identifying them as federal agents for the Justice Department. The intensity of the movement to stifle any criticism of the war was demonstrated when a movie producer, Robert Goldstein, was sentenced to jail for ten years because his movie *The Spirit of '76* showed English soldiers attacking American civilians during the Revolution.

A combination of vigilante mob violence that killed several union leaders, the use of federal troops to break strikes, and government action to jail other leaders for twenty-five-year terms almost destroyed the radical Industrial Workers of the World. Under the leadership of "Big Bill" Haywood, the IWW had rejected both the craft unionism of the AFL and the Socialist party's concern with democratic politics. The IWW stressed direct action by workers to destroy the capitalist system and was successful in organizing many miners, shipbuilders, lumberjacks, and farmworkers in the western states. Government repression against antiwar Socialists and radicals also carried over into persecution of conscientious objectors to military service. The Wilson administration insisted on recognizing only members of the pacifist churches, such as the Quakers and Mennonites, as conscientious objectors who could do noncombat service. Four hundred C.O.s who lacked this religious background were sent to jail. The Supreme Court ruled in *Schenck* v. *U.S.* (1919) that there was no constitutional protection of free speech during wartime. The imprisonment of dissenters by the government, therefore, was constitutional.

WOMEN AND THE WAR

Most middle-class women abandoned their pacifism and supported the war effort. They clearly hoped that this would be, as Wilson claimed, the war to end all wars. Since the president had defined the war as a purity crusade, many suffrage leaders were sure that women would play an active role in making this an exceptional war. Consequently, feminists such as Carrie Chapman Catt and Anna Howard Shaw became leaders of the Women's Committee of the Council of National Defense, formed by the Wilson administration to mobilize the energies of women for the war effort.

The war had cut off immigration from Europe at the same time that it was stimulating economic production. The shortage of labor, which was intensified by the conscription of several million young men, was met in part by 1.5 million women entering the work force as factory workers. Some even took such traditional male roles as engineers on trains. At the end of the war, most women were forced to relinquish these jobs to returning male veterans. Although there had been dramatic economic growth during the war, much of the increase of productivity came from the intensive use of new machinery, which limited the creation of new industrial jobs and reduced postwar opportunities for the skilled labor of women, southern blacks, and European immigrants.

These women munitions workers in New Jersey were among the many women who entered the work force during World War One because of the widespread induction of men into the armed services. Unlike the situation in 1945, most of these women left industrial work at war's end in 1919 and returned to the home. (Sophia Smith Collection/Smith College)

As working women became critical to the wartime economy, the Wilson administration dropped its opposition to women's suffrage, and the Nineteenth Amendment, giving the vote to women, passed Congress in 1920. Earlier in the war, however, Wilson had ordered the arrest of leaders of the Woman's party who picketed the White House. Led by Alice Paul, these feminists contended that World War One was not a war for democracy as long as women did not have the vote. Women dissenters of this kind were treated roughly and force-fed in jail when they went on hunger strikes. But most young middle-class women supported the war effort, and many went into the Army Nurses Corps or the Red Cross, while older women organized Victory Gardens, helped with voluntary food rationing, and made bandages or clothing for the soldiers.

As a purity crusade, World War One provided the context for the passage of the Eighteenth Amendment ending the sale of alcoholic beverages. Food shortages made it appear frivolous to use vital grains in unnecessary beers and whiskeys. Prohibition long had been attractive to many Anglo-Protestants as a way of demonstrating their power to influence or control the lifestyles of the more recent Catholic and Jewish immigrants. The war had intensified the desire to "Americanize" the new immigrants and to bring national unity and a common purpose to the diverse American people. Wartime economic mobilization also underscored the need for productive efficiency by a sober and healthy workforce, and since most of the large breweries had been built by German-Americans, prohibition would most directly demonstrate the ability of Anglo-Protestants to dominate German-American culture.

To ensure that the war properly reflected the ideals of the purity crusade, the women leaders of the American Social Hygiene Association persuaded the secretary of war to establish a Commission on Training Camp Activities. This commission was responsible for seeing that prostitutes did not gather around army camps and that the soldiers received information about venereal disease and had regular medical exams.

The young middle-class men who had grown up within the traditional male ethos were confused, therefore, by the presence of women in a war situation. Their uniformed, militant sports in school, their experience in the Boy Scouts, and their reading of the westerns of Owen Wister and Zane Grey all strongly indicated that war was the perfect arena for demonstrating masculine qualities of aggressiveness while protecting passive, gentle, and virtuous women remaining at home.

But by 1918 many women were in the work force and no longer at home. More confusing, many women wanted to redefine the nature of war and to challenge the male double-standard of sexuality. Most confusing, however, was the behavior of many middle-class young women as nurses, as Red Cross workers, as friends and sweethearts. Progressively since the 1890s, the discipline of the Anglo-Protestant middle class in chaperoning its young women before marriage had been breaking down, and premarital virginity had been decreasing. Increasingly, young women were competing with one another at dances and parties to attract young men through their charm and their willingness to pet without "going all the way." Now the tensions and pressures of the war accelerated the collapse of chaperoning and encouraged more intense sexual relationships. Middle-class women were challenging the exclusive right of men to have premarital sex when women did not have that right for themselves. The war aroused moral anxieties over the maintenance of sexual propriety and the traditional role of middle-class women.

BLACKS AND THE WAR

Southern blacks comprised the other major group that filled the labor shortage caused by the closing of immigration from Europe and the creation of a large army. During the war years, several hundred thousand blacks went North, accelerating the migration of surplus agricultural workers into northern cities since 1900. For the first time since the 1890s, there were many opportunities for blacks to get jobs in industries such as steel and meatpacking. As the need for manpower increased, the Wilson administration reaffirmed the citizenship of blacks by conscripting them into the army, although the marines accepted no blacks and the navy enlisted them only as a noncombat servant class of mess boys. The original intention of the Army Chiefs of Staff was to use blacks

Black soldiers, like this one being welcomed home, were rigidly segregated during World War One. White American leaders believed that blacks were not capable of effective combat service and thus most black military units worked in supply. Some black regiments, however, were permitted to enter combat along side French troops and received decorations from the French army. (Amistad Research Center)

regiments and divisions, and the top commanders of these units were white. The first black regiments sent to France fought as part of the French army, although American generals insisted that their white troops fight as an independent American army commanded by neither the English nor the French.

The French army decorated many black soldiers, but no Medals of Honor were forthcoming from the American army. French officers and civilians often entered into social relations with black officers and soldiers, while white American officers refused any social contact with black officers. In fact, the Anglo-American commitment to segregation went so far that General James Erwin warned the French army and civilians not to associate with black troops.

But for the 400,000 young black men who served in the army, the war experience liberated them from situations of local segregation and taught them to fight against white men, the Germans. Some had been accepted as social and sexual equals in France. It is not surprising, then, that when race riots broke out across the country in 1919, blacks fought back against white aggression. The bloody summer of 1919 brought riots to twenty-five American cities and death to 78 blacks. In Chicago alone, 38 whites and blacks died in street fighting and 578 were injured. The racial violence of 1919 stemmed from fears by lower-income whites that blacks were taking away scarce jobs and that the expansion of black ghettos would destroy white neighborhoods. Whites also feared the sense of pride that accompanied returning black veterans. Blacks, in turn, resented white efforts to deprive the black community of jobs and housing. These conditions and attitudes produced mass movements of black pride and separatism among low-income blacks in the cities during the 1920s.

only as noncombat laborers. But pressure from the NAACP and other black groups forced the army to organize combat units and to establish an officers' training camp for black soldiers. Yet the caste system was preserved because no black officer ever commanded a white man. Black officers commanded black troops in segregated

WILSON AND
PEACE NEGOTIATIONS

The success of economic and military mobilization ensured the Allies' defeat of Germany by November 1918. But the war years had intensified deep social confusions and divisions at home. And soon President Wilson was to discover that similar divisions affected international relations. Most of the voters who had supported peace and global isolation in 1916 were silenced by the pressures of patriotism to support the war. But through their votes for Republicans in the congressional elections of November 1918, many voters expressed restlessness with the war and Wilsonian internationalism. Republicans won smashing victories and established strong control of both the House of Representatives and the Senate in the 1918 election.

Wilson, however, maintained the policy of

President Wilson was greeted as a savior by many of the people of Europe in 1919 when he went to France to negotiate the treaty to end World War One. People everywhere hoped that Wilson could arrange a peace settlement that would prevent the horrors of World War One from being repeated. (National Archives 111-SC-62979)

John Reed

1887-1920

John Reed became the best known of the group of middle-class college students who were attracted to socialism just before World War One. Born and raised in Portland, Oregon, he was sent by his father, a wealthy businessman, to a boarding school in New Jersey and then to Harvard University. Fathers from every section of the country who wanted their sons to be part of a national elite felt the need to enroll their children in eastern preparatory schools and then in Ivy League universities.

At Harvard, Reed enjoyed being part of the youth culture of prolonged adolescence. His most serious thoughts seemed to focus on his role as a cheerleader, in which he led "great crashing choruses during the football games." After graduation he traveled to Europe, supported by an indulgent family that gave him, he wrote, "freedom and understanding as well as material things."

When he returned, Reed drifted into journalism in New York City. There he began to associate with young men, like Walter Lippmann, who had been serious intellectuals in his Harvard class of 1910. They were Socialists and they persuaded Reed to see that "my happiness is built on the misery of others." Reed talked with them in their apartments in Greenwich Village, worked with them on magazines such as the Masses, and went with them to the elegant salon of Mabel Dodge, who shared her wealth and sexual favors with bright young radicals.

Reed went back to Europe when the war began in 1914 and was horrified at the bloodshed of what he saw as a capitalist civil war. He wanted to believe that capitalism was about to disappear. Lincoln Steffens, an older muckraking journalist, reassured Reed that this was true, and together they went to write about the revolution in Mexico, which might mark such *a moment. Then Reed heard about the revolution in Russia and he traveled there. He arrived just in time to witness the bloody victory of the radical Bolsheviks over the moderate revolutionists. Reed returned to the United States with a stirring and optimistic book-length report,* Ten Days That Shook the World, *on the beginning of the worldwide revolution.*

But in 1919 he was aware that no revolution was occurring in the United States. Socialist leaders had been put in jail for opposing the war, and magazines like the Masses *had been suppressed. And now American radicals were more confused as to how to relate to the Bolshevik revolution. Moderates remained Socialists while radicals split into the Communist and Communist Labor parties.*

In 1919 Reed returned to Russia to seek help in ending these divisions. He was bitterly disappointed by the inflexible and unfriendly revolutionary bureaucracy he found there. When he died of typhus in Moscow in 1920, the final irony was that these bureaucrats buried him at the Kremlin Wall as a hero of the Bolshevik revolution.

presidential initiation in foreign policy begun by McKinley and Theodore Roosevelt. Hoping that the United States was emerging from isolation, Wilson became the first president to go overseas, and he appointed himself the chief American diplomatic negotiator at the Paris peace conference. He took along personal adviser Colonel Edward M. House, Secretary of State Robert Lansing, General Tasker Bliss, and a State Department career diplomat, Henry White, as fellow negotiatiors. But the president failed to recognize the advisability of consulting with Republican leaders from the Senate, the very leaders who would be responsible for consideration and passage of any treaty brought back from France.

Wilson carried with him a plan for peace that he had outlined in a speech to Congress in January 1918. He had enunciated fourteen necessary points for a just and lasting peace. The Fourteen Points included freedom of the seas, no barrier to the free flow of trade or passengers on the oceans, disarmament, increasing self-determination of the people in the colonial empires, and self-determination for the peoples of Europe. Most important to Wilson, however, was the creation of a League of Nations to enforce this new world order.

German political leaders had compelled the Kaiser's exile and surrender before German armies had retreated from Belgium and France because they believed that Wilson could achieve a peace not vindictive toward the German people. Wilson, however, lacked the power to force David Lloyd George, George Clemenceau, and Vittorio Orlando, the prime ministers of England, France, and Italy, to accept his vision of world order. In Paris, the European Allies insisted that Germany accept guilt for causing the war and pay $35 billion in war reparations to England and France. England, France, and

MAP 5.3   AMERICAN INTERVENTION IN RUSSIA, 1918

Japan divided the German colonies among themselves and refused to consider ending their own empires. Germany and Austria lost control of non-German peoples in Europe who had been part of the German and Austro-Hungarian empires at the same time that many German-speaking people were placed in the newly formed countries of Central Europe and in Italy.

The only bargaining force that Wilson had in Europe in 1919 was his personal appeals to the people of England, France, and Italy. He believed that the peoples would like his ideas so much that they would pressure their leaders to accept them. This policy had seemed to work in Germany, where popular pressure had forced the end of the war sometime before German

armies had lost their ability to fight. But although Wilson was enthusiastically received in Europe, the political leaders of the Allies did not respond to popular pressure.

The successful Communist revolution in Russia during 1917 further limited Wilson's options in regard to the Allies. During the summer of 1918, the president had sent American troops into European Russia with English and French troops and into Siberia with Japanese troops. Like the leaders of England and France, Wilson hoped to destroy the Bolshevik revolution. V. I. Lenin, the head of this revolution, had declared that the future of the industrial world belonged to communism. In Lenin's analysis, capitalist nations would continue to fight wars among themselves as they competed for overseas markets and raw material until the working class would take control of these countries and institute a cooperative and peaceful world order.

Lenin's vision of an eventual Communist world order challenged Wilson's vision of a peaceful capitalist world order in which European nations would give up their empires. But as American and Allied troops withdrew from European Russia in the summer of 1919 and from Siberia in 1920, the United States and its Allies recognized the failure of their effort to support anti-Communist forces in Russia. And in the chaos that followed the German surrender, Communist uprising spread throughout eastern and central Europe. Wilson believed that communism had to be contained within Russia and not allowed to spread west. His overriding concern with communism forced the president to seek solidarity with the Allies, despite their rejection of the American plan to end restrictive empires and not punish Germany in the peace settlement.

The Treaty of Versailles that Wilson brought home from Paris was opposed by four groups. Both Republican and Democratic liberals criticized the obvious failing of the treaty to create a just peace. Another group of Republican and Democratic liberals represented by Herbert Hoover was not enthusiastic about the League of Nations. Disillusioned by the failure of efforts to use political and military power to achieve a world marketplace, they preferred to rely on the strength of the American economy to break down future trade barriers. Adhering to the principles of the Open Door policy, such leaders feared that the league committed the United States to the continued use of political and military force to freeze the status quo in Europe.

The major group of Republican senators, led by Henry Cabot Lodge, chairman of the Senate Foreign Relations Committee, was quite hospitable toward a peace that punished Germany and was willing to consider a League of Nations. But the Lodge group wanted to make modifications that demonstrated Republican participation in the making of the treaty. Most important, it wanted to strike Article X from the League of Nations charter, a clause that compelled each member of the league to come to the defense of any other member in case it was attacked. Lodge argued that Article X restricted the independence of the United States. Finally, a small group of midwestern and western progressive Republicans, headed by William Borah of Idaho and Robert LaFollette, the Irreconcilables, would not accept the league even with modifications. For these anticorporate progressives, the league sustained the reactionary and unjust imperial structures of England and France.

Wilson could have obtained Senate acceptance of the treaty with the league if he had been willing to compromise with the Lodge Republicans. But he refused to compromise. Once more he went to the people on a long and exhausting speaking tour, asking citizens to pressure the Senate to accept the treaty without modifications. In September 1919, on this trip, Wilson collapsed of a stroke. He remained crippled for the rest of his life and communicated with the government and the public only through his wife. During the final year of his presidency, Wilson continued to oppose compromise on the league. The United States never signed the Treaty of Versailles and never joined the League of Nations. Later in the 1920s, a separate peace treaty was signed with Germany.

SUGGESTED READINGS

The peculiar fascination that China held for the American imagination in 1900 is the subject of Paul A. Varg, *The Making of a Myth: The United States and China, 1879–1912* (1968). The dynamic role of Theodore Roosevelt in American expansion is described in Howard Beale, *Theodore Roosevelt and the Rise of America to World Power* (1956), and David Burton, *Theodore Roosevelt, Confident Imperialist* (1968). The continuity of American expansion under Republican and Democratic administrations is analyzed in Dana G. Munro, *Intervention and Dollar Diplomacy in the Caribbean, 1900–1921* (1964), and Walter and Marie Scholes, *The Foreign Policies of the Taft Administration* (1970).

Richard D. Challener, *Admirals, Generals, and American Foreign Policy, 1898–1914* (1973), E. Berkeley Tompkins, *Anti-Imperialism in the United States: The Great Debate, 1890–1920* (1970), and Warren Kuehl, *Seeking World Order: The United States and World Organization to 1920* (1969), describe the various responses of the White Protestant elite to the increasing competition of the industrial nations of Europe, Japan, and the United States. Continued establishment complacency, however, is the subject of John M. Cooper, Jr., *The Vanity of Power: American Isolationism and the First World War, 1914–1917* (1969).

The cultural and economic forces leading to American entry in the war are discussed in Ross Gregory, *The Origins of American Intervention in the First World War* (1971), John G. Clifford, *The Citizen Soldiers* (1972), and John A. S. Grenville and George Berkeley Young, *Politics, Strategy, and American Diplomacy* (1966).

Robert Osgood, *Ideals and Self-Interest in America's Foreign Relations* (1953), and Ernest Tuveson, *Redeemer Nation* (1968), present one aspect of the ideological outlook that Woodrow Wilson brought to World War One. Another aspect is presented in the essays by Martin J. Sklar, "Woodrow Wilson and the Political Economy of Modern United States Liberalism," and by Murray Rothbard, "War Collectivism in World War I." These essays are in Ronald Radosh and Murray Rothbard, eds., *A New History of Leviathan* (1972). Specific studies of the developing military-industrial complex are Robert D. Cuff, *The War Industries Board: Business-Government Relations during World War I* (1973), and David F. Noble, *America by Design* (1977).

Wartime conformity is analyzed by Russell Weigler, *The American Way of War* (1973), Joan M. Jensen, *The Price of Vigilance* (1968), George T. Blakey, *Historians on the Home Front* (1970), Carol S. Gruber, *Mars and Minerva: World War I and the Uses of Higher Learning in America* (1975), and Walter Preston, *Aliens and Dissenters: Federal Suppression of Radicals, 1903–1933* (1963).

An excellent analysis of Wilson's ideas about the peace settlement is N. Gordon Levin, Jr., *Woodrow Wilson and World Politics* (1968). Other important books dealing with American hopes and fears in 1919 are Arno J. Mayer, *Politics and Diplomacy of Peacemaking: Containment and Counter Revolution at Versailles* (1967), and John M. Thompson, *Russia, Bolshevism, and the Versailles Peace* (1966). Ralph A. Stone, *The Irreconcilables: The Fight Against the League of Nations* (1970), clarifies the motives of Wilson's critics.

American frustrations in 1919 and the search for scapegoats are discussed in Robert K. Murray, *The Red Scare* (1955), Stanley Coben, *A. Mitchell Palmer* (1963), David Brody, *Labor in Crisis: The Steel Strike of 1919* (1965), and William Tuttle, Jr., *Race Riot: Chicago in the Red Summer of 1910* (1965).

Spotlight: The Red Scare

In May 1919 a man refused to stand for the playing of the "Star Spangled Banner" at a public gathering in Washington, D.C. His actions enraged most of the people there to the point that one spectator shot him three times. The crowd cheered this attacker. Across the country in 1919, juries acquitted "patriots" for attacking and sometimes killing "un-Americans." This violence was part of the "Red Scare" that swept the nation throughout 1919. The worst of the hysteria was over by 1920, although it was still possible for a clerk in a clothing store in Connecticut to be jailed for making an unpatriotic statement. His crime was to tell a customer that he believed that V. I. Lenin, the leader of Communist Russia, was "one of the brainiest of world leaders."

Ordinary Americans as well as leaders in the Wilson administration were bewildered and frightened in 1919. After the United States had entered the war in

(*Above*) In July 1917, these copper miners were marched out of Bisbee, Arizona, into the desert where they were held by the army in a stockade for several months. Although members of conservative AFL unions, the miners had cooperated in a strike with the radical IWW. Business leaders accused the IWW of being pro-German and used both vigilantes and federal troops to destroy by violence the IWW and many other unions as well. (Brown Brothers)

1917, American military and naval strength made it possible for the Allies to win a quick military victory over Germany in 1918. By 1919, however, it seemed impossible to conclude a peace that would express American war aims.

Throughout the country, people had been told by their newspapers that a new world order of harmony under American leadership would be the result of the war. At the beginning of the war in 1917, for example, the *Des Moines Register* rejoiced in the future: "It was the American flag that has brought about the peaceable revolution in Russia; and it is the American flag that will bring about the revolution in Germany, peaceable or violent, for that revolution is bound to come. It is American ideals that dominate the world."

But in October 1917 the middle-class revolutionists in Russia were overthrown by Marxist revolutionists. These Bolsheviks, under the leadership of Lenin, numbered only a few thousand. They had, however, intense ideological commitment and discipline. American Socialists, following the teaching of Marx, believed that socialism had to follow the development of an industrial work force. They were surprised and delighted, therefore, when a small Marxist group captured control of Russia, an agricultural country without widespread industrialism. Eugene Debs, imprisoned by Wilson for antiwar activity, declared, "From the crown of my head to the soles of my feet, I am a Bolshevik and proud of it." Discouraged by government repression and demoralized by the wartime splintering of the Socialist movement, Debs wanted to believe that worldwide Socialist revolution had begun.

But a number of Socialist leaders, especially those who were Anglo-Protestants, had chosen to leave the party and support Wilson. For them, Debs and other antiwar Socialists were un-American. "They should be driven out of the country," declared Charles E. Russell, a prowar Socialist, "or shot at once without an hour's delay." The defection of Anglo-Protestant leaders from the Socialist party gave added party influence to the foreign-language federations. But when the immigrant federations voted to associate with a worldwide Communist movement, the Third International, with headquarters in Moscow, Debs refused to accept the decision. The foreign-language federations then left the Socialist party and created the Communist party. As a result, membership in the Socialist party dropped from 110,000 to 40,000. A group of Anglo-Protestant radicals also broke from the Socialist party and formed the Communist Labor party.

Despite the splintering of the radical political movement in 1919, members of the foreign-language federations still felt both optimism and a special responsibility to disseminate information about the revolutionary process from Soviet Russia through their new Communist magazines. By engaging in revolutionary violence, perhaps they could overthrow the capitalist establishment in America just as a small minority had overthrown the ruling groups in Russia.

A few of the radicals hoped that selective bombing of the centers of American politics and business might encourage a mass uprising of American workers against the capitalist system. These radicals misinterpreted the widespread labor unrest of 1919, in which four million workers participated in four thousand strikes. Economic interest, not political radicalism, lay at the root of postwar labor activism. As inflation spiraled in 1918 and 1919, wage earners desperately sought to win pay raises that matched the pace of rising prices. Other workers, encouraged by the growth of union membership during the war, wanted to unionize their industries. This was true in steel, where 350,000 employees began the largest strike thus far in American history in September 1919.

Just as the radicals misread the meaning of the strikes, so did middle-class leaders. If Wilson could not spread the ideals of American capitalism throughout the world, was it possible that Communist ideals could be successful a alternative? The most popular magazine in America, the *Saturday Evening Post,* warned against "a propaganda which is tending to undermine our most cherished social and political institutions and is having the effect of producing widespread unrest among the poor and the ignorant, especially those of foreign birth." Middle-class leaders focused their major fears of Communist power on the steel strike, a strike by police in Boston in an attempt to win recognition for their union, and a strike by thirty-five thousand shipyard workers in Seattle who asked for the support of all other workers through a general strike that would close down the city.

These fears were summarized by the head of U.S. Steel, Elbert Gary: "The contemplated progress of trade unions if successful would be to receive the control of the shops, then of the general management of business, then of capital, and finally of government." A middle-class lynch mob killed some of the strike leaders in Seattle, and federal troops joined the repression. In Boston all the police were fired. The federal government also joined with the large steel corporations to break that strike. Leaders of the national government joined corporate leaders in defining this outburst of labor activity, most of it led by procapitalist AFL leaders, as part of a Communist conspiracy to begin a violent revolution.

In Massachusetts, Governor Calvin Coolidge achieved national publicity with his adamant insistence that the Boston police had no right to strike against the public interest and that "red" agitators were leading the police astray. But the leading perpetrator of the 1919 Red Scare was Attorney General A. Mitchell Palmer, a Quaker and liberal member of the Wilsonian team. Palmer built a policy of government repression against alleged subversives on the wartime precedents already established by the Wilson administration against German-Americans.

By 1919 the federal government identified American radicals with both "un-American" Germany and Russia. These radicals, a government official declared, were "connected with Russian Bolshevism, aided by Hun money." *The Saturday Evening Post* reinforced this idea by calling communism "a Russo-German movement that is now trying to dominate America."

Palmer initiated a federal crusade to eliminate the threat of revolution by staging raids in twelve cities to arrest radicals in November 1919. Many of those arrested were anarchists who were totally opposed to what they saw as the political tyranny of Lenin's communism. And many were opposed to the use of violence. Nevertheless, within one month Palmer used willing federal courts to deport 249 immigrants, including the anarchist leader Emma Goldman, because they were dangerous aliens. Palmer brought the Red Scare to a climax in January 1920 by arresting six thousand people he claimed were subversive. Most were arrested without warrants and held without bail; many were beaten during arrest and while in jail. Finally, however, all but five hundred were released. The remaining five hundred were deported as dangerous aliens, a practice permitted through wartime legislation.

Palmer also established a General Intelligence Division in the Department of Justice under the leadership of a young lawyer, J. Edgar Hoover. The unit later became the Federal Bureau of Investigation (FBI). This national police force focused on the elimination of political radicalism and labor and radical unrest. By 1920 the Department of Justice defined almost all labor activism, even by the AFL, as dangerously radical and un-American. Despite its long commitment to participation in the democratic political process, federal officials also defined the Socialist party to be as dangerous as the revolutionary Communist parties. The House of Representatives twice denied a seat to the Milwaukee Socialist Victor Berger, an antiwar dissenter who had been jailed under the Espionage Act. The state legislature of New York also refused to seat five Socialists in 1919, although Socialists had held political offices throughout the state for twenty years.

Since much of industrial labor was made up of new Slavic and Italian workers, these ethnic groups came into the 1920s under the cloud of being un-American. The pressure on non-English-speaking Americans to conform to Anglo-Protestant standards became intense, as the elite conducted an "Americanization" campaign among ethnic minorities. "This Americanization movement," a Harvard University administrator proclaimed, "gives men a new and holy religion of one country, one language, one flag." But the effect on immigrant culture was disruptive. The continued use of newspapers and other literature not written in English was seen by Anglo-Protestants as a sign of un-American activity. Not only did Jewish, Slavic, Italian, and German-Americans feel pressure to give up their ethnic heritages, but even Scandinavian-Americans felt compelled to sacrifice their rich ethnic traditions. Poetry, novels, philosophy, and theology had been written in Danish, Norwegian, and Swedish in the centers of Scandinavian culture in Wisconsin, Iowa, Minnesota, and the Dakotas during the half century from 1870 to 1920. But much of the vitality of these ethnic cultures disappeared in the 1920s. The wartime pressures for conformity climaxing in the Red Scare of 1919 were to make many Americans vulnerable, therefore, to the persuasiveness of advertising in the 1920s to become part of a standardized society.

By 1920, postwar inflation ceased to be a major problem, and returning soldiers had re-entered the civilian work force. As the major social and economic dislocations faded, so did the fears of a successful Communist revolution in the United States. The collapse of the great Red Scare frustrated the political ambitions of Attorney General Palmer, who failed to win the presidential nomination of the Democratic party. No longer was it sufficient for Palmer to make speeches in which he declared, "I am myself an American and I love to preach my doctrine before undiluted one hundred per cent Americans, because my platform is one hundred per cent American." But the Red Scare had reduced the number of avowed Communists from sixty thousand to ten thousand. Most American Marxists had gone underground to protect themselves from local vigilante violence as well as government repression. The final irony, however, was that Lenin ordered American Communists to surrender their hope for revolution and to begin to work with Progressive forces in the American labor movement and in American politics to bring a gradual, evolutionary change in the American economic system.

Chapter 6

THE NEW ERA OF THE 1920s

The decade following World War One provided a preview of the modern era of conspicuous consumption and the rise of corporation technology and bureaucracy. The energies released by economic growth were stupendous. But as Americans attempted to make peace with the twentieth century, many were threatened or hurt by the changes associated with corporate capitalism and its disruption of traditional life.

NEW ERA PROSPERITY

A strengthened United States emerged from World War One as a creditor nation for the first time in its history. War loans to the Allies,

a stimulus to European buying of American military goods and foodstuffs, amounted to $12.5 billion at the start of the decade. As the nation experienced a spectacular boom between 1922 and 1929, confident corporate and business leaders proclaimed a "new era" in human affairs, an epoch of permanent prosperity and social peace guaranteed by mass production and consumer spending. National income mushroomed from $60 billion in 1922 to $87 billion in 1929. Since prices remained stable, real annual earnings increased by nearly 11 percent. The combined physical production of agriculture, manufacturing, mining, and construction increased by more than one-third between 1922 and 1929. Meanwhile, unemployment rates remained low in most industries.

The unparalled prosperity of the new era

was characterized by a dramatic rise in industrial efficiency and an outpouring of investment into profitable durable goods. Productivity per worker hour jumped 70 percent between 1919 and 1929. Scientific management of the industrial labor force may have accounted for some of that increase. More important were cost-saving innovations in electrical technology and mass production assemblies. Administrative efficiency also improved through such innovations as addressing machines, metered mail, dictaphones, form letters, and payroll checks.

The growth in durable goods began with the construction industry, frustrated during wartime mobilization. Plant expansion, public utility development, highway and public construction, and a housing boom all contributed to one of the greatest building sprees in American history. Construction spending reached $12.8 billion during 1926 alone.

But new era enthusiasm focused on scientific technology. Sophisticated research laboratories in the larger corporations not only pursued productive efficiency but sought to expand the choice of commodities for the mass market that industrialists were just learning to tap. The burgeoning petroleum industry, which produced one billion barrels of crude oil in 1929, learned to synthesize petrochemicals such as acetate and Dacron, as well as highly marketable plastics, cosmetics, and synthetic tires. Rayon, a synthetic fiber made by dissolving wood chips in a chemical solution, became popular in clothing of the twenties. The Dupont corporation also developed cellophane for packaging mass-produced goods.

Electronic communications became one of the nation's major industries in the expansive new era. By the end of 1930 there were twenty million telephones in the United States, in contrast to the 1.3 million of 1900. Electrical ap-

pliance producers such as General Electric and Westinghouse found receptive buyers for mass-produced lamps, home washing machines, refrigerators, electric irons, toasters, and vacuum cleaners. Prodding by the electrical appliance industry led to the establishment of commercial radio stations and networks by the late twenties. The radio age began on election night of 1920, when returns were broadcast from a two-story garage by Pittsburgh's KDKA. By 1931 two radio networks extended to 150 affiliates, more than twelve million American families owned radio receivers, and the radio industry had increased its market value forty times.

Of all the mass-market commodities of the new era, the automobile was the most important stimulus to investment and total output. Henry Ford's Model T, which sold for as little as $295 in 1928, made the dream of mobility a reality for millions of Americans of modest means. The automobile gave immediate status to all buyers. Just under two million cars were sold in 1919, but by 1929 the industry was producing over 5.6 million automobiles a year. When the decade closed, two of every three households in the nation owned a "flivver."

Automobile manufacturing accounted for one-eighth of all industrial activity in the 1920s. Millions of additional jobs were created in auxiliary industries from steel and rubber to fuel and road construction. Expenditure on highway construction reached $1 billion a year by the late twenties, made possible by the Federal Highway Act of 1921, which provided matching funds to the states for road building.

Henry Ford called machinery the "new messiah." Standardization of parts, industrial research, scientific management, long-range budgeting, and mass production were celebrated as keys to industrial progress by Ford and other new era polemicists. Business spokesmen be-

160

In the 1920s, even small towns could have traffic jams. Automobiles were one of the mainstays of new era prosperity. (Brown Brothers)

lieved that these advances created mass markets by lowering prices and raising wages. They argued that the leisure time provided by technology would relieve drudgery, reduce economic conflict, and ensure the good life through a healthy accumulation of goods and services. Their theories were substantiated when outlays for consumer services rose from $21 billion in 1920 to $32 billion in 1929. By the late twenties, installment buying helped to stimulate the mass consumption on which the economy depended. Based on the insights of behavioral psychology, the growing advertising industry studied ways to stimulate consumer buying. Advertising spent $15 per capita in 1929 to persuade Americans that emotional needs such as excitement and security could be satisfied through the purchase of mass-produced items. Popular magazines of the period unabashedly equated success with money, status, and power.

BUSINESS PROGRESSIVISM

Urban and corporation leaders in the Progressive era had promoted a democracy of consumers committed to impersonal and universal standards of doing business and administering

Twenties technology and affluence were not universal. A Native-American home in South Dakota in about 1920 indicates just how remote certain areas of the country were from the prevailing prosperity of this period. (Amistad Research Center)

government. The growth of large corporations underscored the need to replace rigorous competition and individualism with progressive virtues of cooperation and rational planning. World War One tested the new concepts of industrial management and cooperation, as the War Industries Board mobilized a peacetime economy for massive military support. "Our industry came re-born out of the intense experience of the war," board chairman Bernard Baruch later recalled.

Once the fighting ended, upper-middle-class professionals and corporate spokesmen quickly embraced the concept of a new economic era in which harmony, abundance, and progress replaced class and social conflict. In this version of the progressive society, a "new generation" of business leadership had emerged as "trustees" for the public and employees. Dedicated to

ethical standards and long-range administrative planning, the modern corporation manager would combine the spirit of service and social responsibility with the insights of science and group dynamics. Corporate progressives such as Harvard economist Thomas Nixon Carver contended that the corporations had demonstrated their superiority over politics by introducing economic democracy through technology. The vacuum cleaner and the electric iron, asserted the *Magazine of Business,* were prized more than women's suffrage by "the average woman." To new era polemicists, expansion of profits and healthy increases in wages and salaries seemed to indicate that prosperity had permanently conquered the downturns of the business cycle. Enjoying a virtual monopoly over the imagination and rhetoric of the urban middle class, new era leaders won widespread acceptance for their point of view. By the twenties, corporation leaders had succeeded in defining their interests in universal rather than class terms.

Despite rhetoric about new era economic democracy, however, corporate consolidation marked the prosperity of the 1920s. While centralization advanced economic growth, mergers brought the extinction of nearly five thousand manufacturing and mining firms during the decade. Monopolies consolidated domination over aluminum, salt, sugar, and Central American fruits. In petroleum, copper, tobacco, and meatpacking, oligopolies of two or three corporations continued to rule. Mergers and the growth of chain banks consolidated control over capital, while three automobile companies produced 83 percent of the nation's cars as the decade closed. In the retail field the Great Atlantic and Pacific Tea Company revolutionized the grocery industry through the national distribution of packaged foods in A & P supermarkets. The number of chain stores in the nation jumped from below 30,000 at the Armistice to 160,000 by 1929, forcing thousands of small stores out of business. By 1930 the two hundred largest corporations in the United States controlled just under half of all nonbanking corporate wealth. The "top 200," in turn, were controlled by two thousand members of the traditional Anglo-Protestant elite.

With the exception of isolated individualists such as Henry Ford, corporate managers and board chairmen who were oriented to bureaucratic stability set the tone for big business in the twenties. The trend toward long-range planning received impetus from trade associations, which organized entire industries and insulated large firms from the competitive tactics of new entrants. Large corporations had worked with competitors in the commodity committees of the War Industries Board, where they had shared information, divided markets and resources, fixed prices, and established common labor policies. Following the war, business leaders formed trade associations independent of government involvement. Often dominated by the major corporations in each industry, the nation's four thousand trade associations engaged in collective research and market-extension campaigns, strove to improve productive efficiency, and cooperated to frame codes of business ethics. Quick to learn the newly developed art of public relations, twenties corporations expanded upon wartime emphasis on service and goodwill. "Service always pays better than selfishness," Henry Ford insisted, reflecting a commonly held notion that the goodwill of the buying public was essential to the long-range success of a large corporation. As part of the effort to professionalize business management and present a favorable image of corporate institutions and products, 750 business firms subscribed to the Chamber of Commerce's national code of ethics by 1925.

THE SEARCH FOR LABOR HARMONY

Labor relations proved the most difficult challenge for the new management. Wartime tolerance for conservative trade unions had evaporated during the labor strife of 1919, when Anglo-Protestant leaders feared that the immigrant working class was dangerously susceptible to the appeals of international communism. Furthermore, corporation leaders who viewed themselves as trustees for the economic order were reluctant to relinquish traditional Anglo-Protestant authority or managerial prerogatives.

"I will not permit myself to be in a position of having labor dictate to management," Charles Schwab of Bethlehem Steel declared. Schwab's reasoning found support among the smaller corporations that participated in the "open shop" campaigns against trade unions promoted by the National Association of Manufacturers. An open shop is a place of employment where workers are not required to join a union.

Although most twenties business leaders discouraged or bitterly fought independent trade unions, management hoped that class antagonism could be ameliorated through "welfare capitalism" and a "human approach to industry." Seeking a stable and contented working class, the Chamber of Commerce warned that "Where there is no tinder, no fire can start." The war had taught business leaders the importance of morale to labor stability and productive efficiency. New era managers claimed that increased sensitivity to employee problems accounted for a reduction of labor turnover by half in the twenties. Likewise, Henry Ford continually lectured industrialists on the connection between economic prosperity and widely diffused purchasing power.

The human approach to industry in the new era stressed higher wages, improved working conditions, employee representation, fringe benefits, and profit sharing. U.S. Steel spent $10 million a year in safety, medical services, sports, self-improvement classes, and land for employee gardening. Large manufacturers instituted clean and well-lit factories, low-cost cafeterias, employee social clubs, locker rooms, showers, libraries, and swimming pools. Half the nation's large corporations had industrial relations departments. Industrial psychologists applied themselves to problems of worker depersonalization and unpredictability, although efforts often were limited to palliatives such as

cheerful wall coloring or piped-in music. Henry Ford's Sociological Department administered social services to company employees, but it also spied on union organizers and insisted that assembly line workers refrain from drinking and smoking at home. By 1922 paternalistic corporations were spending $10 million a year on company magazines designed to boost employee morale by seeking to foster identification with corporate goals. Large corporations also provided group insurance, private pension plans, and stock ownership through payroll deductions.

Employee representation plans, or company unions, constituted the heart of welfare capitalism advanced by major employers. Shop committees, company councils, and other in-house associations flourished in the twenties. Although such elements were promoted as experiments in industrial democracy, management in the new era rarely delegated responsibility and power, and it prohibited most company unions from dealing with wage and hours issues. *Labor Age* complained in 1927 that General Electric pampered employee committee members with steaks while refusing to discuss issues such as pay increases for day workers.

SHIFTS IN THE WORK FORCE

Although wages rose in the twenties, the new era did not produce a more equitable distribution of wealth. Profits and dividends tripled between 1920 and 1929, far outpacing minimal wage increases. The top 5 percent of American income receivers increased their share of total income from 22 percent to 26 percent in the new era. But more than two-fifths of the nation's consumer units closed the decade at what the Brookings Institution described as a "sub-sistence-and-poverty" level, while another 36 percent lived at "minimum comfort level."

Technological changes and the growth of consumer services considerably altered the composition of the American work force. Although manufacturing output increased by half, mechanization and scientific management resulted in no increase in factory employment. Technological unemployment also hurt workers in coal mining, railroads, forestry, and agriculture. Older workers were particularly affected, since scientific management translated efficiency into terms of unit costs and output. As a result, speed and nimbleness replaced experience and judgment as necessary qualities on the assembly line, and factories began insisting on age limits for hiring. The replacement of skilled labor with unskilled assembly line workers changed the nature of industrial work. Critics commented that factory workers increasingly resembled dehumanized automatons, endlessly repeating specific tasks, losing all control over work rhythms and routines. Silent-film comedies of the twenties portrayed the futility of the "small-man hero" in coping with the dehumanizing power of machinery in mass production.

While industrial employment stagnated in the twenties, white-collar and service employment in growing corporations and bureaucracies increased by nearly half. These occupations constituted nearly one-fourth the national labor force by the end of the decade. The twenties brought millions of Americans an entry into middle-class styles of work, although salaries often were not commensurate with increased occupational status. On the whole, however, higher wages, private insurance plans, and expanded public services such as free education, libraries, and parks contributed to an improvement in the lives of working people during the decade. Most Americans hoped to share in the fabulous fruits of new era prosperity. Significantly, the Socialist Norman Thomas was moved to comment that the American worker of the twenties was "drunk with prosperity."

UNION CONSERVATISM

Shifts in the work force, union cautiousness, and business and government hostility contributed to a dismal decade for the organized labor movement. In 1920 over five million Americans belonged to unions. By 1933 there were less than three million union members across the nation. The American Federation of Labor of the twenties was dominated by conservative craft unions, traditionally composed of older, white, skilled workers in manual trades. William Green, who succeeded Samuel Gompers as president in 1924, supported the AFL conversion from the militancy that characterized 1919 to respectability. Green saw organized labor as an auxiliary to business and stressed concord rather than conflict. Committed to increased output and industrial peace, he reiterated Gompers's advocacy of capitalist order and enmity to bolshevism.

Craft unions were not equipped to take advantage of the new era shift from manual to white-collar work. Since office workers and service personnel believed themselves to be new members of the middle class, they were not attracted to trade union activity. Organized labor was also affected by the rise of new mass production industries that by-passed the craft worker. Assembly line industries such as automobile manufacturing drew heavily upon Russians, Poles, Croats, Hungarians, and Italians, semiskilled immigrants whom organized labor ignored until the 1930s.

The AFL also had great difficulty recruiting southern migrants who worked in textiles, autos, and rubber, since rural traditions of individualism acted against worker cooperation. Furthermore, few industrial or craft unions welcomed blacks or women. Less than 3 percent of all working women were organized by 1929, as opposed to 11 percent of men. Blacks were directly excluded by the constitutions or rituals of twenty-four international unions. The Urban League estimated black union membership to be below eighty-two thousand in the later twenties. Black workers had no choice but to seek employment in open-shop industries such as autos, steel, and meatpacking or to take work as strikebreakers. They were so used during coal strikes in Pennsylvania and Ohio in 1927 and 1928 and in the Boston longshore walkout of 1929.

Hostility to unionism was particularly strong in newly industrialized areas such as the South, mountain states, and southern Midwest. The AFL quickly abandoned an attempt to organize the southern textile industry when a strike at the cotton mills in Danville, Virginia, was crushed by police and state militia in the late twenties. Communist organizers led millworkers in fighting speed-ups in the Piedmont mills of North Carolina, but AFL leadership played little role in such crusades. Strikes in Piedmont textile towns in North Carolina and Tennessee led to antiunion injunctions, troop invasions, and vigilante action against unionists. Since northeastern textile firms had migrated southward to escape unionism, they dealt harshly with it when the threat arose in their new homes.

New industries such as automobiles, utilities, chemicals, and rubber, based in growing industrial centers such as Detroit and Los Angeles, were bitterly antiunion during the new era. The postwar period was characterized by a national open shop campaign. Labor leaders denounced such arrangements as union busting, since workers were not required to pay union dues to receive the fruits of collective bargaining. Initially organized by local employers to combat the Seattle general strike of 1919, open-shop campaigns quickly spread throughout the country. By 1920 the National Association of Manufacturers endorsed the open-shop program, portraying collective bargaining as alien to American traditions.

Courts in the twenties supported the campaign against trade unions. The Supreme Court in 1921 upheld the use of injunctions against unions for purposes of "equity" and ruled that all union picketing was illegal when more than one person was involved. A decision the following year held unions liable for damages when strikes affected interstate commerce or involved the destruction of property. Despite an $8 million legal effort by the United Mine Workers, federal courts upheld injunctions enforcing "yellow dog" contracts in West Virginia coal mines. These contracts prohibited union membership. The injunctions enforcing them made union officers liable to contempt of court if they induced miners to strike.

Despite difficulties, craft unions remained strong in the AFL building trades and the railway brotherhoods, while industrial unions staggered through a troubled era in coal and textiles. A strike of 400,000 AFL shopcraft workers, the largest walkout of the decade, brought rail transportation to a halt in 1922, in the first railroad strike since the Pullman conflict of 1894. Claiming that the railroad unions were "Bolshevik dominated," Attorney General

Harry Daugherty won a federal injunction that prevented union officers from "encouraging any person to leave the employ of a railroad." The 1922 strike failed, but four years later the Watson-Parker Act recognized collective bargaining for railroad workers. Although the new law prohibited railroad strikes for a sixty-day negotiations period, it was a milestone in federal recognition of union bargaining rights.

In an industry decimated by competition from petroleum, the United Mine Workers tried to hold the line against falling wages in anthracite and soft coal. A 1922 strike in hard coal brought out 155,000 miners before President Warren Harding arranged a temporary truce that resulted in an eight-hour day and UMW collective bargaining rights. But when UMW president John L. Lewis refused to revise a 1924 wage agreement with northern soft-coal operators, mine owners moved to destroy the union. Labor war broke out in western Pennsylvania, as miners evicted from company housing fought hired guards. By the end of the decade, UMW membership had tumbled from 450,000 to 150,000, and wages had nearly halved.

Like the soft-coal industry, the garment trades lacked corporate structure and suffered from competition aggravated by the popularity of synthetic fibers and short dresses. The Amalgamated Clothing Workers, led by Jewish socialists, tried to cooperate in saving the troubled needle trades by working to set production standards and maintain shop discipline. The union also built cooperative housing projects, established a bank to aid struggling clothing firms, and created an industrial engineering program to help employers increase efficiency and modernize methods. But garment unions were compelled to supervise layoffs in a declining industry. The International Ladies Garment Workers Union, a force for prewar progressive unionism, saw its predominantly female membership plummet from 120,000 to 45,000 by 1932. Not since the 1890s had the organized labor movement experienced such widespread difficulty.

OLD-STYLE FARMERS

Agriculture, like industry, consolidated and mechanized in the new era, but the results often were disastrous for independent farmers and rural laborers. Small farmers were old-style competitors in an economy that required corporate farms to absorb costs and invest capital in large-scale cultivation. Because agricultural distribution was controlled by major processors, independent farmers could not pass on increased mechanization expenses, interest rates, and taxes to consumers.

Farmers' problems began when government price supports and patriotism prompted the expansion of cultivation of foodstuffs and cotton during World War One. While farmers bought Ford tractors and expensive machinery, the wartime boom converted the vast ranges of the Great Plains to wheat acreage. With conversion to a peacetime economy, however, the government abandoned price supports, demand slackened, and farm prices sank. Wheat farmers who received $2.57 a bushel in 1920 earned less than $1.00 a bushel by the end of 1921. Large staple growers and dairy and truck farmers near urban centers shared in the return of prosperity in 1922. But overproduction, aggravated by foreign competition, plagued most independent farmers throughout the twenties. Farmer bankruptcy averaged nearly 18 percent in the decade, and total farm mortgage debt rose by $2 billion. Unable to hold their land, many small farmers became tenants. By 1930, 42 percent of the agricultural labor force leased farm land as tenants or sharecroppers, and a million farm families had left the land altogether.

As agriculture consolidated, large farm operations began to use wage laborers. In the Southwest, Mexican-Americans worked as field hands on large cotton and vegetable farms. About a half million Mexicans entered the United States with permanent visas in the twenties and subsidized big agriculture through the low wages paid for their farm labor. Mexican-American field workers attempted to organize unions in the California vegetable and fruit industry, but massive arrests, threats of deportation, and AFL disinterest doomed their efforts by the end of the decade.

Independent farmers tried to compete with agribusiness through cooperative marketing, an idea spread across the nation by Aaron Sapiro, a young California lawyer. By 1923 a half million American farmers belonged to marketing associations that handled a volume of $400 million. Under Sapiro's system, growers signed a contract to deliver all marketable produce to the association. The co-op was required to accept all farm produce, market it, and return proceeds to members after deducting costs. Marketing associations were most popular among tobacco, wheat, and cotton growers in the South and West and among fruit, grain, and dairy producers in the Northwest. By the mid-twenties, however, many marketing associations had overextended themselves through poor management, and the farm-cooperative movement waned. By then, farmers were calling for federal price supports to ensure market survival.

HARDING MODERATION

New era philosophy minimized the government's role in the economy. Yet corporate progressives of the 1920s insisted on a dependable judiciary, responsive federal agencies, and "responsible" tax and labor policies as instruments of the harmonious social order they sought. Although a twelve-year ascendancy of Republican presidents retreated from the legislative innovation of the Progressive years, important precedents in national planning emerged during the new era.

The presidential nomination of Warren G. Harding in 1920 arose from a compromise between progressive and conservative Republicans. Harding pictured himself as "a white-haired progressive." To insure geographic balance and an upright tone to the ticket, rank-and-file delegates selected Calvin Coolidge for the vice presidency. Coolidge was a bitter opponent of the League of Nations and had won national recognition for breaking the 1919 Boston police strike.

Harding's campaign involved a nostalgia for prewar stability. In his most quoted speech, Harding set the tone for the campaign and his administration:

America's present need is not heroics but healing, not nostrums but normalcy, not revolution but restoration, not agitation but adjustment, not surgery but serenity, not the dramatic but the dispassionate, not experiment but equipoise....

Harding may have summarized accurately the mood of a postwar middle class overwhelmed by the emotional excess of the military crusade, the debate over the League of Nations, and the strains of the Red Scare. The

*A woman prepares food in an early "modern" kitchen (1925), while listening to the radio.
(Minnesota Historical Society and Minneapolis Star-Journal)*

electorate of the 1920s seemed unmoved by purely political issues and uninspired by lackluster presidential contenders. Eligible voter participation never surpassed 52 percent in new era presidential elections, only two-thirds the level that characterized presidential voting in the late nineteenth century. Voting was even lower in the large industrial cities where working-class ethnics were concentrated. The voting statistics reflected the fact that newly enfranchised women were not casting ballots in large proportions, particularly in immigrant neighborhoods where patriarchal cultural traditions discouraged political participation by wives and daughters. Harding's relaxed middle-class benevolence brought the Republicans 61 percent of the popular vote in 1920, overwhelmingly defeating James M. Cox, an Ohio governor of little ideology, and vice presidential candidate Franklin D. Roosevelt, a Democratic cousin of Theodore.

Neither Harding nor the country, however, was prepared for the postwar depression of 1920–1922. Unemployment averaged 12 percent in 1921, and industrial output was cut by half as decreased government spending and a glutted agricultural market dampened postwar confidence. Through the insistence of Secretary of Commerce Herbert Hoover, Harding arranged a Washington Conference on Unemployment during mid-1921. It was the first time an administration had ever called national attention to joblessness. As a result, local emergency committees and voluntary relief groups were established in 225 cities. Congress refused to pass appropriations for a federal employment service, but the government allotted $450 million for state and local public works as well as repairs for federal facilities. The president's Conference on Unemployment also commissioned an analysis of business cycles by the National Bureau of Economics Research. Released in 1923, the unprecedented report suggested that economic slumps were created by the waste, extravagance, speculation, inflation, and inefficiency developed during booms.

Although the Conference on Unemployment reflected a sense of national planning, its effects were mainly symbolic. Much as Harding hoped and predicted, however, business recovery returned early in 1922, and the administration moved toward more traditional economic policies. Harding accepted the supremacy of corporation business in the new era. Newspaper editor William Allen White noted that "businessmen crowded into the White House until the luncheon guest-list looked sometimes like a chart of interlocking directorates of high finance." Harding reflected more conservative business opinion by supporting high tariffs, nonrecognition of the Soviet Union, collection of Allied war debts, and intensified concerns over continued immigration.

Partially in reaction to Woodrow Wilson, Harding saw the presidency in limited terms. He hoped to achieve consensus and reduce political strife through international peace and business prosperity. "Too much has been said of Bolshevism in America," he proclaimed, resisting a political ploy that others found advantageous. The president pardoned Socialist leader Eugene V. Debs, imprisoned under the wartime Sedition Act, and invited Debs to visit the White House. "I cannot hope to be one of the great presidents," Harding once confided, "but perhaps I may be remembered as one of the best loved." It was a shock to the nation when the White House suddenly announced in August 1923 that the president had died in San Francisco of complications arising from pneumonia and a stroke.

ELECTION OF 1924

Only weeks after assuming the presidency, Calvin Coolidge earned a reputation for political astuteness during a protracted anthacite-coal strike. Though New England congressmen urged government intervention against the United Mine Workers to prevent a winter without fuel, Coolidge chose to wait out the crisis. When the president refused to act, Governor Gifford Pinchot of Pennsylvania, a newly elected progressive Republican, intervened to settle the coal strike on terms favorable to the miners. The coal companies quickly passed the resulting price increase on to consumers. Unlike 1922, when Commerce Secretary Hoover had vigorously exposed price profiteering in coal, the Coolidge administration took no action in 1924. Pinchot received the onus for the price increase and thereby discredited the progressive wing of the party. Politically, Coolidge's inaction appeared the common-sense option. The president did flirt with progressive insurgents in the Republican party by publicly embarrassing U.S. Steel into abandoning the twelve-hour day late in 1923. But by the election of 1924, Coolidge had taken personal control of party machinery and made a conservative imprint on national politics.

Ironically, Coolidge's position within the Republican party strengthened as scandal allegations began to mount against the Harding administration. Senate hearings in 1923 revealed outright collusion between government and corporate power in the oil industry. During the early years of the Harding presidency, Secretary of the Interior Albert B. Fall had leased valuable government petroleum reserves, including the Teapot Dome area of Wyoming, to private interests. In return, Fall had received more than $300,000 in bribe payments. A special government prosecution team also discovered both multimillion-dollar graft in the newly created Veterans Bureau and the involvement of Attorney General Daugherty in a questionable payment of millions of dollars to some German businessmen. By 1924 the secretary of interior was in prison, the attorney general had resigned in disgrace, the secretary of the navy

had barely escaped conviction, and two other Harding officials had committed suicide. Coolidge tried to please the Republican old guard by postponing action against the Harding appointees. But progressive Republicans pushed the matter, and Coolidge emerged as the only public figure with an unscathed reputation. Newspapers described the president's "quiet New England courage" in the face of corrupt politicians and self-serving muckrakers. Much as Coolidge had anticipated, Americans quickly tired of Teapot Dome as the Senate investigation dragged on without new revelations. Corporate rhetoric to the contrary, few Americans were shocked over sleazy business deals in the bull market of the new era.

Coolidge was easily nominated at the 1924 Republican convention. After offering the vice presidency to progressive Senator William E. Borah, Coolidge selected Charles G. Dawes, a midwestern banker and the budget director. In contrast, the Democrats held a bitterly divided convention at New York City's Madison Square Garden. Ever since the Bryan campign of 1896, the party had been split between those who looked to the city and the immigrants, and southerners and westerners who identified with rural Protestantism and Anglo-Saxonism. With convention proceedings broadcast for the first time by radio, furious debates raged over Prohibition and the League of Nations. Police officials physically had to separate gallery partisans from delegates when a resolution to condemn the nativist Ku Klux Klan failed to pass by five votes. In the battle for the presidential nomination, Governor Al Smith of New York, a Roman Catholic and a "wet," faced William Gibbs McAdoo, heir to the Bryan leadership of the rural "drys." After 102 ballots, the Democrats finally compromised on John W. Davis, a conservative Wall Street lawyer. As a gesture

Fiorello LaGuardia

1882-1947

Fiorello LaGuardia was a short and stocky man with a loud voice. His mother was Jewish; his father, an Italian-American Protestant. LaGuardia spoke six foreign languages. He broke into politics as a Theodore Roosevelt progressive. To win support for a campaign to Congress, LaGuardia offered free legal services to immigrant pushcart peddlers, icemen, and shopkeepers; mobilized letter carriers and garment workers; and pulled flophouse voters out of bed before Tammany Hall was awake on election day. LaGuardia won the Italian-Jewish district of East Harlem by 257 votes and went to Washington in 1916.

LaGuardia was an urban evangelist, the first Italo-American to serve in Congress. Like all successful members of Congress, he knew his district. Immigrants from southern and eastern Europe had no tradition of rural individualism in their village heritage. Victimized by a demanding industrial system in America, they sought government protection. Ten years before the New Deal, LaGuardia agitated for old-age pensions, unemployment insurance, shorter workdays, workmen's compensation, and laws against child labor. The Norris-LaGuardia Act of 1932 banned the use of injunctions to prevent strikes and abolished "yellow dog" contracts that obligated workers to shun unions. LaGuardia also campaigned against high prices levied by corporate middlemen. Rising to speak during a House debate over rising profits in the meat industry, LaGuardia pulled a lamb chop from his pocket, then a steak, then a three-dollar roast. "What workman's family can afford to pay three dollars for a roast of this size?" he screamed.

The fiery congressman was not a successful Republican. By 1923 LaGuardia joined rural progressives in denouncing administration friendliness toward corporate monopoly and in *opposing tax benefits for the wealthy, high tariffs, and instant labor injunctions. LaGuardia led the House attack on Coolidge's plan to sell the Muscle Shoals Dam to Henry Ford, suggesting that "this proposition makes Teapot Dome look like petty larceny." He joined with Senator Norris to campaign for public power, supported Senator Borah's opposition to the marine occupation of Nicaragua, and demanded the impeachment of Treasury Secretary Mellon. "I would rather be right than regular," he quipped in 1923.*

Not surprisingly, the Republican House leadership stripped LaGuardia of all committee assignments in 1924. LaGuardia attended the Progressive party convention that year, rising to tell the followers of LaFollette that "I speak for Avenue A and 116th Street, instead of Broad and Wall." Denied the Republican nomination in 1924, he sailed back to Congress on Progressive and Socialist ballots.

LaGuardia was the first urban progressive to sit in Congress. Although he worked with rural insurgents on economic and political issues, he broke with the progressive coalition to fight immigration restriction and federal censorship of movies. LaGuardia also dramatized ethnic resentment toward Prohibition by manufacturing beer at his Capitol office and defying police to arrest him. But LaGuardia's unique contribution was his understanding that the immigrant working class of the large cities constituted a vital component of a new coalition for reform. The man who munched peanuts on the floor of Congress and whose favorite word was lousy instigated the separation of progressive reform from the Protestant elite purity crusade. By the time LaGuardia became mayor of New York City in 1933, urban ethnics were anticipating a "new deal" in Washington.

to the rural wing of the party, delegates selected Charles Bryan, brother of William Jennings Bryan, to run for vice president.

The platforms of the Democrats and Republicans provided no alternative to new era reliance on corporate initiative and antiunionism. As a result, the Coolidge-Davis contest left both rural and urban reformers without a party. Yet two strains of progressive dissidence remained important in the twenties: (1) the movement of independent farmers and small businesspeople against the growth of large corporations and (2) efforts by trade unionists and urban professionals to use government power to protect consumers and workers. Robert LaFollette, who had led the crusade for noncorporate progressivism for two decades, refused to cooperate with plans for a Farmer-Labor party in the early twenties, fearing radical and socialist domination. Instead, LaFollette accepted the presidential nomination of the newly created Progressive party in 1924 and agreed to Senator Burton Wheeler of Montana as his running mate.

Unlike Theodore Roosevelt's Progressives of 1912, the 1924 movement directed an attack against the large corporations. "The great issue before the American people today," the platform declared, "is control of government and industry by private monopoly." Accordingly, the Progressives condemned the administration's procorporate tax program, denounced the protective tariff for manufactured goods, and criticized "mercenary" foreign policy. The Progressive party also appealed to farmers and urban liberals by calling for government ownership of the railroads and water power resources. Seeking a nonsocialist farmer-labor coalition, LaFollette's movement demanded the abolition of government labor injunctions and sought congressional recognition of collective bargaining.

In turn the party not only won support from the railroad brotherhoods but received the first official endorsement of the AFL in federation history.

Despite the well-reasoned attempt to build a third-party movement, the Progressives lacked nationwide organization and funds. Furthermore, LaFollette's rhetoric, like Bryan's in 1896, harked back to the evangelical roots of agrarian moralism and ignored the urban working and middle classes. LaFollette took 16 percent of the national vote in 1924, carrying only his home state of Wisconsin. Coolidge simply stood on his record, ignored the Democrats, and pictured LaFollette as a bolshevik agent. The only issue of the campaign, remarked Coolidge, was "whether America will allow itself to be de-

graded into a communistic or socialistic state or whether it will remain American." Republicans called for "Coolidge or Chaos," dismissing Progressive hostility to the corporate order as either the height of irrationality or malignant subversion. The election results gave five million votes to LaFollette, eight million to Davis, and fifteen million to the president.

COOLIDGE ECONOMICS

With the election over, Coolidge was free to shape the administration in his own image. "The chief business of the American people is business," he once proclaimed. Accordingly, the

MAP 6.1   THE ELECTION OF 1924

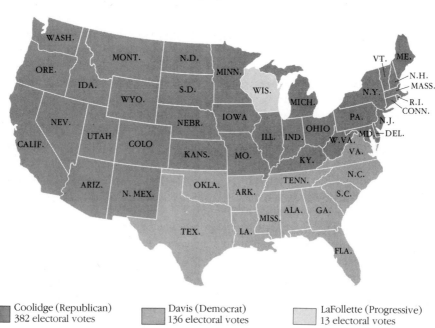

Coolidge (Republican)
382 electoral votes

Davis (Democrat)
136 electoral votes

LaFollette (Progressive)
13 electoral votes

president gave a free hand to millionaire financier and industrialist Andrew Mellon, appointed by Harding as secretary of the treasury. Mellon had worked with Budget Director Dawes on reductions in government expenses and tax programs designed to relieve business and the wealthy. "I have never viewed taxation as a means of rewarding one class of taxpayers or punishing another," Mellon explained. But the treasury secretary did believe that lower taxation would free corporations and the wealthy to invest their capital and create jobs and prosperity. By 1921 Mellon had persuaded Congress to repeal the wartime excess-profits tax and cut maximum income surtaxes to 50 percent. To compensate for lost revenue, Mellon prevailed on Congress to raise postage rates, increase excise and stamp taxes, initiate a two-cent tax on bank checks, and establish a federal licensing fee for motor vehicles.

Operating with the security of a firmly entrenched Coolidge presidency, Mellon's Revenue Act of 1926 wiped out the gift tax, cut the estate tax in half, and trimmed the surtax on income to 20 percent. Two years later Congress reduced taxes by over $220 million and provided treasury refunds to corporations, awarding U.S. Steel $15 million in 1929. By the end of the decade, government expenditures had been halved, and national debt reduced by one-third. Mellon carried out his program of budget, debt, and tax reduction with admirable efficiency, freeing about $350 million of tax monies a year, but the government's refusal to promote income distribution placed the new era boom on weak foundations.

Coolidge not only embraced Mellon economics but continued Harding's policy of placing procorporate Republicans on government regulatory agencies. Presidential appointments to the Federal Trade Commission, the Depart-

ment of Justice, and the federal courts reflected new era emphasis on business consolidation and corporate planning. Under Coolidge, government attitudes toward trade associations changed from harassment over price fixing to enthusiastic acceptance. The Supreme Court finally accepted trade association exchange of statistics in 1925, provided no price or production control was involved. Reflecting the transition from a competitive economy to a corporate system, the Court ruled that traditional concepts of free competition were less important than the circulation of statistics needed to prevent overproduction and economic crises. The Court accepted the trade association argument that technology had forced individuals to depend on large corporations for the necessities of life and that corporations must be free to engage in cooperative efforts to improve industrial efficiency.

Under the leadership of Herbert Hoover, the most energetic member of the Harding-Coolidge cabinet, the Department of Commerce actively promoted the growth of trade associations. Hoover believed that through trade groups, new era business could impose the self-discipline needed to eliminate industrial waste, develop ethical standards, and avoid "destructive competition." The Commerce Department also promoted self-government in agriculture through cooperative marketing associations. The Capper-Volstead Act of 1922 exempted agricultural organizations from antitrust legislation and permitted them to process and market staples in interstate commerce. Hoover authorized $300 million in government loans to farm associations between 1921 and 1924.

Coolidge's Federal Trade Commission also reflected new era aversion to antitrust sentiment. After 1925 the commission investigated only cases in which unfair practices were explicitly detrimental to the public interest, and then settled matters privately. The FTC referred informal agreements, or "stipulations," to trade practice conferences in which corporations were left to "self-rule." An FTC summary in 1927 described the agency's task as "helping business to help itself."

While regulatory agencies in the twenties worked to consolidate corporate power, the Supreme Court under Chief Justice William Howard Taft (1921–1930) began widening the use of federal power. The Court continued to reject child labor prohibitions, minimum wage laws, and other social legislation, citing the due process clause of the Fourteenth Amendment. But the Taft Court bolstered congressional power through the commerce clause of the Constitution. Ruling on the Transportation Act of 1920, the Court sustained the regulation of railroad rates inside a state and approved the federal government's right to establish a revolving fund to distribute railroad profits to weaker lines. Four years later the Court approved congressional regulation of grain exchanges in order to prevent fraudulent and manipulated prices. Taft's majority opinion stipulated that Congress had the right to regulate interstate commerce when it was obstructed and that Congress had to power to determine when that happened.

HOOVER AND THE ASSOCIATIVE STATE

Hoover's Department of Commerce most effectively carried out the implications of new era business philosophy in government. Hoover spoke of an American System, hoping to use the federal bureaucracy to reconcile the nation's corporate structure and liberal-democratic heritage. He envisioned a coordinated program of national development based on voluntary organizations and "associated individualism." Trade associations, professional societies, farm marketing organizations, and labor groups would be encouraged to strive for efficiency and cooperation. Hoover's cooperative capitalism sought to preserve individual initiative and private enterprise by minimizing the domination of single corporations, powerful cartels, and government bureaucracies.

Aside from endorsing trade and marketing associations, Hoover expanded and reorganized the Bureau of Foreign and Domestic Commerce along commodity lines in order to promote collective purchase of raw materials and agricultural produce at cheaper prices. The bureau became a clearinghouse for the collection and dissemination of commercial statistics. Beginning in July 1921, *A Survey of Current Business* published monthly data on current production, prices, and inventories, much of it supplied by trade associations. Hoover also expanded the Bureau of Standards to promote his campaign to standardize industrial weights, measures, sizes, and designs.

Hoover's penchant for industrial efficiency brought him into the fight for a law to control oil pollution in coastal waters. The secretary convened a conference of fish commissioners from Atlantic and Gulf Coast states in 1921. He argued that 90 percent of oil pollution came from coastal shipping. Over resistance from the American Petroleum Institute and Standard Oil, Congress passed an Oil Pollution Act in 1924, but the law merely provided modest fines for polluting coastal ships and tankers. Despite Hoover's systemic approach to the nation's resources, pollution control did not capture public or governmental imagination in the new era.

Nevertheless, a great flood of the Mississippi

River in 1927 brought a dramatic opportunity to put the principles of the associative state into practice. Hoover chaired the Special Mississippi Flood Committee, which coordinated relief efforts by scores of government agencies and private groups such as the Red Cross. With the river swollen to a fifty-mile width at points, Hoover relied on grassroots voluntarism to construct 150 refugee camps to house 325,000 people. The committee coordinated fund raising through the use of statewide credit corporations. In turn local chambers of commerce were encouraged to invest in the credit corporations, so that $17 million of the $20 million spent by the flood committee came from private sources. The secretary of commerce believed that the project demonstrated the combination of bureaucracy and individualism that accounted for the superior quality of life in America, and never forgot its lessons. Although midwesterners continued to settle on the dangerous flood plains, the Mississippi disaster stimulated Congress to appropriate $300 million for levees, drainage basins, and spillways in the Jones Reid Act of 1928, an early step toward government management of river ecology. Hoover's popular blend of corporate planning and voluntarism made him the logical Republican successor to Coolidge when the president indicated he would not run for re-election in 1928. As new era business boomed, Herbert Hoover earned a reputation as "boy wonder" of the Coolidge cabinet and the Republican party.

PERSISTENT PROGRESSIVISM

Hoover's innovations in the Commerce Department reflected the persistence of Theodore Roosevelt's brand of corporate progressivism. That was not sufficient, however, for midwest-ern and far western progressives who identified with Robert LaFollette's attack on corporate privilege. Seeking regulation of monopoly practices and federal help for aggrieved farmers, a farm bloc of nine western senators sought to hold the balance of power in the Senate by the mid-twenties. Led by Borah of Idaho and Nebraska's George Norris, the coalition also sought more influence for the West in the Republican party. Western progressives were responsible for a 1921 law extending federal loans to agricultural marketing associations, as well as the Packers and Stockyards Act, which prohibited meatpackers from monopolizing markets, controlling prices, or establishing territorial pools. A 1921 Grain Futures Act established similar controls over dealers in wheat and grains. Progressives showed their political clout in 1925 when Charles B. Warren, an ultraconservative lawyer for the sugar trust, failed to win Senate confirmation for appointment as Coolidge's new attorney general.

The farm bloc of the twenties constituted the most powerful agricultural lobby in the nation's history. Between 1923 and 1928, farm progressives agitated for a McNary-Haugen bill to provide government price supports for basic crops. A mandatory equalization tax on farmers would compensate the government for losses sustained in dumping surplus crops overseas. Meanwhile a high tariff would keep out agricultural imports. Given the drop in farm prices and increasing agricultural bankruptcy, McNary-Haugen meant to small farmers what free silver had signified for the Populists of the 1890s. Defeated in 1923, the legislation passed Congress in 1927 and 1928, but Coolidge vetoed twice, citing the equalization tax as an unconstitutional levy. Farmers did not win any relief until the Agricultural Marketing Act of 1929, a $500 million appropriation for farm cooperative loans that created a Federal Farm

Board to supervise marketing associations. By the end of the decade, most rural progressives had come to the conclusion that federal taxing power should be used to subsidize agriculture and provide economic security to the farming community. However, some anticorporate progressives, led by Borah, continued to oppose the compulsory equalization tax as an unwarranted extension of government power.

Congressional progressives were more unified over the need for public power, an issue that combined lower costs for farmers with hostility to monopoly. Henry Ford had offered to take a one-hundred-year lease on a group of government nitrate plants located on the Muscle Shoals section of the Tennessee River in 1921. But Senator Norris began a single-handed campaign to stop private leasing of the wartime plants and the adjoining Wilson Dam. Calling for government-owned hydroelectric plants for cheap power, Norris castigated the power trust as "the greatest monopolistic corporation that has been organized for private greed." His proposals for a Tennessee Valley project passed Congress in 1928 and 1929 but were vetoed twice. Nevertheless, Norris and the progressives managed to save Muscle Shoals for public use, and it was incorporated into the New Deal's Tennessee Valley Authority in 1933.

BUSINESS INTERNATIONALISM

Despite popular distaste for the League of Nations and international diplomacy, new era prosperity depended heavily on overseas investment and trade. American corporations increased their foreign holdings by seven times in the 1920s, as the nation's overseas investment reached $7.5 billion. Commerce Secretary Hoover and the twenties State Department shared Woodrow Wilson's desire to provide a market alternative to socialist internationalism by breaking down national empires and creating an "open door" for American business opportunity. But unlike Wilson, new era foreign policy planners were willing to rely far more on business internationalism than on political or military approaches to overseas affairs. In the Middle East, American diplomats worked to win oil concessions or at least equality of treatment for American corporations. But Standard Oil of New Jersey, the leading American company in the area, preferred to conduct private diplomacy or infiltrate European firms already on the resource site.

In reaction to Wilsonian interventionism, new era diplomats proceeded along lines of independent internationalism. Hoover and Secretary of State Charles Evans Hughes believed that the United States could protect its national interest without joining the League of Nations or entering bilateral agreements. The general idea was to work out a concert of power among the United States, Great Britain, France, Germany, and Japan, based on acceptance of the Open Door policy and an aversion to nationalist revolutions. The peaceful expansion of American economic power was to be promoted through settlement of European war debts and multilateral agreements with the great powers.

American policy called for a reintegration of a healthy Germany into a Western community led by the United States. Under the Dawes Plan of 1924, devised by American financier Charles G. Dawes, the Allies agreed to a reduced schedule of the reparations that Germany owed the victors of the war. At the same time J. P. Morgan and other private bankers agreed to substantial loans to Germany to stimulate economic reconstruction. American banks lent over \$1.2 billion to Germany between 1924 and 1930. German reparations then allowed the Allies to repay public war loans owed the United States. These loans also were renegotiated, so that Allied debts shrank by about 43 percent and were repaid at low interest. The Young Plan of 1930, a creation of industrialist Owen D. Young, reduced German reparations further, spread the payments over fifty-eight years, and involved private American banks as sponsors. In essence, credits from American investors were exported to Germany, where they found their way into German reparations payments. Eventually the same capital returned to the United States as part of Allied payment of American war loans. Not only had the United States replaced Britain in dominance of international finance and commerce, but American capital now stimulated European purchase of American commodities and farm produce.

Despite these patterns, high tariffs discouraged trade in the new era. The Fordney-McCumber Tariff of 1922 provided high protective rates for imports of rayon, china, toys, and chemicals, considered to be infant industries. Dyes, cotton textiles, and agricultural produce were subjected to the high tariff as well. But trade barriers erected for special interests at home did not accord with the nation's creditor status, discouraged repayment of foreign debts, and inhibited expansion of overseas markets. The Hawley-Smoot Tariff of 1930 raised rates even further. It was not until Congress passed the Reciprocal Trade Agreement Act of 1934 that the president was freed from the obligation to equalize differences in cost of production between domestic and foreign goods.

The United States's rejection of its membership in the League of Nations and the World Court did not rule out more conventional diplomatic agreements. The Washington Armaments Conference of 1921–1922, a reassertion of American diplomatic leadership following the failure to ratify the Treaty of Versailles, fixed the ratios of large ships of the United States, Britain, and Japan at 5:5:3. The conference also drafted a Nine-Power Treaty, which reaffirmed support for the Open Door to an independent China and pledged to uphold the status quo in east Asia. The United States hoped that economic power would be able to confine Japanese actions in Asia within limits defined by Washington.

The business community led most Americans in support of the arms limitations of the Washington Armaments Conference, since reduced government spending meant possible tax reductions. As no comprehensive plan for world disarmament emerged, however, concerned business leaders welcomed the Harding-Coolidge shift to industrial preparedness and a strong navy. The National Defense Act of 1920 involved business leaders in the War Department's systems of supply and procurement. From then on, industrialists customarily served as assistant secretary of war, with particular responsibility for supervising army supply bureaus. Beginning in the 1920s, corporation industrialists and military leaders shared control of contingency plans for wartime mobilization. Supported by a business community concerned about protection for overseas trade, new era Congresses consistently approved increased appropriations for the navy. The United States also opposed all international attempts to control or limit the private production of munitions in the twenties. As a result, few Americans saw a contradiction between industrial preparedness and the signing of the Kellogg-Briand Pact in 1928. That agreement, negotiated by Secretary of State Frank B. Kellogg and the French foreign minister, expressed a desire to outlaw the use of force in settling international disputes, but the pact included no instrument of enforcement. Its sentiments were to be crudely caricatured in subsequent years.

While economic diplomacy involved the United States in attempts to maintain the Open Door in Europe, the Middle East, and Asia, Latin America became the major outlet for United States capital in the new era. Investment grew in Latin American petroleum, minerals, and agriculture but found more sophisticated outlets by mid-decade in manufacturing, public utilities, and agricultural processing. Loans to cooperative Latin American nations, often tied to purchase of United States goods or services, totaled $1.6 billion between 1924 and 1929. By the end of the decade, Latin Americans bought nearly half their imports from the United States. In turn Americans purchased almost 40 percent of Latin American exports. By 1930 the American ambassador to Chile predicted that the United States would have "first place in South America whether we consciously promote trade and finance or whether we indifferently leave them to take their planned course."

The United States insisted on a closed door to foreign competition in Latin America, where new era presidents inherited a legacy of Wilsonian intervention. Cuba, Panama, Nicaragua, Haiti, and the Dominican Republic were American protectorates receiving support for conservative dictatorships. Troops were withdrawn from the Dominican Republic in 1924, but that country remained a financial protectorate until 1941. The military left Nicaragua in 1925, but the marines returned in 1926 to spend seven years assuring an orderly transition to a military

government trained by American forces. Honduras was occupied by the marines in 1924 when the State Department feared the development of "a condition of anarchy." Haiti remained under military occupation from 1915 to 1934. During the Pan-American Conference of 1923, Uruguay attempted to make the Monroe Doctrine multilateral by placing enforcement powers on all nations in the hemisphere and by outlawing unilateral intervention into any state's internal matters. But the United States forced the tabling of the proposal.

The turning point in American policy in Latin America came with Mexican attempts to nationalize oil fields and mines in the mid-twenties. While some oil corporations began to talk of a bolshevik threat, American bankers warned that continued United States militancy in Mexico would "injure American interests," arguing that the United States had "advanced from the period of adventure to the period of permanent investment." Instead of sending troops, Coolidge dispatched Dwight Morrow, an attorney for J. P. Morgan, to negotiate with the Mexican government in 1927. Morrow's friendly diplomacy won a Mexican promise to respect American oil and mine rights that predated the Mexican Constitution of 1917. Meanwhile Coolidge sent Henry Stimson, another corporate attorney, to work out political differences with Nicaragua.

Coolidge's conciliatory approach was echoed in President-elect Hoover's goodwill tour of Latin America in 1928. Hoover talked of the "relation of good neighbors" and hoped to substitute economic and technical cooperation for traditional policies of American arrogance and intervention. This shift in policy reflected Hoover's view that intervention was expensive and ineffective. The Hoover administration recognized all de facto governments in Latin America and began to withdraw marines from Nicaragua and Haiti. Hoover also refused to intervene in the Cuban Revolution of 1929–1930. "We cannot slay an idea or an ideology with machine guns," he declared. Hoover insisted that economically underdeveloped nations honor the "sanctity of contracts" and "perform international obligations." But neither the president nor Secretary of State Henry Stimson believed that the United States should collect ordinary contract debts by force. Rather, they limited Latin American policy to discouraging rebellion, preventing confiscation of American property, protecting commerce, and promoting political and legal institutions similar to those in the United States.

Hoover's Latin American strategy was expanded during the 1930s. Franklin D. Roosevelt announced a Good Neighbor policy in 1933, coinciding with United States support of a Pan-American resolution that denounced intervention. Roosevelt called for a hemispheric partnership in which good neighbors respected each other's rights, and accelerated the military withdrawals that Hoover had initiated. The last marines left Nicaragua in 1933. In Haiti Roosevelt advanced the marine withdrawal to 1934, although the United States maintained a customs receivership until 1941. After hostility to previous nationalist governments, the Roosevelt administration recognized the Batista coup in Cuba in 1934 and agreed to abandon the interventionist Platt amendment in return for continued rights to the navy base at Guantanamo. A treaty with Panama consolidated American ownership of the Canal Zone but provided for joint maintenance and protection and eradicated the right to intervene.

The United States formally agreed to settle inter-American disputes by arbitration in 1936 when it signed the Buenos Aires Convention at that year's Pan-American Conference. The convention also condemned collection of debts by force. Seeking to win Latin American goodwill in a world increasingly affected by instability in Europe and Asia, Roosevelt refused to intervene in Mexico during 1938 when a dispute between American oil corporations and the Mexican government resulted in expropriation of oil company holdings.

Roosevelt's Good Neighbor policy removed the threat of military and financial intervention but did not erase economic domination of Latin America by the United States. In return for the president's cordiality, Latin American republics were expected to establish stable governments, honor political as well as economic obligations, and use American standards of due process for treating American citizens and property. The Roosevelt administration saw the southern market as a key to the vital export trade. The Reciprocal Trade Agreements Act of 1934 gave the president the right to halve tariffs on Latin American goods in return for tariff reductions from the nations concerned. The Export-Import Bank, created in 1934, lent government funds to Latin American republics in exchange for agreements to purchase the products of American corporations. By 1935 the United States was sending half its cotton and steel-mill exports to Latin America, as well as large quantities of leather, silk, paper, and electrical products. The Good Neighbor policy was a profitable extension of new era business internationalism.

SUGGESTED READINGS

An excellent summary of new era economics can be found in Jim Potter, *The American Economy Between the World Wars* (1974). For descriptions of structural weaknesses in the twenties economy, see John K. Galbraith, *The Great Crash, 1929* (1961), and the relevant sections of Gabriel Kolko, *Main Currents in Modern American History* (1976). Business ideology is examined in the fourth volume of Joseph Dorfman, *The Economic Mind in American Civilization* (1959), but a more detailed view of new era management emerges in the relevant chapters of Morrell Heald, *The Social Responsibilities of Business: Company and Community, 1900–1960* (1970). A thoughtful essay bringing these themes together is Paul W. Glad, "Progressives and the Business Culture of the 1920s," *Journal of American History,* 55 (March 1969).

Conditions of industrial labor and the plight of the unions are described in rich detail by Irving Bernstein, *The Lean Years: A History of the American Worker, 1920–1933* (1960). The agricultural depression is outlined by Gilbert C. Fite, "The Farmers' Dilemma, 1919–1929," in John Braemen, Robert H. Bremner, and David Brody, eds., *Change and Continuity in Twentieth-Century America: The 1920s* (1968). For the response of farmers, see the appropriate chapters of Theodore Saloutos and John D. Hicks, *Twentieth Century Populism: Agricultural Discontent in the Middle West, 1900–1939* (1951).

An overview of twenties politics is Hicks, *The Republican Ascendancy, 1921–1933* (1960), but it should be supplemented by Robert K. Murray, *The Politics of Normalcy: Governmental Theory and Practice in the Harding-Coolidge Era* (1973). Specific examinations of new era presidencies are Murray, *The Harding Era: Warren G. Harding and His Administration* (1969), Andrew Sinclair, *Available Man: The Life Behind the Masks of Warren Gamaliel Harding* (1965), and Donald B. McCoy, *Calvin Coolidge: The Quiet President* (1967). The Harding scandals are described in Burl Noggle, *Teapot Dome: Oil and Politics in the 1920s* (1962). For an informal portrait of Coolidge and his time, see William Allen White, *A Puritan in Babylon* (1938). The continuities of southern progressivism are examined in the relevant chapters of George B. Tindall, *The Emergence of the New South, 1913–1945* (1967), while David Burner, *The Politics of Provincialism: The Democratic Party in Transition, 1918–1932* (1967), describes the twenties conflict between rural and urban Democrats. Republican insurgents receive attention in LeRoy Ashby, *The Spearless Leader: Senator Borah and the Progressive Movement in the 1920s* (1972). Relevant sections of James Weinstein, *Ambiguous Legacy: The Left in American Politics* (1975), describe the influence of Soviet bolshevism on the postwar socialist movement.

Hoover's social philosophy is thoroughly synthesized by Joan Hoff Wilson, *Herbert Hoover: Forgotten Progressive* (1975). For two explanations of Hoover's approach to government activity, see the appropriate sections of William A. Williams, *The Tragedy of American Diplomacy* (1962), and Murray N. Rothbard, "Herbert Hoover and the Myth of Laissez-Faire," in Rothbard and Ronald Radosh, eds., *A New History of Leviathan: Essays on the Rise of the American Corporate State* (1972). Evolving government response to trade associations and business consolidation is examined by Robert F. Himmelberg, *The Origins of the National Recovery Administration: Business, Government, and the Trade Association Issue, 1921–1933 (1976). For the persistence of the Open Door in twenties foreign affairs, see Williams, *The Tragedy of American Diplomacy* (1962). But Wilson, *American Business and Foreign Policy, 1920–1933* (1971), presents a more thorough account of the financial aspects of American diplomacy. A brief guide to Latin American affairs is Edwin Lieuwen, *U.S. Policy in Latin America* (1965).

Chapter 7

THE CONFLICT OF CULTURES IN THE TWENTIES

Despite new era attempts to erect a unified culture based on the rationality of corporate prosperity, Americans of the 1920s found themselves in bitter disagreement over profound social issues. A cultural schism dominated the twenties, pitting large segments of the Anglo-Protestant population against cosmopolitan and liberal tendencies in urban America. As upper-class Protestants began to abandon the progressive purity crusade in the postwar years, Protestants of rural upbringing refashioned the purity movement into a strident attempt to rid American society of alien ideologies, behaviors, and groups. At issue was the secular rootlessness of consumer society, with its dissolution of community and traditional morality, and the new generation of immigrants, radicals, and rebellious youth who defied the core values of

American culture. Nostalgia for a religiously and ethnically homogeneous society defined twenties society as much as did the cult of corporate progress.

URBAN-SUBURBAN BOOM

The 1920 census reported that for the first time in American history, more than half the population lived in communities of more than 2,000 persons. By 1929 there were ninety-three cities with more than 100,000 people. New York City's population increased by 23 percent in the twenties to nearly 7 million, Chicago's jumped 25 percent to 3.4 million, Detroit's leaped 57 percent to 1.5 million, and Los Angeles's more than doubled to 1.2 million. Western cities far outpaced eastern and midwestern centers in growth, increasing in population by nearly a third. "The trend of business," Josephus Daniels observed in 1928, "has been to a great degree towards the cities and city ways so that America has unconsciously been virtually transformed."

More astounding than the growth of central cities was their expansion into suburban areas, where they absorbed small towns, obliterated old distinctions between city and country, and formed supercities. Nearly 71 percent of the nation's population growth in the decade occurred in metropolitan areas. Twenties population growth in the New York "megalopolis" equaled the population gains of twenty-eight states. Metropolitan Los Angeles grew to 2.3 million by 1930. Industrial suburbs prospered as the automobile, rapid transit, telephone communication, cheap electric power, and lower tax rates increased suburban utility for factories and service installations.

The population of suburban residential areas increased more than four times in the twenties, reflecting an escape to the rural ideal of isolated family living. These neighborhoods usually were middle class and homogeneous in ethnic or religious composition. Increasingly they included out-of-town shopping complexes easily accessible by automobile. But the older cities paid a heavy price for suburbanization. Compelled to maintain roads and services for commuters, city administrations lost retail revenues to outlying areas, while the tax base shrank. Newer cities such as Dallas, Kansas City, and Los Angeles avoided this problem because their suburbs grew within expansive central cities.

Metropolitan land values skyrocketed in the new era. The total value of land in cities over 300,000 population doubled in the first half of the decade to $50 billion. In contrast, American farmland dropped by nearly a third in value. Inflated urban land values encouraged the building of skyscrapers to conserve ground space. By 1929 the nation could point to 377 buildings that soared twenty or more stories, a monumental symbol of new era technical progress, but another feature of growing impersonality and uniformity in economic life. Capital investment in suburbanization in outlying areas and skyscraper development in the central core led to the deterioration of inner-city residential areas located between the two. The 1930 census revealed that six million homes in cities, or one-fourth the urban total, did not meet minimum living standards. Urban rents, nevertheless, continued to rise.

City sprawl led to the demand for expanded services and encouraged the growth of city planning commissions and zoning regulations to control land use and building size. Land specialization often encouraged division of residential neighborhoods by race and class. In growing southern cities, New South progressives used zoning ordinances to reinforce the racial segregation they believed essential to orderly industrialization. Smaller cities across the nation adopted the council-manager system, a progressive innovation that entrusted administration of policy to professional city managers. Large cities such as New York also felt compelled to participate in regional planning commissions, a reflection of the increasingly metropolitan character of American society.

Highway and school construction brought a tremendous expansion to new era state governments. Southern states increased highway expenditures by 157 percent in the twenties, as middle-class progressives learned that good roads opened new markets for farmers. New South leadership, for example, made North

Carolina the "Wisconsin of the South" as the state university at Chapel Hill became the leading public institution in the region, and the state embarked upon an ambitious program of highway construction, education, public health, and welfare. Public expenditures in North Carolina leaped 847 percent between 1915 and 1925. In addition, all thirteen of the southern states adopted some kind of budget system between 1918 and 1928. Administrative and tax reforms enabled bureaucracies to expand services, but the rate by which state debt leaped in the South far exceeded that in the rest of the nation.

AUTO CULTURE

Suburbanization and the growth of state highway services were directly linked to the tremendous impact of the automobile on twenties society. "It would be folly to ignore that we live in a motor age," Warren Harding remarked. "It long ago ran down simple living and never halted to inquire about the prostrate figure which fell as its victim."

The automobile revolutionized American life. Its major impact came in the twenties when car registration leaped from 6.7 million to over 23 million. Working people not able to afford new cars were able to take advantage of the blossoming market in used autos. Los Angeles had 20,000 registered cars in 1910 and 100,000 by 1920. By 1930, 800,000 automobiles were owned by Los Angelenos.

Individualized transportation gave people a sense of liberation and exhilaration, setting them free from community standards and opening up options for personal choice. A famous magazine advertisement for the Jordan Playboy de-

picted the car as "the cross of the wild and the tame" and encouraged potential owners to "start for the land of real living with the spirit of the lass who rides, lean and rangy, into the red horizon of a Wyoming twilight." In the South the automobile helped to transport rural blacks outside the restrictions of white-dominated communities. Geographic mobility, status, and pleasure were generated by this technological embodiment of the American dream. Urban historian Lewis Mumford suggested that the auto was a "compensating device for enlarging an ego which has been shrunken by our very success in mechanization." To the American working class, automobile ownership appeared more important than title to a home.

The consequences of the automobile revolution were felt in every aspect of the nation's life. Beginning in Oregon in 1919, gasoline taxes were implemented to finance nonurban highways in every state, perhaps the most uncontested tax ever legislated by government authority. Cities were compelled to pay for street lights and signs, traffic control equipment, and the resurfacing and widening of main thoroughfares, an expense that averaged $400 million a year during the decade. With little public debate, American cities adjusted to the needs of the automobile. Business leaders argued that the auto would create new channels of commerce and, by opening surrounding areas to development, would reduce congestion in central cities. The effect was quite the opposite. Older homes were torn down for new roads, while filling stations, dealerships, garages, and parking lots began to dominate city outskirts and suburbs. Traffic congestion, exhaust, noise, and lack of adequate parking plagued the central city.

Moralists linked the automobile to a rising crime rate and accused it of altering sexual mores, shattering bonds of family life, and undermining community standards of decency. Joyriding on the Sabbath, for example, was upsetting to traditional Americans. Response to the auto culture was particularly ambiguous in the South, where the progressive purity crusade still maintained great influence. In a culture clinging to Protestant fundamentalism and rural virtue, New South progressives welcomed the auto but distrusted its disruptive influence. An investigation by an Atlanta grand jury in

1921 suggested a link between the auto and moral deprivation. Nashville's Salvation Army estimated that the majority of unwed mothers in the organization's maternity homes could blame their condition on "the predatory drivers of automobiles."

In the insular communities of the nation's small towns, social patterns changed when people left on automobile holidays and weekends. Cars also enabled young people to conduct a social life independent of their elders. Although

A 1928 hurricane devastates West Palm Beach. Such destruction ended the frantic boom in Florida real estate that had steadily accelerated throughout the 1920s, as more and more speculators entered the scene. (Wide World Photos)

auto advertisements, budgeted at $10 million a year by the end of the decade, told Americans that cars could "hold the family together," the recreational aspects of automobility stressed pleasure and individual whim, not family or social solidarity. An Indiana lecturer at a twenties Chautauqua meeting noted that the once-sacred family had degenerated into "a physical service station." Automobiles contained no systems for coordinating their movements with others. Consequently their fusion of individuality and technology produced a perfect symbol of American life.

Car mobility led to land speculation in suburbs and auto tourist centers, particularly in sunny Florida. Estimates claimed that twenty million lots were sold in Florida during the booming twenties, as eager speculators bought housing space of questionable value on the installment plan. In 1925 one Miami tract purchased for $8 million sold for $11 million two weeks later. But the Florida land boom collapsed when a severe hurricane devastated Miami during the fall of 1926, and overextension of credit led to bank failures two years later. While automobile culture contributed to urban sprawl and land speculation, it also decimated public transit. Interurban electric streetcars in small communities and local steam trains were no competition for auto commuting by the middle class. Cars, trucks, and buses also helped to reduce rail passenger traffic by one-third and contributed to the stagnation of the railroad freight industry.

NEW MORALITY

Corporate technology and urban-suburban culture wrought revolutionary changes in American social values. In a consumer society manufactured goods such as the automobile determined social status. As a result, traditional faith in the wisdom of age and experience seemed to be supplanted by a new belief in the promise of youth, innovation, and technology. If wartime pressures for conformity prepared the urban middle class for twenties advertising, the temptations of new era consumerism also distracted cosmopolitan Anglo-Protestants from the progressive purity crusade. The movement to purify American life had combined dreams of social efficiency with traditional American values of frugality, temperance, and personal morality. But thrift and frugality were discounted in a marketplace that depended on mass consumption through installment buying. Furthermore, young Anglo-Protestants in large northern cities had been attracted to the Afro-American rhythms of dance-hall ragtime since the 1890s. The disintegration of traditional culture was propelled by Prohibition, which made drinking a status symbol for those who could afford bootleg prices. After 1920 the children of "nice" families enjoyed the adventure of illegal speakeasies and the intrigue of commerce with bootleggers.

The most controversial of the cosmopolitan cultural values centered on a new morality in sexual behavior. Relaxation of sexual codes during the war had only dramatized the gradual abandonment of chaperoning since the 1890s. Throughout the 1910s Margaret Sanger had popularized the use of the diaphragm as the most effective method of contraception. By the twenties the American Birth Control League led the fight to limit the family size of immigrants, but it also taught middle-class women that sexual intercourse need not be restricted to procreation. Twenty-two states restricted or forbade dissemination of contraceptives during the decade, but a 1929 study reported that three-fourths of married women in their early thirties used them. The birth control crusade reached a minor turning point in 1931 when a committee of the Federal Council of the Churches of Christ endorsed artificial contraception. By then family size had declined from 4.6 in 1900 to less than 3.8.

The "flapper" was the perfect symbol of the sexually independent American woman of the post-war period. Coined by journalist H. L. Mencken in 1915, the term referred to brazen and volatile young women who sought sexual satisfaction, social participation, and freedom of choice. Flappers wore bobbed hair that concealed the forehead, and showed off their legs with knee-length skirts. Equally short dresses flattened chests, hid waists, and narrowed hips. The visual effect suggested boyish and single women in energetic motion. To prove their emancipation, flappers unabashedly smoked in public, wore rouge and lipstick, used slangy language, and joined men in speakeasies, jazz clubs, and dance halls.

The disaffection of middle-class cosmopolitans from traditional codes of feminity proved highly unsettling to establish arbiters of taste. Church groups, educational leaders, and college editors attacked the rampant "demoralization" of the country. One critic noted that respectable women had not exposed the naked flesh of lower limbs since the Fall of Rome. The Young Women's Christian Association issued a modesty appeal for lower skirt lengths, and a Utah bill proposed to fix hems three inches above the ankle. Moralizing authorities tried to attack jazz as "cheap, common, tawdry music," connecting the wriggling movements of "hot" dancing to sexual stimulation and "moral ruin." As large dance halls and ballrooms attracted six million admissions during 1924 in New York City alone, the Ladies Home Journal called

for the "legal prohibition" of jazz dancing.

Traditional Anglo-Protestant critics associated jazz, drinking, and hot dancing with sexual promiscuity and the dissolution of the family. Statistics substantiated their fears. Divorce doubled between 1914 and 1929, and studies showed that women born after 1900 were twice as likely to experience premarital sex as those born before that date. A critical change in sexual behavior accompanied the generation of cosmopolitans who reached maturity during World War One and the early 1920s. With the collapse of cultural cohesion over purity and sexual propriety, magazine articles approving easy divorce, sexual freedom, and birth control increased dramatically in the postwar era. In the highly controversial The Revolt of Modern Youth (1925), Judge Ben Lindsey celebrated the movement toward sexual directness by calling for "companionate marriage" based on intimate affection, birth control, and simplified divorce.

Postwar families of the urban middle class tended to be small, planned, child-oriented units that stressed affectionate relations instead of Victorian respect and authority. In a society in which social identity was shaped increasingly by consumerism, urban impersonality, and technological regimentation, the family satisfied important emotional and expressive needs. Despite the emphasis on regularity and orderliness in twenties childrearing manuals, the more relaxed family of the urban middle class allowed for more personal attention to children.

The breakdown in Victorian parental authority and the need to socialize children in schools created greater peer influence for postwar youth. High school enrollment multiplied six times between 1900 and 1930, and college and university attendance tripled to over one million. Providing an entry into careers and marriage, college life set styles of convention for young Anglo-Protestants of the upper middle class. But instead of abandoning sexual morality, as critics charged, campus subculture established new distinctions in sexual relationships. Peer-group propriety, expressed through fraternities, sororities, and campus social life, combined sexual freedom and a sense of limits into increased dating and "petting" practices. Sexual intercourse, in contrast, was condoned only for those couples preparing for marriage. Although college students engaged in drinking, smoking, and casual styles of dress and language, commitment to the family and sexual morality continued to be strong throughout the period. But moral leaders frequently failed to see the new distinctions being fashioned on campus and castigated youth for a total abandonment of morality.

Dialogue over the new morality found its most direct expression in the burgeoning movie industry. Capitalized at over $1 billion, Hollywood films attracted audiences reaching 100 million a week. One survey found that young women between the ages of eight and nineteen attended movies an average of forty-six times a year. National polls revealed that movie stars had replaced political, business, and artistic leaders as the favorite role models of twenties youth.

Prewar films had originated from immigrant culture and specifically appealed to the urban working class. But in the twenties, Hollywood sought profits by mass-producing fantasies for the largest possible audience. As a result, silent film comedians such as Harold Lloyd, Harry Langdon, and Buster Keaton satirized clumsy aspirations toward middle-class respectability but seldom questioned the legitimacy of social mobility or the middle-class world order.

Moviemakers also tread a thin line between

An exhausted couple barely move at a marathon dancers' contest in Chicago. "Hot" dancing became a major controversy in the twenties. (THE GRANGER COLLECTION, New York)

new era fascination for alternative sexual morality and the traditional moral conventions espoused by evangelical leaders and small-town America. Advertisements for films such as *Sinners in Silk* (1924) or *Alimony* (1924) raved about "beautiful jazz babies, champagne baths, midnight revels, petting parties in the purple dawn," but usually managed to reconcile husband and wife by the last reel. Cecil B. De Mille provided audiences with tales of extramarital temptation, titillating moviegoers without offending their conventional standards. His religious epics, *Ben Hur* (1925) and *King of*

Kings (1927), managed to combine moral preaching and orgiastic fantasy. Occasionally, unabashed eroticism dominated the silent screen, as in the intense sexuality of Rudolph Valentino in *The Sheik* (1921) or Greta Garbo's sultry passion in *The Mysterious Lady* (1928). But both Valentino and Garbo were Europeans, and their sexuality was no threat to the notion of American innocence. More often, movies portrayed the independent new woman of the postwar era who could use her toughness to protect purity as well as dispose of it. Actresses such as Clara Bow, Joan Crawford, and Gloria Swanson expressed a vital sexuality in their silent roles, but their characters were best defined by their confident gait and unrestrained energy. The classic sequence of the era may have been Crawford's frantic version of the Charleston in *Our Dancing Daughters* (1928).

The "moderns" of the silver screen conveyed the flapper model to national audiences and trained American women of all classes in new styles of femininity. Movies helped to acculturate both rural Americans and immigrant families to the new ways of the cosmopolitan middle class. They also served as a form of sex education, instructing young people in kissing, eye movement, and techniques of flirtation. Yet stories often concentrated on the winning and holding of husbands. The gold digger scenario taught that marriage was the escape from the dull life of the working girl, even though heroines such as Crawford and Swanson expressed cynicism toward men and their intentions. Moviegoers also learned to associate sexiness with apparel, makeup, and perfume rather than the body itself, as Hollywood contributed to the corporate argument that consumerism could satisfy human needs. The sociologist Edward A. Ross commented in 1928 that the silver screen had made young people "sex-wise, sex-excited and sex-absorbed." Despite its attempt to mediate the nation's cultural dialogue, no cultural force as strong as the movies ever had established itself so independently from the traditional proprietors of American taste. Following a series of Hollywood drug and sex scandals in 1921, thirty-two state legislatures debated movie censorship bills. The industry immediately responded with formation of the public-relations–oriented Motion Pictures Producers and Distributors Association.

LITERARY BOHEMIANS

The cosmopolitan morality of the postwar world was easily discernible in the lifestyles and creations of the more outspoken twenties artists and intellectuals. The intelligentsia imagined themselves the disinherited sons and daughters of the traditional middle class. For the younger dissidents the mindless brutality of World War One symbolized destruction of the spiritual and cultural strivings of the Progressive years. The historian Carl Becker noted in 1920 that the war was "the most futile, the most desolating and repulsive exhibition of human power and cruelty without compensating advantage that has ever been on earth." Ernest Hemingway's *The Sun Also Rises* (1926) and *A Farewell to Arms* (1929) depicted a generation's reaction to the ideological sham and cant of its elders. War "kills the very good and the very gentle and the very brave impartially," Hemingway wrote in terse prose. He confessed to be "always embarrassed by the words 'sacred,' 'glorious,' and 'sacrifice.'" Only death was an absolute in a world view devoid of political ideology.

Hemingway, F. Scott Fitzgerald, John Dos

Passos, Malcolm Cowley, Gertrude Stein, and others drifted to postwar Paris, where they called themselves the "lost generation." Fitzgerald, who chronicled the crash of illusory values in *The Great Gatsby* (1925), spoke of a "new generation... grown up to find all Gods dead, all wars fought, all faiths in man shaken." Since World War One had not been the unifying experience the nation had hoped for, the political cynicism of the lost generation made sense to many Americans.

Bohemian enclaves in Paris and New York reasserted the artist's alienation from mainstream culture in the postwar world. The bohemians struggled against the standardized society, a result, they believed, of the twin evils of materialism and puritanism. "Everybody was hoping to make a killing and get away," the essayist Cowley wrote of new era commerce. Sinclair Lewis's *Babbitt* (1922) drew an unforgettable portrait of a complacent booster in a small town hidden in the monotonus Midwest. The literary dissidents condemned the Anglo-Protestant middle class for making money into a religion and a morality and for arrogantly assuming that economic success gave them cultural privilege and immunity from criticism. H. L. Mencken relentlessly pursued the "boob-oisie" in satirical commentary in the *American Mercury*. And Lewis portrayed the struggle to overcome the conventions of small-town tribalism in *Main Street* (1920), a novel that sold 400,000 copies during its first months of publication.

For the new generation of artists and intellectuals, the heartland of the nation was no longer a garden but a wasteland of conservatism, piety, hypocrisy, and spiritual poverty. They viewed the guardians of middle-class culture as hopelessly stupid and comical parodies of human nature, philistines unable to separate art from morality. One of the Paris expatriates described their exile as an "attempt to recover the good life and the traditions of art, to free themselves from organized stupidity." Placing themselves in opposition to mainstream culture, social critics such as Edmund Wilson, Harold Stearns, Van Wyck Brooks, and Lewis Mumford questioned the technological progress of the new era and feared that the assembly line and skyscraper portended a terrible monotony in American life. Postwar poets such as Ezra Pound, T. S. Eliot, and Hart Crane did the same thing in more indirect fashion.

Many of the bohemians and intellectuals followed what they believed to be the teachings of Sigmund Freud. They hoped to liberate themselves from repression so that their children "could develop their own personalities," and "blossom freely like flowers." The goals, as Malcolm Cowley outlined, were momentary gratification, individuality, creative work, and self-expression. Artists would accomplish them, he wrote, even if it meant breaking every law, convention, or rule of art. Significantly, the outpouring of twenties literature created a golden age in American letters.

WOMEN CONSUMERS AND REFORMERS

Although cosmopolitan Anglo-Protestants shared in the new morality of the flappers, twenties society provided only limited role changes for women. The number of women in the labor force grew by more than one-fourth in the twenties, but women constituted only 21 percent of American workers by 1929. The proportion of women who worked remained constant at one in four, a ratio that barely changed between 1910 and 1940. As in the prewar years, one-third of female labor worked as servants and another fourth in low-paying jobs in factories and mills. But the growth of white-collar services furthered the prewar expansion of clerical and stenographic positions. Married women in the middle class began to take advantage of these income opportunities in the new era, increasing their participation in the work force from 1.9 million to 3.1 million. Women who sought professional work, however, usually found themselves in the "female" professions of nursing and schoolteaching. Medical schools maintained a 5 percent quota on female admissions, while most professions and the great majority of civil service exams excluded them altogether.

At home traditional ideas about women as the moral guardians of the family fit into a corporate economy in which middle-class wives became family business managers. As the urban home of the twentieth century became a center for buying goods instead of making them, middle-class women became the primary consumers of the American family. The role was underlined by new era mass production of household appliances. Postwar advertising directed its appeal to middle-class women, linking consumption with achievement and sexual success and providing women with a sense of importance in their work at home. Psychologists, educators, clergymen, and advertisers continued to tell women that their natural place was in the home and their real job motherhood. Consequently, education for women in high schools and colleges stressed home economics and childrearing.

Unlike industrial and clerical labor, however, housework did not undergo specialization and routinization. It was task oriented, not geared to clock time and not always a full-time occupation. Advertisers boasted that technological innovations would liberate women from household chores, but twenties psychologists and sociologists described "nervous" housewives who felt useless and bored. Cultural values also dictated that women spend the free time produced by technology to perfect the household arts. As a result, middle-class housewives used labor-saving devices to raise standards of household care, but for many the work load remained heavy and tedious.

Flapper emphasis on female sexuality never disputed the belief that normal fulfillment came only through marriage and motherhood. Young middle-class women of the twenties rebelled against the sexual repression and self-denial embodied by both nineteenth-century culture and the progressive purity crusaders and suffragists. In the perspective of a generation immersed in popularizations of Freud's theories of psychoanalysis, the sublimation of energies into social reform was evidence of sexual maladjustment. The new feminism, therefore, worked against the sisterhood of working- and middle-class reformers that some progressive crusaders sought.

Progressive feminists, hoping to purify the social environment of American life, expected the Nineteenth Amendment to end sex prejudice, elevate the nation's morals, and speed passage of social reform. The expectations of these social feminists were fulfilled to some extent in the years immediately following enactment of women's suffrage. Women's reform organizations succeeded in lowering meat prices through support of the Packers and Stockyards Act. A coalition of social feminists worked feverishly to pass the Sheppard-Tower Maternity and Infancy Protection Act of 1921, the first federal venture into social security legislation.

Active in the coalition were women nurtured in the progressive purity crusades, who overcame objections to interference with family life by arguing that the government had to protect the poor from their own ignorance. Showing that one-sixth of the children of impoverished families died within their first year of life, social feminists succeeded in funding public health centers to teach maternity and infant hygiene. Congress responded because it feared the newly enfranchised women's vote, but the controversial law was repealed in 1929. It was not until 1935 that social security legislation included public health care for poor mothers and children.

Scores of women's organizations and pressure groups carried on the moral fervor of the progressive crusades in the years following the war. Social worker Jane Addams headed the Women's International League for Peace and Freedom, organized in 1919, while suffragist Carrie Chapman Catt formed a Committee on the Cause and Cure of War. A Women's Joint Congressional Committee, a coalition embracing nearly every important women's organization in the country, worked with the League of Women Voters as a clearinghouse for social legislation affecting women and children. In the South women progressives helped to institute budget reforms in rapidly growing state governments, coordinated campaigns to publicize the voting records of legislators, worked to protect children through state commissions, and strove to improve working conditions for women in the textile industry.

Due to the nationwide efforts of women progressives, fifteen states passed minimum-wage laws for women between 1912 and 1923. But the Supreme Court invalidated such legislation in *Adkins v. Children's Hospital* (1923), ruling that the Nineteenth Amendment prevented women from receiving special attention. Since women were no longer exempt from rights of contract, the Court declared that no state could interfere with their bargaining rights with employers.

Federal courts also invalidated laws regulating child labor in 1918 and 1922, labeling them undue restraints on interstate commerce. But under pressure from Florence Kelley's National Child Labor Committee, Congress finally approved a child labor amendment to the Constitution in 1924. The amendment gave Congress the right to prohibit or regulate the labor of minors. Anglo-Protestant purity crusaders believed that the state should exercise control of youngsters to improve the moral health of American society and to delay their economic independence from the family. They were joined by activists in the trade union movement who argued that child labor depressed wages and increased adult unemployment. As opposition to maternity and infant care had shown, however, many Americans were not prepared to give the secular state control over family relations and home affairs. In eastern states with heavy Catholic populations, the church campaigned against the amendment as an invasion of parental discretion. Ratification of the child labor amendment failed overwhelmingly, and Congress did not enact child labor legislation until 1938.

Defeat of the child labor amendment brought the disintegration of the National Child Labor Committee and signaled the end of the women's purity coalition. Furthermore, middle-class reformers in the Women's Trade Union League, distraught at the invalidation of the minimum-wage laws, soon began to retreat from their alliance with AFL unionists. The women's movement also split over introduction of an Equal Rights Amendment by the small

National Women's party, a group dedicated to militant feminism. The amendment proposed to extend sexual equality to all areas of law, public policy, and employment, but it frightened reformers who had hoped to use the women's vote as a lever for social welfare programs. Social feminists feared the ERA would eradicate remaining protections for women workers and turn public opinion away from the women's reform movement.

By mid-decade, however, it was clear to most politicians that no women's voting bloc existed. Women who participated in elections seemed to choose no differently from their husbands or fathers, and no overriding issue appeared to move American women as a whole. The new feminism that attracted middle-class women stressed economic independence and satisfying work combined with marriage and motherhood. Women's share of professional workers peaked in the twenties at more than 14 percent, as one-seventh of all academic doctorates were awarded to women. More than three times as many women (55,000) received college degrees in 1930 than in 1920, although the female share of enrollment declined slightly.

Social feminism, frustrated in its legislative efforts, increasingly found expression in professional social work, a field open to participation by women. Many social workers adopted the casework approach to clients, concentrating on the development of personality through adjustment of social relationships. Casework methods stressed individual rehabilitation at the expense of social reform. Yet some reformers still maintained that only social justice could preserve social order and continued to agitate for government activity in education, labor, health, and social security. Their efforts created a bridge to the substantive social reforms of the New Deal.

BLACK METROPOLIS AND THE MINORITIES

While the white middle class moved to post-war suburbs and the outer fringes of northern and midwestern cities, black migrants from the South gravitated to older inner-city neighborhoods. Encouraged by the job opportunities of wartime mobilization and the new era boom, 1.2 million blacks left the rural South between 1915 and 1929. By 1930 New York and Chicago contained black subcities of more than 225,000 people each, and at least two-fifths of the nation's black people lived in cities.

Since blacks were among the last migrants to the industrial cities, most of the available jobs involved menial tasks at low pay. Blacks worked as sweepers and firemen in the Midwest steel industry. In Detroit, where the black population increased six times in the twenties, Henry Ford pioneered the hiring of blacks on the assembly line. By 1930 black Americans held only 2 percent of the white-collar and skilled jobs in the country.

Just as blacks received the worst jobs, they were forced to live in the most dilapidated neighborhoods. Although the Supreme Court outlawed residential segregation ordinances in 1917, white neighborhood associations resorted to restrictive covenants by which property holders agreed not to sell to blacks. Black migrants were pushed into inner-city tenements abandoned by immigrant families moving to better neighborhoods. Confined to a racial ghetto, blacks confronted soaring rents for neglected housing. Whereas whites in New York City, for example, spent one-fifth of their incomes on rent, blacks spent one-third. In East Harlem a community of forty-five thousand Puerto Ricans faced similar conditions.

The combination of high rents and poor

wages led to congested and unsanitary conditions in ghettos teeming with rural blacks unfamiliar with urban health problems. Population density in Harlem was 336 people an acre, about a third more than the average for the borough of Manhattan, and the death rate was 42 percent above that for the rest of New York City. Migration and the struggle for economic survival also disrupted the stability of the extended family of southern tradition, since black women found jobs as domestics, but men had to confront racially conscious employers and unions. As a result, blacks in migrant neighborhoods experienced higher rates of desertion, divorce, and illegitimacy than did whites. Prostitution, gambling, bootlegging, the numbers racket, and narcotics addiction all became part of the impoverished ghetto environment of the twenties.

Although real estate profiteering contributed to the growth of the ghetto, leaders within the black community encouraged development of a "black metropolis." Black pride, habit, and the need for mutual protection led to efforts to "advance the race" by building separate black centers in northern cities. Black businesspeople, politicians, ministers, and journalists worked to create economic self-sufficiency supported by racial clubs, fraternal orders, and mutual-aid societies. But ghetto culture also included storefront "healing" churches that gave southern migrants a sense of self-esteem, respectability, and a tie to home. Just as important to black community life was the numbers game, in which bettors chose a number to be matched by one selected at a central office.

A mass organization known as the Universal Negro Improvement Association received an outpouring of support from working-class blacks in northern ghettos during the early twenties. Founded in 1914 by Marcus Garvey,

a Jamaican, the UNIA enrolled about 100,000 members at the peak of its appeal, although Garvey claimed as many as two million. The Improvement Association espoused black pride. "Up you mighty Race!" Garvey proclaimed, "You can accomplish what you will!" Garvey's eloquence and glorification of blackness inspired poorer blacks to dream of racial freedom and economic independence under black leadership. Garvey called for "Africa for the Africans," describing himself as the "Provisional President of the African Republic." He suggested that a limited number of American blacks might go to Liberia to teach the skills necessary to redeem Africa from European colonialism. He accurately prophesized that a liberated Africa would be an inspiration for black people in the Western Hemisphere. Garvey also preached support of black business in a "buy black" campaign. The UNIA organized grocery chains, restaurants, laundries, a hotel, doll factory, printing plant, and a newspaper called *Negro World*. Its Black Star Steamship Line proposed to establish a commercial link between the United States, the West Indies, and Africa.

Condemned by the entire black national leadership, Garvey's black nationalism brought drama into the lives of a generation embittered by the realities of the urban promised land. By 1922, however, UNIA businesses were collapsing through mismanagement, and Garvey was indicted by the federal government for using the mails to sell fraudulent stock. Although he insisted that trusted associates had betrayed him, Garvey alone was convicted of the charges. After two years in a federal prison, Garvey was deported in 1927 as an alien who had committed a felony. The Universal Negro Improvement Association collapsed, but the fervor of black nationalism never left the ghetto.

While Garvey spoke to the deep-seated feelings of urban blacks, the National Association for the Advancement of Colored People and the Urban League continued to struggle for black justice in the white community. Under prodding by the NAACP, a Dyer Anti-Lynching Bill passed the House of Representatives in 1922, but southern Democrats filibustered the bill to death in the Senate. The ability of the NAACP and the Urban League to mobilize members of black voluntary associations, churches, and mutual benefit societies bore fruit in 1930 when the Senate blocked the nomination of conservative Judge John J. Parker to the Supreme Court. Parker had publicly commented about the unpreparedness of the black for the "burdens and responsibilities of government." The defeat of the Parker nomination, also opposed by the AFL, suggested a powerful coalition among forces of urban liberalism, labor, and civil rights.

On the local level, black communities mounted boycotts against northern school segregation, while students at several southern black colleges organized protests against white paternalism and racism. Meanwhile, blacks in the large cities joined white political machines to win city jobs and protect community interests. Chicago's first district elected Oscar De Priest as the first black congressman ever to come from the north. By supporting the machine of Republican mayor "Big Bill" Thompson, Chicago blacks were able to win one-fourth of the city's postal service jobs by the end of the decade.

Inspired by the potential of the black metropolis, black intellectuals and artists produced a rich literature of race-conscious poetry, prose, and song in postwar Harlem. "I am a Negro — and beautiful" exclaimed the poet Langston Hughes. The verses of Hughes, Sterling Brown, and James Weldon Johnson used the rhythms and moods of jazz and blues and borrowed from the dialect of poor blacks. Novelist Claude McKay published an odyssey of the black working class in *Home to Harlem* (1928). The Harlem Renaissance also stimulated young black painters and sculptors to emulate the grace of African forms. Responding to the growth of a huge market comprising blacks in northern cities, commercial recording companies released "race" records performed by outstanding black blues artists such as Bessie Smith, Ethel Waters, and Louis Armstrong.

Racially progressive whites joined black intellectuals in heralding the Harlem Renaissance and the "new Negro." During 1925 the reform-oriented *Survey Graphic* published a special Harlem issue edited by Alain Locke, the nation's first black Rhodes scholar. The "new Negro," militant and proud, had arrived. White and black intellectuals shared the hope that black cultural creativity would encourage acceptance of blacks by the American people.

Respect for black culture by some whites was a source of inspiration for black writers and artists. But for many whites the Harlem Renaissance meant the nightclubs and revues that made the district a symbol of the Jazz Age in an era of Prohibition. White "slumming" parties considered Harlem to be America's answer to Paris, advertised in handbills as an erotic utopia "where white people from downtown could be entertained by colored girls." Whites were eager to see a "primitive spontaneity" in black life, even when they were entertained by black performers in clubs catering only to white customers. They stereotyped blacks as a "singing race," an "expressive" and "exotic" people who could love and laugh freely in a puritan land. Carl Van Vechten's *Nigger Heaven*, a white view of Harlem orgies and seduction,

A new sense of racial pride among blacks in northern cities helped to sustain a rich variety of expression among black musicians and artists. Here blues coronetist Louis Armstrong plays a set with King Oliver's Band. (Amistad Research Center)

sold 100,000 copies upon release in 1925. While the conditions of the ghetto festered, cosmopolitan Anglo-Protestants enjoyed "a vogue in things Negro."

Like black migrants to the industrial north, Mexican immigrants came to the United States in search of work. Mexican population in the United States doubled in the twenties. By 1930, 600,000 Mexican-born people were in the country, in addition to almost a million more Americans of Mexican descent. Ninety percent lived in Arizona, New Mexico, Texas,

Colorado, and California. Los Angeles had a larger Mexican population than any city except Mexico City itself.

Ignored by the AFL, poorly paid, and deprived of social services and education, Mexican-Americans worked as migratory day laborers in agriculture, transportation, and mining. By 1930, 55 percent of the Mexican immigrant population still could not speak English, and only 5.5 percent of the adults had become citizens. Although demands for restriction of Mexican immigration continually arose from labor, veterans, and nativist groups, southwestern economic interests prevailed in keeping doors open to cheap Mexican labor. A bill for restriction failed in the House during 1925, and Mexicans continued to supply the Southwest with migratory labor for which employers had no responsibilities.

Native Americans experienced similar helplessness in the postwar era. White land grabs and corruption in the government's Indian Bureau contributed to the dwindling of the Indian domain from 138 million acres in 1887 to 47 million by 1934. Despite efforts from white reformers such as the American Indian Defense Association, the new era boom only furthered the economic attacks on Native American property holding. To worsen matters, government policy concentrated on "Americanizing" Indians. Over tribal resistance, the commissioner of Indian affairs ordered the cessation of Native American religious dances that the government considered "pagan." Among them were the Hopi Snake Dance and the Plains Indian Sun Dance. Government authorities reasoned that the abolition of ritual dances was a first step in the Native American's preparation for participation in American society. While the Hoover administration increased aid for Indian education from $3 million to $12 million a year, government boarding schools taught tribal Americans to despise their heritage. Students at some schools were chained to their beds to prevent them from running back to their parents. In protest, the white reformer John Collier led a personal crusade to permit young men to leave the schools for periods of religious rituals, but Native Americans were unable to muster the political power to change oppressive government policies, and cultural and economic stagnation remained the defining feature of reservation life.

ETHNIC ENCLAVES

By 1920 nearly one out of every four white Americans was the offspring of an immigrant. Immigrants and their children constituted a substantial majority of the population of the nation's great cities. The preponderance of ethnic Americans in the industrial work force had contributed to nativist fears of social revolution immediately following World War One. While Anglo-Protestant nativists, industrialists and the AFL strove to limit further immigration, however, millions of immigrant families struggled to find a secure place in their new home.

Immigrants continued to live in the ethnic communities created in the prewar years. Although nativist ideology condemned ethnic exclusiveness, immigrant communities in the larger cities maintained benevolent and mutual-aid societies, as well as their own newspapers. By the early 1920s ten million ethnic Americans read more than one thousand foreign-language newspapers in the United States. Poles, Slavs, Hungarians, and Italians supported ethnic religious and secular organizations in Chicago, a vital center of immigrant culture, and in industrial centers such as New York, Philadelphia, Buffalo, and Cleveland. The cohesiveness of Jewish ghettos, however, began to decline in the twenties, as socially mobile Jews moved to newer residential neighborhoods and second-generation American Jews abandoned religious orthodoxy and Yiddish organizations.

Ever since the 1880s immigrants had comprised the semiskilled labor pool for American industrial expansion. The vast majority of working-class ethnics were factory workers or menial service and clerical operators in the industrial East and Midwest. Italian-Americans, for example, dominated the construction trades.

But by the 1920s some immigrant families had raised enough capital to open neighborhood stores, others had graduated to skilled and supervisory industrial work, and a small percentage had joined the middle class as educated professionals and managers.

For a small number of immigrant entrepreneurs, the road out of the working class lay in machine politics and businesses that thrived on friendly political contacts — construction, utilities, local banking, insurance, and garbage collection. Discrimination against eastern and southern Europeans forced immigrants and their offspring to rely on acquaintances and family connections. As a result, ethnic networks in the larger cities connected politics, labor unions, entertainment, gambling, and organized crime, usually centered in the same districts. The major groups in the organized crime of the twenties were blacks migrating from the South, the Irish, eastern European Jews, and Italians. All of these peoples had left regions deeply suspicious of governmental authority, and each faced massive discrimination. Of the leaders of organized crime in Chicago gambling, for example, 31 percent were Italian, 29 percent Irish, 20 percent Jewish, and 12 percent black.

Up to 1920 Irish-Americans controlled most of the organized crime and machine politics of the large cities. But new sources of immigration from southern and eastern Europe brought fresh struggles for power in the underworld. By the twenties, Jews were major figures in bootlegging in Cleveland and Philadelphia and served other groups as bail bondsmen and defense attorneys. In New York City, where Jews made up one-third of the city's organized labor force, both garment employers and union activists turned to gangs controlled by Jewish syndicate leader Arnold Rothstein during the bitter clothing strike of 1927.

Prohibition provided Italian-Americans with an entry into the organized underworld. Following open gang warfare for control of the bootlegging trade, Al Capone emerged as undisputed leader of the Chicago syndicate in the mid-twenties. Capone consolidated gambling, racketeering, and liquor running and made them into a nationwide industry, while infuriated reformers agonized that friendships and ethnic loyalties tied Chicago gangsters to "legitimate" society and the courts. But there was little that reformers could do to change the system. Black, Polish, German, Czech, and Italian voters returned Republican Thompson to Chicago's city hall in 1927 when they objected to police search of homes during the Democrats' campaign to enforce Prohibition. When the inept Thompson made several remarks ridiculing eastern Europeans, however, he lost the election of 1931 to Bohemian immigrant Anton J. Cermak.

By defeating the Irish-American Thompson, Cermak became one of the first eastern Europeans to rise to political power in the American city. In the 1930s white ethnics still associated with members of their own nationality and retained traditional practices and rituals. But by then, few immigrants were returning to native countries, and the impact of radio, movies, and national politics had done much to acculturate ethnics to American values. From 1928 on, the ethnic vote became a force to reckon with in American politics.

THE NATIVIST RESPONSE

Progressive reformers had hoped to build a homogeneous society of consumer citizens. But from the 1890s on, Anglo-Protestant elites had questioned whether the nation could easily absorb millions of untutored immigrants from southern and eastern Europe. When World War One failed to advance the Americanization of the country's immigrants, nativist leaders attributed labor militance and domestic radicalism to the dangerous influx of foreigners. Antiwar opposition among Irish, German, and Scandanavian-Americans; militant labor agitation by Slavs, Italians, and Jews; and fears of European bolshevism all contributed to the concern about "hyphenated Americans." "Hundred-percent Americanism" became the national standard in the postwar years, as thirty-five states enacted criminal syndicalist laws to discourage subversive activity. Membership in the radical Industrial Workers of the World, for example, constituted a criminal offense in twenty-four states by 1920. An Immigration Act of that year also punished aliens for possessing subversive literature or making financial contributions to organizations that the federal government considered seditious.

The strident crusade for 100 percent Americanism was led by the American Legion, a patriotic veterans group founded in 1919. The Legion quickly recruited one-fourth of the nation's war veterans and exercised considerable local control as a guardian against Communist "influence" and radicalism of all kinds. For example, both the Legion and the Daughters of the American Revolution circulated the infamous "Spider Web Chart," a creation of the Chemical Warfare Service of the War Department, which purported to trace the links of women's peace organizations to bolshevik connections. "Patrioteering" provided beleaguered members of the middle class with an opportunity to demonstrate allegiance to a nostalgic ideal of American unity. Thirty ultrapatriotic organizations thrived in the early twenties, subsisting on private and corporate donations or membership subscriptions.

While Americanization programs in public day and night school continued to teach English in the postwar years, the federal government's Bureau of Americanization strove to help immigrants "renounce allegiance to their old country and prepare to live or die for the glory of the new — America." But confidence in the nation's ability to manage additional immigrants appeared to be waning. "We have put all the sand into our cement that it will stand," lectured General Leonard Wood of the American Legion. The veterans group sponsored an essay contest in 1920 on why the nation should suspend immigration. Typical of nativist sentiment was the comment of Maryland Senator William Bruce that immigrants were "indigestible lumps" in the "national stomach" and "insoluble blood-clots in the national circulation."

Ethnic conflict erupted in 1920 when a nativist mob invaded the Italian district of West Frankfort, Illinois. Reacting to the tensions of a coal miners' strike and several bank robberies attributed to the Italian Black Hand, the mob dragged immigrant families from their homes and burned rows of houses. When the Italian community retaliated against the invasion, five hundred state troopers needed three days to end the fighting.

The Protestant elite's tendency to associate immigrants with radicalism was dramatically illustrated when two Italian anarchists, Nicola Sacco and Bartolomeo Vanzetti, were arrested and convicted on scant evidence for a robbery-murder that took place outside Boston in 1920. The case was appealed through the aid of the American Civil Liberties Union, founded in 1919 to defend victims of the Red Scare. The ACLU protested that the political views of the immigrant anarchists had replaced solid evidence in their trial, and argued that the court had dismissed the testimony of eighteen Italian-American witnesses as unreliable. After long appeals and delays, the governor of Massachusetts referred the case to a special panel headed by the presidents of Harvard University and the Massachusetts Institute of Technology, but the committee supported the findings of the original trial. Sacco and Vanzetti were executed by electrocution in August 1927, although both men defended their innocence up to the last moment. Novelist John Dos Passos later immortalized the incident in his *USA* trilogy. In an ironic reversal of nativist rhetoric, Dos Passos wrote that "America our nation has been beaten by strangers who have turned our language inside out who have taken the clean words our fathers spoke and made them slimy and foul." Although recent scholars tend to conclude that at least one of the men may have been guilty, Dos Passos and other intellectuals were intensely politicized by the case. To the emerging radicals of the late 1920s, the strangers were not the immigrant hordes but the patrician establishment who had turned against the common people.

In their postwar campaign against hyphenated Americans, nativists also singled out Jews as foreign threats to national values. Henry Ford launched a nationwide crusade in 1921 by having car dealers circulate copies of the "Protocol of the Elders of Zion," a fraudulent documentation of an international Jewish conspiracy for world power. Ford's *Dearborn Independent,* distributed through thousands of Ford dealerships, played upon anti-Semitic prejudice by insisting that the American economy was dominated by international Jewish financiers. Meanwhile, quotas regulating the entry of Jews into colleges and medical schools, clubs, residential areas, and businesses continued throughout the decade. In California racial prejudice toward Asians resulted in a campaign against the kimono as a threat to the purity of white women and in continual pressure to exclude Japanese immigration. The Supreme Court ruled in 1922 that immigrants of Japanese birth were ineligible for naturalization.

Nativists in the prewar years had faced presidential vetoes of immigrant restriction bills. But by the early twenties, new era industrialists sought a more integrated labor force, one uncontaminated by foreign ideologies of bolshevism and class consciousness. Industrial managers had supported open immigration in a period of factory expansion. But following World War One, they argued that language and inexperience made foreign-born workers vulnerable to accidents and costly labor turnover. In an attempt to freeze the ethnic proportions of the American population, Anglo-Protestant nativists and many industrialists pressured Congress to pass an emergency immigration law in 1921. The statute limited future immigration from each nation to a percentage of the foreign-born of that nationality residing in the United States in 1910. The Native Origins Act of 1924 set up a gradual timetable for a ceiling of 150,000 immigrants a year, using a 2 percent quota for each national group. In 1929 the quota was divided according to the proportion of national groups living in the United States in 1920.

Immigration restriction discouraged the "new immigration" from southern and eastern Europe (largely Roman Catholic and Jewish) and encouraged migration from northern and western Europe (predominantly Protestant). Although the restriction laws exempted immigrants from the Western Hemisphere and permitted the use of Mexican labor in southwest agriculture, they formalized prohibition of Japanese immigration. By 1929, 32 percent of American immigrants were Canadians. Immigration restriction fixed the national demography, defining it in terms of the existing ethnic components. While implementing the major goal of postwar nativism, however, the quota laws removed the urgency from the anti-immigrant crusade. By the 1930s nativist anxieties concerning the acculturation of European immigrants, Catholics, and Jews had considerably lessened.

Hostility to immigrants and urban culture came together in a spectacular fashion in the revived Ku Klux Klan. Organized in Atlanta in 1915, the second Klan admitted "native born, white, gentile Americans" who believed in white supremacy. Unlike the Klan of the 1860s, its appeal was not limited to the Deep South, but extended to lower-middle-class Anglo-Protestants in the small and growing towns of the Southwest, Midwest, and Far West. The Klan first regained strength over the white suprem-

The political power of the Ku Klux Klan assumed awesome proportions in the mid-1920s. These men were among 85,000 Klan followers who participated in a 1925 march on the Capitol in Washington. (Brown Brothers)

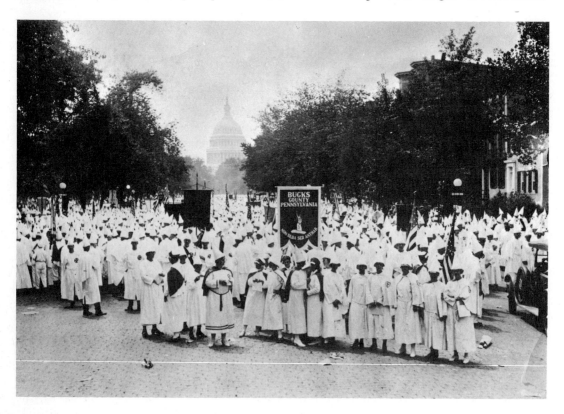

acy issue in the South, mobilizing against the new sense of pride among returning black soldiers and the black migration to southern cities. In a campaign to keep "the nigger in his place," Klansmen paraded in many southern towns on the eve of the 1920 election to discourage black voting. Likewise, black men who "insulted" white women or asserted themselves politically or economically were frequently threatened, whipped, or branded by vigilante action.

The key to KKK growth in the Far West and Midwest, however, was its hostility to the 36 percent of the nation's religious population who were Roman Catholics. "We want the country ruled by the sort of people who settled it," Ohio Klan leaders preached. "Klan-vocations" featured a revival spirit, with "The Old Rugged Cross" the near-official hymn of gatherings. Michigan and Nebraska debated constitutional amendments to ban parochial schools in 1920 and 1921, while Oregon elected a Klan-supported governor in 1922, abolished Columbus Day as a state holiday, and passed an initiative requiring children to attend public schools. A Klan pamphlet proclaimed that schools should be nonsectarian and democratic, "for all the children of all the people," but the Supreme Court struck down the law in 1925, asserting that the state had no right to "standardize its children." In Illinois a Klan mob burned a Catholic church to the ground.

Klan activities also focused on immigrants who refused to "melt" into Anglo-Saxon culture. Immigrants, said KKK leader Hiram Wesley Evans, maintained primary allegiance to their ethnic group and could never be Americanized. Evans proclaimed that the nation lay "disorganized and helpless before the invasion of aliens and alien ideas." Only Anglo-Saxons or Nordics had the inherent capacity for American citizenship, as immigrant lawbreaking and

consumption of alcohol showed. Immigrants also adhered to the detested foreign ideology of bolshevism, with which the Klan associated most forms of political dissent and radicalism. Klansmen also castigated American Jews as both bankers and bolsheviks and as symbols of the urban sins of bootlegging, gambling, and carnal indulgence. Going beyond the Americanization and immigration restriction policies of the Anglo-Protestant elite, lower-middle-class Klansmen proclaimed total opposition to the "Jew, Jug, and Jesuit."

The postwar Klan thrived in boom towns peopled by recent migrants who retained a rural mentality. Uprooted and dislocated, Klansmen sought to define themselves by clinging to traditional values amid the secularization of urban culture. Infuriated by the conversion of upper-middle-class youth to urban cosmopolitanism, Klansmen saw themselves as knights — guardians of the public virtue in a period of bootleggers, speakeasies, gangsters, and prostitutes. Their objections extended to lurid movies, salacious literature, easy divorce, family disintegration, sexy dancing, Sabbath sports, and corrupt politicians. Evans spoke of "drivers of second-hand Fords" who faced "constant ridicule" for their belief in the "sacredness of our Sabbath, of our homes, of chastity." The Klan, said its leading spokesman of the twenties, wished "a return of power into the hands of the everyday, not highly cultured, not overly intellectualized, but entirely unspoiled and not de-Americanized average citizen of the old stock."

Striking out at symbols of urban cosmopolitanism, southern Klansmen organized "whipping squads" for bootleggers, prostitutes, and movie operators and conducted boycotts against Catholic, Jewish, or morally delinquent merchants. Near Birmingham, Alabama, where the county sheriff and most of the city police were

Klan members, Klansmen frequently flashed lights on "parked" cars and ordered couples to move on. "Go Joy Riding with Your Own Wife," one KKK placard read.

Klan membership reached approximately five million by 1925. In some respects the two thousand local Klans reflected the "lodge vogue" shared by the middle-class men of postwar America who joined college fraternities or such organizations as the Elks, Rotary, or the American Legion. Klan revivals and rallies brought relief from the sterility of small-town life and provided social cohesiveness for those in the larger cities. A July Fourth Klan ceremony in Kokomo, Indiana, during 1923 brought 200,000 people to an open-field camp-out, where they waited for the airplane arrival of their leaders. The dramatic growth of KKK strength in the first years of the decade was directed by two Atlanta publicity agents, who received a healthy cut of the $1 initiation fee paid by new members. Seventy-five million dollars may have passed into Klan coffers during the postwar period.

By 1922 the leadership of Hiram Wesley Evans had converted the KKK from a vigilante organization to a highly effective political machine. The Texas Klan elected a United States Senator. The Klan-dominated legislature of Oklahoma conducted a state campaign to impeach the governor when he used martial law against Klan violence. In Indiana, where the Klan had nearly a half million members, Klansmen took over the Republican party, the governorship, and local government and school boards in Indianapolis and Gary. The Klan also elected several congressmen and, through sympathetic delegates to the 1924 Democratic convention, blocked an effort to place an anti-KKK plank in the party platform.

But Klan political power was short lived. In 1925 an Indiana state house secretary poisoned herself after being abducted by the region's Grand Dragon and placed on a train to Chicago. In the lower berth of a pullman drawing room, the Klan official assaulted and mutilated the victim and then held her captive for days in a loft over his garage. The sensational scandal produced a conviction for second-degree murder and a life sentence for the Klansman, David C. Stephenson. When the Klan-supported governor refused to pardon him, Stephenson produced a "black book" with evidence that sent a congressman, the mayor of Indianapolis, a county sheriff, and other Indiana Klan officials to prison. Internal dissension in Klan politics and further moral and financial scandals involving KKK leaders and promoters marked the demise of the organization by the late twenties. By then immigration restriction laws had sapped the momentum of the Klan crusade.

PROHIBITION

The progressive crusade of the Anglo-Protestant purity reformers culminated in Congress's passage of a Prohibition amendment to the Constitution in 1917 and ratification by forty-six states in 1919. Outlawing the manufacture, sale, importing, or transportation of "intoxicating liquors," the Eighteenth Amendment took effect early in 1920. Nativist reformers viewed Prohibition as a means of unifying American culture around traditional values of hard work and Protestant piety. The utopia of the sober Sunday also attacked the saloon, the "breeding place" of immigrant crime, prostitution, and machine politics. While purity reformers and rural traditionalists objected that immigrants and the young legitimized drinking in the corrupt cities, new era businessmen were concerned with the sobriety of the work force in a modernized economy. "Booze had to go out when modern industry and the motor car came in," prohibitionist Henry Ford proclaimed.

National Prohibition brought mixed results. Beer drinking dropped dramatically, halving the consumption of alcohol by the working class. But compliance with the Eighteenth Amendment declined by mid-decade. The use of spirits by middle- and upper-class Americans actually increased, giving vent to charges that Prohibition constituted class legislation that penalized only the poor. The disaffection of upper-middle-class Protestants from traditional standards of piety also enraged those attracted to the moral absolutes of the Klan and evangelical religion. Believing the amendment's blanket condemnation of the liquor trade to be sufficient, the Anti-Saloon League had not pressed Congress for extensive appropriations for enforcement. As a result, the Harding and Coolidge administrations remained indifferent to carrying out the Eighteenth Amendment. By 1927 only eighteen states had appropriated enforcement funds. Prosecutors and juries in the larger cities also were reluctant to challenge the importance of beer and wine to social practices among ethnic Americans.

The emergence of a thriving underworld to meet the demand for bootleg liquor aggravated the threat to lawful order. Such open violation demonstrated the futility of Prohibition as practiced. The Democratic candidate for president expressed his personal opposition to the amendment in 1928, even though he pledged to uphold the law. By then the Association Against the Prohibition Amendment had effectively mobilized the support of wealthy backers such as the Du Pont family and John J. Raskob of

General Motors and was conducting skillful public relations campaigns to discredit the "noble experiment." The Democratic party united on repeal in 1932, and ratification of the Twenty-first Amendment ended Prohibition by the close of 1933. The cultural domination of Anglo-Saxon Protestant America, with its nostalgia for small-town community and moral standards, was no longer absolute, although many southern states referred the matter to local option.

FUNDAMENTALISM AND TRADITIONALISM

Prohibition temporarily erased the feud between Protestant fundamentalists and liberal Protestants who preached the urban social gospel. But as postwar public opinion began to shift from biblical and religious sanctions for behavior to "scientific" authority, fundamentalists reasserted their bitter denunciation of "modernist" interpretations of the Bible. A major cultural battle arose over the teaching of evolution in public schools and universities. Darwinian theory, presented in textbooks as scientific fact, offended fundamentalists who accepted the story of Genesis as the cornerstone of Christian faith. Twenty-one states considered antievolution laws between 1921 and 1929.

In Tennessee an antievolution act was enacted as a symbolic gesture in 1925 with little debate. To the American Civil Liberties Union, however, the law was an infringement on constitutional rights of free speech, and the ACLU found a high school teacher willing to have charges filed against him. The ensuing trial of John Scopes became a spectacle of national drama when William Jennings Bryan

Aimee Semple McPherson

1890-1944

When Aimee Semple McPherson opened a splendid Pentecostal Temple in Los Angeles on New Year's Day 1923, she demonstrated that Protestant fundamentalism was not confined to the southeastern mountains or the isolated countryside. The self-annointed faith healer had been converted at the age of seventeen by Robert Semple, an itinerate preacher. The two married and left for missionary work in China, but Semple died and the young widow returned to the United States. After an unhappy marriage to a grocery salesman, McPherson decorated her "gospel automobile" with evangelical slogans and set out for California.

The "foursquare gospel" of Aimee Semple fell within the pietistic tradition of American Protestantism. It appealed to people of little education and small means, worshipers brought up in the revivalist spirit of the evangelical churches. The majority of McPherson's followers were retirees transplanted from the Midwest and elsewhere. They responded enthusiastically to simple sermons of love and faith healing. McPherson made Los Angeles the headquarters for countless cross-country revival tours, spreading the word in tents, churches, and public auditoriums that the Jazz Age was speeding to hell.

Endorsed by the mayor of Denver in 1921, she filled that city's Coliseum for a month with twelve thousand people nightly. The following year McPherson addressed a secret Klavern of the Oakland Ku Klux Klan. Once the Los Angeles temple opened, her religious enterprise expanded to a Bible college, publishing house, branch churches, and overseas missionary settlements. In 1924 she purchased Los Angeles's third radio station.

The distinguishing feature of McPherson's gospel was her belief that a Jazz Age preacher must "fight fire with fire." She was the first *woman to deliver a sermon over the radio. In San Diego she scattered religious tracts and handbills from an open biplane. The Los Angeles temple provided telephone callers with the time of day as a free service.*

McPherson dressed in long white gowns, dramatically offsetting her cascading blond hair. To portray Bible stories vividly, temple services featured orchestras, choirs, elaborate costumes, and colorful pageantry. McPherson once illustrated a sermon entitled "The Green Light Is On" by riding a motorcycle down the center aisle.

But the evangelist's fusion of traditionalism and modernism brought newspaper outrage when she disappeared in 1926, only to be linked to a Mexican abortion and an affair with the temple radio operator. Still, her following continued to pay homage to Everybody's Sister. After surviving several court suits in the mid-thirties, McPherson died in 1944 from an overdose of barbital sedatives complicated by a kidney ailment. But the Pentecostal movement, spawned by the superficial hedonism of the urban middle class, remained a vital force in American Protestantism. Despite her Jazz Age trappings, Aimee Semple McPherson remained a symbol of Anglo-Protestant nostalgia for the purity of a simpler America.

answered the call of the World Christian Fundamentals Association to assist the prosecution. In turn Clarence Darrow, the most prominent labor defense lawyer of the era and an agnostic, defended Scopes for the ACLU. Bryan called the Dayton, Tennessee, trial a "duel to the death" between Christianity and the doctrine of evolution. Led by H. L. Mencken of the Baltimore *Sun*, the national press advertised the confrontation as a battle between old-time religion and scientific cosmopolitanism, with Mencken deriding fundamentalists as "gaping primates from the upland valleys."

Bryan hoped to show that the doctrine of evolution paralyzed social reform by stressing struggle and conflict instead of Christian love. In this manner, Bryan was midway between the outlook of fundamentalists and social gospel Protestants. But Bryan's attempt to reaffirm spiritual values was clouded by an insistence on village conformity and an effort to suppress free inquiry. The Scopes Trial came to a climax when Darrow called Bryan to the stand. Speaking for traditional faith, the Great Commoner testified that he read the Bible literally. But when asked how long it took to create the earth, Bryan interpreted the Bible by suggesting six time periods rather than days. The close of the sensational "Monkey Trial" found Scopes guilty of the charge, but Bryan had been widely derided and mocked. Five days later he died in his sleep. Although the Tennessee statute remained law until 1966, the Scopes trial ended in national humiliation for the antievolution forces and made the sentiments of traditionalism appear ridiculous.

Traditionalism died slowly in the twenties, clinging stubbornly to all aspects of American life. "Chautauqua" cultural festivals, which combined lectures and entertainment, maintained the nineteenth century's cult of self-im-

Members pose for a group portrait at a Chautauqua gathering in Kansas City. The Chautauqua symbolized the persistence of traditionalism in the 1920s. (The Kansas State Historical Society, Topeka)

provement in small towns across the nation. By 1924 one hundred Chautauqua circuits were reaching thirty million people. Russell Conwell delivered his success-oriented "Acres of Diamonds" speech six thousand times to Chautauqua audiences, while Bryan's "Prince of Peace" lecture was heard on another three thousand occasions. On the radio Pentecostal evangelist Aimee Semple McPherson delivered dramatized sermons that condemned the Jazz Age and stressed the gospel of love.

In Boston an alliance of the Catholic church and the Protestant social elite maintained traditional morality against the protests of urban progressives of the upper middle class. A Boston municipal court found Theodore Dreiser's *An American Tragedy* obscene in 1927, and the district attorney later banned Sinclair Lewis's *Elmer Gantry*. The aristocratic Watch and Ward Society initiated prosecution of those who sold books that the Society had banned. By the later twenties, however, the Catholic church assumed the censorship initiative, finding itself less vulnerable to the attacks of urban liberals. By then book censorship in Boston had become so embarrassing to university intellectuals and society figures that urban professionals mounted an anticensorship campaign against the "backwardness" of the Irish-Catholic working class. But censorship forces held their ground, denouncing the "self-styled intelligentsia" who were "not always sage guides to morality."

As Americans found themselves in a society increasingly dominated by corporate institutions and secular values, they seemed to seek out compensating heroes and heroines. Movie idols provided millions of young people with role models to emulate and cherish. But individual athletes and organized sports offered a vicarious sense of accomplishment and mastery that routinized work and life could not provide. College football, with its tribal ritualism and clockwork precision, dominated campus life in the twenties. The same kind of community spirit pervaded rivalries between small-town basketball teams in rural areas of the Midwest. But the greatest sports heroes were the ethnics and white poor who gravitated to boxing and baseball. Jack Dempsey, an Irish-American, thrilled boxing fans with gutsy and ferocious fighting reminiscent of street brawls. And Babe Ruth, raised in a Catholic orphanage in Baltimore, helped to make baseball the national pastime by hitting sixty home runs for the champion New York Yankees in 1927, as major league attendance climbed to ten million a year.

Of all the individual accomplishments of the twenties, however, Charles Lindbergh's flight across the Atlantic appeared to touch the American people most profoundly. In 1927 Lindbergh flew a single-engine plane by dead reckoning from Long Island, New York, to Paris. The solo, nonstop flight took thirty-three hours and thirty minutes. Lindbergh and his plane, the *Spirit of St. Louis,* were carried back to the United States on a warship sent by President Coolidge. Newspapers across the country splashed front pages with celebrations of the Lone Eagle. An unprecedented ticker tape parade awaited the Minnesotan in New York City, as four million people came out to see the youthful aviator.

Others had flown across the Atlantic in the years since 1919. But Lindbergh had done it alone. To Americans he seemed to symbolize the hope that complex technology and mechanization did not necessarily crush the free, self-sufficient individual. The Lone Eagle dramatized the hope that a highly corporatized society could experience technical progress without relinquishing cherished ideals of individualism. Like Henry Ford, Lindbergh was a hero who combined personal ingenuity with sophisticated machine technology. It did not matter that both Lindbergh and President Coolidge saw the flight primarily as a representation of American aeronautics and industrial cooperation. For Americans in an era when moral certainties were in question, the boyish Lindbergh symbolized the renewal of lost virtue and individual sense of purpose and the hope that youth could be combined with leadership.

CULTURAL CONFLICT AND THE ELECTION OF 1928

Like Charles Lindbergh and Henry Ford, Herbert Hoover embodied both the world of corporate capitalism and the values of traditional America. Although Hoover had made his fortune in mine engineering and investments, he had been born in a small Iowa town, was a Protestant, and supported Prohibition. He represented the old middle class and the agrarian past, as well as the humanizing and organizing talents of progressive business. Hoover had served as wartime food administrator for the Wilson administration and won an international reputation for humanitarianism by organizing European emergency relief. His work as commerce secretary in the Harding-Coolidge administrations had delighted corporate progressives. Once Coolidge declared that "I do not choose to run," Hoover appeared the logical choice for the 1928 Republican nomination for president. After agrarian progressives lost a preliminary test of strength, Hoover took the convention nomination on the first ballot. Republicans chose Kansas Senator Charles Curtis, a

farm-bloc leader, for vice president and called for continued enforcement of Prohibition and maintenance of high tariffs.

By 1928 the Democratic party could no longer ignore its urban-ethnic constituency. Despite Republican support for Prohibition and immigration restriction, the major cities outside the South had been voting Republican since 1896. Seeking support from the cities and the immigrants, the 1928 convention finally accepted New York Governor Al Smith. An Irish-Catholic born in working-class Brooklyn, Smith had risen through the ranks of the Tammany Hall machine and personally favored the repeal of Prohibition. His urban liberalism represented a threat to the evangelical tradition of reform embodied by Bryan and LaFollette. Yet the Democratic platform mirrored the 1924 Pro-

MAP 7.1   THE ELECTION OF 1928

Hoover (Republican)
444 electoral votes

Smith (Democrat)
87 electoral votes

gressives' endorsement of collective bargaining for labor, abolition of court injunctions against strikes, federal aid to support farm prices, and federal regulation of water power. To further balance their ticket, Democrats chose Senator Joseph T. Robinson of Arkansas, an Anglo-Protestant supporter of Prohibition, for the vice presidential nomination.

Both Democrat and Republican platforms agreed on traditional principles of limited government and acceptance of the corporation, as well as on the need to enforce Prohibition as long as it remained law. But the cultural implications of the Smith candidacy were too great for most of the country to swallow. The Anti-Saloon League argued that Smith "appeals to the sporty, jazzy, and liberal element of our population." He was accused of being "New York minded," ridiculed for wearing a derby hat, feared as a representative of "aliens who feel that the older America, the America of the Anglo-Saxon stock, is a hateful thing which must be overturned and humiliated." Kansas journalist William Allen White pictured Smith as the product of a city "maggot-eaten with saloons" and described him as "city born, city bred, 'city broke,' city minded, and city hearted." The first poor boy from a large city to run for president, Smith appeared a defender of the urban immigrant. Opposition to the candidate, wrote Walter Lippman, was "inspired by the feeling that the clamorous life of the city should not be acknowledged as the American ideal." Smith's street origins and urban identification alienated the majority of voters still coming to terms with the American city. A large proportion of urban social workers (including Jane Addams) also opposed Smith for his stance on Prohibition.

The combined effect of Coolidge prosperity, Smith's inability to cultivate farmer discontent, and cultural discomfort with the New Yorker brought a substantial Republican victory. Hoover won 21.3 million votes to Smith's 15 million. A lopsided 444–87 tally in the electoral college reflected Smith's failure to hold the Anglo-Protestant South. One midwestern newspaper rejoiced that Smith's defeat demonstrated that America was "not yet dominated by its great cities.... Main Street is still the principal thoroughfare of the nation."

Although the Smith campaign failed, Democrats doubled their presidential vote of 1924 and emerged as the party of the big cities. In 1924 the Republican plurality in the twelve largest cities had been 1.25 million. But the Democrats captured these cities by 38,000 votes in 1928, extending the margin to an overwhelming 3.6 million by 1936. Smith was the first Democrat to tie the national party to first- and second-generation immigrants. Republicans, in contrast, refused to recognize the urban and ethnic support they inherited at the start of the decade and lost millions of votes through their endorsement of Anglo-Protestant policies of Prohibition and immigration restriction. The Smith political revolution of 1928 represented a new sensitivity to ethnic concerns and suggested that Catholics and Jews would play a far larger role in national politics.

When Hoover took office in 1929, he led a nation that seemed to be resolving many of its ethnic and cultural anxieties. Republicans embraced the new era belief that continued prosperity and corporate rationality would produce a homogeneous society free of class and social strife. "We in America are nearer to the final triumph over poverty than ever before in the history of any land," Hoover proclaimed to enthusiastic cheers. One of the most competent administrators ever to occupy the presidency, Hoover hoped finally to lead the nation to the progressive vision of an American democracy of consumer citizens.

SUGGESTED READINGS

A brief introduction to the cultural conflicts of the new era is Paul Carter, *The Twenties in America* (2nd ed., 1975). William E. Leuchtenburg, *Perils of Prosperity, 1914–1932* (1958), and Gilman M. Ostrander, *American Civilization in the First Machine Age, 1890–1940* (1970), both present overriding interpretations that emphasize twenties technology, youth, and moral innovation. Two exceedingly helpful contemporary studies are Robert S. Lynd and Helen M. Lynd, *Middletown: A Study in American Culture* (1929), and President's Conference on Unemployment, *Recent Social Trends in the United States* (1933).

For a perceptive account of twenties urbanism and suburbanism, see William H. Wilson, *Coming of Age: Urban America, 1915–1945* (1974). Regionalism, technology, and progressivism are related in Blaine A. Brownell, *The Urban Ethos in the South, 1920–1930* (1975). James J. Fink, *The Car Culture* (1975), describes Fordization and social aspects of automobility in the new era. Fresh insights incorporating family history are presented in Paula Fass, *The Damned and the Beautiful: American Youth in the 1920s* (1977), which looks beyond contemporary generalizations about the postwar college generation. An excellent analysis of the social role of twenties film appears in the relevant chapters of Robert Sklar, *Movie-Made America: A Cultural History of American Movies* (1976). The most complete account of the postwar literary renaissance is Frederick J. Hoffman, *The Twenties* (1949), which should be supplemented with Malcolm Cowley, *Exile's Return: A Literary Odyssey of the 1920s* (1951), and Max Eastman, *Love and Revolution: My Journey Through an Epoch* (1964).

The first segment of William H. Chafe, *The American Woman: Her Changing Social, Economic, and Political Role, 1920–1970* (1972), relates the impact of postwar changes on women, and Anne Firor Scott, *The Southern Lady: From Pedestal to Politics* (1970), provides ample discussion of role changes in the South. Social aspects of the new womanhood are treated in Stanley J. Lemons, *The Woman Citizen: Social Feminism in the 1920s* (1973), which can be read with Clarke A. Chambers, *Seedtime of Reform: American Social Service and Social Action, 1918–1933* (1963). A critical view of social feminism is presented by Jill Conway, "Women Reformers and American Culture," *Journal of Social History* (February 1971–September 1972).

The rise of a black ghetto is depicted with great insight in Gilbert Osofsky, *Harlem: The Making of a Ghetto* (1966). Relevant sections of August Meier and Elliot Rudwick, *From Plantation to Ghetto* (3rd ed., 1976), and June Sochen, *The Unbridgeable Gap: Blacks and Their Quest for the American Dream, 1900–1930* (1972), discuss black protest and the Harlem Renaissance. Immigrant cultures are portrayed in the appropriate sections of Richard Gambino, *Blood of My Blood: The Dilemma of the Italian-Americans* (1975), and Richard Krickus, *Pursuing the American Dream: White Ethnics and the New Populism* (1976).

A detailed account of the immigration restriction crusade can be found in the closing segment of John Higham, *Strangers in the Land: Patterns of American Nativism, 1860–1925* (1955). The roots and influence of the Ku Klux Klan are treated in Charles Alexander, *The Ku Klux Klan in the Southwest* (1965), and Kenneth T. Jackson, *The Ku Klux Klan in the City, 1915–1930* (1967). Prohibition as reform is explained by Norman H. Clark, *De-*

liver Us from Evil: An Interpretation of American Prohibition (1976), but a critical portrait of the movement can be found in Joseph R. Gusfield, "Prohibition: The Impact of Political Utopianism," in John Braeman, Robert H. Bremner, and David Brody, eds., *Change and Continuity in Twentieth-Century America: The 1920s* (1968). Norman F. Furniss, *The Fundamentalist Controversy, 1918–1933* (1954), presents a useful study of Protestant evangelicalism and the conflict over religious modernism. For an account of the 1928 election, see Edmund A. Moore, *A Catholic Runs for President* (1956); but the influence of ethnic Americans is defined more clearly in the relevant sections of John M. Allswang, *A House for All Peoples: Ethnic Politics in Chicago, 1890–1936* (1971), and Edward R. Kantowicz, *Polish-American Politics in Chicago, 1880–1940* (1974).

Chapter 8

ROOSEVELT AND THE REGULATED ECONOMY—THE 1930s

When Herbert Hoover assumed the presidency, progressive businesspeople and rural traditionalists shared the hope that he would lead the nation to material prosperity and social harmony. Hoover's experience as a professional engineer and administrator seemed to fulfill the Progressive vision of a planned economy led by technical experts. But as stock prices and corporate profits reached all-time highs during 1929, few Americans paid attention to ominous cracks in new era prosperity. Only in the last ten weeks of the 1920s did corporation leaders begin to understand that the long historic boom brought by territorial expansion, increased population, and technological innovation appeared to be ending.

ECONOMIC COLLAPSE

Elevated stock prices were psychological indicators of investor confidence. But as low interest rates stimulated widespread speculation by the late twenties, some stocks sold at fifty times their earning potential. Large financial corporations benefited from the "bull" market by launching companies that produced nothing, yet brought in millions from stock investment. Meanwhile, middle-class investors aggravated market inflation through "margin" arrangements that allowed them to pay only half the stock price and borrow the rest on paper.

Other problems besides speculation contributed to weaknesses in the twenties economy.

New England, the rural South, and agricultural areas of the Midwest and mountain states never had shared in the twenties boom. Neither had declining industries such as coal mining, cotton manufacturing, shipbuilding, shoe and leather producing, railroads, or agriculture. These weak industries also suffered from the loss of foreign markets that accompanied the high tariffs of new era foreign policy. Business leaders soon learned that restrictive tariffs made economic disaster in Europe and the United States mutually reinforcing.

As productivity gains in industry outdistanced wage costs, investors placed surplus capital in the stock market or overseas plants. The result was declining employment in mining, railroads, and agriculture and stagnation in the manufacturing job market. This technological unemployment particularly hurt older workers and newcomers to the industrial economy such as blacks and European-Americans. Because profit gains far exceeded wage increases in the new era, the top 1 percent of income holders were able to increase their share of national income from 12 percent to nearly 19 percent. With three-fifths of American families earning only enough for "basic necessities," there were not enough consumers to sustain the fever of installment buying that marked twenties affluence.

By 1929 investment seemed to have surpassed the capacity of sales to return profits. Residential construction, a key to new era prosperity, had been declining since 1927. The economy also found itself dependent on the automobile, a durable commodity whose replacement could be delayed by consumer whim. As a result, motor vehicle production and road building were overextended by the end of the decade.

The twenties boom burst during a five-day financial panic, climaxed by a devastating stock market loss of $14 billion on October 29, 1929. As the fall in stock prices fed upon itself, investors were forced to sell securities to pay off loans they had made to purchase stocks in the first place. By July 1933 five-sixths of the value of the 1929 market had been obliterated. Stocks in the Radio Corporation of America, for example, selling for $1.01 a share in 1929, tumbled to less than $.03 a share three years later.

The stock market crash precipitated one of the most horrendous economic declines in American history. Industrial production and national income halved between 1929 and 1933, as annual passenger car sales plummeted from 4.5 million to 1.1 million. Construction spending fell from $8.7 billion to $1.4 billion. Farm receipts dropped from $11.3 billion to $4.8 billion. And investment in capital goods decreased a horrifying 88 percent. Most frightening, however, was the unemployment rate, which leaped from minimal levels to one-fourth the civilian labor force by 1933.

The Depression brought increasing cynicism toward the corporate managers who had directed new era prosperity. Granaries bulged with unsellable wheat as people went hungry; idle coal sat in pits while Americans froze; billions of dollars were locked up in failing banks. A 1932 Senate investigation into Wall Street revealed that the most respected investment bankers had rigged pools, profited by pegging bond prices artificially high, and lined their pockets with fantastic bonuses. Leading financial houses had invited insiders to purchase securities at privately set prices and provided interest-free loans to their officers while the banks were unable to cover their own investments. As pyramids of speculation, financing, and manipulation collapsed, the mighty utility-holding empires folded in bankruptcy. Hatred of bankers was so intense that Senator Carter Glass of race-conscious Virginia observed, "One banker in my state attempted to marry a white woman and they lynched him." Father Charles Coughlin's popular radio commentary continually blamed the Depression on "banksters."

Only in isolated cases did bitterness toward the business community lead to political action in the early years of the Depression. The small Communist party was the first to demand extended relief programs with sit-ins, hunger marches, and City Hall parades. Party organizers in the large cities also provided help to those resisting eviction notices from landlords. The Communists created unemployed councils, which they saw as "a cadre of revolution," and claimed one million participants in International Unemployment Day protests during March 1930. Two years later four demonstrators were killed by Ford security forces when Detroit Communists led three thousand protesters on a march demanding jobs at the company's River Rouge plant.

Discontent was far more pervasive in the farm belt, where independent farmers had been threatened by shrinking markets, disastrous price declines, and mounting foreclosures since the early 1920s. The Crash brought a near-total collapse of the nation's agricultural marketing system. By 1932 Hoover's Federal Farm Board had lost $354 million in loans to crumbling farm cooperatives.

Independent farmers had come to support the idea of federal aid and government price supports during the attempt to enact farm legislation in the late twenties. By 1930 the National Farmers Union had moved beyond cooperative marketing proposals to demands for a guaranteed cost-of-production price and a mora-

torium on foreclosures. As agricultural income halved between 1931 and 1932, Iowa farm leader Mila Reno formed a new organization called the Farmers Holiday Association. Reno urged farmers to withhold produce from market until they were guaranteed costs of production, and issued a stark ultimatum to organized society: "If you continue to confiscate our property and demand that we feed your stomachs and clothe your bodies, we will refuse to function." During the summer of 1932, armed Farm Holiday supporters barricaded midwestern highways with spiked telegraph poles and logs in the effort to stop underpriced produce from getting to market. By early 1933 antiforeclosure activity climaxed with "penny sales" or "Sears Roebuck auctions," in which crowds of farmers gathered to prevent anyone from bidding more than a few cents on farms auctioned for bank sale. Governor William Langer of North Dakota ordered the state militia to prevent county sheriffs from conducting foreclosure sales, while Minnesota Governor Floyd Olson threatened martial law unless the legislature acted to do the same. Nebraska and Iowa legislatures joined Minnesota in declaring foreclosure moratoriums early in 1933. To further dramatize their plight, the Farmers Holiday Association scheduled a national farmers' strike for May 1933.

HOOVER FAILS

President Hoover's first response to the economic setback was to describe it as a "depression," rather than the more frightening "panic" or "crisis." Hoover believed that corporate maintenance of employment, wages, and production would sustain the morale necessary for continued prosperity. Within weeks of the Crash, the president called leading officers of the major corporations to the White House to win promises for such a policy. Voluntarism worked for a time. U.S. Steel, at half capacity at the start of 1931, managed to keep 94 percent of its payroll through work sharing and rotation. Some corporations implemented new era policies by providing loans and direct relief to their unemployed. In March 1930 Hoover told the nation that "the worst effects of the crash upon unemployment will have passed during the next sixty days." But late in 1931, U.S. Steel announced a momentous 10 percent wage cut, ending the hopeful period of industrial wage maintenance. Ford, which had cut its work force by nearly three-fourths, abandoned the $7 day a few weeks later.

Hoover responded to the industrial crisis with public works projects, although the Democratic Congress demanded even more than he approved. Nevertheless, the administration constructed more public works than the federal government had built in the previous thirty years, and the federal budget deficit leaped to an unprecedented $3 billion. During 1931 Gerard Swope of General Electric published a corporate plan for industrial recovery. The Swope Plan reinforced twenties trade association activity with legal sanction. Under federal supervision, trade associations would be immune from antitrust laws and empowered to decide on production, prices, investments, and "unfair" practices. Modified versions of the Swope Plan, supported by the Chamber of Commerce and the National Association of Manufacturers, focused on costly price competition and overproduction among industrialists. But Hoover rejected the Swope Plan's revival

of wartime planning, labeling it "the most gigantic proposal of monopoly ever made in history."

Instead, the president reluctantly supported the creation of a new federal agency in 1932. Modeled on the War Finance Corporation and established in cooperation with the banking community, the Reconstruction Finance Corporation was empowered to make loans to financial institutions, insurance companies, and railroads in order to revitalize the economy. Congress capitalized the RFC at $500 million and authorized it to loan three times that amount. By approving the RFC, Hoover abandoned laissez faire in relation to the business cycle, establishing the convention that prosperity and depression could be publicly controlled by government action. The Emergency Relief and Construction Act of July 1932 nearly doubled RFC capital. The nation's first federal relief legislation, it authorized $300 million in loans to the states for poor relief and public works. The RFC loaned $3 billion in eighteen months, four-fifths to railroads and insurance companies. But by the end of 1932, the agency had advanced only 10 percent of its authorized relief funds to the states, while three times that amount had been forwarded to the Chicago bank headed by RFC chairman Charles G. Dawes.

Hoover's emphasis on public works, voluntary charity, and local agencies proved inadequate in dealing with the effects of massive unemployment. Four New York City hospitals reported ninety-five deaths from starvation in 1931. During the same year 200,000 New York apartment dwellers were evicted for rent delinquency. Meanwhile, the depressed auto industry brought a 41 percent unemployment rate to Detroit by early 1933, as the city de-

Unemployed veterans formed the Bonus Army and spent the summer of 1932 camped out near Washington, D.C. They were finally evicted from their camping place at Anacostia Flats by the army under the personal command of General Douglas MacArthur. Overreaction by the government in this incident helped to undermine President Hoover's authority throughout the nation. (Historical Pictures Service, Inc., Chicago)

faulted its municipal bonds and arbitrarily dropped one-third of its relief families off public assistance. Breadlines and soup kitchens run by municipal agencies or private charities could be found in every major city, but more than one hundred cities had no resources for cash relief. Instead, unemployed workers bought boxes of apples on credit and sold them on street corners for a nickel each. Jobless migrants found empty lots on the edges of industrial centers where they built primitive shelters from packing crates and old metal. Warming themselves before fires of rubbish made in grease drums, the inhabitants of these new American towns christened them "Hoovervilles."

Two million men and boys (and some disguised women) roamed the country in search of jobs or sustenance in the early thirties.

As local resources were exhausted by 1931, twenty-five states established relief programs for the unemployed. Aid for the destitute was "not a matter of charity," preached New York's Governor Franklin D. Roosevelt, but a "matter of social duty," since social and economic factors, not individual character, were responsible for mushrooming unemployment. But Hoover clung to traditional concepts of Anglo-Protestant personal accountability and claimed that federal assistance would invite government mastery and bureaucratic control by distant institutions, as well as bankruptcy of the treasury. "It is not the function of government to relieve individuals of their responsibilities to their neighbors, or to relieve private institutions of their responsibilities to the public," Hoover explained. "You cannot extend the mastery of the government over the daily working life of a people without at the same time making it the master of the people's souls and thoughts."

Hoover considered centralized bureaucracy a "disastrous course" and hoped Americans could maintain the traditions of interclass harmony, voluntarism, and local control that had served so well in the new era. But it was hard for Americans to understand how a president could approve a $45 million appropriation to feed the livestock of Arkansas farmers late in 1930 but oppose an additional $25 million to feed starving Arkansas farm families. Although Hoover expanded public works, approved a Home Loan Act to establish discount banks for emergency credit, and increased the funding of federal land banks, he consistently opposed all schemes for direct federal relief payments. Furthermore, the Hawley-Smoot Tariff of 1930 and the domestic tax increase of 1932 provided the highest external and internal taxes in American history. Herbert Hoover never ceased to believe in the regenerative qualities of the American economy, often blaming the Depression on undeniable instabilities in postwar Europe. But he overestimated the strength of the American economy and underrated the mysterious forces producing contraction. The more the president attempted to reassure Americans that economic recovery was imminent, the more he sacrificed his personal credibility.

Hoover's predicament could be seen in his handling of protesting veterans. Congressional Democrats overrode a presidential veto in 1931 to authorize that half the compensation due

veterans of World War One be paid out in veteran loans. As the economic crisis persisted, however, Democratic congressional leaders proposed that the entire bonus be paid in cash. In a campaign to win congressional approval for full payment of the bonus, veterans from all over the nation descended on the capital during the summer of 1932. By July the Bonus Expeditionary Force had swelled to an estimated seventeen thousand, occupied some abandoned government buildings near the Capitol, and camped out at Anacostia Flats. When the Senate defeated the House bonus bill, the government provided funds to the veterans to return home. But two thousand demonstrators remained in Washington. When local police tried to evict them from government property, rioting erupted.

Hoover responded by summoning federal troops to remove the veterans. Ignoring a presidential order to move cautiously, commanding officer Douglas MacArthur used rough methods to break up the Anacostia camp. Newspaper accounts described bayonet-drawn troops chasing unarmed men, women, and children across the flats while "Hooverville" shacks burned to the ground. Although Hoover had tried to restrain MacArthur, the responsibility for the debacle fell on the president. By election time in 1932, Hoover appeared to be a frightened man who locked the White House doors against the American people and who had lost touch with the catastrophic effects of the Depression on the lives of ordinary people.

ROOSEVELT AND THE NEW DEAL

Sensing victory at the polls, the Democrats successfully united for the 1932 election. The party platform appealed to urban ethnics by calling for repeal of Prohibition and active government help for the unemployed. But the Democrats also satisfied rural conservatives by demanding a 25 percent cut in federal spending. In the attempt to avoid the rural-urban division of the twenties, the party turned to a Wilsonian progressive. Franklin Delano Roosevelt's family were descendants of seventeenth-century landed patricians, but Roosevelt's record as governor of New York State tied him to urban social reformers and the ethnic vote. Governor Roosevelt had sponsored unemployment relief, labor and banking reform, aid to farmers, state hydroelectric power, and conservation measures. The Democratic nominee spoke eloquently of "the forgotten man at the bottom of the economic pyramid" and the need for "bold persistent experimentation." Taking pride in the fact that he was breaking tradition, Roosevelt flew to Chicago to accept personally the convention's nomination. There he pledged himself to "a new deal for the American people."

Always indirect about his political philosophy, Roosevelt described himself as "a Christian and a Democrat." But he did tell businesspeople that his administration would address "the problems of underconsumption, of adjusting production to consumption, of distributing wealth and products more equitably, of adapting existing economic organizations to the service of the people." Roosevelt never presented a clear program to end the Depression, but voters and many business leaders seemed willing to try the Democrats as an alternative to Hoover's impotence. A contributor to a small-town Texas newspaper paraphrased the Twenty-third Psalm to sum up the nation's plight during the summer of 1932: "Depression is my shepherd; I am in want," he wrote. "He maketh me to lie down on park benches; He leadeth me beside still factories.... Surely unemployment and poverty will follow me all the days of the Republican administration; and I shall dwell in a mortgaged house forever."

Republicans had lost eight seats in the Senate and their House majority in the congressional elections of 1930. Now, Hoover warned that should Democrats take the presidency, "the grass will grow in streets of a hundred cities, a thousand towns; the weeds will overrun the fields of millions of farms." But Hoover appeared to be an aloof administrator; Roosevelt, eager to govern. To demonstrate the Progressive belief that the free enterprise system needed overall planning by professionals who could take the problems of the entire economy into account, Roosevelt took on a campaign "brains trust" of experts. They included the lawyer Adolf Berle, Jr., the social work administrator Harry Hopkins, the agricultural economist Rexford Tugwell, and the political consultant Raymond Moley.

Less rebellious than drifting, Americans seemed to respond to Roosevelt's warmth, assertiveness, and sense of experiment. The Democratic nominee promised relief for the unemployed and an energetic approach to economic recovery. When the votes were tabulated, Roosevelt and his running mate John Garner amassed 22.8 million votes to 15.7 million for Hoover and Curtis. The Republicans carried only six states for a total of fifty-nine votes in the electoral college. In swamping Hoover, Roosevelt carried the traditional Democratic South and continued Al Smith's success among urban ethnics in the North.

As Franklin Delano Roosevelt took office in March 1933, the economy sank to its lowest point. Between 1930 and the beginning of the Roosevelt presidency, over five thousand banks with total deposits of $3.4 billion had temporarily or permanently closed. By Inauguration Day twenty-one states had either declared banking moratoriums or drafted special regulations for banks. Organized American finance ceased to function on March 3, 1933, when Federal Deposit banks in New York and Chicago suspended payments. It was clear that the American people no longer had confidence in the banking system. People rushed to withdraw deposits, while corporations and wealthy Americans converted money into gold and hoarded currency.

"This is a day of national consecration," Roosevelt stated in his sober inaugural address. Bidding for the confidence of the American people, the new president assured the country that "the only thing we have to fear is fear itself — nameless, unreasoning, unjustified terror which paralyzes needed efforts to convert retreat into advance." "The money changers have fled from their high seats in the temple of our civilization," he intoned. Roosevelt promised that he would not hesitate to ask for "broad executive power to wage war against the emergency, as great as the power that would be given to me if we were in fact invaded by a foreign foe."

Two days later the president declared a national "bank holiday," closing the banks and halting withdrawal of gold. He also summoned a special session of Congress in an atmosphere of wartime crisis. After thirty-eight minutes of debate, without having seen the bill in question, Congress unanimously passed the Emergency Banking Act. The law gave the president emergency powers to regulate transactions in credit, currency, gold, silver, and foreign exchange. The Treasury Department was to supervise a reorganization of the country's banks, as federal and state banks in the Federal Reserve system reopened under government li-

cense. Loans from the Reconstruction Finance Corporation and new Federal Reserve notes would facilitate the reopening of worthy banks. The president later won the power to devalue the gold dollar, coin silver, and inflate the currency, since Roosevelt hoped to increase prices by buying gold instead of printing more money.

Some businesspeople had expected nationalization of the banks. But Roosevelt even rejected as too radical a proposal by the Morgan interests that federal funds be deposited in state banks experiencing runs. A few days later, sixty million people listened to the president's first "fireside chat" over radio. Roosevelt assured the nation that it was now safe to return savings to the banks. Since the president had said the banks were safe and people believed him, deposits began to exceed withdrawals. One of the greatest gambles in presidential history proved to be a spectacular success. "Capitalism was saved in eight days," Raymond Moley recalled.

100 DAYS

The Banking Act of 1933 began a period of intense legislative accomplishment in the first "100 days" of the New Deal. At stake was government management of the social order, environment, and market relations. The economy was out of balance, said Roosevelt, and defects in the private market system had to be remedied through government action. Assuming unprecedented presidential powers, Roosevelt took the United States off the gold standard during 1933, thereby fulfilling the old Populist demand for inflation. By 1934 the value of the dollar had depreciated 40 percent, a key to the restoration of higher selling prices desperately sought by farmers and industrialists.

MAP 8.1   THE ELECTION OF 1932

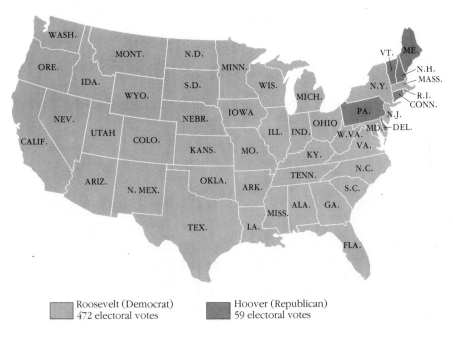

Roosevelt (Democrat)
472 electoral votes

Hoover (Republican)
59 electoral votes

Management of the economy also required stabilization of banking and the stock exchanges, two industries that many Americans blamed for the Depression. The Securities Act of 1933 provided that detailed information concerning stocks be filed with the Federal Trade Commission and that company directors be liable for misrepresentation, fraud, or concealing information. Congress created the Securities and Exchange Commission (SEC) in 1934 to regulate and license stock exchanges. In order to separate the risky investment securities business from commercial banking, Roosevelt signed the Glass-Steagall Act of 1933. The law also created federal insurance on deposits up to $2,500, a reaction against $9 million in personal savings wiped out in three years following the Crash.

A Banking Act of 1935 allowed the Federal Reserve Board to set reserve requirements and review the interest rates of member banks. Like Wilson's Federal Reserve system, Roosevelt's banking reform was supported by Wall Street leaders of the financial community. Stung by the scandals of 1932, leading bankers favored federal intervention to end marginal dealerships in stocks. Federal regulation of securities had been endorsed by the Investment Bank Association since World War One.

Angry farmers had climaxed a half century of agitation by announcing a national farm strike for May 1933. But Congress responded one day before the strike with the Agricultural Adjustment Act. The law assured government price supports or "parity" for basic commodities such as wheat, corn, cotton, tobacco, rice, and hogs. Parity meant that farm prices would bear the same ratio to nonfarm prices that they had between 1909 and 1914. In return for agreements by individual farmers to limit acreage under cultivation, the Agricultural Adjustment Administration (AAA) awarded subsidies financed by a "processing tax" on marketed produce. The idea was to raise farm prices by cutting production to market requirements. "Kill every third pig or plow every third row under," the AAA advised. Under New Deal farm policy, ten million acres of cotton were "plowed under," and six million light hogs slaughtered. By 1935 the price of wheat, corn, and cotton had doubled and farm income was up 53 percent, although consolidation by agribusiness meant that New Deal benefits went to an increasingly smaller number of farmers.

Despite the trend toward agricultural consolidation, New Deal farm policy did attempt to minimize the devastating foreclosures of farm mortgages. A Farm Credit Administration (FCA) provided refinancing for one-fifth of all farm mortgages in the nation. Farm bankruptcy laws in 1934 and 1935 provided for repurchase of defunct farms by owners at low interest. By involving the federal government in the stability of agriculture, the Roosevelt administration eased agrarian discontent, even though large producers benefited most from New Deal encouragement of underproduction.

Concerned with minimal levels of security for frightened middle-class Americans, Congress and the administration also acted to save home mortgages. The Home Owners Loan Corporation (HOLC) issued government bonds to refinance first mortgages. In the attempt to stabilize residential real estate values and support the principle of individual home ownership, HOLC refinanced over one million

homes. But unemployed home owners did not qualify. As a result, HOLC foreclosed 100,000 mortgages during the recession of 1937–1938.

Hoover had lost the presidency because of his failure to provide federal relief for unemployed Americans. But Roosevelt declared that "those suffering hardship from no fault of their own have a right to call upon the government for aid, and a government worthy of its name must make fitting response." The Federal Emergency Relief Administration (FERA) of 1933 inaugurated the era of direct federal aid to the unemployed and destitute. FERA spent $4 billion in cash home relief and emergency work programs and also provided relief payments and rehabilitation loans to one million farm families. Altogether, the massive FERA bureaucracy touched the lives of approximately twenty million Americans.

By June 1933 the Roosevelt administration realized that unemployment relief was not sufficient to stimulate industrial recovery. Prodded by Congress, the president embraced methods of industrial rationalization embodied by the War Industries Board, twenties trade associations, and the 1931 Swope Plan. The National Recovery Administration (NRA) freed corporations from antitrust laws and supervised enforcement of self-regulating industrial codes. Industrywide agreements, sanctioned by government oversight, allowed competing corporations to curtail production, raise prices, regulate business practices, set minimum wages and maximum working hours, and ban child labor. Section 7(a) of the National Industrial Recovery Act compelled participating industrialists to accept collective bargaining rights for workers, a concession to urban liberals and union supporters represented by New York's Senator Robert F. Wagner. Roosevelt soon appointed Wagner to head a National Labor

Board to work out disagreements between management and labor. Although its provisions were difficult to enforce, Section 7(a) gave increasing prestige to the growing Depression union movement and allowed organizers to convince workers that the president and Congress supported unionization.

The Roosevelt administration used the NRA to mount a nationwide campaign in support of the New Deal. Under the enthusiastic leadership of General Hugh Johnson, the NRA resorted to wartime techniques of public relations to "mobilize" Americans for industrial recovery and national unity. In New York City 750,000 people participated in a massive NRA parade of solidarity. Johnson employed brass bands, movie entertainers, and national radio hookups to win mass support for code provisions. Businesses that signed code agreements were awarded blue eagle insignias for display. "We Do Our Part," NRA posters proclaimed. The agency approved 576 separate industrial codes that affected twenty-two million workers. As a result, more than half the nation's industrial work force had won the forty-hour week by 1935.

Roosevelt's 100-day program for economic recovery accelerated Hoover's reliance on public works. The Public Works Administration (PWA) spent $3.3 billion in the first months of the New Deal and nearly doubled that figure by 1935. New Dealers reasoned that government construction programs would compensate for the loss of foreign markets caused by NRA price hikes in manufacturing. Roosevelt had personally conceived an innovative blend of public works, conservation, and unemployment relief during the election campaign. The Civilian Conservation Corps (CCC) hired young men between eighteen and twenty-five in reforesting, road construction, flood control,

land reclamation, range improvement, and soil erosion programs. Organized along military lines, the CCC provided unemployed youth a mixture of discipline, self-respect, and experience in the outdoors. New Dealers also hoped to improve the physical fitness of potential soldiers and to stimulate a public commitment to national service. By 1942, 2.5 million young men had served in the Civilian Conservation Corps.

New Deal interest in long-range economic and ecological planning resulted in congressional approval of a Tennessee Valley Authority (TVA), a public power project embracing a seven-state river basin of forty thousand square miles. TVA's nine government dams produced cheap power for fertilizer and explosives factories and created reservoirs for flood control. TVA planners also promoted regional soil conservation and reforestation. Bitterly opposed by private utility firms through most of the thirties, TVA showed that the Progressive dream of government electric power could stimulate private investment, agricultural development, and market consumption. While thousands of back-country residents became electrical appliance consumers for the first time, TVA provided a yardstick for setting reasonable and fair public utility rates. Government film documentaries such as *The River* (1938) also taught audiences the importance of New Deal programs for soil conservation, reforestation, and electrical power.

Roosevelt's interest in conservation planning prompted him to appoint a Mississippi Valley Committee in 1933. The panel's report made sweeping recommendations for further programs in reforestation, flood and soil erosion control, dams, and hydroelectric power. While some of these suggestions were incorporated in subsequent New Deal legislation, administration conservationists concentrated on the economic potential of natural resources. Roosevelt opposed federal standards for water pollution because of the economic uses of rivers and the high costs of depolluting them. New Dealers continued to place a greater priority on business recovery than on ecological planning. And the president's dream of creating six more TVAs in the great river valleys of the nation never won congressional approval.

NEW DEAL CRITICS

The first 100 days of the New Deal galvanized the nation. Alphabet agencies such as AAA, NRA, TVA, CCC, PWA, FERA, HOLC, and FCA intervened directly in the lives of millions of people bewildered by the economic collapse. Walter Lippmann, no early admirer of Roosevelt, recalled the bleak days of February 1933 when the nation seemed to be composed "of disorderly, panic-stricken mobs and factions." In the 100 days from March to June, Lippmann wrote, "we became again an organized nation, confident of our power to provide for our own security and control our own destiny." Roosevelt had also appealed to Democratic budget balancers by slicing $400 million from veteran payments and cutting the pay of federal employees by as much as 15 percent. Voters responded by providing the Democrats with nine more senators and nine more congressmen during the 1934 elections.

Despite Roosevelt's attempt to bring business, labor, and government together in a corporate society, many Americans remained suspicious of New Deal intentions. Large corporations used the Depression to reduce debts and increase liquid capital, while companies with assets under $100,000 lost money during the

decade. By 1937 six giant corporations (General Motors, American Telephone, Standard Oil of New Jersey, U.S. Steel, DuPont, and General Electric) made nearly one-quarter of the profit earned by the one thousand largest businesses in the United States. Even though car and truck sales plummeted 75 percent in the first years of the collapse, General Motors maintained prices and emerged the leader of the auto industry. Luxury Cadillac sales actually rose in the 1930s.

While industrial giants were consolidating their dominance over small competitors, national chain stores continued to replace small shops and groceries. Lower prices, packaged products, and suburban parking gave the chains nearly 22 percent of all retail business by the end of the decade. But the Depression encouraged grassroots opposition from local interests who argued that chain stores destroyed personal initiative and drained profits from the community. Defenders of small business connected the chains to Wall Street dominance, low wages, and lessening local opportunity. Huey Long's populist administration in Louisiana succeeded in levying prohibitive taxes on chain stores in 1934. By 1939 twenty-seven states had enacted special regulation of the chains.

Discomfort with big government's cooperation with large producers brought attacks from traditional opponents of corporate progressivism, both left and right. At issue were the industrial and agricultural recovery programs of the NRA and AAA. Conservative Democrats such as twenties presidential contenders Al Smith and John W. Davis joined those industrialists and financiers who resented government interference in business to form the Liberty League in 1934. Echoing Herbert Hoover's criticism of federal bureaucracy, the league bitterly attacked New Deal intervention in the marketplace as an unconstitutional departure from American traditions of personal initiative. Meanwhile, intellectuals in the growing Communist party denounced NRA cooperation with business and labeled Roosevelt a "social fascist." The Socialist party, which gathered 885,000 votes for presidential candidate Norman Thomas in 1932, concentrated its attack on AAA neglect of tenants and sharecroppers. The Socialists accurately pointed out that agricultural corporations and landlords qualified for government subsidies by removing tenants and sharecroppers, thereby cutting down on cultivated acreage. As large agricultural producers invested government checks in machinery and tractors, 15 to 20 percent of sharecroppers lost their livelihood by 1936. Many Americans could not understand why AAA was killing hogs and taking food out of production while millions of people went hungry and were forced off the land.

Attacks on the NRA were more numerous. Like the New Deal's agricultural programs, industrial recovery was based on the assumption that the economy was overproducing. Roosevelt's solution was to limit production and raise prices through industrial self-government, conceding to labor the right to organize and promises of a minimum wage. In highly competitive industries such as trucking, garments, and coal, leading corporations saw NRA regulation as a way of preventing price cuts and reckless competition. But in slump-ridden industries such as cotton and lumber, prices declined anyway. Small operators also found it hard to absorb the increased wage rates negotiated by code authorities.

Noncorporate progressives such as Senator Borah of Idaho objected that the NRA sanctioned a cartel structure for the American economy, that big interests dominated code making, and that labor and consumer representatives seldom had voting rights on code authorities. Furthermore, the vast number of codes, which confused procedures, and the reluctance of the administration to antagonize business leaders prevented strict enforcement. Corporations often evaded the labor provisions of industrial codes by establishing company unions or refusing to recognize independent unions as collective bargaining agents. When the Roosevelt administration responded to labor denunciations by tightening codes in 1935, business turned against the NRA, and a bitter feud between the president and the corporate community ensued.

While business, labor, radicals, and anticorporate progressives all attacked the New Deal from different directions, regional leaders began to challenge Roosevelt corporatism from the grassroots. In Minnesota, Farm-Labor Governor Floyd Olson intimidated the state legislature into passing relief for farmers facing foreclosure. If capitalism could not prevent a recurrence of the Depression, Olson vowed, "I hope the present system of government goes right down to hell." Socialist Upton Sinclair, a former Progressive muckraker, won an upset victory in the California gubernatorial primary in 1934, but Roosevelt failed to support his fellow Democrat's "End Poverty in California" campaign. When the Hollywood movie industry donated propaganda newsreels that discredited Sinclair's socialist aspirations, the candidate lost the election to the relief of the White House.

Despite Sinclair's failure, California's large retired population saw welfare for the aged as a major issue that the New Deal was ignoring. Dr. Francis E. Townsend responded by proposing an old-age revolving pension that would

Huey Pierce Long

1893-1935

Louisiana's Huey Long was the New Deal critic Democratic strategists feared the most. Long had the ability to ridicule the Roosevelt bureaucracy from "left" and "right" simultaneously, pitching his sarcasm in the earthy taunts of southern folk humor. At the height of his power, the Kingfish spoke for a nationwide organization of nearly seven million people and threatened to prevent Roosevelt's re-election in 1936.

Long came out of the piny uplands of northern Louisiana, an area of pious Baptists with a long tradition of populism. At the age of twenty-five, Long was elected state public service commissioner and turned the body into an effective regulatory agency by lowering streetcar and telephone rates and disciplining Standard Oil. Benefiting from resentment toward the oil colossus, Long barely missed the governorship in 1924. Four years later, with the Ku Klux Klan no longer splitting the populist vote, Long tried again and won.

Governor Long spent millions on highways and hospitals, provided free textbooks for schools, and created night classes for poor whites and blacks. To finance these reforms, he used deficit spending and levied heavy taxes on the oil refineries. Meanwhile, Long also established an awesome patronage machine. Charged with unauthorized use of state funds, he was impeached by the state House of Representatives in 1929, but the Senate failed to convict. Long claimed Standard Oil was persecuting him and tightened control over the state. By 1934 he had prevailed on the legislature to abolish local government and taken personal control of police and teaching appointments, the militia, courts, election agencies, and tax-assessing bodies.

When he came to Washington as a senator in 1932, Long said he intended to cut the great American fortunes down to "frying size." An *early supporter of Roosevelt, he turned bitterly against the NRA and called the president "a liar and a faker." Like Borah of Idaho, Long believed that the recovery agency only helped large producers to organize a controlled market. He pointed out that AAA crop reductions helped rich landlords force black tenants off the land, and attacked farm corporations as the source of agricultural impoverishment. He praised Roosevelt's "death sentence" for public utilities, but complained "we might as well try to regulate a rattlesnake."*

For Long, the primary challenge was redistribution of wealth. His "Share Our Wealth" program intended to use tax reform and a guaranteed income to meet it. He hoped to bring the issue of wealth distribution to the people in a national presidential campaign. But just a month after he announced his candidacy in August 1935, the Kingfish was shot down in Baton Rouge. Critics may have scoffed at his economic reasoning and condemned his dictatorial methods, but Long was a hero to poor southerners and those who felt left out of the New Deal.

grant $200 a month to every American over sixty, as long as the recipient retired from work and spent the entire monthly sum. The Townsend Plan was to be financed by a 2 percent tax on business transactions, but its creator argued that the program would stimulate spending and end joblessness by cutting the labor force. In an evangelical spirit rooted in the Protestant lower middle class, Townsend promised to put young people to work and stop them from spending time in the pursuit of sex and liquor. Later described as the father of social security, he claimed his movement embraced people "who believe in the Bible, believe in God, cheer when the flag passes by — the Bible Belt solid Americans." Supporters of the Townsend Plan gathered ten to twenty million signatures on nationwide petitions and impelled Roosevelt advisors to consider social security legislation.

A more direct attack on the New Deal came from Father Charles C. Coughlin, a Michigan Roman Catholic with a national radio audience of thirty to forty-five million. An early supporter of Roosevelt, Coughlin began to criticize alleged New Deal connections to both finance capital and communism. Forming the National Union for Social Justice in 1934, Coughlin attracted lower-middle-class support among ethnic Catholics in the urban Northeast and Midwest. His radio commentary denounced conspiratorial bankers and trade unionists while extolling the dignity of working people and small businesspeople. Coughlin's picture of a future society of class harmony without bankers was a vague one, but his massive radio audience attested to widespread discontent with the elitism of New Deal liberalism.

The most effective opponent of the New Deal was Louisiana's Huey Long, the "Kingfish." Arriving in the United States Senate in 1932, the Kingfish inaugurated a "Share Our

Wealth" proposal two years later. Based on the belief that maldistribution of wealth was the key issue before the nation, Long called for the liquidation of all personal fortunes over $5 million through a capital tax. He also planned to use the income tax to prohibit a family from earning more than $1 million a year. Long promised every American family a guaranteed $2,000–$3,000 annual income, enough for a $5,000 homestead, a car, and a radio. Pensions would be distributed to the elderly, and "worthy youth" would receive free college education. Long pledged that a massive public works program would combine with a federal minimum wage and a thirty-hour week to bolster purchasing power. By 1935 twenty-seven thousand Share Our Wealth clubs had sprouted across the country, with a mailing list allegedly surpassing seven million. Long won national support with his folksy ridicule of corporate interests and the urbanity of upper-middle-class New Deal administrators. Calling "Every Man a King," he planned to run for president in 1936. Democratic party tacticians feared Long might take three or four million votes from Roosevelt on an independent ticket. But Long's presidential ambitions were cut down when he was assassinated in September 1935, the apparent result of the Kingfish's extramarital dalliances. With his death, Long supporters joined followers of Coughlin and some Townsendites to form the National Union Party.

ROOSEVELT MILITANCY

By 1935 Roosevelt prepared to respond to the discontent of lower-middle-class Americans. To step up unemployment relief, the president created the Works Progress Administration

(WPA). Under the leadership of Harry Hopkins, an urban social worker, the WPA replaced direct cash relief with a massive government job program. New Deal administrators reasoned that work gave respectability to relief and strengthened individual morale through self-help. Careful not to interfere with private business, the WPA required means tests and investigations to determine eligibility, paid below the prevailing wage, and excluded jobs in manufacturing, merchandising, or marketing. Although the federal government supplied the funds, WPA projects were administered by state and city governments, a response to critics who argued that the New Deal provided federal bureaucracy with too much power.

The WPA spent $10.5 billion in its eight-year lifetime, employing 8.5 million people. By 1936 one-third of all jobless Americans worked for a WPA project. Construction programs involved public buildings and post offices, bridges, airports, storm and water sewers, and 664,000 miles of roads. Through the Federal Theater Project, the Federal Writers Project, and the Federal Artists Project, the government moved into its first sponsorship of the arts. The WPA also included a National Youth Administration to provide jobs and educational subsidies to young people and students.

By the time the WPA moved into action, the NRA was under attack by both businesspeople and union leaders. But the administration was stunned when the Supreme Court unanimously ruled in 1935 that the National Industrial Recovery Act (NIRA) was unconstitutional. Although the Court had expanded use of the Constitution's commerce clause during the twenties, it was not prepared to accept the New Deal's fusion of presidential and corporate power. The Court maintained that the NIRA constituted an invalid transfer of legislative power from Congress to the president and that the attempt to regulate industry within states involved an improper use of the interstate commerce power. Infuriated, Roosevelt claimed that "we have been relegated to a horse and buggy definition of interstate commerce." Eleven months later the court invalidated the Agricultural Adjustment Act. The AAA processing tax, the Court ruled, was part of a system to regulate agricultural production in an artificial manner not within the "welfare" clause of the Constitution.

Invalidation of NIRA increased momentum toward comprehensive labor relations legislation. As a progressive who wished to replace loyalty to economic class with dedication to the national interest, Roosevelt was more concerned about wages and hours than union representation. But widespread strike activity during 1934 had underlined the need for orderly processes of collective bargaining. When it became clear that a labor rights bill introduced by Senator Wagner would pass the Democratic Senate, Roosevelt made it "must" legislation and signed the National Labor Relations Act in 1935. Considered the Magna Charta of organized labor, the Wagner Act upheld the right of workers in interstate commerce to join unions and bargain collectively through their own representatives. Collective bargaining was binding on employers, who were forbidden to impede it in any way or to fire workers for union activity. The law stipulated that the company union, the "yellow dog" contract, employer blacklists, and labor spies were illegal. A National Labor Relations Board would supervise elections to determine which collective bargaining units workers preferred. The board also would investigate "unfair" employer practices and issue cease and desist orders if necessary.

The Wagner Act did not apply to workers in agriculture, domestic service, public employment, or intrastate commerce. But it did initiate a historic shift in the relations between management and labor, making the federal government an active force in the recognition of union representation. Although union leadership never assumed a major role in corporate planning, the National Labor Relations Board subjected arbitrary firings to review and gave labor organizations an institutional legitimacy they had sought since the temporary triumphs of World War One.

To satisfy pervasive demands for economic security and to provide for long-run stimulation of purchasing power among older Americans and others, Roosevelt decided to push for social security legislation in mid-1935. The private charity system developed by Anglo-Protestant elites in the nineteenth century had been designed for small cities with homogeneous populations and workers employed in shops where owners had a sense of personal responsibility. Accordingly, the Progressive party platform of 1912 had acknowledged the inapplicability of private charity to a heterogeneous and corporation-dominated society by calling for a federal system of unemployment insurance and old-age pensions. But plans for social and health insurance met hostility during World War One because Americans associated Germany's welfare state with Prussian collectivism. Throughout the 1920s older Americans in organizations such as the Fraternal Order of Eagles and the American Association for Old Age Security succeeded in enacting pension laws in twenty-nine states. Abraham Epstein's *The Challenge of the Aged* (1928) brilliantly portrayed the connection between old age and dependency in a society in which death rates were declining. By 1930 nearly six million Americans were over sixty-five years of age. Since priorities on efficiency and youth relegated older people to marginal status, old age had become a long-term condition for which savings were rarely adequate. By the mid-thirties, both social reformers and the popular Townsend movement were challenging the Roosevelt administration to do something about old-age dependency.

The Social Security Act of 1935 marked the inauguration of the American welfare state. The law provided those over sixty-five with monthly federal pensions from a self-supporting Social Security Administration. Unlike social welfare plans in other industrial nations, the American system of old-age insurance was contributory, financed by income-tax deductions on employees and payroll taxes on employers. "We put those payroll contributions there so as to give the contributors a legal, moral, and political right to collect their pensions and their unemployment benefits," Roosevelt explained in response to critics. "With those taxes in there, no damn politician can ever scrap my social security program." To meet other problems of dependency, the Social Security Act established federal programs of Aid to Dependent Children, vocational training to the physically disabled, and assistance to homeless and neglected children. Roosevelt's Committee on Economic Security had recommended national health insurance as well, but the proposal was eliminated under pressure from the medical profession and by fears of congressional resistance. Instead, the social security law promoted public health services and provided medical funds for mothers and children in economically distressed areas. Social security also offered federal aid for crippled children.

Social workers argued that New Deal work relief programs failed to complement the vocational aspirations of the unemployed and did not eliminate the stigma of charity. Means tests often delayed assistance until the recipient was destitute. As a result, the Social Security Act provided the nation's first system of unemployment insurance, funded by federal payroll taxes on employers but administered by the states. Only wage and salary workers in commerce and industry were included in the original coverage, but subsequent amendments brought in farmworkers, self-employed farmers, domestic servants, and employees of nonprofit organizations. Although unemployment compensation violated traditional notions of individual responsibility, most Depression-conscious Americans were willing to accept government responsibility for minimal standards of social welfare.

As Roosevelt prepared to sign the Wagner Act and social security legislation, he also began to face the questions Huey Long had raised about redistribution of power and wealth. Earlier in 1935, a presidential order had created a Rural Electrification Administration (REA) to extend electricity to isolated areas not served by private utilities. But in the summer of 1935, Congress passed a comprehensive Public Utility Holding Company Act. The new law set up a three-pronged supervision of the electric and gas industry. A new agency, the Federal Power Commission (FPC), would regulate interstate electric rates and business practices, while the Federal Trade Commission would do the same for gas. The law also gave the Securities and Exchange Commission authority over holding companies that controlled gas and electric transmission. By 1935 the twelve largest utility holding companies controlled almost half the power produced in the United States. Roosevelt's legislation empowered the SEC to obtain information on the corporate structure of all American holding companies. A "death sentence" clause set a term of five years in which each company had to demonstrate that its services were localized and efficient. If no such demonstration were made, the law gave the SEC power to dissolve the company concerned. By threatening dissolution of a group of private corporations, the Public Utility Holding Act ranked as one of the more radical laws to be signed by an American president.

Roosevelt also flirted with a radical bill to redistribute income, commenting that American tax laws had "done little to prevent an unjust concentration of wealth and economic power." But when congressional committees began to weaken the president's wealth tax, Roosevelt took no action to save it. What emerged was not a tax law that distributed income, but a minor revenue-raising bill. The proposed inheritance tax was eliminated, and a greater number of loopholes offset higher tax rates for millionaires.

The New Deal never effectively fought economic concentration, although Roosevelt asked Congress in 1938 to participate in an investigation of monopoly practices. The Temporary National Economic Committee (TNEC) Report found monopoly techniques strengthened in the Depression, and called for antitrust prosecution to decentralize corporate resources and activity. Beginning in 1938, Assistant Attorney General Thurman Arnold initiated a flurry of individual antitrust suits against giants such as General Electric and the Aluminum Company of America, but Arnold made no effort to alter the basic structure of industry, and defense mobilization quickly took the heart out of his crusade. Besides, the Miller-Tydings Enabling Act of 1937 amended the antitrust laws to legalize contracts that maintained the prices of nationally advertised brand names.

THE LANDSLIDE OF '36

Between 1935 and 1936, Roosevelt's pronouncements appeared increasingly hostile to business. The business community, in turn, seemed to view the 1935 reforms as a departure from an earlier move to corporatism. Instead of a program that united labor and management in the search for order and profits, corporation leaders believed Roosevelt was mobilizing Americans on the basis of social class. Roosevelt, however, saw his strategy as conservative. "I am fighting Communism, Huey Longism, Coughlinism, Townsendism," he explained during the 1936 electoral campaign. "I want to save our system, the capitalist system." Roosevelt ignored the Democratic party, presenting himself as "a New Deal liberal fighting not for party success but for a cause," and singled out "economic royalists" who hid behind a professed defense of the nation's institutions to protect their own power.

The "true conservative," Roosevelt told the nation in his first campaign speech in Syracuse, "seeks to protect the system of private property and free enterprise by correcting such injustices and inequities as arise from it." The president repeatedly explained that government had a "responsibility to save business, to save the American system of private enterprise and economic democracy." If necessary, he warned, the administration would act "to protect the commerce of America from the selfish forces which ruined it." Roosevelt, whose legs were paralyzed from a polio attack in the early 1920s, expressed wonder that some big business leaders had so fully recovered from the Depression that they felt "well enough to throw their crutches at the doctor." The forces of "organized money," Roosevelt declared, "are unanimous in their hate for me—and I welcome their hatred."

Charging that regulated monopoly had replaced free enterprise under Roosevelt, Republicans selected Governor Alfred Landon of Kansas as their presidential nominee and another midwesterner, Frank Knox of Illinois, as his running mate. The party platform argued that the New Deal was built on unconstitutional laws, that relief should be returned to nonpolitical local agencies, and that the budget should be balanced. Conservative Democrats in the Liberty League supported the Landon candidacy, while only one-third of the nation's major newspapers endorsed the president. But the Republican press seriously exaggerated discontent with the New Deal when the conservative *Literary Digest* predicted a Landon victory. The actual vote gave every state to the president except Maine and Vermont, and an overwhelming popular vote of 27.7 million to 16.6 million. The Roosevelt landslide also brought awesome Democratic majorities in both houses of Congress. The Union party of Coughlin, Townsend, and Gerald L. K. Smith, nervously watched by administration strategists, attracted less than 2 percent of the popular vote.

Despite vocal opposition to the New Deal, most Americans found confidence in Roosevelt's style. By 1936 the president had forged an effective coalition that tied farmers and southerners to the urban vote of union workers, blacks, white ethnics, and middle-class liberals. Black Americans, traditionally affiliated with the Republican party, began their long association with the Democrats in 1936, despite the absence of any civil rights activity in the Roosevelt administration. Roosevelt's crusade against the monopolies and those business interests who defied government regulation appealed to Americans who believed the New Deal was restoring national prosperity. The president's

inaugural address pointed to "tens of millions ...who at this moment are denied the greater part of what the very lowest standards of today call the necessities of life.... I see one-third a nation ill-housed, ill-clad, ill-nourished." Roosevelt promised to eliminate poverty and make every American the subject of the government's concern.

REFORM, RECESSION, AND RETREAT

Roosevelt hoped to use his second term to extend New Deal reforms to sharecroppers, tenants, and industrial workers. An executive order in 1935 had created the Resettlement Administration (RA), which relocated some tenants and poor farmers in experimental homestead communities. Under the direction of Rexford Tugwell, a member of the president's "brains trust," the RA also established government "greenbelt towns" for low-income city workers. But pressure from southern tenant and sharecropper unions prompted a presidential committee on farm tenancy to recommend stronger measures in 1936. Congress obliged by creating the Farm Security Administration (FSA), which offered long-term, low-interest loans to tenants, sharecroppers, and farm laborers. By 1941 the FSA had loaned $516 million in rehabilitation funds to 870,000 farm families and built county health care facilities and sanitary camps for migrants. Nevertheless, appropriations remained small in comparison to tenant requests, and conservative county committees administered the loan program in the interests of local landlords. By 1945, 1.8 million tenant families still worked the land under conditions of poverty.

Following the Supreme Court's invalidation of the Agricultural Adjustment Administration, Roosevelt spent two years seeking a new law to resume economic planning in agriculture. The second AAA of 1938 guaranteed federal support of farm prices but replaced the unconstitutional processing tax with funding from the federal treasury. The new AAA empowered the secretary of agriculture to establish marketing quotas when surplus threatened the price level and two-thirds of the farmers producing that commodity agreed. Through the Commodity Credit Corporation, farmers were awarded loans if they took surplus crops off the market. Another agency, the Federal Crop Insurance Corporation, provided "social security" for wheat and cotton farmers by accepting crop payments as insurance premiums against future crop loss.

Economic planning in agriculture surpassed that of any segment of the national marketplace, but incentive payments for the great majority of independent farmers were meager, averaging less than $100 a year. Besides, government programs were unable to retire land from cultivation fast enough to overcome increased productivity through mechanization. Farm prices in 1939 still were below 1929 levels, and AAA subsidies only stimulated the long-range trend toward corporatization of agriculture. But farmers did benefit from New Deal conservation policies. Congress created the Soil Conservation Service in 1935, which sent out government teams to promote contour plowing, rotation of crops, fertilizing, and gully planting; and subsequent legislation provided benefit payments for farmers who grew soil-conserving crops.

With the demise of the NRA, Roosevelt pushed for a federal law to regulate wages and hours in industry. But organized labor balked at government interference with wage negotia-

tions. Furthermore, southern congressmen cited their region's cheaper living costs and pressed to conserve the South's lower wage scales. Congress finally overcame the deadlock by passing an extensively amended Fair Labor Standards Act in 1938. Although wage differentials were left to administrative discretion, the law gave industrialists two years to implement a 40¢-an-hour minimum wage and a forty-hour week. Despite the low wage scale and numerous exceptions to its provisions, the Fair Labor Standards Act provided pay increases for over twelve million American workers in interstate commerce and established the principle of national standards for industrial wages. The law also created the first permanent regulation of child labor by prohibiting interstate shipment of most industrial goods produced by minors under sixteen. Workers between sixteen and eighteen also were excluded from occupations declared hazardous by the Children's Bureau. These provisions enshrined public sentiment against child labor in industrial occupations where it was already declining, but children continued to work in agriculture, retail trades, and small businesses.

Despite occasional legislative victories, Roosevelt faced an increasingly hostile Congress in his second term. The president's political problems originated in a bitter controversy over the Supreme Court. Stung by crippling Court invalidation of early New Deal industrial and agricultural regulation, Roosevelt introduced a judiciary reorganization bill in early 1937. The surprise package authorized the president to appoint an additional Supreme Court judge for each justice who did not retire at age seventy. Six Court judges were over that age at the time, and the administration plan could have increased Court membership from nine to fifteen. Roosevelt ruthlessly pushed his bill through

Congress. But the Supreme Court was a symbol of constitutional law, and Democrats joined Republicans to kill the unpopular plan. By asking Congress for unprecedented powers over another branch of government, Roosevelt lent credence to attacks on his dictatorial methods and fed anxieties that a powerful presidential bureaucracy was destroying traditional American freedoms. The acrimonious Court fight helped to destroy the Roosevelt myth of invincibility, divided the Democratic party, and gave anti–New Deal partisans a new lease on life. Never again did the president have full control of congressional Democrats on domestic issues.

By 1939 the anti–New Deal coalition in Congress was strong enough to block administration programs. Congressional conservatives represented rural constituencies and small businesspeople who did not benefit from New Deal assistance to union workers, ethnics, blacks, and relief recipients. Roosevelt adversaries outside the industrial centers of the Northeast and Midwest attacked the "boondoggling" waste of WPA work projects, favored balanced budgets and states' rights, and defended ordinary Americans against the growth of a statist bureaucracy. These conservative congressmen frequently came from rural states or "safe" districts and had built up seniority as ranking members of important committees. The Court controversy showed them that it was possible to oppose the administration without political consequences and reinforced their conviction that the emergency measures of the New Deal had gone far enough. Private lobbying organizations such as the National Committee to Uphold Constitutional Government also lent strength to the anti–New Deal movement by bitterly attacking Roosevelt on the Court issue and mercilessly portraying the president's "dictatorial ambitions."

As Roosevelt cut spending in 1937, a severe economic recession persuaded many Americans that the New Deal had failed. The most precipitous economic decline in history sent unemployment from under seven million early in 1937 to eleven million by 1938, while the stock market lost about two-thirds the ground gained during the entire New Deal. Administration officials accused business leaders of holding back on investment to embarrass the president, but New Deal critics suggested that Roosevelt had engineered a final depression to usher in the overthrow of capitalism. The president reacted by reducing corporate taxes and stimulated purchasing power by appropriating an extra $3 billion for the WPA, FSA, and CCC. For the first time in American history, a president had agreed to use deficit spending as a tool of economic planning. Federal expenditures jumped from $2 billion in 1933 to $5.2 billion in 1939. By fiscal 1942, the federal budget deficit reached $19 billion, and the use of imbalanced budgets had become a hallmark of national political economy.

Inspired into action by the recession and the need for government spending, Roosevelt attempted to alter the character of the Democratic party by turning against conservatives during the congressional elections of 1938. But the recession had made the president only more vulnerable, and any remaining presidential popularity did not carry over into congressional contests. Roosevelt's half-hearted purge resulted in a Republican gain of eighty seats in the House and eight in the Senate and marked the end of the New Deal consensus. The economic crisis of 1937–1938 had created a psychology of New Deal retreat rather than advance. Even when rearmament stimulated economic recovery in mid-1938, a large number of Democratic congressmen remained committed to states' rights, domestic budget retrenchment, and private enterprise. Indicative of congressional conservatism was the formation in 1938 of the House Committee to Investigate Un-American Activities. Chaired by Martin Dies of Texas and empowered to seek out subversive groups in the United States, the House panel began to investigate Communist influence in New Deal agencies.

THE CORPORATE STATE

Despite setbacks between 1937 and 1939, the New Deal left Americans with a government bureaucracy that regularized and stabilized the nation's economic life. Although the demands of a corporate economy had underlined the need for government coordination since the 1890s, the Depression of the thirties tied bureaucratic expertise and federal subsidies to the necessities of national survival. By the end of the decade, the federal government was responsible for maintenance of prices and wages, guarantees of social security, sustenance of purchasing power, protection of home and farm mortgages, underwriting of conservation methods, and widespread regulation of business, banking, and labor practices. But New Deal planning increasingly meant administrative expertise and managerial efficiency in the interests of national stability.

In the new federal system devised by New Deal planners, the states administered and contributed to centrally established policies. State spending doubled under the New Deal. "We are beginning to look to Uncle Sam to be Santa Claus," one Democratic governor remarked in 1935. Yet federal aid did not prevent overwhelming economic pressure on the states.

Budget deficits forced state governments to resort to regressive taxes that burdened consumers regardless of income. As gasoline and sales taxes replaced property and corporate assessments as the mainstay of state income, working- and middle-class Americans found themselves paying heavily for government programs.

With the evolution of the managerial state, the presidency assumed new powers. Roosevelt recreated the modern presidency, giving it central importance after the temporary eclipse of the twenties. Under the New Deal, the White House became the focus of all government, initiating legislation, drafting bills, and lobbying Congress. After a long struggle over the president's "dictatorial powers," Congress finally passed the Administrative Reorganization Act of 1939, which streamlined government agencies under executive command. More important, Executive Order 8248 created the Executive Office of the President, providing Roosevelt with a White House staff and six administrative assistants. Roosevelt also moved the Bureau of the Budget from Treasury to the president's office, setting the precedent for the placement of agencies directly under the president. He ran the first presidential bureaucracy on a "competitive" basis — considering ideas and programs worked out by two or more administrators, but seldom formulating and supervising a coherent policy of his own. The "service intellectuals" who assisted the president normally sacrificed personal interest for loyalty to the administrative team. They prided themselves on not being sentimental, professing a skepticism about utopias and final solutions. Presidential assistants, for example, stressed that relief was not simply a humanitarian gesture but a necessity in stimulating purchasing power and stabilizing the economy. New Dealers shared the president's view that humans, not nature, were responsible for economic laws. This style of centralized rule by government managers and professionals carried over into World War Two, when the demands of national security replaced the mission of economic recovery.

Expansion of the federal bureaucracy also led to increased police powers for executive agencies. The creation of the Federal Deposit Insurance Corporation, for example, meant that robbery of member banks was a federal offense, to be pursued by the Federal Bureau of Investigation. When the son of Charles and Anne Lindbergh was kidnapped and murdered in 1932, Congress included kidnapping as a federal crime. Highly publicized arrests of several Depression bank robbers by J. Edgar Hoover's FBI also accustomed Americans to the idea of a federal police force. While the Federal Communications Act of 1934 made telephone wiretapping illegal, subsequent court decisions refused to ban electronic eavesdropping, or "bugging." Roosevelt requested secret investigations of American Nazis in 1934 and Communists in 1936, permitting government police agents to employ surreptitious methods. By 1939 a Roosevelt memorandum confirmed that the FBI and the military intelligence agencies had responsibility for national security at home.

The reorientation of federal power could not have occurred without consent of the courts. While Roosevelt's "court-packing" plan proved politically disastrous, the Supreme Court never again voted down a New Deal program. Court decisions in 1937 validated the Wagner Act, employing the broadest definitions of the "stream of commerce" concept to rule that "free collective bargaining" between management and labor would benefit the public good. By narrow 5–4 majorities, the Court also approved old-age benefits, federal grants-in-aid, and em-

ployer taxes in the Social Security Act. Another Court decision permitted local officials to acquire private land for federal public housing programs.

The "constitutional revolution" of 1937 marked the abdication of the Supreme Court's economic policy making and its acceptance of the government's role in the market. Subsequently, the Court left economic matters to Congress and the Executive in cooperation with the states and private corporations, making economic management by government a political choice rather than a constitutional controversy. By ruling that the due process clause no longer limited legislative power, the Court supervised the change from a Constitution of limits to one of powers. The corporate state no longer maximized individual liberty but insured conditions for minimal well-being. While corporations could no longer function without government subsidies or regulation of the marketplace, the New Deal assisted labor, agricultural, and professional groups as well.

New Deal reform amounted to an effort to preserve the existing system of corporate capitalism according to amended rules of constitutional democracy. It institutionalized the corporate economy and society, but many conservative businessmen and politicians continued to hold to traditional Anglo-Protestant notions of individual enterprise and personal responsibility, seeing government welfare and union bureaucracy as ever-growing parasites on profits and private investment. Some members of the upper class were outraged by Roosevelt's flirtation with class rhetoric and referred to the president as "That Man," unwilling even to utter his name. But Roosevelt saw government as an aid to business. "To preserve," he remarked cogently in 1937, "we had to reform."

The New Deal was far from a revolution.

It did accept the participation of white ethnics and some women and blacks in the union movement and the federal bureaucracy. But the managerial state did not redistribute income, nor did it build a new political base among the poor, unemployed, tenant farmers, or racial minorities. And only the stimulus of war brought economic recovery after 1938. Nevertheless, Roosevelt had personally restored confidence and faith in the American system amid the most devastating economic collapse in the nation's history and haphazardly constructed the administrative apparatus for government management of the economy. A Gallup poll in 1940 found that 64 percent of the public agreed that the American form of government was "as near perfect as it can be and no important changes should be made in it."

SUGGESTED READINGS

The most comprehensive account of the New Deal era is Arthur Schlesinger, Jr., *The Age of Roosevelt*, 3 vols. (1957–1960). Among one-volume studies, William E. Leuchtenburg, *Franklin D. Roosevelt and the New Deal* (1963), is unsurpassed. Two brief but provocative volumes are Paul K. Conkin, *The New Deal* (1967), and George Wolfskill, *Happy Days Are Here Again!: A Short Interpretive History of the New Deal* (1974).

The economic history of the Depression is set forth in the fifth volume of Joseph Dorfman, *The Economic Mind in American Civilization* (1959), and Jim Potter, *The American Economy Between the World Wars* (1974). Hoover's plight is explored in Gene Smith, *The Shattered Dream: Herbert Hoover and the*

Great Depression (1970), and Albert U. Romasco, *The Poverty of Abundance: Hoover, the Nation, the Depression* (1968). See also Richard Hofstadter's perceptive portraits of Hoover and Roosevelt in *The American Political Tradition* (1948). Robert F. Himmelberg, *The Origins of the National Recovery Administration: Business, Government and the Trade Association Issue, 1921–1933* (1976), describes Hoover's opposition to the Swope Plan. Midwestern agricultural discontent is probed in John L. Shover, *Cornbelt Rebellion: The Farmers Holiday Association* (1965).

Ellis W. Hawley, *The New Deal and the Problem of Monopoly: A Study in Economic Ambivalence* (1966), provides an excellent analysis of the Roosevelt administration's approach to big business, while the relevant sections of Otis L. Graham, Jr., *Toward a Planned Society: From Roosevelt to Nixon* (1976), explore the origins of government centralization and planning. The limitations of New Deal ecological planning are summarized in the relevant chapters of Joseph M. Petulla, *American Environmental History: The Exploitation and Conservation of Natural Resources* (1977), and Walt Anderson, *A Place of Power: The American Episode in Human Evolution* (1976). The best Roosevelt biography is Frank Freidel, *Franklin D. Roosevelt*, 4 vols. (1952–1973), but it should be supplemented by the critical James M. Burns, *Roosevelt: The Lion and the Fox* (1956).

James T. Patterson, *The New Deal and the States: Federalism in Transition* (1969), shows the increasing conservatism of the states during the thirties, while Patterson's *Congressional Conservatism and the New Deal: The Growth of the Conservative Coalition in Congress, 1933–1939* (1967), traces the origin of anti–New Deal politics. The Court controversy is described by Leonard Baker, *Back to Back: The Duel Between FDR and the Supreme Court* (1967). Two reassessments of the "Share Our Wealth" crusade are Hugh D. Graham, *Huey Long* (1970), and Thomas H. Williams, *Huey Long* (1970).

A brief section of Arthur S. Miller, *The Modern Corporate State: Private Governments and the American Constitution* (1976), provides a brilliant analysis of the New Deal's constitutional revolution. William Leuchtenburg, "The New Deal and the Analogue of War," in John Braeman, Robert H. Bremner, and Everett Walters, eds., *Change and Continuity in Twentieth-Century America* (1964), argues that New Deal rhetoric and institutional responses borrowed heavily from the World War

One experience. A careful analogy to nazism is constructed by John A. Garraty, "The New Deal, Nationalism, and the Great Depression," *American Historical Review,* 78 (October 1973).

Several New Left interpretations stress the compatibility of New Deal policies with corporate capitalism. Among the best are Barton Bernstein, "The New Deal: The Conservative Achievements of Liberal Reform," in Bernstein, ed., *Towards a New Past* (1968), Ronald Radosh, "The Myth of the New Deal," in Radosh and Murray N. Rothbard, eds., *A New History of Leviathan: Essays on the Rise of the American Corporate State* (1972), and relevant sections of William A. Williams, *The Contours of American History* (1961).

Spotlight: The Fireside Chat

The Great Depression enabled Franklin D. Roosevelt to refashion the presidency. Never before had administrative agencies intervened so directly into the lives of individual Americans. Reference to "the Government" in the thirties came to suggest the federal government. Always in the news, President Roosevelt personified the state as protector. People frequently gave him personal credit for saving their homes, for old-age pensions, for emergency relief. Poor Americans saw Roosevelt as a friend who did not patronize. "Franklin D. Roosevelt is the only man ever in the White House," one factory supporter explained in 1936, "who understands

(Above) "The Man of the Hour" — this contemporary Roosevelt clock pictures the president standing without crutches before the ship of state.

that my boss is an s.o.b." Others believed that the president's polio-crippled legs enabled him to empathize with the sufferings of those in need.

Roosevelt took pride in his intimate understanding of public grievances. His personal adviser Louis Howe initiated daily presidential press digests, but Roosevelt insisted on closer contact with the American people. He customarily pumped news correspondents, officials, and other White House visitors for information and impressions. The president also received up to eight thousand letters a day, ten times Hoover's average. A mailroom staff of fifty tabulated results in the first use of presidential polling. Roosevelt occasionally used excerpts in public speeches.

The president's most effective means of communication came through informal radio addresses. Radio and politics had crossed paths several times in the twenties. The first scheduled preadvertised program was a Pittsburgh broadcast of the 1920 Harding-Cox election returns. When chain broadcasting assured a national constituency, Harding delivered the first mass audience radio speech in mid-1923, a St. Louis address opposing American participation in the World Court. Coolidge, whose enunciation was particularly clear and distinct, went on the radio once a month during the first half of the 1924 election year. He delivered the first presidential message to Congress ever broadcast. Twenty-one stations carried the president's inaugural address in March 1925, reaching an estimated fifteen million people. Americans rated Calvin Coolidge the fourth most popular radio personality in the mid-twenties.

Radio helped to change the style of national politics. A memorandum from the Republican National Committee explained in 1924 that radio speeches required "a new type of sentence. Its language is not that of the platform orator." Political talks were to be brief and succinct. William Jennings Bryan, traditional Democratic war-horse, came across poorly on the air because his sentences were too long and he wandered away from the microphone. Al Smith, who, as governor of New York, had used the radio to pressure opponents of a tax cut, found that his East Side accent hurt him in national broadcasts.

Following the Crash of 1929, Hoover did not use the radio well. The president noted that radio "physically makes us literally one people upon all occasions of general public interest," but his Depression broadcasts were too general or concerned with trivial subjects.

Radios were in twelve million American homes when the Depression began. But technical developments after 1930 decreased size and cost. An industry estimate of 1935 claimed seventy-eight million regular listeners. By the end of the decade, 86 percent of the population had access to home radios. Surveys indicated that Americans trusted the radio more than the daily newspaper for accurate news. A 1935 brochure promoting radio advertising even claimed that voices of affection and authority made people do what they were told.

Coolidge had rejected "casual talks" to the American people. But Roosevelt had a far more ambitious view of the presidency than his predecessors, describing it as "pre-eminently a place of moral leadership." Following the declaration of a national banking moratorium in March 1933, President Roosevelt scheduled an informal radio address that broadcasters and the press termed a *fireside chat*. Working with several drafts and technical advice from radio specialists, the president took to the air to calm a nation's anxieties. "I want to tell you what has been done in the last few days," Roosevelt said of the national bank holiday, "why it was done, and what the next steps are going to be." He then explained the government's plan to inspect the banks before they resumed business. "I can assure you that it is safer to keep your money in a reopened bank than under the mattress," the president promised. "Let us unite in banishing fear."

Roosevelt delivered sixteen fireside chats during his first two terms. They averaged thirty minutes and were broadcast in the evening. The president spoke naturally and casually, intimately addressing the American people as "my friends." Sometimes he referred to "you and I." Roosevelt illustrated key points with folksy anecdotes and concrete detail. He simplified complex issues such as the banking crisis and used an excellent radio voice to emphasize crucial words and convey an impression of sincerity. Even when audiences surpassed sixty million, the president related individually to listeners, referring to "your government." In an address on the WPA, Roosevelt asked Americans to "tell me of instances where work can be done better." As a result, Americans felt he was confiding to each one of them. During one 1933 broadcast, the president interrupted his remarks to ask for a glass of water. He paused, took an audible swallow, and told listeners: "My friends, it's very hot here in Washington tonight."

The president's first fireside chat reached nearly two-thirds of the radio sets in operation. More than forty thousand letters poured into the White House in response. Other talks focused on descriptions of new laws and agencies, explanations of the "managed currency," proposals for improved working conditions, and outlines of soil and water conservation reforms. "We cannot ballyhoo ourselves back to prosperity," Roosevelt said in his second chat of May 1933. "I am going to be honest at all times with the people of the country." He spoke of "what we have been doing and what we are planning to do." The simplest way for Americans to judge recovery, the president suggested in a fireside chat of June 1934, was to ask: "Are you better off than you were last year?" Other radio talks tried to assure Americans that the administration was not proceeding in "any haphazard fashion." The New Deal, said Roosevelt, was like building a ship — one could not tell how it would finally look from merely observing the frame. Trying to restore confidence in 1935, Roosevelt proclaimed that "Americans as a whole are feeling a lot better."

Roosevelt's radio magic was not always successful. The fireside chat of March 1937, which denounced adversaries "opposed to progress," failed to rally the nation behind the plan to reorganize the Supreme Court. But successful or not, Roosevelt expanded the aura of the presidency by attempting to take the American people into a presidential partnership. "It is your problem no less than mine," he told the country during the banking crisis of 1933. "Together we cannot fail." Roosevelt conveyed empathy for Depression suffering, but stressed the inclusion of Americans in a national community, erasing distinctions between ethnic and racial minorities as he did so. The president strove to appear above party politics, to portray a whole nation united against inscrutable nature and an indifferent economic system. "In a physical and property sense, as well as in a spiritual sense," Roosevelt said in a 1936 talk, "we are members one of another." By the late thirties, the president was expanding upon such rhetoric in radio speeches designed to mobilize the American public to challenges overseas.

Chapter 9

THE SOCIAL FABRIC OF THE DEPRESSION

"Yes, we could smell the Depression in the air," a literary historian recalled of the early 1930s. "It was like a raw wind; the very houses we lived in seemed to be shrinking, hopeless of real comfort." A newspaper publisher remembered sitting in his office bathroom following the Crash, bowels "loose from fear." The collapse of new era prosperity was bewildering and overpowering, equivalent to a natural disaster such as an earthquake. Yet many Americans attempted to restore order and security to lives disrupted by the economic catastrophe. Frequently their efforts coincided with twentieth-century trends toward institutionalization and corporate stability.

THE PSYCHOLOGY OF SCARCITY

The psychological effects of economic depression were enormous. Unemployment, a profound attack on traditional notions of personal reliance and productivity, seemed capricious, choosing victims blindly, sparing others. Even those with jobs had no assurance of holding them and gladly accepted menial tasks as a substitute for higher aspirations. While labor and farm unions channeled the bitterness of those who still had work, unemployment did not produce militance. The numbing effect of prolonged idleness seemed to induce shame, anxiety, self-guilt, and apathy. Psychologists reported alarming rates of sexual impotence among men no longer able to assert the masculine role of breadwinner. Studies showed that unemployed people moved more slowly than the employed poor, were more sick more often, more suicidal, more distrustful, and less self-confident. Some jobless businessmen tried to keep up pretenses by taking daily commuter trains to town, but such self-delusion wore thin. In general, Americans tended to blame themselves, not the economic system, for the Depression.

The realities of the somber thirties undermined dreams of self-improvement, but many Americans continued to cling to desperate hopes. Dr. Napoleon Hill's *Think and Grow Rich* (1937) sold five million copies, while manuals such as Dale Carnegie's *How to Win Friends and Influence People* (1936) and Emmet Fox's *Power Through Constructive Thinking* (1940) also sold well. Harry Emerson Fosdick, a liberal New York City pastor whose national radio programs espoused a class-conscious analysis of the economic collapse, nevertheless produced five bestsellers by insisting that practical Christianity demanded cultivation of one's inner resources.

New Deal administrators and social workers tried to tell the American people that unemployment was an impersonal force beyond the control of its victims. But traditional Anglo-Protestant values stressed the connection between productivity and personal worth. Furthermore, new era Americans had found it easy to believe that every deserving worker could find a job; that only the ill, lame, and lazy needed charity or public relief. Even as unemployment mushroomed in the thirties, it continued to be a sign of personal failure. One study showed that only one-quarter of a sample of unemployed people had sought public relief

after two years of joblessness. The stigma of unemployment also propelled conservative attacks on the "make-work" tasks and high costs of public job programs.

In contrast to the middle-class hedonism of the new era, social values were more austere in the depressed thirties. Food became an exercise in nutrition, while economic insecurity even seemed to dampen sexuality. For families unable to make ends meet, children were burdens and pregnancy a disaster. Social anxiety also surfaced in stricter child-rearing methods. As young couples waited to achieve financial independence, marriage rates dropped. Consequently, the Depression not only accelerated the early twentieth-century trend toward smaller families, but also contributed to extended adolescence and a delay in sexual and social independence. Nevertheless, booming contraceptive sales accompanied the lowest birth rate in American history. Even Sears Roebuck mail-order catalogues carried advertisements for contraceptives under "feminine hygiene needs."

Despite lower marriage and birth rates and a doubling of the divorce ratio, Depression Americans re-emphasized the virtues of motherhood and home. Because the psychology of scarcity stressed security instead of innovation, men hoped for dependable jobs and a secure family life. But as economic depression threatened the masculinity of male breadwinners, roles outside the home became more limited for women. One survey of usually independent college women found that three-fifths hoped to marry within a year or two of graduation. Middle-class women were advised to specialize in "feminine" occupations such as home economics or interior decorating, or to stay home and give men badly needed jobs. A 1936 Gallup poll indicated that 82 percent of the sample believed that women should not take jobs if their husbands were employed. Secretary of

Frances Perkins was appointed secretary of labor by President Franklin Roosevelt. The first woman cabinet member in American history, Perkins urged Depression women to leave the shrunken job market to men. (Brown Brothers)

Labor Frances Perkins, the first female cabinet member in history, characterized women who worked without the need as a menace to society. Federal law in the thirties reflected these concerns by stipulating that only one member of a family could work in a civil service job.

With social pressures discouraging careers for middle-class women, the proportion of professionals in the female work force was even smaller than in the twenties. And three-quarters of women professionals continued to be schoolteachers or nurses. In industry, women workers still earned only half or two-thirds the male pay scale, while two-fifths of the women in manufacturing worked in law-paying textile mills and clothing factories. Minimum wage laws and unionization improved wages in textile and garments, but the great majority of working women nevertheless remained at the bottom of the industrial system. In between the industrial workers and few professionals were growing numbers of secretaries and stenographers who served for low pay in the burgeoning white-collar and service centers in the great metropolises.

The Depression emphasis on women's role at home did not encourage independent political activity. Feminism was not fashionable in the thirties, and the political power of individual women and their organizations usually depended on the support of men. Female precinct workers were instrumental in the Democratic landslide of 1936. Eleanor Roosevelt, who acted as the president's personal adviser on human rights and appointments, also served as a symbol of the socially conscious woman. Yet only in the South, where the Association of Southern Women for the Prevention of Lynching continued the evangelical zeal of Anglo-Protestant progressive reform, did women organize politically on the basis of gender. The ASWPL, an unprecedented coalition between white and black middle-class women, condemned the lynching of black men as an indefensible crime and mounted a regionwide campaign against the hypocrisy and violence of southern white men. Other traditional women's reforms such as health care, better working conditions, and the abolition of child labor were incorporated into broader New Deal and union campaigns.

THE ABSORPTION OF WHITE ETHNICS

Americans no longer perceived national character as distinctly Anglo-Protestant by the 1930s. By then, immigration restriction and new era industrial harmony considerably lessened Anglo-Protestant anxieties over the influx of southern and eastern Europeans. In addition, a new wave of anthropological theory initiated by twenties scholars such as Franz Boaz suggested that "racial" characteristics really were culturally learned patterns of behavior. Cultural relativism and reduced class tension encouraged unprecedented toleration toward Irish-Americans and European ethnics in the 1920s, although such attitudes did not extend to Asians or Latin Americans. By the early thirties, popular ethnic figures in sports and entertainment helped to legitimize this cross-cultural acceptance. For example, at least seventeen of the forty-one most popular records of 1930 were written or composed by Jews, including such eminent songwriters as Irving Berlin, George Gershwin, and Jerome Kern. Berlin's "God Bless America," written in 1938, became an unofficial anthem of national unity during World War Two. On the radio, ethnic comedians such as Jack Benny, Eddie Cantor, George Burns, and Jimmy Durante delighted massive audiences, while the Marx Brothers introduced Americans to the zany possibilities of sound movies.

In an effort to acknowledge the broad spiritual roots of the nation's amalgam of cultures, New Deal rhetoric usually referred to "American faiths" and the "Judeo-Christian heritage." Such language aided Roosevelt's attempt to consolidate the American people behind national recovery programs. The president also responded to the large Democratic vote among Irish-Americans and eastern Europeans through political appointments. One out of nine Roosevelt positions went to a Catholic or Jew, as opposed to one out of twenty-five for Hoover. Among the president's key political advisers were Louis Howe, a Jew, and Jim Farley, an

Irish-American. Financial consultant Bernard Baruch and Treasury Secretary Henry Morgenthau, Jr., were Jewish; Joe Kennedy, a successful building contractor and Boston politico, became the first Irish-Catholic to serve as American ambassador to Great Britain. Catholics and Jews also received 30 percent of the president's nominations for federal judgeships, including Supreme Court Justice Felix Frankfurter and Matthew Abruzzo, the first Italian-American to serve on the federal bench.

New Deal politics both reinforced and contested the traditional ethnic political machines of the large cities. In New York, Roosevelt endorsed Fiorello LaGuardia's nonpartisan "Fusion" triumph over Irish-dominated Tammany Hall in 1933. LaGuardia won the support of Protestant liberals, Jews, blacks, and Italians in a broadly based reform crusade that resulted in expansion of city services, honest methods of budget balancing, and disruption of the ethnic patronage system. The fiery mayor also demonstrated his distaste for ethnic stereotypes by barring Italian-American organ grinders from city streets. Meanwhile, New York City's public college system provided free schooling for upwardly mobile ethnics, particularly the Jews.

Unlike Roosevelt's support for reform in New York, the administration cooperated with entrenched leadership in cities such as Boston, Kansas City, and Jersey City. Since New Deal work agencies were administered locally, city bosses assumed the power to select work relief recipients. As a result, New Deal liberalism differed from progressivism by consolidating ethnic political machines. But the growth of federal agencies and recovery programs also encouraged a new generation of Irish corporate executives, professionals, and young attorneys to join local bosses in expanding urban power bases to the national level. In turn, Poles, Italians, and other white ethnics began to make patronage and power demands on Irish political machines in cities such as Chicago.

Despite the number of ethnic successes, upper-middle-class Protestants continued to dominate the corporate community, while immigrant families provided the bulk of the nation's unskilled labor. In Boston, where one-third of the population was foreign born, 80 percent of immigrant labor did manual work. Unskilled and semiskilled workers never recovered from the loss of occupational mobility that the Depression brought. Half the nation's unemployment occurred in states where a majority of Italians, Poles, Lithuanians, and Jews lived. For ethnic Americans just beginning to grasp the dream of equal opportunity, the economic collapse was a disaster. Ethnics continued to maintain those mutual-aid societies and fraternal organizations, first formed in the early years of the century, that promoted family, cultural, and religious traditions. But as the Depression deepened, the importance of job security and better wages prompted many working-class ethnics to join the industrial union movement. Like the New Deal itself, the union movement asked immigrants and their offspring to reject old patterns of identity and see themselves primarily as Americans.

THE TRIUMPH OF INDUSTRIAL UNIONISM

Because immigration restriction limited the number of newcomers to the factory system, the American work force of the thirties was far more cohesive than before the Crash. Millions of white and black migrants from the South

Bethlehem, Pennsylvania, epitomizes a steelworkers' district and the injured economy of 1935. (Walker Evans/ Library of Congress)

also grew accustomed to working with white ethnics in the mass production industries. As a result, ethnic rivalry and regional exclusiveness no longer prevented industrial workers from cooperating to organize labor unions. The union share of the nonfarm work force had halved in the twenties. But economic collapse disintegrated welfare capitalism and induced a sense of betrayal among industrial workers. Weekly earnings averaged less than $17 in 1932, down from a boom high of $25. In response to the new social and economic conditions, union membership jumped from 2.7 million in 1933 to 12 million by 1943. By the time the nation entered World War Two, nearly one-fourth of workers outside agriculture belonged to unions.

For the first time in American history, government itself provided the stimulus to union recruiting through Section 7(a) of the National Industrial Recovery Act, described by the AFL's William Green as the charter of industrial freedom. Because industrial codes incorporated collective bargaining procedures, union leaders told workers that "the President" wanted them to organize into unions to help fight the Depression. By mid-1934, seventeen hundred national and local unions were organized in mass production industries such as automobiles, steel, lumber, rubber, and aluminum.

The NRA proved particularly helpful to union organizers in the troubled coal industry. The United Mine Workers had abandoned a militant strike in Kentucky's Harlan County during 1932, when a pitched battle between miners and company guards brought murder charges against forty-four strikers and widespread attacks on union followers. Nevertheless, the UMW grew from sixty thousand members to a half million by mid-1933. Once the NRA was created, John L. Lewis led miners in a campaign for union recognition under a single code for the entire soft-coal industry. But operators and steel subsidiaries resisted in a sprawling industry in which local conditions controlled wages. When miners erected armed barricades at a U.S. Steel subsidiary in Pennsylvania, Governor Gifford Pinchot brought out the National Guard. Nearly fifty thousand coal miners joined the violent Pennsylvania strike during 1933. President Roosevelt finally intimidated soft-coal operators into drafting a single NRA code with regional divisions and local wage districts. The national soft-coal code also outlawed wage-demeaning child labor and banned compulsory company stores. "You have delivered the miners out of the wilderness," one mass meeting in Pennsylvania wired the president. Operators signed a wage agreement with the UMW that covered 340,000 miners, the largest number of workers ever included in an American labor settlement.

Lewis's UMW campaign stimulated the entire organized labor movement. But NRA enforcement of industry codes was weak, and company unions grew more rapidly than independent unions. As a result, labor leaders quickly lost patience with industrial employers and began to dismiss the NRA as the "National Run Around." Frustrations erupted in 1934, one of the most active and violent years of labor struggle in American history. While a San Francisco general strike won the support of 125,000 workers, a half million strikers closed down the textile industry in twenty states. In Minneapolis, socialist Teamsters leaders led bloody fighting for control of city streets. Following a declaration of martial law, Minneapolis trucking companies agreed to an NRA code for the local industry.

The militancy of 1934 helped to pass the Wagner Act during the following year. Since collective bargaining was now compulsory and company unions illegal, Lewis convinced the AFL to establish a committee to organize the mass production industries. But when the Committee of Industrial Organizations asked the AFL to grant charters to steel, auto, rubber, and radio workers, the federation asked them to disband. Instead, the new union leaders formed the Congress of Industrial Organizations and established recruiting committees to enroll more workers. By doing so, the CIO went beyond the AFL's craft orientation and established the first successful union organization of entire industries.

CIO unions stressed grassroots organization and recruited blue-collar ethnics, southern whites, blacks, and women in all phases of factory and mill work. Sensitive to deep-seated resentments on the mechanized assembly line, the industrial unions responded to grievances with direct and immediate action. CIO mem-

A contemporary painting by Charles Scheeler portrays the mechanized place of the American worker in industry. (Worcester Art Museum, Worcester, Mass.)

bership began with 1 million workers in 1935 and reached 2.8 million by 1941.

The industrial union movement provided a major outlet for Depression militancy. Whereas unemployment produced passivity and demoralization, blue-collar workers resented the arbitrary policies of corporate management. Predictably, when industrial corporations refused to honor the Wagner Act's provisions for collective bargaining, a series of worker rebellions erupted. Between the fall of 1936 and the summer of 1937, a half million industrial workers joined CIO sit-downs, in which strikers stopped production by occupying plant shops and assembly rooms.

The turning point of the sit-down campaign

Auto workers at the Fisher Body Plant in Flint, Michigan, engage in a sit-down strike in 1937. (Library of Congress)

occurred at a General Motors plant in Flint, Michigan, during early 1937. By then, 140,000 workers at fifty GM factories were striking to win seniority rights, better wages, and collective bargaining rights for the United Auto Workers. When GM tried to evict the Flint strikers by cutting off deliveries of food, auto workers drove off police with a barrage of auto door hinges, coffee mugs, and handmade weapons. Meanwhile, Michigan's sympathetic governor refused to send in troops, and Roosevelt emissaries pressured GM to negotiate. By a settlement reached in February 1937, the giant of the auto industry recognized the UAW as a bargaining agent for 400,000 union members and proceeded to negotiate a contract. One week later U.S. Steel, a bitter opponent of industrial unionism in 1919, settled amicably

with the Steel Workers Organizing Committee, providing bargaining for another 300,000 workers.

Unions helped large corporations predict labor costs, provided orderly processes for grievances, and furthered shop discipline. Even though corporate management resented seniority clauses that interfered with decision making in promotion and hiring, union bureaucracy prevented costly wildcats, walkouts, and slowdowns. But smaller firms felt more threatened by union wage demands and managerial interference. When the Steel Workers Organizing Committee turned to the lesser steel corporations, it met brutal resistance and a campaign to stop industrial unionism. The climax to the emotional "Little Steel" strike came when one thousand workers and their families marched on Republic Steel's Chicago plant in May 1937 and were fired upon by city police, who killed ten and injured fifty-eight. Newspaper accounts, by now impatient with union disruption, pictured the Memorial Day Massacre as the result of Communist agitation, although the few radicals involved were not in a position to determine SWOC policy. But CIO unions abandoned the sit-down and mass action after losing the "Little Steel" strike and began to purge Communists from the movement. The Supreme Court finally ruled sit-downs illegal in 1939.

By World War Two most CIO unions had adopted the restrained "business unionism" of the AFL. This meant that in wartime, unions would not permit strikes to interfere with the national military effort. Adopting the Progressive consensus that called for a democracy of consumers instead of a producer's democracy based on worker control, American unions rejected participation in production planning and conformed to managerial imperatives. Through this arrangement, labor unions permitted corporations to pass higher labor costs on to consumers. As the CIO and AFL grew to impressive proportions during wartime, professional union managers and negotiators began to separate the rank and file from crucial decision making, and worker apathy replaced participation in union affairs. Nevertheless, the union movement of the thirties won substantive gains for industrial workers. Government and union machinery now required corporations to show cause in disciplining or discharging employees, a guarantee against the arbitrary firings that Depression workers had come to fear. Seniority also provided job security for older workers frequently victimized by assembly line management. In addition, unions set standards of equity and prodded nonunion firms into competitive wages. Most important, the union movement gave industrial workers a sense of pride and dignity in an era of social chaos.

Although the solidarity experienced by sit-down strikers did not revolutionize American industrial life, it reaffirmed self-respect among assembly line workers outside the traditional crafts of the AFL. By doing so, the industrial union movement helped to absorb rural migrants, blacks, white ethnics, and women into the nation's productive force and gave vent to class frustrations aggravated by the economic collapse. When the industrial demands of World War Two required harmony among social classes and high levels of dependable productivity, most of the labor movement had no difficulty in abandoning strikes to support the war effort and national unity.

BLACKS AND THE DEPRESSION

CIO activity absorbed a half million black Americans into the labor movement. Steel un-ions, for example, successfully recruited eighty-five thousand blacks, a number equivalent to one-fifth the entire steel work force. Black involvement with the CIO was encouraged by civil rights leaders who wished to break down traditional color bars in the union movement. In a historic moment in labor history, NAACP Secretary Walter White personally circled the Ford plant at River Rouge in 1941 to ask black strikebreakers to leave. When the blacks joined white ethnics and others on the picket line, they received specific assurances from the United Auto Workers that no discrimination against black workers would be permitted.

Although the CIO brought large numbers of black Americans into unions for the first time, Depression conditions worsened unemployment among northern blacks and trapped others in the most poorly paid service and manual labor positions. Job mobility for northern blacks continued to lag behind that of the white ethnics, as black workers frequently were excluded even from semiskilled positions in manufacturing and transportation. Meanwhile, black unemployment rates were three times as high as those for whites. About half the nation's black workers held no job during the depths of the Depression. Because employers often believed that no black should hold a job that a white could fill, nearly two-thirds of the black labor force continued to be confined to agricultural and domestic service.

The New Deal had a mixed impact on northern blacks. Because black unemployment was so high, blacks represented a substantial number of relief recipients. Public aid to unemployed blacks in cities was one of the reasons for continued black migration to urban centers, as the exodus from the South continued at about half the pace of the 1920s. As a result, the percentage of urban blacks who received Depression relief was three times that of urban whites. But demoralizing conditions in urban ghettos fostered profound resentment. Lack of job opportunities and hostility to white store owners and police resulted in a major riot in Harlem during March 1935, in which three blacks were killed, thirty hospitalized, and $2 million worth of property damaged in widespread looting and rioting. The bitterness and incipient violence of northern ghetto life were brutally portrayed by the black novelist Richard Wright in *Native Son* (1940).

Although northern ghettos were no Promised Land, it was not hard to understand why blacks continued to join poor whites in leaving the rural South. Cultivation of cotton and tobacco as well as excessive timber cutting already had depleted much of southern soil when the Depression began. The combination of economic collapse and the use of synthetic fibers devastated the market for cotton, the basic crop of the Deep South. By 1932 cotton prices plummeted to barely a nickel a pound, the lowest price since the crisis of the 1890s. As banks and insurance companies foreclosed one-third of southern cotton fields, black farmers found themselves at the mercy of landlords, heavy debt, and high interest rates. It was no surprise, then, when the president's Committee on Farm Tenancy described the sharecropper standard of living as "below any level of decency" in 1937.

AAA benefits to landlords who limited acreage aggravated the condition of black tenants and sharecroppers. Landlords easily evaded government stipulations that sharecroppers be given a portion of benefits by keeping most of the money in payment for debts, real or imaginary. When provisions of later government contracts assured that sharecroppers would receive direct payments, many landlords classified tenants as wage hands and invested government checks in tractors. As the sale of tractors

nearly doubled in the ten cotton states, tenants and sharecroppers were either dispossessed, reduced to dependence on landlords, or converted to low-paid casual labor in an increasingly mechanized industry.

While economic conditions grew worse, racial segregation continued to confine southern blacks to a rigid caste system. Restaurants, restrooms, and public transit continued to be segregated, while blacks attended separate schools and churches. Even movie theaters featured a separate black balcony, derisively referred to as "nigger heaven." Blacks in many southern towns were addressed only by their first name, regardless of age, and were expected to use the rear door when calling on whites. Southern localities traditionally excluded blacks from jury service, while a rigid arrangement of poll taxes and literacy tests prevented black voting.

Ever since the 1890s, southern racial antagonism had occasionally erupted in orgiastic lynching sprees. White men in the rural South continued to believe that black males constituted a threat to the purity of white women and social decorum. During 1931 nine black teenage hoboes in Alabama were falsely convicted of raping two white girls riding the same freight train. The *Scottsboro* case became one of the major civil liberty causes of the era. Initiated by the Communist party, the campaign to save the Alabama blacks taught many white liberals the degree to which white racism permeated southern social structure. But Communist efforts to recruit blacks by advocating national "self-determination" for the "black belt" of the South never succeeded. Black membership failed to exceed 10 percent of the small Communist party in the thirties.

Communists and Socialists, nevertheless, had some success in organizing black tenants and sharecroppers. In some regions the collapse of the cotton economy helped to weaken the social subservience of black "croppers." With plantations bankrupt and absentee ownership increased, the tight network of patrols, penalties, and personal supervision weakened in the thirties. At the same time, increased class militancy among poor southern whites sometimes acted to soften racial animosity. An influx of liberal New Dealers into the South also contributed to political unrest, stimulating the first mass protest involving rural blacks since the Colored Farmers Alliance of the 1890s.

Initiated by white Communists trying to mobilize southern blacks, the biracial Alabama Sharecroppers Union was founded in 1931. The union attacked wage cuts, foreclosures, and forced labor. Because it threatened established dependence on the planters, the Sharecroppers Union met violent repression from growers and local authorities and fought shoot-outs with county deputies in 1931 and 1932. By 1935 the ASU claimed twelve thousand members in several states and had broken the taboo against assertive violence by black men.

In Arkansas a group of local blacks and whites organized the Southern Tenant Farmers Union in 1934. Some of the whites once had belonged to the Ku Klux Klan, and others were affiliated with Norman Thomas's Socialist party. Thomas quickly became the public spokesman for the union and strove to make the plight of tenants, sharecroppers, and field workers a national issue. A successful STFU strike in eastern Arkansas led to cotton wage increases and the spread of the union to other states in the Deep South. By 1935 the STFU had twenty-five thousand members. When the union initiated another strike in 1936, the Arkansas National Guard prevented strikers from using highways for protest marches. Thomas pleaded for federal intervention, but the only government response was the Bankhead-Jones Act of 1937, an attempt to apply the small-homestead philosophy to the tenant problem through farm purchase loans. By 1941, however, Farm Security Administration loans covered less than 1 percent of the tenant-sharecropper population.

The last major action of the STFU involved a 1939 roadside encampment of one thousand black sharecroppers evicted from cotton lands in southeastern Missouri. The demonstration attracted national attention and exposed sharecropping conditions that shocked many Americans. In its brief life, the STFU made a sweeping attack on the system of class and racial peonage in the South, crusading against poll taxes, inferior education, discrimination in relief, and denial of civil liberties. But since its membership was biracial and class oriented, the STFU was extremely threatening to local landowners. Southern conservatives would continue to associate civil rights activity with agitation by white radicals for many decades. But once the STFU was absorbed by the CIO in the late thirties, dues paying and membership forms alienated agricultural workers, and the movement collapsed.

While southern blacks fell victim to the mechanization of agriculture, northern black voters began to support the New Deal with heavy voting majorities by 1936. Yet the Roosevelt administration failed to offer any civil rights program. Tied to a coalition that included southern Democrats, the president never challenged white supremacy or states' rights on racial matters. Accordingly, Roosevelt refused to commit himself to a crusade by blacks and liberal allies for a federal antilynching law. Meanwhile, the NAACP and black leaders condemned racial discrimination in New Deal work programs, fought successfully to include blacks in the CCC, and protested segregation

These quarters for black sharecroppers outside Tupelo, Mississippi (1936) reflect the kind of deprivation suffered by farmworkers during the Depression. (Walker Evans/Library of Congress)

in TVA model towns. The NAACP also continued legal campaigns for black rights in education, voting, and public accommodations. In addition, a new coalition, the National Negro Congress, brought together virtually every national black leader in 1936 to work for "racial progress." Led by union organizer A. Philip Randolph, the NNC encouraged black participation in the labor movement and tried to tie black interests to New Deal liberalism. But a Communist attempt to win control of the organization led to a fatal defection by NNC leaders in 1940.

Although Roosevelt remained cool to civil rights demands, the president's wife was a friendly advocate of black issues. When the Daughters of the American Revolution refused to rent Washington's only concert stage to

Marian Anderson, a black opera singer, Eleanor Roosevelt arranged for a recital on the steps of the Lincoln Memorial. There, on Easter Sunday, 1939, seventy-five thousand people gathered with administration support for the first mass demonstration for civil rights in American history. The previous spring, black heavyweight Joe Louis had defeated the German Max Schmeling with a first-round knockout in a boxing match promoted by Hitler as a test of Nazi racial supermen. The Louis victory not only showed that Americans could accept a black man as a fighter, but demonstrated that unlike German power, American strength derived from the pluralism of its culture. Nevertheless, the Depression provided few opportunities and many difficulties for the millions of black Americans who remained trapped in southern rural poverty or the hopeless ghettos of the North.

MEXICAN-AMERICANS, FARM LABOR, AND THE "INDIAN NEW DEAL"

Migrants from Mexico were not included in the immigration restriction laws of the twenties. But when the Depression brought decreasing job opportunities in southwestern agribusiness and midwestern industries, local pressures mounted in a campaign to "repatriate" Mexican-Americans south of the border. Signs in the Southwest read "No Niggers, Mexicans, or Dogs Allowed." More than a half million Mexican-Americans left the United States during the 1930s, half of them American born. In Los Angeles, the largest Mexican community in the nation, massive police roundups and arrests during 1931 forced barrio inhabitants to flee the country. Local welfare officials in the

Southwest frequently told Mexican-Americans to leave or lose relief checks. In the Midwest, a coalition of civic groups and local authorities subsidized the exodus of nearly half the Mexicans in the area, believing it less expensive to pay transportation costs to Mexico than to continue to pay relief and unemployment benefits. Although leaders of the Mexican community sometimes supported the return home, local officials seldom informed Mexican-Americans of their rights, and the repatriation campaigns often involved racial intimidation.

Mexican-American farmworkers, imported into the Southwest during the booming twenties, were particularly affected by the Depression. As AAA crop-reduction policies and competition from white migrants made agricultural work scarce, large numbers of Mexican workers attempted to leave the fields for relief and the promise of jobs in the cities. But they seldom were welcome. Under a temporary declaration of martial law, for example, Colorado used the National Guard to turn Mexican job seekers away at the New Mexico border. Those who remained in southwestern vegetable and fruit fields faced decreasing wage scales and deplorable working conditions. Like the black sharecroppers and tenants of the South, Mexican-American farmworkers responded by organizing unions in an increasingly mechanized industry. By 1934 a Mexican confederation of field unions embraced fifty locals and five thousand members. A Cannery and Agricultural Workers Industrial Union and a Trade Union Unity League, both organized by California Communists, also provided leadership and counsel for the Mexican farmworker movement.

Responding to the threat of Communist agitation and labor unrest in the perishable citrus and vegetable industry, California growers received financial backing from banks and utilities to form the Associated Farmers. The association worked in cooperation with state and local police to harvest crops in case of strikes, serve as deputies, and distribute propaganda against the agricultural union movement. Through the influence of the large growers, local authorities in California passed scores of antipicketing and emergency-disaster ordinances and succeeded in gaining state prohibitions against sympathetic strikes, relief for strikers, and the Communist party. Consequently, farm union followers frequently faced vigilante attacks and mass arrests. During one strike, 150 Mexican-Americans were arrested for trespassing on a public highway. Likewise, eight leaders of the CAWIU went to prison in 1934 under state criminal syndicalist charges.

Most Mexican-American unions eventually affiliated with the AFL or CIO, but geographic mobility, violent repression, and the size of the agricultural labor force posed too great a challenge. The thirties produced a legacy of agricultural unionism among Mexican-Americans in California, but New Deal labor legislation did not cover field workers, and the situation in farm labor remained bleak. In Texas, Mexican-Americans had even less access to school or health facilities and labored under the harshest agricultural working conditions in the nation. Not until the 1960s would Mexican-Americans succeed in organizing unions in the volatile citrus and vegetable industry. Meanwhile, conditions in the urban barrios of the Southwest began to resemble the impoverishment of the black ghettos of the Northeast and Midwest.

White migrants in California's farm fields fared no better than the Mexican- and Japanese-Americans they sometimes replaced. Massive drought and destructive dust storms forced 200,000 poor whites to flee the Great Plains during the mid-thirties. These dispossessed farmers and tenants, immortalized in John Steinbeck's *Grapes of Wrath* (1939), sought work in California agribusiness. Like the Mexican-Americans, the Plains refugees organized farmworkers unions, but police and growers brutally attacked them as "Oakie" misfits who were dupes for "red" agitators. Talk of a lettuce strike by white workers in the Imperial Valley, for example, brought a wave of "preventive" arrests by local officials in 1935. When the lettuce workers went on strike the following season, the Associated Farmers spent $225,000 to smash the union and save the $12 million crop. In the successful campaign against union activity, the growers' association mobilized all male residents of Salinas between the ages of eighteen and forty-five and deputized twenty-five hundred men with arms. Against such odds, white farmworker unions also failed.

While agricultural field workers, dispossessed farmers, tenants, and sharecroppers suffered under Depression conditions, Native Americans cautiously approached the administration's "Indian New Deal." Under the leadership of Commissioner of Indian Affairs John Collier, the federal government encouraged tribal organization, economic self-sufficiency, and self-management in a campaign for conservation of Native American culture and resources. Collier created an Emergency Conservation Work Program, an "all-Indian CCC," to organize reservation projects in 1933. But the reform commissioner's most important accomplishment was the Indian Reorganization Act of 1934. This law guaranteed the principle of home rule through tribal constitutions written and ratified by each tribe in referendum. The law also provided government financial aid to support college education and promote study of

Native American culture, traditions, and crafts. Its most controversial provision was the reversion of landholdings to tribal title. Since the Dawes Act of 1887, landholding had been individual. But almost half the 1934 holdings were semiarid or desert lands, and only half the Native Americans in the country owned any land. Average Indian income in 1934 was $48 a year.

Most Native Americans distrusted Collier's program, but over two-thirds the tribes voted to participate. White critics condemned the tribal property arrangement as "sovietization" of reservation life and claimed that the Bureau of Indian Affairs was relegating Native Americans to reservation existence. But Collier believed

that tribal cooperative and communal experience provided an alternative to the atomization of urban industrialism. Despite reduced appropriations, Collier directed the bureau to assist self-governing tribal corporations in using conservation techniques on the land and establishing cooperative businesses. Native Americans also won freedom of contract under the New Deal, no longer needing approval by the secretary of the interior for tribal agreements.

Nevertheless, Collier's policies were projections of white aspirations and perceptions onto Native American life. At times his overall conservation goals, which served national and New Deal needs, interfered with tribal autonomy. In New Mexico, for example, Collier's

Depression unemployment among blacks was three times as high as that of whites. (Brown Brothers)

emphasis on herd reduction and range management replaced goals of Navajo self-rule and preservation of tribal culture. The Navajos had rejected the Indian Reorganization Act and bitterly opposed extension of New Deal agricultural policy to their way of life. Furthermore, New Deal programs for Native Americans only affected those on reservations. In Oklahoma, where half the nation's native people lived, poverty resulting from the thirties drought eliminated private land leasing or made it difficult for Native American property holders to collect rent. Government surplus food and clothing did little to alleviate mass destitution among Oklahoma tribes in a state where three-fourths of Native American children were undernourished, and food shortages and tuberculosis increased drastically in the Depression.

THE FAILURE OF RADICALISM AND THE SEARCH FOR ORDER

The Depression provided American writers and artists with the chance to overcome the isolation of the twenties intelligentsia and speak to the needs of ordinary people. Amid economic collapse and rampant insecurity, men and women of letters rejected the self-indulgence of twenties self-expression and began to focus on social and political themes. Believing that individuals were helpless unless they were part of some larger class, movement, or community, thirties intellectuals stressed the interconnectedness of society and the imperatives of social realism. "There is no longer I," the humorist Dorothy Parker explained, "there is WE." When the aviator Amelia Earhart was lost at sea in a venture reminiscent of Lindbergh's flight across the Atlantic, the liberal *New Republic* asked the government to prohibit citizens from engaging in such "useless" exploits.

For many social intellectuals, the Crash provided the opportunity to guide the American people to a reconstruction of society. The economist Stuart Chase wrote widely selling books that suggested that a collectivist economy, neither capitalist nor socialist, could best use technology to distribute wealth. Chase's hopes for a planned cooperative commonwealth were shared by Progressives such as John Dewey, Lincoln Steffens, and the economist George Soule. While the Depression encouraged former Progressives to espouse democratic socialism, younger theorists such as the philosopher Sidney Hook and theologian Reinhold Niebuhr borrowed aspects of Marxism to suggest that the Crash had outdated liberal approaches to political and economic problems. Whatever their politics, most of the leading social theorists of the thirties called for redistribution of wealth and power in a planned economy directed toward the elimination of poverty and the building of a sense of national community.

The obvious failures of corporate liberalism produced a great interest in Marxism and the Communist party in the 1930s. Desiring to re-enter the mainstream of American life, middle-class writers believed they had to be people of action as well as thought. The Communist party informed intellectuals that capitalism faced bankruptcy because its incessant need to expand could never be sustained. Only through an assumption of power by the working class, the party argued, could the decadent ruling class be replaced and the economy geared to human needs instead of profits. Once historical laws brought the achievement of socialism, workers would no longer be exploited, and depressions would be erased forever through a planned economy that eliminated private property.

For intellectuals looking for an answer to the perplexities of the Crash, the "scientific" approach of communism was compelling. Led by literary and social critics such as Sidney Hook, Edmund Wilson, Mike Gold, and Joseph Freeman, fifty-three writers signed an open letter supporting the Communist ticket in the presidential election of 1932. American capitalism "was like a house rotting away," the appeal read, the wreckage "of obsolete social patterns and institutions." Journals such as Gold's *New Masses* and V. F. Calverton's *Modern Quarterly* continually stressed collectivist ideas as a replacement for "bourgeois" individualism and liberal politics. While scholars such as the literary historian Granville Hicks brought academics into the Communist movement, the party's National Student League mobilized college campuses with crusades for academic freedom, fund raising for striking workers, and the introduction of "class struggle" into classroom dialogues. Communists also figured significantly in the major antiwar demonstration of the decade — a national student walkout on April 13, 1934, which attracted between 500,000 and a million students.

Thirties literature reflected the political concerns of intellectuals seeking a new order. Even those outside the Communist movement shared the hope that the working class would bring a revitalized future. Several writers, including Edmund Wilson, Sherwood Anderson, and John Dos Passos, turned to the documentary to present the unadorned facts of daily life and focus on the dialogue and behavior of ordinary Americans. In *Let Us Now Praise Famous Men* (1941), a documentary compiled for the Farm Security Administration, James Agee and Walker Evans put together a moving photo-essay that portrayed the dignity and perseverance of a group of Alabama sharecroppers.

Other middle-class intellectuals achieved a vicarious sense of militancy by incorporating working-class consciousness in "proletarian novels" such as Robert Cantwell's *The Land of Plenty* (1934) and Jack Conroy's *The Disinherited* (1933). Organized labor and industrial workers provided the heroes of these novels, but in order to teach readers the necessities of revolution and class solidarity, proletarian novels usually involved bitterly lost strikes. In a period in which "social significance" provided the criteria for artistic judgment, literature became a weapon of class war for middle-class intellectuals. The lost generation of the twenties had found its social mission.

The literary style of Depression writers aspired toward easy communication. In the effort to re-establish communication with the American people, social novelists preferred substance over images, experience over ideas, situations over symbols. Even Ernest Hemingway rooted his concern for individualism in the social realism of *To Have and Have Not* (1937), a strike novel in which a character explains that "a man alone ain't got no...bloody chance." Hemingway's *For Whom the Bell Tolls* (1941) introduced an allegorical discussion of individual will and solidarity within the context of the antifascist campaigns of the Spanish civil war. The same concern for endurance and personal survival could be found in *Tobacco Road* (1932), Erskine Caldwell's popular story of an impoverished family of Georgia sharecroppers. In the *Studs Lonigan* trilogy (1936), James T. Farrell placed the struggle for survival among lower-middle-class Irish-Catholics in the slums of Chicago.

Although social realism and class conflict defined most of thirties literature, the most lasting novels returned to themes of personal honor and integrity. In his *U.S.A.* trilogy, John Dos

Passos depicted the moral disintegration of the American spirit through the distortion of language and the senseless chatter of public relations rhetoric. Praised by the Communist party and translated in the Soviet Union, Dos Passos's novels borrowed the techniques of film to present a social montage of real-life biographies, multiple protagonists, newsreels, popular songs, and stream-of-consciousness reporting. But the underlying conflict of *U.S.A.* was the struggle between old-fashioned producer-pioneers and the institutional managers of collective capitalism. Confronted with Depression despair, Dos Passos concluded that the only way to preserve the sanctity of the individual was to reject organized society and collective politics.

Like Dos Passos, John Steinbeck focused on human fortitude amid the mechanization and impersonality of corporate institutions. In *The Grapes of Wrath* (1939), the most popular social novel of the period, Steinbeck reiterated the American faith that when people lost roots in the soil, they lost everything else too. Although the novel described union organizing among Dust Bowl migrants in the California fields, its emotional impact hinged on a basic appeal to the poetry of simple language, family love, and the human impulse to help. Admiration for the ordinary people, not militant ideology, characterized Steinbeck's portrait of the will to survive. "We keep a-comin'. We're the people that live," the novel's family matriarch explained. "They ain't gonna wipe us out. Why, we're the people — we go on."

The heroes of many Depression documentaries and novels were not industrial workers but tenant farmers, sharecroppers, and migrant workers who loved the land and were descended from the nation's early pioneers. Radicals hoped that such stories might convert the American people to the ideal of social recon-

struction. Yet the readership for most of the social novels and documentaries was middle class, and thirties literature reflected a persistent traditionalism among writers and intellectuals. Literary radicals were drawn to revolution as an act of individual will rather than economic necessity. Moved by the need for action and commitment, they tended to become obsessed with personal purity, striving to purge themselves of "bourgeois" attitudes and temptations. Concern over personal purity affected attitudes toward literature. While many of the radicals professed a Marxian approach toward literary criticism, they usually evaluated art by the criterion of whether it adopted correct positions on particular issues. At times, the proletarian novels only seemed to provide a ceremonial catharsis for middle-class radicals whose basic goals were cooperation and stability.

The limitations of the radical Left became more explicit when threats of international fascism moved the Soviet Union to espouse a "popular front" between national Communist movements and other political parties in 1935. The new coalition meant that American Communists were to accept New Deal institutions, adopt Roosevelt as the people's leader, and view social change as an evolutionary process. Communists even abandoned "dual unions," an arrangement by which party workers established independent caucuses to shadow the regular unions to which they belonged. By 1939 CIO membership was 10 to 20 percent Communist, but party members never exerted independent influence in union affairs.

The popular front made peace, social progress, and democratic values the leading priorities of the Communist movement; a defensive posture that bolstered the status quo and undermined critical judgment. "Communism is twentieth-century Americanism," party leader

(National Portrait Gallery, Smithsonian Institution, Washington, D.C.)

Asa Philip Randolph

1889-1979

A. Philip Randolph, a dignified and soft-spoken man who was president of a small union of sleeping-car porters, was the single most important black leader of the 1930s. By 1941 Randolph's efforts to build a mass movement of black working people had elicited the first federal proclamation concerning black Americans since the Civil War.

A devout reader of W. E. B. DuBois, Randolph left Jacksonville, Florida, on a steamboat for New York in 1911. Believing himself to be a member of DuBois's "talented tenth," Randolph took night classes at City College and gravitated toward socialism. In 1915 he and friends launched The Messenger, whose first page proclaimed it "the only radical Negro magazine in America." After a futile attempt to organize hotel waiters, The Messenger began to rally blacks to oppose participation in World War One until democracy was achieved at home. Characterizing the magazine as "the most dangerous of all the Negro publications," the Justice Department briefly detained Randolph and his copublisher for violations of the Espionage Act in 1918. Nevertheless, The Messenger continued to be a center of radical thought in the early days of the Harlem Renaissance.

The turning point in Randolph's career came when black railroad porters asked him to organize a union in 1925. Ever since Emancipation, the Pullman Company had hired only black men as porters, believing that subservient and congenial former slaves would accept insults and demands from white passengers. But Pullman was the largest private employer of blacks in the nation, and Randolph hoped to show that his people could build and sustain a movement for their own economic survival and not permit whites to choose their leaders. The Brotherhood of Sleeping Car Porters organized half the Pullman porters and maids within three years, demanding an end to demeaning tipping, *calling for higher monthly salaries, and insisting that porters be treated with respect.*

Randolph's success with the porters catapulted him into national black leadership. As president of the National Negro Congress, he called for a "new deal" for America's "submerged tenth" and urged blacks to join the burgeoning union movement. Randolph reasoned that black struggles for social justice were linked to the efforts of the white working class and liberal allies. But he also pointed out that "the salvation of the Negro, like the workers, must come from within." Accordingly, when the Roosevelt administration failed to heed protests against racial discrimination in government and defense jobs, Randolph prepared to lead a march of 100,000 black working people to the capital in 1941. "Power and pressure," he told the nation's civil rights organizations, "are at the foundation of the march of social justice and reform."

Despite pleas for restraint from white liberals such as Eleanor Roosevelt and Fiorello LaGuardia, Randolph insisted that "there are some things Negroes must do alone." His strategy worked brilliantly. One week before the scheduled march, Roosevelt agreed to issue Executive Order 8802, which forbade discrimination in government and defense hiring and created a Fair Employment Practices Commission. Randolph appreciated the president's action as a substantial gain for blacks and called off the protest. Although enforcement of the government order proved inconsistent, Randolph had opened the way to massive demonstrations by organized blacks. Twenty-two years later, he saw the fruit of his pioneering when he introduced Martin Luther King, Jr. to a crowd of 200,000 at the celebrated 1963 March on Washington. From DuBois to King, Randolph's remarkable career embodied the continuities of black leadership in the twentieth century.

Earl Browder declared in the effort to reduce anxieties about the revolutionary potential of Communist politics. For intellectuals not often attuned to the intricacies of Marxian analysis, the shift to popular front tactics was a welcome one. In *I Like America* (1938), Granville Hicks wrote simply: "I am a Communist, and I want the same things you do."

Many radical intellectuals suspended critical judgment as loyal Communists and as supporters of the popular front. Fearing fascism without an alliance with the middle class, communist sympathizers embraced the Roosevelt coalition's faith in technical expertise, accepting the view that social problems could best be solved through pragmatism instead of ideology. By 1938 the Communist party had recruited fifty-five thousand members. But when the popular front was defeated by Fascists in the Spanish civil war, American Communists began to doubt whether the Left might succeed anywhere. The disillusioning defeat in Spain accompanied news of Josef Stalin's purges of fellow revolutionaries in the Soviet Union and announcement of the Nazi-Soviet Nonaggression Pact of 1939. These developments only heightened the fears of those Americans who associated Communist loyalty with loss of personal freedom and subservience to the national interests of the Soviet Union. By the end of the decade, many American radicals felt sure that capitalism was not dying and that human rights were better preserved in the United States than in the growing number of totalitarian regimes overseas.

The lost fervor of social change brought intellectuals and writers to a rediscovery and reaffirmation of American life. In *The Ground We Stand On* (1941), Dos Passos presented a tribute to the founding fathers. Alfred Kazin's *On Native Grounds* (1942) sought out the vitality of the nation's twentieth-century literature and emphasized how important a role writers and intellectuals play in American values and traditions. The poet Archibald Mac-Leish, one of the most outspoken proponents of the popular front, now wrote lyrical epics of the golden past and argued that a "constructive" literature should be based on the language of acceptance and belief. As the literary historian Malcolm Cowley suggested, writers were "turning back to the great past in order to see the real nature of the traditions that we are trying to save." By World War Two, it was clear that Depression intellectuals and writers had been seeking recovery and stability, not revolt, and that they welcomed the wartime opportunity to affirm and conserve the core values of American life. The political and psychic wounds of the 1930s produced an entire generation of intellectuals committed to the support of an American consensus. No longer willing to mount criticism against the nation's culture and institutions, intellectuals increasingly tied their activities to government programs and support of the status quo.

TOWARD A NATIONAL CULTURE

New Deal arts programs complemented and supported the search for a national culture by writers and artists. Roosevelt believed that Americans were entitled to cultural enrichment as well as economic and social justice. He hoped to use the arts projects of the WPA to provide work relief for visual artists, musicians, actors, and writers. But Roosevelt and WPA Director Hopkins also wished to democratize the arts by creating a nation of cultural consumers. The WPA's public murals, community arts centers, traveling exhibits, and free concerts were designed to involve community participation in the creation of a national art and to provide mass audiences for once-privileged entertainment. The results were widely mixed. Thousands of post office murals left a legacy of bland social realism in painting, but WPA funding also inspired artistic regionalism and the recovery of lost folklore and handicrafts. The composer Aaron Copland, for example, abandoned avant-garde abstractionism to produce *Billy the Kid* and *Rodeo* for the WPA, two suites based on western folk melodies and stories. Through the auspices of government grants, the documentary emerged as a major art form, embracing film, photography, journalism, broadcasting, and even the "living newspapers" of the Federal Theater Project. Although conservatives objected to government subsidy of artists and intellectuals, the New Deal helped to inspire what Alfred Kazin called the "drive toward national inventory" — the search for a national culture and a usable past.

One of the most divisive issues of the late twenties had been the continuing battle over Prohibition. But when Utah ratified the Twenty-first Amendment in late 1933, one more symbol of Anglo-Protestant cultural dominance was erased. While eight states chose to remain dry and fifteen others sold liquor through state monopolies, drinking never again became a national issue. The return of alcoholic beverages gave legitimacy to the cosmopolitan culture of the urban middle class. As large nightclubs blossomed in the big cities, young people flocked to listen to the mellow, self-effacing vocalists of the big bands and to dance to "swing," a white refinement of "hot" black jazz and "boogie-woogie." Jewish bandleader Benny Goodman broke new ground in urban popular music by including black pianist Teddy Wilson in his swing group and performing concerts at New York's prestigious Carnegie Hall. Meanwhile, acculturated city blacks began to replace the country blues of the twenties with more up-tempo urban blues. In turn, the new black idioms of city blues and jazz were presented to interracial audiences by outstanding black musicians such as Duke Ellington and the singer Billie Holiday.

In cities such as New Orleans, Kansas City, and Chicago, a small group of bohemians, writers, and artists began to gravitate to interracial jazz culture. Musicians and jazz enthusiasts frequently found communion in the sharing of marijuana, a mild euphoriant first brought to the United States by Mexican-Americans and sailors. But as marijuana made its way out of big-city ghettos and barrios, the federal government mounted a campaign to protect middle-class whites from the "loco weed." Harry J. Anslinger, the first director of the Federal Narcotics Bureau, lobbied successfully for a 1937 Marihuana Tax Act, testifying that the wild plant "often gives man the lust to kill unreasonably and without motive." Several states followed by outlawing the possession of marijuana. Despite subsequent reports that contested Anslinger's claims that marijuana was addictive and a "national menace," the federal government continued to mount campaigns against marijuana smoking in the 1940s.

While most Americans did not participate in either marijuana culture or jazz night life, the thirties accelerated a long-range trend toward family consumption in extended leisure. Employment cutbacks in the early Depression brought widespread imitation of Henry Ford's five-day week, first instituted in 1926. By 1940 the average work week was forty-four hours, in contrast to sixty-six hours in the 1870s. The advent of the weekend encouraged a search for inexpensive entertainment, particularly in par-

ticipant sports. Accordingly, the number of municipal golf courses, beaches, swimming pools, and ice-skating areas doubled between 1925 and 1935. Bicycling, roller skating, and softball also provided healthy forms of inexpensive play for Depression families. By 1937 the WPA had spent $500 million for recreational facilities in an effort to democratize sports through participation and to further family consumerism.

The most popular form of daily entertainment in the Depression was radio listening. By 1938 there were forty million radio receivers in the United States. Once the initial purchase was made, families could share the networks' free fare of live commentary, music, variety, and adventure shows. Low-income listeners, women, and rural Americans actually preferred the radio to the written press as a source of news. Like thirties news magazines such as *Time* and *Life*, radio news programs familiarized millions of people with common crises and dangers. But they also helped to overcome the disintegrating aspects of modern life and the chaotic insecurity of the economic collapse. As a psychological study in 1935 indicated, radio encouraged Americans to think and feel alike by providing listeners with "an imaginative sense of participation in a common activity." While families gathered to listen to favorite shows, network programming and advertising also tied isolated individuals to a national community.

By creating uniform standards of speech, taste, and humor, radio did much to nationalize ethnics, social classes, and regional groups. Yet the networks used old stereotypes in bringing ethnic and racial minorities into the national consensus. The comical "Amos 'n' Andy," a white portrait of two opportunistic big-city blacks, contributed to interracial communication through shared humor, but some blacks objected to the perpetuation of the minstrel tradition of the "black face." At the same time, the "Jack Benny Show" provided the black valet Rochester with ample opportunity to ridicule the eccentricities of his penny-pinching boss. Jewish stereotypes found their way into a sympathetic account of life on Manhattan's Lower East Side in "Molly Goldberg."

One of the most popular radio shows was "The Lone Ranger," a timeless adventure that pitted the personal justice of the hero and his Indian guide against an inexhaustible supply of outlaws on the open spaces of the Texas frontier. Depression insecurity and government paternalism seemed to create the need for fantasy heroes who employed virile, individualistic approaches to evil and adversity. The same themes appeared in syndicated comic strips in daily newspapers. "Dick Tracy," begun in 1931, represented the detective as avenging angel. "Radio Patrol" pictured crime as disorder and used the latest techniques of scientific gadgetry to combat it. "Buck Rogers," which first appeared in 1930, employed technology to eliminate social problems in the escapist universe of science fiction. Meanwhile, "Tarzan," who began swinging through the jungle in 1929, provided comic strip fans with a man accountable to no one. By 1938, "Superman" was demonstrating that justice could be achieved through personal strength and ruthless efficiency. The conservative message of the comic strips found its way into Walt Disney animated film cartoons such as "Three Little Pigs" (1933), which suggested that the pig who worked hard but used modern materials and tools would be successful if he stuck to society's rules.

Although radio and the comic strips provided enormous cultural influence, Hollywood remained the nation's primary builder of unify-

ing myths and dreams. By 1939 an estimated 65 percent of the American people went to the movies at least once a week. With the advent of sound in the late twenties, Hollywood studios began producing provocative and iconoclastic films that questioned sexual propriety, social decorum, and even institutions of law and order. Sensual European actresses such as Greta Garbo and Marlene Dietrich, as well as the American Jean Harlow, spoke frankly of sex in early "talkies" and even portrayed prostitutes. At the same time, the irreverent comedies of W. C. Fields, Mae West, and the Marx Brothers brought lighthearted vulgarity and lechery to the screen in sardonic parodies of middle-class pretensions.

While sex and comedy seemed to create an immoral universe, gangster and horror movies introduced elements of moral ambivalence in the early thirties. James Cagney in *Public Enemy* (1931) and Edward G. Robinson in *Little Caesar* (1930) portrayed city criminals whose chaotic lives seemed to reflect the instabilities of the Depression, but whose sense of duty and obligation ultimately triumphed over the urge to rebel. Tough-talking gangster heroes reinforced male images of masculinity threatened by Depression economics. But while hard-bitten criminals won admiration for their grace under pressure, they usually surrendered their alienation and rage for love and comradeship. A similar moral ambivalence was expressed in horror movies such as *King Kong* (1933), which suggested both fear for society's survival and pleasure at the rage vent upon it. Films such as *Dracula* (1931) and *Frankenstein* (1931) expressed more conservative themes by suggesting that the true villains were not horrifying monsters, but solitary scientists who wished to tamper with the natural order of things.

Despite the conventional messages of the

gangster and horror films, Hollywood began to re-evaluate its product by 1933, when Depression cutbacks forced one-third of the nation's movie theaters to close. At the same time, the industry's future was threatened by disapproval from the Roman Catholic church. As the campaign to repeal Prohibition gathered steam, the church began to step into the moral leadership abdicated by feuding Protestant authorities. American bishops in the church created the Legion of Decency in 1933 and announced a campaign to boycott movies considered indecent. Within several months, the legion claimed eleven million signatures on boycott petitions. In response, Will Hays of the Motion Picture Producers and Distributors Association created the industry's own self-policing Production Code Administration. The PCA devised a formula to keep movie sex and crime within moral bounds. Elements of "good" in film scenarios were to balance "evil." According to the principle of compensating moral value, bad acts were to be followed by punishment or retribution, reform or regeneration. The code dictated that "evil and good are never to be confused throughout the presentation," that the guilty were to be punished, and that audiences were not to be encouraged to sympathize with crime or sin. The code also prohibited film portraits of homosexuality, interracial sex, abortion, incest, drugs, profanity, and vulgar language — including the word *sex* itself.

Movies began to follow the guidelines of the Production Code Administration after 1934. "Screwball comedies" featuring Hollywood stars such as Cary Grant, Katherine Hepburn, and James Stewart portrayed the zany antics of the rich, but celebrated the sanctity of marriage, class distinction, and the domination of women by men. Films like *Holiday* (1938) stressed how attractive it was to be a person who liked to have fun and parodied the formal decorum of the old aristocracy; but they also emphasized old-fashioned values such as moderation and family love. In a similar vein, a series of films starring Shirley Temple romanticized the innocence and playfulness of childhood. The trend toward affirmative and sentimental films was propelled by director Frank Capra, whose movies presented images of small towns with comfortable, close-knit American families and friendly neighbors. In *Mr. Deeds Goes to Town* (1936) and *You Can't Take It With You* (1938), folksy male heroes inspired "the people" to rally behind them. These idealizations of social relationships suggested that social problems could be solved by placing more neighborly and responsible people at the top of society's hierarchy and that the basic institutions of American life were sound. Sagas such as *Gone with the Wind* (1939) and even *The Grapes of Wrath* (1940) also conveyed the idea that the American people had rich resources to draw upon in time of trouble.

By the eve of World War Two, the majority of American intellectuals, artists, and purveyors of popular culture had arrived at a consensus that stressed a celebration of conformity and an appeal for national unity. This consensus often extended to union leaders and representatives of the various ethnic and racial communities. Instead of ushering in a period of social reconstruction, as many radicals had hoped, the Depression seemed to reaffirm conservative traditions in American life, to engender passivity toward authority, and to bring new emphasis to the importance of material goods and sound family life. A whole generation of Americans would never forget the insecurities of the economic collapse and would strive in the postwar years to make sure they never returned. The profound legacy of the thirties was the obsessive search for security by a people who felt vulnerable in a world of uncertainties.

SUGGESTED READINGS

Charles C. Alexander, *Nationalism in American Thought, 1930–1945* (1969), provides a useful introduction to the cultural themes of the Roosevelt era. For a graceful account of the social effects of the Depression, see Caroline Bird, *The Invisible Scar* (1966). Robert S. Lynd and Helen M. Lynd's *Middletown in Transition* (1937) describes the consequences of economic collapse for the people of a small town. A moving collection of personal reminiscences is Studs Terkel, *Hard Times* (1970). Harvey Swados, ed., *The American Writer and the Great Depression* (1966), presents a rich assortment of Depression portraits and fiction. The loss of Depression opportunities for women is outlined in the relevant chapters of William H. Chafe, *The American Woman: Her Changing Social, Economic, and Political Role, 1920–1970* (1972).

An innovative account of the assimilation of immigrants during the Depression appears in the relevant chapters of Gilman M. Ostrander, *American Civilization in the First Machine Age, 1890–1940* (1970). See also the appropriate sections of Richard Krickus, *Pursuing the American Dream: White Ethnics and the New Populism* (1976). Thirties labor struggles are portrayed in Louis Adamic, *My America, 1928–1938* (1938), and the exhaustive Irving Bernstein, *The Turbulent Years: A History of the American Worker, 1933–1941* (1970).

Blacks in the Depression are described comprehensively in Gunnar Myrdal, *An American Dilemma* (1944). For a portrait of southern segregation, see the relevant chapters of Hor-tense Powdermaker, *After Freedom: A Cultural Study of the Deep South* (1939). Black treatment by New Deal agencies is chronicled in Leslie H. Fishel, Jr., "The Negro and the New Deal," in Richard Resh, ed., *Black Americans: Accommodation and Confrontation in Twentieth-Century America* (1969). Mexican-American repatriation is described in the relevant sections of Rodolfo Acuña, *Occupied America: The Chicano's Struggle Toward Liberation* (1972), while Carey McWilliams, *Factories in the Field: The Story of Migratory Farm Labor in California* (1939), portrays the union struggles of Mexican-American field workers. One example of Native American resistance to the "Indian New Deal" appears in Donald L. Parman, *The Navajos and the New Deal* (1976).

The dilemmas of the radical literary and cultural movement are treated in great detail in Richard Pells, *Radical Visions and American Dreams: Culture and Social Thought in the Depression Years* (1973). Pells may be supplemented by Daniel Aaron, *Writers on the Left: Episodes in American Literary Communism* (1961). Louis Filler, ed., *The Anxious Years: America in the 1930s* (1963), provides a useful literary anthology. For a description of the popular front of the Communist movement, see the relevant chapters of James Weinstein, *Ambiguous Legacy: The Left in American Politics* (1975).

Relevant segments of Robert Sklar, *Movie-Made America: A Cultural History of American Movies* (1976), portray the conservatism of Hollywood in the era, but William Stott, *Documentary Expression and Thirties America* (1973), describes thirties emphasis on social-conscious art and reporting. The best example of the photo-journalist documentary is James Agee and Walker Evans, *Let Us Now Praise Famous Men: Three Tenant Families* (1941).

Chapter 10

WORLD WAR TWO

President Franklin Delano Roosevelt was a master of the media. He thoroughly enjoyed his frequent meetings with the press—by 1945 he had held 998 press conferences—and he relied on his verbal skill and quick wit to win media support for his policies. But Roosevelt's easy style could be deceptive, perhaps deliberately so. After the outbreak of World War Two on September 1, 1939, Roosevelt's public messages increasingly focused on questions of foreign policy. The president repeatedly assured a worried public that the American people were the "best informed" in the world. Yet on December 7, 1941, most Americans were shocked to learn that Japanese aircraft had executed a surprise attack on the United States naval base at Pearl Harbor, Hawaii.

The shock of Pearl Harbor, besides affirming the skill of the Japanese plans, also stemmed directly from Roosevelt's lack of candor about the changing implications of his foreign policy. Though Roosevelt openly admitted his growing commitment to what he called the "democracies" of the world, he continued to insist that his policies were designed to keep the United States out of war. While campaigning in Boston for an unprecedented third term in 1940, Roosevelt won ringing applause when he announced: "Your boys are not going to be sent into any foreign wars." The president assumed —though he chose not to mention it—that an attack on the United States would not be a "foreign" war.

Such duplicity partly reflected the pressure of electoral politics. In Roosevelt's case, it illuminated the president's pragmatic approach to difficult policy questions, his reluctance to be pinned down to a course of action. This type of leadership also revealed the limitations imposed by the historical position of the United States. Roosevelt's options were limited not only by his personality, but also by the interests and values of the nation that were beyond his control. His approach to foreign affairs depended heavily on the attitudes of Congress and the general public. In a radio broadcast on September 3, 1939, Roosevelt announced that the United States would remain "a neutral nation." But unlike President Wilson during World War One, he added, "I cannot ask that every American remain neutral in thought as well. Even a neutral has a right to take account of facts. Even a neutral cannot be asked to close his mind or his conscience."

THE OPEN DOOR

When he came to office in 1933, Roosevelt inherited a foreign policy based on economic expansion and political isolationism. The defeat of the Versailles Treaty and the League of Nations in 1919–1920 had committed the United States to a policy of independent action. Even Roosevelt, who had supported Wilson's internationalism and had endorsed the league in his vice presidential campaign of 1920, moved away from the principle of international cooperation. But though the State Department preferred the idealized rhetoric of the Kellogg-Briand Pact of 1928, which "outlawed" aggressive warfare, American business interests remained vitally concerned with questions of international markets and foreign trade. In Asia, particularly in China, these economic concerns translated into a continuation of the Open Door policy, by which the United States advocated free trade for all nations in place of spheres of influence.

This commitment to the Open Door brought the United States into conflict with Japan and provided the background for the events that ultimately led to Pearl Harbor. At the Washington Arms Conference of 1921–1922, the United States persuaded Japan to agree to the Nine Power Pact, which formalized the Open Door in China. In this treaty Japan agreed to restore to China sovereignty of the Shantung peninsula and promised to remove Japanese soldiers stationed in southern Siberia since World War One. Japanese troops, however, remained in other parts of China. These agreements failed to consider the interests and sentiments of Chinese nationalists, who continued to oppose any foreign exploitation of their country. In 1929, for example, the Chinese Kuomintang, led by Chiang Kai-shek, seized Russian holdings in northern Manchuria, which led to an undeclared war.

Faced with strong Soviet competition in Manchuria as well as threats from Chinese nationalists, Japanese military leaders stationed in southern Manchuria took matters into their own hands. In September 1931 the Japanese army attacked Manchuria, defeated weak Chinese resistance, and by January 1932 converted the province, renamed Manchuko, into a Japanese protectorate. This assertion of Japanese power threatened American access to Chinese raw materials and markets and consequently violated the principles of the Open Door. But President Hoover, preoccupied by the problems of the Depression and reluctant to seek military confrontation, offered no counter-policy. Hoover also rebuffed suggestions that the United States cooperate with the league in exerting economic pressure on Japan.

Hoover's secretary of state, Henry L. Stimson, advocated a firmer response. With the president's approval, he sent a public letter to China and Japan in 1932 that became known as the Stimson Doctrine. In this letter Stimson reaffirmed the United States's commitment to the Open Door and refused to recognize the puppet government of Manchuko. Great Britain and France, like Hoover, were also reluctant to challenge Japan, and so the league merely adopted the American policy of nonrecognition. The Japanese responded to these rhetorical attacks by withdrawing from the league in February 1933, one month before Roosevelt's inauguration.

ISOLATIONISM

As Roosevelt took office in March 1933, Germany also chose a new leader, Adolf Hitler. Like Roosevelt, Hitler promised to end the Depression. His program of national socialism, however, aggravated differences with the United States. To offset a severe slump in German international trade, the German government subsidized German corporations to make them more competitive. These policies, by discriminating against American business, attacked the principles of the Open Door. The conflict of national economic interest prevented the two nations from signing a new commercial agreement in 1935. At the same time, the United States refused to extend the Open Door to Latin America. When German investors tried to penetrate the Western Hemisphere, the Roosevelt administration responded by offering better terms to preserve the United States's

dominance in its own sphere of influence. In 1938, for example, the United States underbid Germany for training of Latin American armies.

This economic competition was exaggerated by fundamental political differences. Hitler's Nazi party pursued an aggressive anti-Jewish program that offended American public opinion. Hitler also threatened the international order by demanding a revision of the Versailles Treaty to restore Germany as a world power. In 1933 the German leader attended the Geneva World Disarmament Conference and insisted on German military equality. When France refused, Germany withdrew from the conference and then from the league in October 1933. The next year, Hitler announced a program of German rearmament in violation of Versailles. While Hitler defied the league powers, the Italian Fascist leader, Benito Mussolini, sought glory and conquest in Ethiopia, using a clash between Italian and Ethiopian troops at a desert oasis in December 1934 as an excuse to make demands for an indemnity. When Emperor Haile Selassie refused, Mussolini prepared for war. As the arms race exploded in Europe, Japan went to the London Naval Conference of 1935 to demand revision of the Washington agreement in order to acquire naval equality. When Great Britain and the United States rejected the request, Japan withdrew from the session and announced it would increase its navy anyway.

These militaristic rumblings reinforced isolationist feelings in the United States. Since the disillusionment of World War One, Americans were suspicious of involvement in foreign affairs. Most congressmen, as well as their constituents, believed that the United States could preserve its unique institutions only by limiting foreign entanglements. These assumptions were supported by a growing belief that the United States had been tricked into participation in World War One. In 1934 a Senate investigating committee, headed by Gerald P. Nye of North Dakota, held a series of public hearings that revealed huge wartime profiteering by munitions manufacturers and bankers and implied close connections between the armaments industry and American policy making. The idea that American businessmen had lured the country into war was the thesis of a 1935 Book-of-the-Month Club selection, *Road to War: America, 1914–1917* by Walter Millis.

These exposures of the "merchants of death," though greatly exaggerated at the time, had important implications for American foreign policy. As early as 1933 the Senate Foreign Relations Committee, led by staunch isolationists, rejected an administration proposal that would have given the president power to stop the trade of arms with selected aggressor nations. When the committee substituted an amendment requiring an arms embargo against all belligerents in any war, Roosevelt reluctantly killed the entire bill. But because war seemed imminent in Europe and as the Nye committee released its findings, the isolationist Congress became less satisfied with Roosevelt's deliberate vagueness. Besides fearing another war, many conservatives in Congress opposed the increase of executive power by allowing the president to determine embargo policies. Over the objections of Roosevelt, therefore, Congress enacted the Neutrality Act of 1935, which required the president to establish an arms embargo against all belligerents and authorized the notification of American citizens that they sailed on belligerent vessels at their own risk. These provisions attempted to eliminate the issues that

had led to American entry in World War One. But the law left little room for the administration to pursue a creative foreign policy to protect the national interest. In signing the measure, Roosevelt warned that its "inflexible provisions might drag us into war instead of keeping us out."

Five weeks after the passage of the Neutrality Act, Mussolini invaded Ethiopia. Though the league declared Italy the aggressor and voted to impose mild economic sanctions, Britain and France refused to challenge Mussolini and continued their policy of appeasement. Roosevelt, however, used the provisions of the Neutrality Act to call for a "moral embargo" on the shipment of oil to Italy and managed to limit the export of other war materiel. Such gestures, in the absence of collective action, could not prevent the conquest of Ethiopia. Mussolini then withdrew from the league and signed a treaty of alliance with Hitler in October 1936.

As Europe seemed to move closer to war, Congress moved closer to isolation. In February 1936 Roosevelt tried to add a discretionary clause to the Neutrality Act that would have allowed the United States to support certain belligerents. But in the face of stiff opposition, the administration settled for an extension of the old policy. In March German armies moved into the Rhineland in violation of the Versailles Treaty. Britain and France froze in fear. The United States, not even a signer of the treaty, did nothing. The 1936 Democratic party platform reaffirmed the principles of neutrality. Roosevelt, in his only foreign policy speech of the campaign, assured Americans, "We shun political commitments which might entangle us in foreign war; we avoid connection with the political activities of the League of Nations...."

We are not isolationists except insofar as we seek to isolate ourselves completely from war."

The decision to remain uninvolved in European political affairs shaped Roosevelt's response to the Spanish civil war. In July 1936 a right-wing coalition led by the Fascist General Francisco Franco rebelled against the republican government. Despite claims of neutrality, Hitler and Mussolini provided crucial military support for Franco, including the air forces responsible for the first major bombing of civilians at Guernica in 1937. Meanwhile, the Soviet Union sent supplies to the republic (Loyalists). Britain and France, fearful that the war might spread and doubly fearful that a Loyalist victory might lead to a socialist government, formed a Nonintervention Committee to halt all arms shipments to Spain. Since Germany, Italy, and the Soviet Union ignored this policy, its main effect was to deny supplies to the legally constituted republic.

In the United States, the Spanish civil war polarized public opinion. Members of the American Left, ranging from New Deal liberals to Communists, saw Spain as a moral battleground between the forces of democracy and the legions of fascism. Besides organizing mass rallies to support the republic, several thousand men formed the Abraham Lincoln Battalion to fight in Spain. Conservatives and Catholics, however, saw Franco as a defender of traditional social order, especially the Catholic church. For them, Franco was a barrier against world revolution and atheism. Though Gallup polls indicated that pro-Loyalist sentiment greatly exceeded pro-Franco support, Roosevelt feared alienating the Catholic electorate or supporting a pro-Communist Spanish regime. Stating that a civil war could be treated the same as an international war, he imposed a "moral" embargo on the shipment of arms to either side. In 1937 Congress extended the Neutrality Act to Spain. Neither Congress nor Roosevelt viewed the survival of the Spanish Republic as vital to American national interest or security.

Most Americans believed that neutrality legislation would avoid involvement in another European war. But there was still a risk that the United States might also have to surrender its foreign trade in nonmilitary goods to avoid direct conflict. The loss of such trade, however, would undermine economic recovery at home. To solve this problem, presidential adviser Bernard M. Baruch suggested a revision of the Neutrality Act on the principle of "cash and carry." As enacted by Congress in 1937, the cash-and-carry formula permitted the sale of nonmilitary products to nations at war. But belligerents had to pay cash (to avoid the debt entanglements associated with American entry in World War One). The goods also had to be transported in non-American ships (to avoid the problem of neutral rights on the high seas). Cash and carry favored nations with strong navies and large cash reserves. Roosevelt understood that Britain and France, not Germany, would benefit by the law's provisions. The Neutrality Act of 1937 also continued the mandatory embargo on arms sales to all belligerents.

While Congress worked to perfect neutrality legislation, decisions made in other capitals undermined the possibility of implementing strict neutrality. In July 1937 Japan moved to extend its control of the Asian mainland by attacking the northern provinces of China. The Japanese promised to create an East Asia Coprosperity Program that would exclude other nations from Chinese markets and resources. Such a sphere

MAP 10.1 JAPANESE EXPANSION, 1937–1942

1. Panay bombed, Dec. 12, 1937
2. Occupied Feb. 10, 1939
3. Occupied N. Indochina Sept. 22, 1940
4. Occupied S. Indochina July 24, 1941
5. Landings Dec. 8, 1941
6. Landings Dec. 10, 1941
7. Landings Dec. 16, 1941
8. Landings Dec. 20, 1941
9. Landings Dec. 24, 1941
10. Hong Kong falls Dec. 25, 1941
11. Singapore falls Feb. 15, 1942

From The Growth of American Foreign Policy *by Richard W. Leopold. Copyright © 1962, by Richard W. Leopold, reprinted by permission of Alfred A. Knopf Inc.*

of influence paralleled Nazi expansion in central Europe, Britain's control of her Commonwealth nations, and United States dominance of Latin America and the Philippines. But from the American perspective, Japan's denial of the Open Door threatened not only current business but also American aspirations to develop trade with China as a long-term solution to economic depression. To protect American interests, Roosevelt decided to by-pass the Neutrality Act of 1937 and support China simply by refusing to acknowledge that a state of war existed. Without invoking cash and carry, Roosevelt could allow American ships to continue to trade with China.

Such technicalities did not alleviate Roosevelt's concern about Japanese expansion nor did it remove his fears about the cementing of a Berlin-Rome-Tokyo alliance. To counteract the prevailing isolationism in the United States, Roosevelt spoke out in October 1937 against the "epidemic of world lawlessness." "War is a contagion," he warned. "We are determined to keep out of war, yet we cannot insure ourselves against the disastrous effects of war and the dangers of involvement." Asserting that neutrality would "minimize our involvement," the president admitted "we cannot have complete protection in a world of disorder." Roosevelt offered no solutions to the predicament — he had none to make — except to propose a vaguely defined "quarantine" against aggressor nations. The liberal press greeted Roosevelt's speech with enthusiasm. But the isolationists, scrupulous about any international commitments, even amorphous "quarantines," condemned the address and forced the president to reconsider any alterations of policy.

When Japanese planes attacked the United States gunboat *Panay* on the Yangtze River in December 1937, Roosevelt accepted a Japanese apology and promise of indemnity. Despite mild public indignation, the president dared go no further. The strength of isolationism could be seen in the popularity of a constitutional amendment, sponsored by Representative Louis Ludlow of Indiana, to require a popular referendum before Congress could exercise its power to declare war. Only after intense pressure from the administration did the House of Representatives reject the measure — by a narrow 209–188 vote.

The blandness of American foreign policy paralleled the impotence of Britain and France. In March 1938 the two nations allowed Hitler to take over Austria. Six months later they refused to stand up to Germany when Hitler demanded the Sudeten province of Czechoslovakia, which was inhabited by a minority of Germans. At the Munich Conference of September 1938, Britain and France forced Czechoslovakia to concede German demands. When Prime Minister Neville Chamberlain returned to England bearing "peace in our times," Roosevelt telegraphed his congratulations. After seizing the Sudeten, however, Hitler remained unsatisfied. In March 1939 German soldiers occupied the rest of Czechoslovakia, and in April Hitler began to threaten Poland. Britain and France now realized that appeasement had failed and they pledged to defend Poland from German aggression. The Soviet Union remained suspicious of British and French intentions, fearful that the Western allies would be quite content to see Nazis and Communists engaged in mortal conflict. Hitler was equally afraid of a two-front war and, to protect his eastern flank, he signed a nonaggression pact with Soviet leader Josef Stalin in August 1939. Then, on September 1, Germany moved against Poland. Two days later Britain and France declared war on Germany.

NEUTRALITY, 1939–1941

The outbreak of World War Two intensified the contradictions in Roosevelt's foreign policy — his desire to see Hitler defeated and his commitment to keep the United States out of war. To reconcile these divergent interests, Roosevelt emphasized that support of the Allies, while preserving the letter of American neutrality, would protect the United States from foreign aggression without embroiling the nation in war. Accordingly, Roosevelt called Congress into special session in September 1939 to repeal the arms embargo.

The summons produced a bitter debate between isolationists and internationalists. Charles Lindbergh, the popular aviator, and ex-President Hoover broadcast fervent appeals to the public, urging a continuation of the isolationist policy. In response, interventionists formed a Nonpartisan Committee for Peace Through Revision of the Neutrality Act, headed by the prestigious Republican journalist William Allen White, which sponsored radio addresses and grassroots protests to repeal the embargo. In the end, the issue hinged on congressional votes — and, because of powerful public pressure, the interventionists obtained them. The revised Neutrality Act of 1939 still prohibited American vessels from entering the war zones. But it revised the old law to permit belligerents to purchase military supplies on a cash-and-carry basis. "We are trying to keep out of war," insisted an administration supporter in Congress, "not to get closer into it." But the law clearly placed the United States in the Allied camp.

German threats to American interests became clearer in the spring of 1940 when Hitler launched a military campaign against Scandinavia, the Low Countries, and France. As German troops blitzed toward Paris, Roosevelt warned the public against "the illusion that we are remote and isolated." He now asked Congress for a multibillion dollar defense appropriation and, despite isolationist objections, obtained its passage. To encourage the administration, internationalists, led by William Allen White and Clark Eichelberger, formed the Committee to Defend America by Aiding the Allies, a grassroots pressure group that claimed nearly one million members by October. Meanwhile, Roosevelt moved to undercut Republican opposition in foreign policy matters by appointing two leading Republicans to his cabinet: Stimson as secretary of war and Frank Knox, Landon's running mate, as secretary of the navy. The fall of France in June 1940 further undermined the isolationists. Public opinion polls showed a dramatic decline of isolationist sentiment and a rising commitment to support Britain. But 82 percent of the people polled still drew the line at American intervention in the war. Like Roosevelt, they believed that military assistance would enable Britain to defeat Germany.

During the summer of 1940, however, the British military situation became more perilous as German planes bombed English cities and German submarines sank vital English shipping. Prime Minister Winston Churchill pleaded for American naval assistance. Roosevelt, in an unusual exercise of presidential power, agreed to trade fifty overage destroyers for British bases in the Western Hemisphere and a promise that Britain would never surrender its fleet to Germany. In announcing the deal, Roosevelt stressed its nonintervention features. "This is the most important action in the reinforcement of our national defense that has been taken since the Louisiana Purchase," he claimed. But even that, Roosevelt suggested, might not be enough. In September 1940 Congress increased military appropriations and also enacted the first peacetime conscription law in American history.

Despite considerable opposition to Roosevelt's foreign policy, the president managed to minimize its importance in the 1940 presidential election. The Republican candidate, Wendell Willkie, an acknowledged internationalist, endorsed the destroyers-for-bases agreement and supported conscription. Both nominees made assurances that they opposed American entry into the war. After the election Roosevelt continued to make a distinction between military assistance for Britain and an outright alliance against Germany.

Roosevelt returned to the airwaves in December 1940 for what he considered his most important public address since the early days of the New Deal. Stressing the importance of a British victory for American "national security," Roosevelt declared that the United States must become "the great arsenal of democracy." In his state of the union address of January 1941, the president continued to lead the nation away from a policy of strict neutrality, condemning the "so-called new order of tyranny which the dictators seek to create with the crash of a bomb." Roosevelt now pleaded for the protection and expansion of the "Four Freedoms"— the freedom of speech and expression, the freedom of religion, the freedom from want, and the freedom from fear.

But with Britain running out of capital resources and the United States forbidden under the neutrality laws to extend credit, Britain could not obtain sufficient supplies to stop the Germans. Roosevelt moved, as he put it, to "eliminate the dollar sign." If your neighbor's house was on fire, Roosevelt explained to reporters, it would be prudent to lend him an old garden hose to put out the fire before it spread to your house. Afterward the neighbor would return the hose or, if it had been damaged, replace it. Such was the logic of the Lend-Lease Act of March 1941, by which Congress authorized the expenditure of $7 billion to keep supplies flowing to Britain and its allies.

Lend-Lease finally destroyed the fiction of American neutrality, though most Americans still hoped to keep out of the fighting. But Lend-Lease could be effective only if American goods actually crossed the North Atlantic. By the spring of 1941, German submarines, operating in wolf packs, were sinking 500,000 tons of Allied shipping a month. In the face of negative public opinion, Roosevelt declined to establish naval convoys to escort Lend-Lease materiel. Instead he devised a new fiction, the idea of "hemispheric defense," which extended a neutrality zone halfway across the Atlantic, almost to Iceland, and ordered the navy to patrol this area to report the presence of "aggressor ships or planes" to the British navy. Roosevelt also signed an executive agreement with the Danish government in exile that allowed the United States to establish bases in Greenland.

Roosevelt's willingness to play loosely with the language of neutrality infuriated his opponents. When Hitler invaded the Soviet Union in June 1941, Roosevelt extended Lend-Lease to Britain's new ally. The decision prompted isolationist outrage. Charles Lindbergh announced that he preferred an alliance with Germany "with all her faults" rather than one "with the cruelty, Godlessness, and the barbarism that exist in the Soviet Union." Even Senator Harry S Truman questioned Roosevelt's motives. "If we see that Germany is winning the war we ought to help Russia," he explained; "if Russia is winning we ought to help Germany and that way let them kill as many as possible." Hitler, however, offered no such options. In May 1941 German submarines sank an American ship that carried a cargo of military supplies. In July Roosevelt extended American convoys to Iceland, interfering with the effectiveness of German submarines. But in September the Germans attacked an American destroyer, *Greer,* which had been helping the British track it on radio. Roosevelt used the attack to condemn the German "rattlesnakes of the Atlantic," and he indicated a new policy that allowed American ships to shoot on sight German ships in the so-called neutral zone. But German submarines continued to attack American ships. In November Congress revised the Neutrality Act to permit the arming of merchant vessels and allow them to enter the war zone.

These decisions effectively terminated American neutrality. Though neither Congress nor the administration was prepared to declare war, it was only a matter of time before naval confrontations would create a crisis similar to that of 1917. Equally significant, the arming of merchant ships demonstrated that the United States saw no advantage to traditional peacetime diplomacy. Yet even at this point, Roosevelt backed away from further commitments. While setting the United States on a collision course, the president waited for Hitler to fire the first shot.

Hitler, however, was too involved with the European war and too afraid of American military potential to take up Roosevelt's challenge. But ironically the German invasion of the Soviet Union encouraged Japanese expansion in a direction that led to Pearl Harbor. Hitler did not intend that result; indeed, he opposed Japanese policies that were likely to draw the United States into the war. But Hitler no more controlled Japanese foreign policy than

did Roosevelt. It was the Japanese military leadership that maneuvered the United States into total war against Germany.

THE ROAD TO PEARL HARBOR

While the United States had protested the Japanese invasion of China and had advanced a $25-million loan to the Chinese resisters, private American business continued to sell crucial neutral resources to Japan. In July 1939, however, American policy makers decided to increase pressure on Japan by serving the required six-months' notice that the United States intended to cancel its 1911 commercial agreement. After January 1940, the United States was free to halt shipping to Japan, if it so desired. But Roosevelt and Secretary of State Cordell Hull were reluctant to create a crisis, especially because they viewed Germany as a greater threat to American interests.

The war in Europe nevertheless had important implications for Asia. When Hitler signed the nonaggression pact with Stalin in August 1939, the Japanese realized that the Soviet Union remained an important rival in northern China. But the German victories in western Europe offered tremendous alternative possibilities for Japan in Southeast Asia at the expense of France, the Netherlands, and Britain. Shortly after the fall of France, Japan forced the French to accept Japanese occupation of Indochina and persuaded Churchill to accept the closing of the Burma Road that was providing military assistance to Chiang Kai-shek's Chinese nationalists.

The United States responded to these advances by exercising its power to embargo crucial natural resources. In July 1940 the administration forbade the sale of aviation gasoline and high-grade scrap iron. The decision failed to prevent Japan from moving more troops into northern Indochina. In September the White House decided to tighten the economic screws by embargoing all iron and steel, but it continued to allow the export of certain petroleum products. By such gradual means the administration hoped to persuade Japan to reconsider its imperial expansion. Within a week, however, Japan signed a tripartite military assistance pact with Italy and Germany. Japan was hoping to neutralize American pressure by creating the possibility of a two-front war for the United States. But Roosevelt responded by adding more items to the embargo list.

These economic pressures led the Japanese to open diplomatic negotiations in the spring of 1941. The talks would continue through December. But neither the United States nor Japan was prepared to offer the significant concessions that would have made agreement possible. The conflict was symbolized by the Open Door and the Coprosperity Program. The United States was not prepared to accept the Japanese conquest of China or restore full trade with Japan; the Japanese were not prepared to withdraw from China or accept deprivation of crucial resources. In these terms war became inevitable when the United States first initiated economic sanctions against Japan.

While conversations between the State Department and the Japanese ambassador dragged on, the German invasion of the Soviet Union altered the Asian balance. Though Hitler pleaded with Japan to attack Siberia and expose the Soviet Union to a two-front war, the Japanese preferred to take advantage of the Soviet Union's predicament by avoiding direct conflict and moving southward into Malaya and the Dutch East Indies, both areas rich in

oil and rubber. The Japanese marched into southern Indochina in July 1941. Roosevelt responded by freezing Japanese assets in the United States. By limiting Japan's ability to purchase supplies, this decision assumed massive proportions.

The Japanese now faced a crucial choice. They could either abandon their plans for Asian expansion or attempt to seize vital oil supplies from the British and Dutch colonies. Given the militaristic values of the Japanese regime, the former alternative hardly existed. The Japanese also realized — and Roosevelt confirmed this to the British — that the United States would not tolerate an attack on British possessions in Asia. In other words, further Japanese expansion might mean war with the United States. Even by their own estimates, Japanese military leaders knew they could not defeat the United States at war. Yet faced with the alternative of humiliating surrender in 1941, that is what they chose.

On Sunday, December 7, 1941, the White House announced that Japanese forces had attacked the naval base at Pearl Harbor. Catching the base by complete surprise (it was 8 A.M. local time), the Japanese destroyed or damaged eight battleships, three cruisers, nearly two hundred planes, and vital shore installations and claimed nearly thirty-five hundred casualties, while sustaining minimal losses. The next day Roosevelt told a joint session of Congress that a state of war already existed, and promised to lead the American people to "absolute victory." Congress responded with a thundering ovation and then, with one dissenting vote by pacifist Representative Jeannette Rankin, voted for a formal declaration of war. Three days later Germany and Italy joined the Japanese by declaring war on the United States, and the same day, December 11, Congress responded

MAP 10.2   THE WESTERN EUROPEAN THEATER, 1942–1945

From **The Growth of American Foreign Policy** by Richard W. Leopold. Copyright © 1962, by Richard W. Leopold, reprinted by permission of Alfred A. Knopf Inc.

in kind. After a decade of diplomatic maneuvering, the United States was again involved in global warfare.

THE GRAND ALLIANCE

The road to Pearl Harbor could be traced back to a fundamental conflict of national interests: the United States's Open Door policy and Japan's desire for a special sphere of influence in east Asia. A similar defense of national interest shaped Roosevelt's policies toward Europe and influenced his decision to wage a "Germany-first" strategy. In August 1941 Roosevelt and Churchill issued a document, known as the Atlantic Charter, that defined America's war goals. Besides disavowing any territorial benefits, the two leaders affirmed the right of all nations "on equal terms to the trade and to the raw materials of the world." In making the statement, Roosevelt attempted to forestall an agreement between Churchill and Stalin to divide Europe into special spheres of influence.

United States entry into the war eliminated some of the mutual distrust among the Allies. But each nation still recognized its own national interest as paramount. The Soviet Union, reeling under the German advance, desperately needed Allied assistance and hoped for the opening of a second front in western Europe. Stalin also wanted a postwar settlement that would protect the Soviet Union from any subsequent invasions from central Europe. Churchill's goals looked toward preserving the colonial empire, particularly Britain's trading advantages with the Commonwealth nations and in the Middle East. As an outspoken anticommunist, Churchill also feared a strong So-

viet presence in central Europe and wished to preserve Britain's status in Europe through postwar alliances with the United States and France. Roosevelt's goal, besides a quick defeat of Germany, was to replace European spheres of influence — whether British or Soviet — with the American Open Door.

These differing approaches had important effects on military strategy. While Stalin pleaded for a second front, Churchill persuaded Roosevelt, against the advice of American generals, to support an invasion of North Africa in 1942. This operation served to eliminate German threats to Middle East oil, protected Britain's Mediterranean shipping, and provided a base for the invasion of Italy. While German and Soviet armies hammered away at each other, Roosevelt and Churchill met at Casablanca in January 1943 and announced a policy of "unconditional surrender." Military advisers criticized the phrase because it might harden enemy opposition and undermine the possibility of a negotiated settlement. But Roosevelt was motivated as much by rhetoric as by a desire to demonstrate his sincerity to Stalin, despite the delay of the second front. The United States still hoped for Soviet intervention in the war against Japan.

With a second front still in question, however, Anglo-American forces invaded Sicily and Italy in the summer of 1943. Soon afterward, Mussolini fell from power and was replaced by Marshal Badoglio, who made a conditional surrender to the Allies in September 1943. In agreeing to negotiate with Badoglio, a conservative militarist, Anglo-American authorities recognized his importance as an anticommunist force in postwar Italy. To make this point clearer, the western Allies excluded the Soviet Union from the Allied Control Commission, answering Stalin's protests by arguing that the Red Army had not participated in the Italian campaign. This decision served as an important precedent for Soviet policy in eastern Europe.

While Soviet armies still bore the brunt of the war, the Big Three — Roosevelt, Churchill, and Stalin — met at Teheran in November 1943. At this meeting Churchill and Roosevelt agreed to open a second front in France in the spring, and Stalin promised to turn Soviet guns against Japan soon after the European war ended. They also agreed on a preliminary division of Germany into zones and accepted the idea of German reparations to compensate for war losses.

As the Allies prepared for the invasion of France, Anglo-American aircraft began "precision" bombing of the Continent, a policy that meant thousands of civilian deaths. Afterward the raids were found to be minimally effective, except insofar as they had the opposite result of strengthening enemy morale. The air war was more successful in destroying the German *luftwaffe*. Air supremacy was also crucial for the successful beachhead landings at Normandy on D Day, June 6, 1944. After tough fighting in northern France, the Allies moved eastward, racing to meet Soviet armies somewhere in Germany. The goal for both sides was Berlin.

As victory appeared imminent, the Big Three met at Yalta in February 1945 to resolve the unsettled questions of the war. Stalin repeated his promise to go to war against Japan after the defeat of Germany. Roosevelt and Churchill agreed to compensate the Soviets with the Kuerile Islands north of Japan as well as economic rights in Manchuria. The Allies also agreed to a temporary partition of Germany, including a three-way zoning of Berlin. But they failed to reach agreement about the amount of

German war reparations or a procedure for collection.

The main problem at Yalta, however, involved Poland — whose invasion had triggered World War Two more than five years before. To protect the Soviet Union's western boundary from future invasion, Stalin demanded recognition of the territory taken from Poland in 1939–1940. In compensation to Poland, Germany would surrender areas of eastern Prussia. Besides the question of boundaries was the problem of Poland's government. Stalin was determined to have a friendly government on his most vulnerable border, an idea that Roosevelt and Churchill accepted in principle. But the Polish government in exile in London was bitterly anticommunist, as apparently was the Polish underground. As an alternative to these two undesirable choices, Stalin established another government of communist Poles at Lublin. At Yalta the western Allies convinced Stalin to broaden the political base of the Lublin government by including some London Poles. They also persuaded Stalin to permit "free and unfettered elections" in Poland as soon as possible. But in Poland, as in Italy, the Allies did not have an equal stake, and Stalin was not yet ready to accept the Open Door in eastern Europe.

Though the Big Three made major international decisions without consulting all the affected nations, the rise of fascist aggression in the thirties convinced Roosevelt of the value of an international organization to oversee the peace. As a disillusioned Wilsonian, Roosevelt believed that collective security was meaningless without the consent of the great powers. Where Wilson had envisioned a league of all nations, Roosevelt suggested that Four Policemen — the United States, the Soviet Union,

Great Britain, and China — would function more effectively. The president also took pains to avoid Wilson's worst mistakes by consulting openly with members of the Senate Foreign Relations Committee. Public opinion strongly supported American leadership in a United Nations, one indication of which was the popularity of the film *Wilson* (1944), which emphasized the mistakes of 1919. Other influential internationalist works were two best sellers, Sumner Welles, *Time for Decision* (1944), and Walter Lippmann, *U.S. War Aims* (1944).

Plans for the United Nations were first drafted at the Dumbarton Oaks Conference in Washington in 1944. Reflecting Roosevelt's distrust of Wilsonian principles, the plan provided for a permanent Security Council that would be responsible for implementing U.N. policy. In the Security Council, the Big Four retained the power of veto. This principle, which differed greatly from the idea behind the League of Nations, helps to explain why even conservative Americans were willing to support the new international body. At Yalta Stalin raised the possibility of using the veto to prevent discussion of controversial matters, but Roosevelt and Churchill persuaded him that the veto should apply only to decision making. Stalin also asked for representation in the General Assembly for the Ukraine and White Russia. The British, with Commonwealth votes in their pocket, readily agreed, but Roosevelt balked — until Stalin pointed out that the United States was sponsoring ten Latin American nations that had not even joined the war.

The Yalta meeting confirmed April 25, 1945, as the opening of the United Nations conference at San Francisco. Roosevelt appointed a bipartisan delegation headed by his new secretary of state, Edward Stettinius. But the president's lack of interest in the General Assembly led him to underestimate its importance in public opinion. The American people were shocked to learn that Roosevelt had consented to three votes for the Soviets, and many became convinced that an ailing Roosevelt had sold out American interests at Yalta. Roosevelt did not live to hear these complaints. He died of a cerebral hemorrhage on April 12.

MOBILIZATION FOR VICTORY

Though Roosevelt's declining health had been a matter of public speculation, his death stunned the nation. For twelve years he had provided confidence in government. During the wartime crisis his presence in the White House had helped to reduce the level of tension. News of Pearl Harbor had produced a mixture of fear and relief. No one who lived through the event ever forgot that peculiar feeling of catharsis. "The war came as a great relief, like a reverse earthquake," explained *Time* magazine. "Japanese bombs had finally brought national unity to the U.S." On December 8, 1941, sixty million Americans tuned in their radios to listen to Roosevelt's war message. That night air raid sirens in San Francisco, Los Angeles, and New York wailed false alarms that revealed a fundamental insecurity.

Despite the catastrophe at Pearl Harbor, the Japanese attack barely touched American military capacity. The key to military success rested on the nation's vast industrial potential. War mobilization involved the conversion of civilian industries to war-related activity, the creation of new plants, the harnessing of raw materials, and the organization of a work force to perform

Audie Murphy

1924-1971

The most decorated American soldier of World War Two was Audie Murphy. Not yet twenty-one at the war's end, Murphy was credited with killing 240 Germans and capturing dozens more in Italy and France, for which he earned the Congressional Medal of Honor as well as twenty-three other military decorations. His postwar autobiography, To Hell and Back (1948), graphically described the trauma and the bravery of the men who did the fighting. In 1955 it was made into a Hollywood film in which Murphy played himself.

Though nearly sixteen million men and women served in the armed services, only one in eight saw active combat duty. By comparison to the other belligerents, the United States's casualties were low; but nearly 300,000 died in action, and other casualties approached one million. From the perspective of the "GI" — a popular abbreviation of "general issue" — the war was a mixture of boredom and, in Murphy's words, "an endless series of problems involving blood and guts."

Murphy's popularity after the war reflected not only his outstanding battlefield achievements but also the cultural values he represented. He was one of eleven children of poor Texas sharecroppers. His father, a victim of the Depression Dust Bowl, abandoned the family, and his mother died soon after. For Audie Murphy the war offered an opportunity to escape from poverty and personal frustration. But at nineteen he was too skinny for the marines and paratroopers and he barely persuaded the infantry to accept him for front-line service.

Murphy's rise from small-town poverty to national heroism seemed to vindicate the traditional values of self-help and tough determination. Yet his youthful features evoked a simpler time of innocence and virtue. These *attributes enabled Murphy to forge a movie career in Hollywood. But with limited acting ability, he settled into dreary roles in westerns and war films.*

He died on the Memorial Day weekend in 1971 in an airplane crash. Murphy's obituary ironically appeared at a time when Americans were confronting a different type of war veteran — the "grunt" soldier of Vietnam — who, unlike GI Joe, was challenging the wisdom of the military leadership.

war-related jobs. One year after Pearl Harbor, the United States was producing more war materiel than were all its enemies combined.

Roosevelt had recognized the importance of preparing American industry for war as early as 1938. But, typical of his earlier New Deal strategy, he was reluctant to commit himself to any one plan or to delegate authority to a single commission. In 1939 he appointed a War Resources Board to study the problem of military conversion, but in the face of anti-intervention public opinion, he decided to ignore its report. After the fall of France in May 1940, Roosevelt became more resolute, asking Congress for large military appropriations and establishing an Advisory Commission for National Defense. As new problems emerged, Roosevelt reacted by creating new bureaucracies: the Office of Production Management (OPM) replaced the Advisory Commission; the Office of Price Administration (OPA) supervised price controls; the Supply Priorities and Allocations Board (SPAB) dealt with the problems of conversion. Despite considerable administrative confusion, these agencies started the economy moving toward a wartime basis. During 1941 arms production increased by 225 percent.

After Pearl Harbor Roosevelt stressed the importance of even greater production, calling in 1942 for sixty thousand planes, twenty-five thousand tanks, and eight million tons of shipping, and for higher outputs in 1943. To tighten government control of the war industries, he also created the War Production Board (WPB), headed by Donald Nelson of Sears, Roebuck. But when Nelson proved ineffective, Roosevelt moved again, creating the Office of War Mobilization (OWM) in 1943 under the supervision of former Supreme Court Justice James F. Byrnes. These agencies, besides overseeing the division between civilian and military production, set production goals and established priorities for the allocation of scarce resources. Other crucial administrative decisions involved coordinating supplies for American military needs and those of Lend-Lease. By the war's end, nearly $50 billion worth of Lend-Lease material was shipped to the Allies (60 percent to Britain; 20 percent to the Soviet Union; the rest to other nations).

In developing a war economy, an early problem was convincing private business to make the necessary adjustments. After nearly a decade of Depression, manufacturers were cautious about building new plants and shifting to military production. Many feared that conversion would lead to overproduction and create a postwar depression. Equally important, with the beginning of war production in the summer of 1940, the civilian economy began to boom as workers had more money to spend. Many business leaders preferred the known profits of the consumer economy to the uncertain advantages of war production.

The Roosevelt administration attempted to restore business confidence in government by appointing business leaders such as Nelson, U.S. Steel's Edward Stettinius, and General Motors' William Knudsen to "dollar-a-year" positions. These administrators adopted policies that helped to reduce the economic risks associated with war conversion. In 1940 Congress authorized government financing of new construction. The WPB later offered generous tax advantages and "cost-plus" contracts that guaranteed a fixed profit for war business. The federal government also began to finance the cost of industrial research and development for war-related materials, a practice that became a critical ingredient of the American economy even after the war ended. To further encourage business cooperation, the Roosevelt administration abandoned antitrust actions in war-related fields.

Such policies generally favored big businesses over small, even after competitive bidding had been dropped. Larger corporations had greater access to government bureaucracies and had greater experience in handling huge procurement contracts. From the government's point of view, it was simpler to deal with one contractor instead of many. Though some New Dealers criticized the disproportionate awarding of war contracts to the largest companies, the prevailing opinion was expressed by Secretary Stimson: "If you . . . go to war . . . in a capitalist country, you have to let business make money out of the process or business won't work." During World War Two, industrial production increased by 96 percent and net corporate profits doubled.

The mobilization of the war economy also depended on the recruitment of an adequate labor supply. Unemployment figures in 1939 still totaled eight million (17 percent of the labor force), but these unemployed were steadily absorbed into the expanding economy. By 1942 other previously unemployable workers — teenagers, the elderly, blacks, and women — also began to find jobs. One source of employment was the armed services, which took over fifteen million men and women during the war. Another seven million jobs opened on the home front.

This rapid expansion of the labor force, although clearly ringing the end of the Depression, raised serious problems of another sort. The most compelling need was finding the right workers for critical defense industries. Not only was there a shortage of skilled labor, but workers revealed a remarkable willingness to leave their jobs. To deal with these problems, Roosevelt created a War Manpower Commission. But this agency lacked the power to enforce its policies and it could never win presidential support for the idea of "work or fight." As a result, absenteeism and job mobility remained common. In 1944 the turnover in manufacturing industries was 82 percent, three-quarters of which was voluntary. As in the Depression, however, losses in the labor force were more than offset by the use of time-saving machinery that increased individual worker productivity. The Department of Agriculture estimated that farmer productivity increased 25 percent per work-hour between 1939 and 1945 because of mechanization, land consolidation, and the increased use of chemical fertilizers.

The shortage of labor provided opportunities for people who had previously been underrepresented in the work force. Black Americans, disproportionately unemployed during the Depression, repeated the World War One pattern of migration to the cities. Yet black workers still confronted racial discrimination in employment and vocational training, even in government programs and within the armed forces. In the private sector, discrimination in employment was unconcealed. "While we are in complete sympathy with the Negro," declared the president of North American Aviation, "it is against company policy to employ them as aircraft workers or mechanics...regardless of their training.... There will be some jobs as janitors for Negroes."

Such discrimination led A. Philip Randolph, president of the Brotherhood of Sleeping Car Porters, to call for a protest march on Washington in the summer of 1941. Deeply embarrassed by the proposal, Roosevelt tried to persuade Randolph to change his plans. But at last the president was forced to take a public stand against discrimination in employment. On June 25, 1941, Roosevelt issued Executive Order 8802, which prohibited job discrimination in defense industries and created a Fair Employment Practices Commission (FEPC) to investigate cases of discrimination. Roosevelt never felt secure enough to order the desegregation of the armed services, however, and the FEPC, despite the intentions of its members, never possessed sufficient power to enforce its policies. Some two million blacks eventually found work in war industries.

More successful in penetrating the labor force were women. Though females comprised 25 percent of the prewar work force, popular opinion disapproved of working women, particularly when they competed with men for jobs. Even as the nation prepared for war, defense contractors preferred not to hire female employees. Pearl Harbor put aside those prejudices. Between 1941 and 1945, 6.5 million women entered the labor force, a 57 percent increase in female employment. By the war's end, 36 percent of all civilian workers were women. Though initially limited to "light" work, women eventually performed a variety of previously "male" tasks, the most publicized female stereotype being Rosie the Riveter.

Despite widespread recognition of women's capabilities, female workers continued to face prejudicial conditions. Although the War Manpower Commission announced that female workers were entitled to the same pay as men for the same work, employers routinely ignored such requirements. Most women earned no more than the minimum wage, and women were usually kept out of high management positions. These practices reflected the generally accepted belief that war work was temporary. Even though a Women's Bureau survey revealed that 75 percent of working women wished to keep their jobs, business policy assumed that women should give way to men.

"Americans may no longer believe that a woman's place is in the home," sociologist Jerome Bruner observed. "But more important, we believe even less that a man's place is on the street without a job." Women nevertheless resisted giving up their jobs at the war's end.

The fear that women workers would supplant men also influenced the attitudes of organized labor. Worried about the possibility of a postwar depression, union leaders discouraged permanent gains for women even though 20 percent of organized workers were female. Such conservative postures partly reflected a growing alienation of union leaders from the rank-and-file membership. As employment boomed, unions demanded double work shifts, but Roosevelt forced them to accept a forty-hour week — later extended to forty-eight hours — and time and a half for overtime. Between 1941 and 1945 union membership increased by nearly 40 percent.

While organized labor made a general "no-strike" pledge shortly after Pearl Harbor, unions continued to press for higher wages. To deal with these disputes, Roosevelt created a National Defense Mediation Board in 1941, composed of representatives of labor, management, and the public. But when CIO members resigned over a dispute involving union jurisdiction, Roosevelt established another bureau, the National War Labor Board, in 1942. As an extension of the president's wartime emergency powers, the NWLB could set wages, hours, and working conditions and had the legal authority to order government seizure of non-complying plants.

The first major labor dispute involved union membership. Organized labor supported the "union shop," in which all workers must join the union, but management insisted on an "open shop." The NWLB finally persuaded both parties to accept a compromise based on the principle of maintenance of membership. Workers did not have to join a union, but union members had to remain within their union; if membership declined because of turnovers, the union could recruit just enough workers to maintain the initial membership figures. After these grievances were resolved, the unions turned to questions of higher wages to compensate for inflation. Here too the NWLB worked out a compromise formula known as Little Steel. Recognizing a 15 percent inflation between January and July 1942, the board allowed a 15 percent cost-of-living increase for that period. Such wage limits did not apply to overtime, however, and while hourly wages increased 24 percent during the war, weekly earnings went up about 70 percent. Moreover, since Little Steel applied only to disputed cases, employers were often willing to pay higher wages, especially in jobs involving cost-plus contracts.

Despite these economic gains, organized labor still opposed government restraints, and by 1943 union members were complaining about the no-strike pledge. Numerous unauthorized strikes occurred, even in critical war industries. The most serious crisis was John L. Lewis's defiance of the Little Steel formula in seeking higher wages for the United Mine Workers. Protesting that Little Steel offered too little for the impoverished mine workers (annual wages averaged $1,700 in 1942), Lewis led the coal miners in a controversial strike in 1943. Congress responded by passing, over Roosevelt's veto, the Smith-Connally Labor Act, which imposed a thirty-day cooling off period before striking, prohibited strikes in defense industries, and banned union contributions to political parties. Lewis nevertheless continued to agitate for the miners, finally winning additional pay that effectively circumvented the 15 percent ceiling.

With business booming and with full employment, the Roosevelt administration worked to prevent runaway inflation. One solution was to set wage controls, but these, as John L. Lewis demonstrated, frequently could be ignored. Another approach was to establish price controls. In 1942 the Office of Price Administration put a freeze on consumer prices based on the highest prices of March 1942. But despite increased production, food prices continued to skyrocket, upsetting the administration's attempt to balance the economy. Though representatives of the farm states welcomed farm prosperity, Roosevelt persuaded Congress to pass an Anti-Inflation Act in 1942 that enabled him to freeze agricultural prices, wages, and rents. During the last two years of the war, consumer prices increased by less than 2 percent.

Besides price controls, the OPA also instituted a rationing program for scarce materials. These included canned goods (because of tin shortages), rubber, gasoline (because rubber shortages limited tire production), coffee, shoes (because of military needs), sugar, meat, butter, and fuel oil. Rationing produced inadvertent inequities, such as the decline of the quality of merchandise and, more serious, an illegal black market.

Another strategy to decrease consumer purchasing power was the sale of war bonds. Through payroll deduction plans and organized bond drives, bond sales reached $135 billion, of which about $40 billion was purchased by small investors. The deflationary effect of these bond sales was significant, absorbing over 7 percent of net personal incomes in 1944, even though many purchasers redeemed their bonds before the war's end.

More effective in soaking up purchasing power was taxation. Despite vast public expenditures, over 40 percent of the total war bill was financed through taxation. The Revenue

To inspire support on the home front, this 1942 poster exaggerated the danger of enemy attacks on civilian property. (National Archives 179-WP-470)

Act of 1942, besides raising tax rates, broadened the tax base to include lower income workers for the first time. It also increased corporation taxes to 40 percent and raised excess-profits taxes to a whopping 90 percent. Loopholes and generous interpretations of the law frequently lowered these rates in practice. Other provisions promised to rebate the excess-profits taxes to corporations after the war to facilitate reconversion to civilian industries. The law also initiated the policy of payroll withholding, ostensibly to simplify the procedure, but also to take tax dollars out of consumer circulation.

These taxes, even when revised in 1944 to lower revenues, brought $138 billion into the treasury. Business interests often managed to avoid heavy taxes by such devices as nonreporting, expense accounts, and deferred salaries. But the taxes on high personal income and excess profits still produced a significant, though temporary, redistribution of personal income, reversing the old adage that the rich get richer and the poor, poorer. The top 5 percent income bracket declined in relative economic worth as its control of disposable income dropped from 23 percent in 1939 to 17 percent in 1945. At the same time full employment and the expansion of two-income families brought greater purchasing power to poorer people. Yet commodity shortages and rationing, though often ignored, cut across class lines: people with money could not always find what they wanted to buy. Additional incomes thus went into savings, providing the necessary capital for postwar spending.

THE HOME FRONT

If personal savings provided the economic basis for a postwar splurge, other aspects of wartime culture provided the incentive. After a decade of Depression, consumers were anxious to spend their wartime paychecks, but desirable commodities were often unavailable. In 1942, for example, the WPB ordered the automobile industry to stop producing cars and light trucks and to switch to manufacturing tanks and airplanes. When unable to satisfy consumer demands, industry resorted to mass advertising to direct attention from wartime shortage to postwar possibilities. "Ordnance Today," boasted

the Easy Washing Machine Company, "Washers Tomorrow." The Cessna Aircraft Company predicted that the "Family Car of the Air" would enable weekend golfers to tee off 500 miles from home "after the war." This involuntary acceptance of the principle of delayed gratification went a long way toward explaining mass consumption in the postwar period.

With a shortage of consumer goods, Americans began spending more money on entertainment. Hollywood was a major beneficiary: movie attendance reached eighty million customers a week in 1942. Hollywood's War Activities Committee donated over forty thousand prints to the armed services, assuring that more than half a million soldiers watched a Hollywood film every night. With an eye on building national morale, Hollywood glorified the exploits of the American soldier, usually described as the boy next door, and defined the war as a crusade for freedom rather than as a defense of national interest. During the war years horror films declined in popularity, perhaps because of the real horrors of war. The war saw the emergence of a new film genre, the nostalgic musical, in which films like *Meet Me in St. Louis* (1944) described a simpler and happier America. Women's films stressed the importance of self-sacrifice while American men were away from home, and even emancipated women like Bette Davis were placed in unrealistically lavish settings to emphasize the fantasy rather than the reality of female independence.

The political content of Hollywood films changed dramatically after Pearl Harbor. During the era of neutrality, the major studios scrupulously censored politically controversial scenes. In *Blockade* (1938), for example, an early film about the Spanish civil war, it was

People of all ages and from diverse ethnic backgrounds supported the war effort by buying United States defense bonds. (Library of Congress)

impossible to tell which side the protagonist supported. In 1942, however, *Mrs. Minniver,* a sentimental story about British resistance to the Nazi blitz, won seven Academy Awards. Public opinion toward the Soviet Union also changed as Communists became military allies. Though most Americans remained suspicious of Soviet intentions, a 1944 poll showed that one-third of the people interviewed had favorable impressions of the Soviet Union and 46 percent believed that the Stalinist government was as good as could be expected for the Russian people. These favorable ideas were reinforced in numerous magazine articles and in two highly acclaimed Hollywood productions, *Mission to Moscow* (1943) and *Song of Russia* (1944). Both films later became severe embarrassments to Hollywood when the Cold War led to the investigation of Communist subversion in the movie industry.

Popular images of the Axis enemies also revealed underlying assumptions that had important wartime ramifications. Italian-Americans, like other Roman Catholic immigrants, had faced traditional discrimination. Within the Catholic church, moreover, Italians resented the dominance of the Irish hierarchy. These negative experiences left many Italian-Americans with ambivalent feelings about the United States. In 1942, 600,000 Italians had not become naturalized citizens. After the outbreak of war, they technically became "enemy aliens." Yet the Roosevelt administration, aware of the ethnic antagonism caused by World War One, attempted to avoid racist hysteria against Europeans. Moreover, Roosevelt appreciated the importance of the Italian vote for the Democratic party in the 1942 congressional elections. On Columbus Day, therefore, Roosevelt revoked the enemy alien status of Italians and facilitated the procedures for naturalization. In a similar electoral situation in 1944, Roosevelt appealed to Italian voters by announcing a loan and relief supplies for the defeated Italian enemy.

The desire to differentiate between the Italian people and the Italian government emerged clearly in Hollywood films. In *Sahara* (1942), for example, which featured Humphrey Bogart as an American desert fighter, an Italian prisoner of war was described contemptuously as a "pot of spaghetti," but the film went on to point out that loyal Italian-Americans probably had helped make the steel for Bogart's tank. "Italians are not like Germans," the film concluded; the Fascist uniform covered only the body, not the soul. Such notions helped prepare the American public for the relatively lenient treatment toward the defeated Italian government in 1943.

While Hollywood portrayed Italians as inadvertent enemies, it depicted Nazis and Japanese as ruthless barbarians. Since the Roosevelt administration played down anti-German feeling at home, Hollywood also distinguished between Nazis and other Germans. The cruel, callous Nazi, however, became a common stereotype on the silver screen. In *Sahara*, the captured German flyer, unlike the Italian, remains intransigent, dedicated to the philosophy of the master race. In another Bogart film, *All Through the Night* (1942), Hollywood revealed another aspect of nazism — its gross stupidity, a recurring screen phenomenon that encouraged audiences to laugh at the world conquerors. Such laughter reduced the Nazis to human proportions. Depictions of the Japanese, however, were utterly humorless. Partly because of the anger created by Pearl Harbor and partly because of anti-Asian racism, Americans were unable to see the Japanese enemy as human. Instead the typical Japanese warrior was a robot-like creature prepared to die for the emperor.

POLITICS IN WARTIME

Though the popular media emphasized the theme of national unity, disagreements between liberals and conservatives undermined Roosevelt's search for consensus, especially after the 1942 elections brought a Republican majority to Congress. Having learned from Wilson's failure the importance of maintaining a working relationship with Congress on matters of foreign policy, Roosevelt decided to abandon the more liberal aspects of the New Deal. At a press conference in December 1943, he announced that "Dr. New Deal" had given way to "Dr. Win the War."

Roosevelt's surrender reflected the realities of congressional power. But it did not weaken the president's hopes for postwar reform. In January 1944 he used his annual state of the union message to propose an economic "bill of rights." "We cannot be content," he declared, "if some fraction of our people — whether it be one-third or one-fifth or one-tenth — is ill-fed, ill-clothed, ill-housed, and insecure." Roosevelt proceeded to throw his weight behind liberal legislation for veterans' benefits. By 1944 about one million veterans had returned from the armed services, many of them injured or otherwise unable to adjust to civilian life. Congress responded to presidential urging as well as a strong American Legion lobby by enacting the GI Bill of Rights, which provided unemployment, social security, and educational benefits to veterans. But a conservative Congress fought back attempts to link this legislation to a broader program of social welfare. In the end, the GI Bill, by providing scholarship, home loans, life insurance, and burial costs, offered traditional middle-class opportunities.

Though Roosevelt envisioned a liberal Democratic program, conservatives continued to grow in strength even in his own party. When the president supported a federal election law to enable soldiers to vote, southern Democrats joined Republicans to defend the principle of states' rights and defeat the measure. In 1944 Roosevelt vetoed an appropriation bill that gave generous depletion allowances to oil and lumber investors and exempted the natural gas industry from excess-profits taxes. Roosevelt's stinging message aroused the hostility of his previously loyal supporters in Congress, and

Democratic votes were essential in overriding the veto.

Roosevelt's problems with conservative Democrats encouraged the Republican party. Wendell Willkie, the Republican candidate in 1940, had returned from a round-the-world goodwill tour as a committed internationalist, enthusiastic about America's responsibilities to the world as well as to social reform at home. The Republican party, more conservative than its titular head, rejected his call and turned instead to Governor Thomas E. Dewey of New York, an energetic but undazzling candidate.

Despite rumors of Roosevelt's ill health, there was never any question of his renomination. The problem for Democrats focused on the vice presidential choice. Henry A. Wallace, the incumbent, had offended regular party bosses as well as conservative southern Democrats by his outspoken liberalism. Wallace's rival, James Byrnes, a southerner, was hated by organized labor. Roosevelt shrewdly picked a compromise candidate, Harry S Truman of Missouri, a loyal New Dealer whose major claim to fame was his chairmanship of the Senate War Investigating Committee, which had assiduously exposed unnecessary government waste and attempted to prevent war profiteering.

Few issues separated the candidates. Dewey readily endorsed a bipartisan foreign policy, including a commitment to postwar internationalism, and also accepted such New Deal policies as social security, unemployment insurance, collective bargaining, and farm price supports. The Democrats benefited greatly by campaign support from the CIO's Political Action Committee (PAC), which brought out the workers' votes. The urban electorate provided Roosevelt's margin of victory: 25.6 million to 22 million popular votes; 432 to 99 electoral votes.

DOMESTIC CONFLICT

While Democrats and Republicans struggled for control of the nation's political institutions, other Americans struggled more simply for survival. Roosevelt's Four Freedoms served as a convenient rallying point for the war effort, and the president's Office of War Information tried to portray the war as a democratic crusade. But members of outgroups — political dissenters, Japanese-Americans, blacks, Jews, Chicanos, young people, and women — discovered basic inconsistencies in the so-called American Creed. Despite Roosevelt's rhetoric, many Americans found themselves excluded from the national identity.

Roosevelt and Attorney General Francis Biddle tried to avoid the rabid hysteria of World War One in dealing with political dissenters. Their task was made easier by the Communist party's unqualified support of a war that put the United States on the same side as the Soviet Union. But the administration remained totally unsympathetic to right wing critics and American Fascists. In 1942 Biddle invoked the Espionage Act of 1917 to prevent the mailing of Father Coughlin's *Social Justice,* an isolationist, Jew-baiting magazine, and when Coughlin protested, the administration persuaded the Catholic hierarchy to silence the priest. Biddle also indicted twenty-six Fascists in a celebrated sedition trial that dragged on for over two years before the administration decided to drop the charges. Under the Hatch Act of 1939, which attempted to eliminate subversives from federal employment, the Civil Service Commission instituted a series of loyalty checks.

The government demonstrated even greater intolerance toward those who refused to comply with the Selective Service Act on grounds of conscience. Though the law allowed for Conscientious Objector status, Selective Service Director Lewis B. Hershey chose a narrow definition, ruling in 1942 that religious conscience implied a belief in divinity. About thirty-five thousand COs were willing to work at alternative government service. But many draft boards refused to recognize CO status, and

Fearing the possibility of subversion, Roosevelt ordered the roundup of all Japanese-Americans, including this girl photographed at Owens Valley, California. These Japanese-Americans, many of them American citizens, were placed in internment camps. (Library of Congress USF-33-13288-M3)

many pacifists refused to compromise with any government service. Over fifty-five hundred men, most of them Jehovah's Witnesses, chose prison over compliance with Selective Service. Jail sentences averaged four to five years. Meanwhile, civilian Jehovah's Witnesses were subject to government harassment and occasionally mob violence.

The most serious attack on civil rights and cultural differences emerged in government policy toward Japanese-Americans. Alarmed by Pearl Harbor and by subsequent Japanese victories in the Pacific, Americans focused their

"Hard hat" workers in defense industries enjoyed unprecedented prosperity as the wartime economy finally brought an end to the Great Depression. (Dorothea Lange/City of Oakland/The Oakland Museum)

fear and then their venom on the Japanese-American population, most of whom lived on the West Coast. In looking for scapegoats, journalists falsely reported that California Japanese had conspired in the attack on Pearl Harbor and were planning further subversion at home. When none occurred, California Attorney General Earl Warren used this demonstrable loyalty as counter-proof. "We are just being lulled into a false sense of security," he told a congressional investigating committee in February 1942, "and the only reason we haven't had disaster in California is because it has been timed for a different date." The commanding general of the area, John DeWitt, analyzed the situation more simply: "A Jap's a Jap.... It makes no difference if he is an American citizen." Even the prestigious liberal journalist Walter Lippmann warned against "the Fifth Column on the Coast."

Roosevelt responded to this public pressure with Executive Order 9066, which ordered the internment and relocation of all Japanese. Of the 110,000 people affected by the decision, two-thirds were American citizens by birth (under the Naturalization Act of 1924, Japanese immigrants were not permitted to become American citizens). Many of these victims, particularly the assimilationists, were anxious to demonstrate their loyalty to the United States and saw compliance as the most convincing proof. Others protested vigorously: "Has the Gestapo come to America? Have we not risen in righteous anger at Hitler's mistreatments of the Jews? Then, is it not incongruous that citizen Americans of Japanese descent should be similarly mistreated and persecuted?"

Forced to sell their private possessions at short notice — usually to unscrupulous white buyers — the Japanese were herded into detention centers and then relocated into ten concentration camps in arid parts of the country. These executive decisions were upheld in a series of Supreme Court rulings in 1944. In the *Korematsu* case, the Court upheld the relocation from the West Coast on grounds of military necessity. But in the *Endo* case, the Court denied that citizens could be detained once their loyalty had been established. By that time the War Relocation Authority already had begun to release loyal Japanese and had announced the termination of the camps on January 2, 1945.

Though surrounded by barbed wire and military guard, the relocation camps were less like Nazi concentration camps than American Indian reservations. Government authorities had relatively little social contact with inmates, who lived in segregated areas. Such straitened circumstances encouraged a revitalization of traditional Japanese culture — similar to the Ghost Dance traditions that emerged when the Plains Indians were forced onto reservations. The internment created severe conflicts between these traditional Japanese and the assimilationists, who wished to break completely with the old culture. Tensions intensified in 1943 when the government attempted to separate the "disloyal" Japanese. The issues were complicated by questions of military service (Japanese volunteers eventually were accepted by the army, fought in segregated units, and proved to be exceptionally tough soldiers), by parental attachment, by fear of reprisal, and by distrust of the government. Those deemed disloyal were moved to the Tule Lake camp, where the renaissance of Japanese culture was seen as a preparation for a return to Japan. During the war nearly six thousand Japanese renounced their United States citizenship and forty-seven hundred Japanese-Americans obtained "repatriation" after the war.

Though wartime necessity rationalized the destruction of Japanese civil rights, the same imperatives of national unity enabled Afro-Americans to challenge traditional race prejudice. Where the theme for blacks in World War One had been W. E. B. DuBois's summons to "close ranks," black leaders in World War Two insisted that "declarations of war do not lessen the obligation to preserve and extend civil liberties" at home. Even after Roosevelt established the FEPC, Randolph's March on Washington movement did not disband but remained as an important all-black, mass-based pressure group. The NAACP also grew during the war, increasing its membership ninefold to 450,000. "Not since Reconstruction," concluded Gunnar Myrdal's massive study of race relations, *An American Dilemma* (1944), "has there been more reason to anticipate fundamental changes in American race relations, changes which will involve a development toward the American ideals."

The changes came slower than Myrdal predicted. In the army, blacks, like Japanese, served in segregated units, while the Red Cross separated "colored" blood from "white." Military policy, as Lewis Hershey explained, "is simply transferring discrimination from everyday life into the Army." Fundamental to that policy was a belief that blacks were too docile to make good fighters. As a result, blacks were initially assigned to labor units, denied opportunity for promotion, and barred from prestigious duties such as flying. Even after proving their battlefield valor, black service remained unrecognized; no blacks were awarded medals of honor in World Wars One and Two. Most humiliating of all to black soldiers was the realization that Nazi prisoners of war could use public eating facilities whereas blacks in American uniforms were denied service. Such treatment did not go unchallenged in the army. Numerous race riots occurred both on and off base, and in one notorious case the black athlete Jackie Robinson was court-martialed for defying Jim Crow policy.

Blacks on the home front continued to face racist policies. The extent of the problem was revealed in a public opinion poll taken at the beginning of the war. As reported by Myrdal, 18 percent of blacks admitted pro-Japanese feelings; in a similar poll, southern white industrialists, when asked to choose between complete racial equality or a German victory, chose the latter by a large majority. Such sentiments were equally strong in the North. In Detroit, white crowds rioted in 1942 to prevent blacks from moving into the federally funded Sojourner Truth housing project. The next year Detroit exploded again as racial tensions produced a two-day race riot that left thirty-five dead and over seven hundred wounded. Major race riots also occurred in Texas; Ohio; Springfield, Massachusetts; and Harlem.

Despite these conflicts, World War Two represented an ideological turning point in American race relations. The repudiation of Nazi racism, reinforced at the war's end by the discovery of the infamous death camps, challenged the validity of America's own racist assumptions. A chapter of Wendell Willkie's best-selling *One World* (1943) criticized "Our Imperialism at Home" and called for an end to "a smug racial superiority, a willingness to exploit an unprotected people." In 1944 the Supreme Court abolished the white primary, which had served to disfranchise black voters in most southern states. The changing attitudes could be seen in popular films, which began to move away from the Sambo stereotypes of the thirties. In the classic *Casablanca* (1943), for example, the black pianist, Sam, portrays a

mature adult capable of deep political conviction, while *Sahara* contrasted the reliability of an African soldier with the brutality of the Nazis. Such changes provided an important bedrock for the civil rights movement of the postwar era.

The experience of blacks was comparable to that of Jews. Though Roosevelt appointed many Jews to important positions in government, it was not uncommon before the war for Jews to face discrimination in business, social life, and education. In Boston young supporters of Father Coughlin roamed the streets to attack Jews and vandalize synagogues. Immigration laws established quotas that discriminated against Jews, even when refugees from Nazi persecution literally faced death as the only alternative. Not until 1944 did Roosevelt move to facilitate the admission of Jewish refugees from Europe. Yet the horror of Nazi anti-Semitism thoroughly discredited American anti-Semitism and, although private prejudices remained, removed the gross forms of discrimination in such areas as education quotas.

While it became relatively easy for Jews to overcome ethnic discrimination, other groups encountered stronger barriers. The Spanish-speaking, brown-skinned Mexican-Americans of the Southwest continued to face overt discrimination. Besides housing segregation, they suffered from unemployment, low wages, and endemic poverty. During the war younger Chicanos formed teenage "pachuco" gangs and dressed in lavish costumes known as "zoot suits." Though zoot suiters hardly differed from other adolescent youths, newspapers exaggerated the threat of gangsterism. In July 1943 rumors that pachucos had beaten a sailor provoked a four-day race riot in Los Angeles. White servicemen raided the barrios, attacked the zoot suiters, and stripped them of their clothing. Though prominent leaders condemned the riot, the situation typified the problems of politically weak ethnic minorities. Like the Japanese, Mexican-Americans lacked the power to protect their communities.

The fear of the zoot suiters revealed not only a persistent problem of ethnic antagonism but also a more general anxiety about youth. "The youngsters of this spontaneous movement are *not* delinquent," insisted psychologist Fritz Redl. "They are normal, growing youngsters." Like other adolescents, zoot suiters adopted a distinctive uniform to reinforce group identity. During the war years there was also a dramatic rise in juvenile delinquency, particularly in sex crimes, and army officials openly worried about a venereal disease epidemic. Contemporaries speculated about the reason for adolescent delinquency, wondering if the war had unleashed some primal antisocial instinct. Yet the "crimes" attributed to the youth culture — premarital sexual relations, drinking, frivolity — were closely related to adult fantasies. "In a society where such strong emphasis is placed upon individual achievements," observed Harvard sociologist Talcott Parsons, "it is not surprising that there should be a certain romantic nostalgia for the time when the fundamental choices were still open." Adults, particularly people whose lives were disrupted by and preoccupied with war, resented the independence and spontaneity of the youth culture. "To label them all delinquents," Redl concluded, "is nothing but self-deception."

Whatever its basis, the concern about youth reflected a growing belief that the American family was disintegrating because mothers were leaving their children to take war work. According to conventional wisdom, marriage was the single most important event in a woman's life. "That determines a woman's fundamental

Two "pachuco" Mexican-Americans display their pegged trousers, slashed by rioting servicemen. (Wide World Photos)

status," explained Talcott Parsons, "and after that her role patterning is . . . a matter of living up to expectations and finding satisfying interests and activities." Career women were supposed to be unmarried. But during World War Two the largest number of new workers were married. It was this group, particularly those past childbearing years, that desired to remain in the work force after the war. Participation in war work thus legitimated women's employment among middle-class families. But the widespread recognition of women's contribution to the war effort failed in the short run to alter traditional expectations.

The tendency for social values to lag behind wartime changes reflected the inability of Americans to confront the vast implications of World War Two. Despite a sense of crisis, most Americans viewed the war as a temporary detour. Where the "doughboys" of World War One were celebrated as heroic adventurers, the soldiers of World War Two appeared as civilians in uniform. "Home," wrote the front-line journalist Ernie Pyle, "the one really profound goal that obsesses every one of the Americans marching on foreign shores." Even the fictional heroes were different. The outstanding novel of World War Two, Norman Mailer's *The Naked and the Dead* (1948), used the device of flashback to accentuate the temporary nature of soldier status. Such attitudes encouraged the notion that things would revert to prewar status after the defeat of Germany and Japan.

The experiences on the home front, however, destroyed those illusions. Shortly after Pearl Harbor, Jonathan Daniels, a journalist who later joined the White House staff, urged a return to America's frontier heritage. "The forties are here in which Americans stand on a continent as men," he exulted. America was "grown magnificently male again.... We are men again in America." The male warrior, like the nineteenth-century pioneer, would restore the national identity. But Daniels's appeal of 1941 neglected the existence of other Americans — women and racial, ethnic, and religious minorities. World War Two brought these groups into greater prominence. By 1945 few would settle for the invisibility implied in Daniels's statement.

TRUMAN AND TRUCE

Roosevelt's successor, Harry Truman, inherited the delicate diplomatic responsibility for settling the peace. Though he lacked Roosevelt's experience and skill, Truman determined to obtain concessions from the Soviet Union. Where Roosevelt had pragmatically accepted the vague language of Yalta, the new president insisted that the Soviet Union adopt the American interpretation of the meeting. Almost immediately he attacked Stalin's foreign minister, Molotov, over Soviet policy in Poland and threatened to cut off American assistance to the Soviet Union. At San Francisco American delegates reluctantly accepted the three Soviet votes that Roosevelt already had conceded at Yalta, but not without forcing other compromises from the Soviets. After the formal German surrender on May 8, 1945 (V-E Day), the United States abruptly halted Lend-Lease, ordering ships in mid-Atlantic to turn around. After British and Soviet protests, however, Truman denied responsibility and reversed the order. Worried about the deterioration of American-Soviet relations, Truman decided to call another summit conference.

Truman's desire to meet with Stalin reflected an important change in the balance of power. Shortly after succeeding Roosevelt, Truman learned about a top-secret military project to build a nuclear bomb. Truman speculated that the bomb might give the United States greater leverage in winning concessions from the Soviets. He accordingly timed the summit meeting at Potsdam for mid-July 1945, the same week the first atom bomb would be tested in New Mexico.

The atom bomb had emerged as a logical outgrowth of modern physics. Its fundamental principles were brought to the United States by scientists fleeing from Nazi Germany. In 1939, at the urging of the physicist Leo Szilard, Albert Einstein wrote to Roosevelt suggesting the possibility of nuclear weapons and warning that German scientists might already be developing them. After initial caution, Roosevelt created a National Defense Research Committee to encourage nuclear research. Because refugee scientists were considered security risks, they were not allowed to work on such top-secret projects as radar; ironically, many turned to the atom bomb instead.

As the atom bomb developed, Roosevelt decided to share its secrets with the British (who had made important early contributions). At Churchill's urging, he refused to divulge the secret Manhattan Project to Stalin, even though he knew that spies already had informed the Soviets of the project. In reaching this crucial decision, Roosevelt assumed that Britain would be a vital postwar ally, especially if isolationism again became a dominant force. But he believed that the Soviets could not be trusted. Since Stalin already knew about the bomb project, however, the decision created mutual distrust. Within the administration there was never any doubt that the atom bomb would be used against the enemy. Fire bombings of Dresden and Tokyo had claimed more victims than would die in atomic bombings. In May 1945 a committee of administrators and scientists agreed that the bomb should be dropped against Japan. The major reason for this decision was the belief that the new weapon would forestall an invasion of Japan and thus save one million American lives. The bomb would also demonstrate — to friend and foe alike — the superiority of American military strength in the postwar world.

The Potsdam conference failed to resolve Soviet-American conflicts. With news of the successful atom bomb test, Truman tried to force Stalin to alter the political arrangements in eastern Europe, where leftist parties prevailed. Stalin refused to change these governments, viewing Truman's request as a betrayal of the principle of spheres of influence reached at Yalta. Those principles had permitted Soviet dominance in eastern Europe, but also had allowed the suppression of Greek Communists and the creation of a pro-Western government in Italy. At Potsdam the Big Three did agree to partition Germany, but again failed to resolve the question of reparations. Final peace treaties were delegated to a subsequent Council of Foreign Ministers.

By the summer of 1945, the Japanese cause seemed hopeless. In July the Japanese premier made overtures through the Soviet Union, indicating a willingness to sue for peace. The Truman administration responded with demands for unconditional surrender and warned that Japan faced imminent destruction. When the Japanese failed to reply, Truman allowed military decisions to proceed. On August 6, 1945, a B-29 dropped a single atom bomb on the city of Hiroshima, killing 80,000–100,000 inhabitants. On August 9 the Soviet Union entered the war. The same day, another atom bomb fell on the city of Nagasaki. The Japanese now sought immediate peace, agreeing on August 14 to surrender, provided only that the emperor be retained. When Truman agreed, World War Two was over.

SUGGESTED READINGS

The most comprehensive treatment of Roosevelt's foreign policy is Robert Dallek, *Franklin*

D. Roosevelt and American Foreign Policy, 1932–1945 (1979). A brief but thorough introduction to the major issues of foreign policy on the eve of World War Two is Robert A. Divine, *The Reluctant Belligerent: American Entry into World War II* (1965). More detailed is a two-volume study by William L. Langer and S. Everett Gleason, *Challenge to Isolation, 1937–1940* (1952) and *The Undeclared War, 1940–1941* (1953). These surveys may be supplemented by John E. Wiltz, *From Isolation to War, 1931–1941* (1968).

The ideological context of United States foreign policy is explained in the relevant chapters of William Appleman Williams, *The Tragedy of American Diplomacy* (1962). These themes emerge in greater detail in Lloyd C. Gardner, *Economic Aspects of New Deal Diplomacy* (1964). Also helpful in understanding the relationship between economic interest and ideology is a brief essay, Thomas H. Etzold, "Why America Fought Germany in World War II" (1973). For studies of isolationism, see John E. Wiltz, *In Search of Peace: The Senate Munitions Inquiry, 1934–1936* (1963), and Manfred Jonas, *Isolationism in America: 1935–1941* (1966). The diplomatic implications of isolationism emerge in two studies of the United States's response to the Spanish civil war: Allen Guttmann, *The Wound in the Heart* (1962), and Richard P. Traina, *American Diplomacy and the Spanish Civil War* (1968). Roosevelt's perception of the national interest is examined in Robert A. Divine, *Roosevelt and World War II* (1969).

A thorough study of the United States's relations with Japan is Dorothy Borg, *The United States and Far Eastern Crises of 1933–1938* (1964), which should be supplemented by Herbert Feis, *Road to Pearl Harbor* (1950). For the Japanese context, see Robert J. Butow,

Tojo and the Coming of the War (1961). The attack on Pearl Harbor is examined in Roberta Wohlstetter, *Pearl Harbor: Warning and Decision* (1962).

The issues of wartime diplomacy are described in Gaddis Smith, *American Diplomacy During the Second World War, 1941–1945* (1965), and John Snell, *Illusion and Necessity: The Diplomacy of World War II* (1963). The relationship between military and diplomatic affairs is emphasized in A. Russell Buchanan, *The United States and World War II*, 2 vols. (1964). More specific is Raymond G. O'Connor, *Diplomacy for Victory: FDR and Unconditional Surrender* (1971). Gabriel Kolko's *The Politics of War: The World and United States Foreign Policy, 1943–1945* (1968) stresses the inherent contradictions of national interest within the Grand Alliance. The origins of the United Nations is well treated in Robert A. Divine, *Second Chance: The Triumph of Internationalism in America During World War II* (1967). For a brilliant analysis of the diplomatic implications of the atom bomb, see Martin J. Sherwin, *A World Destroyed: The Atomic Bomb and the Grand Alliance* (1975).

Domestic issues during World War Two are best described in Richard Polenberg, *War and Society: The United States, 1941–1945* (1972). For Roosevelt's presidential role, see James MacGregor Burns, *Roosevelt: The Soldier of Freedom* (1970). John Morton Blum's *V Was for Victory: Politics and American Culture During World War II* (1976) explores the cultural context of wartime decision making. It may be supplemented by Geoffrey Perrett, *Days of Sadness, Years of Triumph* (1973), Richard Lingeman, *Don't You Know There's a War On?* (1970), and a compilation of "oral" histories, Roy Hoopes, *Americans Remember the*

Home Front (1977). For the movie industry, see Charles Higham and Joel Greenberg, *Hollywood in the Forties* (1968).

The impact of the war on Japanese-Americans is examined by Roger Daniels, *Concentration Camps USA: Japanese-Americans and World War II* (1971), as well as by Edward Spicer et al., *Impounded People: Japanese-Americans in the Relocation Centers* (1969), a report originally written in 1946 for the War Relocation Authority. The experience of blacks emerges in Richard Dalfiume, *Desegregation of the Armed Forces, 1939–1953* (1969). Also illuminating are the memoirs of black soldiers compiled in Mary Penick Motley, *The Invisible Soldier* (1975). The best sources for the impact of the war on women are the relevant chapters of William H. Chafe, *The American Woman* (1972). An excellent comparative study is Leila Rupp, *Mobilizing Women for War: German and American Propaganda, 1939–1945* (1978). For the pacifist movement, see Lawrence S. Wittner, *Rebels Against War: The American Peace Movement, 1941–1960* (1969).

For the Nuremberg trials, see Bradley F. Smith, *Reaching Judgment at Nuremberg* (1977), and Telford Taylor, *Nuremberg and Vietnam: An American Tragedy* (1970).

Spotlight: The Nuremberg Trials

The difficulty in reaching international agreements at Yalta and Potsdam contrasted with the unanimity felt by the Allies about punishing German war criminals. Over the centuries of warfare, an international "common law" had emerged, which prohibited certain wartime behavior, such as the indiscriminate murder of prisoners of war and civilians. These precedents included articles of the Treaty of Versailles that attributed war guilt to Germany after World War One and obligated that defeated country to pay war "reparations" to the victors. During the interwar period, however, many Americans criticized these provisions on the grounds that the victorious nations often had been guilty of similar activities and yet had gone unpunished. Moreover, many of the so-called German atrocities during World War One had subsequently been found to be figments of Allied propaganda.

Such ambiguities were at great remove from obvious German war crimes in World War Two. Besides invading other countries, Nazi Germany had wantonly violated rules of warfare regarding civilian populations. In defeated countries, German armies instituted reigns of terror — robbing, raping, and murdering innocent people. The Germans also implemented Nazi racial policies designed to exterminate "inferior" peoples such as gypsies and Jews. At the war's end, the Allied armies liberated barbaric concentration camps, such as Auschwitz and Dachau, in which millions of civilian captives had been enslaved, tortured, and starved before they were sent to mass deaths in gas chambers and their bodies plundered of hair, artificial teeth, and tattooed skin.

The enormity of German war crimes led Allied leaders to seek an unambiguous criminal judgment. At the Moscow foreign ministers' conference of 1943, the Big Three warned that war criminals would be punished "by joint decision." As victory appeared imminent in 1944, exiled leaders of occupied countries and Jewish refugees called for a more explicit statement to avert last-ditch Nazi atrocities. But Great Britain and the United States feared jeopardizing the lives of Allied prisoners of war and remained doubtful of the atrocity descriptions. But the murder of captured American soldiers at Malmedy during the Battle of the Bulge in December 1944 stiffened the Allied position.

Allied leaders, including such prominent members of the Roosevelt administration as Secretary of the Treasury Henry Morgenthau, proposed the summary execution of Nazi war criminals. But other administration officials, such as Secretaries Stimson and Hull, recognized the importance of establishing legal precedents to discourage future wartime behavior. With Roosevelt's approval, the War Department made elaborate preparations for the creation of a postwar international tribunal to try Germans accused of war crimes. Such a trial would avoid the possibility of making martyrs of German war leaders, establish a clear record of German war guilt, and reaffirm the nature of wartime criminal activities.

The major powers, which after the defeat of Germany included France, agreed to an international tribunal on war crimes at the San Francisco conference of April 1945. Negotiations about the nature of the trial, the definitions of "war crimes," and the list of defendants continued in London through the summer. These prolonged discussions revealed inherent problems within the Grand Alliance, ranging from Soviet demands for mass retribution (German criminality had been particularly severe on the Russian front) to American insistence on prosecution for "conspiracy" to commit crimes (a concept that was alien to continental law) and the inclusion of prewar policies in the indictment. But the Allied leaders at Potsdam, in one of their last demonstrations of wartime unity, recognized the importance of an international trial and broke the deadlock.

The Big Four announced agreement on the International Military Tribunal on German war crimes in August 1945. Each of the Allies would appoint a judge and an alternate; each would prosecute separate aspects of the united case. The defendants would be given rights of counsel and due process to assure a fair trial. The sessions would be held in the Bavarian city of Nuremberg. Its medieval fortress and prison provided one of the few undestroyed facilities in Germany capable of holding the defendants. Moreover, Nuremberg symbolized the former strength of Nazi ideology. It had supported torchlight parades and mass rallies. And a series of laws promulgated at Nuremberg in 1935 stripped the Jews of their political rights, leaving them defenseless for Nazi atrocities.

In drawing up the indictment, Allied prosecutors established four major categories of criminality — conspiracy to commit war crimes, violations of traditional laws of war (mistreatment of prisoners, murder not justified by military "necessity"), crimes against peace (aggressive warfare, violating treaties), and crimes against humanity (racial, religious, and political persecution, extermination). These legal divisions were designed to cast a wide basis for establishing complicity, embracing leaders and followers, and members of both the military and civil government. Since Hitler and other prominent Nazis already were dead, the Allies selected defendants who were most representative of Nazi institutions, though not necessarily the most abominable criminals. Within these guidelines, twenty-two representatives of Nazi Germany were accused of various war crimes. The Allies also charged that certain Nazi organizations, such as the Gestapo (secret police), the SS (paramilitary elite), and the Nazi party leadership, were criminal. A judgment against criminal organizations would extend guilt to members of those groups. This aspect of the charge emphasized the principle of individual responsibility for criminal actions and undercut the defense that a criminal could be excused merely for obeying the orders of superiors.

In presenting its case, the prosecution stressed the universal implications of punishing war crimes. "While this law is first applied against German aggressors," explained Supreme Court Justice Robert H. Jackson, who served as chief American prosecutor, "if it is to serve any useful purpose it must condemn other nations, including those which sit here now in judgment." By establishing a strict rule of international law, the Nuremberg proceedings promised to limit the devastating effects of modern warfare.

Despite such claims, the Nuremberg trials reflected the realities of political power in postwar Europe. Although the London Charter that authorized the proceedings made no distinctions among the Axis enemies, no Italians were charged with war crimes. This omission reflected a general satisfaction that the lynching of Mussolini in 1943 served as sufficient retribution. Equally important, the western Allies who fought against Italy were more concerned with bringing that nation into a Western anticommunist coalition. Similarly, in examining the question of conspiracy to plan aggressive warfare, the Nuremberg Tribunal skirted the sensitive question of the Nazi-Soviet pact of 1939. Though publication of the secret passages of that alliance indicated that Stalin knew about Hitler's plans to attack Poland and had continued to "cooperate" with Nazi aggression, the Soviet representatives forced a rewording of the final judgment to avoid implicating the Soviet leadership.

The defense of national interests by the Allies also led them to apply separate standards in judging German war policies. Evidence used by the prosecution came almost exclusively from captured German documents, material that most governments manage to keep secret for a specified time. Thus the German defendants did not have access to material in the Allied archives that might have demonstrated similar policies executed by the prosecuting countries. In any case, the tribunal ruled that a defense argument based on the Allies having committed similar acts was inadmissible.

These principles enabled the Allies to avoid several embarrassing contradictions in their judgment. One of the grounds for accusing the Germans of waging aggressive warfare was the invasion of neutral Norway in 1940. At that time, however, the Germans captured Allied documents that revealed that Great Britain had been planning a similar invasion. The German defendants thus adopted the defense that the invasion of Norway was designed to forestall British plans. At Nuremberg, the British judges knew that the German evidence was correct, but the British government suppressed such confirmation from other judges. Though the United States and France were prepared to ignore the German allegations, the Soviet judge argued that British invasion plans did exist, but differed qualitatively from the German attack because of military "necessity." This Soviet position indirectly supported the Soviet invasion of Finland in 1939. In the end, the Nuremberg Tribunal dismissed the argument that British strategy justified the German attack. It took no position on similar British attack plans.

A contradictory decision also emerged in the judgment against Admiral Karl Doenitz, commander of the German submarine program, later head of the German navy, and after Hitler's suicide, leader of the Third Reich for twenty days. According to the indictment, Doenitz had authorized violations of international law, such as sinking neutral merchant vessels, establishing naval war zones, and failing to rescue passengers and crews from ships sunk by German submarines. Yet considerable trial evidence, including the testimony of the American naval commander of the Pacific, Admiral Chester Nimitz, demonstrated that the Allied navies had pursued policies nearly identical to those of the Germans. After considerable disagreement within the tribunal (the American judge, Francis Biddle, argued for complete acquittal), Doenitz was nevertheless convicted.

Despite the judgment against Doenitz, the similarities between German and Allied warfare prevented a clear resolution of the legal questions regarding weapons, not only involving submarines, but also aerial bombardment of civilians. The German air forces had initiated programs of terror bombings as early as the Spanish civil war and had blatantly attacked such civilian centers as London and Coventry. But the Allied air forces had retaliated in kind, destroying most German cities, unleashing incredible fire storms in Dresden, and ultimately concluding the war with atomic bombings of Japan. Such a record kept the Nuremberg Tribunal from examining the legality of total warfare tactics.

The Allies nevertheless recognized the importance of mass communications in modern warfare by indicting the Jew-baiting propagandist Julius Streicher. As editor of a German newspaper, Streicher personified the most egregious forms of anti-Semitism, freely advocating the annihilation of all Jews. Yet despite his inflammatory rhetoric, the journalist held no civil or military positions that related to war crimes. He was convicted instead for contributing to a political climate that enabled "crimes against humanity" to flourish. Streicher's case symbolized a widespread repudiation of public racism in the United States. Though race prejudice might remain within people's minds, the Nazi experience undermined its social acceptability.

Despite the attempt to prosecute representatives of all aspects of Nazi society, the Nuremberg proceedings failed to include leading industrialists. The original indictment had listed the patriarch of the Krupp family, whose factories had employed slave labor and had profited by the rearmament of the Third Reich. Yet because of a prosecution error, the named Krupp was not in charge of the family business, but was a senile, incontinent old man who was incapable of standing trial. This prosecution oversight had important implications. First, it left the legal questions of industrial complicity in war crimes unexamined. Second, it assured that the role of multinational affiliates of the Krupp combine, including American corporations, would go unchallenged (some of these corporations later obtained benefits from the United States government as a result of damage caused to their European holdings by Allied attacks). Finally, by leaving the Krupp empire intact, the Nuremberg proceedings indirectly facilitated the rebuilding of the German economy with its heavy industry closely wedded to the anticommunist nations.

Though political power influenced certain aspects of the Nuremberg trials, the judges strove to follow recognized legal precedents regarding evidence and due process. The final verdicts thus reflected the judges' determination of individual cases. Of the twenty-two defendants, twelve were sentenced to hanging, seven received prison terms ranging from ten years to life, and three were acquitted. Three of the six Nazi organizations charged with criminality were so declared. In reaching these diverse verdicts, the Nuremberg Tribunal managed to balance demands for severe retribution with complaints that the proceedings involved laws that were created after the crimes were committed (ex post facto laws). Whatever their political prejudices, the judges emphasized their roles in further defining the nature of international rules of war.

The Nuremberg proceedings provided guidelines for the trial of lesser war criminals in Japan and Germany. These subsequent trials, conducted by military tribunals of the individual victors and by the reconstituted German governments, eventually dealt with several thousand accused war criminals and resulted in hundreds of death sentences and prison terms. In sum, these various proceedings reaffirmed the basic principles of Nuremberg: aggressive warfare, violations of traditional warfare, and inhuman acts constituted crimes; individuals remained accountable for their criminal actions despite superior orders; and individuals accused of war crimes were entitled to judicial trials.

The legal precedents served to institutionalize the moral outrage caused by Nazi war crimes. "The time was ripe to step across the line from conscience to a legal order," explained the philosopher Ralph Barton Perry, "and to create a legal precedent for future times." The past three decades, however, have revealed the limitations of the Nuremberg precedent. During the Vietnam War, for example, proponents of American foreign policy and their critics both cited the Nuremberg conclusions to justify their mutually exclusive policies. Despite the high idealism of the participants, the Nuremberg Tribunal remained a political creature of the Grand Alliance.

Chapter 11

POSTWAR SOCIETY, 1945-1960

The atomic bombing of Hiroshima and Nagasaki ended World War Two much earlier than most Americans had anticipated. The mass jubilation of V-J Day was soon followed by a demand for rapid demobilization of the armed forces. More than one million servicemen had been discharged before the war's end, but nearly fourteen million remained under arms. These veterans viewed themselves as civilians-in-uniform. After an average of three years of military service, they were anxious to go home. But few were nostalgic for the prewar era, a time of general economic hardship. Their prevailing sentiment was expressed in a popular song of 1945: "Gotta Make Up for Lost Time."

Public attention focused on the problems and difficulties of readjustment. In 1945 the nation's divorces leaped to over half a million,

twice as high as prewar figures. Such statistics reflected the haste of wartime marriages, the problems of long separations, and a growing sense of economic independence among women who had entered the labor force during the war. Veterans also faced serious economic problems. Most veterans wanted a job "with a future," but many found their wartime skills of little help in finding any employment. Government benefits under the GI Bill provided one year's unemployment insurance (at $20 per week) to ease the transition. Also vital for the ex-soldiers were their large wartime savings.

Readjustment was especially difficult for certain minority groups. Japanese-Americans, released from concentration camps in 1945, faced pervasive hostility and discrimination on the West Coast. White farmers who had confiscated Japanese agricultural property sometimes refused to surrender it and resorted to arson and violence to intimidate the rightful owners. In the southern states black veterans were reminded of their second-class status by a series of brutal lynchings that captured national attention. And poor veterans, of every nationality, returned to living conditions that reflected fifteen years of economic shortage.

The availability of government-financed scholarships under the GI Bill, however, offered veterans the possibility of attaining better-paying jobs. Between 1945 and 1950 over two million veterans took advantage of these appropriations to enroll in colleges and universities; millions more returned to high schools and vocational training programs. A postwar survey indicated that as many as one-fifth of the college-bound veterans would not otherwise have gone back to school. The heavy influx of students forced colleges to expand their facilities by opening branch campuses and offering evening instruction. Federal funds, by underwriting tuition bills, indirectly served as a catalyst for this expansion.

SCIENCE AND SOCIETY

The growing interest in higher education was stimulated by the achievement of American science during World War Two. The secret development of radar, the use of the pesticide DDT to kill malaria-carrying mosquitoes, the effectiveness of "miracle drugs" like penicillin in treating infection, the emergence of synthetic compounds to substitute for scarce resources like rubber — all testified to the importance of scientific research. In popular imagery, the scientist and the engineer became heroic figures.

These accomplishments were dwarfed at the war's end by the development of atomic bombs. During the war, atomic energy research had been classified top secret for reasons of military security. But the theoretical basis of the bomb had been established by physicists throughout the world. What was secret about the atom bomb was whether it would work. Once the bomb had been dropped over Japan, the secret was revealed. It was only a matter of time before other scientists could develop similar weapons. For this reason, Secretary of War Henry L. Stimson urged President Truman to allow the Soviet Union to share the atomic secrets along with Great Britain. Stimson was overruled, however, and the Truman administration chose to keep the bomb a secret — a symbol of American superiority.

Congress endorsed the policy of secrecy in the Atomic Energy Act of 1946. The law established an Atomic Energy Commission (AEC) and placed control of nuclear research and development in civilian hands. Though the United States held a monopoly of atomic weapons, official policy claimed to be seeking the abolition, or at least the limitation, of further nuclear production. Even proponents of secrecy shared Stimson's fear that modern civilization might be completely destroyed. The decision to keep the bomb secret also represented an attempt to remove atomic weapons from public discussion, where its feasibility might become a subject of political or military pressure.

Though a politically unmentionable subject, the bomb nevertheless unleashed profound fears about the future of scientific investigation. J. Robert Oppenheimer, head of the Los Alamos research team that developed the atom bomb, warned his colleagues in October 1945 that "if atomic bombs are to be added ... to the arsenals of a warring world, ... the time will come when mankind will curse the names of Los Alamos and of Hiroshima." Oppenheimer's concerns were mirrored on a popular level in postwar science fiction. Flourishing as never before, new science fiction writers like Isaac Asimov developed futuristic themes of human beings seeking to avert ultimate catastrophe. In Hollywood films the serious scientist became an ambivalent character, simultaneously capable of bringing salvation or annihilation.

These ambiguities began to disappear after 1949 when the Soviet Union tested its own atomic weapons, and the United States decided in 1950 to develop a hydrogen bomb of even greater destructive capability. Congress appropriated larger budgets to the AEC, which thereby attracted the best academic scientists. Cloaked in secrecy, American scientists no longer appeared as a demonic force, but as technicians in the service of their country. Despite civilian control of atomic energy, nearly all nuclear research and development involved military weapons. Scientists, instead of representing the independent search for truth, became subordinate to the military. These themes dominated the science fiction films of the fifties; invariably military personnel, portrayed as individualistic heroes, saved the scientist from his own confusion.

The popular distrust of atomic research reflected an underlying ambivalence about the alienation of modern society from nature and the physical environment. In glorifying the concept of scientific objectivity, natural and social scientists defined the universe as matter, a material entity that could be manipulated to serve human ends. Instead of seeing the universe as a home for all forms of life, the scientific mind stressed the importance of subduing and conquering nature. "Any addition to our store of adequately established knowledge," ar-

gued sex researcher Alfred C. Kinsey in 1953, "may ultimately contribute to man's mastery of the material universe." Such attitudes justified the scientists' "right to investigate," whatever the opinion of the larger society or the consequences of scientific research.

In advocating mastery of the material universe, however, scientists merely expressed the beliefs of most Americans. The sense of alienation from the environment appeared in such basic areas of life as food, clothing, and housing. "To change every contour of a site is not only to strip it of every root, tree and flower," complained the architect Robert Woods Kennedy. "It is to make an enemy of it." Throughout the postwar period, consumers welcomed inventions in chemistry that accelerated the production of synthetic goods. Fibers made of rayon, nylon, and Dacron were used in place of cotton and wool. In home furnishings, wood and leather increasingly gave way to plastic substitutes. Artificial flavors and food preservatives became staples in the American diet.

The widespread use of synthetic products, besides changing the quality standards of ordinary consumption, had serious side effects on the natural environment. Most synthetics were derivatives of petroleum products. Thus the use of artificial fibers in clothing or vinyl interiors in automobiles drained irreplaceable fossil resources. Yet postwar Americans seldom questioned the corporate or government decisions that irrevocably altered the face of the land. In 1957, for example, to avoid the possibility of a Japanese trade treaty with Communist nations, the Eisenhower administration authorized Japanese lumber companies to cut huge forests in the Tongass National Forest in Alaska. Equally serious, artificial waste products did not readily disintegrate into a natural organic state. Chemical waste products remained in the environ-

Ground zero, Hiroshima, symbolized the awesome power of atomic bombs. (U.S. Strategic Bombing Survey, National Archives 243-H-269)

ment to contaminate and even destroy the ecological balance. Only exceptional cases aroused public attention — such as the belated discovery that radioactive strontium 90, a "fallout" of atomic bomb testing, might be poisoning milk.

The lack of interest in ecological questions reflected a belief in unlimited growth. "The people of America need to be electrified by our limitless possibilities, not frightened into action by prophets of disaster," declared Truman's chief economic adviser, Leon Keyserling. Such optimistic assumptions encouraged needless use of natural resources. Thus when the

automobile industry began developing high horsepower engines, it easily persuaded the petroleum industry to develop appropriate high-octane gasoline. Similar waste appeared in the "planned obsolescence" of supposedly durable products such as automobiles. Two books of 1948, William Vogt's *Road to Survival* and Fairfield Osborn's *Our Plundered Planet*, warned about the limits of resources. "Man must recognize the necessity of cooperating with nature," Osborn declared. "The time for defiance is at an end." But most scientists simply denied the accuracy of such arguments.

The atomic age comes home — the predawn sky is lit by a test explosion 90 miles away, 1952. (UPI Photos)

And less articulate Americans preferred to accept business assurances that technology could solve all technological problems.

The reckless destruction of natural resources could be attributed not only to popular ignorance about the implications of technology but also to the culture's separation from the natural environment. Lacking any attachment to nature, postwar Americans glorified mobility, the use of synthetics, and the indiscriminate consumption of resources. These values encouraged the emergence of a rootless society that was unconnected to nature. The lack of rootedness had profound effects on social and economic relationships.

BUSINESS RECONVERSION

The triumph of rootless social values was facilitated by a new alliance between government and big business. In accepting the scientific values of objectivity and detachment, postwar Americans also acknowledged the importance of expertise in decision making. They assumed that professional experts would render impartial decisions for the betterment of the entire society. Those with such expectations, however, failed to realize that government decisions increasingly reflected the interests of the business community.

During World War Two, the Roosevelt administration had depended heavily on the expertise of business leaders. These dollar-a-year men remained on the payrolls of their private corporations while making crucial economic decisions for the government. Their primary commitment to big business triggered a bitter debate about the reconversion to a civilian economy that began in 1944. As the demand for war production declined, Donald Nelson, chairman of the War Production Board, recommended that small businesses that were losing war contracts be allowed to reconvert to peacetime production. The larger corporations, he maintained, could continue to meet the military demands. This proposal was resisted vigorously within the WPB by big business leaders like Charles E. Wilson of General Electric. Fearing that small businesses would gain an advantage in the transition to civilian production and thereby threaten the prewar patterns of corporate competition, Wilson convinced military leaders to pressure the WPB to defeat Nelson's plan. Claiming wartime necessity, military and big business leaders combined to delay reconversion until 1945. Their resistance effectively protected the wartime expansion of big business; but it resulted in a continued shortage of civilian goods when the war ended.

Government also cooperated with big business in administering veterans' benefits. When only one-fifteenth of the first 1.5 million veterans chose to continue their GI life insurance policies, the military joined with commercial life insurance companies to launch an advertising campaign to reverse the trend. By early 1946 one-third of the veterans opted to continue their policies. The administration of GI mortgages also benefited private business. Though over one million veterans had taken out home loans by 1947, the mortgages were administered by the Veterans' Administration rather than the Federal Housing Authority. Veterans as a result had to satisfy the requirements of private bankers and pay higher interest rates. Moreover, while the VA would guarantee loans for private investors, it was notoriously lax in protecting veterans from unscrupulous builders and real estate agents.

The alliance between government and big business had important repercussions in the postwar economy. As World War Two ended, Chester Bowles, chairman of the Office of Price Administration (OPA), recommended the continuation of wartime economic controls to ease the transition to a civilian economy. Rapid decontrol, he warned, would benefit big businesses that controlled the lion's share of scarce resources; it would seriously undermine small businesses and would cause a severe inflation of prices. But the WPB instead responded to big business pressure and quickly lifted most of its wartime controls. Bowles's prediction proved remarkably accurate. Unable to obtain scarce material, small businesses folded or sold out to larger corporations. Big business also took advantage of the government's generous reconversion sales and purchased government-built wartime plants at a fraction of their costs. The government also offered liberal tax concessions and dropped the wartime excess-profits tax. Such subsidies facilitated business reconversion. They also assured that the biggest corporations would maintain their dominance of the postwar economy.

The abandonment of government controls created serious problems for consumers. Since businesses could obtain greater profits from expensive goods than from cheaper lines, manufacturers mainly produced high-priced goods. The resulting shortage of such necessities as clothing led to skyrocketing prices and an illegal black market. The abrupt lifting of WPB controls of building materials produced a similar crisis in the housing industry. Despite OPA protests, the WPB's reconversion policies encouraged the construction of higher-priced industrial plants without alleviating residential housing shortages. Builders and real estate brokers profited immensely as house prices soared overnight, in some cases even doubling.

Such economic problems forced President Truman to re-establish some of the wartime controls. But the larger businesses continued to monopolize scarce materials, keeping prices high. With the authority of OPA scheduled to end in June 1946, Truman appealed to Congress to extend its life. But when a conservative Congress reacted to business pressure and passed a weak bill, Truman vetoed it. The inflation only became worse, jumping as much as 35 percent in one month. Congress then passed another weak bill that Truman reluctantly approved. The new law extended price controls for one year. But ceilings on meat prices led farmers to withhold their products, creating shortages and a black market. Scarcity and inflation became important political issues in the 1946 elections.

The problems of reconversion were particularly acute for young adults. Many believed that the war had taken, in the words of the Hollywood Academy Award–winning film of 1946, "The Best Years of Our Lives." Two-thirds of the veterans had been unmarried while in uniform and most were anxious to settle down and start families. Such factors stimulated the largest baby boom in modern American history. Despite low levels of foreign immigration, the nation's population leaped from 140 million in 1945 to 152 million in 1950 and exceeded 179 million by 1960. This increase came largely from a high birthrate that grew steadily from 1940 until 1957, when it began to drop. These fertility patterns are particularly noteworthy, since the rate of marriage declined throughout the postwar period. Such statistics indicate that family size was increasing, particularly in the middle- and upper-income brackets.

The growth of population also depended on a declining death rate. Antibiotics such as streptomycin and Aureomycin helped control infectious diseases. The most dramatic breakthrough was the introduction of the Salk vaccine in 1955 to prevent the childhood killer poliomyelitis. As childhood mortality declined, life expectancy rose considerably between 1950 and 1959: for whites, from 69.1 to 70.5; for nonwhites, from 60.8 to 63.5.

POPULATION MOBILITY

The expansion of population accelerated long-term patterns of mobility. Attracted initially by war-related industry, people flocked to the southwestern and western states. In Texas the growth of the petrochemical industry, stimulated by the increased use of fossil fuels, encouraged a population increase of one-third. In Arizona, Tucson and Phoenix mushroomed into sizable cities. The biggest growth came in California, which attracted over five million people between 1940 and 1960. California more than doubled its population in this period and surpassed New York as the most populous state in 1963. This burgeoning population was supported by the expansion of defense-related industries, particularly aircraft, electronics, and machinery. The admission of Alaska and Hawaii into the Union in 1959 — the first new states since 1912 — symbolized the westward movement of population.

While the national population increased and the center of population shifted toward the west, urban populations grew at an even faster rate. Between 1940 and 1960, 22 million people migrated from rural areas to cities, causing the rural population to decline from 11 million in 1940 to 7.4 million in 1960. This trend, part of a long historical process, reflected the reduced need for farm labor due to an increased mechanization of agriculture. Cities throughout the nation also attracted rural southern blacks who were escaping not only impoverished conditions but also more blatant forms of racial discrimination.

HOUSING SHORTAGE AND SUBURBAN DEVELOPMENT

The most immediate effect of this expanding population was a shortage of housing. During the Depression and World War Two, new residential construction had virtually disappeared. By 1945 the total value of American housing was worth 7 percent less than in 1929. The return of war veterans together with the surge of population put great pressure on existing facilities. The problem was aggravated by postwar shortages of building materials and by a related inflation of real estate costs. To solve these problems and cut housing costs, builders began to construct new residential structures on

the fringes of cities, an area that soon became known as suburbia. With apartments unavailable, young families discovered that it was easier to purchase houses by obtaining a home mortgage. Such loans were frequently backed by the federal government under the FHA or VA. New construction soared in the decade after World War Two, stimulating the economy by its consumption of building materials and by creating new employment.

The most dramatic building success of the postwar period was made by Arthur Levitt, who popularized the construction of standardized housing. Using specialized work crews, interchangeable designs and materials, and package deals that included interior appliances, landscaping, and legal fees, Levitt brought single-unit dwellings to lower-middle-class families. To keep prices down, Levitt eliminated dining rooms, basements, and attics as well as unnecessary trim. When critics complained that Levitt's houses were monotonously repetitious, he offered customers different exterior paints, curved streets, and structures placed at slightly different angles. Levitt's mass-produced houses, which were imitated by builders throughout the nation, benefited from a new standardization within the appliance industry. Because postwar houses scrimped on such "extras" as closet space, built-in cabinets with standardized and interchangeable parts became a feature of kitchens and bathrooms.

The creation of suburban neighborhoods accentuated the rootlessness of American society. Remote from city centers, suburban workers had to commute to their jobs. The new housing developments, built in sparsely populated areas, also lacked such community institutions as libraries, schools, hospitals, mass transportation, and shopping facilities. Also absent from many of these neighborhoods were old people, who might have provided a sense of continuity. Even the landscape lacked roots. "The trees are so small," complained one midwesterner.

Suburbanites compensated for the lack of institutions by relying more on the automobile. Registered cars and trucks increased from thirty-one million in 1940 to sixty-one million in 1955. Where housewives were left behind, second cars became necessary to reach the new shopping centers, schools, or medical facilities. Besides consuming vast amounts of gasoline, automobiles produced noxious fumes that polluted the air. In 1947 the journalist John Gunther boasted that Los Angeles, by relying on electricity, would enjoy "clean industry... which in turn means clean towns." Yet within one decade the Los Angeles smog, caused by automobile exhausts, had become a serious health hazard.

The sense of suburban rootlessness was aggravated by a lack of attachment to the new houses. Since home buyers had little choice but to accept the limitations of postwar building design, they were prepared to sell their houses when economic conditions improved. As families grew in size, suburbanites readily moved to larger accommodations. The interchangeableness of residence was closely related to the interchangeableness of jobs. As chain stores proliferated in the new shopping centers, employees were "relocated" at the convenience of management. Store managers, Gunther complained, never became "a real ingredient in the life of a community." Gone too was the intimacy between small businesspeople and their customers. "Ever since the war," complained TV's Alice Kramden, "the butchers don't treat a woman with respect."

Though the withdrawal to the suburbs relieved some of the housing pressure, metropolitan centers remained desperately overcrowded.

Social critics blamed urban slums for encouraging crime, particularly juvenile delinquency. The idea gained popularity from such Hollywood films as *Knock on Any Door* (1949) and *Blackboard Jungle* (1955). When local government seemed unable to solve the urban housing problem, President Truman joined with conservative Senator Robert Taft to persuade Congress to pass the Housing Act of 1949. This legislation, asserting the importance of "decent" housing for all Americans, authorized slum clearance and the construction of 810,000 units of low-rent housing. Despite imaginative plans, however, the federal housing program was sidetracked by Korean War expenditures and further undermined by real estate interests and the unsympathetic Eisenhower administration.

The departure of middle-class taxpayers to the suburbs narrowed the urban tax base at a time when more people needed municipal services than ever before. With increased use of automobiles, mass transit deteriorated for want of funds. In some cities urban officials accepted bribes from bus companies to replace inexpensive electric trolley cars with gas-consuming buses. The resulting traffic congestion, together with air pollution, could not be eased even by the construction of new freeways that surrounded most major cities.

While city dwellers watched the quality of urban life decline, city planners discovered loopholes in the Housing Act that permitted them to destroy old buildings without constructing low-cost housing. Encouraged by the Eisenhower administration, urban renewal saw old neighborhoods, often with homogeneous ethnic populations, uprooted to make way for convention centers, office buildings, parking lots, and other nonresidential units. Such reconstruction brought profits to real estate interests, who accepted the values of rootlessness.

Lost, however, was the sense of urban communities that rooted people to local churches, playgrounds, and small businesses.

RESIDENTIAL SEGREGATION

The problems of urban congestion and housing shortage fell most heavily on racial minorities. Besides the problems of poverty, nonwhites also faced a pattern of organized discrimination that prevented them from finding adequate housing. Through "restrictive covenants," white property owners, with support from real estate brokers, frequently signed legally valid contracts agreeing not to sell or rent their dwellings to minorities. Such practices enjoyed the support of the federal government. "If a neighborhood is to retain stability," advised an FHA underwriting manual, "it is necessary that properties shall continue to be occupied by the same social and racial classes." And the FHA enforced its guidelines by refusing to insure any nonsegregated projects. For minority groups such practices meant overcrowding and high rents.

Patterns of residential segregation could be justified under the principle of "separate, but equal" that the Supreme Court had articulated in *Plessy* v. *Ferguson* in 1896. After World War Two, however, these assumptions increasingly came under attack. In 1947 Truman's Civil Rights Commission condemned the use of restrictive covenants. Black protesters described a federal plan for land clearance in Washington, D.C., as "a concerted drive...to establish a Hitler-like ghetto" and persuaded Congress to reject the plan. In his 1948 book, *The Negro Ghetto*, Robert C. Weaver charged that residential segregation was the major im-

pediment to northern blacks' full participation in American life.

In protesting residential segregation, Weaver not only questioned the legality of restrictive covenants but also suggested that the principle of separate, but equal had inherent limitations. "As long as colored groups are relegated to separate parts of the city," he wrote, "as long as they live in a world apart..., colored Americans are stigmatized in the eyes of the rest of the population." Such stigmas created profound problems for blacks. Some blacks took pride in their blackness and accepted its social inconveniences. But others, who had partially absorbed the values of whites, tried to overcome their racial identity by bleaching their skin, straightening their hair, or, in the case of lighter-skinned people, "passing." These strategies created a hierarchy within the black community: "If you're white, you're all right/if you're brown, stick around/if you're black, keep back." The solution to such problems, most black leaders believed, was to eliminate the institutions that caused racial injustice.

Protests against segregated housing culminated in an NAACP-sponsored lawsuit, *Shelley* v. *Kraemer*. To support the case, the Justice Department argued that restrictive covenants undermined "respect for the dignity and rights of the individual." In 1948 the Supreme Court ruled that government support of such covenants was illegal. In accepting social science testimony that depicted the psychological and sociological damage caused by segregation, the Court laid the basis for a revision of the *Plessy* doctrine. But the *Shelley* case did not overturn the principle of separate, but equal. In throwing out restrictive covenants, however, it enabled blacks in northern cities to move into some previously exclusive neighborhoods.

Despite these advances, residential segregation persisted in most areas, affecting not only blacks but also Spanish-speaking and other minorities. Of the nearly one million Puerto Ricans who lived in New York in 1960, 40 percent were forced to live in inadequate dwellings. Yet their monthly rentals remained high, absorbing as much as one-third of their incomes. Spanish-speaking people in the western states suffered from similar disadvantages. In higher-income brackets, residential segregation affected such groups as Chinese, Japanese, and Jews, who tended to cluster in homogeneous communities. The existence of ethnic neighborhoods in cities, however, frequently reflected a positive assertion of cultural identity. Not all minorities wished to be assimilated in the American melting pot.

ROOTLESSNESS AND ROOTEDNESS

The tension between assimilation and cultural identity appeared most clearly in the case of Native Americans. Prior to World War Two, federal policy toward reservation tribes had wavered between detribalization and protection of Native American rights. In 1946 the Indian Claims Commission Act allowed the tribes to bring legal action against the federal government for violations of previous treaties. But though the law seemed to be protecting Native American culture, it was administered by the Bureau of Indian Affairs to hasten the removal of government services. This policy was made explicit in 1954 when Congress approved a series of termination bills. These laws called for the dissolution of tribal structures, the disbursement of tribal assets, and the ending of federal assistance. Implemented against the Meno-

menie of Wisconsin and the Klamath of Oregon, the policy created severe economic and social problems.

Within the Native American communities, two antithetical processes emerged after World War Two. Native American veterans frequently had trouble readjusting to traditional tribal life. In addition, many tribes were affected by the white technological culture, such as electricity and the mass media it introduced. As a consequence, traditional tribal rituals became less important and the number of Native American languages declined. In the face of this assimilation, Native Americans who were more traditional chose to resist the absorption of white culture. Thus the postwar period also saw a revitalization of Native American religions and a self-conscious attempt to preserve Native American identity. The reassertion of traditional cultures enabled Native Americans to oppose the termination program. In its place they proposed self-determination for each community. Yet the status of reservation tribes remained unresolved in the sixties.

The clash between a rooted society and a rootless one could also be seen in the status of American farmers. Though agriculture flourished through most of the postwar period, the farm population itself continued its historic decline. The application of technology to farming dramatically increased agricultural output by 6 percent per year between 1949 and 1959. But farm production rose chiefly because machines replaced workers. Equally significant, the total number of farms continued to decrease. These trends revealed the impact of technological values on rural America. Benefiting from research and development programs at state agricultural colleges, farmers invested in new equipment and new hybrid crops that could be handled safely by machines. In the Southwest, irriga-

Many elderly Americans found modest housing in trailer camps that sprang up in warm-weather states, such as this one in Florida. (Wide World Photos)

tion brought additional acreage under cultivation. Farmers also greatly increased the use of chemical fertilizers to stimulate growth; chemical pesticides to kill weeds, plant diseases, and insects; and chemical additives to fatten livestock and to assure that fields would ripen uniformly. Such practices involved vast inputs of fossil energy to fuel machinery and to stimulate crop growth. Many of the commonly used pesticides, such as DDT, were later found to be harmful to the ecological balance.

Technological agriculture proved to be extremely profitable. But mechanization and mass production required large capital outlays that small farmers could not afford. Moreover, mechanized agriculture was most efficient on large acreage. These factors encouraged the consolidation of farmlands in gigantic holdings and the shifting of ownership to large corporations. As conglomerates moved into farming, they formed monopolistic agribusinesses that controlled the food industry from seeding the fields to distributing the processed products.

The profitability of corporate agriculture depended heavily on federal government expenditures. Postwar food shortages in Europe provided large markets for American farm surpluses. As those outlets diminished, Congress approved the Agricultural Acts of 1948 and 1949, which provided government price supports for basic crops. Truman's secretary of agriculture, Charles Brannon, also pressed for a program of direct subsidies to farmers to compensate for overproduction. Though the Brannon Plan would have protected farmers from unprofitable markets, it rewarded the largest producers who grew the most crops. Even so, critics denounced the scheme as socialistic and a conservative Congress refused to pass it.

During the fifties, farmers producing agricultural surpluses continued to benefit from government price supports. This program was augmented in 1956 by an Agricultural Act that rewarded farmers for not planting certain crops. The Soil Bank Act of 1956 also reimbursed farmers for converting crop land into noncommercial conservation acreage. Despite such measures farmers continued to produce large surpluses. Moreover, the price support program offered disproportionate subsidies to the biggest farms. "The majority of farm people derive little or no benefit from our agricultural price support legislation," admitted the *Economic Report of the President* in 1959; "those with the higher incomes are the main beneficiaries."

The rise of technological agriculture not only destroyed community patterns of rural society but also imposed mass-produced food on the rest of the nation. Between 1950 and 1959 average per capita consumption of dairy products declined from 29.4 to 25.6 pounds per year, fresh fruits from 107.4 pounds to 101.5 pounds, and fresh vegetables from 139.5 to 125.2 pounds. Consumers made up for these losses by eating greater quantities of processed and frozen foods. Such products relied on nutritional additives, artificial flavoring and coloring, and preservatives to maintain a modicum of food value. These processes added as much as 30 percent to the cost of each edible pound of food.

The proliferation of chain supermarkets offered consumers few alternatives to this mass-produced fare. The inaccessibility of suburban shopping centers discouraged daily food purchases. And the availability of larger refrigerators and freezers, together with the growing use of preservatives, enabled families to store packaged foods for later consumption. Such eating habits also encouraged the expansion of drive-in restaurants and snack shops that offered standardized food throughout the country. Eating in restaurants, however, also introduced middle-class people to new varieties of cuisine. In reaction to mass food, a new interest in gourmet cooking appeared, and the sensuality of eating became an acceptable form of middle-class recreation.

CORPORATE ECONOMY

Government support of corporate agriculture reflected a general pattern of economic relations. During World War Two, business and political leaders expressed concern that reconversion and demobilization would bring another Depression. "We cannot have full employment and prosperity in the United States without foreign markets," Assistant Secretary of State Dean Acheson told a congressional committee in 1944. To obtain such markets, business needed adequate credit. But Acheson admitted that private capital was insufficient for the task. In the postwar years, therefore, government subsidies directly and indirectly bolstered business prosperity.

The likelihood of a postwar depression was initially offset by large wartime savings amounting to $140 billion and a strong desire of consumers to acquire scarce durable goods. This unusual demand, in the face of industrial shortages, produced a serious inflation that lasted through 1947. Business also benefited from huge government-sponsored exports to war-torn Europe. Encouraged by the Marshall Plan of 1947, merchandise exports exceeded imports by $25 billion in the first four years of peace.

By 1949, however, the demand for consumer durables declined and the economy entered a period of recession. Some economists saw this downturn as the end of the postwar honeymoon. But the recession was cushioned by growing expenditures for residential housing. These investments were supported by federal government policies that protected home loans and kept interest rates low while requiring minimal down payments and long-term mortgages. In this manner, government intervention in the economy helped to prevent a serious depression. The recessions of 1954 and 1958 evoked similar government responses. In both cases, federally supported private housing and new public construction increased to ease the problem.

Government intervention in the economy was even more important in the area of deficit spending for military purposes. In 1946 the Pentagon began an elaborate public relations campaign to persuade Congress to maintain American military strength. But a conservative Congress preferred to cut government expenditures and rejected the program. Despite such failures, military leaders joined business groups in advocating larger defense budgets. By 1947 the official acknowledgment of a "Cold War" with the Soviet Union reinforced these appeals. By that time Congress was prepared to increase military appropriations.

Such expenditures were crucial for stimulating economic growth. "Pressure for more government spending is mounting," reported *Business Week* in early 1950. "The reason is a combination of concern over tense Russian relations and a growing fear of a rising unemployment here at home." The outbreak of the Korean War in June 1950 ended any further debate. In the first year of the war, the military budget leaped from $14 billion to $34 billion, and exceeded $50 billion in 1953, the last year of the war. By then military expenditures represented 13.5 percent of the gross national product, while other defense-related federal government expenditures raised that number to 21 percent. It was no coincidence that unemployment in October 1953 reached a postwar low point of 1.8 percent, with slightly more than one million people out of work.

The continuation of the Cold War after the Korean cease-fire assured that high military budgets would be an integral part of the American economy. During the Eisenhower administration more than $350 billion was spent on defense, and 77 percent of every budget dollar was spent on military-related appropriations. The annual military budgets often meant the difference between corporate profits and losses. These vast expenditures included a program to stockpile strategic material that might be unavailable in time of future war. The program became a bounty for numerous industries.

Such supports to private industry illuminated an inseparable tie between military preparedness and business prosperity. Talk of a thaw in the Cold War invariably brought falling prices on Wall Street. A growing concern about these tendencies led President Eisenhower to devote his farewell address of 1961 to warning against the "military-industrial complex." "We have been compelled to create a permanent armaments industry of vast proportions," the outgoing president observed. "We annually spend on military security alone more than the net income of all United States corporations." Yet Eisenhower offered no solution to the situation, and John F. Kennedy campaigned in 1960 on the false assertion that the Republican administration had been lax enough to create a "missile gap."

The relationship between government and business involved more than the amassing of armaments. Central to the expansion of the economy was government support of research and development. Between 1950 and 1959, expenditures for "R and D" increased about threefold to an estimated $12 billion. Besides helping the defense industry, such appropriations supported university research programs at a rate of $300 million per year. With such incentives academic science readily worked to fight the Cold War. Most of the funding for these projects came from the federal government under the category of defense. For example, aircraft manufacturing, which was one of the largest growth industries of the postwar period, drew 80 percent of its business from military agencies. Employing 1.25 million workers in 1959, the aircraft industry was a major factor in the burgeoning West Coast economy. So too was the electronics industry, which grew 15 percent

a year, becoming the fifth largest industry in 1960. Most electronics sales went to the federal government, primarily for missiles and other military equipment.

Government agencies continued the World War Two pattern of relying on the largest corporations in awarding contracts to private business. Despite efforts of the Small Business Administration to encourage government procurement from smaller businesses, Defense Department awards to small firms steadily declined. The amount of R and D funds that reached small businesses was 4 percent, a figure unlikely to stimulate new corporate growth. Though convenient for government administrators, the support of big business did not bring reduced costs. Most contracts were awarded without competitive bidding, and business "overruns" were readily absorbed by federal budgets. There was little irony, therefore, when Eisenhower's secretary of defense, Charles E. Wilson, remarked, "For years I thought what was good for the country was good for General Motors, and vice versa."

CONSUMER SPENDING

Corporate prosperity reinforced a belief in unlimited growth that in turn stimulated unprecedented consumer spending. "Not only do the younger people accept the beneficent society as normal," reported sociologist William H. Whyte, Jr.; "they accept *improvement*, considerable and constant, as normal too." Despite significant economic recessions in 1948–1949, 1953–1954, and 1957–1958, private consumption steadily increased each year. Even though real wages did not return to World War Two levels until 1955, consumers drew upon savings in the immediate postwar years to acquire such durable goods as appliances, automobiles, furniture, and television sets. This mass consumption was a reaction to the commodity shortages that dated from the Depression. By 1949, however, the demand for durables dwindled and contributed to the recession.

As consumers satisfied their demand for durables, they shifted their interest to other types of commodities. Attracted by seemingly liberal credit policies, purchasers went into debt beyond the prewar highs of the twenties. Consumer installment indebtedness reached $34 billion in 1957, or nearly 10 percent of personal income. Such "conspicuous consumption" may have been an attempt to assert individuality. Though American culture traditionally valued personal uniqueness, the nationalization of the marketplace, together with the mass media, seemed to be homogenizing social differences. By purchasing new innovative products (such as "hi-fidelity" or stereophonic record players), middle-class consumers could reassert their unique personalities. Similarly, larger cars, with exaggerated "fins" on the rear fenders, allowed drivers to appear particularly bigger and bolder. Men's clothing styles began imitating women's fashions by undergoing annual changes that made serviceable wardrobes outmoded overnight. The attempt to live one step ahead of the Joneses, moreover, created an endless cycle of buying.

These consumption patterns closely followed one of the major growth industries of the postwar period: advertising. Though popular exposés like Vance Packard's *The Hidden Persuaders* (1957) explained the underlying techniques of advertising, market research showed that the consuming public remained more responsive to emotional appeals than to product substance. Annual advertising expenditures

soared over the $10-billion mark by 1960. The largest expenditures were in consumer softwares and luxuries such as tobacco, beverages, drugs, amusements, and home furnishings. A significant factor in postwar advertising was its emphasis on national media rather than local outlets. The trend facilitated product identification for a rootless population that migrated at an increasing pace. The importance of advertising was attested by the highly effective TV commercials developed by Batten, Barton, Dursten, and Osborn for Eisenhower's 1952 presidential campaign.

The growth of the advertising industry was part of a larger expansion of all service industries in the postwar economy. Once consumers had purchased their durable commodities, they steadily spent larger sums for such services as rent, insurance, automobile repairs, and medical care as well as for utilities and public transportation. This heavy demand for services, though unable by itself to support a high growth rate in the economy, was a crucial factor in avoiding a downturn. Yet when the rate of military expenditures dropped in 1957, the result was a severe recession.

The expansion of service industries indicated a new dimension of the American labor force. As part of a long historic tradition, technological innovation had increased individual worker productivity. This process in turn diminished the number of blue-collar jobs. Yet technology also created new occupations in white-collar services. Equally important, the growth of corporations led to the expansion of a managerial corps of employees who administered the bureaucracies rather than produced commodities. In 1956 the number of workers in service industries exceeded the number of producers for the first time, thus heralding the postindustrial society.

Indicative of this pattern was the growth of government bureaucracy. Employment in state and local government rose two million between 1950 and 1960, an increase of 52 percent. The federal bureaucracy also expanded in both civilian and military spheres. By 1960 nearly 8.5 million employees were drawing government paychecks, largely for white-collar employment.

LABOR UNIONS AND ECONOMIC STABILITY

Despite the remarkable economic growth of the postwar period, unemployment remained an endemic problem. Worried about the possibility of another Depression, Congress approved the Employment Act of 1946. The law committed the federal government to maximize employment by direct intervention in the economy. It also created a Council of Economic Advisers to help the president formulate policy. Though the act only made explicit what the government had done during the Depression and World War Two, neither Truman nor Eisenhower wholly endorsed its implications of a government-regulated economy.

The feared levels of mass unemployment never materialized. But the sudden termination of war contracts resulted in temporary layoffs and a cut in overtime work. Worker take-home pay dropped just as the lifting of wartime controls stimulated an inflation of prices. Workers responded with a series of prolonged strikes that threatened the entire economy. Though the Truman administration condemned the strikes, workers managed to win substantial wage increases as well as "cost-of-living" adjustments to offset inflation. Businesses passed these raises on to consumers, however, thereby feeding the inflationary cycle. Though the 1946 strikes aroused bitter verbal controversy, John Gunther pointed out that during the large automobile walkout, "there was not one bloody nose." Labor unions continued to seek higher wages, better working conditions, and job security packages. But labor radicalism waned as unions recognized the importance of cooperating with business and government in stimulating the economy. Fundamental to this growing conservatism was the purging of Communists from AFL and CIO unions and the passing of leadership to staunch defenders of capitalism.

The legal guidelines for cooperation between labor and business were established in the Taft-Hartley Act of 1947. To protect the public interest from harmful labor-management disputes, the law allowed the government to seek an injunction against strike action and provided for a sixty-day "cooling-off" period during which federal mediators would try to settle the issues. If disputes remained unsettled, the president could ask Congress for additional legislation. Truman and Eisenhower called for strike injunctions seventeen times between 1947 and 1959.

Taft-Hartley also prohibited "closed" shops (which forced employers to hire only union members) but permitted "union" shops (in which all employees had to join a union after being employed). It prohibited secondary boycotts, jurisdictional strikes, and certain "unfair labor practices." As an additional conservative measure, the law required union leaders to certify that they were not members of the Communist party or other subversive groups. On the level of state government, Taft-Hartley was followed by "right-to-work" laws that permitted "open" shops, in which workers did not have to join a union.

Organized labor viewed Taft-Hartley as an attack on basic workers' rights and vowed to see the law repealed. Yet union membership, which had increased dramatically during the Depression and World War Two, stabilized near the wartime highs. White-collar workers, more numerous than ever before, remained nonunion. Even before Taft-Hartley restricted organizing activities, many unions were ignoring the unorganized segments of the labor force. During World War Two the NAACP battled with racist unions to win admission for blacks, but often failed to persuade all-white locals to change their policies. Many unions also neglected to organize women workers, believing that females were a threat to male union-members' jobs. Instead, rival AFL and CIO unions debated jurisdictional issues and raided each other's membership.

The threat of Taft-Hartley forced organized labor to re-evaluate its goals. In 1951 the CIO expelled eleven member unions for communist leanings, a decision that not only emphasized labor's support of the Cold War but also indicated the similarities between the CIO and the AFL. By the fifties the AFL had accepted the idea of industrial unionism, while the CIO had endorsed labor stability. Such agreement of purposes led to the merger of the AFL-CIO in December 1955.

The resolution of interunion rivalry enabled organized labor to present a united front on political and economic issues. But the AFL-CIO, under the leadership of George Meany, supported the existing pattern of government-subsidized business prosperity and simply tried to obtain its share of the wealth. Union negotiators accepted the importance of cooperating with business by accepting cost-of-living increases, clauses that permitted reopening contracts if economic conditions changed, and long-term settlements. More concerned with economic security than with altering the structure of society, unions increasingly sought such fringe benefits as pensions, paid vacations, paid sick leaves, and medical and hospitalization plans. Even without these extras, the annual real income of wage earners increased about 25 percent between 1946 and 1959.

With priorities on economic stability, however, unions preferred industry-wide agreements that tended to eliminate competition between separate businesses. Such broad settlements also reduced the autonomy of individual unions. In effect, organized labor used its strength to assure worker compliance with agreed-upon business decisions. "We need the union to insure enforcement of the contract we have signed, to settle grievances, to counsel employees in giving a fair day's work for a fair day's pay," acknowledged a business leader, "to help increase productivity." Unauthorized "wildcat" strikes were aimed not only at employers but also at unresponsive union bureaucrats.

The separation of union leadership from rank-and-file workers often encouraged the alliance between labor and business. The amount of worker participation in union elections declined from 82 percent in the prewar period to 58 percent in 1958, a trend that continued through the next two decades. Such patterns enabled the existing leadership to maintain its control of union policy and to suppress dissident rank-and-file movements. Union leaders often drew large salaries and enjoyed executive privileges such as nontaxable expense accounts that put them in the same class as business leaders.

While critics complained about the union leadership's "passion for respectability," congressional investigation unearthed widespread corruption in the management of union funds.

In 1954 a Senate investigating committee, chaired by James L. McClellan of Arkansas, exposed financial abuses and racketeering, particularly in the Teamsters Union. Such revelations led the AFL-CIO leadership to expel the Teamsters as well as other suspected unions. This belated housecleaning failed to prevent further government action. In 1959 the Landrum-Griffin Act required unions to file economic statements with the Department of Labor, a measure the Executive Council of the AFL-CIO viewed as a "severe setback."

POVERTY AND SOCIAL CLASS

Steady increases in annual average wages and the expansion of white-collar employment seemed to justify John Kenneth Galbraith's vision of *The Affluent Society* (1958). But Galbraith's title was unduly optimistic. Despite the appearance of affluence and prosperity, certain groups remained deeply impoverished, even by the government's conservative definitions. As workers lost their jobs to automation, unemployment became a pervasive problem. Rates of unemployment ranged between a low of 3 percent during the Korean War to nearly 8 percent during the recessions of 1948–1949 and 1957–1958. Even in the recovery years of 1956 and 1959, they averaged 4.2 percent and 5.3 percent respectively. These wage losses were not offset by government welfare programs. Unemployment insurance reimbursed only 20 percent of lost worker incomes. Not only were payments low, but many workers were not protected by insurance programs or had exhausted their benefits.

Another class of impoverished people were the elderly, people over the age of sixty-five. A 1960 Senate report admitted that "at least one-half of the aged — approximately eight million people — cannot afford today decent housing, proper nutrition, adequate medical care, preventive or acute, or necessary recreation." Unable to work for reasons of health or mandatory retirement policies, they derived most of their incomes from social security payments, private pensions, or welfare. During the fifties the number of people entitled to social security benefits increased nearly fivefold, to 9.6 million. Yet government assistance provided only a small fraction of their incomes. As a result, more than half of the households headed by people over sixty-five had an income level of less than $3,000 a year in 1960. Even elderly property owners found their standards of living declining as inflation and higher property taxes cut into their fixed incomes. One symptom of this problem was the proliferation of old-people's trailer camp settlements in warm-weather states like Florida.

Nonwhites also suffered disproportionately. As victims of racial as well as economic discrimination, nonwhites earned substantially less than whites in all parts of the nation. Moreover, in the period from 1949 to 1959, the gap between black and white incomes increased. The major problem for nonwhites was obtaining entry into occupations that paid better wages. Consigned by custom and prejudice to menial jobs, blacks experienced upward occupational mobility at a rate far below that of immigrant ethnic groups. A study of occupational patterns in Boston demonstrated that this gap was a function not of education, but of racial discrimination. Black women, for example, concentrated in low-paying jobs such as housekeeping, waitressing, and practical nursing. On these levels their paltry incomes were not significantly different from those of white women. But in factory work, which still paid only poverty-level wages, black women earned substantially less than whites.

Other minority groups, such as Puerto Ricans, Mexican-Americans, Native Americans, Asian-Americans, and rural whites, also obtained extremely low incomes. Most worked in occupations that were not protected by minimum-wage laws. In New York City 80 percent of the Puerto Rican families earned less than the Department of Labor's estimated minimum levels for "modest but adequate" standards of living. Such figures placed Puerto Ricans below blacks in the city's hierarchy. In the western states the income of Spanish-speaking workers ranked higher than that of blacks but substantially below that of whites. In California the average income of Japanese and Chinese families in 1959 was a lowly $3,000, but even that was higher than the income of Spanish-speaking Americans. Poorest of all non-whites were Native Americans, who lived in such severe squalor on reservations that their death rate was three times the national average.

Rural whites also earned less than the national average. In 1959, 1.5 million farmers, five-sixths of them white, earned less than $3,000. Most of them lived in the South in dilapidated housing that lacked electricity and plumbing. Government studies indicated that 56 percent of these low-income farm families suffered from serious dietary deficiencies. During the fifties 1.5 million whites were forced to leave Appalachia, perhaps the most rooted white culture in the nation, to find jobs in the cities. These migrants settled in poor urban neighborhoods, estranged from their rural roots. But they retained their traditional culture and helped to popularize country and western music among urban dwellers much as blacks had carried the blues to the cities in the twenties.

A black schoolhouse in rural Alabama, 1945. The war bond poster contrasts with an otherwise stark interior. (Amistad Research Center)

WOMEN AND THE WORK FORCE

Among the poorest households were those headed by women. Widows, unmarried mothers, and women who were divorced, separated, or deserted headed one-twelfth of American households in 1956. Most worked as secretaries, sales help, or in semiskilled trades—occupations that were generally unorganized by unions. Lacking union support, women were forced to accept lower salaries than men for similar work tasks. Such discriminatory patterns reflected a larger ambivalence about the status and role of women in postwar society.

Many Native Americans, like this woman on an Apache reservation in Arizona, still obtain water from unsafe or contaminated sources. (Office of Information Services, Division of Indian Health, U.S. Public Health Service)

Women's participation in the wartime work force set an important precedent for female employment. Though many women were subsequently replaced by returning veterans, female employment increased sharply in 1947 and returned to the World War Two levels by 1950. This trend continued in the next decade. Between 1940 and 1960 the number of female employees doubled. By 1960, 40 percent of the adult female population was at work, a striking increase from the prewar 25 percent rate.

The persistence of economic discrimination against women workers, however, revealed a new aspect of this burgeoning female employment. The average age of women employees in 1960 was forty-one; and 60 percent of women workers were married. Households in which both husband and wife worked reached the ten-million mark by 1960. These two-income families included a growing number of mothers with young children. Prior to World War Two, working wives and mothers usually came from the poorest classes of society. But in the postwar period, an increasing number of middle-class women found jobs even when their husbands earned substantial incomes.

In explaining their entry into the labor force, most working women emphasized financial necessity as a motive. Yet that response took on a new meaning in the fifties. Since real wages remained lower than wartime earnings until 1955, families needed additional incomes to acquire goods and services they desired to compensate for prewar and wartime deprivation. The soaring birthrate reinforced these felt needs. Moreover, as consumption became an integral part of middle-class culture, the demand for luxury items encouraged two-income families. Finally, at the end of the fifties, an inflation of prices exceeded wage increases, again causing a decline of real income and providing an impetus for wives to work. Yet such economic motives, pervasive though they were, did not persuade employers to offer equal pay for equal work. Working women, it was commonly believed, did not need as much income as working men.

The middle-class status of postwar working women indicated that more than economic necessity was a reason for employment. The desire to purchase luxury items and other consumables satisfied psychological desires that women shared with men. Working wives, like their husbands, also stressed the relationship between work and a sense of personal fulfillment. The higher the level of female education, the more likely it was that women would enter the labor force. Finding satisfaction in occupational roles rather than in traditional domestic situations provided the background for a growing sense of female independence.

The rise of female employment challenged the traditional view that a woman's proper place was in the home. According to accepted psychological theory, women were naturally passive, unassertive, and therefore ill equipped to cope with the problems of business. Women who were competitive or who ventured into public life were by definition unnatural. "I Denied My Sex," a popular-magazine story about a woman's career in police work, typified a pulp literature that advocated domesticity. The most popular television comedy of the fifties, "I Love Lucy," consistently parodied the housewife's craving to become a success outside the home. Middle-class magazines like *Good Housekeeping* and *Mademoiselle* urged women to accept the satisfaction of raising children and supporting their male breadwinners. "A family is like a corporation," declared a journalist. "We all have to work for it."

FAMILY RELATIONS

This celebration of domestic tranquillity nevertheless concealed a basic tension in American family relations. Many housewives, frustrated by domesticity but afraid to challenge traditional values, turned to alcohol, tranquilizers, or psychiatrists for solace. The desire to make some "contribution" to the family income impelled some well-to-do housewives to become shoplifters, even though they had sufficient money to purchase the goods they stole. TV programs with titles like "The Honeymooners," "Make Room for Daddy," and "Father Knows Best" ostensibly portrayed marital bliss. But the plot structures emphasized intense family conflicts, often characterized by verbal aggression. TV commercials also appealed to an unceasing battle of the sexes. Such evidence helps to explain why, despite all the propaganda for domesticity, marriage rates steadily declined while divorces increased.

The disintegration of traditional marriages also reflected a conflict between sexual values and sexual behavior. In 1948 Alfred Kinsey and a group of researchers at Indiana University published *Sexual Behavior in the Human Male,* followed five years later by a similar study of females — both of which became best sellers despite an esoteric format and a mass of statistical charts. At a time when popular magazines advocated premarital virginity, the Kinsey report revealed that most men and nearly 50 percent of women had experienced premarital intercourse. Kinsey also discerned that many people were reluctant to discuss sexual immorality, considering it "a religious obligation to impose their codes upon all other segments of the population." Yet half the men and 26 percent of the women interviewed had experienced extramarital sexual relations. In addition, 37 percent of the men and 28 percent of the women had some overt homosexual contacts. Kinsey concluded that two-thirds of the marriages studied had serious sexual disagreements and he speculated that 75 percent of the divorces were caused by sexual incompatibility.

The erosion of the traditional family was seen by conservatives as the cause of a new national malaise — juvenile delinquency. President Truman joined a chorus of politicians who saw the cure for juvenile crime in women staying at home. But statistical surveys in Detroit indicated that the children of working mothers had a lower-than-average rate of delinquency. Social workers and economists pointed to the relationship between poverty and juvenile crime, suggesting that slum clearance and social welfare programs would solve the problem. Newspapers were particularly interested in juvenile sex crimes, luridly describing teenage sex clubs, prostitution, and rape. This emphasis on adolescent sexuality fit a statistical pattern described by the Kinsey report. According to Kinsey, males reached a peak of sexuality in their late teens (women, Kinsey found, peaked in their thirties), but the existing values denied them a legitimate sexual outlet. Kinsey suggested that teenage sexuality was normal and healthy, and he urged parents and law enforcement authorities to be more understanding and more tolerant.

Kinsey's advice reinforced the messages that adults were receiving from the most popular pediatrician of the postwar era, Dr. Benjamin Spock. His *Baby and Child Care,* published in 1946, sold over twenty-two million copies. The book's popularity indicated that postwar adults, having migrated away from their own parents, felt a need for expert counsel on so fundamental a matter as child rearing. "Trust yourself," Spock told these anxious parents. "Don't take too seriously all that the neighbors say. Don't be overawed by what the experts say. Don't be afraid to trust your common sense." Where earlier government child-rearing pamphlets had emphasized a strict regimen in nurturing, Spock called for flexibility. His respect for children led critics to denounce his "permissiveness." Yet Spock advocated firm parental control based on a spirit of love and understanding.

The reliance on child-rearing expertise and the general concern about juvenile crime shared a common basis: adults lacked confidence in their ability to understand and to guide the young. Hollywood films like *The Wild One* (1953) and *Rebel Without a Cause* (1954) portrayed a youth culture that rejected the materialistic values of their parents. "I love people with kids," scoffed a gangster in *Desperate Hours* (1955). "They don't take no chances." The caution of adults toward their children led to an emphasis on "social adjustment" and "conformity," a trend symbolized by the growth of Little Leagues that replaced the spontaneous play of childhood with adultlike uniforms, schedules, and scorecards. "No longer is it thought to be the child's job to understand the adult world as the adult sees it," complained David Riesman in his classic study, *The Lonely Crowd* (1950). Instead, children reacted to a media-built world that depicted appropriate childhood models.

YOUTH CULTURE

The separation between adults and children culminated in the emergence of a unique youth culture. More concerned about peer approval, adolescents formed clubs, cliques, and gangs that experimented with cigarettes, alcohol, and sex. From the mid-fifties, their music was rock and roll. The language of their songs complained about parents who pried into their private lives, warned people not to step on their territory, and boasted that rock and roll was here to stay. Their hero was Elvis Presley, who mixed pelvic thrusts with knowing grins. And they swayed romantically to songs like "Love Me Tender" and "Earth Angel." Though the rate of premarital sexual intercourse increased during the fifties, teenagers avoided public sexuality lest they acquire a "reputation." The introduction of a new dance, "The Twist," by Chubby Checker in 1959, however, turned suggestive dancing into a national fad. But it was

not until the next decade that adolescents discarded all conventional dance steps and found communal rhythms by dancing en masse.

Adults claimed to be shocked by the rock-and-roll generation and its flaunting of convention. But to a remarkable degree, the youth culture simply imitated middle-class adult models. Though delinquents might dress in black leather jackets and motorcycle boots, most teenagers aspired to "dress up" like their parents. Teenagers also borrowed their parents' attitudes toward consumption, forming a multibillion dollar adolescent market for records, clothing, jewelry, automobiles, and entertainment. Marriage also remained a major goal for most, so much so that teenage girls were known to sacrifice academic grades to avoid appearing exceptional and therefore unpopular. So pervasive were these values that truly exceptional youth, such as the poet Sylvia Plath, felt they were suffocating inside a "bell jar" of conformity. This mood of acceptance dominated college campuses, where a "silent generation" expressed a distinct preference for courses in business administration and education.

PUBLIC EDUCATION AND EDUCATIONAL GOALS

Despite this youthful conservatism, parents worried about the next generation and hoped that public schools could compensate for the deficiencies of home. School buildings were strained beyond capacity, however, as the arrival of the first baby-boom students forced school districts to open makeshift quarters and adopt "split-session" instruction. As more parents became concerned about the quality of education, school budgets increased, making teaching an attractive occupation for college graduates. The academic content of the curricula largely reflected the pedagogical philosophy of John Dewey and progressive education. Education, according to progressive theories, should discard rote learning and instead emphasize the individuality and life experiences of the students. Progressive educators went further to suggest that vocational training, social guidance, and "hygiene" were appropriate subjects of instruction.

Such goals were not always implemented. "The best thing about contemporary education," wrote psychologist Paul Woodring in 1952, "is that a great many classroom teachers ignore the gobbledygook and the pedagoguese and go right ahead and do a sensible job of teaching." These sentiments reflected a growing belief that American public schools, by emphasizing such amorphous goals as a student's social adjustment, were failing to provide basic education. Right wing anticommunists claimed that certain textbooks were "un-American" and, in many cases, succeeded in purging so-called subversive material. Educators like the historian Arthur E. Bestor challenged the lack of intellectual development in the public schools and suggested taking education out of the hands of academic professionals. Such comments had little effect on the public school system.

The optimistic belief that Americans had created a superior educational program, however, was rudely destroyed in 1957 when the Soviet Union launched Sputnik, the first artificial satellite. Shocked by this Cold War defeat, educational reformers scurried to make amends. As Admiral Hyman Rickover stated, the proper sphere of education was *"the intellect alone."* For most people this philosophy meant rejuvenating mathematics and the sciences and de-emphasizing "softer" subjects in the humanities. Spurred by the crisis, President

For white middle-class youth, the 1950s were a time of affluence, with more people attending high schools and colleges than ever before. (Elliott Erwitt/Magnum)

Eisenhower persuaded Congress to pass the National Defense Educational Act in 1958. The law, which provided the first major federal aid to education, offered funds to encourage the study of science, mathematics, and foreign languages. This government support, which later was extended to include such subjects vital to the "national defense" as history, stimulated the vast expansion of higher education in the next decade.

EDUCATIONAL SEGREGATION

The extraordinary faith that Americans placed in public education vividly contrasted with the social caste system that excluded minority groups from equal educational opportunities. Under the doctrine of separate, but equal, seventeen states required segregated public schools in 1951. But the problem involved more than separate facilities. In 1945 the southern states spent twice as much to educate white children as blacks; in 1947 four times as many whites as blacks finished high school. Such statistics belied the fiction of separate, but equal.

Determined to challenge these policies, the NAACP, under the direction of lawyer Thurgood Marshall, initiated a series of legal suits to end discrimination in education. Benefiting by postwar antipathy to racism, Marshall won significant victories against segregated law schools and graduate schools by arguing that the alternative black institutions were unequal in quality to white schools. Such arguments failed to confront the negative effects of segregation itself.

In a bold departure, Marshall decided to attack public school segregation by denying the concept of separate, but equal. Using psychological evidence demonstrating that "prejudice and segregation have definitely detrimental effects on the personality development of the Negro child," Marshall persuaded the Supreme Court to reconsider the *Plessy* doctrine. In a historic ruling, *Brown* v. *Board of Education of Topeka,* delivered May 17, 1954, the Su-

preme Court acknowledged that to segregate children "because of their race generates a feeling of inferiority...that may affect their hearts and minds in a way unlikely ever to be undone." In public education, the Court concluded, "'separate but equal' has no place. Separate educational facilities are inherently unequal."

The *Brown* decision, which was written by Eisenhower's first appointee to the Supreme Court, Chief Justice Earl Warren, heralded a new era in race relations. Most liberals, including the NAACP attorneys, believed that institutional segregation was the cause of racial prejudice. They therefore believed that the new legal principle would establish a society based on racial equality. In 1955 the Supreme Court reaffirmed that idea by ordering immediate compliance with the *Brown* ruling. Other segregated institutions, such as restaurants, movie theaters, toilets, and transportation, seemed likely to fall.

The southern states, however, refused to accept the Court's decision. Some opposed any alteration of traditional race relations; others bitterly resented this new expansion of federal power over states' rights. Southerners then launched a determined and bitter program of "massive resistance" to public school integration. Inspired by White Citizens' Councils, some areas, such as Prince Edward County in Virginia, closed all the public schools rather than integrate. Mobs attacked black schoolchildren and physically blocked their attendance at white schools. In 1957 Eisenhower federalized the National Guard and sent paratroopers to Little Rock, Arkansas, to protect black students at Central High School. Even with such dramatic efforts, public school integration proceeded at a snail's pace. In 1960 less than 1 percent of black children attended integrated schools in the southern states. In the North, a pattern of de facto segregation remained unaffected by the Supreme Court's decision.

SPORTS, ENTERTAINMENT, AND SEXUALITY

The antipathy to integration, besides reflecting traditional racist feelings, had a psychological basis in a fear of physical contact between the races. Throughout American history, blacks had symbolized body activity in work, in dance, in sex. Proximity to blacks threatened to expose whites to their own elemental passions. One stereotyped answer to proposed integration — "Would you want your daughter to marry one?" — reflected this underlying fear. The destruction of the principle of separate, but equal eliminated what white racists considered the only alternative to racial and sexual chaos.

The fear of body contact was first attacked in the area of sports. Joe Louis, heavyweight boxing champion during World War Two, carefully avoided challenging the principles of white supremacy. But in some southern states it was illegal for white boxers to meet blacks in the ring. Blacks were permitted to play football on northern college campuses, but were conveniently left behind when their teams played against southern colleges. Blacks were excluded from playing basketball on Big Ten teams. "This is an indoor sport," John Gunther explained, "and taboos are strong...against any contact between half-clad, perspiring bodies, even on the floor of a gym." Major league baseball was not integrated until Jackie Robinson broke the color line with the Brooklyn Dodgers in 1947. But even then, Robinson was forbidden by his managers to argue with umpires or

express any aggression toward whites. By 1960 baseball, basketball, and football were racially integrated industries, though it was observable that nonstarring players were usually white.

The acceptance of black athletes was facilitated by the emergence of mass spectator sports in the postwar period. As personal consumption grew, so too did expenditures for recreation, which increased from $11.3 billion in 1950 to $18.3 billion in 1959 to $21.6 billion in 1962. This pattern was dramatized by the expansion of major league baseball to the West Coast in 1957, a process that helped to nationalize professional sports while destroying local minor league teams. TV revenues became increasingly important as a source of capital, and these monies depended on high viewer ratings. Black athletes helped to expand the size of this spectator base.

A major consumer of sporting equipment, however, was not teams, colleges, or athletes, but rather big business. Concerned about worker morale, large corporations bought recreational facilities for their employees and encouraged the formation of company teams. Such expenditures helped establish corporate loyalty and supported the fiction that corporations were happy families. From the employers' point of view, such benefits linked higher productivity to social reward. Yet organized sports, particularly company-sponsored programs, did not increase free time. By planning recreation, these programs eliminated spontaneous leisure. Such organized entertainment became more common in the postwar decades, culminating in the TV sports spectator culture.

The emergence of television represented a major innovation in mass entertainment. In 1947 there were ten TV broadcasting stations in operation; TV sets numbered about 20,000, and manufacturers were producing about 7,000

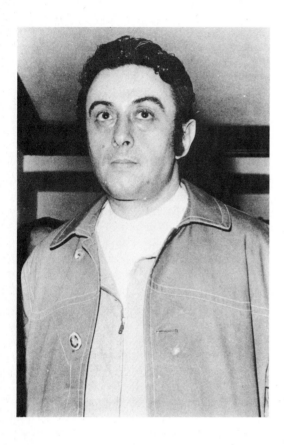

Lenny Bruce

1926-1966

The most controversial comedian of the postwar era was a stand-up nightclub performer named Lenny Bruce. Using a jazz soloist's style, Bruce blended plain street talk with Yiddish idiom to satirize and demystify social convention. His favorite subjects were religious hypocrisy, the artificiality of traditional sexual relationships, and racial chauvinism. He dedicated his autobiography, How To Talk Dirty and Influence People (1972), to "all the followers of Christ and his teachings; in particular to a true Christian — Jimmy Hoffa — because he hired ex-convicts as, I assume, Christ would have."

Born Leonard Schneider in New York, he joined the Navy at the age of sixteen and saw active service in the Mediterranean. After the war Bruce hustled as a con-artist for mock charities before drifting into comedy work in sleazy nightclubs. By the mid-fifties Bruce's type of humor won national attention. He appeared on national television, made popular records, and captivated audiences at top nightclubs across the country.

Bruce's comic routines illuminated the unspoken anxieties of fifties culture. While middle-class ethnic groups embraced homogenized suburban values (including, as in Bruce's case, the changing of ethnic names), the comedian's sketches reaffirmed the vitality of ethnic, religious, and racial identity. As middle-class Americans celebrated traditional monogamous marriages, despite a soaring divorce rate, Bruce spoke about alternative premarital, extramarital, and homosexual relationships. He attacked middle-class consumption patterns, raged against bureaucracy, and pointed to the absurdity of a Christian country waging endless war.

Bruce's insistence on artistic sincerity led him to attack legal censorship of free speech. His use of explicit language brought police repri-

sals, and he faced a series of arrests and court trials in several cities on charges of obscenity. The endless litigation drained his energy, and the subject of legal harassment came to dominate his nightclub act.

As police departments worked with municipal courts to silence the "sick" comedian, Bruce died of an overdose of heroin. His obscenity conviction, however, was overturned posthumously. Bruce's quarrel with the censorship of language provided an important basis for the free speech movements that later spread over many college campuses.

sets each year. In 1948 sales suddenly skyrocketed as consumers discovered a durable household means of entertainment. Set ownership became a status symbol. Each year, the number of TV sales rose as households clamored to buy not only one set, but often two. By 1957 Americans owned forty million TV sets and could select programs from as many as seven broadcasting channels at a time.

TV, as a new industry, was controlled by the same corporations that dominated radio. Programming was determined not by the content of the shows but, as in radio, by the ability of a broadcast to attract commercial sponsors. In the early years of TV broadcasting, when its commercial abilities remained unproved, networks often bought packaged programs manufactured by advertising agencies. In 1951, however, TV advertising sales exceeded those of radio for the first time. With sponsors convinced of the profitability of TV advertising, the problem was only to create programs that attracted wide audiences. Searching for the common denominator that would boost ratings, TV turned to variety programs, situation comedies, and quiz shows. Missing from these audiences, however, were adult men. TV solved that problem by increasing coverage of sports. With a captive audience, the three major networks offered nearly identical fare.

The rise of television severely damaged the other popular media — radio, magazines, and motion pictures. During the immediate postwar years, Hollywood had examined such controversial subjects as racism (*Home of the Brave*, 1948); anti-Semitism (*Crossfire*, 1947; *Gentleman's Agreement*, 1947); alcoholism (*The Lost Weekend*, 1945); and mental illness (*The Snake Pit*, 1949). The investigation of Hollywood for Communist subversion in 1947, however, sent a chill through the industry that discouraged social protest. As TV challenged the motion picture industry, Hollywood also sought bland subjects to win back its audiences, relying on technological innovations that were unavailable on TV screens — 3D, wide screens, and color.

Sex, moreover, was one subject banned from the airwaves. Though still bound by its own industry code that prohibited nudity or overt sexuality, Hollywood exploited the pseudosexuality of symbols like Marilyn Monroe. Women in fifties films were remarkably sexless, despite big bosoms and deep cleavages. This fascination with imaginary sexuality had important social implications. In his study of male sexuality, Kinsey observed that better educated men were more stimulated by erotic objects and stories than the lesser educated. In addition, they were less embarrassed by nudity. Kinsey also discerned that socially mobile males adopted the standards of the group into which they moved. The rise of white-collar employees in the fifties may explain the sexual revolution that began in that decade.

Erotic literature had flourished underground for centuries. But in the fifties it began to surface in such "soft-core" magazines as *Playboy*. Explicit language, still "bleeped" on TV, could occasionally be heard in motion pictures. The best seller of 1957 was a racy suburban novel, *Peyton Place,* by Grace Metallious. In 1948 Norman Mailer's *The Naked and the Dead* had to use the nonword "fug" to get past the censors. But in 1959 the Supreme Court denied the censorship of D. H. Lawrence's *Lady Chatterly's Lover* on grounds of free speech. The decision, though ambiguously enforced, opened the door to other nonconventional sexual literature.

The growing acceptance of eroticism indicated a general reconciliation to the human body, a trend that would later change American attitudes toward sex, food, dance, illness, and death. But in the fifties such possibilities were subsumed by corporate-consumer values. Sexual expression, as defined by Hollywood, *Playboy,* and their imitators, was a reward for the affluent. For example, airline stewardesses who served businessmen their meals and drinks were hired by criteria of beauty and sex appeal. In other words, sexual women, as opposed to stereotyped housewives, were expensive. Such attitudes linked the new sexuality not with social liberation, but with institutional conformity. Women's liberation would require a different constituency.

ALTERNATIVE VOICES

The relaxing of sexual standards of the wealthier classes contrasted with the moral conservatism of most Americans. The postwar era witnessed a resurgence of church membership in all denominations. This interest in spiritual security reflected the underlying anxieties of rootlessness and a pervasive fear of nuclear annihilation. Responding to these secular insecurities, religious leaders offered less a promise of salvation hereafter than a sense of identity and solace on earth.

The titles of best-selling religious books reflected these limited concerns: Rabbi Joshua Loth Liebman's *Peace of Mind* (1946), Bishop Fulton J. Sheen's *Peace of Soul* (1949), and the Reverend Norman Vincent Peale's *The Power of Positive Thinking* (1952). "Believe in yourself!" Peale proclaimed. "Have faith in your abilities! Without a humble but reasonable confidence in your own powers you cannot succeed." Evangelicals, like the Baptist

Billy Graham, also flourished in this religious renaissance.

These conservative tendencies troubled social critics who warned about the stultifying effects of conformity. "By and large," observed Will Herberg, author of *Protestant Catholic Jew* (1956), "the religion that actually prevails among Americans today has lost much of its authentic...content." These patterns accentuated a larger problem of alienation. "When white-collar people get jobs," cautioned C. Wright Mills in *White Collar* (1951), "they sell not only their time and energy but their personalities as well." Similar warnings came from such works as David Riesman's *The Lonely Crowd* (1950), Herbert Marcuse's *Eros and Civilization* (1955), William H. Whyte's *The Organization Man* (1957), and John Keats's *The Crack in the Picture Window* (1957). The publication of these works, however, belies the image of the silent fifties as a time of mass amnesia.

Alternative voices emerged in art, music, and poetry. Though most Americans preferred the representational painting of Thomas Hart Benton, Grant Wood, or Grandma Moses, a new group of "abstract expressionists" turned New York into an international center of non-representational Action Painting. Jackson Pollock, Willem de Kooning, and Mark Rothko painted with vigorous line and color that compelled viewers to seek their own meaning in the work. In music teenagers might shuffle to the refrains of rock and roll while their parents worked and shopped to the tune of Musak. But the "bebop" sound of Charlie Parker and Dizzy Gillespie brought new vitality to jazz. Nightclubs like New York's Birdland and San Francisco's Hungry i mushroomed around the country, offering hard-driving rhythms that shook the walls.

These alternative voices required a consciousness that leaped beyond the dominant values of society. "Once science has to serve, not truth, but the interests of a class, a community, or a state," warned the refugee economist Friedrich A. Hayek in *The Road to Serfdom* (1944), "the sole task of argument and discussion is to vindicate and to spread still further the beliefs by which the whole life of the community is directed." After the development of the atom bomb, American science could only reinforce humanity's separation from nature. Technology was destroying the earth itself, forcing people to abandon traditional communities, to become strangers to each other and to themselves.

The strongest voice of protest came from a group of "Beat" poets and writers who congregated in San Francisco in the fifties. Jack Kerouac, Alan Watts, Gary Snyder, and Gregory Corso decried the alienating effects of American culture and called for a new spiritualism that merged the spirit and the flesh. Most eloquent was the poet Allen Ginsberg. In *Howl*, published in 1956, he indicted a society that watched "the best minds of my generation destroyed by madness." Strong, rolling cadences condemned "the scholars of war" with their "demonic industries" and "monstrous bombs." His vision in the poem "America" reached to the core of the postwar identity:

America when will we end the human war?
Go fuck yourself with your atom bomb.

SUGGESTED READINGS

A thorough social history of the postwar period is Geoffrey Perrett, *A Dream of Greatness: The American People, 1945–1963* (1979). Also useful are Joseph C. Goulden, *The Best Years: 1945–1950* (1976), and Douglas T. Miller and Marion Nowak, *The Fifties: The Way We Really Were* (1977).

The relationship between government and the economy is illuminated in the relevant chapters of Gabriel Kolko's *Main Currents in Modern American History* (1976). For the immediate postwar years, see two articles by Barton J. Bernstein: "The Debate on Industrial Reconversion," *American Journal of Economics and Sociology,* 26 (1967); and "The Removal of War Production Controls on Business, 1944–1946," *Business History Review,* 39 (1965). Also enlightening are Fred J. Cook, *The Warfare State* (1962), and the final chapters of Walter Millis's *Arms and Men: A Study in American Military History* (1956).

A thorough examination of economic trends is provided by Harold G. Vatter, *The U.S. Economy in the 1950's* (1963). For a study of the disparities of wealth, see Herman P. Miller, *Rich Man, Poor Man* (1964). A valuable study of poverty is Michael Harrington's *The Other America* (1962).

For the housing problem in the postwar years, see Richard O. Davies, *Housing Reform During the Truman Administration* (1966). There is a vast literature on suburbia. A good starting point is Robert C. Wood, *Suburbia: Its People and Their Politics* (1959), but it should be supplemented with Scott Donaldson, *The Suburban Myth* (1969).

The status of women is explored in the appropriate chapters of William H. Chafe, *The American Woman* (1972). For popular images of women in film, see Molly Haskell, *From Reverence to Rape* (1974), and Brandon French, *On the Verge of Revolt* (1978).

The struggle to end racial discrimination is brilliantly described in Richard Kluger, *Simple Justice: The History of Brown v. Board of Education and Black America's Struggle for Equality* (1976). It should be supplemented by Donald R. McCoy and Richard T. Ruetten, *Quest and Response: Minority Rights and the Truman Administration* (1973), and Anthony Lewis and the *New York Times's Portrait of a Decade: The Second American Revolution* (1964).

Popular culture may be explored through Erik Barnouw, *The Image Empire* (1970), which examines television; Gordon Gow, *Hollywood in the Fifties* (1971); and James Gunn, *Alternative Worlds: The Illustrated History of Science Fiction* (1975). For the Beat writers, see Lawrence Lipton, *The Holy Barbarians* (1959).

Chapter 12

THE TRUMAN ADMINISTRATION, 1945-1952

The expansion of the American economy after World War Two exceeded the most optimistic expectations of wartime leaders. In 1945 the Truman administration had been more concerned that reconversion would produce mass unemployment and Depression conditions. These fears reflected the failure of the New Deal to eliminate unemployment until the nation began preparing for war in 1940. It was from this perspective that President Truman formulated not only a domestic program, but a foreign policy as well.

Truman's sole distinction prior to obtaining the vice presidential nomination in 1944 had been his support of New Deal legislation. In September 1945 he reaffirmed that commit-ment, telling Congress that "the ultimate duty of Government" was "to prevent prolonged unemployment." The president called for "full-employment" legislation, as well as such reform measures as a permanent Fair Employment Practices Commission (FEPC), public housing, higher minimum wages, and urban redevelopment. This ambitious program soon collided with a conservative Congress that disagreed with the president about the importance of government intervention in the economy. Though Congress acknowledged government responsibility for avoiding a depression in the Employment Act of 1946, it refused to allow automatic government expenditures to assure economic stability.

THE PROBLEMS
OF RECONVERSION

Truman's immediate domestic problems, however, related less to unemployment than to inflation. Within one week of V-J Day, the administration began lifting wartime controls on civilian production, triggering a sudden increase in consumer demand and soaring prices. In this crisis Truman failed to exert adequate leadership. Consumers attacked the administration's unwillingness to establish workable controls, while conservatives denounced Truman's half-hearted efforts as "creeping socialism." In the absence of a coherent government program, prices continued to climb until mid-1948, when consumer demand for durable goods finally began to slacken.

The postwar inflation created serious problems for workers who suffered a real loss of wages at the end of the war. To offset such economic imbalances, organized labor initiated a series of strikes for higher wages in such industries as automobiles, steel, meatpacking, coal, and transportation. In the first year after V-J Day, nearly five million workers were involved in over forty-five hundred work stoppages that resulted in the loss of nearly 120 million workers' days of labor. Truman feared that an increase of wages would lead to a rise in prices, feeding the inflationary spiral and resulting in economic collapse. He therefore urged industry leaders to grant wage increases while maintaining price lines. When they refused, the president could only acquiesce to continued inflation.

Truman, frustrated by the numerous strikes, was convinced that organized labor was threatening the economic structure of the nation. In May 1946 the railroad workers went on strike, despite the president's seizure of the railroads. Facing a major transportation crisis, Truman presented a dramatic appeal to Congress in which he requested legislative authority to allow the army to operate the trains, to authorize court injunctions to keep workers on the job and punish uncooperative union leaders, and finally to permit the president to draft striking workers into the military services to force them to work. Though labor leaders settled the strike before Congress could act on the president's request, Truman's proposal provoked bitter attacks from organized labor. Conservative Senator Robert A. Taft, a Republican presidential contender, condemned Truman for challenging basic civil liberties. Despite such rhetoric, Congress approved the use of court injunctions to stop certain strikes.

Truman soon used these powers to end a coal strike that threatened to disrupt the economy. In April 1946 John L. Lewis led a strike by the United Mine Workers — which previously had violated labor's "no strike" pledge during World War Two. When contract negotiations failed, Truman seized the mines and ended the strike by accepting an inflationary settlement. In November, however, Lewis again called a strike in defiance of the government. Unlike Roosevelt, who in wartime had met Lewis's demands, Truman obtained an injunction and a $3.5 million fine against the UMW, which forced the union to surrender.

Truman's failure to maintain price controls and his brusque treatment of labor unions alienated liberal support. Republicans, on the other hand, attacked Truman's commitment to the New Deal. With a simple campaign slogan, "Had Enough?" Republicans won a landslide victory in the congressional elections of 1946, obtaining a legislative majority for the first time since 1928. Among the victors were freshman congressmen John F. Kennedy, Richard M. Nixon, and Joseph R. McCarthy. The latter two candidates added an ominous note to the campaign by accusing their Democratic opponents of serving as Communist agents in government.

Once in control of the Eightieth Congress, Republicans established a working alliance with southern Democrats by agreeing to thwart civil rights legislation. This conservative coalition then proceeded to block other liberal measures, such as public housing, federal aid to education, higher social security payments, and certain farm legislation. Reflecting their opposition to organized labor, the conservatives joined in passing the Taft-Hartley Act of 1947, which limited the right to strike. Truman, hoping to win back his labor supporters, denounced the bill as "a clear threat to the successful working of our democratic society." Congress nevertheless overrode the president's veto. But Truman's defense of unions helped return organized labor to the Democratic camp.

The success of conservative Republicans in 1946 persuaded Truman to reassess his domestic program. Within a week of the election, he ended all wage controls and retained only a few price controls, thus acknowledging government's inability to control inflation. Truman also began to move in a liberal direction on civil rights. Though he had advocated a permanent FEPC in his first message to Congress, Truman had subsequently backtracked in supporting equal rights for blacks. Prior to the election, civil rights leaders pressed the president to take a public stand against an epidemic of lynching. But Truman feared antagonizing the South. Instead he decided to pursue a cautious policy by creating a special commission

on civil rights, which he staffed with liberals. Yet he waited until after the election before announcing the commission, which was charged with recommending policies to protect civil rights.

While Truman bowed to liberal pressure for civil rights for blacks, his administration was taking the first steps toward curtailing the rights of political minorities considered disloyal or subversive. On the eve of World War Two, President Roosevelt had initiated an internal security program designed to protect government from subversive employees. Although wartime conditions existed, Roosevelt's program attempted to protect the civil rights of government personnel by limiting the investigatory powers of the FBI and by requiring adequate proof of subversion. Despite these restraints, the FBI exceeded constitutional safeguards by wiretapping and by burglarizing private offices and homes of suspected employees. Such violations prevented the government from prosecuting the editors of *Amerasia,* a monthly magazine, for possessing documents stolen from the Office of Strategic Services (OSS). Evidence of subversion was reinforced in 1946 by exposure of Soviet espionage in Canada.

These revelations provided ammunition for Republicans to attack the Truman administration for failing to identify and punish suspected subversives. Such allegations were doubly impressive to people who believed that the New Deal was another form of state socialism. In the aftermath of the Republican electoral victory, therefore, Truman created a Temporary Commission on Employee Loyalty to recommend revisions of the government's loyalty program. The announcement of a new program in the spring of 1947 coincided with a new approach to foreign policy.

POSTWAR FOREIGN POLICY

The fear of depression that motivated Truman's domestic policies was also an essential ingredient in the emergence of his postwar foreign policy. "Our international policies and our domestic policies are inseparable," declared Secretary of State James F. Byrnes in August 1945. "Our foreign relations inevitably affect employment in the United States. Prosperity and depression in the United States just as inevitably affect our relations with the other nations of the world." More specifically, the State Department argued that economic prosperity at home and abroad offered the surest protection against another war.

This economic interpretation of international relations partially reflected the social composition of the policy-making elite throughout the postwar period. Leaders of the State Department invariably had deep personal connections with the nation's largest corporations and held powerful positions as corporate lawyers, financiers, or big-business executives. Such personnel, appointed by both Democratic and Republican presidents, imposed their own values with respect to international order on American policy. Defining the "national interest" in capitalist terms, they endeavored to increase American trade and defend private property at the expense of friend and foe alike.

Such assumptions had a long history in the concept of the Open Door. As expressed by State Department officials, American capitalism required an expanding marketplace to sell the products of industry and so assure domestic prosperity. The immense expenditure of natural resources during the war also indicated that the United States required ready access to raw materials. These twin goals, it was commonly believed, could be achieved only by a world system of free trade. A multilateral economic system, in which all nations had equal access to markets and resources, would prevent the emergence of economic blocs that encouraged international rivalry. "Nations which act as enemies in the marketplace," explained one State Department adviser, "cannot long be friends at the council table."

American diplomacy in World War Two attempted to protect the principles of the Open Door in the postwar period. Such programs as the International Monetary Fund and the World Bank, both created by international agreement in 1944, endeavored to stabilize international currency and trade. Since both institutions were financed by American dollars, their policies protected American interests. A related proposal, which was never implemented, called for a general reduction of world tariffs to avoid the catastrophic competition among nations that occurred during the Depression.

The goal of free international trade promised distinct advantages for the United States. Recognizing that Europe would require extensive American investment to recover from the damage of the war, State Department planners hoped to use American economic power to force Great Britain, France, and the Soviet Union to open their trading blocs to American business. In 1945 these nations applied for American loans to replace aid lost at the expected termination of Lend-Lease. But American negotiators deliberately delayed action, hoping to use this economic leverage to obtain trading concessions. This policy was reiterated by Truman in a "Navy Day" speech in October 1945. "We believe that full economic collaboration between all nations, great and small, is essential to the improvement of living conditions all over the world," he declared.

Truman's position conflicted with both the British policy of preferential treatment for Commonwealth nations and Soviet opposition to capitalist penetration. Moreover, the United States did not always implement its own proposals. Congress failed to approve tariff reductions, fearing that foreign manufacturers would threaten the domestic economy. Nor did the administration advocate opening Latin America to European business. Truman expected the nations of the Western Hemisphere to "work together as good neighbors" and he explicitly repudiated "interference from outside."

Despite such contradictions between American free trade policy and practice, the United States agreed to loan Britain $3.75 billion only on condition that the British open their empire to American trade. The war-ravished ally had no choice but to accept. American negotiators also forced France to accept multilateralism before lending nearly $1 billion to rebuild the economy. But the Soviet Union, though desperate after four years of war, refused to capitulate to American demands. The resulting deadlock increased a tension between the two powers that culminated by 1947 in an undeclared "Cold War."

American conflict with the Soviet Union reflected basic ideological differences on the nature of world order. Stated simply, it was a conflict between a capitalist society dedicated to the Open Door in international relations and a socialist society committed to a regulated economy within spheres of influence. Moreover, each system saw the other as inevitably expansive, inevitably a threat to its own integrity. This image of global rivalry had historical roots that extended back to the Bolshevik Revolution of 1917. In the subsequent three decades, such antithetical values affected relations between the two nations. But ideology was not the only factor in creating Soviet-American hostility after World War Two.

The Soviet position, as expressed by Marx and Lenin, insisted that capitalism was doomed to collapse because of its internal contradictions; a socialist society, it was believed, would inevitably replace this outmoded system. Meanwhile, the Soviet Union must strengthen its own society and lend assistance to socialist revolutionaries elsewhere to accelerate the historical process. These principles were modified by Josef Stalin, who seized power in the Soviet Union in the twenties. Though Stalin continued to advocate world revolution, his foreign policy aimed more at protecting the Soviet Union from its capitalist enemies. When Nazi Germany threatened Soviet interests, Stalin sought an alliance with Britain and France; when they rebuffed him, he signed a nonaggression pact with Hitler. The German invasion of 1941, however, brought the Soviet Union into the Grand Alliance. Stalin's major postwar goal, therefore, was to protect his country from invasion through Poland and to rebuild his war-torn land.

American policy makers, however, saw the existence of a Communist state as a threat to capitalist-democratic institutions. Taking Marxist-Leninist rhetoric at face value, they envisioned an aggressive Soviet Union seeking to conquer the world. This image of the Soviet Union as a revolutionary state dominated the thinking of State Department bureaucrats who advised the president on foreign policy. The necessities of a wartime alliance, however, diminished the influence of these ideas. Though suspicious of Stalin, President Roosevelt was willing to treat the Soviet Union as a "normal" state protecting its national interests. Moreover, he preferred to handle international relations outside the bureaucratic structure of the diplomatic corps. Roosevelt's policies consequently lacked an institutional base to survive him.

Roosevelt also failed to develop public support for his foreign policy. Fearful of a resurgence of isolationism, he hesitated to move too far ahead of public opinion. Though mid-war polls indicated that three-fourths of the population favored American participation in a postwar international organization, Americans continued to express suspicion of power diplomacy. Roosevelt therefore did not challenge the popular view that the United Nations, like the League of Nations, would be based on Wilsonian principles of multinational representation. These ideals would be institutionalized in the General Assembly. But Roosevelt believed that the U. N. could succeed where the league had failed only if international order were based on Big Power diplomacy. And in his diplomatic negotiations, Roosevelt assumed that the Big Four, with veto power in the Security Council, would interact on a basis of power relationships.

Roosevelt's public ambiguity produced serious misunderstandings after his death. At Yalta, for example, Roosevelt and Churchill implicitly accepted Soviet predominance in Eastern Europe, while Britain claimed special privileges in the Mediterranean, and the United States controlled Latin America. Such spheres of influence contradicted a Wilsonian world order as well as the economic principles of the Open Door. Roosevelt accepted these limitations because of the realities of Soviet power in Eastern Europe and his recognition of Stalin's desire to prevent another invasion from central Europe.

At Roosevelt's death, however, Truman knew nothing of his predecessor's foreign policy assumptions. Instead the new president viewed the Soviet presence in Eastern Europe merely as a challenge to the Wilsonian order. More-over, where Roosevelt often ignored the State Department's assessment of the Soviet threat, Truman turned to the cabinet bureaucracies for advice. These altered circumstances precipitated Truman's early clashes with the Soviet Union over U.N. representation, the settlement of Eastern Europe, and the question of German reparations.

The change of administrations also affected American policy toward the European colonies, most significantly the French colony of Indochina. After the Japanese occupied the territory, the American OSS provided military support for a national liberation movement led by Ho Chi Minh. Such assistance, besides reflecting the wartime crisis, revealed Roosevelt's belief that the French colony should be placed under an international trusteeship until Indochina achieved full independence. Roosevelt did not intend to restore the colony to France; he did not even envision France, a defeated nation, as one of the trustees. In 1945 Ho Chi Minh drafted a formal declaration of independence based on the principles of Thomas Jefferson's statement of 1776.

The Truman administration soon reversed Roosevelt's policy. Pressured by Churchill, who feared that the breakup of the French empire might lead to the disruption of Britain's, Truman agreed to the restoration of Indochina to France. This decision was closely related to Truman's perception of a world Communist menace. Ho's sympathy to communism alarmed State Department officials who hoped to preserve an Open Door in Southeast Asia, the very area that Roosevelt had refused to surrender to Japan in 1941. Equally important, Truman wished to retain French loyalty in Europe, where France would join Britain as allies against the Soviet Union. The United States implemented its new policy by providing ships and military assistance to transport a French expeditionary force to Indochina in 1945. Ho Chi Minh's repeated appeals for American support were ignored by the State Department.

THE COLD WAR

The Big Three met at Potsdam in July 1945 but failed to resolve their differences. Truman, emboldened by the successful testing of the atomic bomb, rejected Stalin's interpretation of the Yalta agreements. He refused to accept a Soviet sphere of influence in Eastern Europe, and he narrowly defined the promised reparations from Germany, so that the Soviet Union would remain vulnerable to American economic pressure. These questions were postponed to a Foreign Ministers Conference in London in September 1945. Truman also decided to exclude the Soviet Union from participation in the occupation of Japan.

The effectiveness of the atom bomb in defeating Japan encouraged Truman and Secretary Byrnes to remain uncompromising with the Soviet Union. Stalin, fearful about the implications of this new atomic diplomacy, offered the minor concession of postponing elections in Bulgaria and Hungary. But Byrnes's continuing hard line could not produce additional concessions at the London meeting. This failure to reach agreement demonstrated the fallacy of Big Bomb diplomacy; the Soviet Union would not be coerced by threat of attack to accept American foreign policy. Secretary of War Stimson, who had once viewed the bomb as a diplomatic lever, now saw an opportunity to ease international tensions by sharing nuclear secrets with the Soviet Union. "If we fail to approach them now and merely continue to negotiate with them, having this weapon rather ostentatiously on our hip," he warned, "their suspicions and their distrust . . . will increase." But after a high-level policy debate, Truman rejected Stimson's suggestion. "The atomic bomb does not alter the basic foreign policy of the United States," he remarked in October 1945.

Despite his doubts about further negotiations, Truman permitted Byrnes to meet with Stalin in Moscow in December 1945. The sessions proved remarkably successful, producing agreements that allowed greater Western representation in Bulgaria and Rumania, established a joint commission to form a government in Korea, and made preliminary plans for a U. N. Atomic Energy Commission. A gleeful Byrnes returned to Washington. But instead of praise, he was met by an angry president who criticized his concessions. "Unless Russia is faced with an iron fist and strong language another war is in the making," Truman declared. "I'm tired of babying the Soviets."

Truman's belligerent position won reinforcement within the State Department from George Kennan, a prestigious student of Soviet affairs. "We have here," he cabled from Moscow in February 1946, "a political force committed fanatically to the belief that with [the] U.S. there can be no permanent *modus vivendi,* that it is desirable and necessary that the internal harmony of our society be disrupted, our traditional way of life destroyed, the international authority of our state be broken if Soviet power is to be secure." Kennan's "Long Telegram" was enthusiastically endorsed in the administration because it confirmed the president's belief that there could be no compromise with Communist nations.

Though highly influential within the government, Kennan's message did not reflect American public opinion. In March 1946 Truman accompanied Winston Churchill to Fulton, Missouri, where the former prime minister presented a bitter attack on the Soviet Union for drawing an "Iron Curtain" around Eastern Europe. Churchill's position, like Kennan's, suggested that the Soviet Union could not be treated like an ordinary nation within the context of international power. Rather, the Soviet Union represented "a growing challenge and peril to Christian civilization." He therefore called for a "special relationship" between the United States and Great Britain, including maintenance of the atomic monopoly. Churchill's rhetoric, though gratifying to Truman, brought storms of protest from the general public. It nevertheless served the administration's purpose of publicizing a shift in foreign policy assumptions. Other well-placed news "leaks" endeavored to mold public opinion according to State Department perceptions. Such publicity was credited in Congress for obtaining approval of the British loan in the summer of 1946.

As part of its attempt to mobilize domestic support, the Truman administration relied increasingly on public forums to express its antipathy to the Soviet Union. The most prestigious — and the most politically secure — of these vehicles was the U. N. With American dominance in the General Assembly, the United States could wage the Cold War while appearing to be idealistic. But when the U.N. did not serve American purposes, the administration conveniently by-passed that body. Since the United States could not prevent shipment of essential U.N. food relief to Communist countries, the Truman administration decided to withdraw support from the U.N. Relief and Rehabilitation Administration, which theoreti-

cally had been a nonpolitical humanitarian agency.

The first major case before the U.N. involved Soviet occupation of Iran in 1946. Though defined by the United States as a question of territorial integrity, the main problem focused on oil. During World War Two, the Big Three had occupied Iran jointly, promising to withdraw after the war. But the Soviet Union hesitated to leave and demanded oil concessions similar to those won by the British. Stalin also supported a revolt in the northern provinces of Azerbaijan. The Truman administration, fearing a Soviet attempt to control vital oil resources, leaped to Iran's support in the Security Council, where the United States held a preponderance of votes. The State Department also sent a strong protest to the Soviet Union. Such diplomatic pressure forced Iran and the Soviet Union to reach a compromise, providing for oil concessions and Soviet withdrawal. The Iranian government then suppressed the northern revolt and soon thereafter repudiated the oil agreement. The United States, using U.N. institutions, had thwarted Soviet policy.

The U.N. also served to justify the United States's monopoly of atomic weapons. In March 1946 the administration announced the Acheson-Lilienthal plan, providing for the internationalization of atomic energy. According to the proposals, the United States would relinquish its control of atomic weapons in a series of transitional stages. During this time the United States would maintain its monopoly, while other countries would remain open to international inspection. Truman appointed the financier Bernard Baruch to present this program to the U.N. The final Baruch plan added other qualifications, including the surrender of the veto on atomic energy issues and the imposition of "condign punishments" by a majority vote (controlled by the United States) for violations. Unwilling to open its resources to outside inspection and fearful of continued American monopoly, the Soviet Union rejected Baruch's proposal. In its place the Soviets suggested immediate nuclear disarmament and sharing of atomic secrets, while postponing specific controls. The Truman administration scoffed at this solution, considering it a sign of Soviet duplicity.

Truman's inability to see the logic of Soviet objections reflected a moral absolutism that dominated the postwar era. Having defined World War Two as a crusade for "liberty" (rather than national interest), the Democratic administration could contrast America's virtuous commitments with the cynical power politics of its opponents. The Soviet Union's attempt to protect its borders and to rebuild its economy could be seen as Machiavellian and evil. These attitudes were strengthened by the memory of Nazi aggression. Asserting that all totalitarian states sought world conquest, members of the Truman administration disavowed any compromise that might appear to be "appeasement." Standing up to the Soviets, they believed, was the best way to avoid World War Three. "The language of military power is the only language which disciples of power politics understand," Clark Clifford assured the president in the summer of 1946.

The assertion that the United States represented the cause of freedom while the Soviet Union symbolized "red fascism" had important implications for domestic attitudes. Primarily it served to silence criticism of the administration. During World War Two most isolationists had come to accept the importance of American leadership in the postwar world. But some Republicans, like Senator Taft, remained skeptical about certain administration programs such as the British loan. Once Truman defined American policy as the antithesis of evil, however, such opposition vaporized. Instead, Republicans, led by Senator Arthur Vandenberg and foreign policy expert John Foster Dulles, supported the administration under the principle of "bipartisanship."

As the Cold War consensus crystalized in 1946, a major voice of opposition was that of Henry Wallace. Secretary of agriculture in the New Deal, Roosevelt's third-term vice president, and now secretary of commerce, Wallace questioned Truman's rigid policy toward the Soviet Union. Truman simply ignored Wallace's private protests. But in September 1946, with Truman's approval, Wallace presented a public address at Madison Square Garden that called for a reorientation of American foreign policy. Though Wallace reaffirmed the importance of "an open door for trade throughout the world," he nevertheless argued that the United States had "no more business in the *political* affairs of Eastern Europe than Russia had in the *political* affairs of Latin America, Western Europe, and the United States." The statement undermined the position of Byrnes, who was then trying to persuade the Soviets to reorganize the governments of Eastern Europe. When Byrnes threatened to resign, Truman withdrew his approval of the speech and fired Wallace. "The Reds, phonies, and the 'parlor pinks,'" Truman wrote, "seem to be banded together and are becoming a national danger."

The dismissal of Wallace reflected the administration's growing intolerance of positions that had seemed thoroughly orthodox only one year before. After the conservative victories in the 1946 elections, liberals continued to desert Truman's leadership. In December influential liberal groups coalesced as the Progressive Citizens of America (PCA). Complaining that the Democratic party had departed from the tradition of Roosevelt, they urged the Democrats to reaffirm their liberal principles or face competition from a new third party. Wallace, it was suggested, would revitalize the New Deal. The PCA significantly prohibited internal discrimination for political beliefs, including communism.

This question of Communist affiliation soon split the liberal movement. Many liberals not only opposed communism but especially resented the conservatives' accusations that liberals were merely an instrument of Soviet foreign policy. In January 1947 these non-Communist liberals formed the Americans for Democratic Action (ADA). Like the PCA, the ADA endorsed expansion of the New Deal, the U.N., and civil rights. But the ADA explicitly rejected "any association with Communists or sympathizers with communism in the United States as completely as we reject any association with Fascists or their sympathizers."

The logic of the ADA was best expressed by one of its founders, the theologian Reinhold Niebuhr. As an orthodox Protestant, Niebuhr saw the human condition as enmeshed in sin; no human achievement could attain perfection. Yet the Soviet Union, like its Fascist antagonists, believed that science and human reason could transcend sin and create perfection on earth. Such optimism was prideful, Niebuhr suggested, and made communism a particularly dangerous enemy. Niebuhr therefore advocated strenuous opposition to the Soviet Union. "Russian truculence cannot be mitigated by further concessions," he declared, dismissing Wallace's optimism about negotiating with Communists.

Niebuhr thus became a firm supporter of Truman's foreign policy.

THE TRUMAN DOCTRINE

During the winter of 1947, American intelligence detected a relaxation in Soviet policy, ranging from demobilization of its armies to a willingness to negotiate a peace treaty with Germany. The State Department nevertheless believed that such changes were deliberately deceptive, merely another tactic in a larger strategy of world domination. Reinforcing this distrust was a growing concern about the slow pace of economic recovery in Europe. Plagued by food shortages and industrial chaos, the European nations seemed incapable of reconstructing their economies. Impoverished economic conditions, the State Department feared, would provide fertile ground for Communist expansion. Already the Communist parties of Italy and France had achieved significant electoral success. Unsettled economic conditions in Europe also threatened to affect the American economy, which required a flourishing export market. "Peace, freedom and world trade are indivisible," Truman declared. "We must not go through the thirties again."

The problem climaxed in February 1947 when Great Britain notified the State Department that it could no longer provide economic and military support for Greece. Since World War Two, a Greek Communist party supported by Yugoslavia (but *not* by the Soviet Union) had been waging guerrilla warfare against a corrupt, undemocratic, British-backed regime. The United States had supported Britain's policy and had even sent economic aid to the Greek government. Britain's inability to finance her commitments now offered the United States an opportunity to become dominant in the area.

American intervention in Greece required congressional approval. Yet a conservative Congress was eager to reduce taxes and cut government expenditures; and the American public remained uninterested in the Balkan civil war. To overcome this resistance, Truman adopted the advice of Senator Vandenberg: he would "scare hell out of the American people." In March 1947 Truman presented Congress with what became known as the Truman Doctrine, in which he requested $400 million of economic and military assistance for Greece and Turkey. Concealing the economic basis of his policy, Truman instead depicted an emergency crisis that pitted the American way of life against that of the Soviet Union. The United States, he declared, must "support free peoples who are resisting attempted subjugation by armed minorities or by outside pressures."

The Truman Doctrine represented a major turning point in American foreign policy. First, it suggested that the United States must initiate unilateral action without consultation with either the U.N. or the Soviet Union. Though a conference of foreign ministers was simultaneously held in Moscow in March 1947, Dean Acheson, later to become Truman's secretary of state, testified in the Senate that it was impossible to "sit down with the Russians and solve questions." Second, the Truman Doctrine abandoned the idea of effecting changes within the Soviet sphere of influence and instead stressed the importance of containing further Soviet expansion. This decision institutionalized the division of the globe into areas of "freedom" and zones of "terror and oppression." Such dichotomies allowed no room for compromise or for degrees of commitment; all Com-

munists were evil, all Communist threats were equally critical. This idea of containment was elaborated by George Kennan in an anonymously published article, "The Sources of Soviet Conduct," in July 1947. Though sharing Truman's view of a pervasive Soviet menace, Kennan put less emphasis on military strategy and stressed the value of economic pressure in weakening the Communist appeal.

Truman's belief that communism was a monolithic threat placed the United States on the side of authoritarian governments. Viewing the Greek Communists as minions of Moscow, Truman preferred to support the undemocratic status quo. In Turkey the United States readily backed a reactionary regime that not only suppressed internal dissent but also had cooperated with the Germans during World War Two. In justifying these questionable alliances, the Truman administration articulated what later became known as a domino theory. "If Greece and then Turkey succumb, the whole Middle East will be lost," advised one State Department official. "France may then capitulate to the Communists. As France goes, all Western Europe and North Africa will go."

Such logic alarmed conservatives and liberals alike. Senator Taft protested that the president's bold initiative had presented Congress with a virtual fait accompli. Though he eventually agreed to support the Truman Doctrine, Taft emphasized that it was not "a commitment to any similar policy in any other section of the world." At the other end of the political spectrum, Wallace broadcast a scathing critique of Truman's proposal. "There is no regime too reactionary" to receive American aid, he cried, "provided it stands in Russia's expansionist path." A Gallup poll indicated that a majority of Americans favored economic aid to Greece but opposed military assistance.

Arthur H. Vandenberg

1884-1951

"The Old Guard dies but never surrenders," wrote Milton S. Mayer in 1940. "Vandenberg surrenders, but never dies." Senator Arthur H. Vandenberg of Michigan personified the transition among many Americans from prewar isolationism to postwar internationalism. Though Old Guard Republicans, like Senator Robert A. Taft of Ohio, refused to compromise an anti–New Deal, "America first" ideology, Vandenberg easily drifted with the changing assumptions of American voters.

Born in Michigan in 1884, Vandenberg embraced the conservative middle-class midwestern values of his surroundings. As editor of the Grand Rapids Herald, he supported progressive reform, backed Woodrow Wilson's decision to seek intervention in World War One, but opposed portions of the League of Nations charter that seemed to impinge on the constitutional limits of foreign policy. Appointed to the Senate in 1928, Vandenberg supported the Hoover administration's efforts to end the Depression. After the election of Franklin D. Roosevelt, however, Vandenberg backed the Democrats' early New Deal program in the interests of bipartisanship. By 1935, however, he rejected Roosevelt's leadership and became an outspoken critic of the administration.

Vandenberg also dissented from Roosevelt's foreign policy. An opponent of international alliances, he favored strict neutrality legislation, was even willing to sacrifice traditional neutral rights, and worked unsuccessfully to prevent the repeal of an arms embargo in 1939. He also attacked the Lend-Lease plan, arguing that it would hasten American entry into World War Two.

Vandenberg's position changed dramatically after Pearl Harbor. He appealed — unsuccessfully — to Roosevelt to support a bipartisan congressional-executive committee to create a united foreign policy. In January 1945 he presented a widely hailed speech in which he endorsed a postwar international organization. He served as a representative to the United Nations conference in San Francisco and was largely responsible for the adoption of Article 51, which provided for regional alliances. Intended to protect United States influence in Latin America, this article later provided the basis for NATO and other regional pacts.

Vandenberg remained suspicious of the Soviet Union. He was one of two senators to oppose recognition of the Soviet Union, and he distrusted Soviet foreign policy throughout World War Two. Vandenberg was personally vain and easily subject to administration pressure and flattery. Though the leading Republican in the area of foreign policy, he uncritically embraced Truman's anti-Soviet policy, working for Senate endorsement of atomic secrecy, the Truman Doctrine, Marshall Plan, and NATO.

His endorsement of a bipartisan foreign policy contrasted with the Old Guard's suspicion of internationalism. Taft's opposition to Truman's intervention prevented the Ohio senator from capturing the Republican nomination in 1948 and 1952. Yet Vandenberg, whose foreign policy position was more popular, failed to win the personal respect of his colleagues and never became a party leader. He died of cancer in 1951.

Despite such opposition, Truman's shrill presentation had correctly gauged congressional opinion. By May 1947 the president signed the Truman Doctrine into law. Yet American aid neither suppressed the Greek rebellion nor made the government less oppressive. Only the cessation of Yugoslavian aid in 1948 permitted the defeat of the Greek insurgents. The limitations of the Truman Doctrine were well understood. "There is no use in pretending...that for $400 million we have bought peace," admitted Vandenberg. "It is merely a down payment."

The Truman Doctrine, by emphasizing the military threat of communism, diverted attention from the main purposes of Truman's foreign policy. Despite the president's rhetoric, the administration primarily desired to stabilize the European economy to prevent the spread of communism and to protect the flow of American trade. Military assistance comprised only one part of that program. Yet the administration believed that was the only language Congress and the public would understand.

The second aspect of the program was revealed by Secretary of State George Marshall in June 1947. Using the Harvard University commencement as a forum, Marshall described the severe economic problems that afflicted Europe and called for a program of economic assistance that would provide for the permanent reconstruction of European stability. To accentuate the humanitarian dimension of his proposal, the secretary suggested that the European nations initiate a formal request. He also claimed to offer American assistance to all nations, including Communist. "Our policy is described not against any country or doctrine," he maintained, "but against hunger, poverty, desperation, and chaos."

In inviting Soviet participation, however, Marshall was less than candid. Though Molotov attended a European conference in June 1947 to formulate a response to Marshall's address, he soon discovered that the American-controlled plan would threaten the independence of each nation's economy. Moreover, the program seemed to envision a return to a prewar economy that left Eastern Europe far less industrialized than Western Europe. To satisfy American requirements, the Soviet Union, instead of receiving reparations to rebuild its economy, might actually have to contribute food to other nations. Finally, as Molotov complained, the plan would revitalize Germany and lead to German integration in the Western economy.

The State Department correctly predicted the effects of these objections: the Soviet Union refused to participate in the Marshall Plan. Molotov then offered alternative economic assistance to Eastern Europe and effectively prevented those nations from participating in the Marshall Plan. Besides tightening its economic grip on Eastern Europe, the Soviet Union also eliminated anti-Communist groups from the government of Hungary. By the autumn of 1947, the Soviet Union announced the creation of Cominform, the successor of the prewar Comintern, to assure the ideological unity of Communist parties throughout the world. Such action, though viewed by American leaders as proof of a global Communist conspiracy, could also be seen as a response to American attempts to create an anti-Communist bloc in Europe. Fearing "capitalist encirclement," the Soviet Union sought to solidify its own position. Yet by having to reject what ostensibly was an innocent American gesture of assistance, the Soviet Union acquired the onus of dividing postwar Europe into armed camps.

The Soviet response merely facilitated the implementation of the Marshall Plan. The remaining sixteen nations drafted a four-year program based on increased production, stability of currency, lowered tariffs, and economic cooperation. They also requested over $20 billion of American aid to pay for imports from the United States; but the Truman administration cut that figure to $17 billion. While negotiations continued, the United States began to rebuild German industry as a precondition for European recovery. These measures alarmed the French, who had industrial hopes of their own. But the United States effectively used its economic power to overcome French resistance. Earlier, that same power had been used to persuade the French and Italian governments to drop the Communist party from their coalitions.

The anti-Communist aspects of the Marshall Plan helped create a more favorable reception in Congress. But the conservative majority remained suspicious of executive power and questioned the necessity of economic aid. These problems reinforced a general apathy. In November 1947, 40 percent of the American people had never heard of the Marshall Plan. To overcome this inertia, the Truman administration launched a systematic drive to mold public opinion. The State Department joined with corporate lawyers and big-business leaders as well as organized labor, ADA, and the Farm Bureau to lobby for congressional approval. This issue crystalized when the Truman administration realized that interim assistance was necessary before Congress could act on the full program. Summoning a special session of Congress in October 1947, the president played down the economic basis of his foreign policy and instead returned to the militant anti-Communist rhetoric of the Truman Doctrine.

The strategy worked. By November Truman signed an interim assistance bill into law.

MOBILIZING A
DOMESTIC CONSENSUS

The American anti-Communist foreign policy paralleled an anti-Communist crusade at home. Nine days after enunciating the Truman Doctrine, the president created a Federal Employee Loyalty program to eliminate subversive employees from government. Truman's announcement reflected the political pressures of the conservative Eightieth Congress as well as anti-Communist feelings within the administration. In January 1947 the House Un-American Activities Committee (HUAC) had resumed its investigation of Communist infiltration of government, the Hollywood motion picture industry, education, and labor unions. Meanwhile, Truman's temporary commission heard testimony from such experts as FBI Director J. Edgar Hoover and Attorney General Tom Clark, who advocated strong safeguards against disloyal employees and warned of dire consequences for the national security.

Responding to these pressures, Truman's executive order established loyalty investigations of all government employees and of all people seeking government jobs. In attempting to preempt congressional action, Truman ordered the dismissal of any worker for whom there were "reasonable grounds" for suspicion of disloyalty. Though permitting a loose definition of *loyalty*, Truman nevertheless attempted to protect the rights of individuals by requiring proof (not just suspicion) of disloyalty and by limiting the investigating powers of the FBI and the Loyalty Review Board. Such safeguards, however, were later sacrificed in the interests of administrative efficiency.

The attack on the American Communist party reflected an attempt to assure ideological conformity. The Communist party, though politically vocal, had steadily declined in numbers since 1939. And despite the headline revelations of Communist espionage, no one was convicted of espionage under Truman's loyalty program. Communism represented less a political threat than an unacceptable cultural alternative. Eastern European ethnics within the United States, for example, resented the loss of nationality of their homelands as well as Soviet attacks on their traditional churches. These groups supported a strong domestic anti-Communist program. In 1947 J. Edgar Hoover published a widely circulated article, "Red Fascism in the United States Today," which articulated a fear of totalitarianism in America. The next year, Hollywood produced *The Iron Curtain,* the first of many movies that depicted Communists as puppets of Moscow. In 1949 George Orwell's *1984* was condensed in *Reader's Digest,* while *Life* magazine compared the futurist tyranny with Soviet Russia. Such popular media described communism as a threat to individual liberty, as a pervasive Big Brother stifling all emotional relationships in the name of scientific socialism. The image of the cold-hearted bureaucracy, which in many ways mirrored Americans' fears about their own society, fueled the anti-Communist crusade.

Besides implementing loyalty checks of government employees, Truman also ordered Attorney General Clark to publicize a list of "subversive" organizations. This list, which in 1947 comprised ninety-one groups that Clark considered dangerous, served to stigmatize opponents of government policy. Other branches of government, defense industries, and private organizations accepted the list at face value and used it to discriminate against members. Clark also began a campaign to deport aliens accused of subversion. In a series of headline-grabbing arrests, Clark violated individual civil rights on flimsy charges of subversive activity. Clark's fervor resulted in unprecedented cooperation between the Justice Department and HUAC in the investigation of Hollywood screenwriters who refused to testify about their political affiliations.

The concept of "national security," which Truman used to justify the attack on communism, also stimulated a reorganization of the military elite. In July 1947 Congress passed the National Security Act, which placed the armed services within the Department of Defense, legalized the Joint Chiefs of Staff, created the National Security Council, and established the Central Intelligence Agency. Intended to coordinate military strategy and eliminate interservice competition, the new administrative machinery only intensified rivalry between the military branches for appropriations. The main issue focused on whether the navy or the air force would be the primary line of defense. In January 1948 a presidential commission, headed by Thomas Finletter, concluded that air power and polar route defense should be the basis of American military policy.

The decision to rely on air power had been supported by a massive public relations campaign by the faltering aircraft industry. "Since we are living in a world of peril," editorialized the sympathetic *Fortune* magazine, "it is not too much to say that the present state of the aircraft industry represents as grave an industrio-economic problem as exists in the U.S. today." Such promotional devices were not limited to private industry. In 1946 Truman

had called for Universal Military Training (UMT) as a way of maintaining American defense and to inculcate patriotism in young Americans. The Pentagon promptly initiated a massive public relations effort to win congressional approval; in that year, the army became the third largest advertiser in the United States. Despite such pressure, Congress rejected UMT in 1947. A congressional investigation then attacked the army for seeking to manipulate public opinion. "Government propaganda distorts facts with such authority that the person becomes prejudiced or biased in the direction which the Government propagandists wish to lead national thinking." This criticism failed to deter the military lobby, however, and the Pentagon public relations budget continued to grow, approaching $10 million by 1950.

TRUMAN AND MILITARY CRISIS

The attempt of the military to create a sense of crisis served to inflate not only Pentagon budgets but also the presidential ambitions of Harry Truman. In November 1947 Clark Clifford, the president's counsel, drafted a memorandum that assessed Truman's chances in the next election. In this paper Clifford argued that the president could successfully rebuild the New Deal coalition by appealing to the big-city labor vote and to minorities. To accomplish that task, Truman would have to undermine Wallace's support among liberals. Clifford therefore recommended that Truman "identify him and isolate him in the public mind with the Communists." As for foreign policy, the memorandum emphasized the importance of presidential leadership. "There is considerable political advantage to the Administration in its battle with the Kremlin." The creation of "a sense of crisis," stopping short of real war, Clifford suggested, would rally public support.

Clifford's strategy provided the background for presidential decision making. Despite its approval of the Truman Doctrine and the interim aid to Europe, Congress continued to debate the funding of the Marshall Plan. Taft, hoping to secure the Republican nomination, criticized the program as a "European TVA" and spoke about budget cutting. Wallace, who announced his candidacy in the Progressive party in December 1947, chastised the president for by-passing the U.N. and for provoking the Soviet Union. In January 1948 Truman requested a larger budget to underwrite American air power, but Congress seemed uninterested.

Soviet action suddenly disrupted the domestic scene in February 1948. The crisis began in Czechoslovakia, the nation that symbolized the futility of prewar appeasement. Though the Soviet Union had been willing to accept a coalition government that included non-Communists, it had forced the Czechs to reject participation in the Marshall Plan. The United States then assumed that Czechoslovakia, as a Soviet satellite, could not obtain American assistance without first adopting political changes. The Czechs therefore had to seek economic aid from the Soviet Union. The American decision to rebuild Germany also alarmed the Czechs, who had been early victims of Nazi expansion. These policies weakened the position of non-Communist Czechs. When an internal power struggle began in February 1948, the Communists managed to seize power. Americans reacted to this change with horror, viewing the episode as proof of Soviet aggression. Though newspapers spoke about the "fall" of Czechoslovakia, high admin-

istration officials had already assumed that Czechoslovakia was part of the Soviet bloc the previous year.

Truman nevertheless responded to the crisis with a determination not to repeat the 1938 sellout at Munich. When General Lucius Clay, the American military leader in Germany, reported "a subtle change in Soviet attitude," Truman sensed the imminence of war. On March 17, 1948, Truman addressed a joint session of Congress on the perilous situation. "Since the close of hostilities, the Soviet Union and its agents have destroyed the independence and democratic character of a whole series of nations in Eastern and Central Europe," he declared. "It is this ruthless course of action, and the clear design to extend it to the remaining free nations of Europe, that have brought about the critical situation in Europe today." Truman then requested passage of the Marshall Plan, enactment of UMT, and the resumption of selective service.

The president's somber appeal proved effective. Within one month, Congress voted to approve the Marshall Plan and passed a new selective service act. Conservatives once again managed to defeat UMT. But the legislature proved more than generous in allocating $3.5 billion for military purposes (25 percent more than the administration requested). Such funds revitalized the aircraft industry and reinforced the coalition between business and the military. The emphasis on military preparations also represented a rejection of the principles of the Marshall Plan, which had seen economic coercion as the key to victory in the Cold War.

The shift toward military confrontation in 1948 was dramatized by the Berlin blockade. Since the end of World War Two, the United States and the Soviet Union had been unable to agree on a final peace settlement. The disagreement initially had reflected different attitudes toward German reparations. The Soviet Union, devastated by war, had wished immediate payments from current production. But the United States, hoping to use economic pressure to create an Open Door in Eastern Europe and fearing Soviet strength, was reluctant to meet that demand. The State Department countered the Soviet argument by stressing the importance of economic stability in Germany and by suggesting that reparations be paid only after Germany had financed its imports from the United States.

The controversy over Germany in 1948 was complicated by a mutual fear that a rearmed Germany would support one of its former enemies against the other. Committed to containing Soviet communism, the United States could not tolerate a Soviet ally in central Europe. Similarly, the Soviet Union feared a renewed "capitalist encirclement." As the United States and Great Britain began to plan for the economic integration of their zones, the Soviet Union became more conciliatory, offering to negotiate on Lend-Lease, Austrian currency reform, and reparations. But the Western powers ignored these gestures and continued on a program of German currency reform.

Stalin correctly perceived that the currency question was but a preliminary to the creation of an independent German state, firmly wedded to the Western camp. One day after the West announced a new currency, the Soviet Union closed overland routes into Berlin, a city that was jointly occupied by the wartime allies. The United States military immediately prepared for war. Truman, fearful of capitulating to the Soviets, decided to support Berlin. The decision precipitated a gigantic airlift of food and supplies that lasted for nearly eleven months. Unwilling to go to war, Stalin was forced to accept the Western fait accompli in Germany.

The Berlin blockade emphasized the importance of military preparations. "We are playing with fire while we have nothing with which to put it out," declared Secretary of State Marshall. In July 1948 Truman ordered B-29 bombers to England. These were the only American planes capable of dropping atom bombs in Europe, though they were not modified for such work until 1949. The Soviet Union had not yet developed nuclear weapons. But for the first time, atomic weapons had become an instrument of American foreign policy. Truman, who had ordered the atomic bombing of Japan, was prepared to act again.

The repetition of Truman Doctrine rhetoric in the spring of 1948 enabled Congress to reverse administration policy in Asia. The corruption of the regime of Chiang Kai-shek, together with the growing success of the Communist Mao Tse-tung, had persuaded the State Department to allow the Chinese civil war to run its course. But the Truman Doctrine had suggested that *any* Communist expansion threatened American interests. Though the administration was prepared to overlook that inconsistency, conservatives in Congress, known as the China Lobby, insisted on a literal application of the Truman Doctrine. In approving the Marshall Plan, therefore, Congress appropriated funds for the Chiang regime. Thus the United States became committed to a reactionary, but non-Communist, Chinese government in a manner that influenced Asian foreign policy for three decades.

The original decision to abandon Chiang also shaped American policy toward Japan. Recognizing the advantage of Japan as an ally, the United States moved to establish a "democratic," non-Communist government for its former enemy. In 1947 the United States extended economic assistance to bolster Japanese industry and trade. These economic measures were matched by a strengthening of American military bases in Japan. Such policies would protect American interests in Asia, even after Mao had defeated Chiang.

Shifting to a military strategy, the United States moved to solidify its own sphere of influence in Latin America. Though the Truman administration condemned Soviet power in Eastern Europe, the United States had assumed that it would control Latin America. In 1945 the State Department had promoted Articles 51 and 52 of the U.N. Charter, which allowed regional defense pacts. It also had supported U. N. membership for such overtly Fascist countries as Argentina. In 1947 the United States endorsed the Rio Pact, which provided for collective self-defense of the Western Hemisphere. The following year, the Bogotá Treaty created the Organization of American States, which facilitated hemispheric consultations through a regional defense committee. The United States also accepted a clause disavowing intervention in the internal or external affairs of another state.

In creating this hemispheric alliance, the United States avoided any economic commitments to this impoverished portion of the world. Unlike its policy toward Europe, the State Department pressed for private economic development rather than government programs. Yet in a series of bilateral agreements, the United States agreed to provide Latin America with military assistance, including the training of military officers. Such military support served to protect the reactionary status quo throughout Latin America. The United States readily accepted the fiction that social protest in Latin America was Communist inspired.

THE ELECTION OF 1948

Truman's militant foreign policy in 1948 worked, as Clifford had predicted, to increase the president's popularity. Truman also used the Czech crisis to read Henry Wallace out of the Democratic party. The former vice president had scored well in early public opinion polls, indicating that he might drain enough liberal support from Truman to assure a Republican victory. In a St. Patrick's Day speech, however, Truman followed Clifford's advice about isolating Wallace from non-Communist liberals. "I do not want and I will not accept the political support of Henry Wallace and his Communists," he declared. By identifying Wallace with the Soviet threat, Truman kept many liberals from supporting the third-party candidate.

The split between liberals seemed to ensure a Republican victory. To assure that success, the Republicans passed over Taft, whose midwestern conservatism might alienate the eastern vote, and nominated the 1944 standard-bearer, Thomas E. Dewey of New York. The party platform was moderate, if not liberal. The Republicans criticized the postwar inflation, for which they blamed high government expenditures. The party also called for federal support of housing, farm payments, the abolition of the poll tax, a permanent FEPC, and increases in social security allotments. On matters of foreign policy, Republicans shared Truman's Cold War outlook. Endorsing the spirit of a bipartisan foreign policy, the platform advocated "stopping partisan politics at the water's edge." This bipartisan strategy, designed to allow Republicans to share responsibility and glory in the Cold War effort, freed the incumbent party from having to explain the origins of the controversy with the Soviet Union.

The Democratic party approached the election with considerably less confidence. The ADA, skeptical of Truman's liberal credentials, attempted to persuade General Dwight D. Eisenhower to run for president, but he refused the invitation. With Truman controlling the party machinery at the national convention in July 1948, his nomination was assured. In accepting the candidacy, the president revealed an ingenious campaign strategy. He would call the Republican-dominated Eightieth Congress into a special session to allow his opponents to enact their party platform. Then the public could ascertain the sincerity of the Republican candidates.

Though Truman dominated the party convention, he could not prevent a major split over the party platform. The president had joined a southern coalition in supporting a weak position on civil rights. But the ADA, having lost in its attempt to obtain a liberal candidate, now determined to win a liberal platform on civil rights. Led by Minneapolis Mayor Hubert H. Humphrey, the liberals carried the platform fight to the floor of the convention. "The time has arrived for the Democratic party to get out of the shadow of states' rights," Humphrey declared, "and walk forthrightly into the bright sunshine of human rights." The speech galvanized liberal support, and a strong civil rights plank was voted part of the Democratic platform.

The Democrats' stand on civil rights alarmed southern delegates, who bolted from the convention. Three days later, dissidents from thirteen southern states convened in Birmingham, Alabama, to form a States' Rights party and nominate Governor Strom Thurmond of South Carolina for president. The Dixiecrats, as they were called, opposed such civil rights measures as eliminating the poll tax, a permanent FEPC,

and a federal antilynching law. This position reflected more than a refusal to extend civil rights to blacks. It also attacked the growth of the federal government bureaucracy, seeing federal legislation as a threat to local government on such basic matters as voting and law enforcement. The Dixiecrats never expected an electoral victory. They failed to attract such prominent southern leaders as Harry Byrd of Virginia and Richard Russell of Georgia, who remained within the Democratic party. But the Dixiecrats did hope to weaken the Democratic slate to emphasize their importance to the national party.

The supporters of Henry Wallace met in late July to organize the Progressive party and to nominate Wallace and Senator Glen Taylor of Idaho as running mates. Though Communists held important positions within the party, the Progressive platform represented a commitment to liberal principles. Offering a genuine alternative to Truman's Cold War and Dewey's bipartisanship, the Progressives insisted that "responsibility for ending the tragic prospect of war is a joint responsibility of the Soviet Union and the United States." Quoting Wallace's statement that "there is no difference which cannot be settled by peaceful, hopeful negotiation," the Progressives denounced "anti-Soviet hysteria as a mask for monopoly, militarism, and reaction."

On domestic issues the party endorsed a strong civil rights position, and Wallace refused to speak to any segregated assembly. In internal matters the Progressives adopted party rules that based representation on population rather than as a reward for party power. Yet the Progressives could never overcome their association with communism. "Politicians of both major parties have tried to pin the Communist tag on the followers of Henry A. Wallace," acknowledged pollster George Gallup in July 1948. "Apparently their efforts have succeeded." The Wallace campaign was hampered by systematic harassment, which included mob violence and the denial of public meeting places.

While Dixiecrats and Progressives sniped at Truman, the special session of the Eightieth Congress convened. Republican party leaders resented Truman's election strategy. If they enacted their platform promises, the president would get credit for forcing their hands; if not, they would appear hypocritical. Amid much futile discussion, they chose the latter path and adjourned without enacting significant legislation. This decision provided Truman with plenty of campaign ammunition. Not only was the Eightieth Congress reactionary, the president charged, but it was a "do-nothing" bunch. Truman carried this message in a strenuous "whistle-stop" campaign in which he delivered hundreds of speeches throughout the land.

Truman's intent was to recapture the New Deal supporters. His stinging veto of the Taft-Hartley law in 1947 had won him the endorsement of organized labor. This support was reinforced by the purging of Communists from the CIO leadership. As the big unions worked to prove their non-Communist orthodoxy, Truman appeared as their only logical choice. Wallace, whose New Deal credentials were as sound as Truman's, could not overcome the Communist taint. Meanwhile, Truman appealed to the farm vote by blaming Republicans for weakening the support program at a time when food prices had begun to slip.

Truman also benefited from the departure of the Dixiecrats. Though he had accepted the report of his civil rights commission in 1947, Truman had been slow to implement its proposals. Wallace's attack on racism forced the president to act. With southern Democrats nominally out of the party, Truman had less to lose by taking a bold stand on civil rights. In July 1948 he prohibited discrimination in federal employment and ordered the end of segregation in the armed services. Truman also campaigned in Harlem, where he promised support of civil rights legislation. Unlike Wallace, Truman never launched a full-scale attack on Jim Crow laws. Yet black voters remained faithful to the Democratic party.

While Truman castigated Republican conservatism, Dewey coasted toward what appeared an easy victory. He failed to challenge Truman's foreign policy, despite the crisis of the Berlin blockade. He also ignored the startling testimony of Whittaker Chambers, a former editor of *Time* magazine, who told HUAC that a State Department official, Alger Hiss, had been a member of the Communist party. Dewey's self-confidence was based on pre-election public opinion polls that forecast a Republican victory.

These prophecies were overturned in November when Truman defeated Dewey by more than two million votes. In the electoral college Truman's 304 votes topped Dewey's 189 and Thurmond's 34. Wallace, who gathered only 1.1 million votes, half of them in New York, gained no electoral votes. Truman's upset victory reflected the accuracy of Clifford's pre-election strategy. Truman did best in areas of New Deal strength as voters adhered to their party identities and voted on party lines. This pattern of party voting meant that Truman was most successful in northern cities, where he attracted the votes of labor, Jews, Catholics, and blacks. He also won over midwestern farmers who had abandoned the Democratic party in the late thirties. Declining prices in 1948 renewed farmer anxieties about an agricultural depression.

THE FAIR DEAL

Truman's victory also returned a Democratic majority to Congress. In January 1949 the president eagerly greeted the Eighty-first Congress with an ambitious legislative program. "Every segment of our population and every individual," he declared, "has a right to expect from our Government a fair deal." Truman's Fair Deal was an extension of Roosevelt's New Deal. It called for increased social security and minimum wages, civil rights legislation, federal aid to education, a program of national health insurance, and a repeal of Taft-Hartley. But Truman overestimated his political strength.

The Fair Deal soon encountered stiff resistance from the true majority in Congress — a conservative coalition of southern Democrats and midwestern Republicans. By controlling the congressional committee system, these groups prevented serious consideration of Truman's proposals. In May 1949 Truman agreed to scrap most of the Fair Deal. Though he remained committed to repealing Taft-Hartley, neither he nor heavy pressure from organized labor could persuade Congress to act. The legislature did extend social security benefits and raise minimum wages. But these benefits were usually insufficient even by the government's standards of living. Congress also enacted a Public Housing Act in 1949 that provided for urban slum clearance and government-funded construction of low-income dwellings. The measure was narrowly passed only because of a severe housing shortage. Yet most of the authorized buildings were never constructed, and the Truman administration was unwilling to challenge an uncooperative real estate lobby.

Truman's drive for civil rights legislation also stalled in Congress. After unsuccessfully attempting to liberalize the Senate's rules regarding filibusters, the administration watched its program languish in committee. Truman demonstrated his commitment to civil rights by rejecting a southern compromise that would have left enforcement powers in the states. But the president recognized the power of the congressional committee system and chose to avoid a hopeless skirmish. The Eighty-second Congress, elected in 1950, failed even to consider a civil rights bill out of committee.

Truman's support of civil rights within the executive branch was also inconsistent. Despite his 1948 order desegregating the armed forces, the military evaded enforcement of the president's decision. In Truman's inaugural parade of 1949, black soldiers marched with whites, but the army blocked full integration by segregating platoons. This pattern of quasi-integration persisted during the Korean War. Moreover, white military officers frequently court-martialed black soldiers on dubious charges. In Europe the military did not even begin desegregation until 1952.

Truman's Department of Justice supported civil rights suits by filing friendly briefs with the Supreme Court. But the FHA continued to accept residential segregation, even after the Court disallowed restrictive covenants. Truman also proved slow to re-establish the FEPC after the outbreak of the Korean War. When he finally created such a committee, he offered no enforcement powers to halt discrimination in war industries. Despite this spotty record, Truman received praise from black leaders. "No occupant of the White House since the nation was born," wrote the NAACP's Walter White in 1952, "has taken so frontal or constant a stand against racial discrimination as has Harry S. Truman." And after deciding not to seek renomination in 1952, Truman became more

General Eisenhower reviews black troops in 1945. The armed services remained segregated until the Korean War. (Dwight D. Eisenhower Library)

outspoken in defense of equal rights for blacks. "The full force and power of the federal government must stand behind the protection of rights guaranteed in the federal Constitution," he told the graduating class of Howard University.

The limitations of Truman's Fair Deal reflected a significant shift in liberal thinking. After the defeat of Wallace, liberals repudiated political association with communism, and in 1950 Wallace himself rejected the Progressive party. The move away from the Left was articulated by Arthur M. Schlesinger, Jr., in *The Vital Center,* published in 1949. Like his mentor, Reinhold Niebuhr, Schlesinger perceived communism and fascism as indistinguishable threats to freedom. Seeking a perfect society, Schlesinger argued, was naive and self-deceptive. Now he called upon Americans to become political "realists," to shun the idealism of perfectionist movements. Such attitudes justified the removal of Communists from public positions. By 1949 the CIO had completed the expulsion of eleven unions.

A BIPARTISAN FOREIGN POLICY

Schlesinger's defense of power as an instrument of policy translated in foreign affairs to a justification of Truman's Cold War. The administration also obtained valuable support in June 1948, when a bipartisan Senate passed the Vandenberg Resolution, which permitted the United States to participate in a military alliance with the nations of Western Europe. Spurred by the Berlin crisis, the State Department proceeded to negotiate the North Atlantic Treaty Organization (NATO) treaty. In January 1949 Truman announced that the United States would provide military aid to Western Europe; three months later the NATO pact was signed in Washington. Meanwhile, the United States worked feverishly to create a new West German state; and in May 1949 the Federal Republic emerged as a member of the Western alliance.

The NATO pact institutionalized the division of Europe into spheres of influence. Though the treaty obligated the United States to send military assistance to its European allies, State Department planners anticipated no imminent war. Nor did the treaty add to American military power, since the United States still had a monopoly of atomic bombs. The purposes of NATO were primarily political. It forced the nations of Europe to abandon diplomatic independence and to align with the United States. It assured American dominance in Western Europe. "The Atlantic Pact is but the logical extension of the Monroe Doctrine," explained the chairman of the Senate Foreign Relations Committee. The Senate quickly ratified the treaty, but the House proved reluctant to appropriate funds for its implementation.

Then, in September 1949, Truman announced that the Soviet Union had exploded an atom bomb. Within a week the House provided funding for NATO.

The realization that the Soviet Union possessed an atomic bomb demonstrated the futility of atomic secrecy. Yet the political climate of 1949 discouraged cooperation with the Soviet Union. Instead, American policy makers now moved to consider the development of an even more deadly weapon, the hydrogen bomb. Though the Atomic Energy Commission and its civilian advisory committee recommended against building a thermonuclear device, Truman decided to proceed with its manufacture in January 1950. The nuclear arms race continued. By 1951 the United States had successfully tested its hydrogen bomb; within two years the Soviet Union did the same.

The decision to create bigger armaments had important political consequences. In seeking congressional approval of NATO, the administration had given assurances that the defense pact would not alter the status of Germany. By November 1949, however, the army had developed plans for rearming Germany. In 1950 the United States recommended the creation of ten German divisions. This proposal acknowledged a major reversal in European power arrangements since the end of World War Two. France, however, was horrified at the thought of a remilitarized Germany and protested vehemently. The United States overcame these objections by promising to station troops in Europe and by providing economic and military aid. Such assistance was sent to France under the guise of NATO defense. But the French also used this materiel to wage war against liberation movements in the colonies of Indochina and Algeria.

American indifference to economically oppressed peoples was further revealed by the Point Four program, an idea introduced in Truman's inaugural address. Asserting American responsibility to spread "the benefits of our scientific advances and industrial progress" to the "underdeveloped areas" of the world, the president called for a new foreign aid program. Despite the rhetoric, Point Four offered no alternatives to the existing pattern of international economic relations; the "underdeveloped areas" were seen as suppliers of raw materials and consumers of industrial goods. Nor did the program offer to alleviate the endemic poverty of these areas. Even so, the administration could not persuade Congress to appropriate more than a token $27 million in 1950. In practice, Point Four focused less on humanitarian assistance than on providing expert studies to facilitate private business investment. The emphasis on potential profit meant that more Point Four money was invested in industrializing areas like Canada than in impoverished nations like India.

While Americans resisted sending aid to "underdeveloped areas," conservative congressmen criticized the administration for failing to supply adequate assistance to Chiang Kai-shek. Though the State Department opposed such aid, the logic of the Truman Doctrine had obliged the United States to send hundreds of millions of dollars to the Nationalist regime. But the armies of Mao Tse-tung steadily hammered away at Chiang's crumbling forces, capturing American-supplied equipment and winning defections from the Nationalist government. By August 1949 the State Department saw the inevitability of a Communist victory and halted further assistance. "The only alternative open to the United States," asserted a State Department "White Paper," "was full-scale intervention in behalf of a government which had lost the confidence of its own troops and its own people." In December Chiang abandoned the mainland and fled to Taiwan.

Given the logic of containment, the Communist victory could be seen only as a devastating defeat of American foreign policy. The congressional China Lobby attacked the administration for failing to support an anti-Communist ally. Such criticism prevented Truman from seeking an accommodation with Mao. Instead, the United States adopted a policy of nonrecognition that lasted for more than two decades. The debate over military assistance to Chiang also shattered the bipartisan alliance in foreign affairs. After Chiang's defeat, the administration foreign policy was no longer immune from serious Republican attack.

Partisan suspicions were aggravated in February 1950, when Americans learned that Mao had signed a mutual assistance pact with the Soviet Union. Such revelations called for explanations. The "loss" of China and the Soviet explosion of an atom bomb indicated some serious errors of policy. But another ingredient was soon added to the story. In January 1950 Alger Hiss, a former State Department official, was convicted of perjury in his libel suit against Whittaker Chambers, who had accused Hiss of being a spy. The previous discovery of Soviet spies in Canada and the United States, together with the Hiss case, now reinforced the image of the Soviet Union as an internal menace. Republican leaders, believing that the Hiss case was only one strand in a complicated espionage network, condemned the "soft attitude of this Administration toward Government employees and officials who hold or support Communist attitudes."

MCCARTHY AND SUBVERSION

In February 1950 an obscure Wisconsin Republican, Senator Joseph R. McCarthy, discovered a strategy for bolstering his political career by attacking communism in government. "I have in my hands," he told the Women's Republican Club in Wheeling, West Virginia, "a list of 205 [government employees] that were made known to the Secretary of State as being members of the Communist party and who nevertheless are still working and shaping policy in the State Department." In later versions of that speech, McCarthy changed the number of alleged Communists in government, but he stuck to the rest of his story. Drawing considerable attention, McCarthy presented his evidence to the Senate. In a long, rambling speech based on irrelevant files, McCarthy maintained his exaggerated claims.

McCarthy's accusation of Communists in government appealed to the conservative Republican leadership that was looking for grounds to attack the Truman administration. Prestigious politicians like Robert Taft rallied to McCarthy's defense. Such partisan attitudes enabled McCarthy to flourish, even after a Senate investigatory committee, chaired by Millard Tydings, found no evidence to support his charges. In accepting the Tydings report, which described McCarthy's allegations as "a fraud and a hoax," the Senate voted along strict party lines. The pre-eminence of party loyalty defused the effect of the Tydings report and enabled McCarthy to remain a powerful force in the 1950 congressional elections. Taking to the campaign trail, McCarthy reiterated his accusations of "treachery and incompetence" in government. In Maryland he joined the Republican candidate in smearing Tydings with alleged Communist affiliation that contributed to the incumbent's defeat. In California McCarthy helped Nixon destroy Helen Gahagan Douglas, whom he dubbed the Pink Lady. Florida's Claude Pepper, an early critic of Truman's foreign policy, became the Red Pepper and went down in defeat. Illinois's Scott Lucas, Senate majority leader, fell to the conservative Everett Dirksen. McCarthy's impact on these contests remained unclear. But the 1950 elections resulted in a Congress controlled by conservative Republicans.

McCarthy's rash outbursts against communism reflected the political climate in 1950. Two years earlier Senator Karl Mundt and Congressman Nixon had unsuccessfully sponsored legislation for controlling the activities of domestic Communists. Their bill provided for the registration of all Communist organizations, creation of a Subversive Activities Control Board, banning of Communists from defense employment, and denial of such traditional privileges as passports and the use of the U.S. mail. In 1950 the measure was revived as the McCarran Internal Security bill. The new measure authorized the president to declare an "internal security emergency," which permitted the detention of suspected dissidents. Truman promptly vetoed the bill, "because any governmental stifling of the free expression of opinion is a long step toward totalitarianism." Congress nevertheless overrode the veto.

After the 1950 elections HUAC and McCarthy's Internal Security subcommittee continued to investigate disloyalty in government. The major target of their accusations was the State Department, which was blamed for deliberately subverting American foreign policy. Though critical of McCarthy, the administration reacted to these charges not by defending the civil liberties of the accused but by affirming its own anti-Communist credentials. Fearful of provoking further attacks, Truman vacillated on the question of disclosing confidential records to congressional investigators, finally offering some documents but not others.

McCarthy's popularity worried the president. Hoping to prevent further legislation, he decided to appoint a special commission, headed by Admiral Chester Nimitz, to review the government's internal security program. But when Congress delayed authorization of the commission, Truman acted independently. The rules established in 1947 required "reasonable grounds" for dismissal of suspected subversives. In April 1951, however, Truman issued an executive order that introduced a new standard for dismissal. According to the new policy, an employee could be fired when there was "reasonable doubt" about the person's loyalty. The shift in language effectively moved the burden of proof from the accuser to the accused.

Truman's innovation ironically lent credence to McCarthy's charge that existing procedures had been insufficient for preventing subversion. Thus, despite the changes, criticism of the administration persisted. Such pressure led Truman to broaden his loyalty program in 1952 to include civilian consultants in government. Truman also tightened the procedures for classifying government information. In taking these steps, Truman seemed as much interested in thwarting congressional attacks as in preventing actual disloyalty. This yielding to public pressure had the effect of legitimating McCarthy's inquisition.

The willingness of Americans to support the anti-Communist crusade reflected a series of interrelated values. After the high optimism of World War Two, the emergence of a Cold War was unexpected and alarming. These fears were aggravated by a dread of nuclear annihilation; the victims of London, Dresden, and Hiroshima had been innocent civilians. Instead of soothing these fears, the Truman administration intensified them in justifying its foreign policy.

Communism was seen not merely as a political system, but as a threat to the American way of life. Novelists like Mickey Spillane, Hollywood films like *Red Planet Mars* (1952), and a host of popular magazine articles portrayed communist values as a threat to American liberty. Atheism, bureaucracy, and totalitarianism were seen as the antithesis of American religion, family, individualism, and sense of community. Yet these social values already were threatened from within by the rootlessness of American society. "The unity we seek is more than material," declared Thomas Dewey in his 1948 acceptance speech. "Our problem is not outside ourselves. Our problem is within ourselves.... Spiritually, we have yet to find the means to put together the world's broken pieces, to bind up its wounds, to make a good society." To conservative Americans, the anti-Communist crusade seemed a logical defense against the disintegration of modern society. Such feelings justified blacklists, loyalty oaths, and public harassment.

THE KOREAN WAR

The sense of crisis provided the background for a reformulation of American foreign policy in 1950. At Truman's request the National Security Council prepared a comprehensive analysis of the world situation in a document labeled NSC–68. The paper reiterated the values that had influenced State Department decision making since 1945. "The Soviet Union, unlike previous aspirants to hegemony," it asserted, "is animated by a new fanatic faith, antithetical to our own, and seeks to impose its absolute authority over the rest of the world." The United States, NSC–68 declared, must be prepared to halt Soviet expansion and to reimpose American-oriented governments throughout the world.

Such lofty goals made it imperative for the United States to establish a global defense system that included hydrogen bombs, the expansion of conventional military forces, and a series of American-dominated alliances. To finance this ambitious program, NSC–68 recommended a quadrupling of the $13 billion national defense budget. This costly plan, however, would face considerable opposition from administration critics in Congress. Moreover, the Soviet Union had avoided any action to justify American intervention. Then, on June 25, 1950, North Korean troops invaded South Korea.

MAP 12.1   THE KOREAN WAR, 1950–1953

1. Maximum advance of North Koreans, Sept. 1950
2. Maximum advance of United Nations, Nov. 1950
3. Armistice Zone, July 1953

The territorial division of Korea reflected the larger conflicts of the Cold War. According to agreements made at the end of World War Two, the Soviet Union disarmed the Japanese armies north of the 38th parallel, while the United States occupied the area to the south. Both powers spoke about unifying Korea, but neither side wished to risk the dominance of the other. Instead, each global power supported a friendly regime in its sphere of influence. Though the United States extended aid to the South Korean government of Syngman Rhee, the State Department did not view the area as vital to American national security. In January 1950 Secretary of State Dean Acheson specifically excluded Korea and Taiwan from the American defense perimeter in the Pacific.

This statement may have emboldened the North Korean government, headed by the pro-Communist Kim Il Sung. When spring elections indicated the general unpopularity of the Rhee regime, North Koreans began a campaign for national elections that would lead to unification. These national goals may have coalesced with the objectives of the Soviet Union, which feared that the United States was rebuilding Japan as an Asian bulwark against communism. In any case, after a series of mutual border violations, North Koreans, supported by Soviet-built materiel, crossed the 38th parallel.

As the North Korean army advanced quickly through South Korea, Truman moved to halt the offensive. He immediately ordered American assistance to South Korea and directed the navy to sail between China and Taiwan to avoid an invasion of the Nationalist-held islands. The next day the United States called an emergency session of the U.N. Security Council, which, in the absence of the Soviet delegate, branded North Korea as an aggressor and demanded its retreat. As South Korean troops continued to collapse, however, Truman ordered American forces into action. "The attack upon Korea," he declared, "makes it plain beyond all doubt that communism has passed beyond the use of subversion to conquer independent nations." The U.N. subsequently approved Truman's independent action, giving international sanction to American foreign policy.

Truman's decision — as at the times of the Berlin blockade and the Soviet explosion of the atomic bomb — was made without consultation with congressional leaders. Most Americans nevertheless supported the president's action. Truman's claim that he was merely enforcing U.N. policy won the favor of liberals. Sixteen nations eventually participated in the war, but most of the resources came from the United States. Moreover, the American military commander, General Douglas MacArthur, took orders directly and exclusively from United States headquarters.

American forces arrived in Korea just in time to stop a complete North Korean victory. After hard fighting near the southern port of Pusan, the U.N. allies turned the tide of battle, forcing North Korean troops to retreat. At the start of the war, the United States insisted that it was fighting "solely for the purpose of restoring the Republic of Korea to its status prior to the invasion from the north." By September 1950, however, the temptation of wresting territory from Soviet dominance became overwhelming, and the administration authorized an American advance north of the 38th parallel. With the Soviet Union back in the Security Council, the United States resorted to its dominance of the General Assembly to win U.N. endorsement. MacArthur, supremely confident, promised a complete victory by Christmas. But 80 percent of America's 142,000 war casualties followed from this decision.

The invasion of North Korea raised serious questions about the limits of American intervention. In October Truman flew to Wake Island to confer with MacArthur and agreed to allow American troops to proceed to the Yalu River, which bordered China. The decision alarmed the Chinese government, already frustrated by the American defense of Taiwan. China warned the United States not to threaten its borders. When Truman ignored

that statement, Chinese troops crossed the Korean border to halt the American invasion. The bloodiest fighting of the war now forced the U.N. armies into a deadly retreat, driving them south of the 38th parallel.

Confrontation with China raised the possibility of another world war, including the use of nuclear weapons. But Truman exercised his power as commander-in-chief to restrain MacArthur's bellicosity and prevented an attack on Manchuria. Truman also responded to international pressure and decided not to use atomic

President Truman and General MacArthur meet at Wake Island to discuss Korean War strategy, 1950. It was the only time the two men met. (Department of State/Courtesy Harry S. Truman Library)

weapons. Yet the administration rebuffed proposals for international mediation of the dispute. Viewing the Chinese as pawns of a Soviet-dominated conspiracy, Truman articulated a domino theory of power that forced him to hold fast in Korea.

By 1951 the battle lines had again stabilized around the 38th parallel. But MacArthur chafed at the limits of American involvement and publicly criticized the president for refusing to wage all-out war. "There is no substitute for victory," he declared. Exasperated by MacArthur's arrogance, Truman fired his general. The decision provoked the wrath of conservatives, who welcomed MacArthur home with extraordinary parades and a unique address to a joint session of Congress. The general took the opportunity to condemn the idea of a limited war. The administration responded, first by reiterating the importance of civilian control of the military, and then by arguing that the Korean War needed to be seen in the context of a broader foreign policy. With Europe uppermost in their minds, American policy makers did not want to provoke Soviet intervention; nor did they wish to alienate their allies in Western Europe. By halting Communist expansion in Korea, the administration could claim a major Cold War victory.

The removal of MacArthur also paved the way for the opening of truce negotiations in June 1951. They lasted for two years, while the fighting continued. The two sides nearly reached agreement on a new boundary line in 1951. But then they disagreed about the repatriation of prisoners of war. The Chinese, following international law, insisted on the return of all prisoners. But the United States, unwilling to return anti-Communists to a Communist state, demanded voluntary repatriation. The impasse was breached only after the inau-

guration of President Dwight Eisenhower in 1953.

The Korean War provided an opportunity for a more aggressive foreign policy throughout the world. Recognizing that the U.N. had approved the Korean action only because the Soviet Union had boycotted the Security Council, the United States moved in 1950 to circumvent the veto power. In a "Uniting for Peace" resolution, the General Assembly announced its right to recommend military intervention in cases of veto in the Security Council. This provision altered the basic assumptions of Big Power diplomacy that had been established at Yalta and in the U.N. Charter. In effect, the United States was announcing the futility of negotiation as a way of establishing world order. Instead, it would use the General Assembly to legislate diplomacy. This situation assumed that the United States would be able to control a majority in the U.N.

The Korean War also committed the United States to supporting reactionary regimes in Asia. Though State Department officials had been prepared to accept a Chinese invasion of Taiwan in early 1950, the outbreak of Korean hostilities provided an excuse to send the Seventh Fleet to protect the besieged island. War with Communist Chinese in Korea exaggerated American fears of a "yellow peril." The prevalence of these attitudes troubled liberals at home. "We will never win the political war in Asia," warned the NAACP's *Crisis*, "as long as Koreans and Asiatics are 'gooks' in the eyes of our fighting men." Yet the specter of a densely populated anti-American Communist China served as a convenient rationale for maintaining an alliance with less perilous Asians in Taiwan and Japan.

These attitudes converged in the formulation of American policy toward Indochina. After the

United States refused to recognize his independence movement, Ho Chi Minh commenced a war of liberation against the French empire. Lacking alternatives, Ho reluctantly accepted assistance from Vietnam's traditional enemy, China. In January 1950 Mao's revolutionary government recognized that of Ho; two weeks later the Soviet Union did the same. Ho's cooperation with Communist nations persuaded the United States to offer additional aid to the French to suppress the liberation movement. After the outbreak of the Korean War, Truman extended this assistance to include military personnel.

In justifying this decision, the Truman administration followed the logic of NSC–68, which saw Indochina as the "key area of Southeast Asia." Besides being a source of "vitally important raw materials" such as rice, rubber, and tin, Indochina had extraordinary strategic value. "If Indo-China went," testified a State Department official in 1951, "the fall of Burma and the fall of Thailand would be absolutely inevitable." These would be followed by Communist victories in Malaya and India.

The State Department was also concerned about the ideological impact of the "fall" of Indochina. The success of a Communist-oriented liberation movement would suggest that world communism was invincible and so create a sense of defeatism in other parts of the globe. Finally, the State Department saw Indochina as the only non-Communist area for Japanese economic expansion. Just as the United States had opposed Japanese restrictions on the Open Door on the eve of World War Two, now American policy makers feared that unless Japan had extended trade opportunities in Southeast Asia, it would be forced into an economic arrangement with Communist China and the Soviet Union. Yet a capitalist-oriented Japan

was an essential aspect of America's containment of Asian communism. These assumptions led to increasing American commitments in Southeast Asia that culminated in the Vietnam War.

The desire to reinforce relations with Japan produced a new treaty in 1951. The pact restored Japanese control of the home islands but allowed American occupation of Okinawa. Japan also agreed to the stationing of American troops on her territory. When Japan's former victims in the Pacific raised the question of reparations, the United States warned against the higher danger of driving Japan into an alliance with Communist nations. The United States nevertheless offered assurances to protect Australia and New Zealand from future attack. These were formalized in the ANZUS treaty of 1951. With such alliances the United States established an anti-Communist barrier against Chinese and Soviet expansion.

American support of Japan as a bulwark against communism paralleled a realignment with the United States's former enemies in Europe. After the outbreak of the Korean War, the United States proceeded with its plans to rearm Germany. To overcome European objections, however, the United States had to agree to station American troops under the NATO command. This policy already had been recommended in NSC–68. But the Adenauer government of West Germany objected to the second-class status implied in the American plan for rearmament. In 1952 a meeting in Lisbon reached a compromise agreement that allowed German forces to enter a multinational European Defense Community (EDC). But the plan was never implemented.

The willingness to establish alliances with former enemies led to American support of Italy and Spain. In 1951 the Western allies agreed to lift military restrictions imposed on Italy in 1945. American policy toward Franco's Spain underwent a dramatic transformation. During World War Two Franco had supported the Axis powers who had helped him come to power in 1939. After the war the United States continued to oppose the Fascist regime. But by 1950 a coalition of conservative congressmen and military officers urged the administration to accept Franco as an anti-Communist ally.

In 1950 the United States extended its first loan to Spain; in 1951 Truman sent an ambassador to Madrid; in 1953 the United States signed a treaty allowing American military bases in Spain in exchange for American economic and military assistance. Like other recipients of American aid, Franco used these funds to suppress domestic revolutionary protest. Meanwhile, within the United States the Veterans of the Abraham Lincoln Brigade, whose members had fought against Franco in the Spanish civil war, was put on the attorney general's list of subversive organizations.

In supporting Spain, Italy, Germany, and Japan against China and the Soviet Union, the United States had radically reversed the Great Power alliance of World War Two. Secretary of State Dean Acheson summed up this transformation in 1952: "We are standing on the threshold of a New Europe and a New World."

SUGGESTED READINGS

The major issues of the Truman years are explored in great detail in Alonzo L. Hamby, *Beyond the New Deal: Harry S. Truman and American Liberalism* (1973). A detailed study of Truman's first administration is Robert J.

Donovan, *Conflict and Crisis: The Presidency of Harry S. Truman,* (1977). Also useful as an introduction to the period is an anthology, Barton J. Bernstein, ed., *Politics and Policies of the Truman Administration* (1970). A convenient collection of primary sources is Barton J. Bernstein and Allen Matusow, eds., *The Truman Administration* (1966).

The domestic policies of the Truman administration are examined in the works by McCoy and Ruetten and by Davies listed at the end of chapter 11. On farm policies, see Allen Matusow, *Farm Policies and Politics in the Truman Years* (1967); for labor, see R. Alton Lee, *Truman and Taft-Hartley* (1966). The Wallace candidacy is described in Richard J. Walton, *Henry Wallace, Harry Truman, and the Cold War* (1976), which contains many primary sources, and Norman D. Markowitz, *The Rise and Fall of the People's Century: Henry A. Wallace and American Liberalism* (1973). James T. Patterson's *Mr. Republican: A Biography of Robert A. Taft* (1972) details the career of the leading conservative.

The domestic anti-Communist crusade is described by Athan Theoharis, *Seeds of Repression: Harry S. Truman and the Origins of McCarthyism* (1971), and Alan D. Harper, *The Politics of Loyalty* (1969). For Joseph McCarthy, see the works listed at the end of chapter 13. A suggestive essay is Les K. Adler and Thomas G. Paterson, "Red Fascism: The Merger of Nazi Germany and Soviet Russia in the American Image of Totalitarianism," *American Historical Review*, 75 (1970). The close relationship between domestic anticommunism and foreign policy is presented in Richard M. Freeland, *The Truman Doctrine and the Origins of McCarthyism* (1972). For the split between liberals and radicals, see Mary Sperling McAuliffe, *Crisis on the Left* (1978).

A sensible and readable introduction to postwar foreign policy is Walter Lafeber, *America, Russia, and the Cold War, 1945–1975* (1976). Also valuable for exploring the origins of American policy is Daniel Yergin, *Shattered Peace: The Origins of the Cold War and the National Security State* (1977). For international economic affairs, see Fred L. Block, *The Origins of International Economic Disorder* (1977). A useful anthology of dissenters from Truman's policies is Thomas G. Paterson, ed., *Cold War Critics* (1971). The Korean War is examined by David Rees, *Korea* (1964) and Ronald Caridi, *The Korean War and American Politics* (1968). Also insightful is Ernest R. May, *"Lessons" of the Past: The Use and Misuse of History in American Foreign Policy* (1973). For a thorough analysis of the Rosenberg case, see Walter and Miriam Schneir, *Invitation to an Inquest* (1973).

Spotlight: The Case of Ethel and Julius Rosenberg

In June 1953, two New York Jews in their mid-thirties — Ethel and Julius Rosenberg — died in the electric chair for passing secret atomic bomb information to the Soviet Union during World War Two. "I consider your crime worse than murder," Judge Irving Kaufman told the young parents in imposing the death penalty. Their treason, he concluded, "caused . . . the Communist aggression in Korea, with the resultant casualties exceeding fifty thousand and who knows but that millions more of innocent people may pay the price." President Dwight Eisenhower echoed Kaufman's reasoning in rejecting a last-minute plea for executive clemency. "By immeasurably increasing the chances of atomic war," he declared, "the Rosenbergs may have condemned to death tens of millions of innocent people all over the world."

Throughout the lengthy legal proceedings, however, the Rosenbergs maintained their innocence, even rejecting an offer of clemency from the Eisenhower administration in exchange for a full confession. Instead, the convicted spies insisted that they were victims of a government conspiracy provoked by their leftist political beliefs. There was a political "frame-up," Julius Rosenberg declared, "to establish a fear paralysis among outspoken progressives and to stifle criticism and opposition" to the Cold War. "We are the first victims of American Fascism," alleged Ethel Rosenberg in her last letter. These claims aroused passionate debate at home and abroad, leading thousands of Europeans to protest outside American embassies and to flood the White House with petitions for mercy.

Eisenhower, like his Democratic predecessor Harry Truman, remained unmoved. He argued that a show of compassion would reinforce a Communist belief that the United States was "weak and fearful." Such intransigence reflected the immense symbolic importance of the Rosenberg case. As a symptom of the Cold War, the trial and sentence dramatized the political changes that had occurred in the United States since the Grand Alliance of World War Two. For the Rosenbergs had been found guilty of passing secrets not to the enemy, but to a wartime ally.

Imposing the death sentence also served notice to political dissenters about the consequences of radical opposition. That the Rosenbergs were convicted largely on the testimony of confessed spies who had turned state's evidence to obtain lesser punishments alarmed other radicals who feared similar reprisals from former comrades. Such threats, as Julius Rosenberg predicted, helped to undermine the American Left, especially the Communist party. Fearing further attacks, many leaders of the Communist party went "underground" to prevent a complete destruction of the radical movement. Others simply deserted the party. Both strategies seriously weakened the Communist organization and facilitated the creation of an anticommunist consensus.

The political intensity surrounding the Rosenberg case was closely related to popular fears and misunderstandings about atomic energy. During World War Two, the Office of War Information conducted a successful publicity campaign warning civilians of the importance of secrecy in matters of war production and troop movements. The explosion of atomic bombs over Japan in 1945 seemed to vindicate the lessons of wartime secrecy. At the war's end, military leaders urged that atomic energy remain under military control to preserve an American monopoly over atomic secrets. This position soon met indignant reaction from the nation's leading scientists, who emphasized that the theoretical basis of the atomic bomb was well understood by physicists throughout the world. Congress reacted to a scientists' lobby by establishing civilian control over atomic energy.

Though scientific leaders predicted that other nations could develop atomic bombs in less than a decade, political and military leaders preferred to believe that the Soviet Union lacked the technological expertise to produce atomic weapons for another generation. Such beliefs encouraged the Truman administration to flaunt American atomic power during such crises as the Berlin blockade. These illusions were rudely broken in September 1949 when President Truman announced that the Soviet Union had exploded an atomic bomb. The president emphasized that the Soviet success had been expected by American scientists. But critics of the administration soon charged, in the words of Senator Karl Mundt, that "Communist espionage" had permitted the Soviet Union to acquire "the secrets of our atomic bomb."

These assertions of communist espionage reflected a naive appraisal of Soviet technology, the belief that Soviet science could not compete effectively with capitalist industry. Moreover, as the United States moved quickly to develop a more powerful hydrogen bomb, the idea of American technological superiority was especially comforting. From these assumptions, the only explanation of the Soviet atomic achievement was that spies had passed information to the enemy. Such conclusions ironically were shared by the Rosenbergs' defense attorneys. During the trial, the Rosenberg defense urged that prosecution testimony about the bomb be impounded by the court to prevent the dispersal of "secret" information. (Such trial errors may have resulted from the refusal of other lawyers to enter the case for fear of political reprisal. Significantly, after the trial, disbarment proceedings were begun against the Rosenbergs' lawyer, Emanuel Bloch.)

Suspicions of espionage activity had been nourished in the postwar years by the elaborate confessions of two self-admitted spies, Elizabeth Bentley and Whittaker Chambers, who testified that Soviet agents had infiltrated the United States government. Despite detailed FBI investigations, Bentley's charges led to no indictments. But Chambers's allegations culminated in November 1949, two months after the Soviet explosion, in the second trial of Alger Hiss, a State Department official accused of spying, and resulted in Hiss's conviction for perjury in January 1950. The following month, the British government announced the arrest of Klaus Fuchs, a British scientist who had worked on the atomic bomb, for espionage. Within a week, Senator Joseph McCarthy claimed to have evidence of communist subversion of the State Department.

The Hiss conviction and the arrest of Fuchs seemed to substantiate McCarthy's charge of the existence of an espionage ring in the United States. Government officials began an intensive search for communist spies. The temper of the times may be gauged from a warning of Columbus, Ohio, police officers to local teenagers to be suspicious of "any new member of a group whose background is not an open book" and by a Birmingham, Alabama, ordinance that banished from the city "anyone caught talking to a Communist in a 'nonpublic place,' or anyone who passed out literature that could be traced, even remotely, to a Communist hand." In this atmosphere of distrust, the FBI announced the arrest of Fuchs's American accomplice, a chemist named Harry Gold, in May 1950.

Gold's arrest was followed by several others, including that of a Brooklyn machinist, David Greenglass, who worked at the wartime atomic bomb project in Los Alamos. The outbreak of the Korean War in June 1950 underscored the seriousness of Greenglass's offense and, after intensive FBI questioning, he named as coconspirators his sister and brother-in-law, Ethel and Julius Rosenberg. Other accused accomplices included several of Rosenberg's acquaintances, including a college classmate, Morton Sobell.

Besides an interest in left-wing politics, the members of this alleged spy network shared a common ethnic heritage: they were all Jewish. The idea of an international Jewish conspiracy had been widely circulated among right-wing American groups since the beginning of the twentieth century. The Gold-Greenglass-Rosenberg-Sobell alliance seemed to fit a stereotype of subversive Jews. Government officials therefore took special care to avoid the appearance of anti-Semitism. Chosen as presiding judge was a Jew, Kaufman, as were the chief prosecuting attorney, Irving Saypol, and his assistant Roy Cohn (who later achieved notoriety as chief counsel for Senator Joseph McCarthy). Despite such efforts, however, critics of the case argued that Kaufman, Saypol, and Cohn represented a type of American Judaism different from that of the defendants. Whereas the court officials symbolized the melting-pot tradition of Jewish assimilationism, the Rosenbergs remained closer to their Old World roots, identifying strongly with the victims of Nazi racism, interspersing their language with Yiddish, and living near their childhood homes on the Lower East Side. Moreover, there were no Jews on the jury.

The Rosenbergs were accused of no overt act, merely of "conspiracy" to commit espionage, a crime difficult to substantiate. The government's case hinged primarily on the testimony of their alleged accomplices, Gold and Greenglass. Many states, including New York, limited the applicability of such accomplice testimony, but the federal courts applied no restrictions. Moreover, government officials used the press as a forum in which to assert the guilt of the defendants. During the trial, Judge Kaufman overruled defense objections and permitted questioning of the Rosenbergs' political beliefs, presumably to demonstrate a connection between their left-wing sympathies and their willingness to spy. Such rulings enabled the prosecution to benefit from widespread anti-Communist sentiment and to reinforce the image of an international conspiracy.

The evidence against the Rosenbergs nevertheless remained open to various interpretations. Greenglass claimed, for example, that the Rosenbergs had been rewarded by the Soviet Union with expensive gifts, including a valuable table. The defendants emphasized their relative poverty, however, and insisted that they had purchased an inexpensive table at a New York department store. Not until after the trial was the table located; its markings seemed to corroborate the Rosenbergs' testimony. Similarly, the prosecution attempted to prove that the Rosenbergs had contemplated flight from the country by introducing alleged passport photographs; the government failed, however, to introduce other evidence that implied that the photos were *not* for passports. Subsequent studies also suggest that a hotel registration card, introduced only in photostat, might have been forged in the original.

Despite such problematical evidence, the appellate procedure prevented a re-hearing of the trial. Though the Rosenbergs' attorneys carried their pleas to the Supreme Court, they could appeal only judicial *procedures,* not trial evidence. A few days before the execution date in June 1953, however, Supreme Court Justice William O. Douglas stayed the sentence pending further examination of certain legal technicalities. Aware that the Eisenhower administration was negotiating a Korean War truce, Douglas may have hoped that a more peaceful political climate would result in a lesser sentence. But the Eisenhower administration intervened to persuade Chief Justice Fred Vinson to recall the Court to a special unprecedented session, which vacated Douglas's stay. Within two days, the Rosenbergs were dead.

This haste in implementing the death sentence revealed unusual cooperation between the judicial system and the executive branch. Documents released under the Freedom of Information Act indicate that Judge Kaufman consulted with prosecuting attorneys before imposing sentences. The judge also drafted elaborate denials of defense motions prior to even hearing those arguments. He refused to examine new evidence, such as the mysterious table. And to avoid the Rosenbergs' death occurring on the Jewish sabbath, he accelerated rather than delayed the time of execution.

Kaufman's resolution stemmed from his perception of the Cold War. "This country is engaged in a life and death struggle with a completely different system," he declared in rhetoric that had become familiar since the end of World War Two. "All our democratic institutions are ... directly involved in this great conflict.... The punishment to be meted out in this case must therefore serve the maximum interest for the preservation of our society against these traitors in our midst."

These ideological imperatives justified loyalty oaths, blacklists, preparation of concentration camps for political prisoners, increased armaments, an aggressive foreign policy, and the execution of the only atomic spies who maintained their innocence. Morton Sobell, accused of indirect complicity and who also maintained his innocence, received a thirty-year sentence (he served eighteen years). David Greenglass faced fifteen years (he served ten); his wife, a confessed coconspirator, was never indicted. (Gold, convicted in another court, received a maximum thirty-year sentence). This pattern of punishment indicates that, Kaufman's language notwithstanding, the severity of the Rosenbergs' sentence reflected not the crime, but their refusal to admit guilt. In a war of moral absolutes — a conflict between American capitalism and Soviet communism — Ethel and Julius Rosenberg remained conscientious objectors.

The ambiguities of the Rosenberg case continue to attract wide interest. There are at least three novels based on the case: Helen Yglesias's *How She Died,* E. L. Doctorow's *The Book of Daniel,* and Robert Coover's *The Public Burning*; a play, Donald Freed's *Inquest*; and a documentary film, "The Unquiet Death of Julius and Ethel Rosenberg." These works emphasize the uncertainties of the evidence and the shadows of doubt that might have led to acquittal in calmer times. They argue strongly that the political climate of the early fifties prevented a fair trial. In 1974, the Rosenbergs' children, Michael and Robert Meeropol, formed a National Committee to Reopen the Rosenberg Case. "To be writing an opinion in a case affecting two lives after the curtain has been rung down upon them has the appearance of pathetic futility," wrote Supreme Court Justice Felix Frankfurter three days after the execution. "But history also has its claims."

Chapter 13

THE EISENHOWER ADMINISTRATION, 1952–1960

By 1952 the Truman administration had lost control of its foreign and domestic policies. Truman's adoption of the principles of containment had wrecked earlier State Department hopes for an international Open Door. Even worse, containment had bogged down in the military quagmire of Korea, a "limited" war that promised neither victory nor an early end. On the home front, Truman's Fair Deal lacked the political base to overcome the opposition of congressional conservatives. In the Senate, Joseph McCarthy continued his campaign to expose alleged Communists in government, capturing headlines by his brash condemnations. Republican leaders, hoping to embarrass the administration, supported McCarthy's actions. Truman's difficulties were compounded by revelations of corruption by high administration officials.

THE ELECTION OF 1952

These problems provided the Republicans with a campaign slogan for 1952 — "K_1C_2": Korea, Communism, Corruption. But despite the Democrats' vulnerability, the Republicans feared a repetition of the disastrous election of 1948. Senator Robert Taft, the leading Republican conservative, worked feverishly to win his party's nomination, believing that the liberal wing offered a poor alternative to the "socialistic" New Deal. "The greatest enemy of liberty," declared Taft in 1952, "is the concentration of power in Washington." Taft also questioned an internationalist foreign policy, believing that heavy expenditures abroad would cause economic collapse at home. These Old Guard attitudes were challenged by Republican liberals such as New York's Thomas Dewey, who accepted a Cold War foreign policy and recognized the impossibility of dismantling the New Deal. They saw Taft's brand of Republicanism as inevitably doomed.

Liberal Republicans turned their attention to a man who claimed to have no interest in presidential politics: General Dwight David Eisenhower. As supreme commander of NATO forces in Europe, Eisenhower refused to take a public political stand. His political beliefs were sufficiently ambiguous for Truman to offer him the Democratic nomination in 1952. Eisenhower was too conservative to run as a Democrat. But unlike Taft, Eisenhower believed in the importance of American military presence in Western Europe. In June 1952 Eisenhower returned from Europe to seek the presidential nomination. The general's immense popularity soon swamped the Taft candidacy. After a brief convention skirmish, Eisenhower captured the Republican nomination in July. As a concession to Taft's supporters, Eisenhower chose the right wing Californian, Richard Milhous Nixon, as his running mate.

The Republican party platform expressed the K_1C_2 formula. "There are no Communists in the Republican Party," the platform boasted, but the Democrats "shielded Traitors to the Nation in high places." Such subversive infiltration had caused the defeat of Chiang Kai-shek and had embroiled the nation in the Korean War. Denouncing the policy of containment as "negative, futile, and immoral," the platform promised to bring "genuine independence" to the "captive peoples" of Eastern Europe. In offering an alternative to containment, this plank appealed to the Eastern European immigrant voters, who traditionally had been Democrats. When linked to the McCarthyite attack on communism, it strengthened Republican support among Catholics. The platform

also adopted a conservative position on civil rights. Though condemning bigotry, Republicans insisted that the state governments had primary responsibility to protect civil rights. This defense of states' rights broadened the party's appeal in the South.

While Eisenhower promised "to lead a great crusade . . . for freedom," the Democrats searched for a party leader. Having announced his own retirement, Truman supported Governor Adlai Stevenson of Illinois. But Stevenson steadfastly refused the candidacy, partly because he wished to remain independent of the incumbent president, and partly because he recoiled from challenging Eisenhower's enormous popularity. While Stevenson hesitated, the contest centered on Georgia Senator Richard B. Russell, an archconservative; Averell Harriman, a liberal Cold Warrior of New York; and Tennessee Senator Estes Kefauver, who had gained national attention through a televised investigation of organized crime. But Russell's conservatism had little support outside the South, Harriman's liberalism threatened to create another Dixiecrat secession, and Kefauver's attack on crime brushed too closely to the big-city political bosses. The Democratic National Convention then turned to the noncandidate Stevenson, who promised to "talk sense to the American people." To balance the party in the South, the Democrats gave the vice presidential nomination to John Sparkman, a segregationist senator from Alabama.

Though Stevenson recognized the handicap of association with the Truman administration, the Democratic campaign revealed a continuity of principles and policies. "In Korea," Stevenson declared, "we took a long step toward building a security system in Asia," and he expressed pride in American "courage to resist that ruthless, cynical aggression." Stevenson also echoed the president's position on domestic communism. Though criticizing McCarthy's attacks on "faithful public servants," the Democratic candidate applauded a "healthy apprehension about the communist menace in our country." Describing communism as the "strangulation of the individual," Stevenson argued that American Communists "have surrendered their right to our trust."

Trying to rid himself of Truman's political liabilities, Stevenson remained cautiously conservative. Despite pressure from Truman, Stevenson took a moderate position on civil rights, emphasizing the importance of state sovereignty. Only after intense criticism from liberals did he endorse a permanent Fair Employment Practices Commission (FEPC). This belated ges-

ture cost Stevenson significant support from blacks, while alienating southern Democrats. Stevenson further aroused southern Democrats by opposing state control of offshore oil wells, a stance that led powerful southern leaders to repudiate his candidacy. Stevenson's hesitancy to attack the Taft-Hartley labor law also offended a traditional Democratic labor constituency, and he nearly lost the support of labor unions. Stevenson's attempt to rise above party strife brought him closer to the Republican camp, blurring the differences between the parties.

While Stevenson struggled to chart an independent course, Eisenhower posed as a candidate above parties. After making a postconvention peace with Taft, Eisenhower scrupulously

MAP 13.1   THE ELECTION OF 1952

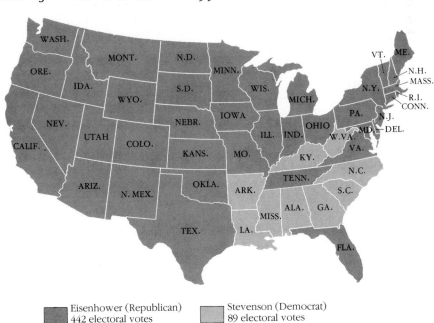

Eisenhower (Republican)
442 electoral votes

Stevenson (Democrat)
89 electoral votes

avoided antagonizing Old Guard Republicans. Though personally insulted by McCarthy's attacks on General George Marshall, Eisenhower's former superior, the nominee quietly deleted a defense of Marshall when speaking in McCarthy's home state of Wisconsin. Eisenhower also avoided direct attacks on Truman, leaving the bitter campaign oratory to Nixon. Eisenhower adopted the beneficent role of great crusader, promising to restore morality to government. He allowed his running mate to hammer away at "Adlai the appeaser . . . who got a Ph.D. from Dean Acheson's College of Cowardly Communist Containment."

Nixon's role as Eisenhower's shotgun suddenly backfired when newspapers reported that the vice presidential candidate possessed a secret "millionaire's" fund to defray political expenses while serving in the Senate. Democrats immediately used the issue to reply to Eisenhower's accusations about a "mess in Washington." To avoid further embarrassment, Eisenhower's advisers urged him to drop Nixon from the ticket. But while Eisenhower delayed, Nixon seized the initiative. Using Republican party funds, he bought television time to take his case to the public. Sitting behind a desk, a portrait of Lincoln on one side, his wife, Pat, on the other, Nixon explained the sources of his funds and defended his personal honesty. Adopting the folk metaphors of Lincoln, he emphasized that his family had not profited from politics, that his wife still wore a "plain Republican cloth coat," and that despite the criticism he would not return a gift that his daughter had received, a cocker spaniel named Checkers.

The performance was sentimental, but effective. Public opinion rose in Nixon's favor, and Eisenhower decided to keep him in the campaign. The Checkers speech also demonstrated the immense political significance of television.

It highlighted the importance of a politician's public image. It suggested that a politician could effectively appeal over the heads of party leaders to the people. For Nixon, the speech not only proved his usefulness to Eisenhower but also gave him a supreme confidence in the medium. In later years he returned to television to win vindication for other aspects of his career, though seldom with the success of his 1952 effort.

Eisenhower tried to avoid direct statements about foreign policy. Though he supported the basic premises of Truman's Cold War, Eisenhower rejected the president's request for a bipartisan approach to foreign policy. Eisenhower endorsed the Republican party platform, drafted by John Foster Dulles, which promised to liberate Communist-dominated peoples. But the candidate avoided militant rhetoric, allowing Dulles and Nixon to speak for him. Eisenhower's position on Korea was equally murky. He approved Truman's intervention, just as he shunned MacArthur's call for all-out war. Yet the war was unpopular, and the Republican candidate blamed the Democrats for bungling the war effort.

Stevenson justified the administration's war policy, arguing that the only "answer" was to "keep it up as long as we have to." But Eisenhower hinted at alternative policies. "If there must be a war," he maintained, "let it be Asians against Asians, with our support on the side of freedom." Eisenhower's military experience enabled him to speak with authority and confidence. Though he possessed no specific proposal for ending the war, he created an image of superior wisdom. Speaking in Detroit on October 24, Eisenhower reiterated his commitment to terminate the war. "That job requires a personal trip to Korea," he declared. "I shall make that trip. . . . I shall go to Korea." Eisenhower's promise touched the fears and aspirations of a war-weary nation. The strategist of D Day would end the bloodletting of Korea.

Eisenhower's image as a nonpartisan soldier, aloof from the world of crass politics, proved the basis for a landslide victory. Eisenhower captured nearly thirty-four million votes to Stevenson's twenty-seven million and swept the electoral college 442 to 89. Stevenson carried only nine states — all southern or border states. But Eisenhower won in four southern states, breaking the Democrats' "solid South" for the first time since Al Smith's defeat in 1928. Eisenhower also attracted the traditional Democratic vote in the big cities — blacks, Catholics, and immigrants. And on his coattails, he pulled a Republican majority in both houses of Congress.

Republicans exulted in the destruction of the New Deal coalition. The victory of conservatives like McCarthy and the defeat of several of his critics seemed to vindicate the anti-Communist crusade. But the voting statistics also indicated that Eisenhower ran far ahead of other Republicans, including McCarthy. The election of 1952 was an Eisenhower victory, not a Republican one, and the party controlled the House by only eight seats, the Senate by one. During the fifties, voting behavior generally followed party lines. Voters seemed to be less interested in a general political ideology and more sensitive to short-term issues or party affiliation. Even new voters identified strongly with one of the major parties. Eisenhower's ability to avoid a coherent philosophy enabled him to attract a large proportion of independent voters and Democrats. These crossovers supported Eisenhower, but not necessarily other Republicans. The willingness of Democrats to vote for Eisenhower also reflected a consensus of purpose within the two parties. In the South, Republicans attracted newcomers to the region and uprooted voters who held no loyalty to the entrenched Democratic elite and who appreciated the sense of stability promised by the Republican platform.

WAGING THE COLD WAR

The K_1C_2 slogan, too easily seen as a cynical formula for getting votes, revealed deep-seated fears within American society. By 1953 the dread of nuclear war permeated the country. The federal Civil Defense Administration, created in 1951, disseminated booklets entitled "Survival Under Atomic Attack," which explained the fundamentals of civil defense. Congress appropriated $3 billion for bomb shelters, but an administrator admitted that less than 1 percent of the population would be protected. In New York and San Francisco, school officials routinely issued dog tags to children to facilitate identification of nuclear victims. Radio stations prepared for emergency broadcasting. "I cannot tell you when or where the attack will come or that it will come at all," President Truman admitted. "I can only remind you that we must be ready when it does come." Such oblique warnings fed a remarkable popular interest in flying saucers and mysterious invaders. The Hollywood science fiction film *The Thing* (1951) ended by advising audiences to "Watch the skies!"

Eisenhower's inaugural address spoke to these fears. His words echoed the vision of an earlier president, Abraham Lincoln. (Eisenhower's celebration of Lincoln would later be seen when he chose the sixteenth president's portrait for the basic postage stamp of the period.) Just as Lincoln saw the American nation as the "almost chosen people," Eisenhower also recognized a special relationship with God. As he had done throughout the campaign, the president began his inaugural address with a prayer, beseeching God's guidance during this "time of tempest." Like Lincoln, Eisenhower saw the nation confronting trials and tribulations that would test the divine character of the people. "Are we nearing the light — a day of freedom and of peace for all mankind?" he asked. "Or are the shadows of another night closing in upon us?" For Eisenhower the epochal struggle between light and shadow had brought the United States into inevitable conflict with world communism, a faith that knew "no god but force." "In the final choice," the soldier-president announced, "a soldier's pack is not so heavy a burden as a prisoner's chains."

The metaphors of morality and struggle reflected the new administration's approach to foreign policy. Like the leaders of the Truman administration, Eisenhower and his secretary of state, John Foster Dulles, believed that the Soviet Union was an aggressive nation, seeking to destroy a unique American way of life. Since 1949 the Soviets had enlisted a new, even more dreadful ally: Communist China. In the face of this menace, the Democrats had adopted a defensive strategy that endeavored to contain further Communist expansion.

Eisenhower and Dulles now sought to shift the initiative to the United States. In June 1952 Dulles wrote an article for *Life* magazine, entitled "A Policy of Boldness," that explained the new strategy. Containment, Dulles argued, was designed to protect the status quo, to enable the United States to coexist with the peril of communism. This approach, however, held slim possibilities of eliminating the threat altogether; it was a "treadmill" policy. Moreover, containment was a costly program, requiring heavy expenditures of economic and military assistance to allies throughout the world. Even the peripheries of the struggle, such as Korea, drained resources from the nation. As an alternative, therefore, Dulles proposed a policy based on principles that became known as "massive retaliation." Instead of waiting for the next Communist advance, the nations of the "free world" should prepare "to retaliate instantly" against the Soviet Union itself, "by means of our choosing." Nuclear weapons aimed at the Kremlin — not at some border area — would deter further Communist expansion.

The doctrine of massive retaliation presupposed American military superiority over the Communist enemy. "Our nation must stand as a solid rock in a storm-tossed world," declared Dulles. In nearly all their public addresses, the leaders of the Eisenhower administration reiterated the importance of strength and power. Such values reflected the traditional warrior code of toughness. But Eisenhower and Dulles added a moral ingredient to the formula. It was not simply that the United States must match the military strength of the Soviet Union, but rather, Dulles and Eisenhower believed, that Communist strength was essentially a façade: as a "godless" people, the Communists were morally rotten at the core. A tough foreign policy based on moral righteousness, therefore, must inevitably defeat the morally weak foe. Eisenhower, moreover, described massive retaliation as a "punishment to be visited upon Russia." The United States, as a Christian country, would implement the wrath of God.

The belief in moral superiority also had a nonmilitary dimension. The United States could wage the Cold War merely by demonstrating its virtue to the "captive peoples" of the world. To carry this message behind the Iron Curtain, the United States established Voice of America broadcasts, which presented American versions of international news. To supplement these pro-grams, Eisenhower advocated the creation of Radio Free Europe in 1949. Ignoring legal re-strictions on broadcasting, RFE used propa-ganda and polemics to agitate for insurrection in Communist countries. Funds for RFE came primarily from the secret budgets of the Central Intelligence Agency. A Free Europe Press, es-tablished in 1953, floated propaganda-filled bal-loons into Communist territories. These activi-ties assumed that moral support would ignite an inherent desire for freedom among "en-slaved" peoples. More often, however, the mes-sages exaggerated the United States's commit-ment to alter the structure of power.

Besides its implications for world affairs, the idea of massive retaliation had distinct domestic advantages. Conservative Republicans, led by Senator Taft, had long dissented from the soar-ing military budgets of the Truman administra-tion. Eisenhower shared their sentiments. Such budget cutting, however, could not be allowed to compromise the nation's military strength. The emphasis on air power and nuclear weap-ons provided a prudent solution to the military-budget equation. The "New Look" in military policy enabled the administration to reduce the size of military forces while retaining "massive retaliatory power." This decision enabled Eisen-hower to cut $7 billion from Truman's projected military expenses. But Eisenhower's unwilling-ness to reduce the budget even further aroused the anger of staunch conservatives.

The Republican Old Guard also criticized the president's handling of the Cold War. The Republican party platform had promised to "re-pudiate all commitments contained in secret understandings such as those of Yalta which aid Communist enslavements." This position reflected a fear of executive independence in foreign policy. But though Eisenhower accepted

The introduction of family bomb shelters revealed the pervasive dread of holocaust in the 1950s. (Wide World Photos)

the statement as a useful campaign strategy, he was reluctant to compromise his own presi-dential powers. Eisenhower, moreover, did not wish to threaten American claims to Berlin by repudiating the wartime agreements that legit-imated the division of Germany. To avoid jeopardizing the European situation, the ad-ministration introduced a resolution in Febru-ary 1953 that renounced diplomacy sacrificing the independence of "captive peoples," but that also ignored the question of Yalta and the deci-sions of previous presidents. This compromise failed to satisfy Republican conservatives and caused congressional dissent. While Eisenhower was forced to look to Democrats for support, the sudden death of Josef Stalin in March 1953 promised to alter the international situa-tion. The administration took the opportunity to retreat from direct confrontation with congressional conservatives, and the motion never came to a vote.

Eisenhower's success at diverting a controversy failed to alter the conservatives' conviction that executive powers threatened constitutional government. In 1954 Senator John Bricker of Ohio proposed a constitutional amendment requiring that international agreements be approved by Congress before becoming law. This measure challenged not only executive powers but also the internationalist nature of American foreign policy. Supporters of the Bricker amendment pointed out that the U.N. Charter, by affirming human rights, potentially influenced domestic legislation. Eisenhower strongly opposed the Bricker amendment. But because the president believed in a rigid separation of powers, he exercised minimal leadership to defeat the proposal in Congress. Senate Democrats, led by Lyndon Baines Johnson, again saved the president from his own party's conservatives. Though the Bricker amendment obtained a 60–31 majority, it fell one vote short of the necessary two-thirds required for constitutional amendments.

Congressional conservatives also opposed a compromise settlement of the Korean War. They had criticized Truman's initial decision to limit the war, charging the president with appeasing the Communists. But Eisenhower's enormous prestige as a military leader as well as his electoral popularity enabled him to accomplish what the previous Democratic administration was reluctant to suggest. In December 1952 Eisenhower fulfilled his campaign promise to go to Korea. After analyzing the stalemate situation, the new president recognized that a continuation of the ground war would only add to the imbalanced budget. Secretary Dulles joined conservatives in supporting a war for

complete victory. But Eisenhower shunned the use of atomic weapons for several reasons. First, he feared they would provoke Soviet intervention in the war. Second, the United States's atomic arsenal was too small to dissipate in a remote corner of the Cold War. Third, the possible ineffectiveness of such weapons threatened to undermine the immense advantages of atomic diplomacy. As in World War Two, the Korean War had demonstrated the severe limitations of aerial bombardment.

Eisenhower determined to use American military power not for victory but to persuade the Communist People's Republic of China to negotiate a settlement. In his inaugural address, the president announced he was removing the Seventh Fleet from the area separating Taiwan from the mainland, hinting that he was removing an obstacle from an invasion by Chiang Kai-shek. Eisenhower also used diplomatic channels to notify China that the United States might resort to nuclear weapons to drive the enemy to the truce table. After nearly three years of fighting, the Chinese shared American war-weariness. Stalin's death, which introduced the possibility of a shift in Soviet foreign policy, added to China's uncertainty. In March 1953 the Chinese indicated a willingness to resume negotiations.

Peace talks began in Panmunjom, Korea, in April. Both China and the United States accepted the limits of the military struggle. But they still disagreed about the return of prisoners of war. To force the issue, Dulles again introduced the threat of atomic weapons, while the State Department offered a slightly altered proposal. Within three weeks the Chinese accepted, confirming Dulles's faith in tough diplomacy. But Syngman Rhee, the dictatorial leader of South Korea, violently opposed a peace treaty that left his country divided near the 38th parallel. To undermine the settlement, Rhee released twenty-seven thousand prisoners, who vanished into the countryside. American officials quickly intervened, first to assure the People's Republic that the United States had negotiated in good faith, and then to convince Rhee to reconsider his objections. Desirous of an early peace, the Chinese overlooked Rhee's obstructionism and agreed to a final armistice in July 1953.

The end of the Korean War brought most Americans not a sense of celebration, but plain relief. Thirty-three thousand Americans had died to defend an area that State Department officials had admitted was beyond a strategic defense perimeter. Yet congressional conservatives protested that the compromise treaty was actually a vindication of Communist aggression. Republican Senate Majority Leader William Knowland called the settlement a truce without honor, while Taft, then dying of cancer, considered it "extremely unsatisfactory." Eisenhower nevertheless viewed the treaty as a necessary expedient to halt the drain on American resources.

The administration was careful, however, to distinguish the Korean settlement from any semblance of weakness. As a warning to its Communist enemies, the United States joined its allies in stating that further aggression in Korea would have consequences "so grave that in all probability it would not be possible to confine hostilities to Korea." Such threats of massive retaliation were reinforced by the retention in Korea of American military bases, including nuclear-armed missiles. The United States also adopted a multibillion-dollar program of economic and military assistance to shore up the South Korean government. Despite the reactionary internal policies of the Rhee regime, Eisenhower was determined to

stop Communist advances at the 38th parallel. The effect of the Korean treaty, therefore, was to institutionalize the Truman policy of containment in Asia.

Eisenhower's policies toward Europe also revealed basic continuities with those of his predecessor. Though the administration spoke grandiosely about liberating the peoples of Eastern Europe, the principles of massive retaliation were too inflexible to respond effectively to minor crises. When East German workers staged anti-Communist protests in June 1953, Dulles could offer only moral encouragement and $15 million worth of free food. The United States, in effect, accepted the reality of Soviet power in Eastern Europe. Despite its claims to have seized the initiative in foreign policy, the Eisenhower administration could only react to changes elsewhere. Yet this realization of Soviet strength did not produce a desire to negotiate differences. When Stalin's successor, Georgi Malenkov, proposed a treaty to first neutralize Germany and then hold free elections, Dulles rebuffed the idea, arguing that elections must come first. Committed to their world view, Eisenhower and Dulles believed that Soviet power would dissipate because of its own internal weaknesses. While that deterioration proceeded, the United States would watch cautiously and wait.

Eisenhower's reluctance to enter negotiations over Germany reflected the persistence of the containment policy. In seeking to reduce American military expenditures, Eisenhower hoped that the European allies could be persuaded to assume some of the costs. Following the policies of the Truman administration, Dulles pleaded with the allies to ratify the European Defense Community (EDC), an agency that would supplant NATO and permit the arming of Germany without a German general staff. It was this desire to bring Germany into the Western alliance that led Dulles to rebuff a neutralization of the former enemy.

The proposed EDC troubled American allies in Europe. Besides the question of national jealousies, the European nations feared a defense alliance based on massive retaliation and atomic warfare. Such a strategy left ultimate authority on the use of nuclear weapons with the United States. European leaders were also dismayed by Eisenhower's cool response to the apparent moderation of Soviet policy after the death of Stalin. Above all, the French detested the idea of a rearmed Germany. When France delayed acting on the proposed EDC, Dulles attempted to exert additional pressure, suggesting that unless EDC was approved, the United States might undertake an "agonizing reappraisal" of its entire policy toward Europe. Such heavy-handed language, instead of coercing European compliance, underscored Western Europe's dependence on American military strength. Such factors convinced the French to reject EDC in August 1954.

The failure of EDC, however, did not deter American policy makers. Since the United States and Great Britain believed that Germany was essential to the defense of Western Europe, they chose an alternative policy that enabled Germany to rearm under NATO. By 1955 France faced a rearmed Germany that was not limited by the regulatory controls of EDC. "These agreements are founded upon the profound yearning for peace which is shared by all the Atlantic peoples," Eisenhower declared. "The agreements endanger no nation." But the entry of Germany into NATO assured a permanent division of central Europe. In 1955 the Soviet Union initiated the Warsaw Pact, a military alliance that attempted to balance the power of NATO.

SECRET FOREIGN POLICY

The willingness of the United States to dismiss the objections of France, an avowed ally, revealed the self-righteous basis of Eisenhower's foreign policy. Believing that communism was an absolute evil, the United States unilaterally acted on behalf of friendly nations. In the case of other nations, the United States did not hesitate to violate international law when American interests appeared to be threatened. Yet such threats often reflected not a Communist menace but a disagreement over national interest. The Eisenhower administration usually blurred that distinction, claiming that all challenges to the national interest had a Communist base. Such a view could be attributed to a fundamental inability to see the world outside the polarities of what Eisenhower called "light" and "shadow." But in certain situations, there is evidence that the Eisenhower administration deliberately deceived the American people about the nature of international conflict. In concealing their motives, the nation's leaders believed — as in the case of France — that their vision was in the best interests of all.

A major instrument in implementing American policy in unfriendly areas was the Central Intelligence Agency (CIA). Founded in 1947 exclusively as an intelligence-gathering body, the CIA possessed a multibillion-dollar top-secret budget that absolved it of accountability to Congress or the public. In 1953 Eisenhower appointed Allen Dulles, formerly of the Office of Strategic Services and brother of the secretary of state, to head the CIA. Between 1950 and 1955 the CIA tripled in size to fifteen thousand personnel. Besides establishing spy networks throughout the world, the CIA performed secret operations outside the law that facilitated the formal policy of the State De-

394

partment. The CIA, for example, regularly supported raids from Taiwan to the Chinese mainland. When CIA activities were discovered by other countries, the United States denied the allegations and used the episodes to denounce its enemies as international liars. Several CIA agents languished in Chinese prisons while their employers disavowed their actions. Such dishonesty was justified by the belief that the United States was engaged in mortal struggle against a ruthless, unscrupulous foe. Unsurprisingly, other governments could see the United States in the same light.

The CIA was intimately involved in a coup d'état in Iran in 1953. Two years earlier, the premier of Iran, Dr. Mohammed Mossadegh, had attempted to end British exploitation of the impoverished country by nationalizing the nation's oil wells. The Western-owned oil companies retaliated by instituting a boycott on Iranian oil. Mossadegh appealed to the United States for assistance, but Eisenhower rebuffed him, claiming that "it would not be fair to American taxpayers." The United States did not support a return of the oil wells to Britain; it wanted them for itself.

After Eisenhower's rejection, Mossadegh sought assistance from the Soviet Union. The CIA then stepped in to prevent an Iranian-Soviet alliance. In August 1953 American agents provided crucial military support that enabled the shah to topple the Mossadegh regime. The shah then appointed a premier who was friendly to American interests. In the ensuing negotiations, the nationalized oil wells were replaced by an international consortium, in which American-owned companies held 40 percent interest. By overthrowing the Mossadegh regime, the United States not only broke the British oil monopoly but also placed Iran safely in the non-Communist camp. This realignment was strengthened by American economic assistance to the new Iranian regime.

American intervention in Iran was duplicated in Guatemala in 1954. As in Iran, a popular leader, Colonel Arbenz, attempted to improve economic conditions in his country by enacting land reform and by nationalizing the vast holdings of the United Fruit Company. Arbenz offered a small compensation for the expropriated property, but United Fruit, with the backing of the State Department, rejected the sum. The United States government then began planning to overthrow the Arbenz regime. Through formal diplomatic channels, the State Department urged Arbenz to settle the dispute at the World Court at The Hague. Simultaneously, a secret CIA group began to train an invasion army in nearby Nicaragua and Honduras.

To justify this new version of Dollar Diplomacy, the State Department tried to demonstrate that Arbenz's policies were an opening wedge for "international communism," which would imperil the entire hemisphere. In March 1954 the United States sponsored a resolution at the Tenth Inter-American Conference that declared that Communist control of "any American State" endangered "the peace of America." The motion passed 17–1, with Guatemala alone voting against this new interpretation of the Monroe Doctrine. In May 1954 Arbenz received a shipment of arms from Czechoslovakia, confirming the State Department's worst fears. One month later the CIA-backed army, led by the exiled Colonel Carlos Castillo Armas, invaded Guatemala and defeated Arbenz's forces.

The deposed leader appealed to the U.N. for assistance. But the United States effectively quashed any help by arguing that the Organization of American States, not the Security Council, had proper jurisdiction. "The situation is being cured by Guatemalans themselves," maintained Dulles. After the coup succeeded, however, Dulles took credit for having thwarted "the traitorous tools of foreign despots." In labeling Arbenz a tool of Soviet policy, the Eisenhower administration obtained bipartisan approval. "There is no question here of United States interference in the domestic affairs of any American state," insisted Senator Lyndon Johnson. "We are concerned only with external aggression."

Having argued that the United States had saved Guatemalans from an international conspiracy, the Eisenhower administration arranged to support the new Armas regime with $90 million of economic and military aid. "The United States pledges ... to help alleviate conditions in Guatemala," assured Dulles, "which might afford communism an opportunity to spread its tentacles throughout the hemisphere." Yet Armas soon returned the nationalized land to United Fruit, provided tax benefits for the large corporation, crushed the labor union movement, and took the vote away from illiterate people, who comprised 70 percent of the population. By defining Arbenz's nationalism as a form of international communism, the Eisenhower administration mustered the political support to restore conditions favorable to American capitalism. But it also aligned itself with the forces of reaction in Latin America.

DOMESTIC CONSERVATISM

American opposition to radical social reform in other countries paralleled the administration's attitudes toward economic development at home. Like most Republicans, Eisenhower initially believed that the swollen budgets of pre-

vious Democratic administrations reflected a general "mismanagement" of government. Eisenhower's secretary of the treasury, George Humphrey, was dedicated to a balanced budget by curtailing government expenses. But Eisenhower soon recognized that the administration could not dismantle the social welfare programs of the New Deal. To balance the budget, therefore, the administration reluctantly delayed a tax cut and extended the wartime excess-profits tax to 1954. Despite Humphrey's most frugal efforts and the sharp criticism of Old Guard Republicans, government expenditures remained a basic prop of the American economy.

Eisenhower's economic conservatism emerged more clearly in the debate over control of offshore oil deposits. For more than a decade, the federal government had contested the claims of several coastal states, particularly Texas, Louisiana, and California, to jurisdiction over tideland oil. Since the major oil companies expected beneficial legislation from the state governments, they supported these state claims. In 1946 Congress moved to transfer control to the states. But Truman vetoed the measure, arguing that offshore oil belonged to the nation. In 1947 and 1950 the Supreme Court upheld Truman's position. The Court ruled nevertheless that Congress did have the power to give control of offshore oil to the states.

Conservative Republicans opposed federal control of private business and supported the states' claims. So too did southern Democrats, who saw state control of oil not only in their economic interests, but also as a defense of states' rights. In 1952 these forces pushed through another bill granting jurisdiction to the states. Again Truman vetoed the measure. And before leaving office, Truman reserved offshore oil for the use of the navy.

The new Republican administration determined to reverse Truman's position. Working with southern Democrats, Republicans passed a measure giving control of offshore oil to the states in 1953. Liberals opposed the bill, and Senator Wayne Morse of Oregon staged a twenty-two-hour filibuster in a futile attempt to prevent its enactment. The passage of the Tidelands Oil Act revealed the laissez faire assumptions of the Eisenhower administration. The president personally favored an even more extensive giveaway, but agreed to support his attorney general's defense of federal claims to the continental shelf.

The administration also joined congressional leaders in resisting legislation to alter oil depletion allowances and other tax benefits for the oil industry. This alliance reflected the political strength of southern Democrats from the oil states, especially Speaker of the House Sam Rayburn and Senate Majority Leader Lyndon Johnson, both of Texas. The coalition worked to remove federal controls of natural gas. In 1950 Congress enacted the Kerr bill, exempting natural gas producers from regulation of prices. Encouraged by liberals, Truman vetoed the measure. Eisenhower, however, supported such legislation. But a 1956 bill, which would have removed federal controls, became enmeshed in scandal when an oil lobbyist tried to bribe a senator. To avoid embarrassment, Eisenhower vetoed the bill. The administration, however, relied on a probusiness Federal Power Commission to protect the natural gas industry from strict regulation.

THE ANTI-COMMUNIST CRUSADE

Eisenhower's belief in the separation of powers influenced his reaction to congressional attempts to purge Communists from government. During the 1952 campaign Eisenhower avoided controversy with such arch-conservatives as Senators McCarthy and Arthur Jenner and endorsed all Republican candidates. After the election Eisenhower continued to appease the conservative wing by naming Scott McLeod, a staunch anti-Communist and McCarthy supporter, to head the State Department's personnel program. Such an appointment, the president felt, would remove conservative accusations that American foreign policy was subverted from within.

Eisenhower also moved to revise Truman's loyalty program. In April 1953 the president issued Executive Order 10450, which decentralized the government's review of employees and placed final responsibility with the separate departments of government. Eisenhower also established a new standard for dismissal. Where Truman required evidence of disloyalty or subversion, the Republican president authorized dismissal on the vague grounds that an individual's employment "may not be clearly consistent with the interests of national security." Under these new guidelines Eisenhower claimed to have removed twenty-two hundred "security risks" in his first year of office. But few were actually charged with disloyalty.

The administration's definition of security risks revealed other underlying assumptions within the Cold War consensus. Besides obvious cases of negligence or criminal acts, Eisenhower's standards for dismissal included "notoriously disgraceful conduct, habitual use of intoxicants to excess, drug addiction, or sexual perversion," as well as insanity. Persons practicing such acts were "risks" because they were vulnerable, weak, and dependent. The Cold War required tough soldiers who would not be dependent on others.

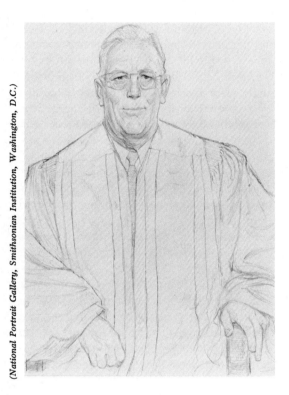

(National Portrait Gallery, Smithsonian Institution, Washington, D.C.)

Earl Warren

1891-1974

"The biggest damfool decision I ever made," Eisenhower remarked of his eight years in the White House, was the appointment of Earl Warren as chief justice of the Supreme Court in 1953. In making the choice, Eisenhower had fulfilled a political debt. As governor of California, Warren represented the liberal wing of the Republican party. He had been Dewey's running mate in 1948 and an important "dark horse" candidate in 1952.

Prior to his Supreme Court appointment, Warren had earned a reputation as an assiduous law enforcement officer in his role as California district attorney and state attorney general. During World War Two, he had advocated confinement of Japanese-Americans. Elected governor in 1943, Warren supported liberal legislation in such areas as health insurance, but had consistently advocated state control and states' rights.

Warren's position on the Supreme Court led to dramatic reversals of precedent. In his first major decision, Brown v. Board of Education (1954), the chief justice dismantled the doctrine of separate, but equal and paved the way for fundamental changes in race relations. The attack on undemocratic practices by the states also led to a Court order for the reapportionment of legislative districts according to the one-person, one-vote principle in 1962 (Baker v. Carr). These rulings altered a traditional political structure that enabled rural elites to ignore numerical majorities.

Warren also became a strong defender of individual rights. In the Yates decision (1957), he concurred in reversing the conviction of leading Communists by differentiating between the theory of subversion and its actual practice. This position led to the eventual overthrow of certain loyalty oaths and state laws against Communists. Under the principle of due process of law, he defended the rights of criminals to legal counsel and fair treatment by police. The Warren-led Court tightened the interpretation of obscenity to limit censorship of speech and the press. In 1962 the Court supported a rigid separation of church and state in denying prayers in public schools. Such opinions earned Warren the hatred of right wing groups such as the John Birch Society, which demanded his impeachment.

Despite the unpopularity of some of his rulings, Warren was widely respected for his personal integrity. President Johnson therefore named him to head a commission to investigate the assassination of President Kennedy. Warren's personal reputation helped persuade political leaders to accept the commission's controversial report. Warren's retirement in 1969 heralded the end of a liberal era of an "activist" judiciary.

Frequent victims of the warrior code were alleged homosexuals. In a single case in 1960, the National Security Administration fired twenty-six employees for sexual deviation. Given the frequency of homosexual contacts reported by Dr. Alfred Kinsey, persecution of homosexuals seemed particularly severe. During the 1952 presidential campaign, Stevenson, who had recently been divorced from his wife, took special care to remain in female company to counter rumors that he was a homosexual. Stevenson's vacillation about running for office reinforced a sense of his weakness. *Life* magazine criticized the candidate's "Softness Toward Communism." Similarly, the anti-Communist *New Leader* praised the political "hards" who were "willing to risk reaction and war... to fight Communism." In a culture that defined courage in terms of hardness and strength, homosexuals symbolized the "soft" side of all males. Unwilling to accept these characteristics within themselves, political leaders saw nothing wrong in suppressing "weak" men.

The desire to suppress deviant lifestyles closely paralleled an attack on deviant opinion in all levels of government. Shortly after moving into the State Department, Dulles removed several career diplomats, including a group of prestigious China experts who had predicted Mao's victory in 1949. These officers had been accused not of disloyalty but of indiscretion. Dulles also encouraged the departure of George Kennan, viewed as the architect of Truman's containment policy. To replace Kennan as ambassador to the Soviet Union, the administration supported Charles E. Bohlen, an expert on Soviet affairs. But rigid anti-Communists questioned the nomination, pointing out that Bohlen had served Democratic presidents at Yalta and Potsdam. The administration nevertheless decided to stand behind Bohlen. A compromise was reached when Senators Taft and Sparkman examined Bohlen's confidential FBI file. Their favorable report led to senatorial confirmation of the appointment. But Taft indicated the implications of the controversy when he told the president, "No more Bohlens."

The suppression of alternative opinions was revealed dramatically in the case of J. Robert Oppenheimer, the celebrated physicist who had directed the development of the atomic bomb. By 1950 Oppenheimer had expressed serious reservations about further nuclear armament and had opposed the decision to manufacture a hydrogen bomb. Oppenheimer's known association with leftists had aroused suspicions about his loyalty, but the scientist had passed numerous investigations and had maintained his security clearance. In July 1953, however, Eisenhower's director of the Atomic Energy Commission, Admiral Lewis Strauss, began to remove classified documents from Oppenheimer's custody, and in December Strauss asked for the scientist's resignation. Oppenheimer demanded an investigation, which was completed in April 1954. By a 2–1 vote, a special review panel lifted Oppenheimer's security clearance. The scientist was forced to leave the government service.

The attempt to stifle dissenting viewpoints had profound consequences on individual lives, but the administration remained insensitive to these problems. Upon assuming the presidency, Eisenhower inherited a delicate legal case involving the convicted atomic spies Julius and Ethel Rosenberg. Though the only defendants to insist on their innocence, the Rosenbergs had been sentenced to death. Such a punishment revealed a popular but erroneous belief that the Soviet Union lacked the intellectual sophistication to develop atomic weapons without American help. In upholding the sentence, the federal courts cooperated with government prosecutors to assure that unrepentant Soviet sympathizers would receive ultimate punishment. Facing execution in June 1953, the Rosenbergs appealed to Eisenhower for clemency. But the president refused to intervene, charging that the atomic spies "may have condemned to death tens of millions of innocent people all over the world."

"In America," protested the playwright Arthur Miller in *The Crucible,* a 1953 version of the Salem witch trials, "any man who is not reactionary in his views is open to the charge of alliance with the Red hell." Foremost in making such accusations was Senator Joseph McCarthy. "There is only one real issue for the farmer, the laborer, and the businessman," he declared during the 1952 campaign, "— the issue of Communism in government." Such statements proved useful in the election campaign, but members of the Eisenhower administration were concerned when the senator continued his charges after the inauguration.

McCarthy's position as chairman of the Senate Subcommittee on Government Operations provided a forum for his persistent attacks on Communist influence in government. In the spring of 1953 McCarthy and his legal aide, Roy Cohn, staged a series of hearings about the Voice of America, claiming that the organization was a front for leftist groups. McCarthy also meddled in State Department affairs, seeking to "negotiate" a reduction of Greek shipping to China. In April 1953 Cohn and his friend, G. David Schine, embarked on a chaotic investigation of the United States Information Agency in Europe. Their scrutiny of USIA libraries revealed over thirty thousand "subversive" authors, a category that included writers like Theodore Dreiser, Archibald MacLeish, and Arthur M. Schlesinger, Jr. Despite complaints about these absurd charges, the USIA quickly removed several thousand volumes from library shelves.

These attacks finally provoked a presidential response. "Don't join the book-burners!" Eisenhower advised a Dartmouth College commencement audience in June 1953. "Don't be afraid to go into your library and read every book as long as that document does not offend your own ideas of decency." But when asked by the press to elaborate on his comments, the president maintained that he was not referring to McCarthy. Eisenhower was reluctant to clash with McCarthy, fearing a split within Republican ranks and worrying about lending dignity to the senator's crusade. "I will not get into the gutter with that guy," the president declared. The McCarthy problem, he hoped, would wear itself out.

McCarthy's power ended, however, only when he finally outraged the political leadership that had tacitly supported him. In early 1954 McCarthy began an investigation of alleged communism at Fort Monmouth, New Jersey. He soon clashed with General Ralph Zwicker, chastising the officer for his defense of "Communist conspirators." The White House tried to stop McCarthy's criticism, but the senator sidestepped administration pressure. The army responded by releasing documents that revealed McCarthy's attempt to obtain special privileges for Cohn's friend, Private David Schine. Shouting "blackmail," McCarthy insisted on a full investigation of the army. Democratic Majority Leader Lyndon Johnson now saw an opportunity to ruin McCarthy. Like other Democrats, Johnson had avoided a confrontation with the Wisconsin senator, fearing a vicious counterattack. "Joe will go that extra mile to destroy you," he remarked. But Johnson believed that public exposure would also lead

McCarthy to destroy himself. He therefore urged that the Army-McCarthy hearings be televised. For thirty-six days the nation was treated to a spectacle of McCarthy's erratic, irrational behavior. While the senator stormed at witnesses and ignored legal procedures, his public-opinion ratings steadily dropped. In May McCarthy added one year to his denunciation of "twenty years of treason," thus implicating the Eisenhower administration in a coverup of communism. He had gone too far.

In June Republican Senator Ralph Flanders of Vermont introduced a resolution calling for McCarthy's censure by the Senate. In a carefully orchestrated proceeding, a panel of conservative senators recommended censure of McCarthy for conduct that "tended to bring the Senate into dishonor and disrepute." McCarthy continued to rage against the Senate, accusing that body of serving the Communists. But half the Republicans joined the unanimous Democrats in voting McCarthy's censure. Vice President Nixon, presiding in the Senate, deleted the word *censure* from the final document. It was a formality that made no difference. McCarthy's power was broken. He remained in the Senate, politically ineffective, until his death in 1957.

The elimination of McCarthy created an illusion that the Communist witch hunts had ended. But the attack on communism extended far beyond the chambers of Congress, revealing the power of systematic political repression. Libraries removed "controversial" books; school boards and universities dismissed leftist teachers; industries established blacklists to prevent employment of suspected Communists. Such activities won wide support, even from liberals. Minnesota's Hubert H. Humphrey, an early defender of civil rights, supported legislation to prohibit the Communist party. "We liberals," added Illinois's Paul Douglas, "must destroy the Communists if this dirty game is to stop."

THE POLITICS OF CONSENSUS

Despite McCarthy's problems in 1954, therefore, Republican leaders expected the anti-Communist crusade to be an effective campaign weapon in the congressional elections. Eisenhower avoided the emotionally charged issue and contented himself with a nationwide speaking tour on behalf of Republican candidates pledged to his administration. But Nixon, repeating his performance of 1952, attacked the Democrats for their toleration of "the Communist conspiracy in the United States." Neither Eisenhower's prestige nor Nixon's rhetoric could overcome the political effects of an economic recession. More significant was the president's inability to attach his popularity to other Republican candidates. Though Eisenhower could attract a large independent vote, other politicians were linked in the public mind with traditional party labels. In the end, the Democrats won small majorities in both houses of Congress.

The Democratic victories of 1954, instead of creating partisan conflict between the branches of government, actually encouraged cooperation. Rayburn and Johnson, the congressional leaders, shared a conservative outlook that differed only slightly from the president's. Their power in Congress reflected the strength of southern Democrats. Since committee assignments depended on seniority, southerners from the one-party region enjoyed obvious advantages. The patterns of congressional representation also strengthened the conservative group. Urban areas, which traditionally supported liberal candidates, were underrepresented in Congress because state legislatures gerrymandered voting districts to suit local political needs. The imbalances in legislative apportionment were not corrected by the principle of one-person, one-vote until a Supreme Court ruling in 1962.

Reflecting this conservative consensus was Eisenhower's articulation of a philosophy of "modern republicanism." Rejecting the Old Guard Republicans who had criticized Eisenhower's foreign policy and his minimal social legislation, the president suggested that the federal government "must do its part to advance human welfare and encourage economic growth with constructive actions." Such ideas departed from the laissez faire principles of the Republican right wing. But they did not commit the administration to a major program of social welfare legislation. Eisenhower's vision of politics was well summarized by Arthur Larson in his 1956 book, *A Republican Looks at His Party,* a work that the president endorsed. "This is no time to harry the American public from crisis to crisis," Larson advised, "nor to drive breaches between groups for transient political advantage."

This belief in a political consensus encouraged the emergence of an intellectual consensus that dominated the social sciences. The major historians of the fifties, Louis Hartz, Richard Hofstadter, and Daniel Boorstin, described the American past as a homogenized culture without significant class, ethnic, or racial conflict. Racism, for example, became an aberration from the American mainstream that was peculiar to the antebellum South. In sociology and political science, academic scholars stressed the "pluralism" of American society, an interaction of groups that lacked ideological tensions. These trends encouraged the proliferation of American Studies programs that taught the uniqueness and, by implication, the superiority of American culture. The sociologist William Whyte observed in 1956 that most social scientists held a "bias against conflict." Such terms as "disharmony, disequilibrium, maladjustment, disorganization," he remarked, were considered "bad things."

A major unifying force was the Cold War. Democrats and Republicans alike shared a belief in the Communist menace and agreed that the United States had to maintain its military strength. A 1956 survey indicated that there was no correlation between political opinions on domestic issues and support of a tough stand against international communism. Thus Eisenhower's popularity remained high, even though voters might reject other Republican candidates. The relationship between Cold War expenditures and economic prosperity also assured minimal resistance to the administration's budgetary requests for military purposes.

FOREIGN POLICY IN ASIA

Support of the Cold War, however, did not imply a bipartisan foreign policy. Democratic opposition to the principles of massive retaliation led to a major defeat of the State Department's policy for Vietnam in 1954. Since the outbreak of the Korean War, the United States had supported the French attempt to suppress the Viet Minh rebels led by Ho Chi Minh. By 1954 the United States had spent $1.2 billion on military assistance and was financing nearly 80 percent of the total war costs. These expenses included several hundred "technical" advisers. Such intervention was justified by the belief that Vietnam was a valuable source of raw materials as well as a vital strategic link in the attempt to halt Communist expansion.

Despite American aid, France was unable to defeat the Viet Minh. French opinion, moreover, began to doubt the validity of the war. In April 1954 the French garrison at Dien Bien Phu was surrounded by Vietnamese forces. France faced a major military defeat and appealed to the United States for assistance. Eisenhower had no interest in committing the United States to a ground war in Southeast Asia. Given the doctrine of massive retaliation, however, American assistance would be limited to an air attack, perhaps with atomic weapons. While the French garrison lay under siege, policy makers in Washington debated American foreign policy.

For Eisenhower, Vietnam held the future of Asia. At a press conference in April 1954, the president explained the "falling domino" theory: "You have a row of dominos set up, you knock over the first one, and what will happen to the last one is the certainty that it will go over very quickly." The fall of Vietnam would mean that "many human beings pass under a dictatorship that is inimical to the free world." It would interfere with the acquisition of precious resources. And it would imperil Japanese trade, forcing that ally "toward the Communist areas in order to live." Eisenhower never wavered from this belief that the Viet Minh represented not an anticolonial force, but an instrument of world communism.

The president received differing advice from his closest aides. Dulles and Admiral Arthur W. Radford, chairman of the Joint Chiefs, advocated air attacks to relieve the French, and Air Force General Nathan Twining went so far as to promote an atomic bombing of the Vietnamese countryside. But Army Chief Matthew Ridgway, who as MacArthur's replacement in Korea well remembered the futility of limited warfare, spoke strongly against intervention. Eisenhower then consulted congressional leaders. "Where do the British stand?" asked Richard Russell. The administration admitted that it lacked the support of its allies. The congressmen urged Eisenhower not to act unilaterally.

An international conference to discuss Indochina was scheduled to convene at Geneva in April. British Prime Minister Winston Churchill was unwilling to jeopardize that meeting by supporting American military operations, though Dulles suggested that an air attack would strengthen the allied negotiating position. The administration then used Nixon to send up a trial balloon, proposing American intervention on behalf of the French. Public reaction was highly critical. Meanwhile, the French military position continued to deteriorate. On May 7 the forces at Dien Bien Phu surrendered. "American foreign policy has never in all its history suffered such a stunning reversal," complained Lyndon Johnson in the Senate. "We have been caught bluffing by our enemies." Eisenhower still considered entering the conflict, but the French had lost the will to fight. In June the administration formally rejected the French request for assistance.

The fall of Dien Bien Phu made a diplomatic settlement imperative. In July France signed the Geneva Accords that ended eight years of colonial warfare. According to the agreement, France acknowledged the independence of Vietnam, Laos, and Cambodia. Vietnam was divided temporarily at the 17th parallel, but this division did not imply a political separation of that country. National elections, supervised by an international commission, would be held within two years to unify the country. In the interim, neither zone was to

enter military alliances or allow foreign military bases to be established. These terms required the Viet Minh to surrender portions of the country under their control. But since Ho Chi Minh anticipated an easy electoral victory, he viewed the retreat as a temporary concession.

By acknowledging the validity of a Viet Minh government, if only for the northern portions of Vietnam, the Geneva settlement represented a serious defeat for American foreign policy. Though the United States formally announced that it would respect the Geneva Accords, it refused to sign the agreement. Meanwhile, the Eisenhower administration initiated immediate actions to continue the war against the Viet Minh. Dulles worked to establish a Vietnamese alternative to Ho Chi Minh and succeeded in having Ngo Dinh Diem, an American-educated Catholic seminarian, appointed premier of the French-controlled portion of the country. The administration also rushed a military mission to Vietnam. Headed by Colonel Edward G. Lansdale, who had gained experience fighting Communist Huk guerrillas in the Philippines, the mission performed acts of sabotage and launched a propaganda campaign to discredit the Viet Minh government.

The United States pursued a similar policy through traditional diplomatic channels. Determined to supplant France's role in Vietnam, the State Department by-passed French colonial administrators and transmitted aid directly to the Diem regime. This procedure freed the United States from accusations of supporting European colonialism. But it also had the effect of forcing France to withdraw from Vietnam prior to the 1956 deadline. The United States quickly stepped into the power vacuum. American advisers began to train a large Vietnamese army "to deter Viet Minh aggression by a limited defense of the Geneva Armistice demarkation line." The United States, in effect, was forestalling the possibility of national unification under a Viet Minh government.

These policies were made explicit in July 1955 when Diem announced that he would not honor the Geneva agreement calling for national elections. France and Great Britain protested this decision, but the United States backed Diem. "While we should certainly take no positive step to speed up the present process of decay of [the] Geneva Accords," Dulles declared, "neither should we make the slightest effort to infuse life into them." The United States continued to pour over $1 billion of economic and military aid into Vietnam, financing most of Diem's government expenses. Eisenhower also welcomed Diem in Washington, where the two leaders reaffirmed the struggle against "continuing Communist subversive capabilities."

American support enabled Diem to suppress his political rivals in Vietnam. Diem's soldiers made mass arrests of Communists and non-Communists alike. In 1955 he rigged elections that made him president with 98 percent of the vote. Diem also subverted a land reform program begun by the Viet Minh. Such policies triggered a guerrilla revolt. Though the Viet Minh supported such attacks, the anti-Diem movement originated in the south. In 1959, however, Viet Minh insurgents, many of them native to the south, returned to challenge the Diem regime. To preempt this movement, the United States urged Diem to institute political and social reforms. But Diem refused, leading the American ambassador to notify Washington that "it may become necessary ... to begin consideration of alternative courses of actions and leaders." This predicament was inherited by President Kennedy in 1961.

While taking unilateral action to support Diem, the United States attempted to use collective security to prevent the further spread of communism in Asia. Learning from the loss of Dien Bien Phu, the administration sought to obtain precommitments from its allies. In September 1954 Dulles signed a Southeast Asia Treaty Organization (SEATO) pact with Great Britain, France, Australia, New Zealand, Thailand, Pakistan, and the Philippines. This treaty provided for mutual defense against either armed attack or subversion and indirect aggression. "An attack on the treaty area would occasion a reaction so united, so strong, and so well placed," boasted Dulles in the language of massive retaliation, "that the aggressor would lose more than it could hope to gain."

The SEATO agreement, however, had inherent limitations that made Dulles's words seem like bombast. Such pivotal nations as India, pursuing a policy of neutrality, refused to cooperate. Moreover, the treaty obliged the eight nations only to consult and then follow normal constitutional procedures. Finally, it was unlikely that massive retaliation would be effective against indirect subversion. The Senate nevertheless ratified the treaty with little dissent. It was never invoked, however, and the agreement was ended in 1977.

The façade of SEATO was soon revealed when the United States made a unilateral decision to defend Chiang Kai-shek's control of the islands between China and Taiwan. Until World War Two, Japan had claimed Taiwan (Formosa) but recognized China's historic claims to Quemoy, Matsu, and the Tatchens. In fleeing the mainland, Chiang maintained control of all these islands. At the outbreak of the Korean War, Truman had ordered the Seventh Fleet to protect these territories from an expected Chinese invasion. But Eisenhower

405

had removed the fleet in 1953, hinting that he was "unleashing" Chiang to attack the mainland. With American support, Chiang also reinforced the island outposts.

In September 1954, while Dulles was flying to Manila to negotiate the SEATO pact, Chinese shore batteries began to bombard Quemoy, and the Peking government called for the "liberation" of Taiwan. The Joint Chiefs of Staff immediately began planning a counteroffensive, including an atomic attack on China. Great Britain opposed such action, viewing Chiang's control of the offshore islands as provocative. Eisenhower recognized that the islands were not crucial to the defense of Taiwan, but he insisted that the Chiang government was part

MAP 13.2   TAIWAN

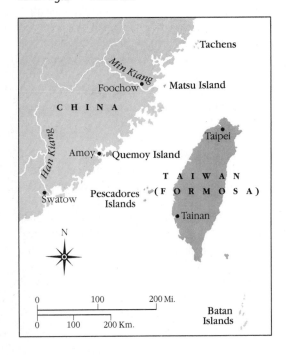

of the "backbone" of American security in the Pacific. In December Dulles negotiated a mutual defense pact with Chiang, but it made no mention of the disputed islands.

After the Chinese captured one of the Tatchen Islands, however, Eisenhower determined to clarify his defense of Taiwan. In January 1955 he asked Congress for authority to use armed forces "to assure the security of Formosa and the Pescadores" as well as "closely related localities." This request for discretionary power to declare war coincided ironically with the Senate's consideration of the Bricker amendment, which would have required legislative cooperation with executive decisions. Yet Congress treated the president's request uncritically, approving Eisenhower's blank check by nearly unanimous votes in both houses. Nor was Eisenhower opposed to using this unprecedented power. As China continued to bomb the offshore islands, the administration prepared for war. But pressure from Asian neutrals persuaded China to relax the tensions. By late spring the crisis had passed.

In supporting the Taiwan government in 1955, however, Eisenhower allowed Chiang to maneuver the United States into supporting a dubious claim to the offshore islands. In subsequent years Chiang took the opportunity to strengthen his fortifications on the disputed territory. But in August 1958 the People's Republic reopened the problem by launching a steady bombardment of Quemoy. Dulles responded to the crisis by reiterating a domino theory that justified defense of the islands, if necessary with atomic power. This position alarmed ally and enemy alike; both Britain and the Soviet Union advised the United States against military intervention. The administration's saber-rattling also brought stern criticism at home. Such pressure forced Dulles to admit that the

United States had no legal obligations to defend Quemoy and Matsu. This position soon eased the crisis. But in defending his bellicose posture, Eisenhower scrupulously insisted that the Formosa Resolution of 1955 granted the president sole responsibility for judging an "appropriate . . . defense of Formosa."

EUROPEAN DIPLOMACY

Eisenhower's assertion of executive prerogatives in 1958 contrasted with his attitudes about presidential diplomacy during his first years in office. Doubting the value of personal negotiations, Eisenhower allowed Dulles to negotiate on his behalf. Eisenhower's hesitancy stemmed from a belief that individual leaders would not significantly alter national policies. Moreover, he feared that a failure of summit diplomacy would only aggravate world tensions. For these reasons Eisenhower preferred to issue broad policy statements and await normal diplomatic responses. In December 1953, for example, Eisenhower addressed the U.N. General Assembly, presenting a dramatic "atoms for peace" proposal that urged international control of atomic weapons. When the Soviet Union reacted unfavorably, however, the president settled for the propaganda advantages and made no counteroffer.

Eisenhower also tried to avoid a meeting of world leaders proposed by Winston Churchill in 1955. He insisted that as a precondition for meeting with Soviet leaders, the former allies adopt a peace treaty with Austria. By 1955 Stalin's successors were anxious to nullify the rearming of Germany by stabilizing central Europe and, to Eisenhower's surprise, agreed to an Austrian treaty. The president's excuse for

opposing a summit conference thus disappeared. In July 1955 Eisenhower attended a meeting with leaders of the Soviet Union, Great Britain, and France in Geneva. The main topics on the agenda — the status of Germany and disarmament — could not be settled. But Eisenhower captured international attention by proposing an "open skies" plan that would allow each nation to observe the other's armaments to prevent surprise attack. The Soviet Union rejected the scheme, viewing it as a threat to its sovereignty.

The Geneva sessions produced no tangible results. The Soviet Union now accepted the division of Germany and took the final steps to establish a separate East German government. But the summit meeting did abate world tension, and the press hailed the peaceful "spirit of Geneva." In his state of the union message of January 1956, Eisenhower acknowledged a new facet to the Cold War. "Communist tactics against the free nations have shifted in emphasis," he declared, "from reliance on violence to reliance on division." To counter this strategy, the president counseled unity and strength. Secretary Dulles was more blunt. In an interview with *Life* magazine, he boasted about the salutary effects of a tough foreign policy. "We walked to the brink and we looked it in the face. We took strong action."

The limits of "brinksmanship" were revealed in two related crises in 1956. In February, the new Soviet leader, Nikita Khrushchev, greeted the Twentieth Congress of the Communist party with an astounding speech that denounced the policies of Stalin. In attacking the "cult of the individual," Khrushchev suggested that Stalin had erred in trying to build a monolithic Communist bloc in Eastern Europe. It was possible, Khrushchev implied, for communism to adapt to local conditions, separate from Soviet control. Two months later, the Soviet

Union dissolved Cominform, the instrument of international Communist conformity.

These liberalizing tendencies encouraged the Communist parties of Eastern Europe to seek independent positions. In the summer, riots in Poland against the Stalinist regime enabled independent Communists, led by Wladyslaw Gomulka, to come to power. With popular support Gomulka negotiated with Soviet leaders and won important concessions for national autonomy. Spurred by Poland's success, mass demonstrations erupted in Hungary, demanding removal of the Stalinist leadership. Despite opposition from conservatives within the Kremlin, Khrushchev accepted the rise of an independent Communist, Imre Nagy. But when Nagy announced that he was taking Hungary out of the Warsaw alliance, Khrushchev felt compelled to restore the solidarity of the Communist bloc. Ordering Soviet tanks into Budapest, Soviet leaders crushed the Hungarian uprising, despite the gallant resistance of poorly armed rebels.

The American response to these dramatic events was negligible. Though Radio Free Europe broadcast moral support, perhaps even exaggerating the United States's commitment to intervene, the Eisenhower administration settled for pious condemnations of Soviet cruelty. The United States introduced a resolution in the Security Council calling for withdrawal of Soviet forces, but the Soviet Union vetoed it. The United States then turned to the General Assembly. By then the rebellion had been broken. Having done nothing to help the rebels, Eisenhower decided to provide sanctuary for thousands of "freedom fighters" who sought asylum in the United States. Eisenhower's failure to act revealed the illusion of an easy "liberation" of Eastern Europe as well as the futility of relying on massive force as an exclusive instrument of policy. American impotence also betrayed serious divisions within the Western alliance.

CRISES IN THE MIDDLE EAST

The importance of oil in the postwar world underscored the economic and strategic value of the oil-rich Middle East. Though the United States supported the independence of Israel, it also took pains to maintain friendship with the Arab states. As part of its professed anticolonialism, the United States encouraged the departure of British forces from Egypt, which was accomplished by treaty between 1954 and 1956. In 1955, however, a successful Israeli attack had demonstrated Egypt's military weakness. The new Egyptian leader, Gamal Abdel Nasser, now sought outside assistance to strengthen his country economically and militarily. While Nasser negotiated with Czechoslovakia to purchase arms, Dulles moved to win Egyptian friendship by offering to finance the Aswan Dam, a giant hydroelectric project that promised to modernize Egypt. Nasser accepted the offer and made a formal application for American assistance.

Dulles's scheme soon ran into congressional opposition. Questioned about the implications of a Middle East arms race, the secretary admitted the possibility of a war between Israel and the Arab states. These fears were aggravated by the formation of an Arab military alliance in April 1956. One month later, Nasser announced his recognition of the People's Republic of China. This decision, together with the Czech arms purchase, lessened the possibility of obtaining congressional approval for Nasser's dam. In July Dulles decided to withdraw his offer to construct the project. "Do nations which play both sides get better treatment than nations which are stalwart and work with us?" asked Dulles piously.

The American reversal humiliated Nasser. One week later the Egyptian leader took revenge by nationalizing the Suez Canal. The seizure alarmed Great Britain and France, who were dependent on the canal for oil. Both nations hinted about the possibility of military reprisal. Dulles opposed such a reassertion of colonialism, fearing that it would drive the Arabs irrevocably into the Communist camp. He proposed as an alternative the creation of an independent canal commission to protect each side's interests. But the idea was unacceptable to all parties. Dulles's refusal to support the Western allies angered them, and they decided to take independent action. While the United States issued a bland statement condemning the use of force in the Middle East, Great Britain and France met with Israel to develop secret plans of attack.

In October Israel launched a surprise attack on Egypt. This conflict provided Great Britain and France with an excuse to intervene to protect the independence of the Suez Canal. The invasion coincided with the Soviet attack on the Hungarian rebels. Faced with a double crisis, the furious Eisenhower demanded that Great Britain and France withdraw from Egypt. So too did Khrushchev, who warned the Western nations about the possibility of a retaliatory attack. The Soviet leader also proposed that his nation join the United States in settling the controversy. This suggestion alarmed Eisenhower, who believed that the Soviet Union would use the conflict as an excuse to acquire power in the Middle East. The United States then rushed to avoid Soviet intervention by unilaterally demanding British and French withdrawal. To strengthen this demand, the

United States halted oil shipments from Latin America to its allies. Such pressure forced a capitulation. By December the allies had removed their forces from the Middle East. The entire episode demonstrated the growing influence of small nations on Big Power diplomacy.

Nasser's successful defiance of the European nations created a power vacuum in the Middle East. Eisenhower moved quickly to prevent the Soviet Union from taking advantage of the situation. In January 1957 the president asked Congress to approve a resolution, known as the Eisenhower Doctrine, "to deter Communist aggression in the Middle East area." Besides requesting a special appropriation for economic and military assistance, the resolution announced that "overt armed aggression from any nation controlled by international Communism" would be challenged by American military forces. As with the Formosa resolution, the president was seeking blanket authority for future executive action.

The proposal instigated a major debate in the Senate. J. William Fulbright of Arkansas denounced the administration's attempt to manipulate congressional opinion by surreptitious news leaks and secret meetings "in an atmosphere of suspense and urgency." He challenged the administration's unusual claim of executive powers and pointed out that Eisenhower offered no specific policy goals. Majority Leader Johnson, however, managed the bill through the Senate, but not before he weakened some of the president's discretionary powers.

The Eisenhower Doctrine became a convenient rationale for United States intervention in the Middle East. In April 1957 the regime of Jordan's King Hussein was threatened by pro-Nasser rebels. The king claimed, however, that the rebellion was really a Communist attack. Understanding the duplicity of language, Eisenhower nevertheless invoked his doctrine and sent the Sixth Fleet into the area to protect the political status quo. In July 1958 a similar distortion of events led the president to order the marines into Lebanon. This dramatic gesture served notice to Arab nationalists that the United States was determined to protect its access to Middle East oil.

THE POLITICS OF MODERATION

The willingness of Democrats to support the administration's foreign policy paralleled a prevailing consensus about domestic politics. Though liberals like Hubert Humphrey and Paul Douglas spoke eloquently about social reform, the Democratic leadership worked closely with Eisenhower's "modern" Republicans to enact minimal welfare legislation. Surveying the political spectrum in 1956, Adlai Stevenson aptly concluded that "moderation is the spirit of the times."

The limitations of this conservative consensus could be seen in the cautious approach to minimum wages, public housing, and health benefits. In 1955 Eisenhower proposed a 90¢-an-hour minimum wage, 35¢ less than organized labor desired, and extension of coverage to include unorganized retail and service workers. Democratic leaders wished to preserve the support of labor unions. But conservatives opposed broadening the coverage to unskilled workers, most of whom were members of racial minorities. Political leaders then agreed to a compromise that raised the minimum wage to $1 an hour but ignored unorganized laborers.

Though the Public Housing Act of 1949 had authorized the construction of nearly one million dwellings, subsequent appropriations had drastically reduced that figure. The shortage of adequate housing remained critical, especially in the cities. But in 1954 Eisenhower requested only 140,000 units. Congress responded by cutting that number to 75,000 over a two-year period. In the area of health care, political leaders in both branches of government dismissed proposals for national medical insurance as "socialized" medicine. In 1955 the administration endorsed the principle of providing free distribution of the new Salk vaccine to prevent poliomyelitis. But the Department of Health, Education, and Welfare drew a storm of criticism for failing to prepare an adequate program of supply and distribution.

Eisenhower's desire to minimize government involvement in the economy led him to reverse the Democrats' approach to public control of electric power projects. In 1954 the president recommended a revision of the Atomic Energy Act to allow private manufacture and operation of atomic reactors. This legislation led to the first privately run atomic power plants. More controversial was the administration's decision to by-pass the Tennessee Valley Authority in providing electricity for AEC facilities. Eisenhower endorsed an AEC contract with the Dixon-Yates Combine, believing that the federal government should not compete directly with private industry. The idea clashed with the very existence of TVA, long a symbol of New Deal liberalism. Amid charges of corruption, Eisenhower stood by the project. But in 1955 the city of Memphis independently decided to build a power plant that made Dixon-Yates a dead issue.

Despite such squabbles on domestic issues, Eisenhower remained extremely popular. But confidence in the administration was shaken in September 1955 when the president suffered a heart attack. With Eisenhower temporarily disabled, the public worried about the succession of the conservative vice president. Once Eisenhower's recovery seemed assured, the cabinet adopted administrative procedures to minimize Nixon's access to power. The administration also worked to coordinate government operations to avoid a semblance of internal dissension. Eisenhower recovered rapidly, but his health remained an important issue in the election of 1956.

Eisenhower was nevertheless confident about his abilities and resolved to seek a second term. There was no question about his receiving the nomination. In his acceptance speech the president forecast a time of peace and prosperity,

but warned that "it will not be attained by revolution [nor] by the sordid politics of pitting group against group." As president of all the people, Eisenhower would campaign on the principles of consensus. Eisenhower introduced an element of uncertainty for the Republicans when he hesitated to support Nixon as his running mate. The vice president fought back stubbornly and thwarted a weak "dump Nixon" movement.

With Eisenhower's nomination, the Democrats' chances seemed slim. But the race for the nomination saw stiff competition between Stevenson, Kefauver, and Harriman. Stevenson won a first-ballot decision and chose Kefauver as his running mate. The party then adopted a

MAP 13.3   THE ELECTION OF 1956

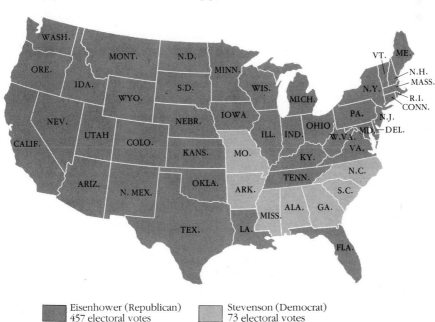

Eisenhower (Republican)
457 electoral votes

Stevenson (Democrat)
73 electoral votes

moderate, noncontroversial platform. Hoping to regain the South, the Democrats wavered on support of the Supreme Court's school desegregation decision. The party's position on foreign policy echoed the Cold War values of the Republican administration.

Stevenson introduced two controversial proposals in the campaign. He called for the end of the military draft and a moratorium on hydrogen bomb testing. These issues played directly to Eisenhower's strength, for the president appeared as an unquestioned authority on military affairs. The outbreak of the Suez crisis and the Hungarian revolt in October provided the Democrats with late-campaign ammunition. But the crisis in foreign policy merely reinforced Eisenhower's appeal as a leader in world affairs. "The butchers of the Kremlin," scoffed Nixon, "would make mincemeat of Stevenson over a conference table."

Eisenhower's margin of victory exceeded that of 1952. He captured 58 percent of the popular vote and carried all but seven states. But in an unusual situation, other Republican candidates fell far behind the president's pace, and the Democrats regained control of both houses of Congress. This anomalous situation reflected the persistence of party voting habits (there were 50 percent more registered Democrats than Republicans in 1956). Eisenhower could win Democratic support, but lesser Republicans lacked that advantage. The importance of foreign policy issues in the campaign reinforced that trend. Unlike domestic issues, which touched voters personally, international affairs remained distant for most people. Thus voters could follow their personal inclinations to support Eisenhower without upsetting any commitment to specific issues. In 1956 Eisenhower attracted voters in all political spectrums because issues were relatively unimportant.

DOMESTIC DEBATE

Despite his attempt to present a middle-of-the-road program, Eisenhower's second administration was marked by sharp discord with Congress. The first controversy erupted when the president presented a $71.8 billion budget request for 1958. Eisenhower claimed that this figure, the largest peacetime budget ever presented, represented a minimal estimate. But the president's calculations were undermined by Treasury Secretary George Humphrey. "If we fail to economize over a longer period of time," he told a press conference, "I predict...a depression that will curl your hair." Eisenhower weakened his position further by urging Congress to cut government expenditures as much as possible. These remarks fueled a bitter legislative "battle of the budget." Spurred by conservatives, Congress began to pick apart the president's budget, threatening the administration's entire program. Though Eisenhower attempted to rally public support, Congress held the power of the purse. In the end, the budget was shaved by $4 billion, including $1 billion in foreign aid.

The reduction of government expenditures, instead of strengthening the economy, had the opposite effect. By mid-1957, industrial production had dropped, unemployment increased, and members of the administration were worrying about the economic recession. Eisenhower remained skeptical about the value of government spending to stimulate the economy. But Congress had fewer reservations. Increased appropriations, including public works projects, added over $8 billion to the budget. By September 1958 these funds had halted the recession. But continued government spending also fed an inflation and resulted in large budgetary deficits.

This segregated laundromat epitomized the belief that black people were naturally unclean. (Leonard Freed/Magnum)

While Congress and the president wrangled over the economy, the nation approached a profound crisis over civil rights. During the fifties, major political candidates avoided taking a strong stand on civil rights legislation, lest they offend conservative voters. In his first year in office, Eisenhower promised to end segregation in the armed forces, the federal government, and the nation's capital — all policies that had been initiated by Truman — but otherwise stressed the role of the states and cities in resolving these questions. The Supreme Court desegregation decision of 1954, however, created a new climate of opinion.

The strongest movement for civil rights began in the streets of Montgomery, Alabama, in December 1955. Rosa Parks, a black seamstress, refused to obey a Jim Crow law requiring segregated seating in public buses. Her protest soon mushroomed into a citywide bus boycott led by a Baptist minister, Reverend Martin Luther King, Jr. This direct action not only won the immediate issue, but also demonstrated the advantages of organized black protest.

While whites resisted efforts at desegregation, Eisenhower tried to ignore the problem. "The final battle against intolerance," he remarked in 1956, "is to be fought — not in the chambers of any legislature — but in the hearts of men." The president firmly rebuffed suggestions that he take a strong stand in support of the desegregation of public schools. He did propose legislation that year to protect the voting rights of blacks. A weak measure passed the House, but was quickly killed in the Senate.

In 1957 Eisenhower again requested legislation to protect the right to vote. This proposal now won the support of Lyndon Johnson, who wished to demonstrate his liberal credentials and so enhance his chances for the presidential nomination in 1960. Working behind the scenes, Johnson persuaded southern leaders to drop the filibuster in exchange for a diluted bill. The majority leader then introduced amendments that weakened the administration's proposal. The new bill called for a powerless Civil Rights Commission and authorized the attorney general to seek injunctions for violations of voting rights. Johnson's strategy succeeded, and Congress passed the first significant civil rights legislation since Reconstruction.

The significance of the new law was soon dwarfed by a major defeat of segregation through direct action. In September 1957 Governor Orval Faubus of Arkansas mobilized the National Guard to prevent the integration of Central High School in Little Rock, an action that violated a federal court order. While armed soldiers prevented black students from attending the school, Eisenhower hesitated to act. Faubus's defiance of federal authority raised serious questions about the limits of federal power. These considerations, together with a growing concern about his personal prestige, finally moved the president to action. "Law can not be flaunted with impunity by any individual or mob of extremists," he declared. Three weeks after Faubus challenged federal authority, Eisenhower federalized the National Guard and ordered paratroopers to enforce the court decision. Despite continued mob protest, black students began attending the school.

The school integration case represented more than the breakdown of Jim Crow. In confronting white mobs, blacks learned that personal confrontations could be an effective weapon in the quest for equal rights. In 1957 Martin Luther King helped to organize a coalition of black activists in the Southern Christian Leadership Conference (SCLC). King also led a March on Washington in 1957 that attracted fifteen thousand protesters, a forerunner of later mass demonstrations. Such protests revealed a profound dissatisfaction among blacks at the lack of government response to their grievances. These feelings exploded in a series of spontaneous "sit-in" protests that began in February 1960. Instead of waiting for legislative or judicial sanction, young blacks simply violated Jim Crow laws. Such actions won mass support among northern whites who joined blacks in a national crusade for civil rights. This alliance between white liberals and blacks culminated in mass protests in the next decade.

Disillusionment with traditional institutions was intensified by the astounding news of October 4, 1957: the Soviet Union announced that it had launched an artificial satellite. "The Soviets have beaten us at our own game," declared Lyndon Johnson, "—daring scientific advances in the atomic age." Besides the philosophical shock waves caused by the triumph over the earth's gravitation, the launching demonstrated that the Soviet Union possessed superior rocket technology. The military implications of this superiority were impressive. The dreaded Soviet enemy had developed the capability of delivering intercontinental ballistic missiles (ICBMs) armed with nuclear weapons before the United States possessed sufficient retaliatory power. Within the administration, these fears were confirmed by a secret report prepared by Rowan Gaither. Eisenhower remained calm, however, and rejected Gaither's proposal to begin a national fallout shelter campaign.

The perceived sense of a missile gap fed popular fears of nuclear annihilation. Best-selling books like Nevil Shute's *On the Beach* (1957) and Walt Miller's *A Canticle for Leibowitz* (1959) dramatized the imminence of holocaust. These tensions help to explain the popularity of so-called sick comedians such as Mort Sahl and Lenny Bruce, who poked fun at the precariousness of contemporary institutions. The Eisenhower administration tried to alleviate these fears by denying any military deficiencies. But Democratic leaders took the occasion to criticize the Republican leadership. In the Senate, Johnson backed legislation to create a civilian-controlled space agency, the National Aeronautics and Space Administration (NASA), with expensive facilities in Johnson's home state of Texas. Senator John F. Kennedy of Massachusetts, looking toward the 1960 elections, began a sharp verbal campaign against the administration's handling of the missile gap.

The combination of Sputnik, Little Rock, and the recession, together with a conservative Republican stand on labor legislation, produced landslide victories for the Democrats in the elections of 1958. Democrats controlled the House by a margin of 283–153 and the Senate by 65–35. This majority confronted the administration with powerful opposition to its program. Democrats increased government spending for defense. The party also enacted the admission of Alaska and Hawaii in 1959, but carefully reversed the administration's priorities by welcoming the Democratic state first. Congress also embarrassed the president by denying the nomination of Lewis Strauss as secretary of commerce. Despite these disagreements, however, the administration worked with Congress to

Physicist Werner Von Braun explains the Saturn missile to President Eisenhower, during whose administration the United States strove to bridge the "missile gap." (Dwight D. Eisenhower Library)

enact aid to education, increased support of state unemployment programs, an anticorruption labor law, and a reorganization of the Pentagon.

PRESIDENTIAL DIPLOMACY

Eisenhower's last years in office saw the president increasingly concerned with foreign affairs. Dulles died in 1959, creating an opening for personal diplomacy. In 1958 Eisenhower had sent Nixon on a "goodwill" tour of Latin America. But the vice president had been met by hostile crowds that protested United States economic and political exploitation of the area. The administration dismissed these demonstrations as examples of Communist infiltration. But Adlai Stevenson returned from a trip to Latin America in 1960 with an alternative assessment. "It is foolish ... to attribute anti-Americanism just to Communist agitation," he maintained. The problem was that the Eisenhower administration "has been basically concerned with making Latin America safe for American business, not for democracy," especially by supporting "hated dictators."

Stevenson's analysis had a small impact on Eisenhower's relations with Cuba. After backing the right wing Fulgencio Batista since 1952, the United States reacted cautiously to the revolutionary government of Fidel Castro that seized power in 1959. Though the administration offered economic aid to Castro, it soon came to distrust the Cuban's anti-American posture and his open acceptance of left wing politics. In May 1959 Cuba enacted agrarian reform laws that nationalized some private American holdings. Eisenhower quickly cut off aid to Cuba and demanded immediate compensation. American antipathy to Castro increased when the Cuban leader summoned the United States to provide massive assistance for Latin American economic reform.

Eisenhower re-evaluated his policy toward Castro in 1960 with an eye toward reversing the Cuban's popularity in Latin America. But relations between the two nations became even worse. In February 1960 Castro announced the sale of sugar to the Soviet Union in exchange for economic and military assistance. Eisenhower feared a Soviet presence in this Amer-

ican sphere of influence. He then launched a two-pronged attack. In March Eisenhower ordered the CIA "to organize the training of Cuban exiles, mainly in Guatemala against a possible future day when they might return to their homeland." In public, the president exerted economic pressure by ordering a cut in American sugar purchases. Castro correctly protested that the reduction of sugar purchases was a preparation for an invasion. Khrushchev promptly announced that the Soviet Union would protect the Cuban government. Frustrated by Castro's audacity, Eisenhower severed diplomatic relations in January 1961, leaving the problem for his successor.

While protecting the United States's traditional dominance in Latin America, Eisenhower moved to reduce tension with the Soviet Union without jeopardizing American strength. Since his "atoms for peace" proposal of 1953, Eisenhower had emphasized inspection and control as a precondition for disarmament. In 1956 he had sneered at Stevenson's call for a halt in nuclear testing. But subsequent negotiations between American and Soviet scientists indicated that controls could be instituted. In 1958 the president announced that the United States was ending further nuclear testing. The Soviet Union inaugurated a final series of tests before it too halted similar explosions. The moratorium, however, did not indicate a significant shift of policy, for both powers remained committed to what Churchill called a "balance of terror."

Though liberals pressed for a reduction of the arms race, Eisenhower continued to pursue a Cold War strategy. In 1958 the United States assured West Germany that it would maintain its military obligations in Europe. The rearmament of Germany alarmed the Soviet Union, and Khrushchev decided to use his apparent

416

lead in ICBMs to demand that the Western powers remove their forces from Berlin. He issued a six-month deadline for compliance. Eisenhower rejected Khrushchev's demand, and both leaders spoke about the possibility of World War Three.

These tensions were eased in 1959 when Khrushchev and Eisenhower agreed to engage in personal diplomacy. The Soviet leader toured the United States and met amicably with the president at Camp David. Though substantive issues remained unresolved, Khrushchev quietly lifted his deadline for resolving the Berlin issue and invited Eisenhower to visit the Soviet Union. Encouraged by these trends, Eisenhower began a series of goodwill tours to Asia, Europe, and Latin America.

But in the spring of 1960, relations with the Soviet Union reached crisis proportions. The status of Germany remained a serious problem. A summit conference was scheduled to open in May 1960. The heads of state expressed optimism, but the diplomatic rift remained great. Then on May 5, Khrushchev announced that the Soviet Union had shot down an American spy plane, the U-2. The United States immediately denied the charge, claiming that a "weather plane" strayed from its course. But then Khrushchev produced the CIA pilot, Francis Gary Powers, revealing the American lie.

In seeking to clear his reputation, Eisenhower proceeded to make a series of diplomatic blunders. The State Department replied to the latest evidence by acknowledging the U-2 mission. It also justified such flights by affirming the importance of the "open skies" formula that the Soviet Union had rejected at Geneva in 1955. Khrushchev then lodged a formal protest of American violation of Soviet air space. Working through established diplomatic channels, Eisenhower still hoped to salvage the sum-

Moscow citizens view some incriminating evidence recovered from a U-2 spy plane piloted by Francis Gary Powers and downed by the Russians in May 1960. This incident and the American government's response were later used by Soviet Premier Khrushchev as an occasion for breaking up the Paris summit conference between him and President Eisenhower. (Dwight D. Eisenhower Library)

mit conference with Khrushchev. By claiming ignorance of the U-2 program, the president could rise above the crisis. But Eisenhower's disavowal of knowledge of the spy missions implied that subordinates had taken control of the administration. Such a situation, especially in an election year, threatened the president's power. Eisenhower therefore was forced to acknowledge his complicity. "It is a distasteful but vital necessity," he declared, reminding the

American public of the lessons of Pearl Harbor. Eisenhower's admission destroyed the summit meeting. At the Paris session, Khrushchev denounced the president and refused to negotiate. The Cold War came alive with tension.

The intensification of the Cold War had a profound effect on public opinion. Democratic politicians attempted to lay the blame exclusively at Eisenhower's door. Though careful to maintain a Cold War stance, Stevenson condemned the president for handing Khrushchev "the crowbar and the sledgehammer" to wreck the summit conference. More fundamental, however, the U-2 affair shocked the American public by revealing the duplicity of its government. Eisenhower, who strove to rise above parties, had lied not only to Khrushchev, but also to American citizens. The notion of a credibility gap between the people and their government would haunt American politics for the next two decades.

SUGGESTED READINGS

A comprehensive treatment of the Eisenhower administration is provided by Herbert S. Parmet, *Eisenhower and the American Crusades* (1972). Also helpful is a biography by Peter Lyon on *Eisenhower: Portrait of a Hero* (1974). A detailed collection of primary sources is Robert L. Branyan and Lawrence H. Larsen, *The Eisenhower Administration*, 2 vols. (1971).

The political issues are described in James Sundquist, *Politics and Policy: The Eisenhower, Kennedy, and Johnson Years* (1968). For insights into congressional power, see Rowland Evans and Robert Novak, *Lyndon B. Johnson: The Exercise of Power* (1966). Stevenson's career is described favorably in Stuart Gerry Brown, *Conscience in Politics* (1961), which includes many original sources, and the more detailed study, John Bartlow Martin, *Adlai Stevenson of Illinois* (1976). For Nixon, see the superb analysis by Garry Wills, *Nixon Agonistes* (1970). Voting behavior in the fifties is explained in Norman H. Nie et al., *The Changing American Voter* (1976).

A detailed study of southern politics is Jack Bass and Walter DeVries, *The Transformation of Southern Politics: Social Change and Political Consequence Since 1945* (1976). For the Warren Court, see the relevant chapters of Paul L. Murphy, *The Constitution in Crisis Times: 1918–1969* (1972). Works relating to the civil rights movement are listed at the end of chapter 11.

The best study of McCarthyism is Richard H. Rovere, *Senator Joe McCarthy* (1959). Also helpful on McCarthy's support are Michael Paul Rogin, *The Intellectuals and McCarthy* (1967), and David M. Oshinsky, *Senator Joseph McCarthy and the American Labor Movement* (1976). For McCarthy's relationship to the Senate, see Robert Griffith, *The Politics of Fear* (1970).

A good introduction to Eisenhower's foreign policy is Walter Lafeber's *America, Russia, and the Cold War* (1976). It should be supplemented by Townsend Hoopes, *The Devil and John Foster Dulles* (1973). For the secret foreign policy, see David Wise and Thomas B. Ross, *The Invisible Government* (1964), and Victor Marchetti and John D. Marks, *The CIA and the Cult of Intelligence* (1974).

Chapter 14

The Cold War loomed large in the 1960 presidential election. For eight years Eisenhower had extolled the warrior virtues of strength and power. But at the age of seventy, Eisenhower was the oldest man ever to hold the nation's highest office. He now seemed impotent against Khrushchev's indignation, the eruption of liberation movements in Asia and Africa, and anti-American protests in Latin America and Japan. Popular jokes referred to the "Eisenhower doll—wind it up and it does nothing for eight years." In the Senate, John F. Kennedy attacked the president for failing "to maintain the minimum conditions for our survival." "This is not a call of despair," he added. "It is a call for action."

The Massachusetts senator used the theme of Republican immobility in his bid for the presidency. As the youngest candidate (only forty-two when he announced his intention), Kennedy symbolized strength, vigor, and energy. "We've got to get this country moving again," he insisted. But Democratic leaders felt that Kennedy's youthfulness might be an electoral handicap. More problematic was the candidate's Roman Catholic religion. Only one Catholic, Al Smith, had run for president, and he had suffered a devastating defeat in 1928, losing even the "solid" Democratic South.

To remove these doubts, Kennedy entered a series of primary contests against his major rival, Senator Hubert H. Humphrey of Minnesota.

As a native New England, Kennedy easily won in New Hampshire. He also triumphed in Wisconsin. But voting analysis revealed that Kennedy carried Catholic voters, whereas Humphrey attracted Protestants. Kennedy's appeal as a national candidate thus hinged on his performance in West Virginia, an impoverished state with a 95 percent Protestant population. Confronting the religious issue directly, Kennedy's expensive campaign overcame traditional Protestant prejudices. He went to the Democratic convention with a clear advantage over his rivals. At the last moment, supporters of Adlai Stevenson tried to draft the two-time loser. But Kennedy held firmly to his delegate support and won a first-ballot nomination. Then, to balance the slate in the conservative South, he chose Majority Leader Lyndon Johnson of Texas as his running mate.

KENNEDY VERSUS NIXON

While the Democratic candidates captured national headlines in their race for the nomination, Vice President Richard M. Nixon quietly called in a dozen years of political debts to cement his support within the Republican party. New York's Governor Nelson Rockefeller briefly challenged the vice president, but Nixon easily won the nomination. The lack of serious opposition cost Nixon national publicity. But he tried to take advantage of the situation by posing as a candidate above party faction. He chose as his running mate Henry Cabot Lodge, who had served as the United States ambassador to the United Nations, where he had earned a popular reputation as a defender of "captive peoples." Republicans expected Lodge to appeal to the anti-Communist ethnic minorities, perhaps to undermine some of Kennedy's Catholic support.

Kennedy's Catholicism remained a controversial subject. He decided to bring the issue to the forefront at the Houston Ministerial Association, a gathering of Methodists that held national interest. "I am not the Catholic candidate," he announced. "I am the Democratic Party's candidate . . . , who happens also to be a Catholic." Kennedy carefully delineated his commitment to the separation of church and state, expressing disbelief that "40 million Americans lost their chance of being President on the day they were baptized." The effect of Kennedy's speech was difficult to determine. But Kennedy rose in favor among black Protestants in mid-campaign when he telephoned support to Martin Luther King, who had been arrested in Georgia. Black evangelicals overcame their doubts about Kennedy's religion and remained faithful to the Democratic party.

Despite Kennedy's handicaps, Nixon recognized that the number of registered Democrats exceeded Republicans. He hoped to attract independents and Democratic crossovers by emphasizing his relationship to President Eisenhower. Contrasting his own experience with Kennedy's youth, Nixon suggested that he had provided leadership within the Eisenhower administration. Yet the president resented such exaggeration. When asked by reporters about Nixon's participation in key administration decisions, Eisenhower replied, "If you give me a week, I might think of one." The negative effects of this statement were aggravated by Eisenhower's minimal activity in support of Nixon's candidacy. At the same time, however, Nixon was forced to defend Eisenhower's policies, including the president's handling of the U-2 affair. Kennedy thus enjoyed the advantage of attacking the party in power. "Mr. Nixon says 'We never had it so good,'" Kennedy remarked. "I say we can do better."

The differences between the candidates were less substantive, more a question of emphasis. In his acceptance speech to the nominating convention, Kennedy proclaimed that the nation stood "on the edge of a New Frontier — the frontier of the 1960's — a frontier of unknown opportunities and peril — a frontier of unfulfilled hopes and threats." Such rhetoric appealed to a national fascination with mobility, with a pervasive sense of rootlessness. Kennedy's willingness to use these metaphors instead of

the traditional Catholic emphasis on roots and a sense of place reflected his commitment to melting pot assimilation. Thus his language easily merged with Nixon's. The vice president's frenetic mobility was symbolized by his decision to visit all fifty states during the campaign. As the race drew to a close, Nixon also embraced the imagery of frontiers and rootlessness. "This country has always been full of the great spirit of conquering new frontiers," the Republican declared.

The substantive similarities between the candidates emerged in a series of nationally televised debates that attracted over 100 million viewers. On domestic matters, both candidates agreed about such goals as economic growth,

MAP 14.1   THE ELECTION OF 1960

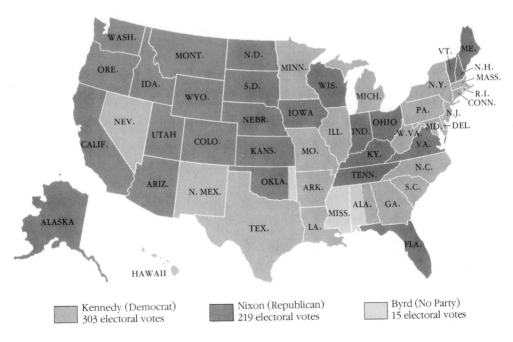

| Kennedy (Democrat) 303 electoral votes | Nixon (Republican) 219 electoral votes | Byrd (No Party) 15 electoral votes |

aid to the poor, and material progress. They both defended the records of their predecessors, with Kennedy summoning the memory of Roosevelt and Truman, and Nixon boasting about Eisenhower. In foreign policy, the candidates shared the vision of Cold Warriors. The only significant difference was whether to defend Quemoy and Matsu. Kennedy suggested that the islands were not essential to the security of Taiwan; Nixon warned that a retreat from such areas of freedom would "start a chain reaction."

Despite these common assumptions, television highlighted not the candidates' words but their manner of presentation. Radio listeners, who were not distracted by visual appearances, reacted favorably to Nixon's speeches. But the television cameras accentuated the vice president's heavy "five o'clock shadow" and dark eye sockets. His makeup dripped, and his body movements seemed stiff. Suffering from a severe cold, he looked unhealthy, if not unsavory. In contrast, Kennedy brought a dramatic flair to the television screen. He seemed comfortable and confident. The television format, by projecting the candidates as equals, added to Kennedy's national reputation. Subsequent polls indicated that the debates may have influenced as many as four million voters; of these, Kennedy gathered three-quarters.

Such intangible factors had immense significance, for the balloting was extremely close. With nearly sixty-nine million people voting, Kennedy obtained a popular majority of only 118,000 — a margin of one-tenth of 1 percent. Kennedy's electoral victory was a decisive 303–219, but these figures concealed paper-thin majorities in such key states as Illinois and Texas. A switch of only thirty-five thousand votes could have reversed the final decision. Kennedy

also trailed behind Democratic congressional candidates. Though the Democrats maintained control of both houses of Congress, the freshman class of new legislators formed a majority in opposition to the presidential victor. Since southern Democrats frequently aligned with Republicans, the administration lacked a working majority in Congress.

Kennedy's narrow victory revealed significant political trends. In the South, Kennedy's Catholicism reduced his support. But the presence of Lyndon Johnson on the ticket offset this deficiency. Nixon failed to match Eisenhower's success in that region. Yet Republicans carried Virginia, Florida, Kentucky, and Tennessee. Members of the electoral college from Alabama and Mississippi, nominally Democratic, cast their ballots for Harry F. Byrd of Virginia. These patterns suggested a renaissance of the two-party system in the South. In the North, Kennedy captured 78 percent of the Catholic vote. He also won the support of blacks and Jews. The return of these predominantly urban groups to the Democratic party indicated that Eisenhower's popularity was a personal, not a party, phenomenon.

THE KENNEDY PRESIDENCY

With his slender majority, Kennedy was not about to initiate bold departures of policy. He immediately showed his orthodoxy by reappointing J. Edgar Hoover and Allen Dulles to their positions as heads of the FBI and CIA. Kennedy's cabinet appointments also represented the same corporate elites that had served in previous administrations. The president intended to maintain personal control over foreign policy. For secretary of state, he passed over Adlai Stevenson, who was considered too weak a warrior, and chose the hawkish but unassertive Dean Rusk. To head the Department of Defense, Kennedy selected the president of the Ford Motor Company, Robert McNamara, an energetic believer in administrative efficiency and technological expertise. Douglas Dillon, a Wall Street financier and member of the Eisenhower administration, became Kennedy's secretary of the treasury. The most controversial appointment was Kennedy's nomination for attorney general: his brother Robert F. Kennedy. In making this choice, the president not only brought his major political adviser directly into the administration, but also established tight control of the sensitive area of executive law enforcement.

The Kennedy leadership extolled the values of scientific management and cold reason. "Most of the problems...that we now face are technical problems, are administrative problems," Kennedy declared in 1962. "They are very sophisticated judgments which do not lend themselves to the great sort of 'passionate movements' which have stirred this country so often in the past." Matters of foreign policy, the president suggested, "are so sophisticated and so technical that people who are not intimately involved week after week, month after month, reach judgments which are based on emotion rather than knowledge of the real alternatives." Such assumptions not only justified reliance on technical experts, but also allowed the administration to ignore popular opinion.

This optimism about executive leadership reflected a growing acceptance of an activist government. Though conservatives condemned the expansion of government services, a large pub-

lic consensus had become confident that careful management could solve basic social and economic problems. "There is a recurring temptation to feel that some spectacular and costly action could become the miraculous solution to all current difficulties," admitted President Eisenhower. This confidence in public affairs contrasted with older fears about big government. The inclusion of private questions in the census, for example, had aroused bitter controversy in 1940 and 1950. But in the year of Kennedy's election, such complaints had given way to a silent acquiescence in government intrusion.

Kennedy's promise of dynamic leadership alarmed the outgoing president. In a farewell address to the American people, Eisenhower warned against the temptations of "unrealistic programs." Citing the emergence of a "military-industrial complex," the civilian-soldier urged the nation to be vigilant against "the disastrous rise of misplaced power." He also pointed to the dangers of plundering natural resources and thus jeopardizing the material abundance that had nourished a unique American heritage.

Eisenhower's caution contrasted with the grandiose optimism of Kennedy's inaugural address. "Let the word go forth," Kennedy announced, "that the torch has been passed to a new generation of Americans—born in this century, tempered by war, disciplined by a hard and bitter peace, proud of our ancient heritage." Avoiding the domestic questions that might provoke disagreement, the president spoke to the problems of world affairs. Like his predecessor, Kennedy repeated the warrior virtues of strength, warning of the temptation of "weakness," yet "racing to alter that uncertain balance of terror that stays the hand of mankind's final war." To the rhetoric of the Cold War, the

A youthful President-elect Kennedy listens to outgoing President Eisenhower, the oldest man to hold the nation's highest office. (Wide World Photos)

president added an apocalyptic dimension, describing the nation at "its hour of maximum danger."

During the recent campaign Kennedy had insisted that there was no difference between a Protestant and a Catholic president. Yet the new leader added a distinct, if subtle, Catholic perspective to the Cold War. Like his predecessors, Kennedy defined communism as a total threat to American life. But where earlier Cold Warriors envisioned a dramatic transformation of the forces of evil, Kennedy spoke more about the "burden" of "relentless struggle" with no early or simple resolution. "I do not shrink from this responsibility," he boasted, "I welcome it." Such work "will not be finished in the first one hundred days," he admitted. "Nor will it be finished in the first one thousand days, nor in the life of this Administration, nor even perhaps in our lifetime on this planet." Insisting that the moment of spiritual conversion for the American people would not be easy or instantaneous, Kennedy stated more simply, "Let us begin."

NEW FRONTIERS

Kennedy's world view of steady struggle culminated in his famous appeal: "Ask not what your country can do for you — ask what you can do for your country." To the familiar military summons, Kennedy added the possibility of alternative service. Adopting an idea of Hubert Humphrey, Kennedy established the Peace Corps to bring American technological skills to impoverished areas of the world. Such service, the president hastened to add, "will not be easy." Like American businesspeople and military service men and women, members of the Peace Corps acted as missionaries of the American way of life. By 1963 Kennedy could boast that over one million citizens, including ten thousand Peace Corps volunteers, lived outside the territorial frontiers of the United States, where they served "on a mission of freedom."

The creation of the Peace Corps reflected Kennedy's recognition that the nations of Asia, Africa, and Latin America held the key to the global struggle against communism. The new president pledged his "best efforts" to assist the new nations "to break the bonds of mass misery." Kennedy established a Food for Peace program that shipped surplus food to poor countries. He claimed to be motivated not by international politics, "but because it is right." Unlike Eisenhower and Dulles, Kennedy did not publicly insist that neutral nations take sides in the Cold War. In the former Belgian colony of the Congo, for example, the administration supported a U.N. peace mission that backed a neutralist government. Yet Kennedy expected U.N. intervention to keep the Soviet Union out of Africa. He therefore allowed the CIA to provide secret cash payments as well as military aid to friendly Congolese politicians. No less than Eisenhower, Kennedy was not prepared to "lose" areas of freedom to communism.

Kennedy's approach to economically underdeveloped nations revealed an inability to understand the dynamics of social change. In his inaugural address, Kennedy called for "a new alliance for progress" in Latin America. Two months later he announced "a vast cooperative effort ... to satisfy the basic needs of the American peoples for homes, work and land, health and schools." Promising to bring technical expertise and capital investments, the president envisioned major agrarian reform and public welfare within the context of democratic institutions. These promises were institutionalized at a conference at Punta del Este in August 1961. Pledging $20 billion over ten years, the Kennedy administration predicted rapid economic development that would alleviate the endemic poverty of Latin America while bringing social reform. Such assistance had the indirect advantage of boosting the United States's sagging prestige in the area.

Despite Kennedy's rhetoric about linking social reform to economic growth, the United States had no intention of redistributing wealth and power in Latin America. Fearful of triggering a mass revolution in the image of Castro's Cuba, the administration expected to work through the established elites and business interests. But these groups, though desirous of assistance, had no wish to participate in democratic reform sponsored by North American "Yanquis." Promises of agrarian reform thus

A Peace Corps volunteer teaches students in Nigeria, one of many Americans of all ages who responded to Kennedy's call for active service. (Marc Riboud/Magnum)

brought minimal gains to impoverished peasants.

United States business interests were equally reluctant to risk investment in Latin America. In 1962 Congress approved the Hickenlooper Amendment, which prohibited foreign aid to countries that nationalized or excessively taxed United States corporate property. The next year, the Foreign Assistance Act established an Investment Guaranty program that required recipients of United States aid to insure investors against losses due to nationalization. These requirements protected a conservative economic program. Most aid to Latin America came in

the form of loans, rather than grants, that had to be repaid with interest and other service charges (usually amounting to half the face value of the loans). Even these limited funds had to be spent within the United States at prevailing prices. The Alliance for Progress merely protected the United States's traditional markets in the Western Hemisphere.

The Alliance for Progress also promised to blunt the revolutionary appeal of Fidel Castro. During his last days in office, Eisenhower had broken diplomatic relations with Cuba and had encouraged the CIA to plan a military coup.

As a presidential candidate, Kennedy endorsed the overthrow of Castro, describing Cuba as "a hostile and militant Communist satellite." Central to Kennedy's reasoning was the belief that Castro did not represent the Cuban people. These assumptions were reinforced by CIA reports, based on interviews with Cuban refugees, suggesting that anti-Castro sentiment could topple the regime. To increase pressure on Castro, Kennedy persuaded business leaders to boycott Cuban dealings; in March 1961 he prohibited the importation of Cuban sugar.

These efforts culminated in a CIA-planned invasion of Cuba at the Bay of Pigs in April 1961. Using Cuban exiles, the CIA had trained a military force at secret bases in Guatemala. On the eve of the invasion, however, Kennedy received information suggesting that Castro knew about the plan. The president nevertheless approved the scheme. But the CIA planned badly, landing the invaders at an indefensible position and losing critical supplies. At the last moment, Kennedy canceled United States air support, dooming the mission. Most serious, the administration had failed to realize the strong political base of the Castro government.

Though American newspapers had received unofficial leaks about the Bay of Pigs operation, the administration had prevailed upon the major publishers to suppress the story. This policy was encouraged by deliberate lying in official circles. "There will not be, under any conditions, an intervention in Cuba by the United States Armed Forces," the president told a press conference five days before the futile mission. On the morning of the invasion, Dean Rusk issued an equally unreliable statement. "The American people are entitled to know whether we are intervening in Cuba or intend to do so in the future," he maintained. "The answer to that question is no. What happens in Cuba is for the Cuban people to decide." Nevertheless, the administration steadfastly refused to believe that that was exactly what had happened at the Bay of Pigs.

In justifying the invasion, Kennedy defined Castro in the context of the Cold War. "We are opposed around the world by a monolithic and ruthless conspiracy," he told the nation's leading news editors, "that relies primarily on covert means for expanding its sphere of influence." This "rising din of Communist voices," Kennedy concluded, had to be matched by strong counter-insurgency. The president regretted not the launching of the invasion force but the failure of its mission. The situation also required "self-discipline" at home to "match the iron discipline" of the Communists. Embarrassed by the premature disclosure of the Bay of Pigs operation, Kennedy urged the news media to limit their reporting of world events. "Every democracy," he claimed, "recognizes the necessary restraints of national security."

In the aftermath of the Bay of Pigs, the president moved to strengthen his control over the CIA. Following a McNamara proposal, he established a Defense Intelligence Agency to coordinate military intelligence as a check on civilian operations. Kennedy did not oppose illegal CIA activities against foreign governments. But he limited CIA operations to paramilitary activities that were "plausibly deniable." In 1962 he replaced Allen Dulles with a Kennedy-style technician, John McCone.

In shifting responsibility to the CIA, Kennedy failed to realize the inherent fallacy of his counterrevolutionary assumptions: that Castro, in fact, spoke for the Cuban people. Eighteen months after the Bay of Pigs, the president broadcast an appeal to "the captive people of Cuba" and described their leaders as "puppets and agents of an international conspiracy." Kennedy continued to exert economic pressure on the Castro regime, prohibiting trade with the island. The CIA also endeavored to disrupt Cuban commerce with the Soviet Union, in one case deliberately contaminating a shipload of sugar with bad-tasting chemicals. Secret CIA operations included support of anti-Castro exiles and underworld gangsters who returned to Cuba as guerrillas and assassins.

COUNTER-INSURGENCY IN SOUTHEAST ASIA

Kennedy's inability to understand the Cuban revolution and the nature of the defeat at the Bay of Pigs embroiled him in the political struggles of Southeast Asia. "Thank God the Bay of Pigs happened when it did," Kennedy told Theodore Sorensen six months later. "Otherwise we'd be in Laos now." The Cuban fiasco had taught the president about the risks of ill-prepared military adventures. But he had not grasped the political implications of indigenous revolutionary movements. Laos, instead of spelling a new direction in American foreign policy, proved to be merely a prelude to Vietnam.

As Eisenhower handed the reins of office to Kennedy, the outgoing president apologized for the "mess" in Laos. "You might have to go in there and fight it out." A political coalition established in 1954 had collapsed four years later. The Eisenhower administration had then moved to support an anti-Communist regime. But when the pro-American government used rigged elections in 1960 to exclude both Communists and neutralists, the dissidents organized a coup that triggered a three-sided civil war. As the United States supported one faction, the Soviet Union backed the Pathet Lao.

Upon entering office, Kennedy announced his support for "an independent country not dominated by either side." Unable to see the Laotian crisis as a domestic problem, however, the president warned about the influence of "outside" forces. "We cannot . . . accept any visible humiliation over Laos," he declared. The new administration soon began preparations for military intervention. But the Soviet Union, fearful not only of the United States but also of China, wanted no controversy. Kennedy and Khrushchev agreed to reconvene the Geneva Convention and work for a political settlement based on Laotian neutrality. In reaching this decision, the president overruled the advice of military leaders who favored the use of force. With removal of the great powers, the competing Laotian factions agreed to form a neutralist government in 1962.

Despite the formal settlement in Laos, however, the Kennedy administration decided to create a pro-American regime. Using the foreign aid program, the United States pressured the neutralist government to exclude the Communist faction. Meanwhile, the CIA provided assistance to anti-Communist guerrillas to escalate the military struggle against the Pathet Lao. In 1963 these pressures exploded into open warfare on the Plain of Jarres. United States involvement steadily increased, leading to secret bombing raids against the local Communists. As in Cuba, Kennedy failed to realize the strength of indigenous revolutionary sentiment.

The Laotian controversy soon blurred into the larger United States commitment to South Vietnam. In both countries Kennedy saw Communist aggression "nibbling away" at the forces of freedom. "The complacent, the self-indulgent, the soft societies are about to be swept away with the debris of history," Kennedy warned at the time of the Bay of Pigs. "Only the strong, only the industrious, only the determined, only the courageous, only the visionary who determine the real nature of our struggle can possibly survive." By 1961 the Vietnamese regime of Ngo Dinh Diem was rapidly losing ground to the pro-Communist Viet Cong as well as to non-Communist dissidents. Kennedy believed that the United States had to intervene in Vietnam to halt the erosion of power on the peripheries of the "free world."

MAP 14.2   VIETNAM AND SURROUNDING INDOCHINA

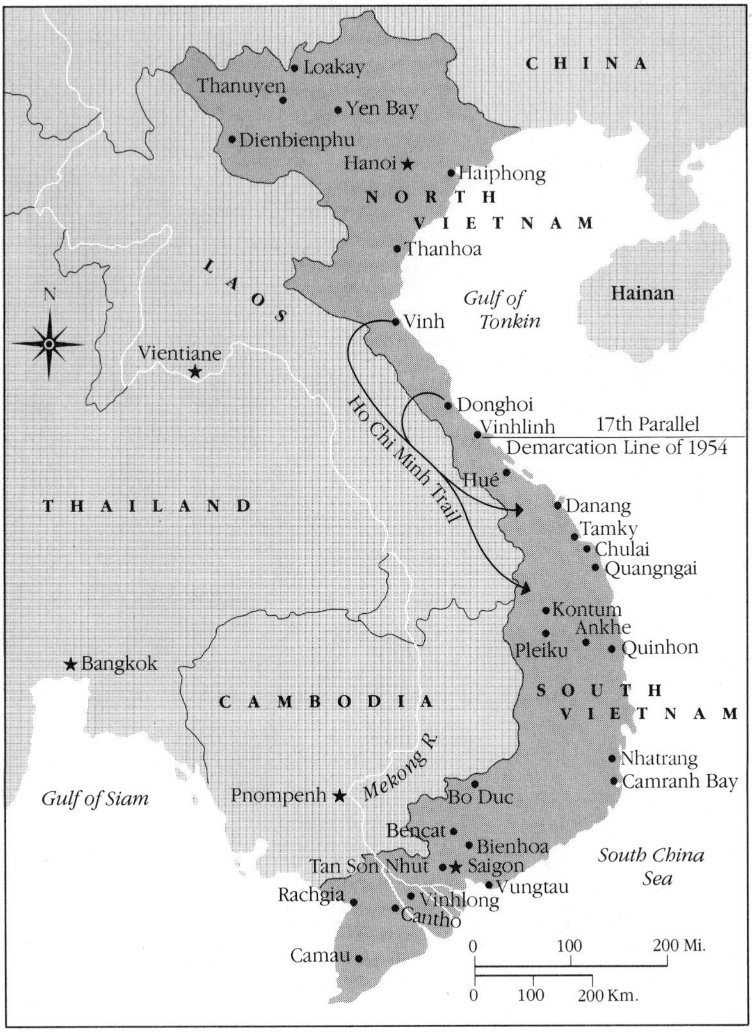

The president supported a policy of counter-insurgency. Where the Eisenhower administration had emphasized the strategy of massive retaliation aimed at the Soviet Union, Kennedy stressed the importance of conventional arms for "brush-fire" wars and guerrilla activity. These beliefs led Kennedy not only to increase American ground forces but also to develop the elite Special Forces (Green Berets), counter-insurgent training centers, and specialized guerrilla equipment. All these forces converged in Vietnam. As General Maxwell Taylor explained in 1963, Vietnam was "a going laboratory" for the study of "subversive insurgency."

Humiliated by his public defeat at the Bay of Pigs and cautious about involvement in Laos, Kennedy decided to act decisively in Vietnam in the spring of 1961. While Vice President Johnson consulted with Diem in Saigon, Kennedy authorized an increase in the number of military advisers and dispatched Green Berets and intelligence agents to engage in covert warfare. The president also invited Diem to request additional ground forces. But the Vietnamese leader opposed American pressure to initiate political reforms and waited until October 1961 to apply for more troops. Kennedy's decisions were reinforced by the vice president's report from Vietnam. Failure to help Diem, Johnson maintained, "would say to the world ...that we don't live up to our treaties and don't stand by our friends."

As Diem's position continued to deteriorate, Kennedy sent another advisory team, headed by General Taylor and the economist Walt W. Rostow, to Saigon in October 1961. They reported that Diem required massive military assistance, including ground troops. The president, however, was reluctant to commit conventional forces and risk a repetition of the Korean War. Kennedy instead viewed Vietnam from the perspective of the Philippines and Malaya, in which counter-insurgency had proved effective. At the end of 1961, therefore, he authorized an increase of military assistance, including "support troops" and technical advisers. The CIA also began recruiting and training Montagnard mercenaries to fight the anti-Communist crusade. These military activities were augmented by an attempt to pressure Diem to make basic political reforms to win the loyalty of the Vietnamese people. As in Latin America, however, American efforts to promote democratic reform proved futile. Diem remained committed to his own power.

As American aid poured into Vietnam, the level of violence steadily increased. Helicopter warfare initially terrorized the Viet Cong, forcing them to withdraw from exposed positions. In 1962 the National Liberation Front, which represented primarily southern Vietnamese opposed to Diem, indicated a willingness to negotiate a neutralization of South Vietnam. But the Kennedy administration, optimistic about military victory, rebuffed the approach. Meanwhile, the United States persuaded Diem to experiment with political counter-insurgency based on "strategic hamlets." Assuming that guerrilla armies required a popular base, the scheme proposed the physical separation of the peasants behind barbed wire encampments. Lacking contact with the people, the guerrillas would lose their support and disappear. The Diem regime embraced the idea, for it facilitated control of the population. But Vietnamese peasants resented the forced uprooting as well as the pervasive corruption of the government. Nor did the hamlets provide safety from Viet Cong attack.

Despite the failure of the strategic hamlet

program, members of the Kennedy administration remained optimistic about a final victory. "Every quantitative measurement we have," declared McNamara with his typical faith in numbers, "shows we're winning this war." In his 1963 state of the union message, Kennedy boasted that the "spearpoint of aggression has been blunted in Vietnam." The State Department confirmed this optimism by announcing that thirty thousand Viet Cong had been killed in 1962; that figure, however, was twice as large as the estimated size of the entire Viet Cong organization at the beginning of the year. "We can't win," said a GI parody of administrative double talk, "but it's not absolutely essential to pick today to lose."

Exaggerated administration claims stemmed not only from naiveté or poor calculation. They also reflected a determined effort to deceive the American people about the nature of the United States commitment. Government officials systematically avoided publicizing their operations in Vietnam. As in the Bay of Pigs affair, the administration misled the press, offering government news briefings in place of first-hand coverage. Kennedy also tried to suppress unfavorable stories, personally asking the *New York Times* to reassign its Saigon reporter, David Halberstam.

The bad news could not always be silenced. By 1963 the Viet Cong had taken the military initiative, stepping up terrorist attacks against the Diem regime. Equally serious was Diem's refusal to offer political reform. The issue climaxed in 1963 when Buddhist militants protested against Diem's dictatorial policies. South Vietnamese soldiers fired on the crowd, precipitating further demonstrations and bloody reprisals. In June a Buddhist priest dramatically set himself on fire to protest the abuses of power. Though Americans were horrified by a series of self-immolations, Diem's supporters remained unmoved, scoffing at the "barbecue show" and intensifying a reign of terror.

Such reactions embarrassed the Kennedy administration, but the president took refuge in the domino theory. "For us to withdraw from that effort," he told a press conference, "would mean a collapse not only of South Vietnam, but Southeast Asia. So we are going to stay there." The administration nevertheless began seriously to consider the removal of Diem. When the Vietnamese leader refused to institute political changes, the administration encouraged a military coup. On November 2, 1963, Diem was captured by his own army officers and killed.

Diem's death shocked Kennedy. But the president did not live long enough to revise his commitment to Vietnam. On September 2 Kennedy had acknowledged that the United States could not win the war for the Vietnamese people. "In the final analysis," he said, "it is their war." In the same interview the president rejected the possibility of withdrawal. One month later, however, Kennedy announced that one thousand soldiers would return from Vietnam by the end of the year and that the major United States commitment would end in 1965. Kennedy's decision may have reflected the same misplaced optimism that characterized American policy toward Vietnam throughout the sixties. Yet Kennedy never rescinded his order. Moreover, a high-level meeting in Honolulu on November 20, 1963, agreed to an "accelerated plan" for the withdrawal of American forces. Such shadowy evidence suggests that with Diem out of the way, Kennedy was thinking about a political solution to the war.

KENNEDY AND KHRUSHCHEV

The limitations of Kennedy's policies in Africa, Latin America, and Asia confirmed his world view of "relentless struggle." In the European arena, however, Kennedy spoke a simpler language of military strength. Having campaigned on the issue of Soviet military superiority, the Democratic president did not reverse his position when he learned, shortly after taking office, that there never had been a missile gap. Nor did the new president respond to a cordial letter from the Kremlin or to the friendly gesture of releasing several imprisoned American fliers.

Kennedy instead devoted his first state of the union message to exaggerating the "national peril." Warning that a monolithic Communist conspiracy sought "world domination," the president called for extensive investments in American military defense. Two months later, Kennedy made the first of three military budget requests, asking Congress to appropriate $2.4 billion. Though aware of American missile superiority, he earmarked most of the funding for missile programs. In May, barely a month after the Bay of Pigs disaster, Kennedy requested additional appropriations for conventional weapons and counter-insurgency.

This extensive military buildup reflected the president's belief that the Cold War could be ended — by victory over the Soviet Union. "Let us never negotiate out of fear," he had said in the inaugural address. "But let us never fear to negotiate." Knowing that the Soviet Union trailed far behind the United States in weaponry, Kennedy hoped to create a preponderance of power that would force the Kremlin to accept American terms. In this spirit, he agreed to meet Khrushchev in Vienna in June 1961.

Kennedy underestimated the Soviet position. Though Khrushchev had made conciliatory gestures and was keenly aware of American military superiority, he would not sacrifice Soviet national interest to the bellicose president. The two leaders could easily agree to neutralize Laos, because neither perceived that country to be of vital national concern. But the question of Berlin was less open to negotiation. Reminding Kennedy that World War Two had been over for sixteen years, the Soviet leader demanded that the Western powers sign a final peace treaty that recognized the two Germanys and ended the military occupation of Berlin. Otherwise, he warned, the Soviet Union would sign a separate treaty with East Germany, leaving the Western powers to settle with the de facto regime. Kennedy refused to consider Khrushchev's proposal, insisting that the United States could not abandon its allies in West Berlin. Khrushchev argued that Berlin had no military significance and that he wished only to legitimate the European status quo to reduce further tension. Kennedy remained adamant. "It will be a cold winter," he remarked.

The president returned from Vienna bearing "sober" news for the American people. In a televised speech, Kennedy reaffirmed his intention to maintain American forces in Berlin. This inflexibility, following on the spring military buildup, alarmed Khrushchev. He now capitulated to Kremlin hard-liners and announced a Soviet military buildup to counter American increases. This decision, though a reaction to Kennedy's policies, merely confirmed the administration's view of an aggressive Soviet Union.

Kennedy brought his case to the American people in a grim television broadcast in July

1961. "We do not want to fight — but we have fought before," the president warned in militant rhetoric. "Those who threaten to unleash the forces of war on a dispute over West Berlin should recall the words of the ancient philosopher: 'A man who causes fear cannot be free from fear.'" Kennedy then asked Congress for $3.25 billion, increasing his military requests to $6 billion in his first six months in office. He also increased the size of the armed forces, calling up reservists and extending the draft. Finally, in a gesture that flashed horror through the land, the president asked for increased appropriations for civil defense and bomb shelters. With no consultation, Kennedy was implementing his inaugural promise to "pay any price" to force the Soviet Union to back down on Berlin.

While Americans worried about nuclear holocaust, Khrushchev moved to defend the Soviet position. On August 13, 1961, he authorized the erection of a military barrier to separate East Berlin from the western zones. The Berlin Wall abruptly ended a flood of refugees that was undermining the East German economy. Equally important, the physical barrier symbolized the reality of two Germanys. Despite an extreme crisis atmosphere, Kennedy determined to test the limits of Soviet strategy. He ordered fifteen hundred battle-ready troops to drive from West Germany into West Berlin and commissioned Vice President Johnson to meet them there. Khrushchev decided not to aggravate the situation. American soldiers entered West Berlin peacefully, demonstrating Kennedy's resolve. By September the two powers agreed to negotiate. Having finally managed to bring the United States to the conference table, Khrushchev scrapped his deadline for settling the Berlin question. The crisis passed,

though the talks continued for another ten years. Kennedy's rigidity had brought the world to the brink of nuclear war.

The intensity of the Cold War was dramatized when Khrushchev announced on August 30 that the Soviet Union was ending its three-year moratorium on nuclear bomb testing. Within a week Kennedy declared that the United States had "no other choice" but to resume underground tests. Two days later, *Life* magazine published an article, endorsed by Kennedy, that asserted that a national program of fallout shelters would assure a 97 percent survival rate in case of nuclear war. These grim forecasts precipitated the first major protests against nuclear testing. Peace organizations like the National Committee for a Sane Nuclear Policy (SANE) and the Student Peace Union (SPU) organized mass demonstrations to protest the arms race.

While Soviet tests escalated to the fifty-megaton level (equivalent to fifty thousand tons of TNT), the Kennedy administration aggravated the situation by revealing to Khrushchev that United States intelligence knew the extent of Soviet military weakness. This knowledge enabled Kennedy to propose the resumption of a Geneva Disarmament Conference that would enable the United States to maintain its nuclear advantage. However, France, a nuclear power since 1960, refused to participate, and the Soviet Union introduced its familiar objections to international inspection. With no prospect for a test-ban treaty, Kennedy ordered the resumption of atmospheric tests in April 1962. At the same time, the administration encouraged American scientists to perfect methods of analyzing nuclear explosions as a precondition for a subsequent test ban.

THE CUBAN MISSILE CRISIS

In notifying Khrushchev that the United States had determined the extent of Soviet missile deployment, the Kennedy administration aroused Soviet fears about the imbalance of power. The United States then intensified these concerns by announcing a shift in nuclear strategy in June 1962. Hereafter, American missiles would be aimed not at Soviet cities but at nuclear missile sites. Such targets meant that an American first-strike attack could obliterate Soviet power to retaliate. Khrushchev eventually expected stockpiles of intercontinental ballistic missiles (ICBMs) to reach a level of parity. But in the immediate future, the Soviet leader recognized his vulnerability to American power.

Khrushchev decided to offset this disadvantage by placing less-expensive short-range missiles in Cuba. In the aftermath of *Sputnik,* the United States had pursued a similar policy by establishing missile bases in Turkey and Italy. Khrushchev also anticipated a secondary advantage of bolstering the Castro regime. During the summer of 1962, therefore, the Soviet Union began preparing for the construction of missile sites in Cuba. Word of these preparations reached the United States through Cuban refugees. Senator Kenneth Keating, seeking election in New York in November, publicized these reports and criticized the administration for allowing Communist expansion in the Western Hemisphere. To such charges, the Kennedy administration replied that there was "no evidence of...significant offensive capability either in Cuban hands or under Soviet direction." These assurances reflected a private Soviet promise to do nothing that might affect the congressional elections.

Continued surveillance by U-2 aircraft, however, indicated that the Soviet Union was indeed constructing missile sites with a striking range as far as two thousand miles. Kennedy promptly summoned a top-level executive committee to consider an appropriate response. The choices ranged from a military attack, advocated by Dean Acheson, Maxwell Taylor, and the Joint Chiefs of Staff, to a diplomatic retreat, supported by Adlai Stevenson, that involved the trading of outmoded American bases in Turkey for those in Cuba. Within this spectrum a consensus eventually emerged that considered armed intervention only a last resort. Yet the administration rejected the possibility of negotiating the removal of the missiles; Soviet power in the Western Hemisphere, it was believed, was not negotiable.

Kennedy finally accepted a third strategy that did not completely rule out the other two. On October 22, 1962, he presented the situation to the American public. Describing the Soviet intervention as "deliberately provocative," Kennedy demanded "withdrawal or elimination" of all missiles. "We will not prematurely or unnecessarily risk the cost of worldwide nuclear war in which the fruits of victory would be ashes in our mouth," he promised, "— but neither will we shrink from that risk at any time it must be faced." As the world rushed toward nuclear holocaust, Kennedy announced he was establishing a "quarantine" — actually a warlike blockade — to exclude offensive weapons from Cuba. The administration estimated that the missile bases would become operative within ten days. The president appealed to Khrushchev to withdraw "this clandestine, reckless, and provocative threat to world peace."

In confronting Khrushchev publicly, Kennedy avoided traditional diplomatic channels that might have lowered the level of tension. The president also rebuffed a U.N. proposal for a three-week moratorium and determined not to consult with American allies. Such rigidity exaggerated the nature of the crisis. As McNamara pointed out, nuclear warheads in the Soviet Union could inflict much greater damage than the weapons in Cuba. Moreover, Cuba surely would not launch a suicidal attack against the United States. To the contrary, official explanations later claimed that Cuba needed the missiles to prevent an American invasion. But the idea that the missiles did not represent an immediate threat contradicted Kennedy's insistence on a deadline for their removal. A more likely explanation was his desire to settle the crisis before the November elections. In taking his firm position, the president shifted the initiative — and the responsibility — to Khrushchev.

The Soviet leader had not anticipated Kennedy's outraged reaction. Nor had he expected the public humiliation of a diplomatic retreat. In a private letter to Kennedy, Khrushchev protested the demand for an unconditional surrender. Calling American policy "outright banditry," he refused to recognize the naval blockade. But Khrushchev was not about to provoke a war that "would not be in our power to stop." In another emotional letter to the president, the Soviet leader emphasized that the Soviet ships in mid-Atlantic carried nonmilitary goods and that the missiles already were landed in Cuba. He then proposed to remove the weapons, provided the United States ended the blockade and agreed to respect Cuban independence. "Only a madman," Khrushchev wrote, "can believe that armaments are the principal means in the life of a society."

The next day, however, the president received still another message from Khrushchev that stiffened the terms for removal of the missiles. The Soviet leader now demanded the withdrawal of missiles from Turkey in exchange for those in Cuba. This new position, like Kennedy's outrage at the Cuban missiles, was more symbolic than real, for the Turkish missiles were outmoded and the United States already had more deadly weapons aimed at the Soviet Union. Months earlier, the president had even ordered the State Department to negotiate the removal of those missiles from Turkey, but Turkish leaders had been unenthusiastic about losing the profitable bases. Yet in October 1962, Kennedy refused to negotiate the question, partly fearing the effect on American allies in Europe, partly concerned about appearing to compromise with a Communist country on the eve of the elections.

Robert Kennedy proposed a solution to this new dilemma. The United States should ignore Khrushchev's second letter and answer only the first. Kennedy's reply, therefore, made no mention of the Turkish bases. Yet when the Soviet ambassador questioned this omission, the administration explained that Turkey was beyond negotiation; nevertheless, the United States made an informal agreement to remove the missiles from Turkey and Italy. Having preserved its public image, the Kennedy administration was prepared to relinquish the substance of the issue. Khrushchev accepted the arrangement, and the crisis passed. In December Kennedy admitted that the Cuban missiles would not have changed the *military* balance of power. "But it would have politically changed the balance of power. It would have appeared to, and appearances contribute to reality."

TOWARD DÉTENTE

Kennedy's preoccupation with the appearances of power cloaked a more subtle realization about the limits of force. Though Khrushchev's timely withdrawal enhanced the president's reputation, the global position of the United States became worse. Kennedy's victory over the Communist superpower obscured the administration's inability to alter power within a revolutionary society. Castro, Kennedy's Communist nemesis, remained firmly entrenched in Cuba, and the administration had agreed to respect his sovereignty. (Kennedy actually allowed the CIA to continue its anti-Castro activities in violation of his pledge to Khrushchev.) In Europe, France's Charles de Gaulle viewed the missile crisis as the epitome of American arrogance. Appalled by Kennedy's unilateral action, the French leader began to separate from NATO, vetoed British participation in the Common Market, and attempted to create a rapprochement with the Soviet Union.

The brush with nuclear war had a sobering effect within the administration. "One mistake," Kennedy conceded, "can make this whole thing blow up." Yet Kennedy waited for Khrushchev to take the initiative to prevent a recurrence. In December 1962 the Soviet leader suggested the two nations end further nuclear testing. But subsequent negotiations soon bogged down over the question of on-site inspection. In previous discussions this issue served as a convenient excuse to avoid disarmament and a reduction of Cold War tensions. The Eisenhower administration had rejected assurances from American scientists that satellite photographs and distant seismographs could provide adequate detection of nuclear explosions. But Kennedy, more confident about American technology and more fearful of catastrophe, determined to reach agreement.

The president introduced a major re-evaluation of the Cold War in a dramatic speech at American University in June 1963. Assuring the world that the United States did not seek "a Pax Americana enforced . . . by American weapons of war," he urged Americans "not to see only a distorted and desperate view of the other side, not to see conflict as inevitable." The United States could not overlook its differences with the Soviet Union. But "we can help make the world safe for diversity," he declared.

The president announced that the United States and Great Britain were sending representatives to Moscow to discuss a test-ban treaty. In addition, he was halting American testing as an act of "good faith." Having set aside the question of inspections (and underground testing), Soviet and American negotiators quickly initialed a treaty banning nuclear tests in the atmosphere. In July 1963 Kennedy presented a summary to the American public, heralding the new treaty as a "first step — a step towards peace — a step towards reason — a step away from war." Kennedy's hopeful rhetoric, however, still had to win approval from the American people, the "military-industrial complex," and a hawkish Congress. Earlier efforts by McNamara to streamline the Department of Defense by curtailing certain military production and closing superfluous military installations had aroused deep public concern. In one Long Island community, for example, the cancellation of a fighter-bomber contract threatened thirteen thousand employees, who protested so loudly that the administration reversed its position. These pressures reflected not just cynical self-interest, but also sincere ideological suspicion of Soviet intentions.

The administration therefore emphasized that the test-ban agreement was a victory for the United States. Since the United States held an undisputed lead in nuclear weaponry, the ban on atmospheric tests would protect that superiority. Nor would the American lead in underground testing be threatened. To win support from his military advisers, Kennedy made assurances that the United States would conduct "comprehensive, aggressive, and continuous" underground nuclear tests. These promises were fulfilled after the Senate ratified the treaty in September 1963. Underground nuclear testing reached a higher level after 1963 than before.

Despite these concessions to the military, Kennedy continued to express interest in reaching a détente with the Soviet Union. "If this pause in the Cold War merely leads to its renewal and not to its end," he warned in an address to the U.N., "— then the indictment of posterity will rightly point its finger at us all." With joint support from the United States and the Soviet Union, the General Assembly passed a resolution condemning the placement of nuclear weapons in outer space. On a bilateral level, the two powers agreed to install an emergency "hot-line" telephone to prevent an accidental conflict. In October the administration announced that the United States would sell surplus wheat to the Soviet Union, a decision that helped the American economy without jeopardizing national security. It represented a symbolic reduction of international tension.

The signs of détente did not indicate a rejection of the Cold War. Though Kennedy welcomed the test-ban treaty, he rebuffed Khrushchev's proposal in July 1963 to formulate a nonaggression pact between NATO and the Warsaw Pact nations. Such an agreement would have undermined the Western alliance and perhaps threatened American dominance in Western Europe. To bolster American influence, the president journeyed to Europe in the summer of 1963, where he reiterated the Cold War polarities first stated by President Truman.

Kennedy emphasized the global dimension of the American commitment in a speech in West Berlin. "Two thousand years ago the proudest boast was 'civis Romanus sum' [I am a Roman citizen]," the president declared, quoting the words of another apostle, Paul. "Today, in the world of freedom, the proudest boast is 'Ich bin ein Berliner.'" Like the early Christians, Kennedy reaffirmed the impossibility of compromising with atheistic evil. In 1959 Khrushchev had expressed his faith in the historical inevitability of a communist victory when he told Eisenhower, "We will bury you." Kennedy remained wedded to a similar, though opposite, belief. In a speech intended for delivery in Dallas on November 22, 1963, the president defined his sense of historical destiny: "We in this country, in this generation, are, by destiny rather than choice, the watchmen on the walls of world freedom."

POLITICS AND THE DOMESTIC ECONOMY

President Kennedy's willingness to seek global confrontation contrasted with his position in domestic matters. Certain of American strength in world affairs, Kennedy did not negotiate "out of fear." But at home, the administration lacked a firm base of power. Kennedy's slim electoral victory reflected the divided opinion of the electorate. A Gallup poll in January 1961 indicated that 42 percent hoped the president would pursue moderate policies; 24 percent hoped he would be more conservative; 23 percent desired a liberal position. Within Congress, an old conservative leadership, backed by the seniority system, jealously guarded its power and its prerogatives. This cautious mood was

Betty Friedan

1924-

"Is that all?" By popularizing and legitimating that simple question, Betty Friedan stimulated a fundamental re-examination of the fifties truism that the American woman would achieve maximum fulfillment as wife and mother, as housewife and homemaker. Her book of 1963, The Feminine Mystique, which challenged the prevailing mythology of domestic bliss, sold three million copies and reached an estimated readership five times as large.

Born to immigrant Jewish parents in Peoria, Illinois, Friedan studied psychology and social science at Smith College and the University of California, Berkeley. "I didn't want to be like my mother," she later recalled. Friedan worked as a journalist during World War Two, but lost her job to a returning war veteran. She was fired from another job because of pregnancy, in violation of a union contract. In 1949, she explained, there was no term to describe "sex discrimination."

During the fifties, Friedan lived in various suburbs of New York, raising three children. She continued a free-lance journalist career and wrote articles for such magazines as Harper's, Good Housekeeping, Redbook, and Mademoiselle. For a piece about her Smith College classmates fifteen years after graduation, Friedan conducted a survey of their attitudes and feelings. It revealed a profound unhappiness among college-educated, middle-class women. But the article was rejected by the editors of women's magazines.

Friedan turned instead to her book. "Something is very wrong with the way American women are trying to live their lives today," she began. "It is no longer possible to...dismiss the desperation of so many American women." Friedan proceeded to demolish the "happy housewife" syndrome of postwar society and argued that middle-class women required a *sense of* personal *fulfillment to be truly satisfied.*

Having identified a major social problem, Friedan joined other feminists in seeking its resolution. In 1966 she helped found the National Organization for Women (NOW) "to bring women into full participation in the mainstream of American society now" and served as its first president until 1970. She also helped establish the National Women's Political Caucus in 1971, but split publicly with other feminist leaders over political strategy. Friedan described her career after 1963 in It Changed My Life *(1976).*

revealed prior to inaugural day when Vice President–elect Johnson, recently the efficient Senate majority leader, offered to lead the Democratic caucus. Johnson's former colleagues rebuffed the idea and reaffirmed the separation of powers. Congress had served notice that it would be reluctant to follow the new administration's leadership.

Kennedy's precarious position reflected the legislative strength of southern Democrats who, though nominally members of the president's party, frequently joined with Republicans to thwart consideration of liberal measures. To overcome the conservatism of the House leadership, Speaker Sam Rayburn proposed an expansion of the Rules Committee to increase its liberal membership. By threatening House traditions, the scheme aroused deep southern resentment, but Rayburn managed to pass the measure on an extremely narrow vote. The victory removed only one obstacle, however, and southern legislators continued to crush or dilute such liberal administration proposals as an increase in minimum wages and federal aid to education.

Kennedy's major concern was to rejuvenate the economy. Believing that a healthy capitalist structure was essential to effective rivalry with world communism, Kennedy had criticized the Eisenhower administration for failure to stimulate economic growth. Never doubting the possibility of unlimited expansion, the Democratic president promised to bring the economy to a 5 percent growth rate per year. These political concerns were made especially acute by a severe recession that was causing 7.7 percent unemployment by January 1961. To combat the recession, Kennedy proposed increased unemployment benefits, depressed-area development programs, and additional public housing. Congress moved slowly to enact these measures.

Meanwhile, the economy showed signs of improvement.

Kennedy's economic advisers, particularly the liberal Walter Heller, urged more vigorous federal spending. But the administration was unwilling to challenge a conservative Congress on that issue. Fearing that deficit spending would antagonize the business community, Kennedy instead proposed a tax credit for new investment in plant equipment. By stimulating business expansion, this measure would simultaneously attack unemployment and provide the basis for long-term growth. To compensate for the loss of tax revenue, however, Kennedy also requested tax reforms that would close such corporate loopholes as expense accounts, earnings on dividends, and foreign income. But these changes attacked the interests of the wealthiest and most powerful groups, and Congress delayed action until 1962. Meanwhile, heavy government spending for military defense boosted the sagging economy.

As the recession passed in 1961, Kennedy turned his attention to controlling inflation. In January 1962 the president's Council of Economic Advisers issued a series of "wage-price guideposts" that recommended noninflationary increases. Though business leaders resented the administration's desire to manage the economy, the wage-price formula made no effort to alter the existing patterns of corporate wealth. The guidelines for price increases remained imprecise and subject to corporate manipulation. But wage increases were directly linked to corporate production. The administration did not envision employees obtaining a larger share of corporate profits. "Forcing wages up ahead of productivity," Kennedy asserted, "can only weaken our efforts to expand the economy."

Despite this conservative outlook, the wage-price controls produced a major clash between the president and the nation's largest industry — steel — in the spring of 1962. As part of its anti-inflation program, the administration had persuaded the United Steelworkers Union to accept a modest pay increase. Central to the arrangement was the steel industry's promise to hold the price line. But in April 1962 Roger Blough, president of U.S. Steel, notified the president that he was raising steel prices an inflationary $6 per ton. Other steel companies announced they would follow Blough's lead.

"My father once told me that all steelmen were sons of bitches, and I did not realize until now how right he was," Kennedy remarked. He then launched a strenuous campaign to force the steel industry to rescind the increases. Administration officials pleaded with friendly steel executives to hold the old price line. McNamara instructed the Defense Department to purchase only from low-price manufacturers, and Robert Kennedy ordered the Justice Department to investigate the possibility of illegal price fixing. These pressures led Inland Steel Corporation to reject a price increase, creating a domino effect within the industry. Kennedy had ably defended his economic strategy.

The president's assertion of the government's economic power aroused the hostility of business leaders. These negative feelings were reinforced by a slumping stock market. In May 1962 Wall Street prices touched the lowest point since the Crash of 1929. This trend reflected the belated impact of the recession of 1960–1961, which had reduced corporate earnings. But the president's stand on steel prices disheartened the business community, which blamed the administration for the downturn.

Kennedy responded to this crisis in confidence by emphasizing his support of business. At the Yale University commencement in June 1962, the president pleaded for an end to "sterile acrimony." The interests of government and business, he insisted, were the same. Kennedy proceeded to challenge certain fallacies in popular thinking. He argued that the government was not too large and that its growth since World War Two had been slower than other sectors of the economy. The president also denied the evils of deficit spending, pointing out that federal government indebtedness had increased less than private and local government debts. Finally, Kennedy minimized the economic importance of business confidence in government, observing that previous recessions had come during popular administrations. "What is at stake is not some grand warfare of rival ideologies," the president maintained in the language of consensus, "but the practical management of a modern economy."

The Kennedy administration moved quickly to demonstrate its commitment to business prosperity. A lowering of margin requirements on the purchase of securities stimulated the stock market. In July 1962 the Treasury Department liberalized the scale of depreciation allowances for business equipment, thus encouraging the replacement of older machinery. Congress also enacted the proposed tax credit on new investments as well as a diluted tax reform package that maintained specific benefits for business. Kennedy endorsed new legislation for the marketing of drugs that proved favorable to the pharmaceutical industry. In the field of space technology, the administration favored private control of a communications satellite corporation, thus permitting private business to benefit from the government's space program.

The commitment to business interests culminated in Kennedy's support of foreign trade. Since the latter part of the Eisenhower administration, the United States economy had suffered a serious imbalance of foreign payments, largely because of heavy spending for foreign military bases. In 1961 Kennedy created a special position in the Defense Department to encourage the sale of American arms to foreign nations. Besides bringing profits to arms manufacturers, this policy linked business prosperity to American foreign policy. Kennedy also continued Eisenhower's policy of trying to persuade the NATO nations to pay a larger proportion of the common defense. As an inducement, Kennedy proposed the creation of a Multilateral Nuclear Force (MLF) in 1962. But United States insistence on an absolute veto over the use of nuclear weapons offended the allies, and the idea was never implemented.

Indicative of the erosion of the Western alliance, the European nations also thwarted Kennedy's hope for expanded international trade. In 1962 the president presented a trade expansion bill as his major legislative concern. Such a law, Kennedy declared, "could well affect the unity of the West, the course of the Cold War, and the economic growth of our Nation for a generation to come." In response to intense administration pressure, Congress enacted a measure in 1962 that permitted the president to negotiate across-the-board tariff reductions. In the tradition of the Open Door, Kennedy expected this legislation to increase American trade with the European allies. His hopes were rudely assaulted, however, when France vetoed British participation in the Common Market, and the prospects of Atlantic economic unity diminished.

In seeking ways to strengthen the economy, Kennedy discarded his initial belief in a balanced budget and embraced the "new economics" of John Maynard Keynes. In 1961 the president had rejected the advice of his Council of Economic Advisers to cut taxes to stimulate economic expansion. By 1962, however, Kennedy accepted the theory that a tax cut would increase consumer spending, lift the "fiscal drag," and thus increase the rate of economic growth. Kennedy's willingness to experiment with deficit spending aroused conservative opposition, and he waited until January 1963 to submit his proposal to Congress. Kennedy's plan called for a $13.6 billion reduction of taxes, most of it on individual incomes, as well as significant tax reforms to shift the tax burden toward the upper brackets. But the president clearly was more committed to the tax cut than to reform, and he offered little protest when Congress whittled away the reform provisions. The measure, not enacted until the Johnson administration, provided the basis for an extraordinary surge of economic growth.

THE CIVIL RIGHTS CRISIS

Kennedy's reluctance to challenge congressional conservatives influenced his stand on the question of civil rights. Recognizing the political strength of southern Democrats, the administration tried to appease the conservative leadership. Kennedy responded quickly to southern patronage demands, awarded federal construction projects to southern states, and raised the level of price supports on cotton. More important, the president declined to introduce civil rights legislation or issue strong executive orders.

Shortly after taking office, Kennedy created a Commission on Equal Employment Opportunity (CEEO), headed by Vice President Johnson, and charged it with ending discrimination on work done under government contract. But the CEEO preferred voluntary compliance and seldom punished violators. During the 1960 campaign Kennedy claimed that Eisenhower could eliminate federal support of segregated housing "with the stroke of the presidential pen." But the Democratic president became remarkably silent when that power passed into his own hands. Hoping to win congressional approval for a Department of Urban Affairs, Kennedy refused to challenge segregated housing. Not until 1962, after Congress defeated his efforts, did Kennedy act to end segregation in federally funded housing. More than previous administrations, however, Kennedy appointed blacks to government positions and allowed them to work in areas other than race relations.

Kennedy's limited support of equal rights for blacks reflected more than a fear of southern power. Like other liberals, the president believed that changes in race relations could not be forced on the nation. He placed his hopes for racial justice not on new legislation but on enforcement of the voting rights provisions of the Civil Rights Acts of 1957 and 1960. According to his premises, Attorney General Robert Kennedy would file suits on behalf of black plaintiffs, thereby guaranteeing black suffrage and providing the basis for black political power. He believed that other changes would follow from these beginnings. But Kennedy's inertia, after acquiring 70 percent of the black vote in 1960, belied his premises. Moreover, he weakened even the minimal possibilities of obtaining favorable rulings by appointing segregationist judges to federal courts in the South. One Kennedy appointee openly referred to blacks as "niggers" and "chimpanzees."

The administration's failure to support civil rights reform angered the black community. Instead of waiting for government action, black activists determined to force legal change by

A black minister protects his house from night riders after becoming the first black to register to vote in his Louisiana parish in sixty years. (Bob Adelman/Magnum)

violating segregationist laws. Following the nonviolent, direct action of Martin Luther King and the sit-in demonstrators of 1960, the Congress of Racial Equality (CORE) launched a series of "freedom rides" in 1961 to force integration of interstate commerce and transportation. Busloads of freedom riders were met by angry white crowds who attacked them while FBI agents looked on. The administration justified its refusal to intervene by stressing its lack of jurisdiction in matters of state and local control.

The public violence nevertheless forced Kennedy to act. The administration sent federal marshals into the South and obtained court injunctions against interference in interstate bus travel. At the same time, Robert Kennedy called on the freedom riders for a "cooling-off period." An indignant Martin Luther King agreed only to "a lull." "We had been cooling off for 100 years," protested James Farmer, organizer of the freedom rides. "If we got any cooler we'd be in a deep freeze." Meanwhile, Attorney General Kennedy petitioned the Interstate Commerce Commission to issue an order prohibiting segregation in interstate travel.

After an initial rebuff, Kennedy exerted behind-the-scenes pressure that led to the desired ICC ruling in September 1961.

In reacting to the freedom rides, the administration revealed its preference for avoiding direct confrontation outside the legal framework. This tendency emerged clearly in a lengthy power struggle over the integration of the University of Mississippi in September 1962. James Meredith, a black air force veteran, had obtained a federal court order allowing him to register at the all-white school. But Governor Ross Barnett spoke for the southern leadership when he announced his refusal to comply with the ruling. The Kennedy administration determined to enforce the law. Following the precedent of Eisenhower in 1957, Kennedy federalized the National Guard and sent regular army troops and federal marshals to the area. But the administration was especially careful not to threaten local authority. Even when bloody riots erupted, Attorney General Kennedy allowed state officials to maintain their power. Nor did the government attempt to punish Barnett for violating the law.

While the administration sought to heal the breaches caused by the civil rights movement, liberal activists began a voter registration campaign in the South. Such activities brought them into contact with a police and legal system that violated basic constitutional rights with impunity. As in the case of the freedom rides, civil rights workers discovered that the federal government was reluctant to provide adequate protection. Denying its jurisdiction, the administration refused to confront traditional southern power. This failure to act aroused widespread indignation among blacks and stimulated further mass protest. To quiet this dissent, Kennedy proposed a civil rights bill in February 1963. "We are committed to achieving true equality of opportunity," he declared, "because it is right." Yet the president's message called only for accelerating prosecution of voting rights violations, the authorization of federal funds to encourage school desegregation, and the extension of the Civil Rights Commission. Unmentioned were the broader questions of equal rights or the extralegal protests sweeping the land.

Black leaders rejected Kennedy's caution. In the spring of 1963, King's Southern Christian Leadership Conference (SCLC) carried the civil rights crusade to Birmingham, Alabama, purportedly "the most thoroughly segregated big city" in the nation. King's nonviolent strategy aimed at producing so much "creative tension" that segregationist leaders would feel compelled to negotiate a peaceful settlement. The American Gandhi was not mistaken. After several weeks of noisy but relatively peaceful demonstrations, the local police chief, "Bull" Connor, attempted to end the movement by attacking the protesters with clubs, fire hoses, and dogs. This violence steeled the nerves of black demonstrators and, because of wide television coverage, sent waves of outrage throughout the country. The Kennedy administration at last intervened, pressing Alabama business leaders to settle the issues. In May a shaky truce was reached.

The Birmingham confrontation—and the many other demonstrations it spawned—convinced Kennedy to stand behind strong civil rights legislation. "We face...a moral crisis as a country and as a people," he told a television audience in June 1963. "It cannot be met by repressive police action. It cannot be left to increased demonstrations in the streets." Kennedy then introduced a new civil rights bill that prohibited racial discrimination in public accommodations, authorized the attorney general to initiate suits to desegregate public schools, sought to improve black employment opportunities, and incorporated the administration's earlier proposal to protect voting rights. Black activists questioned some of the legal loopholes that remained in the bill. But few doubted the clarity of Kennedy's moral position.

While Congress began to consider Kennedy's civil rights package, black leaders decided to stage a show of strength by organizing a March on Washington. The president initially discouraged such a demonstration, fearing that it would inflame passions and embarrass the administration. But the civil rights leadership refused to retreat. On August 28, 1963, 250,000 marchers converged in the nation's capital to affirm their commitment to civil rights. "I have a dream," Martin Luther King told the assemblage. "I have a dream that...the sons of former slaves and the sons of former slave-owners will be able to sit together at the table of brotherhood." King's passionate language electrified the crowd.

Other voices in Washington, however, presented an alternative vision of the black future. John Lewis, head of the Student Non-Violent Coordinating Committee (SNCC), attacked the Kennedy administration for its "immoral compromises" with conservative politicians. "If any radical social, political, and economic changes are to take place in our society," he maintained, "the people, the masses must bring them about. In the struggle, we must seek more than mere civil rights; we must work for the community of love, peace, and true brotherhood." Three months later, Lewis's language was echoed in a speech by the black nationalist leader, Malcolm X. Calling for a revolutionary consciousness, he scoffed at the limited horizons of racial integration. "A revolutionary," he asserted, "is a black nationalist."

RADICAL POLITICS

These broad statements, transcending the traditional dialogue of political parties, perplexed the political leadership. "Extremism," as it was called, aroused the specter of Communist subversion. Conservatives like Ross Barnett accused civil rights organizations of acting as "Communist fronts," while liberals like Arthur M. Schlesinger, Jr., identified black radicals with Mao Tse-tung. Such labeling reflected an inability to perceive or understand indigenous radical activity; it was the same logic that saw Fidel Castro and Ho Chi Minh as mere puppets of Moscow.

The confusion of radicalism with communism permeated the political establishment. As the Kennedy administration became committed to supporting Martin Luther King, it strove to purge radicals from the civil rights movement. Secret wiretaps of King's telephone by the FBI indicated that one of his associates may have been sympathetic to communism. President Kennedy personally warned King of such associations and persuaded the black leader to break relations with this supporter.

Kennedy's fears about Communist influence reflected not so much his concern about national security as his dread of Communist taint. Long after Joseph McCarthy was dead, communism still conjured up visions of ultimate evil. Prominent Communists continued to face economic and political discrimination. Leftist entertainers like the singer Pete Seeger were denied access to television programs and college campuses. At Queens College in New York, school officials simultaneously banned speeches by the Communist leader Ben Davis and Malcolm X, precipitating the first major student strike for free speech in 1961. The next year, the same college administration placed the en-

Malcolm X, addressing a Black Muslim audience in 1961, emphasized the importance of preserving a black identity in white America. (Eve Arnold/Magnum)

tire student editorial board on probation for attacking HUAC. Kennedy's support of international diversity had made few inroads at home.

The attack on student radicalism reflected the perpetuation of an academic philosophy called *in loco parentis* (in the place of the parent). Under its principles, university officials claimed the right not only to guide students' intellectual development, but also to supervise their personal lives. Student involvement in the civil rights movement stimulated strenuous protests against these paternalistic

values. Attacks on the university system merged with a broader vision for a humane society in the radical organization Students for a Democratic Society (SDS). In a position paper known as the Port Huron Statement (1962), SDS founder Tom Hayden condemned the "poverty, waste, elitism, manipulation" that characterized mainstream politics. Ironically, until 1966 SDS bylaws banned affiliation with Communists.

The awakening of student protest on the Left mirrored the emergence of a radical poli-

446

tics of the Right. As liberal Democrats and "modern" Republicans joined in a political consensus that accepted government participation in the economy and minimal social welfare legislation, orthodox conservatives condemned the betrayal of such traditional American values as individualism and laissez faire. Equating social reform with alien "un-American" forces, extreme conservatives concluded that "Communist influences are now in almost complete control of our Federal Government." In 1958 Robert Welch, a wealthy business leader and former director of the National Association of Manufacturers, founded the secret John Birch Society to agitate against the alleged "Communist conspiracy." Funded largely by small-business executives, such right wing organizations not only opposed domestic liberalism but also objected to an internationalist foreign policy, including participation in the U.N., foreign aid, or negotiation with the Soviet Union. Though numerically weak, the radical Right was particularly vocal.

Conservative opinion was also enjoying a renaissance within the major political parties. As the administration endorsed a more aggressive civil rights movement, the conservative ideology spread through the South. "This is like a dictatorship," Mississippi's Ross Barnett protested against federal authority. "It looks like we're being kicked around." Southern Democrats spoke loudly about deserting the national party. Taking advantage of these resentments, Republican Senator Barry Goldwater of Arizona offered an orthodox alternative. In his best-selling book, *The Conscience of a Conservative* (1960), Goldwater criticized "the encroachment of individual freedom by Big Government," defended states' rights, attacked forced school desegregation, called for the return to a "free" marketplace, and urged a more

vigorous waging of the Cold War. The program promised to create a new conservative coalition.

Kennedy's advisers feared that Goldwater would drain the president's support in the South and Southwest. A popular bumper sticker — "Kennedy for King — Goldwater for President" — indicated the liability of civil rights. In Texas the Democratic party had split into warring camps, threatening the party's electoral chances. For this reason Kennedy decided to keep the Texan Johnson as his running mate in 1964. Yet Texas remained a hotbed of anti-Kennedy sentiment. In October 1963 U.N. Ambassador Stevenson had been pushed and spat upon by an angry crowd in Dallas. With an eye on the next presidential election, Kennedy decided to go to Texas in November to mend his political fences and reunite the state's Democratic party.

SUGGESTED READINGS

A brief survey of the Kennedy years is Jim F. Heath, *Decade of Disillusionment: The Kennedy-Johnson Years* (1975). Two Kennedy workers have written extensive but uncritical studies: see Arthur M. Schlesinger, Jr., *A Thousand Days* (1965), and Theodore Sorensen, *Kennedy* (1965). More insightful of Kennedy's policies is Bruce Miroff, *Pragmatic Illusions: The Presidential Politics of John F. Kennedy* (1976).

The election of 1960 is described in Theodore H. White, *The Making of the President: 1960* (1961). For a more detailed statistical analysis of voting patterns in the fifties and sixties, see Norman H. Nie et al., *The Changing American Voter* (1976). Kennedy's problems with Congress are explored in Tom Wicker, *JFK and LBJ: The Influence of Personality upon Politics* (1968). The Kennedy administration's relationship to the civil rights movement is analyzed critically in Victor S. Navasky, *Kennedy Justice* (1971), and more favorably in Carl M. Brauer, *John F. Kennedy and the Second Reconstruction* (1977). The problems of economic policy are described in Jim F. Heath, *John F. Kennedy and the Business Community* (1969).

A critical analysis of Kennedy's foreign policy is Richard J. Walton, *Cold War and Counterrevolution* (1972). The main issues of the Cuban missile crisis are discussed in an anthology, Robert A. Divine, ed., *The Cuban Missile Crisis* (1971), and David Detzer, *The Brink* (1979). Kennedy's attitude toward Vietnam is explored in portions of Ernest R. May, *"Lessons" of the Past* (1973). For the CIA, see the works listed at the end of the chapter 13. A detailed study of the German question is Curtis Cate, *The Ides of August: The Berlin Wall Crisis, 1961* (1978).

There is a vast literature on the Kennedy assassination. The best starting point is an anthology, Peter Dale Scott, Paul L. Hoch, and Russell Stetler, eds., *The Assassinations: Dallas and Beyond* (1976). Extremely provocative in relating Kennedy's assassination to American foreign policy is Carl Oglesby, *The Yankee and Cowboy War: Conspiracies from Dallas to Watergate and Beyond* (1976). For the social context, see Bradley S. Greenburg and Edwin B. Parker, *The Kennedy Assassination and the American Public* (1965).

Spotlight: The Kennedy Assassination

Kennedy's mission ended abruptly under a hail of bullets in Dallas on November 22, 1963. As the presidential motorcade passed near the downtown area, Kennedy was shot and killed by sniper fire. In the ensuing confusion, eyewitnesses disagreed about the sequence of events. Dallas police quickly arrested a mysterious character named Lee Harvey Oswald, who claimed to be a "patsy" for unknown conspirators. Before he could be tried, however, Oswald was killed by a Dallas nightclub owner, Jack Ruby, who allegedly had connections with the criminal underworld. Lyndon Johnson, who had accompanied Kennedy to his politically divided home state, took the presidential oath of office in Texas before returning to Washington with the slain president's body.

The assassination of John Kennedy had a profound impact on American society and culture. Because of its suddenness, news of the killing wrenched the American people from the routines of their daily lives. People would later remember exactly what they were doing when they first heard the news. As word of the shooting spread from Dallas, people everywhere crowded around televisions and radios seeking further information. The sophistication of the public media made the assassination a national event, an experience that was shared simultaneously throughout the country and the world. Surveys later revealed that 92 percent of all Americans learned of the assassination within two hours and that more than half of all Americans watched the same television coverage of the event. Millions of citizens were glued to their television sets on November 24 and watched Jack Ruby murder the suspected assassin. As Pearl Harbor had shocked an earlier generation of Americans, the assassination of Kennedy and its aftermath touched the lives of the entire nation.

This shared experience created a unique moment in American history, a time when normal activities stopped because of the weight of the tragedy. On the day of the president's funeral, schools and businesses were closed to enable all people to share in the national ritual. As a Catholic, Kennedy received the last rites of the church. But even the hoary traditions of the Catholic church paled before a dramatic display of national symbols — a riderless black horse, a military cortege, the playing of taps. This secular pageantry brought people together on an emotional level, reinforcing a sense of national identity.

A fundamental ingredient of these unifying themes was Kennedy's public image. Where previous presidents emphasized their wisdom and experience, Kennedy celebrated youth and energy. His family's touch-football games were noted for their vigor and intensity. The president boasted about physical fitness, encouraging people to embark on fifty-mile hikes. The Kennedy family, with its young children, suggested growth and strength. The president projected these attributes in his frequent television appearances. He was a master of the visual media, combining physical grace with sharp wit. "Washington had . . . become the Hollywood of the upper middle class," chided critic Roger Hagan. "Through the slick media, every mannerism of the first family . . . reverberates through the suburbs of the land."

Kennedy's vigor starkly contrasted with the impotence of death. His assassination symbolized the imminence of everyone's death and intensified a pervasive death fear within American culture. Despite the obvious knowledge that all people die, American society traditionally tried to ignore the inevitability of death. Jessica Mitford's exposé of the funeral industry, *The American Way of Death* (1963), illuminated some of the strategies Americans used to avoid confronting death and dying. In Dallas, for example, the funeral parlor that provided Kennedy's coffin possessed a "Slumber Room" where survivors could view the dead. Makeup devices were designed to conceal ugly wounds and bodily disintegration. The Kennedy assassination undermined these charades. Kennedy was not in "slumber" and his head was too badly mutilated to be exposed; he was dead.

The death anxiety within American society had intensified during the Kennedy administration. Since the atomic bombing of Hiroshima in 1945, Americans had lived in close proximity to annihilation. Kennedy had admitted that "a simple clash could escalate overnight into a holocaust of mushroom clouds." He had taken the nation to the brink of nuclear calamity during the Cuban missile crisis, acknowledging that "American citizens have become adjusted to living daily on the bull's-eye of Soviet missiles." Despite Kennedy's claim of adjustment, Americans dreaded the possibility of mass death. "We may be the last generation in the experiment with living," protested the Port Huron Statement. And conservatives complained, in the words of Senator Goldwater, of "a craven fear of death."

This fear of human annihilation was accentuated by a new image of the global condition. As part of his Cold War strategy, Kennedy had committed the United States to an elaborate program for the exploration of outer space. In 1961, after America's first astronaut, Alan Shepard, rode a missile three hundred miles, the president announced a bold and costly program to place human beings on the moon by the end of the decade. "No single project," he explained, "will be more impressive to mankind." One year later John Glenn became a national hero by circling the earth three times. "This is the new ocean," Kennedy proclaimed, "and I believe the United States must sail on it."

Though he defined space exploration as a competition with the Soviet Union, Kennedy appreciated the implications for the rest of mankind trapped by the earth's gravity. Distant photographs of earth demonstrated the smallness and frailty of the blue planet. Despite the rhetoric of new frontiers and new oceans, Kennedy realized that the earth was mankind's only home. "We all inhabit this planet. We all breathe the same air," he declared in his American University speech of 1963. "We all cherish our children's future. And we all are mortal."

The imminence of global death was closely related to concern for the living environment. The discovery of radioactive fallout in the form of strontium 90 had initially perplexed scientists. In 1955, however, the Atomic Energy Commission assured the public that only animals who ate contaminated grasses would be endangered. Human beings, the AEC insisted, were exempt from the radioactive chain. Such statements clashed with the emerging science of ecology, which stressed the interrelatedness of all life. In a carefully documented book, *Silent Spring* (1962), the biologist Rachel Carson described the pervasive danger of the uncontrolled use of pesticides. "The question is whether any civilization can wage relentless war on life without destroying it," she warned.

The ecology movement, the space program, the rumblings of the Cold War — all spoke to a culture preoccupied by cataclysm. The killing of Kennedy reduced

this imminence of mass death to human proportions. The slain president personified what could happen to anyone and to everyone. This sense of heightened
vulnerability helps to explain the popular fascination with the Kennedy assassination and the Kennedy family survivors. The thirst for information, as evidenced
by the proliferation of newspaper and magazine articles, reflected a psychological
attempt to master the events by learning about them. It also betrayed an unwillingness to accept the finality of death.

Anguished by the Kennedy assassination, Americans sought appropriate ways
to commemorate the dead president. Kennedy memorabilia — pictures, charms,
jewelry, and books — found ready customers, even in the gloomy Christmas season that followed the assassination. Local governments named and renamed public
buildings after Kennedy. The space center at Cape Canaveral became Cape Kennedy (later changed back under the Nixon administration); New York's Idlewild
Airport switched to JFK; and a new arts complex in the nation's capital was called
the Kennedy Center. The president's grave at Arlington National Cemetery became an overnight shrine. These monuments attempted to provide an earthly
immortality to ease the nation's psychic loss.

To explain the national trauma, President Johnson created a nonpartisan commission, headed by Chief Justice Earl Warren, to investigate the circumstances of
the assassination. Though he selected the most prestigious political leaders, Johnson imposed one serious handicap. He insisted on a final report before the elections of 1964. This rigid timetable resulted in a sloppy report that failed to answer
basic questions about Kennedy's death. Released in October 1964, the Warren
Report concluded that Kennedy had been killed by the dead assassin, Oswald,
who had acted alone and who in turn had been killed by Ruby, acting alone. A
1966 Gallup poll found that a majority of American citizens doubted the validity
of the report, and yet a majority also opposed reopening the case.

In assessing Oswald's motives, the Warren Commission stated simply that the
assassin was a "loner" who suffered from an "inability to enter meaningful relations with people." As for Ruby, the report attributed his actions to extraordinary
grief at the Kennedy assassination. Such flimsy explanations encouraged the proliferation of alternatives. Oswald's interest in Cuba led to two mutually exclusive
possibilities. The first explanation saw Oswald as a Communist agent, taking
revenge on Kennedy for the Bay of Pigs and for CIA attempts to assassinate
Castro. A second scenario saw Oswald as an enemy of Castro, working with Cuban refugees and international criminals and seeking to eliminate Kennedy because
of his refusal to support further anti-Castro operations. Few students of the
Warren Report, however, accepted the finding that Oswald acted alone.

Though Oswald's motives remain unexplained, the willingness to ascribe his
actions to insanity or mental disturbance reflected a dominant attitude toward po-

litical violence. Even Oswald's legal defender, Mark Lane, described the unknown assassins of Kennedy as "motivated by diseased minds." Throughout American history, presidential assassins like John Wilkes Booth and Charles Guiteau have been dismissed as insane. Later assassins such as Sirhan Sirhan (who shot Robert Kennedy), Charles Bremer (who attacked George Wallace), and Lynette Fromme (who tried to kill Gerald Ford) have equally been silenced by claims of insanity. Another assassin, James Earl Ray (who killed Martin Luther King) pleaded guilty and avoided political testimony. This pattern of enforced silence minimized the significance of assassination as a political act.

Kennedy's assassination triggered a wave of similar crimes that included (in addition to the ones mentioned above), the murder of Malcolm X and the American Nazi George Lincoln Rockwell. These murders reflected political polarities that could not be resolved within the existing political institutions. But to avoid an examination of the need for such extralegal politics, American leaders ruled these acts, by definition, to be insane. Political assassination nevertheless had an internal logic as well as a rational (if unpleasant) objective. The failure of the government to confront these issues assured the perpetuation of popular conspiracy theories about the rash of political violence in the sixties.

The political ramifications of the Kennedy assassination were intimately related to the emotional power of the tragedy. "For me this one act has made all other acts irrelevant and trivial," declared one student. Such sentiments may have had a significant effect on the traditional patterns of voting. In the three presidential elections before Kennedy's assassination, voting behavior indicated that most people ignored the content of political issues and expressed a simple preference for one of the two major parties. Between 1960 and 1964, however, there was a sharp increase in the proportion of voting according to issues and a simultaneous decrease in the importance of party affiliation. This shift in voting habits became a clearer trend in subsequent elections.

The growing emphasis on political issues rather than party labels reflected the political style of a new generation of voters who reached their majority during the Kennedy and Johnson years. Unlike older voters, these newer constituents perceived politics as immediate and personal. Such moral questions as the arms race and civil rights touched deeply in the lives of ordinary citizens. Viewing politics as a system rather than as a random series of events, the new voters formulated politically consistent responses. Such changes remain difficult to explain. But the impact of Kennedy — both in life and in death — on young people illuminates one level of motivation. As a source of idealism, Kennedy's stature was magnified by his tragic death.

For the Kennedy assassination, above all, was an emotional event. In reacting to the murder, Americans spontaneously created an idealized sense of community, an idealized feeling of national harmony. Sharing their shock and their fear, Americans believed they could transcend the differences that separated them. For this reason, they responded favorably to Johnson's call for a consensus. Such idealized hopes, however, were impossible to obtain in the political world of American society. Yet Americans continued to measure their political problems against idealized standards of community. The disillusionment of subsequent years, particularly among young people, could be traced to the high level of early aspiration. In death, Kennedy created what had eluded him in life — a broad affirmation of community that transcended the differences of established politics.

Chapter 15

Five days after the assassination of John F. Kennedy, Lyndon Baines Johnson appeared before both houses of Congress. "All I have, I would have given gladly not to be standing here today," he said quietly. The former vice president and Senate majority leader pledged to lead the nation to a consensus in domestic affairs and singled out civil rights legislation as a fitting tribute to the late president. "Let us here highly resolve that John Fitzgerald Kennedy did not live or die in vain," Johnson stated. "Let us continue."

KENNEDY LEGACY

The new president moved quickly to assure an orderly and smooth transition of power in a na-

tion traumatized by the events of the Kennedy assassination. To win national confidence in his leadership, Johnson telephoned the fifty governors, consulted with former Presidents Truman and Eisenhower, and conferred with business, labor, and civil rights leaders. He also insisted that Kennedy's aides remain in the new administration. New Frontier appointees such as Secretary of State Rusk, Defense Secretary McNamara, and National Security Adviser McGeorge Bundy continued to play central roles in the foreign policy of the Johnson years.

By early 1964 Johnson chose three legislative priorities — a tax cut, civil rights, and antipoverty legislation. Tutored by Economic Adviser Walter Heller, Kennedy had asked for a $10 billion tax cut in 1963. The request marked a deliberate attempt to use deficit spending to stimulate private spending, and Heller predicted that higher tax revenues would accompany increased consumption. Although the House passed Kennedy's proposal two months before his assassination, fiscal conservatives in the Senate and business leaders remained uneasy over large deficits. Johnson won the tax cut through personal persuasion and by slicing Kennedy's proposed budget to under $100 billion. Passed in February 1964, the $11.5 billion personal and corporate income tax cut was the new president's first legislative triumph. It marked the institutionalization of the deficit and stimulated a 7 percent boost in the gross national product in 1964. National production continued to rise through 1966, while both unemployment and inflation sank to 3.8 percent, a dramatic indication of fiscal success.

Kennedy's second legacy was the call for a civil rights bill to prohibit racial discrimination in voting, public accommodations, and employment. Before his death Kennedy had lined up sufficient congressional support to pass a civil rights law, but expected southern members of Congress to weaken some of its provisions and reject others. Johnson succeeded in prevailing upon the House to pass an uncompromised bill in February 1964, but faced a seventy-five-day filibuster in the Senate. In mid-June, Illinois Republican Senator Everett Dirksen decided to support Johnson's civil rights bill as "an idea whose time had come." With the added strength of northern Republicans, two-thirds of the Senate voted to invoke cloture, ending debate and killing the southern filibuster. It was the first time the Senate had ever voted cloture on a civil rights issue. The Civil Rights Act of 1964 gave the federal government the power to sue to desegregate accommodations and public schools. It attempted to outlaw the denial of equal job opportunity in all but the smallest businesses and unions and allowed the federal government

to monitor state voting records. For black Americans and their supporters, the Civil Rights Act was a step toward the dream of equal opportunity, but conservatives such as Senator Barry Goldwater objected to extending the power of federal government to local and community affairs.

Johnson's third priority in 1964 was poverty legislation. In a commencement address at the University of Michigan, the president asked students to join "in the battle to build the Great Society." America could be more than rich and powerful, Johnson preached, and he committed the nation to "an end to poverty and racial injustice." The president believed that medical care, education, job training, and racial equality could complete the New Deal by finally assuring equal opportunity for all Americans. The Economic Opportunity Act, signed in August 1964, focused on training programs for the young and loans and grants for self-help projects initiated by local communities. The bill's Community Action program was important to the president because it called for "participatory democracy" of the poor to break the cycle of poverty. The law also established a Job Corps for youth, and VISTA (Volunteers in Service to America) — a domestic Peace Corps. Sargent Shriver, Kennedy's Peace Corps director, headed the Office of Economic Opportunity (OEO), which administered the multibillion-dollar program. Beginning in 1966, OEO also created Headstart, a "prepackaged" program for local agencies that provided intensive preschool training for the children of the poor.

When Congress adjourned for the fall election campaign of 1964, most of the president's legislative goals had been fulfilled. They included a $1 billion housing program, federal grants for mass transportation, extensive loans to college students, and massive aid for college construction. Johnson also expanded a Kennedy pilot project into a full-scale food stamp program for the working poor. Much of Congress's work was based on Kennedy concepts, but it was Johnson's legislative skill and his rapport with southern conservatives that translated New Frontier intentions into political accomplishments. LBJ also benefited from a "honeymoon" relationship with Congress, stimulated in part by election-year restlessness.

THE LANDSLIDE OF '64

As Johnson's programs were signed into law, Barry Goldwater emerged as the Republican candidate for the presidency. The conservative senator's followers mounted a grassroots campaign to select convention delegates from nonprimary states and reverse a thirty-year domination of the Republican party by eastern liberals. Like the Taft movement of the 1950s, Goldwater partisans sought a break with party acceptance of the New Deal and managerial liberalism. The climactic point in the Goldwater drive came in the California primary, where the senator won a tight victory over Governor Nelson A. Rockefeller of New York. Rockefeller symbolized eastern liberalism and corporate power, and had recently divorced his wife and then married a younger woman, herself divorced. At the Republican Convention in San Francisco, Rockefeller was roundly booed by Goldwaterites, while a liberal resolution renouncing "extremist groups" such as the John Birch Society was decisively defeated. Following his first-ballot nomination, Goldwater selected William Miller, a conservative New York congressman, as his running mate. In his acceptance address, Goldwater responded to charges that his views on defense, race, and anticommunism mirrored those of the right wing Birch Society. "Extremism in the defense of liberty is no vice," he inserted in the middle of the routine speech, "...moderation in the pursuit of justice is no virtue." The convention came alive with boisterous chanting, but to many Americans the specter of political fanaticism appeared unsettling.

Goldwater enthusiasts, particularly in Anglo-Protestant areas of the South and Southwest, insisted that lawlessness was the major domestic issue of the era. The Goldwater candidacy was the first to embrace the "social issue," the discomfort experienced by many Americans over personally frightening aspects of social change in the sixties. Violence in the streets, political corruption, aimlessness among youth, anxiety among the elderly, and loss of spiritual meaning in the culture were themes that Goldwater articulated. Refashioning the traditional call for personal accountability, Goldwater held social permissiveness responsible for a "growing menace" to "personal safety, to life, to limb, and property." He also opposed the Civil Rights Act because it required government to interfere with social and personal relations. "In Your Heart, You Know He's Right," Goldwater bumper stickers proclaimed.

Goldwater extended his critique of mainstream liberalism to the administration's handling of the hostilities in Southeast Asia. "Failure in the jungles of Vietnam," he cried, "proclaims lost leadership, obscure purpose, weakening wills, and the risk of inciting our sworn enemies to new aggressions and new excesses." The senator held out the use of nuclear defoliants as a possible option for cutting insurgent supply lines and called for increased air power. He even labeled the president "soft on communism." But Goldwater's "cowboy" style of from-the-hip commentary frequently got him into trouble. Soon he was clarifying remarks about social security, TVA, and nuclear warfare. Goldwater's mercurial style inspired a television commercial, sponsored by the Democratic party, that showed a little girl picking petals from a daisy in a mock countdown and was followed by a quick shot of a nuclear explosion. The narrator assured that Lyndon Johnson was for peace and military restraint. Republican protests subsequently banned the advertisement from TV screens, but it did point to Goldwater's vulnerabilities.

Johnson did not enter the Democratic primaries. National attention focused on Governor George C. Wallace of Alabama, who took 34 percent, 30 percent, and 43 percent of the vote against Johnson stand-ins in Wisconsin, Indiana, and Maryland. Political commentators described the Wallace vote as a "backlash" against civil rights agitation and integration, but the conservative Democrat directed most of his rhetoric toward liberal paternalism and big government. Wallace's surprising success revealed lower-middle-class restlessness with the consensus of managerial liberalism and its disregard of their own struggles for survival.

It was black activism, however, that obsessed Johnson with the dangers of strife and violence at the Democratic Convention. Earlier that summer the Student Non-Violent Coordinating Committee (SNCC) had invited one thousand white activists to participate in a voter registration campaign in Mississippi. But the integrated crusade met with violent repression from vigilantes and local authorities who resented outside interference. "Mississippi Summer" brought one thousand arrests, numerous church burnings, bombings, and beatings, and the murder of three civil rights workers. Although only twelve hundred blacks were registered during

the summer's bloody events, a contingent of SNCC workers and new black voters came to Atlantic City to demand political representation. Calling themselves the Mississippi Freedom Democratic party, they argued that the all-white delegation from Mississippi should be unseated because black citizens were unable to participate in their selection. When both sides refused to compromise, the regular delegates, most of whom supported Goldwater, stalked out of the convention, and the embittered Freedom Democrats sat-in at the vacant seats.

Johnson had hoped for a unified convention. But concern with party harmony and fears of another assassination prompted presidential aides to request the FBI to eavesdrop on Martin Luther King and SNCC. Johnson's worried assistants also received minute-by-minute phone calls concerning "potential trouble" from confidential informants who had infiltrated the civil rights camp. While the president agonized about racial strife in Atlantic City, he also withdrew Attorney General Robert Kennedy from consideration for the vice presidency. Anxious to move beyond his predecessor's shadow and easily intimidated by intellectuals and the chic Kennedy people, Johnson announced his decision to leave Kennedy off the Democratic ticket by shrewdly revealing that no member of his cabinet would be selected. Instead, the president nominated a liberal of good standing in the party, Minnesota Senator Hubert Humphrey.

Johnson and Humphrey proclaimed an electoral politics of consensus by defending civil rights legislation and calling for moderation in Vietnam. "We seek no wider war," the president responded to Goldwater's plea for military escalation, as he denounced those who would "supply American boys to do the job that Asian

Lyndon Johnson used the politics of consensus to construct a 61 percent plurality in the 1964 presidential election. Johnson won over 90 percent of the black vote. (Frank Wolfe/Lyndon Baines Johnson Library)

boys should do." But, significantly, Johnson added that he had not "chosen to retreat" and turn Vietnam over to the Communists. The Johnson-Humphrey ticket scored a record 61 percent plurality in the 1964 election, amassing 43 million votes. Goldwater and Miller carried only Arizona and five states in the Deep South, while the Democrats won over 90 percent of the black vote. Similar to Roosevelt's victory in 1936, the Johnson landslide provided the president with better than two-to-one majorities in both houses of Congress. The election also inflated Johnson's conception of presidential au-

thority and bolstered his consensus view of the nation and the world. With an overwhelming electoral mandate, Lyndon Baines Johnson had achieved political independence and a unified nation.

Facilitated by a procedural change that allowed new legislation to by-pass the conservative House Rules Committee, the liberal Eighty-ninth Congress passed aid to education, Medicare, and a Voting Rights Act in 1965. The education bill overcame a controversy about assistance to private schools by basing aid on the number of low-income families in each school district, while a Higher Education Act, passed later in the year, provided college scholarships and fellowships. But these laws enabled the federal government to influence local political decisions. As early as April 1965, the commissioner of education ruled that school districts had to show a "good faith substantial start" toward desegregation or lose federal funding. A year later the Office of Education issued tighter guidelines, declaring an end to "paper compliance with desegregation orders." As appropriations for education reached $10 billion by the late sixties, therefore, conservatives objected that federal aid was threatening local control over schools.

Johnson also pushed for the health care bill for older Americans that Kennedy had feared pressing. With the president's approval, congressional leaders put together a compromise that incorporated Republican demands for voluntary medical insurance to cover doctors' fees and drug costs. But the heart of the Medicare package provided for hospital and nursing home care for Americans over sixty-five through payroll taxes administered by social security. In addition, the bill provided "Medicaid" grants to states that enacted health programs for poor and indigent people of all ages. By 1970 the cost of state health care nearly equaled that of Medicare. But although the Great Society medical programs were a step toward the comprehensive health scheme that Harry Truman had proposed in 1948, the government had no control over service fees, and medical costs increased drastically for all patients.

The most dramatic Great Society reform was the Voting Rights Act of 1965. The twenty-third Amendment to the Constitution, ratified early in 1964, outlawed the poll tax in federal elections, long a barrier to black voting in the South. But as "Mississippi Summer" and Mar-

tin Luther King's marches in Selma, Alabama, demonstrated, white resistance to black balloting remained violent in the Anglo-Saxon South. Accordingly, Johnson summoned a warlike joint session of Congress in March 1965 to request federal protection for blacks who tried to register to vote. The president's words were astounding. First, he compared the Selma demonstrations to Lexington, Concord, and Appomattox as turning points in "man's unending search for freedom." Then, borrowing the language of the civil rights movement itself, the first southern president since Woodrow Wilson told the nation that "All of us ... must overcome the crippling legacy of bigotry and injustice — and we *shall* overcome."

Signed in August, the Voting Rights Act abolished the literacy test and empowered the attorney general to assign federal examiners to register voters in those states still practicing political discrimination. Applied to state and local elections as well as federal, the law marked a revolution in southern political life. Over 400,000 new black voters were registered by examiners in the next year. By 1968 one million southern blacks had been added to the voting lists.

The Great Society reached its apex in 1965. The president approved a $1 billion Appalachia Assistance program, most of which went to road building in the economically depressed region embracing eleven states. A $7.8 billion housing bill included rent supplements to low-income families, but that part of the appropriation was postponed because of strong Republican opposition. Johnson also made the Department of Housing and Urban Development a cabinet-level office, and followed that with approval of the Demonstration Cities and Metropolitan Development Act. The latter appropriated $900 million for intensive attacks on urban blight and established "incentive" grants to encourage metropolitan planning. While Congress more than doubled funding for OEO, it also provided federal grants and loans for public works in "depressed" areas. The consensus approach of the Great Society was symbolized by congressional abolition of the national-origins quota system for immigration. Although immigration was limited to 390,000 a year, close relatives of American citizens and those with special talents and skills were now favored instead of particular nationalities. By 1972 immigrants accounted for 23 percent of the nation's population growth.

RACIAL TURMOIL IN
THE CITIES

The Great Society brought dramatic gains for blacks in national affairs. Robert Weaver was appointed the first black cabinet member in history when he assumed directorship of the Department of Housing and Urban Development. Johnson also named the first black woman to a federal judgeship and appointed Thurgood Marshall, former counsel of the NAACP and the great-grandson of a Maryland slave, as the first black ever to serve on the Supreme Court. In 1966 Massachusetts elected Republican Edward Brooke the first black senator since Reconstruction. Despite these gains, however, moderate leadership found it increasingly difficult to contain the mixture of impatience, rage, and black consciousness that accompanied heightened aspirations and unchanging realities for most black Americans.

Passage of the Voting Rights Act marked the last triumph for the nonviolent and integrated civil rights movement. After 1965 national at-

tention shifted to the 53 percent of the black population that lived outside the South. Many of these Americans lived in decaying ghettos in the older industrial cities of the Northeast and Midwest. The very areas to which southern blacks had migrated since World War One were those in which technology was replacing low-skilled service jobs and from which factories were leaving for the suburbs and the South and West. The exodus of manufacturing plants from the old rail centers and the transition to a sophisticated service economy were disastrous for the black labor force. For example, the Department of Labor reported in 1968 that black Americans were more than three times as likely as whites to be in poverty and twice as likely to be unemployed. Unemployment among black youths in 1966 was 27 percent, compared to 12 percent among young whites; median income for blacks was $4,481 and $7,517 for whites.

As demands for welfare and social services increased in the inner cities, middle-class whites and businesses undermined the needed tax base by moving to the suburbs. By the sixties, America's great cities increasingly were inhabited by the segregated, unemployed, poor, and the elderly. Welfare, housing, and jobs all were inadequate in such a setting. Mothers receiving Aid to Dependent Children, the fastest growing welfare program of the decade, were allotted 21¢ a meal per person in Chicago in the early sixties. Despite the Johnson poverty program and OEO rhetoric, life for most ghetto Americans remained depressingly unchanged throughout the decade.

Shortly after the signing of the Civil Rights Act of 1964, the powder keg exploded. One hundred ghetto rebellions occurred between 1964 and 1967 in the most violent period in American history since the Civil War. Property damage from the disturbances approximated $750 million. The riots began in New York's Harlem, when an off-duty white policeman shot and killed a black youth who allegedly drew a knife. The result was an angry rampage by blacks that destroyed over one hundred businesses, brought hundreds of arrests, and left over one hundred injuries. The Harlem Riot was followed by similar outbreaks in Brooklyn, New Jersey, Philadelphia, Chicago, and Rochester. The following summer, Watts went up in smoke. Watts was a corner of Los Angeles with high dropout rates, 30 percent unemployment, and a long tradition of police harassment. Rioting, arson, shooting, and looting resulted in thirty-six deaths, one thousand injuries, four thousand arrests, and massive property destruction in August 1965. As young blacks chanted "burn, baby, burn," twenty-three thousand National Guardsmen occupied Watts during the six-day riot. But a new sense of power and pride in black identity seemed to emerge from the Watts Rebellion.

By 1966 militant black leaders such as Stokely Carmichael of SNCC were predicting another "long hot summer." Not surprisingly, Carmichael was arrested for inciting a riot when the mayor of Atlanta was toppled from the roof of a car. In Chicago, Martin Luther King had just begun an "open city" campaign when three nights of rioting resulted from a police decision to turn off fire hydrants used for relief from the stifling heat. At King's request, Mayor Richard Daley agreed to set nozzles on hydrants and obtain federal funds for ghetto swimming pools. Later in the summer King led marches for integrated housing into the white ethnic neighborhoods of southwest Chicago, where he and his followers were jeered and pelted with rocks and bottles.

King warned in 1967 that at least ten major cities were ready to explode in racial violence. The summer brought 150 separate riots. In Detroit one week of devastation resulted in forty-three deaths, two thousand injuries, five thousand homeless people and $50 million property damage. Sociologists described the Detroit disturbances as a "commodity riot" in which both whites and blacks helped themselves to goods, but indiscriminate shooting by police and the inexperienced National Guard aggravated racial tension. In Newark, New Jersey, one of the first northern cities with a black majority, severe economic competition with whites and the worst housing in the nation set the stage for the 1967 riot. Twenty-six people died in what the governor's Select Commission later described as "excessive and unjustified force" by police and National Guardsmen. Reports indicated that law enforcement personnel vandalized black businesses and shot ghetto residents indiscriminately. The following year a poll of Newark rioters indicated that 58 percent did not believe the United States worth fighting for. The racial mood of 1967 was conveyed by SNCC leader H. "Rap" Brown, who urged black demonstrators in Cambridge, Maryland, to "burn this town down if this town don't turn around and grant the demands of Negroes."

The riots of the mid-sixties frightened and angered many Americans, particularly white ethnics living in adjoining communities to the blacks. Reacting to the violence, President Johnson appointed a National Advisory Commission on Civil Disorders in 1967, chaired by Governor Otto Kerner of Illinois. The commission's report, issued in February 1968, declared that the United States was "moving toward two societies, one black, one white, separate and unequal." The riots, concluded the distinguished and biracial panel, resulted from white racism and ghetto conditions created, maintained, and condoned by white society. The commission urged a massive commitment to housing, education, welfare, and jobs, as well as better law enforcement techniques. But the president, by then preoccupied by issues of foreign policy, remained silent on the Kerner Commission findings.

CORPORATE WEALTH AND EMPIRE

Despite increased activity in education, housing, and health, federal spending on goods and services barely kept pace with the rising gross national product of the sixties. Income distribution remained lopsided in the prosperous decade. For example, the wealthiest fifth of American families received over 45 percent of the nation's personal income in 1966, whereas the lowest fifth took in a bare 3.7 percent. Tax loopholes underlined the pattern. More than 150 persons with income surpassing $200,000 paid no taxes in 1968. Outstanding tax-exempt bonds, a refuge for wealthy investors, amounted to nearly $86 billion in 1963. Oil-depletion allowances also worked to the advantage of corporations like Atlantic Richfield, which paid no taxes out of a $145 million income in 1967. The percentage of federal revenues coming from corporate income taxes actually dropped from 20 percent in 1955 to 12 percent in 1970.

The sixties produced booming prosperity for American corporations. Profits jumped $12.5 billion, or 57 percent, between 1960 and 1964, as technology continued to play a vital role in American capitalism. Pneumatic conveyors, copying machines, videotape recorders, piggyback freight, jet aircraft, and containerization in ocean shipping were sixties innovations that increased efficiency and profit making. Furthermore, corporations provided a wide variety of low-cost items with new synthetics in textiles and construction, plywood, and freeze-dried foods. Lucrative military and space contracts, particularly in the "sun belt" extending from Southeast to Southwest, also stimulated corporate prosperity and consolidation. By the end of the decade, 71 percent of the profits in manufacturing went to the four hundred largest producing firms in the nation, and half of premium stock was held by large banks, insurance companies, and financial brokers.

The scope of corporate enterprise became an issue of public policy in the sixties. Critics charged that the interaction of private business with public officialdom, an American reality since World War Two, did not always benefit the nation. Personnel shifted easily between corporate management and the federal regulatory boards that set industry standards. When companies with federal contracts got into financial trouble, government assistance frequently assured continued operation, and few government officials attempted to protect consumer interests. But Ralph Nader, a private citizen, worked to publicize the problems facing the ordinary consumer. His book, *Unsafe at Any Speed* (1965), chronicled the vulnerabilities of General Motors' Corvair. Senate hearings in 1966 revealed that the world's largest corporation had investigated Nader's personal life in order to discredit his work. A jury award brought Nader $280,000, which he used to establish research centers to monitor the varying quality of American consumer products. The young lawyers attracted to the campaign called themselves Nader's Raiders, and also investigated mining safety, radiation hazards, pollution, union corruption, and tax inequities.

Sixties prosperity relied substantially on overseas activity. As investment in the Common Market countries of Europe doubled, the total value of American-owned plants and equipment overseas surpassed $100 billion by the end of the decade. Standard Oil of New Jersey, for example, sold more oil in Europe than in the United States. While American firms exported $35 billion worth of goods each year by mid-decade, foreign subsidiaries of American "multinationals" annually sold another $45 billion. By 1967 American corporations funded 80 percent of the vital European computer business and owned half of all modern industry in Britain. As the decade closed, the United States controlled nearly three-fourths of the world's oil and produced most of its machinery, electronics, and chemicals. Through the dissemination of technological products and practices, sophisticated corporations had assumed the mission of "Americanizing" the rest of the planet.

One of the most effective tools of American corporate prosperity was foreign aid, which surpassed $6.6 billion a year during the sixties. Aided by a 1968 "additionality" clause, which required foreign-aid recipients to "buy American," four-fifths of overseas assistance came back to the United States in spending on American products. Loans through government bodies such as the Agency for International Development (AID) and the Export-Import Bank helped underdeveloped nations meet the interest required by congressional foreign aid, but kept these nations in financial subservience to the United States. American assistance also maintained contracts for corporations based at home, as when food shipments to famine-stricken India were held up in 1966 while American oil companies negotiated to establish fertilizer plants in that nation. Military aid, particularly in Latin America, accustomed foreign governments to American products and

technology, and trained police and military forces. Such assistance helped to maintain social structures in which conservative elites exerted power and preserved investment stability for American corporations.

The conservative approach to foreign policy was clearest in Latin America, where Johnson adviser Thomas C. Mann proclaimed that the United States hoped to foster economic development and private investment, not social reform. As a result, Kennedy's Alliance for Progress floundered, and land reform, literacy, and distribution of wealth barely increased in the impoverished region. American preference for stability at any cost surfaced when the United States quickly recognized a repressive military regime after a Brazilian coup in 1964. Significantly, the coup officers who overthrew the constitutionally elected government had been trained under AID military assistance.

Johnson's Latin American policy crystalized with the invasion of the Dominican Republic in 1965, when constitutionalists took to arms to restore a president overthrown by the army. Already the beneficiaries of a $5 million American loan, the Dominican generals asked for American military assistance to "help restore peace." Johnson decided to intervene on the frantic advice of his Dominican ambassador, who alleged that fifty-three Communists were leading the constitutionalist movement. On television, the president explained that he was sending in the marines to save American lives and to prevent a "band of Communist conspirators" from wreaking disorder in an explosive situation. Enunciating a Johnson Doctrine, the chief executive proclaimed that "the American nations cannot, must not, and will not permit the establishment of another Communist government in the Western Hemisphere." Eventually, twenty-four thousand American troops supervised the creation of a new provisional government, but the hasty Dominican intervention seemed an overreaction by a great power to a minor dispute not central to its interests. Unilaterally, Johnson had decided that another Castro-type revolution in the hemisphere would not be tolerated.

The major instrument of American foreign policy in Latin America was not the military, but the Central Intelligence Agency. With little hindrance the CIA practiced "covert interference" in the internal affairs of poor countries that the United States wished to control or influence. Techniques included blackmail, bribery, forgery, bombing, sabotage, daily espionage, propaganda, disinformation (deliberate circulation of false information), psychological warfare, military training, and paramilitary activities. Financial support to individuals, political parties, private organizations, unions, and businesses also was common practice. American foreign policy advisers believed that the Cuban Revolution had stirred the forces of instability in the hemisphere. Their intention was to use the CIA to promote stability through assisting local governments to build up security forces and put down the violent Left. If economic growth and political stability were to continue, friendly governments needed time in which to effect the reforms that would prevent communism.

The CIA financed mass urban demonstrations against the leftist government in Brazil shortly before the 1964 coup. In Ecuador agency operatives worked to strengthen non-Communist trade unions and disrupt the revolutionary Left. Through agency auspices the State Department and AID funneled up to $20 million into the Chilean elections of 1964, where they were successful in contributing to the defeat of Salvador Allende, the Marxist candidate. In Peru the CIA secretly loaned helicopters, arms, and Green Beret training to the government effort to head off a guerrilla insurgency in the eastern jungles. During 1967 agency special operations officers assisted the Bolivian army in tracking down world revolutionary Che Guevara, who was quickly executed by the Bolivian government.

The same philosophy led to CIA intervention in the Congo in 1964, where agency mercenaries used American B-26 bombers to carry out regular missions against insurgents, while CIA money and arms supported the pro-Western government. In Laos, where American troops were prohibited by the 1962 Geneva Accords, the CIA maintained a private army of thirty-five thousand mountain tribesmen and recruited and financed another seventeen thousand Thais. Bombing and supply missions were flown by pilots hired through Air America, the agency's proprietary company in Southeast Asia. The secret program, not revealed until 1971, cost about $70 million a year.

By the end of the decade, American military power was awesome. The United States had 429 major and 2,972 minor military bases across the globe in thirty countries, and one million American service men and women were based overseas. The nation's military arsenal included one thousand nuclear-armed intercontinental missiles and seventy nuclear-powered and armed submarines. In fact, America's nuclear storehouse amounted to the equivalent of fifteen tons of TNT for every person in the world. The total tonnage of its navy was greater than that of all other nations combined. Costs for the military establishment ran to $216 million a day. Between 1945 and 1970, American taxpayers spent $1 trillion (one million millions) on defense. Yet, the late sixties brought the United States to the worst military and political

disaster in its history, as military and technological power proved impotent in Southeast
Asia.

VIETNAM

One of Lyndon Johnson's first acts as president
was to confer with Ambassador to South Vietnam Henry Cabot Lodge. Lodge delivered the
grim news that attacks from the guerrilla arm
of the National Liberation Front (NLF) had
increased sharply. Johnson, who had presented
Kennedy with a glowing firsthand report on
American prospects in Vietnam in 1961, told
Lodge that he was "not going to be the President who saw Southeast Asia go the way China
went."

The nature of Johnson's commitment in Vietnam, however, differed significantly from that
of Kennedy. In the last days of his life, Kennedy had ordered a reduction of American
forces in Vietnam and had indicated a dissatisfaction with a military solution. But he had not
publicized the changing direction of his policy.
Moreover, prominent members of the New
Frontier, such as Secretary Rusk, continued to
favor full military operations.

After meeting with Lodge, therefore, Johnson canceled the withdrawal of troops and approved a program to accelerate covert attacks
against North Vietnam and operations into
Laos. Under secret plan 34A, implemented February 1964, hired Asian sabotage teams para-
chuted into North Vietnam, conducted commando raids against transportation targets, and
kidnapped Vietnamese to gain intelligence information. American destroyers also patrolled
the Gulf of Tonkin, while PT boats bombarded
North Vietnamese coastal installations.

As Johnson continued to speak publicly
against American military involvement in Vietnam, he proceeded with a covert war. He promised economic aid to both Vietnams if Hanoi
would keep within the temporary border erected
by the 1954 Geneva agreements. If not, he
warned, the United States would devastate
North Vietnam. In May 1964 the State Department secretly drafted a congressional resolution for a declaration of war. A CIA National
Intelligence Estimate predicted that no other
nation, with the possible exception of Cambodia, would succumb to communism if Laos and
Vietnam fell. But Johnson, like his three predecessors in the White House, believed in the
domino theory and in the need to maintain
American credibility.

South Vietnamese ships began bombarding
several North Vietnamese islands in the Gulf
of Tonkin in July 1964. American destroyers,
fit for electronic intelligence, accompanied
them. When three North Vietnamese PT boats
fired on one of the destroyers in what the
United States described as international waters,
four American fighter planes strafed the at-
tackers. On August 4 the Americans claimed a
second attack on the destroyer and a sister ship,
although a subsequent report blamed "freak
weather effects, and an overeager sonar man"
for that impression, and the North Vietnamese
vehemently denied the allegation.

Johnson, nevertheless, ordered an air reprisal
on PT boat bases in North Vietnam. Addressing the American people on national television,
the president assured that a "positive reply" was
"being given as I speak to you tonight." Although American commitment would "be re-
doubled by this outrage," the president said,
"we still seek no wider war." On August 7
Johnson went to Congress with a reworded
version of the May declaration of war. The

MAP 15.1   SOUTH VIETNAM

© 1966 by the New York Times Company. Reprinted by permission.

Tonkin Gulf Resolution stated the "Congress approves and supports the determination of the President as commander-in-chief to take all necessary measures to repel any attack against the forces of the United States and to prevent further aggression." The resolution passed the House 416–0 and the Senate 88–2, with only Wayne Morse of Oregon and Ernest Gruening of Alaska dissenting. A Harris poll also showed 85 percent approval of the air strikes against North Vietnam. The administration had stopped short of a full declaration of war, careful not to antagonize China or the Soviet Union. But Johnson had won a free hand to conduct a war by presidential discretion, and he continued to cite the Tonkin resolution as the legal basis of his Vietnam policy. This interpretation had a precedent in the Formosa Resolution of 1955.

As the United States increased its opposition to North Vietnam, street fighting by students and Buddhists erupted against the increasingly authoritarian regime in South Vietnam. On Christmas Eve 1964, an American billet in the heart of Saigon was blown up, killing two GIs and injuring eight. Johnson refused the strong response called for by the Pentagon. The turning point instead came in February 1965, when a company of NLF insurgents attacked an American base at Pleiku in the central highlands, killing 9 Americans and wounding 140. "They are killing our men while they sleep at night," a disturbed president told a congressional briefing. Johnson then announced Operation Flaming Dart, a program of retaliatory air strikes against North Vietnam. The president believed that the Pleiku attack was directed from Hanoi, perhaps even Peking, and vowed that he would not be scared out of Vietnam.

In response to American bombing raids, the Soviet Union and North Vietnam announced a "mutual aid" treaty in which the Soviets would supply antiaircraft weapons. A few days later the American barracks at Qui Nonh was blown up, killing twenty-three Americans. At this point the State Department retreated to a fixed position and rejected a French offer to arrange negotiations. Placing the conflict within the context of Cold War balance of power, Defense Secretary McNamara told a House committee that the United States would not leave Vietnam because China was making it a test of the Sino-Soviet rivalry. But McNamara's assistant secretary, John McNaughton, privately estimated that only 20 percent of American war aims concerned Chinese expansion and that merely another 10 percent involved a better life for the Vietnamese. The remaining 70 percent, McNaughton conceded, incorporated the necessity of avoiding a humiliating defeat for the United States. No doubt should ever be left, McNaughton stated in a top-secret Pentagon memorandum, "regarding American policy, power, resolve, and competence."

By March 1965 Operation Rolling Thunder began a full-scale bombing of North Vietnamese military installations. Poor accuracy marked the air force strikes, as North Vietnamese antiaircraft quickly discovered the direct routes flown by pilots anxious to add to their number of sorties. The result was a high loss of planes and indiscriminate bombing of schools, hospitals, and other civilian targets. Meanwhile, 3,500 recently arrived marines, still classified as "advisers," took the offensive for the first time in the American involvement on the ground, and Johnson authorized an additional 100,000 troops for Vietnam duty. The president explained his position at an address at Johns Hopkins University. We do not seek territory in Vietnam, he stated: "We fight because we must fight if we are to live in a world where every country can shape its own destiny." Johnson spoke of the commitment of the United States "to strengthen world order," to sustain the confidence of those who depend on America. "To withdraw from one battlefield means only to prepare for the next," the president explained. In conciliation, he proposed a $1 billion "Marshall Plan" for the Mekong Valley of South Vietnam. A Gallup poll showed that 61 percent of the sample approved the increased troop allotments. Johnson's decision to use ground troops in offensive action was designed to maintain enough force to prevent the Communists from winning, but not enough to antagonize China into full participation. The president was demonstrating that a limited war could be fought with conventional weapons.

By the summer of 1965, however, the war was no longer limited. American ground troops began their first full-scale combat offensive, engaging in "search-and-destroy" missions. In the air, B-52s flew three thousand miles from Guam to drop 750-pound bombs on suspected Viet Cong strongholds in South Vietnam. By the end of the year, American and South Vietnamese air attacks on the South surpassed seventy thousand strikes. December brought the first air strikes against industrial targets in the North, including a power plant just outside the chief North Vietnamese port of Haiphong. At Christmas Johnson declared the beginning of a thirty-seven-day bombing halt and sent emissaries around the world to explore possibilities for peace. But the stumbling block to negotiations was the refusal of the United States to recognize the National Liberation Front as a political force independent of North Vietnam. The administration contended that the North Vietnamese had invaded South Vietnam, and thereby denied that the United States had become embroiled in a civil war. When North Vietnamese infiltration continued during the bombing pause, American attacks on the North resumed.

Johnson would go no further than an offer to withdraw troops and end the bombing once a peace settlement was achieved.

Just as Congress approved a $14.7 billion supplemental expenditure for Vietnam, Johnson flew to Honolulu to embrace South Vietnamese leaders Nguyen Cao Ky and Nguyen Van Thieu and to pledge "social revolution" for the South and 385,000 more troops. Meanwhile, the resumption of bombing early in 1966 brought public hearings on Vietnam policy by the Senate Foreign Relations Committee. Led by Committee Chairman J. William Fulbright of Arkansas, several senators questioned the legality of the undeclared war and listened to retired Lieutenant General James A. Gavin become the first military man to oppose the war. Former State Department troubleshooter George F. Kennan, author of the containment policy toward the Soviet Union, testified that he felt "bewildered" by the commitment to defend a nonessential South Vietnam. In contrast, Ambassador to South Vietnam General Maxwell Taylor maintained it was essential to demonstrate the failure of "wars of liberation." It was clear that the administration had staked its reputation at home and abroad on the successful conclusion of the Vietnam War.

"We do not seek to enlarge this war," Johnson insisted in May 1966, "but we shall not run out on it." He testily predicted there would "be some Nervous Nellies and some who will become frustrated and bothered and break ranks under the strain." But bringing consensus to Vietnam was no easy task. In Danang and Hue, South Vietnamese marines were compelled to put down antigovernment demonstrations, as Ky led the forces capturing Buddhist pagodas. A new program of "pacification" began with the training of South Vietnamese cadres in the spring of 1966, but NLF control only increased in the northern provinces. Furthermore, elections promoted by the United States only proceeded when "neutralists," "pro-Communists," and areas under insurgent influence were excluded.

Starting in June 1966, the United States began to bomb central Hanoi. "We must continue to raise the price of aggression at its source," Johnson explained in the language of militant retaliation. The goal of American bombing had changed from breaking the enemy's will to cutting supply lines. But the CIA and Defense Intelligence Agency reported that sixteen months of bombing had brought "no measurable direct effect on Hanoi's ability to mount and support military operations in the South." One pilot in every forty sorties was lost in the bombing program. Johnson promised that the United States would stop bombing if the North Vietnamese pledged to send no more troops south, but Hanoi responded that peace depended on withdrawal of all American troops and bases and peaceful reunification of the two Vietnams. In turn, Johnson informed American allies in Asia that South Vietnam must be preserved. The president also made a surprise visit to a military base in Vietnam, where he gave a rousing speech urging American soldiers to "come home with that coonskin on the wall." The warrior mentality still prevailed. Back in the United States for the congressional elections of 1966, the president reminded Americans that they were "outnumbered fifteen-to-one" in the world and that "we have what they want."

But Johnson's efforts were to no avail. Military advisers repeatedly made the error of assuming that lessened Viet Cong combat operations indicated diminished capability, when the VC only were adapting new strategies after American escalations. Furthermore, American denial of civilian damage from the bombing in North Vietnam was belied when the *New York Times* published firsthand reports by correspondent Harrison Salisbury that described the destruction in central Hanoi. By the fall of 1966, Defense Secretary McNamara, disillusioned by plane and pilot losses, rejected a Pentagon troop request for the first time and privately called for a new initiative toward a political settlement. When McNamara vetoed General Westmoreland's plea for 300,000 more troops early in 1967, the defense secretary commissioned a systematic study of Vietnam policy, later to be called the Pentagon Papers, to re-examine the original strategies behind the war. McNamara eventually settled on fifty-five thousand more troops, assuring a half-million-man ground force for 1968. But by December 1967, Johnson's impatience with the ambivalence of his Pentagon chief led to McNamara's resignation and appointment to the World Bank.

As Americans confronted regular North Vietnamese troops, casualty figures jumped feverishly. In one battle a mistaken air force strike against an American position killed thirty GIs. Meanwhile, the NLF controlled the timing and terms of nearly four-fifths of the military engagements in the southern provinces by mid-1967. In turn, pacification in the South became increasingly bloody.

Beginning as a counter-insurgency program to win "hearts and minds," pacification evolved into a terror campaign that herded refugees into "strategic hamlets" for "protection" from guerrilla insurgents. To destroy Viet Cong hideouts, bases, and sources of food, American planes dropped napalm, defoliants, and herbicides in South Vietnam. Napalm burned everything it touched, including the skin of human beings, while fragmentation bombs hopelessly destroyed internal organs with millions of tiny particles that could not be detected by X rays.

MAP 15.2   THE TET OFFENSIVE, 1968

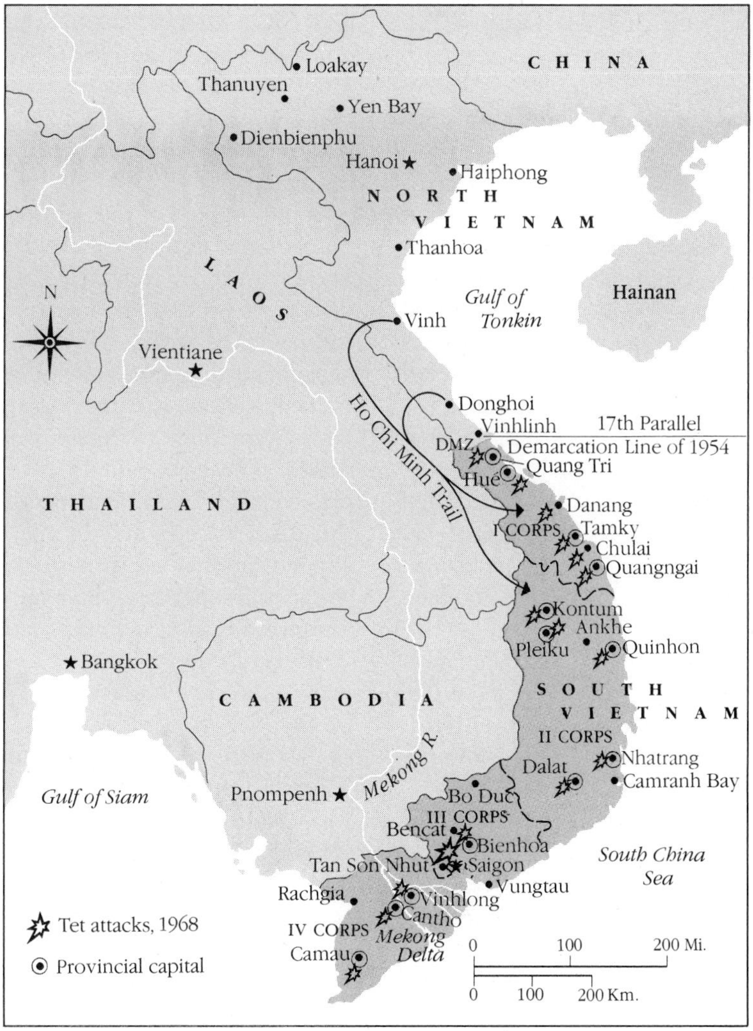

Loakay
Thanuyen
Yen Bay
Dienbienphu
Hanoi ★
Haiphong

CHINA

NORTH
VIETNAM

Thanhoa

LAOS

Gulf of
Tonkin

Hainan

N

Vinh

Vientiane ★

Donghoi
Vinhlinh
17th Parallel
DMZ Demarcation Line of 1954
Hué Quang Tri

Ho Chi Minh Trail

THAILAND

Danang
I CORPS Tamky
Chulai
Quangngai

Kontum
Ankhe
Pleiku Quinhon

★ Bangkok

CAMBODIA

SOUTH
VIETNAM

II CORPS

Dalat
Nhatrang
Camranh Bay

Gulf of Siam

Mekong R.

Pnompenh ★

Bo Duc
III CORPS
Bencat Bienhoa
Tan Son Nhut Saigon
Rachgia Vungtau
Vinhlong
Cantho
IV CORPS Mekong
Camau Delta

South China
Sea

✪ Tet attacks, 1968
◉ Provincial capital

0   100   200 Mi.

0   100   200 Km.

Reprinted by permission from TIME, The Weekly Newsmagazine; Copyright
Time Inc. 1968

Bombing in the South was indiscriminate and lethal to civilians who often were listed in "body counts" as "suspected Viet Cong." After villages were bombed, peasants were relocated, a strategy promoted by American social scientists as "forced urbanization." These campaigns also involved the arrest and interrogation of suspected members of the "Viet Cong infrastructure." Aided by a central computer in Saigon that assigned "neutralization" quotas for each province, teams of Vietnamese "Revolutionary Development" units conducted systematized kidnapping, torture, and assassination programs in the villages. The CIA, which trained and supervised the Vietnamese cadres, estimated the death toll from this Operation Phoenix to be at least twenty thousand.

The futility of the American effort in Vietnam was brought home by the Communist Tet Offensive in February 1968, a coordinated attack on every major city in South Vietnam planned in conjunction with internal revolutionary uprisings. In Saigon a commando attack on the United States Embassy brought five American deaths and a six-hour battle with marine guards and military police. For twenty-eight days, the Communists held Hue, the capital of old Vietnam, where they executed police officials and pro-Americans, while block-by-block fighting, bombing, and shelling continued incessantly. The South Vietnamese, in turn, executed Buddhists, students, and teachers as "VC collaborators." An estimated thirty-two thousand insurgents were killed during Tet, while over four thousand Americans lost their lives and nearly twenty thousand were wounded. Although the Communists withdrew from the major cities they had captured, the Tet Offensive destroyed any war optimism still surviving in the United States, and more than half the American people turned against the

war for the first time. Despite Pentagon claims of victory, Tet demonstrated that the Viet Cong and North Vietnamese only had to survive in order to prevent the United States from "winning" the war. It also revealed the impotence of a South Vietnamese Army unable to defend positions without American air or artillery assistance.

Several aspects of the Tet confrontation were particularly disturbing. At Khe Sanh three hundred marines were killed in a seventy-seven day siege by surrounding North Vietnamese regiments. Following the battle, the Americans abandoned the position as of no value. In the Mekong Delta one thousand pro-Saigon villagers were killed by American artillery and air strikes. The commanding air force major explained that "it became necessary to destroy the town to save it." In the village of Son My, an untested company in the Americal Division was unable to find an NLF batallion that army intelligence had located in the area. Tense and under pressure to build up the VC body count, Lt. William L. Calley's men lined up over four hundred villagers, mostly old people, women, and children, and shot them all. The My Lai massacre, not disclosed until 1969, was reported in army records as an important victory involving enemy sniper attacks and fierce fighting. By the end of March 1968, however, Pentagon and presidential credibility concerning the war were exhausted.

THE WAR AT HOME

As dissent against the Vietnam War escalated, the Johnson administration adopted measures to impose a consensus by force. Beginning in 1968, the FBI applied its counterintelligence capacities to further what Bureau Director J. Edgar Hoover saw as a crusade "to expose, disrupt, and otherwise neutralize the activities of the New Left." Records of "black-bag jobs" (burglaries) against "domestic subversive targets" were placed in a special "Do Not File" file. COINTELPRO, as the Bureau called its program, also attempted to widen the rift between radical organizations through falsely attributed letters and undercover agents. In California, COINTELPRO agents hired a prostitute infected with venereal disease to seduce New Left leaders and discredit them with campus followers.

But the FBI's major target was Martin Luther King. Hoover feared the civil rights movement might produce a "black messiah" who would unite American blacks in a movement to disrupt society. When Attorney General Robert Kennedy authorized wiretaps on King's telephones in 1963, the FBI went further and placed "bugs" (electronic recording devices) in his bedroom. Kennedy desired to ascertain Communist influence on King and approved the taps on a trial basis. But stung by the minister's attacks on Bureau handling of civil rights cases, the FBI conducted a full-scale public relations vendetta to discredit and intimidate King.

FBI activity was duplicated by other intelligence agencies. Following the Watts riots in 1965, army intelligence began to gather information to be used when troops were called to police civil disturbances. A "domestic war room" in the Pentagon treated campus and urban demonstrators as "insurgents" whose actions aided the Communists. By 1968 the army had compiled 100,000 dossiers on antiwar activists and elected officials and employed one thousand undercover agents to spy on American citizens. During the summer of 1967, Johnson also established a Special Operations Group in the CIA. "Operation Chaos" kept files on seventy-two hundred Americans and trained agency recruits by assigning them domestic surveillance of dissidents, demonstrators, and even "suspicious" members of Congress. The program also instituted wiretaps and break-ins against radicals and featured a computerized index that included the names of 300,000 individuals and organizations. Since the CIA charter prohibited agency domestic operations, Operation Chaos was blatantly illegal. But when the CIA attempted to convince Johnson that domestic dissent was independent of foreign funding, the president was reluctant to accept the findings.

Johnson had hoped to finance the war without cutting Great Society funding. But as war costs rose to $2 billion a month by 1966, Johnson admitted that "guns and butter" were not always compatible. In a year of record federal spending overseas, Congress abolished the school milk program and sliced money for education. While Democrats defeated Republican attempts to dismantle OEO, Congress required that community action funds be channeled through public officials, and the antipoverty agency struggled along on half its projected funding.

Despite the need to cut spending, Johnson desired to forestall social strife by keeping the Great Society alive. Korean War veterans won educational aid in 1966, while the president signed a bill that raised minimum wages by one-fourth and covered farmworkers for the first time. The 1967 school aid bill was the largest in history and was followed the next year by an urban development package that provided the most generous housing allotment since 1949. Johnson also approved creation of a cabinet-level Department of Transportation and signed a $330 million model cities bill. A

Robert Francis Kennedy

1925-1968

The death of Robert Kennedy signaled the end of hope in a turbulent era desperately in need of conciliation. Kennedy had served as the New Frontier's principal power broker — presidential campaign manager in 1960, attorney general, and personal adviser to his brother's presidency. A tough Irish-American who believed in Cold War vigilance, he helped to fashion counter-insurgency in Vietnam and personally supervised the CIA's covert campaigns in Cuba and elsewhere. But Dallas tore his world apart, and Kennedy began a new career in 1964 as the junior senator from New York.

Affected by his own personal tragedy, Kennedy used his Senate prestige to push for greater commitments toward those without privilege or power. He visited Cesar Chavez's grape strikers in California, took testimony on malnutrition in Mississippi, conducted hearings on the squalor of reservation life in New Mexico. In an eloquent denunciation of American materialism, he warned in 1967 that "We cannot measure national spirit by the Dow-Jones Average, nor national achievement by the gross national product."

Kennedy was not among the first to question the Vietnam War. But early in 1966 he issued a cautious call for a coalition government in Saigon. A year later Kennedy took the Senate floor to condemn the administration's bombing: "We are all participants.... We must also feel as men the anguish of what it is we are doing." In November 1967 he delivered a spontaneous tirade on national television against American slaughter of the Vietnamese. Commentators began to speculate on his availability for the presidency, but Kennedy was too much of a professional Democrat to risk splitting the party in a personal vendetta against an incumbent president. Once again, however, he was moved by events beyond his control.

The eighty-five-day campaign of Robert Kennedy stirred an emotional groundswell never before seen in American politics. Kennedy proposals for a draft lottery, corporate ghetto development, and Vietnam negotiations were modest. But "Bobby" symbolized the lost idealism of the New Frontier, the flickering hope that all classes and races really could share in the American Dream. He campaigned on the streets, jacket off, tie loose, and sleeves rolled up. Excited crowds swarmed along the primary trail just to touch his hand.

When Martin Luther King was assassinated in April 1968, Kennedy went directly to a ghetto street gathering in Indianapolis and shared his own feelings of loss by quoting the Greek poet Aeschylus. A nearby graffiti explained his remarkable following among American blacks: "Kennedy white but alright./The one before, he opened the door." But the secret to the Kennedy campaign was the compassion he expressed toward all the nation's working people and dispossessed. Despite his stance against the war, the tough-minded senator scored heavy primary pluralities in white districts that had previously supported George Wallace.

Robert Kennedy was the only leader of his era who might have united white working people, antiwar students, and the racial minorities in a coalition for change. At the Democratic Convention in Chicago, members wept and sang the "Battle Hymn of the Republic" in his memory.

truth-in-lending bill, signed in 1968, required that consumers be told the costs of loans and installment plans in terms of annual rates.

Although these were substantial accomplishments for a nation at war, ghetto and campus rioting hurt further liberal proposals. When Johnson followed King's "open city" campaign in Chicago with submission of an equal housing bill in 1966, two attempts to end a Senate filibuster failed, and the administration settled for a $40 million appropriation for rat control in city slums. Congress responded to campus antiwar disorders in 1968 by stipulating that students convicted of disruptions could not receive federal funds.

Congressional uneasiness with domestic programs also reflected the soaring inflation precipitated by spending for the war. By 1968 the defense budget reached $70 billion. Johnson had prevailed upon Congress to suspend Kennedy's investment tax credit and had accelerated depreciation allowances in 1966, but these minor tax increases proved insufficient. The president suffered a severe legislative setback the following year when Congress refused to accept his war tax surcharge, preferring either spending cutbacks or tax reform. Johnson finally won a 10 percent surcharge on individual and corporate income taxes in 1968. But to satisfy fiscal conservatives, he was forced to accept a restriction on domestic spending and federal employment of civilians. The delay in taxing inflated profits and incomes. This inflation combined with war spending to bring a phenomenal rise in the federal deficit. From $3.8 billion in 1966, the deficit leaped to $8.7 billion in 1967 and a catastrophic $25.2 billion in 1968. As a result, the consumer price index rose 5 percent in 1968 alone.

Wartime inflation was particularly harmful to the elderly and others on fixed incomes, as well as to the forty million Americans who constituted the working class. But Americans of modest income feared tax increases that would aggravate their financial burdens, while the banking community worried that raised interest rates would discourage installment buying and home purchases. Given the widespread reluctance to cut defense in wartime, public opinion responded to the threat of inflation by calling for cutbacks in liberal welfare programs. Deficit spending under Kennedy and Johnson actually had stimulated business activity more than government programs. But as the financial pressures of the Vietnam War built up after 1965, many Americans began to resent reforms that seemed to benefit professional program administrators, dissatisfied students, and rebellious minorities. Although statistics continued to emphasize the poor standing of blacks in income and employment, many working-class and middle-class whites believed that hard-earned tax dollars were benefiting blacks while they were left to face an intolerable economic squeeze on their own.

The conservative backlash to the Great Society surfaced in the congressional elections of 1966. Stressing "crime in the streets" and the need for "law and order," Republicans gained forty-seven seats in the House and three in the Senate. Democrats warned that education, jobs, better housing, and an end to discrimination were needed to eliminate domestic strife, but were hampered by the realization that Great Society spending had to be reduced in the face of war costs. In Georgia, segregationist Lester Maddox, who had defied the Civil Rights Act of 1964 by chasing blacks from his restaurant with a pistol, was elected governor in a runoff in the state assembly.

"Law and order" meant that voters were sensitive to the increase in offenses against persons, which more than doubled between 1960 and 1968. In New York City a special election defeated by a 2–1 margin the creation of a civilian review board to monitor police. Concern over crime also resulted in the Crime Control and Safe Streets Act of 1968, which provided grants to upgrade local law enforcement, authorized wiretapping with a warrant, and banned interstate shipment of handguns and their sale to minors. As a response to urban rioting, the law disqualified from federal employment anyone convicted of a riot-related felony. Most important, the omnibus bill attempted to reverse *Miranda* v. *Arizona,* the Supreme Court decision of 1966 that ruled that police must inform criminal suspects of their rights. The Crime Control Act responded to conservative ire about "permissiveness" toward criminals by providing that voluntary confessions were admissible in federal trials.

This concern over social and economic disorder enabled Alabama Governor George Wallace to attract a massive following by 1968. Wallace won extensive working-class support in rural and small-town areas of the South, but elsewhere his support was divided equally between working people and the middle class. A large segment of the Wallace movement also consisted of noncollege youth, polarized to the Right by the confrontation politics of campus radicalism. Wallace articulated deeply held resentments toward liberal government programs, ghetto rioting, and student rebellion, but also emphasized the importance of property rights and local government. When he announced his presidential candidacy in the American Independent party in February 1968, Wallace promised to maintain social peace with "30,000 troops with two-foot-long bayonets." He called for repeal of civil rights laws and a forceful pursuit of the war in Vietnam. To emphasize his confidence in the military, Wallace chose former Air Force Chief of Staff Curtis Le May as his running mate. Le May dampened the Wallace upsurge with a thoughtless quip about bombing North Vietnam back to the Stone Age. But the campaign also spoke to grassroots impatience with the two major parties.

Despite Wallace's prowar appeal, blue-collar support of the war was only 1 percent above that of the rest of the nation in 1966. Late in 1967 a national sample disapproved of Johnson's handling of the war by a 68–22 percent margin, but also viewed peace demonstrations as "acts of disloyalty against the boys fighting in Vietnam." Those who defended the war felt the president had the facts. Even if he did not, sentiment to support the troops was very strong. A New York City march "supporting our men in Vietnam" attracted seventy thousand people in 1967.

THE CHAOS OF '68

Although the administration put on a bold front, the Tet Offensive brought an end to the Johnson war policy and ushered in the most calamitous year in American political history since the Civil War. Westmoreland continued to request at least 200,000 more troops and mobilization of the reserves. His proposal would have added $12 billion to war costs already reaching $30 billion a year. But Clark Clifford, who had replaced McNamara as defense secretary, found extensive "dove" sentiment among top Pentagon civilians. Poring over pessimistic military and CIA reports, Clifford discovered that the past year's bombing had only tripled North Vietnamese infiltration rates. Beginning in February 1968, Clifford quietly rallied sup-

port within the administration for a reduction of the costly war effort. On March 12 antiwar Senator Eugene McCarthy astounded the nation by taking 42 percent of the vote in the New Hampshire Democratic primary. Four days later Robert Kennedy announced his candidacy for the presidential nomination. On March 18, 139 members of the House called for a congressional review of the administration's war program. Four days later Johnson relieved Westmoreland of the Vietnam command and summoned a meeting of the Senior Informal Advisory Group.

The March 22 conference included twelve of the most prestigious members of the nation's foreign policy, business, and law establishment, men who constituted the cream of the American corporate elite. Nearly all had approved the escalation of bombing in 1967. But present policy, a majority concurred, could not achieve its objectives without the use of unlimited resources for another five years. This was impossible, the group counseled, without citizen support and budgetary sacrifices. Former Treasury Secretary Douglas Dillon, former Undersecretary of State George Ball, former Deputy Defense Secretary Cyrus Vance, and Wall Street luminary John McCloy, all of whom saw Europe as the proper arena for American economic expansion, emphasized the strain on the dollar abroad and the threat to international monetary stability. Generals Omar Bradley and Matthew Ridgway vacillated in support of the bombing. But the climax to the meeting came when former Secretary of State Dean Acheson, whom Johnson deeply respected, argued that the bombing was more damaging to the administration in Washington than the regime in Hanoi. Acheson described the Joint Chiefs of Staff as "mad" and said the president's speeches were so out of touch with reality that "nobody could believe them." The war had brought a loss of national purpose, Acheson warned, and eclipsed the "most critical priority of all"—the home front.

Johnson and his advisers had believed that wars of national liberation were Communist efforts to wear down the West and eventually surround the United States and Europe with hostile forces. They had faith that American power and idealism could stop Communist revolts, even when they occurred against corrupt and authoritarian regimes. Strong leadership, Johnson believed, could overcome obstacles at home and abroad. He hoped to be remembered as a great president. But the twelve "wise men" whom Johnson had summoned buttressed Senator Fulbright's 1965 observation that the nation was "losing its perspective on what exactly is within the realm of its power and what is beyond it." Following the meeting, Clifford told Johnson that a "peace speech" was in order for the television talk the president had scheduled to precede the Wisconsin primary. Johnson resisted, but the polls had turned against him, the press spoke of a "credibility gap," and hostile demonstrators greeted him at every turn. On March 31 Johnson stunned the nation when he explained that "I shall not seek, and I will not accept, the nomination of my party for another term as your president." He also announced suspension of bombing above North Vietnam's 20th parallel and indicated a willingness to include the NLF in peace negotiations.

Johnson hoped that his withdrawal from the presidential race would encourage peace prospects and lead to the healing of bitter wounds at home. But the difficulty of achieving domestic peace was underscored when Martin Luther King was assassinated by a self-proclaimed white racist on April 4, the day after the North Vietnamese had agreed to peace

talks. Riots immediately erupted in black ghettos across the country. Whole blocks between the White House and the Capitol were burned out after three days of looting and arson in predominantly black Washington. In Chicago, Mayor Daley ordered police to "shoot to kill arsonists and shoot to maim looters." All told, rioting occurred in 168 cities and towns, producing forty-three deaths and two thousand arrests. But within a week of King's death in Memphis, Congress passed Johnson's long-delayed open housing bill. The Civil Rights Act of 1968 banned racial discrimination in the sale and rental of about four-fifths of the nation's housing. It also outlawed crossing interstate lines with intent to incite riot or disorder.

Johnson's withdrawal opened up the possibility of an antiwar Democratic candidacy. Minnesota Senator McCarthy had announced his intention to test rising sentiment for a negotiated settlement late in 1967. When college and peace volunteers presented him with an awesome organization, McCarthy broadened his criticism with attacks on an arrogant military and an overextended presidency. Government's role was to liberate people, not to organize them, he preached, as young activists flocked to the "get clean for Gene" crusade. Conservatives also responded to McCarthy's emphasis on limited government, lessened expectations, and personal honesty.

Robert Kennedy, who was elected senator from New York in 1964, moved more slowly to an antiwar stance. Up to 1968, Kennedy was reluctant to split the Democratic party by challenging an incumbent president. But following the New Hampshire primary, Kennedy told Clark Clifford that he would seek the nomination if the president did not create a special commission to explore a wider peace approach. Johnson vehemently rejected the proposal. Kennedy then announced his candidacy, believing that the McCarthy crusade had demonstrated the political futility of the president's position. He called for a Vietnam peace settlement based on political compromise, arguing that the nation should not subordinate the national interest to an "incompetent military regime," and linked Vietnam to neglect of domestic issues. Kennedy's compassion and enthusiasm attracted a wide spectrum of minorities, working-class Catholics, labor supporters, and students. On June 4 he won the California primary. But minutes later, Kennedy was assassinated by Sirhan Sirhan, a Palestinian who opposed Kennedy's pro-Israel position.

The assassinations of Kennedy and King had a devastating effect on the majority of the American people. It seemed that only death awaited young men of vision and energy, that attempts to stop the killing in Vietnam were futile. As it became clear that Vice President Humphrey, who entered the presidential race late in April, would take the nomination, peace activists and young radicals went to Chicago to demonstrate at the Democratic Convention. Inside the convention hall, Mayor Daley had erected the most elaborate security measures in American political history. A private security force issued electronically scanned passes to delegates and used force to control reporters, delegates, and visitors. A minority platform report, sponsored by Senators McCarthy, George McGovern, and Edward Kennedy, called for an unconditional end to the Vietnam bombing,

MAP 15.3   THE ELECTION OF 1968

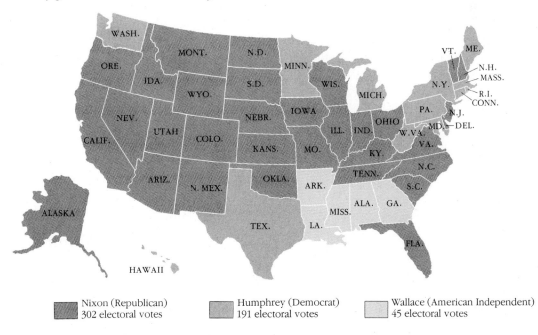

Nixon (Republican)
302 electoral votes

Humphrey (Democrat)
191 electoral votes

Wallace (American Independent)
45 electoral votes

negotiated withdrawal, and a Saigon coalition with the NLF. But the doves were unable to overcome administration pressure, and the measure failed by a 3–2 margin. While clubbed and Maced demonstrators on Chicago streets chanted "The whole world is watching!" the presidential balloting proceeded on the convention floor. Rising to nominate George McGovern of South Dakota, who had won the endorsement of Kennedy's California delegates, Senator Abraham Ribicoff denounced "Gestapo tactics on the streets of Chicago." Daley shot to his feet, shouting obscenities at the speaker, and the hall erupted in pandemonium.

Backed by organized labor and the party professionals, Humphrey easily won the nomination. But the Democrats were so badly split that the vice president's chances seemed slim. Humphrey's major problem was achieving an independence from the Johnson war policy that would not offend the party mainstream. For Americans sickened by the war, Humphrey's enthusiastic support of the hawk position was unforgivable. In October he finally broke with Johnson, announcing in Salt Lake City that he would risk an unconditional cessation of all bombing. From then on, Humphrey and running mate Edmund Muskie rose dramatically in the polls, but it was too late. Even Johnson's last-minute announcement on October 31 that he had completely stopped the bombing was not enough to erase the image of chaos and violence that voters associated with the Chicago convention.

While the Democrats wrestled with the war, Richard Nixon sailed to an easy Republican nomination. Overcoming the image of "loser," the former vice president took primary after primary, cultivating a new aura of maturity and mellow reflection. Although he did not provide details, Nixon pledged new leadership to "end the war and win the peace in the Pacific." He hinted at a Great Power settlement of the conflict and the creation of a new global balance of power. Nixon pictured the strongest nation in the world tied down in an endless war, unable to manage its economy, and overwhelmed by lawlessness. He promised to "bring the American people together," and chose Maryland Governor Spiro T. Agnew for the vice presidency.

On election day Nixon and Agnew won by less than a percentage point. Wallace's Independent party, which hoped to deprive anyone of an electoral college plurality and send the contest into the House of Representatives, amassed nearly 14 percent of the vote. Surprisingly, much of the Democratic coalition of labor, blacks, Catholics, Jews, and urban voters held together in 1968. But in the South, Humphrey scored less than 30 percent, and Nixon and Wallace carried 57 percent of the national electorate.

The turbulent events of the sixties shook faith in the political system. A government credibility gap and violent dissent brought widespread alienation from conventional politics. Accordingly, independents rose from 22 percent of the electorate in 1965 to 30 percent by 1969. But alienation was not necessarily helpful to the youthful insurgents of the Democratic party and the Movement Left. By decade's end, six-sevenths of all voters were over the age of thirty and the great majority of voters, as conservative political analysts indicated, were "unyoung, unpoor, and unblack." As 1968 ended, the American death toll in Vietnam passed thirty thousand, and a half million troops remained in that distant outpost of national aspirations. A weary nation looked to Richard Nixon to restore tranquillity at home and a dignified peace abroad.

SUGGESTED READINGS

A thorough synthesis of the politics of the Great Society appears in the relevant chapters of Jim F. Heath, *Decade of Disillusionment: The Kennedy-Johnson Years* (1975). Segments of Alexander Kendrick, *The Wound Within: America in the Vietnam Years, 1945–1974* (1974), trace the connections between Johnson foreign policy and domestic developments. A useful history of the sixties is William L. O'Neill, *Coming Apart: An Informal History of America in the 1960s* (1971). Two anthologies that address the political controversies of the era are Jerome M. Mileur, ed., *The Liberal Tradition in Crisis: American Politics in the Sixties* (1974), and Marvin E. Gettleman and David Mermelstein, eds., *The Great Society Reader: The Failure of American Liberalism* (1967). Peter Joseph, *Good Times: An Oral History of America in the Nineteen Sixties* (1974), offers excellent material from interviews with prominent Americans of the decade.

The economics of the corporate state are analyzed in John K. Galbraith, *The New Industrial State* (1967). A useful synthesis that includes material on sixties business consolidation is Robert L. Heilbroner and Aaron Singer, *The Economic Transformation of America* (1977). G. William Domhoff, *Who Rules America?* (1967), presents considerable data on the economic elite, while urban renewal and ghetto problems are addressed in several essays in Alexander B. Callow, Jr., ed., *American Urban History: An Interpretive Reader with Commentaries* (1969).

Johnson's domestic political problems are analyzed by Eric Goldman, *The Tragedy of Lyndon Johnson: A Historian's Personal Interpretation* (1969), and Thomas Powers, *The War at Home: Vietnam and the American People, 1964–1967* (1973). The brief essay on Johnson in William A. Williams, *Some Presidents, from Wilson to Nixon* (1972), combines New Left analysis with sympathies toward the president as a southerner. See also George E. Reedy, *The Twilight of the Presidency* (1970). Johnson's political opponents are described in Richard Rovere, *The Goldwater Caper* (1965), David Halberstam, *The Unfinished Odyssey of Robert Kennedy* (1968), and Lewis Chester, Godfrey Hodgson, and Bruce Page, *An American Melodrama: The Presidential Campaign of 1968* (1969).

The Vietnam War is placed into the perspective of the battle against communism in the relevant chapters of Walter LaFeber, *America, Russia, and the Cold War, 1945–1971* (1972). Walt W. Rostow, *The Diffusion of Power* (1972), presents an overview of foreign policy from the standpoint of the Kennedy-Johnson administrations, while *The Pentagon Papers* (1971) presents the documents instrumental in American decision making in Vietnam since 1945. Richard J. Barnet, *Roots of War: The Men and Institutions Behind U.S. Foreign Policy* (1972), places Vietnam within the context of national security management. For a critique of liberal intervention in Vietnam, see Halberstam, *The Best and the Brightest* (1972). Johnson's abandonment of escalation in 1968 is treated by former Pentagon official Townsend Hoopes, *The Limits of Intervention* (1972). Relevant chapters in Gabriel Kolko, *Roots of American Foreign Policy* (1969), offer a radical critique of the war and can be supplemented by segments of the more informal Felix Greene, *The Enemy: What Every American Should Know About Imperialism* (1970). The most informative work on the CIA is Victor Marchetti and John D. Marks, *The CIA and the Cult of Intelligence* (1974).

Chapter 16

FRAGMENTATION OF AMERICAN SOCIETY, 1960-1980

"We stand on the edge of a New Frontier," President John Kennedy proclaimed in 1961. "It would be easy to shrink from that frontier —to look to the safe mediocrity of the past." Like Theodore Roosevelt in 1901, Kennedy asked young Americans to reject a life of comfort and personal pleasure for one of hardship and military discipline. "I am asking each of you," the president continued, "to be new pioneers on that New Frontier." And Kennedy pleaded for young people to "pay any price, bear any burden, meet any hardship" to make that New Frontier a success.

The nation's first Catholic president thus attempted to revitalize the urban-industrial frontier first conceived by Roosevelt and the Progressive leadership. By involving standards of sacrifice and collective heroism, Kennedy also

recalled the pattern of social values established by middle-class Anglo-Protestants during the Progressive years. So too did another Catholic, Vincent Lombardi, coach of the professional football team, the Green Bay Packers. In the 1960s Lombardi became the most important spokesman for football as the game that taught the virtues of military discipline. Like Kennedy, Lombardi stressed the necessity of victory. "Winning," he declared, "isn't everything. It is the only thing."

THE CRISIS OF ADOLESCENCE

The emergence of Catholic leaders such as Kennedy and Lombardi in the 1960s demonstrated that the prosperity brought by World War Two had lifted many Catholics out of working-class and into middle-class status. By the sixties, Irish Catholics had achieved levels of income and education approaching that of such Anglo-Protestant groups as Episcopalians and Presbyterians. But the rise of Catholic leaders not only signified Catholic assimilation to Anglo-Protestant middle-class values; it also revealed underlying weaknesses in that middle-class structure. Such figures as Kennedy and Lombardi were popular precisely because established middle-class people as well as recent entrants into that class were apprehensive that their children were losing a sense of discipline and ambition.

The first signs of a youth rebellion were directed against a social pattern constructed at the end of the nineteenth century. The white Protestant upper middle class in the 1890s had pressured American children into embracing a new pattern of adolescence. This pattern reflected basic economic changes in post–Civil War society. By the beginning of the twentieth century, most young members of the upper middle class could no longer expect to become independent businesspeople. Instead, job opportunities for them increasingly were found in large corporations or in government bureaucracies. Economic success increasingly depended on advanced education. But lengthy schooling extended the time of a child's dependence on parents and schools. Consequently, social, sexual, and economic independence for upper-middle-class youth was to be delayed at least until the age of twenty-two. To fill the years between fourteen and twenty-two, a special youth culture, centered on competitive sports, gradually evolved under the guidance of adults.

At the beginning of the twentieth century, the most important of these sports was football.

The game had developed in the late nineteenth century as an elite activity for the 5 percent of young men who went to college. In football, a successful play required every member of the team to move at the same time. The young men who played football frequently became corporate executives who had the responsibility to get thousands of employees to start work at the same time. Football reflected the rhythms of corporate competition, not mere rivalry as between independent farmers or small businessmen. Team cooperation and precision approximated the discipline of competing armies. Unlike baseball, a sport in which the length of innings was unpredictable and the pace frequently was relaxed, football involved the pressure of playing against the clock.

The upsurge of professional football after 1945 coincided with the rapid increase in the number of American college students. In 1940 only one-sixth of the eighteen-year-old population went on to college. But the dramatic increase of automation in industry and the mechanization of agriculture meant that most new jobs were to be found in the white-collar sector. As a result, young people were encouraged to go beyond high school in preparation for the changing job market. By expanding state teachers colleges into more diversified institutions and establishing new state colleges and junior colleges, it was possible by 1965 to enroll 50 percent of all teenagers into higher education.

As many children of Catholic blue-collar workers moved up to white-collar status between 1945 and 1965, however, the offspring of the Anglo-Protestant establishment were reacting to a profound contradiction of values. The growth of a corporate economy since 1920 had fed upon the stimulation of consumer demand. Consumerism accelerated as the baby boom of 1940 to 1958 increased average family size to almost four children. As larger numbers of young people began to move through high schools and colleges in the early 1960s, advertisers quickly turned to this vastly expanded youth market. To take advantage of the affluence of so many middle-class children, corporate advertisers stressed how separate the young were from parents and encouraged youngsters to buy products designed especially for them.

The marketing of these special records, clothes, food, and movies intensified the problem of identity for young men. Under the pattern of adolescence developed in the 1890s, youngsters were expected to learn discipline to contain their energies before they left home to compete successfully for careers. Young men were supposed to avoid all kinds of pleasures that might weaken that discipline. They were encouraged to dress in scout uniforms and march in the woods under the direction of adults and were urged to train for uniformed competitive sports under the same kind of leadership. But advertising told them to enjoy pleasure and relax at home as their mothers and fathers did. By the 1960s, mass media suggested that almost everyone was going on to college and that careers were easily available. Why then should American youngsters discipline themselves in preparation for a world of ruthless competition when there was a world of plenty?

Much of the development of a generation gap in the 1960s, therefore, came from a rebellion by upper-middle-class children against the late-nineteenth century idea of adolescence held by their parents. But it is clear that this counterculture built on attitudes that had been causing contradictions within the lifestyle of the middle class since at least the 1920s.

Most of the young men and women of the upper middle class during the 1960s rejected the delay of social and sexual independence demanded by the old style of adolescence. They had begun to identify in the late 1950s with Elvis Presley because they saw him as a representative of lower-income whites and blacks who still became socially and sexually independent at an early age. By 1964 the Beatles, a musical group whose members were raised in the slums of Liverpool, England, had become a much more powerful and explicit symbol of teenage sexuality. By the mid-sixties, sexual expression by rock musicians on stage was much more explicit than that of Elvis Presley or Chubby Checker at the end of the fifties. The total liberation of the body became a major objective of the counterculture in the 1960s.

WOODSTOCK NATION AND THE NEW ADOLESCENCE

As many middle-class youths rebelled against the restraints or inhibitions that characterized the old model of adolescence, they began to claim the right to sexual and social independence during their college years. This rebellion radically changed college lifestyles. Until the 1960s college administrations acted on the philosophy of *in loco parentis*. The administrators, especially the deans of men and women, had the responsibility of seeing that the students did not act like adults in making social and sexual decisions. Strict dormitory regulations were established. Both male and female students were required to be in their rooms at a certain hour in the evening. Sexual mixing was strictly forbidden. All of these regulations broke down in the 1960s to the point where at some

With the great increase in national wealth after World War Two, middle-class Americans from every part of the country began to visit Reno and Las Vegas, Nevada, where gambling was legal. The emergence of Las Vegas as a center of middle-class recreation indicated how dramatically patterns of middle-class morality and economic values had changed since 1900. (UPI Photos)

colleges male and female students shared the same dormitories.

The majority of middle-class young people compromised their rebellion and accepted continued economic dependence on their parents until graduation from college and entrance into the work force. A minority, however, "dropped out" of college; some even dropped out of high school and refused to enter the "straight" economic lifestyle of the "establishment." Many of those who remained in school occasionally used drugs, especially marijuana, as a sign of their rebellion. The old principle of adolescence had insisted that no consciousness-altering drugs, including alcohol, should be available to the young. Yet the lifestyle of the suburban middle class from 1920 to 1960 increasingly included "cocktails" as an important part of social life, especially parties. Drinking was well established among college youth by the 1950s, so another form of consciousness-altering drug was necessary to show independence from the ways of the older generation. For the dropouts, something stronger than marijuana was needed to prove independence, and they often found it in LSD or heroin. Yet some of the drug takers were motivated by more than the desire for independence from their parents. The Beat poets of the 1950s, for example, had used drugs to free themselves from the consciousness of "square" society and to find a higher and more spiritual reality. A significant number of young people used drugs for this purpose as they searched for new religious inspiration throughout the 1960s and 1970s.

From 1965 to 1969 high school and college students, most of them still economically dependent on their parents, provided the audience for "hard" and "acid" rock music bands like the Rolling Stones. Long-haired rock performers symbolized a dropout way of life that completely rejected the morality and discipline of the older generation. "You can't trust anybody over thirty," they shouted. Jim Morrison of the Doors explained that "We make concerts sexual politics" and boasted that he could sustain an erection through a two-hour concert. It was support from college students that made a public figure of the Harvard psychologist, Timothy Leary, who advocated freedom through drug taking. "Remember, man," he insisted, "a natural state is ecstatic wonder. Don't settle for less." And it was attention from college students seeking new values that made the novelist Ken Kesey and his Merry Pranksters a focus

of national controversy as his group traveled across the country in its psychedelic bus, liberating people with music, drugs, and sex. Janis Joplin, a successful rock singer who died of a drug overdose, proclaimed, "I never hold back, man. I'm always on the outer limits of probability." Dropping out as a fantasy for college students reached a climax in August 1969 when 400,000 gathered at a rock festival in rural New York before returning to classes in the fall. This Woodstock festival seemed to be filled with a spirit of love and gentleness, drugs, sex, and music. For many it marked the end of a materialistic, war-loving America and the birth of a spiritual, peace-loving "Age of Aquarius."

But another festival in 1969 at Altamont, California, featuring the Rolling Stones, ended in violence when one member of the audience was kicked to death. At the same time, a dropout group headed by Charles Manson murdered several affluent people, including a pregnant movie star, Sharon Tate. By the end of the 1960s it was becoming clear that the most important community of dropouts, the Haight-Ashbury district in San Francisco, was overwhelmed by violent crime that fed on extensive drug taking. It was also becoming clear that corporate advertisers were profiting handsomely by exploiting fantasies of dropping out. Rock music itself was big business, and producers, record companies, agents, and some rock stars rapidly became wealthy. So did the importers and manufacturers of drugs. Corporations also profited by selling love beads, head bands, blue jeans, and even "hip" cosmetics and hair accessories. Likewise, the producers of movies that celebrated the rebellion of the young against the establishment — *The Graduate, Easy Rider, Alice's Restaurant, Bonnie and Clyde* — expected to make money and did.

By 1970, then, some of the excitement of dropping out had lost its appeal. But conservatives, many of whom believed that the turmoil over competing lifestyles in the 1960s was caused by a few misguided young people who would straighten out when they had to earn a living, were still uneasy during the 1970s. While no coherent movement of cultural and political dissent survived the seventies, significant signs of social breakdown characterized the decade. Consumption of drugs, including marijuana, angel dust, cocaine, and heroin, increased, while use of alcohol spread even into grade school.

The seventies also witnessed a rapid rise in the number of illegitimate children, most of whose mothers were in the ten-to-fourteen-year age group. As girls became sexually active at earlier ages, delinquency and crime rates rose dramatically among them. Most disturbing, the suicide rate for young people tripled during this period.

The fact that the youth rebellion of the 1960s reflected the changing values of adult culture is suggested by the confusion of the courts in defining obscenity and pornography. Departing drastically from the purity crusade of the late nineteenth century, the Supreme Court had ruled at the end of the 1950s that underground literary classics such as D. H. Lawrence's *Lady Chatterly's Lover,* Frank Harris's *My Life and Loves,* and *Fanny Hill* could no longer be barred from the mails or confiscated by American customs officers. Grove Press immediately became a major publisher of books that formerly would have been classified as pornographic. Pornographic movies came out from underground and were shown openly. Nudity and sexual language also became a standard part of movies made by major Hollywood studios. Yet government officials continued to cen-

sor "hard-core" pornography and attempted to maintain a distinction between good and bad sexuality.

Younger men in the "square" middle class of the 1950s participated in this sexual revolution by making *Playboy* magazine a success. The magazine featured photographs of nude young women. Playboy clubs provided sexual titillation for successful young businessmen. Businessmen also were customers in restaurants featuring "topless" waitresses and lingerie shows at lunch time. By the 1960s Las Vegas, Nevada, became established as a center to which businessmen from every part of the nation came to relax. They watched shows featuring Hollywood stars, gambled, and were entertained by the many attractive young women in the city.

The rejection of traditional middle-class morality by young people who remained within the economic system was dramatized by the new lifestyle practiced by professional athletes in the 1960s. Professional football proved so popular on television that the American Football League was organized to challenge the National Football League for lucrative contracts from the major TV networks. This expansion led to a bidding war for college stars. A quarterback from the University of Alabama, Joe Namath, was signed in 1964 to a $400,000 bonus to play for the New York Jets of the new league. Namath's bonus and salary began a trend to higher salaries as professional athletes in all sports realized that they worked in show business. Hiring lawyers and business managers, they rejected the tradition that players never questioned team owners or the discipline set by managers. A new emphasis on personal expression and personal fulfillment replaced spartan loyalty to the team. Namath led this change by emphasizing his personal hair and clothing style and by leading a lifestyle more like that of a movie star than of the traditional professional athlete. Soon Namath was making more money from TV commercials, linking his personal image as a "swinger" to a variety of products, than he did from his football salary. Another athlete, Jim Bouton, a former major league baseball player, changed the public image of athletes considerably when he wrote *Ball Four* (1970), a humorous account of the game that revealed the off-the-field pleasure seeking of his teammates.

The trend from self-discipline to self-indulgence among professional athletes was another indication of the confusion of values among middle-class Americans. Professional athletes were grown men who were supposed to remain socially dependent on their leaders as long as they played the game. Until the 1960s they were seen as permanent adolescents. Under the patterns of adolescence that prevailed between the 1890s and the 1960s, young people were to show their dependent status by leaving all important decisions to their elders. But these attitudes were altered in the 1960s, and professional athletes demanded recognition of their adult dignity and formed players' associations to bargain with team owners.

ANTIWAR PROTEST AND
A NEW LEFT

The rebellion of college students against the traditional pattern of adolescence went beyond the rejection of *in loco parentis,* which had given college administrators the right to regulate students' sexual lives. It extended to politics as well. The leaders of Students for a Democratic Society (SDS), for example, saw the major difference between the "New Left" and the "Old Left" of the 1930s as the attitude toward discipline. Adults of the various Marxist parties of the 1930s expected college students to follow their leadership blindly and accept a military discipline of unquestioning loyalty within the party. SDS, however, which criticized universities for not allowing students to participate in making decisions, was equally critical of the absence of participatory democracy in the parties of the Old Left. SDS leaders also were inspired by writers such as Paul Goodman, Norman O. Brown, and Herbert Marcuse who berated the way modern capitalism forced people to repress their imaginations, the capacity of their bodies to experience pleasure, and their instinct for play. But Goodman, Brown, and Marcuse argued that Soviet Russian communism was as repressive as capitalism and that Old Left organizations in the United States encouraged this kind of repressiveness.

SDS leaders expected the economic slowdown and rising unemployment of the Eisenhower administration to continue under President Kennedy. They expected increasing numbers of poor people to join them in a reform movement that would bring a decentralized economy run cooperatively by local groups. These local groups would make decisions through participatory democracy. But the depression did not come and the white and black poor in the urban slums and impoverished countryside did not become involved in radical actions. Nevertheless, the growth of anti–Vietnam War attitudes among middle-class students and their parents between 1964 and 1968 led SDS to believe that a major new radical movement was developing in America.

The first massive student protest of the sixties came in Berkeley, California, in the fall of 1964 when the Free Speech Movement

(FSM) arose over a university prohibition of on-campus recruiting and fund raising for the civil rights movement. Eight hundred students were arrested at a sit-in at Berkeley's Sproul Hall. After FSM, middle-class students began to see themselves as an oppressed class whose training was designed to place them in the bureaucracies of the corporate order. "There's a time when the operation of the machine becomes so odious," FSM leader Mario Savio told the Berkeley students, "that you can't take part.... And you've got to put your bodies upon the gears... and you've got to make it stop."

By early 1965, students concerned with domestic issues such as racism, poverty, corporate power, and the military-industrial complex began to connect overseas military activities with social injustice at home. SDS shifted its focus from participatory democracy for working people to the Vietnam War. Student radicals saw the war in Asia as a pilot project of counterinsurgency designed to demonstrate that the United States would not tolerate change in economically underdeveloped areas. But SDS changed antiwar protest by placing responsibility for Vietnam on liberals tied to the corporate structure. Weeks before the bombing of North Vietnam began in March 1965, SDS had planned a small April march for Washington, D.C. To everyone's surprise, twenty thousand people attended the demonstration. By then, teach-ins on the war had begun at major universities. At Berkeley twelve thousand students and faculty participated in a Vietnam Day teach-in.

As draft calls rose to forty thousand a month in mid-1966, rallies, marches, teach-ins, and draft-card burnings increased. Young men refused induction orders, thousands deserted the armed forces, and more fled to Canada or Europe to avoid the draft. At Fort Hood, Texas,

three men refused orders for duty in Vietnam. Protesters sat-in at military induction centers and harassed on-campus job recruiters for the military, CIA, and defense contractors such as Dow Chemical, which produced napalm.

While the Johnson administration remained aloof from criticism, Vietnam protest became massive. In 1967, "Stop the Draft Week" at the Oakland Induction Center, led by the pacifist group Resistance, resulted in a battle of several hours between police and twenty thousand demonstrators. That November over 100,000 protesters surrounded the Pentagon, while in New York City 300,000 people marched to protest the Vietnam War. Weeks later a new phase of the antiwar movement commenced when Father Philip Berrigan and three other members of the Catholic Ultra-Resistance poured ox blood on draft files in Baltimore. The following year Berrigan, his brother Daniel, and six other Catholic radicals burned the draft files of a Maryland town with homemade napalm. The Catonsville Nine submitted to voluntary arrest and revealed that they had followed napalm instructions from a Special Forces handbook. All nine were convicted in the fall of 1968. At Fort Jackson, South Carolina, army doctor Captain Howard Levy was court-martialed for refusing to train Green Berets in dermatological warfare.

BLACK AND WHITE RADICALS

White radicals and antiwar activists hoped that their cause would benefit from the simultaneous rebellion of black college students against racism. Up to 1964, the nonviolent civil rights movement in the South had won the support of both established black organizations such as the NAACP and CORE and the white liberal community. But by the mid-sixties, signs of stress were apparent in this coalition. Little had been done to desegregate schools in the South after the Supreme Court decision of 1954 and segregation was increasing in northern schools. The rise of black voting had not affected politics in the southern states. Major liberal newspapers in the North, like the *New York Times*, criticized the sit-ins and freedom rides. Young blacks began to see — just as SDS leaders had insisted — that there was a very strong and unresponsive establishment. President Nathan Pusey of Harvard University, for example, when challenged about the university's lack of a concern for social justice, replied, "Our purpose is just to invest in places that are selfishly good for Harvard. We do not use our money for social purposes."

Many young blacks who wanted to reject this establishment, however, perceived white liberals and white radicals as part of it. Antagonism toward whites on the part of young black activists reached a deep intensity by 1966. As murders of blacks who defied southern racial taboos continued, James Meredith, who had been the first black student at the University of Mississippi, began a "March Against Fear" into Mississippi to enroll the state's 450,000 potential black voters. As soon as Meredith crossed the state line from Tennessee, he was wounded by a sniper. The disrupted march was resumed by a broad spectrum of national black leadership.

Earlier that year the Student Non-Violent Coordinating Committee had abandoned nonviolence, excluded whites from membership, and chosen the militant Stokely Carmichael as director. While Martin Luther King and his followers continued to preach nonviolence on the March Against Fear, Carmichael took up

the rhythmic cry of "Black Power, Black Power" and predicted another "long hot summer." The new phrase electrified the media and frightened whites throughout the nation, although to most blacks its purpose was to instill a sense of pride and identity. "If we are to proceed toward true liberation," Carmichael stated, "we must set ourselves off from white people."

Throughout the rural South in the 1960s, most blacks, like this cottonpicker, remained economically dependent on white landowners and were kept isolated from political participation. (Bruce Davidson/Magnum)

WE ARE BEAUTIFUL

In the growing black ghettos in the cities, in contrast to many areas in the rural South, blacks worked to liberate their children from psychological dependence on whites by teaching black pride, as in this school in Harlem. (Charles Gatewood)

Even a black novelist like James Baldwin, who had many white friends, explained the riots and violence of the 1960s as a response to the terrible history of the exploitation of blacks by whites. "To be a Negro in this country," Baldwin said, "is to be in a rage all the time." Eldridge Cleaver, then emerging as a Black Panther leader, voiced agreement with whites in the New Left that Americans needed to be liberated from the repressive discipline that robbed the human body of its freedom. In his best-selling book, *Soul on Ice* (1968), Cleaver found that blacks still had that freedom, expressed by the spontaneity of sexual life in the black community. But Cleaver had little hope whites could share that liberation.

Malcolm X was a major black leader who did call for the cooperation of radicals of every race against the establishment. Malcolm Little became a convert to the Black Muslim faith while in prison. To symbolize his liberation from white domination, he changed his name to Malcolm

X. A persuasive speaker and organizer, Malcolm began to question the Black Muslim doctrine of voluntary black segregation from "evil whites." He broke from the Black Muslims after he came to believe that the great oppressive force in the world was capitalism and that the economically oppressed of all colors, including whites, must work for a socialist alternative to capitalism. But Malcolm X was assassinated in Harlem in 1965. His killers probably were blacks who opposed his ideology, although white law enforcement never satisfactorily explained the circumstances.

The spirit of Malcolm's teachings, however, resurfaced in the Black Panthers, organized in Oakland the following year. Founded by Bobby Seale and Huey P. Newton, the Panthers monitored ghetto police and addressed the needs of poor blacks by providing free breakfasts for schoolchildren and establishing health clinics. To dramatize their right to bear arms against police "occupying" black communities, the Panthers marched into the California legislature with loaded rifles and shotguns. When Newton was arrested for murder in an Oakland confrontation with police, the Panthers began a long and insistent "Free Huey" campaign. By 1968 the Black Panther party had devised a ten-point program embracing Marxist concepts of self-determinism and the end of "welfare colonialism."

The FBI and local police forces harassed all black radicals, but they were most eager to destroy the Black Panthers. By 1969 two of the major Black Panther leaders, Eldridge Cleaver and Bobby Seale, had fled the country to escape legal harassment. Another leader, Bobby Hutton, had been killed, and the last, Huey Newton, was in prison. In December 1969 Chicago police officers staged a late-night raid on the headquarters and living space of the city's Panther party. The attack, directed with FBI assistance by Illinois State Attorney Edward V. Hanrahan, resulted in the killing of Panther leaders Fred Hampton and Mark Clark. Although none of the occupants of the house fired a shot and Hampton was hit by bullets while sleeping, a county court subsequently acquitted Hanrahan and thirteen others of conspiracy to obstruct justice. But the Chicago murders and other police raids against Panthers enraged black activists and white radicals.

Black leaders often were torn between the philosophy of separate black power and their desire to stop the Vietnam War by cooperating with white antiwar activists. They were aware that young blacks suffered casualties in Vietnam in greater proportion than whites. SNCC was the first black organization to oppose the war, initiating the "Hell, no, we won't go!" chant in daily demonstrations at the Atlanta induction center. Julian Bond, SNCC's communications director, twice was denied his seat in the Georgia legislature for antiwar statements before the Supreme Court ordered his reinstatement. By the spring of 1967, Martin Luther King proposed that the civil rights and antiwar movements merge, calling the American government the "greatest purveyor of violence in the world." Meanwhile, heavyweight boxing champion Muhammad Ali was arrested for refusing induction in the army after he claimed conscientious objector status as a Black Muslim minister. "No Viet Cong ever called me 'nigger,'" he explained in defense of his refusal to fight. Boxing authorities quickly stripped Ali of his crown.

The Chicago "New Politics" Convention of 1967 provided an opportunity for a coalition between black power advocates and antiwar activists. But although the convention platform

Eldridge Cleaver

1936-

Eldridge Cleaver was the most powerful symbol of revolutionary change in America in 1968. Cleaver had been paroled from prison only two years earlier. But it was his history as a juvenile thief, as an alienated man of senseless violence, and then as a political prisoner that gave Cleaver much of his power as a critic of the establishment. Raised in the Los Angeles ghetto, he fell into trouble with the law for petty theft and the sale of marijuana before he was out of grade school. Cleaver received a long prison term for assault with intent to rape and murder in 1958. In prison, he began to read the writings of Malcolm X. Imitating this new-found hero, Cleaver converted to the Black Muslim faith and rejected the anarchy of his early life. While still in prison, he began to study Afro-American history. He also began to write about his personal life, placing it within the context of the white racism that he saw as the dominant force in American society. When Malcolm X left the Black Muslims and began to preach that capitalist exploitation of whites and blacks must lead to a coalition of the oppressed of every color, Cleaver made the same change in emphasis.

Some of his writing, which showed great artistic skill, was smuggled out of prison and published in Ramparts, a journal of radical lay Catholics. Cleaver's literary talents were quickly recognized, and he signed a contract to write a book for a major publisher. With backing from members of the white literary community, he was paroled in 1966, and his book, Soul on Ice, published in 1963, became a best seller. But Cleaver came out of prison searching for the kind of political radicalism suggested by Malcolm X. He found this radicalism in the Black Panthers. The Panthers had started in Oakland, California, hoping to lead young ghetto blacks out of a life of apathy and petty crime *into a life of political and economic radicalism. Like Malcolm X, the Panthers were ready to work with radical whites dedicated to social revolution.*

Cleaver was an excellent speaker and soon was reaching large white audiences in opposition to the war in Vietnam. A group of white radicals in California persuaded Cleaver to be the presidential candidate of their Peace and Freedom party in 1968. The nomination gave him further opportunity to speak against American colonialism. Governor Ronald Reagan put pressure on the parole board to warn Cleaver to stop his political speeches. He refused. But J. Edgar Hoover had ordered the FBI to harass the Panthers, and local police were encouraged to suppress Panther activity. In April 1968, police in Oakland moved against a group of Panthers including Cleaver. Two policemen were wounded when the Panthers resisted, and a Panther leader, Bobby Hutton, was killed while Cleaver and another leader were wounded. Appeals by his lawyers kept Cleaver out of jail until November 1968, but he fled the country rather than return to prison. After seven years in exile in Cuba, Algeria, and France, Cleaver returned to the United States to face court proceedings. His return in 1975, he said, was prompted by his loss of faith in Marxist materialism and his conversion to Christianity.

called for "revolutionary change" and "open draft resistance," the gathering split over Panther demands that blacks be given half the leadership positions. The following year, the Panthers managed to win the support of white radicals through the Peace and Freedom party. The party ran Eldridge Cleaver, the Panther author, for president and stressed peace in Vietnam as well as self-determinism for blacks.

Cooperation between black and white radicals also came at Columbia University in the spring of 1968, when separate groups of black and white students took over two university buildings for several days. The students were protesting both university ties to the war through the Institute for Defense Analysis and the proposed construction of a gymnasium in a park separating Columbia from Harlem. SDS leaders who mobilized the white protesters saw the Columbia confrontation as an opportunity to promote the radicalization of students. The occupation, which ended with seven hundred arrests and rough handling by New York police, set the tone of confrontation for more than three thousand campus protests during 1968. Although most concerned Vietnam, student issues and demands for black studies also figured heavily, and for the first time arson and bombings marked student protests. SDS, which hoped to use the university as a stepping-stone to revolution, claimed 100,000 members in 1968. When President Johnson's Committee on Student Disorders, headed by Harvard law professor Archibald Cox, made its report that year, it described the college generation of the period as "the best informed, the most intelligent and the most idealistic this country has ever known." But the committee noted that the university had become the "surrogate for all the tensions and frustrations of American policy in Vietnam."

Despite instances of cooperative activity, however, there was no major national coalition of white and black radicals by the end of 1968. Nor had SDS been able to persuade most college students to become politically active. The majority of young people expressed their rejection of the establishment through the development of alternative lifestyles rather than through politics. Most antiwar activists, young or middle-aged, believed that the economic and social system was sound and could be brought back to health by ending the war. And the overwhelming majority of antiwar activists as well as most of the youth in the counterculture were strongly critical of the violence on the campuses in 1968. It was not surprising, then, that SDS membership declined after 1968.

The turn toward radical violence in 1968 came partly from the assassinations of Martin Luther King and Robert Kennedy and from the Chicago convention of the Democratic party. Because the New Left was unable to bring a strong economic radicalism to challenge established Democratic leaders, dramatic protests in Chicago came from the Yippies, a New York–based group devoted to irreverent anarchism and cultural revolution. These activists called for a "Festival of Life" to counter the August "Convention of Death." Most peace groups declined to join the Chicago demonstrations, but Mayor Richard Daley's refusal to accommodate any form of protest attracted media attention. Stressing law and order, Daley directed Chicago police to prevent protesters from camping out in city parks. Tension between police and demonstrators mounted until the evening of August 27, when crowds of protesters surged toward the convention headquarters. Blocked from marching on a convention busily ratifying the war, some of the protesters began to pelt police with sticks, bottles, and sexual taunts. The police charged furiously into the crowd with clubs, tear gas, and Mace. The president's National Commission on the Causes and Prevention of Violence later described the Chicago battle as a "police riot" involving "unrestrained and undiscriminate" attacks against many people "who had broken no law, disobeyed no order, made no threat." But most Americans blamed the demonstrators for the chaos in Chicago.

Increasingly isolated from mainstream opinion, political radicals became more violent after 1968. The Weathermen, a remnant of SDS that included newly radicalized women, came to Chicago in October 1969 to take part in "Days of Rage." Protesting government prosecution of the leaders of the 1968 convention protests, they "trashed" cars, banks, and businesses. The police used their guns to restore order and arrested three hundred persons. After Chicago, Weather leaders such as Mark Rudd and Bernadine Dohrn became underground fugitives.

Organized in secret "affinity groups," the Weather Underground initiated a series of dramatic bombings to demonstrate the vulnerability of the social system. The most controversial of the bombings killed a graduate student in August 1970 at a research facility at the University of Wisconsin. No longer could radicals claim that bombings were directed only against property. Such radical activity aroused the opposition of leaders of organized labor, who rejected both economic radicalism and the antiwar movement. "We are members of the capitalist society," George Meany, the head of the AFL-CIO declared. "We are dedicated to the preservation of the system, which rewards the workers." During the 1960s many young blue-collar workers, wearing hard hats, disrupted peace marches as they chanted, "God bless the establishment."

White blue-collar workers, who often had Catholic or evangelical Protestant backgrounds, had difficulty relating to New Left leaders, who usually were raised in families connected to established Protestant churches or to the Jewish community. Many blue-collar workers came from families that had been struggling to reject their ethnic backgrounds and to be accepted as Americans. They could not understand the New Left leaders whose families were part of the American establishment and who now wanted to reject that Americanism. In May 1970 construction workers attacked a peaceful demonstration of college students on New York's Wall Street, injuring about forty. A few days later twenty thousand supporters of the "hard-hats" paraded down Broadway in a show of support for the war. President Nixon subsequently met with a delegation from construction and longshoremen's unions, confiding that he found their actions "very meaningful." But the president's courting of labor leaders was not fruitful. By 1972, Gallup polls indicated that blue-collar workers were more critical of Nixon's war policies (44 percent opposed) than the general public (39 percent opposed).

As campus protest abated, disaffection and antiwar activity began to penetrate the armed forces, where most soldiers came from low-income families. In such an atmosphere, career soldiers in Vietnam were openly ridiculed, and rumors spread of widespread murder of officers. The army eventually created separate companies for those who refused to go into action. Readily available Asian heroin contributed to sixteen thousand drug-abuse-related military dismissals in 1969 and 1970. At home, twenty-seven military prisoners were tried for mutiny at the San Francisco Presidio. Antiwar activists provided support and meeting places for GI dissenters by establishing coffee houses close to military bases. A Concerned Officers Movement spoke out against the war, and twelve thousand men joined Vietnam Veterans Against the War (VVAW). In April 1971, two thousand Vietnam veterans rallied in Washington, as scores of decorated soldiers, some in wheelchairs, threw their medals on the steps of the Capitol. By then, a Gallup poll indicated that 61 percent of the American public believed Vietnam to be a "mistake." "How do you ask a man . . . to die for a mistake?" VVAW spokesman John Kerry asked the Senate Foreign Relations Committee in testimony that accompanied the powerful demonstration.

Discontent also reached the nation's prisons by the early seventies, particularly among blacks tutored by the street-wise Black Panthers. In 1970 three black California "Soledad Brothers," including the political writer George Jackson, were charged with the slaying of a white prison guard. Jackson's young brother attempted to kidnap the trial judge as a hostage. The resulting shoot-out, in which the judge and the younger Jackson were killed, only led to the arrest of communist philosopher Angela Davis, who was accused of supplying the weapons. After spending sixteen months in jail, Davis was acquitted by an all-white jury in June 1972. But George Jackson had been killed the previous August in an alleged escape attempt from San Quentin. Increased politicization and racial consciousness also contributed to a rebellion at New York's Attica prison during September 1971. Over one thousand inmates at the overwhelmingly black and Puerto Rican institution took ten guards as hostage in response to crowded conditions and bitter charges of racial abuse. Inmates insisted on personal negotiations with Governor Nelson Rockefeller, but when the governor refused, nine guards and thirty-one prisoners were killed in the ensuing attack by fifteen hundred armed state troopers. Attica remained a bloody symbol of brutality and racial hostility in seventies America. Ten weeks later a similar outbreak at New Jersey's Rahway prison ended peacefully when Governor William Cahill assured prisoners that their demands would be considered.

Despite the failure of radical movements to bring substantive social change, activists had successfully underscored the moral bankruptcy of the Vietnam War and contributed to pressures for withdrawal of ground troops. But violent and disruptive tactics, no matter how effective in unsettling the nation's leaders, appeared to most Americans as the irresponsible acts of a handful of unrepresentative "crackpots." These attitudes were dramatized in 1974 when members of the secret Symbionese Liberation Army (SLA) kidnapped San Francisco communications heiress Patricia Hearst. The SLA won considerable publicity when it demanded free food for the poor as part of Hearst's ransom. The group then released tapes in which Hearst claimed that she had converted to the revolutionary crusade. Indeed, the heiress participated in a dramatic robbery of a San Francisco bank. When leaders of the terrorist organization subsequently were killed by Los Angeles police, Hearst escaped, only to be captured by the FBI in September 1975. Back in the protection of her family, she pleaded that the traumatic kidnapping had destroyed her sense of individual will. After serving twenty-two months in prison for the bank robbery, Hearst was pardoned in 1979 and resumed her place in San Francisco society. The SLA affair only re-emphasized the isolation of remnants of the revolutionary Left from the American people.

BLACK POWER AND AFRO-AMERICAN CULTURE

By 1969 there seemed little hope for an easy and quick revolution that would instantly convert all Americans to the counterculture of the dropouts or to the decentralized communal economics and participatory democracy of the New Left. But the groups who wanted to return to what they believed was the unity and optimism of the liberal establishment under President Kennedy were equally disappointed. Liberal historians and sociologists in 1960 used a melting pot theory to explain the development of American history. They argued that all groups that were different from the Anglo-Protestant middle class — blacks, Native Americans, Chicanos, Catholic and Jewish immigrants from Europe — were in the process of being assimilated to the Anglo-Protestant middle-class lifestyle. The advocates of black power challenged this view. Although blacks had been stripped of their African languages and forced to speak and write English for hundreds of years, black intellectuals insisted in the 1960s that there was a vital Afro-American culture. While this was most obvious in music, they argued that there also were survivals of African culture in the way in which American blacks understood religion, defined family values, and saw the nature of the world.

As he lost the ability to identify himself with the white culture for which he had written his early plays, the black dramatist LeRoi Jones changed his name to Imamu Baraka. In his books of essays, *Home* (1966) and *Raise Race Raze Rays* (1970), he spoke of giving up the white ideal of being an independent artist to accept the African ideal of the artist as a spokesperson for the community. Other major black writers such as John Oliver Killens joined this movement to Afro-American unity. In Killens's novel *And Then We Heard the Thunder* (1962), the hero rejects the goal of making it as a leader in white society. He too rejoins the black community as he affirms his roots. "This is me. Proud black American me, whose ancestors came from great Africa." Other black novelists in the 1960s and 1970s who celebrated the Afro-American community, stressing its values of communal sharing in contrast to Anglo-Protestant competitive individualism, included John William (*Captain Blackman*, 1973) and Ernest J. Gaines (*The Autobiography of Miss Jane Pittman*, 1971).

Black college students used confrontation tactics to force college authorities to establish black studies departments or programs where black literature, history, and family patterns could be seen as alternatives to white culture rather than as inferior forms of white culture. The students were supported by the scholarship of both black and white professors who concluded that there was a history of a strong, separate Afro-American culture. These scholars had to become sensitive to oral tradition before they were able to understand how African cultures were passed from one generation to another. One of the scholarly discoveries was the existence of an African tradition of an extended family among American blacks that was different from the tradition of the nuclear family among whites. The extended-family tradition stressed cooperation rather than competition. Unlike the white nuclear family, in which parents had total responsibility, cousins, uncles, aunts, and grandparents were encouraged to help raise children. There was also evidence of a separate black English with different rules of grammar. Afro-American tradition stressed the interrelatedness of all things in contrast to the white middle class, which divided things into separate parts.

Black English encouraged children to think in terms of this interconnectedness.

CHICANO CULTURE AND ACTIVISM

The example of black power inspired other Americans to seek identity in their social and ethnic groups. The founding rally of the Italian-American Civil Rights League attracted fifty thousand people to New York's Columbus Circle in June 1970. In Brooklyn, New York, working-class Jewish youth organized a Jewish Defense League (JDL) to protect synagogues and schoolchildren in a racially tense neighborhood. And elderly Americans sought to advance their social and political needs by forming the Gray Panthers. The closest replica of the black power movement, however, surfaced among Mexican-Americans, the most rapidly growing group of Americans. While the birthrate of blacks remained slightly higher than that of whites, it tended to follow the major population pattern of American society and had dropped since 1958. But the Chicano birthrate remained high, as did the birthrate in Mexico. Population growth and poverty in Mexico continued to encourage immigration to the United States after World War Two. Between 1945 and 1965, five million Mexican workers, or braceros, were brought into the United States to cultivate and harvest vegetable crops. Under the labor contracts, they were expected to return to Mexico when the harvest ended. Many did not and many more crossed the border as illegal aliens. In the ten years following World War Two, four million were apprehended by American authorities as they crossed the border and were sent back to Mexico. These figures indicate the

Cesar Chavez was a leader of the 1960s effort to unionize migrant farm workers. Chavez believed that the many Chicano workers could gain economic strength only as they liberated themselves from psychological dependence on Anglos (white Americans) by developing pride in their Mexican-American heritage. (Paul Fusco/Magnum)

massive scale of the illegal immigration and point to the probability that millions were not apprehended. By 1970 Chicano population counted in the census approached ten million, but estimates were much higher, and migration from Mexico continued with equal intensity throughout the 1970s.

This Spanish-speaking population was joined by a million Puerto Ricans. Concentrated in New York and Chicago, Puerto Ricans were pushed toward the United States by a high birthrate and the poverty of that American colony. Miami, Florida, also developed a huge district of Spanish-speaking people who had fled the Communist revolution in Cuba. Spanish-speaking radio stations were popular in Miami, New York, and Chicago as well as in every major city in the Southwest. Public schools in Spanish-speaking communities also established bilingual education.

Organized in a similar fashion to the NAACP, a League of United Latin American Citizens (LULAC) had begun to work for the civil rights of Spanish-speaking Americans before World War Two. Both the NAACP and LULAC represented middle-class groups who hoped for assimilation in white society, and both turned to the courts to end patterns of segregation in the schools and denial of citizenship rights. Chicanos in the Southwest, for example, like blacks in the South, were not allowed to serve on juries. As blacks became more active in politics and moved to challenge Jim Crow patterns, Chicano leaders such as Edward Roybal in Los Angeles worked to get their people involved in politics and social action through the Community Service Organization. This activity led by 1960 to the Political Association of Spanish-Speaking Organizations (PASO).

About the same time that young black-power advocates were questioning efforts by moderates to end discrimination and integrate into white society, young Chicanos began to choose brown power over integration. The Brown Berets, like the Black Panthers, carried weapons to show that they would not retreat before the threat of Anglo violence. Using confrontation tactics, young Chicanos forced college administrations to establish Chicano studies programs or departments. Magazines like *El Grito, Bronze, El Machete,* and *La Raza* were published to raise social and ethnic consciousness. The scholarly journals *Aztlan: Chicano Journal of the Social Sciences and the Arts* and the *Journal of Mexican-American History* began publication to serve as a foundation for college programs throughout the country. The renaissance of black novelists, poets, and dramatists was paralleled by a renaissance of Chicano novelists such as Raymond Barrio, Richard Vasquez, and José Antonio Villarreal; poets such as Miguel Ponce, Tomás Rivera, and Roberto Vargas; and painters such as Malaguias Montoya and Esteban Villa.

Another major parallel between the development of black and brown power was the similar style of leadership expressed by the Chicano leader Cesar Chavez and the black leader Martin Luther King, Jr. At the time of his assassination in 1968, King had turned his attention from civil rights to the problems of poverty facing so many blacks. He had gone to Memphis, where he was killed, to encourage a strike of the city's sanitation workers. That spring, as thousands of blacks camped out near the Lincoln Memorial, SCLC carried out King's plan for a poor people's demonstration in Washington. Fifty thousand people, half of them white, then participated in a "Solidarity March" to reaffirm the slain minister's dream.

Like King, Chavez was able to appeal to the conscience of middle-class whites by reminding them of the exploitation of his people and by using Christian imagery to challenge the complacency of the establishment. Chavez, a deeply religious man who used the Virgin of Guadalupe as the symbol of his struggle for social justice, emerged as a national figure in 1965 for his leadership of Mexican-American grape pickers in California. Like King, Chavez preached nonviolence as he moved his National Farm Workers Association to improve the working conditions and pay of farmworkers throughout California. And, like King, he did reach the conscience of many white Protestants. But unlike the black minister, Chavez was able to appeal to many newly middle-class Catholics who had left the problems of the poor behind when they moved from the slums of the central cities to the suburbs.

Still another parallel between the two movements was the increasing rejection of the nonviolent positions of King and Chavez by young radicals. Reies Lopez Tijerina, a Chicano from New Mexico, shared the attitudes of black leaders who had become impatient with the possibility of reform through the legal system or with the appeal to the conscience of middle-class whites. Tijerina asked Chicanos in New Mexico to remember the outrage of the 1890s when they had been cheated out of their land. Emphasizing especially the return of the land that villages held in common before the coming of the Anglos, Tijerina armed his followers and urged them to take back what belonged to them. Like many black militants, Tijerina was jailed for his challenge to the establishment.

Deep bitterness developed in Texas where José Angel Gutierrez developed a political party, La Raza Unida, to win Chicano control of the twenty counties in south Texas in which they were the majority. This bitterness was similar to that which developed throughout the South in the 1960s as blacks started to win political control in those counties where they were the majority. The fierce efforts of Anglos (white Americans) in the Southwest and South to retain control of rural counties where either Chicanos or blacks were the majority was similar to efforts by whites in northern and southwestern cities to keep growing black or Chicano populations from getting political power.

Rudolfo "Corky" Gonzales was a Chicano urban leader in Denver, Colorado, in the 1960s. Chicanos were not the majority in Denver, but through his organization, the Crusade for Justice, Gonzales encouraged the Chicanos to use their political power as a large minority to bring about changes in the school and welfare system.

All the major Chicano political and cultural leaders of the 1960s, like the blacks, contrasted their social system of extended families, with less stress on individual achievement and more emphasis on social justice, to that of Anglo-Protestant competitive capitalism. Militant Chicano leaders conveyed a sense of a separate culture with deep roots in an ancient past. They noted with pride that Spanish culture had been absorbed and reshaped by the Aztec culture of northern Mexico and what was now the southwestern part of the United States. These notions led Chicanos to distinguish themselves sharply from the Catholic culture that had come to America from modern Europe. They pointed to the separate styles of church architecture and art and to separate traditions such as that of the Virgin of Guadalupe with different festivals and feast days. By the 1960s the hierarchy of the American Catholic church, largely Irish-American, was forced to admit that it had underestimated the cultural strength of the Chicanos and it began to appoint, for the first time, Chicanos as bishops in such states as Texas and New Mexico.

NATIVE AMERICAN CULTURE AND MILITANCY

Young American Indians in the late 1960s joined young blacks and Chicanos in rejecting the melting pot ideal. Their affirmation of red power mirrored declarations of black and brown power. Communication among Native American groups had been increasing since 1944, when the National Congress of American Indians (NCAI) was formed. Using this network, Native American leaders intensified their pressure on the national government to end the presence of the Bureau of Indian Affairs (BIA) on reservations. True local government, they argued, had not been achieved because of continued interference by BIA agents in tribal life. By the 1960s younger Indians were growing impatient with the inability of the NCAI to win more tribal autonomy and formed the more militant National Indian Youth Council. After 1966 some adopted confrontation tactics, marching on the BIA in the nation's capital and sitting-in on college campuses to force the establishment of American Indian departments or programs.

Native American militancy in the 1970s partly resulted from the doubling of Indian population to one million between 1945 and 1975. Once the United States Public Health Service replaced the BIA in providing Indian medical services at the end of World War Two, improved health care permitted Native Americans to experience a higher birthrate than that of the rest of the nation. Despite the persistence of higher mortality rates among Indian infants than among other American infants, the nation's Indian population grew. Half the population was concentrated in settlements in cities such as Los Angeles, San Francisco, Chicago, and Minneapolis by 1970. Here urban Indians

In 1973, American Indian Movement (AIM) leaders seized Wounded Knee, South Dakota, by force and held it for several months against armed pressure from the FBI. As in the case of dramatic acts by black and Chicano leaders, the purpose of this seizure was to help liberate American Indians from their psychological dependence on whites. (UPI Photos)

formed Native American centers that emphasized pride in cultural traditions.

Although urban settings provided opportunities for cultural cohesion, unemployment and poverty characterized Native American life in the city. Average yearly income for urban Indians was $1,500 in 1960. And because of poor food and bad living conditions, the average life span of an Indian was forty-four years compared to sixty-six for a white. These circumstances encouraged the growth of urban radicalism among Native Americans in the early 1970s. Groups such as the American Indian Movement (AIM) demanded greater economic and political activity for Indians in the cities and on the reservations. Led by urban Indians such as Clyde and Vernon Bellecourt and Russell Means, AIM members seized Wounded Knee, South Dakota, in 1971 to dramatize demands for autonomy. For two months before they surrendered, the warriors exchanged gunfire with the FBI who surrounded their outpost. The FBI had worked closely with local police forces to suppress radicalism among Native Americans as well as among Chicanos and blacks.

While Native American radicalism captured the imagination of young Indians in the cities, some of the traditional tribes found it difficult to follow their lead. The Navaho, for example, at 150,000 members the largest tribe in the nation, rejected radical politics because they had resisted white influence on their reservations and sought no demands from the white power structure. The Pueblo followed a similar pattern. But even off the reservations, most Indians held to tribal traditions. The Cherokee of Oklahoma, whose reservation had been destroyed in the 1890s, continued to demand that their children speak the native language at home, despite the pressure of public schools.

ECOLOGY AND THE LIMITED FRONTIER

Although a much smaller group than blacks or Chicanos, Native Americans probably had a greater impact on the imagination of young white people in the 1960s and 1970s. Seeking ties to a tradition of mysticism and the use of hallucinogens, the counterculture began to explore Native American sources. In *The Teachings of Don Juan: A Yaqui Way of Knowledge* (1968) and several sequels, Carlos Castaneda portrayed a "separate reality" of magic and spiritual enchantment conveyed to him by an ancient desert medicine man. But countercultural youth also wanted to redefine America as a peaceful home. They hoped to end the tradition that Americans were warlike conquerors of new frontiers. The pattern of adolescence developed around 1900 asked young people to find their heroes among winning football players, winning soldiers, or winning cowboys. Many of the songs, stories, and movies of the counterculture, however, celebrated antiheroes, losers who refused to find fulfillment in the wars of conquest by the establishment. For the counterculture, Native Americans had represented admirable values in defending their homes but had been defeated by evil men for three hundred years. The counterculture hoped to learn from Indian experience how to survive defeat by the establishment.

In questioning militant heroes, young people found support in Joseph Heller's 1960 novel, *Catch-22*. Heller presented World War Two as an absurd experience. In the senseless context of insane bureaucracies, there was no possibility of heroism as young men had been taught to believe in it. The only sane act for the hero, Yossarian, was to drop out and row away on a life raft. The successful movie

M*A*S*H and the TV program with the same name also presented a war without heroic action against the enemy. The only heroism came from small acts of kindness to and support of the people who shared personal suffering, trapped in a way of life they didn't believe in.

The cowboy as a hero who conquers frontiers collapsed as a believable figure both in the movies and on the TV screen during the 1960s. Movies of the 1960s and 1970s such as *The Ballad of Cable Hogue, McCabe and Mrs. Miller, Ride the Whirlwind,* and *Little Big Man* removed the glamour of the conquest and replaced heroes with confused and sometimes evil men. The TV western also became absurd in the 1960s. The first TV westerns for children at the beginning of the 1950s such as the "Lone Ranger" presented heroes who lived outside of society in the open spaces of the frontier. Holding to a personal code of honesty and justice, the hero drew strength from nature to ride into towns and overcome the corrupt elements there. Then he rode back into boundless prairies and mountains. By the end of the 1960s, however, the most important TV westerns like "Bonanza," the "Big Valley," and "High Chaparral" had heroes who were protecting the boundaries of their property. As long as the western hero was presented as someone who rode away from society, the lack of women on the frontier did not seem odd. But when a group of men, as in "Bonanza," were living as a permanent society without women, the situation became absurd.

The Indian political leader and writer Vine DeLoria, Jr., argued in *God Is Red* (1973) that the frontier experience of whites was ending and that they must learn from the Native American to live with America as a home. DeLoria agreed with Chief Luther Standing Bear that "the white man does not understand America. The roots of the tree of his life have not yet grasped the rock and the soil. But in the Indian, the spirit of the land is still vested."

DeLoria appealed to the sciences of biology and physics developed in the white man's universities to show the falseness of the social, economic, and political life of the whites. White science, he argued, taught that the earth is our home and must be conserved, but white economics and politics considered the earth as a frontier to be conquered. DeLoria was correct about white science. By the 1960s biologists such as Paul Ehrlich in *The Population Bomb* (1969) argued that endless population growth was based on the hope of a limitless frontier. But with the closing of that frontier, Ehrlich and others called for an end to population growth. An organization, Zero Population Growth, attempted to persuade American political leaders to work for population control. By the late 1960s, environmentalists began to emphasize that humans live within the circle of the earth's atmosphere and must limit the pollution discharged into the air from industry and cars. Congress and state legislatures soon passed laws to control air, water, and land pollution. The national government and the states also created environmental protection agencies.

Although such legislation was enforced haphazardly, government concern with the environment won endorsement from ecologists. In *The Closing Circle* (1971), Barry Commoner argued that since nature works in vast cycles to regenerate the earth's air, water, and land, human economy must adapt to the cycles. Straight-line economic growth or progress conflicted with natural cycles. Some major economists such as Nicholas Georgescu-Roegen, who wrote *The Entropy Law and the Economic Process* (1971), were converted to the views of the biologists and physicists and rejected the possibility of continued economic growth. A group of scientists from many nations published a study in 1972, *The Limits of Growth,* that warned that the growth economy was rapidly exhausting the earth's resources. According to their computer analysis, catastrophic breakdown would come by the end of the century if limits to growth were not set by human beings.

This "subversive" science of ecology gave intellectual authority to Afro-Americans and Chicanos as well as to Native Americans because their traditions, like ecology, emphasized that everything was interconnected. It also gave authority to those in the Anglo-Protestant counterculture who, in the 1960s, followed the leadership of the Beat poets of the 1950s. Allen Ginsberg and Gary Snyder expressed the sense of being within nature in their poems. They were attracted to Asian philosophy because it taught humanity to find truth within the universe rather than to seek to analyze the universe by standing outside it, as modern Europeans and Americans believed possible.

Ironically, the landing of an American astronaut, Neil Armstrong, on the moon on July 20, 1969, served to dramatize the ecological perspective that humans live within the circle of the earth. President Kennedy had included the sending of men to the moon as an important part of his New Frontier philosophy. Although President Eisenhower declared that "anybody who would spend $40 billion in a race to the moon for national prestige is nuts," Kennedy persuaded Congress to fund the Apollo project. Dr. James E. Webb, the director of the National Aeronautics and Space Administration (NASA), expressed Kennedy's motivation when he remarked, "With a billion people already allied against us, and the emerging nations weighing events . . . the United States must present the image of a can-do nation, with which they can confidently align their futures."

NASA was encouraged to ignore problems of safety in an attempt to reach the moon by 1967, the fiftieth anniversary of the Russian Revolution. On January 27, 1967, the astronauts Virgil I. Grissom, Roger B. Chaffee, and Edward H. White died in a rocket malfunction. But when Armstrong walked on the moon in 1969, President Nixon declared it was "the greatest week since the Creation."

The moon landing, however, did not inspire most Americans to see traditional frontier heroes conquering the vast expanses of space. Instead, looking back at the blue and living earth from the dead moon in the black coldness of outer space, many people felt for the first time that their planet was an island home. Viewed from the moon, the earth was an exceptional and precious gift to be preserved.

WOMEN'S LIBERATION

Unlike Afro-Americans, Chicanos, and Native Americans, women of the white Protestant middle class did not bring a sense of oppression into the 1960s. The ethnic and racial minorities kept alive traditions that told of ancestors who had not been dominated by whites and of cultures that hoped to be liberated from that domination. But middle-class women, who shared the wealth, security, and status of fathers, husbands, and sons, had no such memories or awareness of a shared culture. Nevertheless, a strong sense of women's liberation emerged by the end of the sixties and continued to grow in the 1970s.

Middle-class women had proved their strength during World War Two when they worked in vital industries. Then, after the war, popular novels and films encouraged women to relinquish their jobs to men and return to their homes. But as establishment institutions were called into question by the counterculture and the minority cultures in the 1960s, middle-class women became aware of the way in which they had been taught to see themselves as weak and helpless.

The first major statement of this middle-class women's liberation was Betty Friedan's *The Feminine Mystique* (1963). The large sales of the book showed that many women could see, with Friedan, the contradiction between the ideal middle-class woman as "young and frivolous, almost childlike; fluffy and feminine; passive, gaily content in a world of bedroom and kitchen, sex, babies, and home" and the way in which most women, as members of the lower-income majority, held the least rewarding jobs in the economy.

Many middle-class women became angry as they discovered how they had been persuaded since 1920 not to seek professional careers. Unlike the feminists of the Progressive era, however, they also demanded a place in business as well as in the professions. And they were not satisfied to be an example of purity for male politicians. They wanted to share leadership with men in important political institutions. Agitation by a small group of professional women led President Kennedy to establish a National Commission on the Status of Women. Soon every state had established such commissions. Under the Civil Rights Act of 1964, women, like blacks, were to be protected against discrimination in hiring and in wages. It was now against the law to deny a woman a job because of her sex or to pay her less than a man for the same work. The Equal Employment Opportunity Commission (EEOC), however, moved very slowly to protect women under these provisions.

But some middle-class women grew impatient and organized the National Organization for Women (NOW) in 1966. NOW focused its energy on the passage of the Equal Rights Amendment (ERA) to the Constitution, which would prohibit sex discrimination. NOW also worked to end sex discrimination in private industry. Middle-class women showed their concern for lower-income women by asking for maternity leave rights for working women and government-financed day-care centers for preschool children. Like middle-class men, women of the middle class believed that each individual could find justice in the marketplace if equal educational facilities were provided and racial and sexual discrimination was ended. These women reformers did not share the hostility to the marketplace held by the counterculture and the New Left and did not accept the concern for social, rather than individual, justice in the traditions of the Chicanos, Native Americans, and Afro-Americans. Middle-class women who were college faculty members organized a Women's Equity Action League (WEAL) to protect their interests, as did the women in national government with their organization of Federally Employed Women (FEW).

The National Women's Political Caucus worked to have women accepted as leaders of the major political parties, and both the Republicans and the Democrats moved to include more women as delegates to their conventions. Congresswomen Shirley Chisholm and Bella Abzug initiated reforms in the Democratic party to increase the percentage of female convention delegates from 10 percent in 1968 to 40 percent in 1972. During the 1970s an increasing number of women were elected to state legislatures, governorships, and Congress, although their numbers remained far below the proportion of women in the national population.

The goals and successes of middle-class women reformers were very different, therefore, from those of women reformers during the Progressive era. So were the goals and successes of women radicals. Some college women from the middle-class establishment participated in the development of the New Left and joined the civil rights movement to destroy the Jim Crow system in the South. As they became sensitive to the injustice of established institutions in the early 1960s, many women radicals also became sensitive to "sexism." They angrily objected to the "male chauvinism" that denied them a leadership role in radical movements, just as they were denied a leadership role in the establishment. Women activists frequently were told by male radicals that their major contribution to the cause was to provide sex for the male leaders. These men, wrote Elizabeth Janeway, still believed that it was a "man's world" and there was a "woman's place" apart from that world. Kate Millett wrote *Sexual Politics* in 1969 to show how all men held women in contempt.

Radical women were able to come together quickly and powerfully because their work for the New Left or civil rights in the early 1960s had brought women from every section of the country in contact with each other. As the counterculture developed its own magazines such as the *Berkeley Barb, Village Voice,* and *Rolling Stone,* the radical women began to publish their own journals: *Off Our Bodies, Ain't I a Woman,* and *Majority Report.* A magazine that tried to provide a common ground for middle-class and radical women was *Ms.,* which became a financial success after it began publication in 1972.

One radical group, Redstockings, insisted that "We identify the agents of our oppression as men. Male supremacy is the oldest, most basic form of domination. All other forms of exploitation and oppression (racism, capitalism, imperialism) are extensions of male supremacy." By the early 1970s these radicals seemed to have experienced the same kind of frustration that the male-dominated New Left had developed by 1969. They were not able to recruit a large group of followers committed to the belief that women must segregate themselves from men. Neither had the radicals from middle-class backgrounds found a way to communicate with women from lower-income groups or from the black, Chicano, and Native American cultures.

A third group of women, represented by Elizabeth Janeway, Carolyn Heilbrun, Alice Rossi, and Gloria Steinem, seemed to suggest another alternative for women. These women looked to an "androgynous" society in which men would be free to develop their feminine characteristics and women, their masculine attributes. In such a world, there would not be a sharp distinction between home and marketplace. Both men and women would feel comfortable and competent at home, in rearing children, and in making a living.

GAY LIBERATION

The youth rebellion of the 1960s directed much of its energies against the patterns of traditional adolescence that placed rigid definitions on the behavior of men and women. Traditional roles dictated that men were strong and competitive and that women were weak and passive. But a decade of role questioning made it possible for homosexuals to consider making their identities public and to develop movements for gay pride and gay power. Homosexuals, an estimated 10 percent of the population, had been under special pressure in the 1950s to hide their identities. The anticommunist crusade led by Senator Joseph McCarthy had associated homosexuals with communism. In the federal civil service in Washington, D.C., and in the artistic community in Hollywood, the two areas under greatest pressure from McCarthy, one could be fired from a job for no other reason than suspected homosexual tendencies. As recently as 1964, Walter Jenkins, an official in the Johnson administration, was forced to resign because it was revealed that he had a homosexual experience.

But the Kinsey reports had indicated that 37 percent of all males and 28 percent of females had had at least one homosexual experience some time during their lives. Homosexuals were reassured by these reports that they were a significant part of the population. During the 1950s, middle-class homosexuals began to develop organizations such as One Inc., the Mattachine Society, the Society of Individual Rights, and the Daughters of Bilitis to protect their civil rights and to provide psychological support for their members. Like early black civil rights organizations, they tended to work quietly through the courts. An aggressive public demand for gay rights, however, emerged among young homosexuals at the end of the 1960s. The development of this gay rights movement had many parallels with the development of women's liberation.

Many women's liberation leaders had become rebels against the establishment by participating in the civil rights movement for blacks, in the antiwar movement, or in the New Left. They had become angry, however, when these movements for social change declared that they were interested only in changing relationships between men and not in changing the traditional roles of women and men. Many homosexuals had the same frustrating experience in the 1960s. They had participated in the civil rights and antiwar movements and had called for economic change; young lesbians had participated in women's liberation. But none of these movements, including women's liberation, had questioned the traditional relations between "straight" and "gay" people. All had assumed that being gay was abnormal and unnatural. All had declared that liberation was for "straight" people, not for "queers." By the end of the 1960s, young gays had developed anger against both the establishment and the various reform movements. They also had developed skills of organization and political activism through participation in protest movements.

By the end of the decade, therefore, the situation was ripe for an explosive demand by gays for their own rights. When police raided a gay bar, the Stonewall Inn, in New York City in June 1969, homosexual patrons no longer accepted police brutality as customary and fought back for the first time. Gays in New York and many other cities used this event to declare the beginning of gay power as they shouted, "Out of the closets, into the streets." With some success, gays began to pressure states to end laws against sex acts by consenting adults of the same sex. They also asked city and state governments to include homosexuals in civil rights legislation that barred discrimination in jobs and housing. On the second anniversary of the Stonewall Inn raid, the New York Gay Activists Alliance held a commemorative march in which ten thousand paraded from Greenwich Village to Central Park. Marches were also held in Boston, New Orleans, and San Jose. By 1971, when Jack Baker, a law student and affirmed homosexual, was elected president of the student association at the University of Minnesota, student homophile groups had been established on seventy campuses.

Gay lifestyles also influenced seventies youth culture. By the end of the decade, both working-class and middle-class young people were dancing to "disco" music, a fusion of persistent Afro-American or Latin rhythms accompanied by electronic synthesizers. The "discotheque" had originated with exclusive nightclubs for the "jet set" wealthy in New York City during the late sixties. By the early seventies, gay clubs in New York had adopted the format in which glamorously attired clients responded to recorded music with precise and expressive dance movements. As heterosexual couples were attracted to the disco beat, the music, dance, and clothing became a hallmark of American culture and were celebrated in the popular film *Saturday Night Fever*. By the late seventies the disco beat provided the background for television commercials, police serials, and even network sports coverage. Despite disco's origins in gay culture, however, the end of the decade also witnessed the birth of an antihomosexual movement. Led by Florida singer Anita Bryant and a number of major evangelical leaders, local citizens' groups succeeded in 1978 in eliminating homosexuals from inclusion in the civil rights ordinances of Miami, St. Paul, and Wichita, Kansas.

MIDDLE AMERICA AND MORAL CRISIS

The upsurge of social conservatism at the end of the 1970s continued the themes stressed by George Wallace and Richard Nixon in 1968.

Another limitation on seventies conservatism

Lower-middle-class and blue-collar workers in the South, who were largely evangelical Protestant, and in the North, where many were Catholic, were confused by the social ferment of the 1960s. Under pressure to send their children to college, these "middle Americans" especially felt the need for young people to discipline themselves if they were to win a white-collar job. They were bitter, therefore, when they saw upper-middle-class college students setting bad examples, as campus agitators called for an increase in student administrative leadership and a furthering of sensual pleasure. Americans from the lower middle class and from blue-collar industries became even more bitter when they saw the major institution of establishment authority, the Supreme Court, accept this "permissiveness." The Court, for example, had voted against compulsory prayers and Bible reading in the public schools. Other Court decisions seemed to accept pornography and obscenity. These Americans believed that the Court was protecting criminals when it moved to protect the rights of people accused of crimes. The Court also appeared permissive to conservatives in ruling that laws restricting the sale and distribution of birth control methods were unconstitutional. As reported crime rates rose rapidly in the late sixties, criminal activity was associated with the permissiveness of the Supreme Court and the Anglo-Protestant establishment. Early seventies television featured a host of serials that celebrated the courage and wit of law enforcement officials upholding moral order.

By the mid-1970s, however, President Nixon's appointments to the Supreme Court had reversed the trend toward protecting the rights of the accused and the rights of privacy against police searches. The Nixon majority also seemed to reverse the Court's liberal tradition concerning civil rights. In the Bakke decision of 1978, the Court ruled against the use of racial quotas in the affirmative action admission policies of medical schools. Since 1965, it had been the policy of the national government to encourage such programs to overcome historical patterns of racial, ethnic, and sexual discrimination. Now some black leaders, such as Jesse Jackson, wondered if the Bakke decision marked the final collapse of efforts to establish greater social justice in the United States.

As mass media became open to gay and feminist critiques, a number of women with leaders such as Phyllis Schlafly banded together to preserve the traditional role of women as homemakers. They focused their efforts on blocking passage of the Equal Rights Amendment (ERA). Playing upon widespread resentment toward the middle-class cosmopolitans of the women's liberation movement, these activists succeeded in delaying, and perhaps defeating, passage of ERA by state legislatures in the late 1970s. When the Supreme Court ruled that laws against abortion were unconstitutional, these women attempted to enact a constitutional amendment that would permit legislation to bar abortions. And by 1980 they had succeeded in getting many state legislatures to cut back funding of abortions for poor women and had won severe restrictions on the use of federal funds for low-income women who wanted abortions.

Evangelical ministers such as the Reverend Carl McIntire and the Reverend Billy James Hargis had been attempting since the 1950s to build a political movement to stop social permissiveness. But although many Americans were drawn to social conservatism in the 1970s, the spread of the Charismatic and Pentecostal movements among Protestants and Catholics focused the energies of such conservatives on personal conversion, not social action.

Another limitation on seventies conservatism in middle America was the acceptance of new forms of birth control such as the pill by young women of southern Protestant background and northern Catholics. This change caused a special crisis of authority among Catholics, since the church hierarchy in Rome and the United States remained firmly against both "artificial" means of birth control and abortion. Surveys revealed, however, that while 40 percent of Catholic women used unapproved forms of birth control in 1960, the proportion had increased to 70 percent in 1970. The Catholic church, therefore, failed to function as a foundation of social conservatism in the 1960s and 1970s. Furthermore, the Catholic community faced considerable disarray in the 1960s as five thousand priests and forty-five thousand nuns left their callings and the number of young men preparing for the priesthood dropped from fifty thousand to eighteen thousand. Weekly attendance at Mass fell from 70 percent to 50 percent of Catholic parishioners, and participation in monthly Confession dropped from 37 percent to 17 percent. More dramatically, acceptance of the Pope's authority dropped from 70 percent to 40 percent.

The strongest academic criticism of permissiveness in the 1960s and 1970s came from Jewish intellectuals who had been accepted by the Anglo-Protestant academic community in the 1940s and 1950s. Writing in such magazines as *Commentary*, these critics attacked the way in which establishment leaders made concessions to the counterculture and the black, Chicano, and Native American minorities. Meanwhile, Jewish religious and social organizations focused increased energies on moral and financial support for Israel. The Jewish retreat from political liberalism took a different form in the 1970s when a number of young

Jewish intellectuals joined with young white Protestants and blacks to develop a neo-Marxist interpretation of American society. The academic professions of history, political science, sociology, anthropology, economics, and philosophy no longer were able to stop young professionals in those fields from becoming Marxists. Other young Jews were attracted to Asian religions. Still others turned back to ancient Judaism to find communal traditions and ethnic identity.

Given these deep confusions in the Protestant, Catholic, and Jewish communities, it was not surprising that no organized movement of social conservatism developed in the United States in the 1970s. Some sociologists in the late sixties had predicted a "blueing of America." They believed that the breakdown of the 1900 pattern of adolescence among the children of the white Protestant elite would open the door of upward economic mobility for the children of lower-middle-class and blue-collar workers. Symbolized by their love of President Kennedy and Coach Lombardi, these children were still willing to accept the discipline of delayed social and sexual maturity. They were still willing to compete hard. They still thought it was worthwhile to win a place in the establishment. But the "blueing of America" never completely arrived. Studies of young noncollege workers in the early 1970s found them moving rapidly toward some of the values that emerged on college campuses in the mid-sixties.

While only one out of ten college students identified with the New Left in 1967, many young people on campus had lost a great deal of respect for authority, police, and institutional religion. Two-thirds of the students believed that the country was run by big business and not by Congress or the president. And between 1967 and 1971, a very strong antiwar attitude

developed. While half of those polled were ready to support a war to protect national interest in 1967, only 30 percent supported that kind of war in 1971. One of three believed in war for national honor in 1967, but that ratio dropped to one out of five in 1971.

Between 1965 and 1971, polls indicated a steady movement toward permissiveness among college students. The trend was toward the acceptance of premarital sex, the use of marijuana, and the toleration of homosexuals. Further studies revealed that young noncollege workers, who constituted three-fifths of those between the ages of eighteen and twenty-two, resisted these changes until 1969. But young workers began to shift rapidly away from the old adolescence between 1969 and 1973. In 1960, one out of five young blue-collar workers wanted more sexual freedom; this ratio increased to one out of two by 1973. Two out of three had found premarital sex to be morally wrong in 1960, but only one of three did in 1971. In 1973, half of the noncollege youth accepted homosexual relationships between adults, although in 1969, three out of four had condemned that activity. Two of three had opposed abortions in 1960, but this had dropped to one of two in 1973.

Blue-collar youth had disagreed with college students on the value of organized religion, patriotism, and hard work in 1969. But by 1973 they shared the skepticism of college students on these issues. Support for organized religion among noncollege youth dropped from 65 percent in 1969 to 40 percent in 1973. Support for patriotism also fell from 60 percent to 40 percent during those four years. Belief that hard work always pays off dropped even more sharply, from 80 percent to 50 percent.

For young men and women in blue-collar jobs, the loss of blind loyalty to authority made them question the lack of worker participation in making decisions in the plants where they were employed. Job satisfaction became as important as wages. Polls indicated that many wished workers owned the businesses and factories where they spent so much of their lives. This discontent forced some business executives to become more sensitive to the feelings of their employees and to develop more flexible working schedules. No major changes occurred in the 1970s, however, toward significant participation of workers in decision making about the jobs they performed.

Despite the popularization of certain values and practices introduced by sixties counterculture, however, most of the nation's forty million working-class people continued to cling to many of their own traditions and outlooks. For example, several hundred thousand Americans in campers and pickup trucks continued to flock to the annual auto races at the Indianapolis Speedway. Camping out with ample supplies of hamburgers, beer, and country music, these vacationers conducted communal celebrations that rivaled the intensity and shared feelings of Woodstock. While disco music pervaded radio, television, and the movies by the late seventies, transplanted southerners, westerners, and other urban workers continued to listen to recorded country music. Based in music centers such as Nashville, Tennessee, and Austin, Texas, country music lamented the loss of family and community roots while simultaneously exploring the urban experiences of adultery, divorce, drinking, and alienating work.

The 1970s witnessed renewed sensitivity toward working-class culture and ethnic identity. By the end of the decade, Hollywood had produced successful films such as *Blue Collar, Norma Rae,* and *The Deer Hunter* that portrayed both the frailties and courage of those who worked the assembly lines, mills, and blast furnaces. As white ethnics began to organize for political power and cultural influence in the major industrial cities, films such as *The Deer Hunter, Rocky, The Godfather* and *The Godfather, Part II* depicted vital religious and social traditions among the nation's eastern and southern Europeans. Prodded by books such as Michael Novak's *The Rise of the Unmeltable Ethnics* (1971), major universities in urban centers began to establish programs in ethnic studies.

THE NEW AGE

The loss of social cohesion in American life in the 1960s and 1970s prompted many young people to search for spiritual alternatives. Because of the loss of faith in established religious institutions, the spiritual searching of young people often took them toward Oriental mysticism. Zen, Tibetan Buddhism, Yoga, I Ching, and other Asian philosophies and disciplines grew in popularity, particularly among middle-class youth. Much of the Charismatic movement within Catholicism shared the rejection of modern materialism in favor of increased spirituality. Such concern also appeared among "Jesus Freaks." These young Christians criticized the lack of spirituality among established Protestant denominations. They also were less willing to give their loyalty to the national government, capitalism, and the nuclear family than were the older group of evangelical Protestants. Like some of the counterculture and radical political experimenters of the early seventies, many of these groups established live-in communes in both rural areas and large cities.

While such religious developments were not threatening to the majority of the nation's people, the growth of spiritual cults disturbed American notions of individual free will. Groups such as Esalen, the Church of Scientology, the Hari Krishnas, and the disciples of the Korean Sun Myung Moon demanded total commitment and involvement by their members. By the late 1970s the parents of some cult members had turned to professional "deprogrammers" to reverse the brainwashing allegedly perpetrated by these organizations. The worst fears of anticultists were confirmed, however, when over nine hundred members of the California-based People's Temple committed mass suicide in 1978 in Guyana under orders from their spiritual father, Reverend Jim Jones.

Although the Jonestown suicides pointed to the dangers of cultism, the rampant concern for spirituality in the seventies went beyond fads and charismatic leaders. Writers such as William Irwin Thompson (*At the Edge of History*, 1971) spoke of a "planetary consciousness" that tied intuitive speculation to the experiments of the modern physical sciences. Novelist Tom Robbins, whose *Even Cowgirls Get the Blues* (1976) infused descriptions of counterculture antics with Oriental mysticism and biophysics, proclaimed that such "holistic" synthesis marked the dawn of a "new age." Holistic thinkers were particularly critical of the way in which modern medicine separated the mind from the body, treating the body as a machine. The mechanical tendencies of the medical establishment also treated one part of the body in isolation from the other parts. Holistic medicine accused the medical establishment of neglecting both the role of nutrition and exercise and the importance of the mind and spirit in individual health. George Leonard's *The Ultimate Athlete* (1975) provided an example of the attempt to combine body, mind, and spirit. Leonard argued that true athletics was spiritual and involved "entering the realm of music and poetry, of the turning of the planet, of the understanding of death." The 1970s produced widespread acceptance by middle-class Americans of natural pathology, Chinese acupuncture, meditative techniques for treating illness and disease, and body exercises such as jogging.

Asian philosophies of wholeness gained new prestige when scientific experiments confirmed that the mind could influence such bodily states as the pulse and breathing rate. Scientific equipment also suggested that half the brain had artistic and imaginative qualities that were neglected or repressed by the educational system. Psychologists such as Robert Ornstein in *The Psychology of Consciousness* (1972) and Paul Watzlawick in *The Language of Change* (1978) called on modern psychology to give up its materialistic approach to human behavior because of this evidence.

Young physicists such as Fritjof Capra in *The Tao of Physics* (1975) also argued that the major developments of twentieth-century physics had broken down the distinction between spirit and matter. For Capra, the logic of physics was similar to that of Oriental mysticism. These changes in psychology and physics toward a more spiritual definition of reality were paralleled in popular culture by two very successful movies in 1977 and 1978, *Star Wars* and *Close Encounters of the Third Kind*. These films were very different from most of the science fiction movies of the 1950s that portrayed the invasion of Earth by hostile aliens from outer space. The heroes of the fifties movies had been scientists who produced atomic weapons for the military to use against aliens. In *Star Wars* and *Close Encounters*, however, evil was represented by military power that used atomic weapons. The heroes, who did not represent centralized power, gained strength from a sense of unity with a spiritual universe. "The Force be with you" was the religious statement of *Star Wars*. And for Americans torn apart by nearly two decades of social and cultural ferment, *Close Encounters* concluded with the promise that "We are not alone."

SUGGESTED READINGS

Two useful overviews of the 1960s are Ronald Berman, *America in the Sixties* (1968), and William O'Neill, *Coming Apart* (1972). Joseph Kett, *Rites of Passage,* and Kenneth Keniston, *The Uncommitted* (1965) and *Youth and Dissent* (1971), analyze the crisis of adolescence. The first major study of the youth rebellion is Theodore Roszak, *The Making of a Counter Culture* (1969). Richard King, *The Party of Eros: Radical Social Thought and the Realm of Freedom* (1972), describes some of the philosophic heroes of the youth culture, as does Robert Hunter, *The Storming of the Mind* (1972). Another excellent description of the new values is Philip Slater, *The Pursuit of Loneliness* (1970). The new religious perspectives of the decade are discussed in William Braden, *The Age of Aquarius* (1970), Robert Wuthnow, *The Consciousness Reformation* (1976), and Charles Glock and Robert Bellah, eds., *The New Religious Consciousness* (1976). The most recent study of the major cultural expressions of the 1960s is Morris Dickstein, *Gates of Eden* (1977).

Cultural confusions in the white Protestant establishment are explored in E. Digby Baltzell, *The Protestant Establishment* (1964), Peter

Schrag, *The Decline of the WASP* (1976), and Ralph Brauer, *The Horse, the Gun, and the Piece of Property: Changing Images of the T.V. Western* (1975).

The factors leading to the emergence of a New Left after the sterility of the Old Left in the 1940s and 1950s is the subject of John P. Diggins, *The American Left in the Twentieth Century* (1973), Peter Clecak, *Radical Paradoxes: Dilemmas of the American Left, 1945–1970* (1973), and Irwin Unger, *The Movement* (1974).

The major principles of the ecology movement and its challenge to technology and economic growth can be found in Paul Sheperd and Daniel McKinley, eds., *The Subversive Science* (1969), Barry Commoner, *The Closing Circle* (1971), Nicholas Georgescu-Roegen, *The Entropy Law and Economic Process* (1971), and Victor Ferkiss, *The Future of Technological Civilization* (1974).

Vine DeLoria, Jr., *God Is Red* (1973), uses these ecological principles to criticize white Protestant values. Other studies of the recovery of cultural confidence by Native Americans are Helen Hertzberg, *The Search for an American Indian Identity* (1971), Stuart Levine and Nancy Lurie, *The American Indian Today* (1965), and Stan Steiner, *The New Indians* (1968). Matt Meier and Feliciano Rivera, *The Chicanos* (1972), and Rudolfo Acuna, *Occupied America: The Chicano's Struggle Toward Liberation* (1972), describe the resurgence of Chicano culture.

An overview of changes in the black community is Benjamin Muse, *The American Negro Revolution: From Violence to Black Power* (1968). Excellent descriptions of the dramatic changes in black literature are Addison Gayle, Jr., *The Way of the New World: The Black Novel in America* (1976), and

Eugene B. Redmond, *Drum Voice: The Mission of Afro-American Poetry* (1976).

Barbara Deckard, *The Women's Movement* (1975), Betty Gorburg, *The Changing Family* (1973), and Gayle Graham Yates, *What Women Want: The Ideas of the Movement* (1975), discuss the patterns of change among women. An excellent oral history of the origins of the women's movement can be found in Sara Evans, *Personal Politics* (1979).

Michael Novak, *The Rise of the Unmeltable Ethnics* (1971), Richard Krickus, *Pursuing the American Dream: White Ethnics and the New Populism* (1976), and Daniel Yankelovich, *The New Morality* (1974), analyze the stresses and confusions among blue-collar Americans.

Chapter 17

THE SEARCH FOR AUTHORITY, 1968-1980

Despite the major cultural changes of the 1960s, President Richard Nixon attempted to create a political administration based on traditional values of order, discipline, and strength. Elected amid the social chaos of 1968, Nixon represented the attempt to restore the discipline that Anglo-Protestant culture expected of its youth. The president's critique of permissiveness and his personal enthusiasm for the collectivized competition of football set the tone for an administration that sought to counter the pleasure seeking of the middle class with renewed respect for authority and national power.

NIXONIAN SOCIAL MANAGEMENT

Conforming to a pattern originally set in the New Deal, the Nixon White House moved to centralize policy making at the expense of Congress, the cabinet, and the permanent regulatory agencies. With Roy Ash of Litton Industries at the helm of a key reorganization task force, the Nixon administration began to adapt techniques of corporate management to national planning. Ash assumed responsibility for the Office of Management and Budget (OMB), which monitored the managerial practices and performance of the federal agencies. Under "Management by Objectives" procedures, borrowed from private corporations, all agencies listed their annual goals so the president might choose the highest priorities. Nixon also appointed presidential counselor John Ehrlichman to head a new Domestic Council. Modeled on the National Security Council, the DC formalized the transfer of policy making to the White House by acting as the president's planning board.

Ehrlichman's Domestic Council used cabinet officials to chart national policy, but Nixon went outside the cabinet system to appoint Harvard's Daniel Moynihan to lead an Urban Affairs Council. Moynihan's systems approach to urban policy prompted the president to maintain Great Society programs such as Model Cities and OEO, and encouraged Nixon to endorse the idea of a nationwide growth policy. Through Moynihan's influence, the president also created a controversial commission on population growth and family planning. Nixon's desire to fuse national planning with management efficiency was evident in his 1971 message on government reorganization, which recommended that bureaucratic overlapping be ended by consolidating domestic policy making in four broad categories — natural resources, community development, human resources, and economic affairs. But reorganization threatened vested interests accustomed to working with congressional oversight committees, and Congress never followed through on the idea.

Although Nixon had been elected as a budgetary conservative, he understood that government management could encourage social stability. Accordingly, federal spending, as a percentage of the gross national product, continued to rise during the Nixon years. By 1975 government outlays for income maintenance surpassed defense costs for the first time in history. Rising government assistance was reflected in the expansion of Aid to Dependent Children (ADC), a welfare program that covered two million youngsters in 1960 and twelve million in 1975. By the mid-1970s, thirteen million American families were receiving government food stamps. Nixon and Moynihan hoped to reduce the cumbersome welfare bureaucracy and channel money directly to the poor. Accordingly, the president introduced a $6 billion Family Assistance Plan in 1969. In order to satisfy Republican conservatives, Nixon denied that FAP was a guaranteed income program and misleadingly labeled it "workfare." But the president's bill did not include strict work requirements, and conservatives objected to its provision of at least $1,600 a year to every poor family. Ironically, the plan was killed in the Senate when liberals feared inadequate support levels for the poor and objected to Nixon's rhetoric. In reprisal, the president made major cuts in Great Society programs such as Head Start, the Job Corps, and OEO. By 1975 twenty-five million Americans still lived below the poverty line.

While centralizing procedures in the federal bureaucracy, Nixon attempted to revitalize state and local governments. The president's 1971 State of the Union message called for a "New American Revolution" through revenue sharing between the federal government and the states, a proposal first made by a Lyndon Johnson task force. Despite much rhetoric over the "New Federalism," however, general revenue sharing provided no more than 5 percent of state and local funds, while the federal government continued to control spending through larger outlays for "special programs." Although conservatives hoped to reverse the erosion of local control that had marked federal policy making since the New Deal, problems of inflation distracted the Nixon administration from that goal.

Several developments contributed to the inflation that characterized the years after 1965. Between 1965 and 1975 the nation spent $600 billion on weapons. But massive foreign aid and overseas investment brought a resulting troublesome export of dollars, in annual balance-of-payment deficits of $20 billion. So great was the flow of capital abroad that by 1974 the foreign earnings of American multinational corporations constituted 30 percent of all corporate profits after taxes. This "dollar drain" reduced the supply of gold reserves in the United States and contributed to rising corporate debt, which reached $1.3 trillion in 1974. Corporate debt, in turn, increased the competition for credit and accelerated interest rates and further inflation.

Inflation disrupted the social stability that Nixon sought, as it reduced spending power and eliminated savings. The national median housing price, for example, had been within reach of two-fifths of the nation's families in 1965. By 1971, however, only one-fifth could afford such a price. Inflation also aggravated relations between labor and management, since both worker productivity and real wages began to decline after 1966. A wildcat strike by 100,000 Teamsters tied up trucking in the Midwest and West Coast during the winter of 1969–1970 and was followed by a long strike of auto workers. But civil servants, teachers, and hospital workers also joined unions to strike for better pay against the government itself. A spontaneous walkout of postal workers, for example, briefly disrupted mail deliveries in 1970; but the president threatened to use troops and the strike was abandoned.

Nixon began to fight inflation by extending Johnson's 10 percent tax surcharge, vetoing a bill to expand public works in the cities, and declaring a ninety-day freeze on wages, prices, and rents in 1971. The president also created a Cost of Living Council to monitor rising costs. Nixon's freeze marked the first peacetime price control in history, but by the end of the year he was forced to devalue the dollar to stop further inflation. Fearful that stringent economic control might slow the economy and boost unemployment, the president relaxed wage and price regulations in 1973. But a government-subsidized sale of 8.5 million tons of grain to the Soviet Union contributed to a 20

percent leap in retail food prices that year, and Nixon resorted to another freeze. When that proved ineffective as well, the president conceded that inflation was beyond the immediate control of the government, and a discouraged administration allowed economic controls to expire in 1974.

Just as the administration gave up its war on inflation, it found itself confronted with an energy squeeze. In 1973 one-third of the nation's oil was imported, a proportion that approached one-half by the late seventies. Estimates suggested that half the 12 percent leap in the 1974 consumer price index stemmed from dwindling energy resources and soaring fuel costs. Nixon appointed Colorado Governor John Love to a newly created Energy Policy Office in June 1973 and allotted $100 million for energy research. But in October, Middle East oil-producing nations declared an export embargo against the United States to weaken American support for Israel. The embargo dramatized American dependence on foreign oil sources, and the price of imported petroleum quadrupled in three months. By February 1974, motorists lined up for hours to buy gasoline, as the major oil distributors held back on supplies. Americans who paid 35¢ a gallon in mid-1973 paid 50¢ a gallon by early 1975.

Nixon responded to the escalated energy crisis by replacing Love's office with a new Federal Energy Administration, headed by Deputy Treasury Secretary William E. Simon. He also signed legislation that permitted construction of a pipeline from northern Alaskan oil fields owned by the major oil producers. Opposed to rationing, Nixon sought a symbolic commitment to energy conservation by lowering the maximum speed limit to 55 mph. Although energy consumption did not decrease dramatically, slower speeds reduced traffic fatalities by one-fifth, and Congress made the speed reduction permanent late in 1974. The president also announced Project Independence, an effort to make the nation self-reliant in energy. But estimates placed the costs of energy independence at $1 trillion. When Nixon vetoed a bill to tax oil profits in March 1974, most Americans suspected that the "energy crisis" was a ruse to pad corporate dividends. Not until the later seventies did automobile manufacturers respond with production of smaller and more efficient vehicles. Whatever the size of their cars, Americans remained skeptical about the energy crisis and continued to insist on individualized forms of transportation.

Despite a strong beginning, the Nixon administration pulled back from concepts of national planning. The president created an Environmental Protection Agency (EPA) in 1970 to consolidate the government's antipollution programs and later asked Congress to establish various controls over private resources. But the Nixon presidency failed to meet the twin challenges of inflation and energy conservation and never followed up on initial interest in growth and population policy, land-use planning, and explicit national goals. All that remained of Nixonian innovations in social management were the reforms that strengthened the president's control of the federal bureaucracy and that consolidated power in the White House.

THE REVIVAL OF
SOCIAL CONSERVATISM

Throughout the sixties, liberal cosmopolitans had defined the issues and solutions to national problems with little sensitivity to lower-middle-class and working-class people. Exaggerating the

political influence of minority voters, the professional middle class, and the young, New Frontier and Great Society administrators had attempted to erect a homogeneous society built upon corporate precepts of cooperation and goodwill. But liberal social programs seemed to suggest that the government was concerned only with the rich and the very poor. And by this time millions of ethnic Americans had internalized traditional values of hard work, obedience to law and order, respect for authority, self-reliance, and patriotism. As welfare spending, ghetto rioting, illegal antiwar protests, and youth rebellion crescendoed in the late sixties, ethnic and lower-middle-class Americans found their conventional lifestyles and values ridiculed by the media and the liberal intelligentsia.

Many white Americans resented the attention given to black demands in the late sixties and expected blacks to adhere to white standards and values. Like George Wallace, Nixon played upon these sentiments in appeals for law and order and in suggestions that "black capitalism," not political activism or cultural independence, would bring equal opportunity. In a policy that Domestic Adviser Moynihan described as "benign neglect," the Nixon administration discouraged the use of federal power to ensure racial integration in the work force and the schools. When the Labor Department prepared to order minority representation on federal construction jobs in 1972, Nixon characterized quotas as "a dangerous detour away from the traditional value of measuring a person on the basis of ability." Twelve days later the department announced that "proportional representation" was a goal, not a requirement, of federal contract compliance.

School integration provided a more complex issue for the administration. While Nixon gave verbal support to equal opportunity, he opposed cutting off funds for school districts that did not comply with judicial orders for integration. Nevertheless, the Department of Health, Education, and Welfare began to withhold funds from certain northern communities and ordered hearings on racial discrimination in Boston schools. Meanwhile, the Supreme Court unanimously approved school integration through busing, although Chief Justice Warren Burger also indicated that racially balanced schools were not required in all cases and that "unwarranted" decisions for busing had been made in the past.

Opposition to busing combined elements of racial prejudice with sincere concern for neighborhood schools and community stability in working-class districts of the inner cities. Nixon felt compelled to respond to these sentiments by publicly reaffirming his personal distaste for busing. The president also proposed a judicial moratorium on busing directives, during which Congress could consider whether to deny the courts further power to order them. While the NAACP accused Nixon of bringing Jim Crowism back to the nation's schools, a federal court

City police escort school buses at the peak of the busing controversy in the Boston school district. Bunker Hill Monument appears in the background. (Nick Passmore/Stock, Boston)

postponed the busing of 300,000 students in Detroit. Yet school desegregation proceeded at an increasing pace in the Nixon years, and the president's resistance proved largely symbolic.

While Nixon failed to slow the pace of school integration, he attempted to show that the Democratic Congress was "soft" on crime. The administration introduced a controversial court reorganization bill for Washington, D.C., labeling it a model for national crime legislation and a warning to "criminal forces." Although the bill provided police and judges with no more power than they already possessed, it legitimized "preventive detention" and certain warrantless searches. To constitutionalists such as Senator Sam Ervin of North Carolina, the bill clearly violated four of the ten amendments in the Bill of Rights. But Congress shared the president's sensitivity to law and order and passed the package in a surprise move in 1971.

Nixon attracted social conservatives by placing blame for society's permissiveness on the liberal Supreme Court. Court decisions involving abolition of prayer in public schools, reapportionment of state legislatures, and protections for criminal suspects had encouraged sixties conservatives to support Nixon's promise to appoint nonactivist justices. When Chief Justice Earl Warren retired in 1969, Nixon chose Warren Burger, a moderate Minnesota Republican, as Warren's replacement. But when a second vacancy occurred that year, the president followed Attorney General John Mitchell's "southern strategy" and nominated Georgia Judge Clement Haynsworth. When the Senate questioned a conflict of interest in Haynsworth's judicial record, however, he became the first Supreme Court nominee in forty years to be rejected. Nixon responded by appointing another southerner, Harold Carswell. But Senate inquiry revealed that Carswell

had made white supremacist statements in a 1948 election campaign, and his nomination was rejected as well. Infuriated, Nixon lambasted the Senate for "regional discrimination" and claimed that his power of appointment had been abrogated by liberals hostile to a strict interpretation of the Constitution. Yet the president eased the tension by selecting another Minnesota moderate, Harry Blackmun.

The Court fight demonstrated Nixon's determination to attack liberal institutions with conservative principles. By the end of his first term, the president succeeded in appointing two more conservatives to the increasingly cautious Supreme Court. Although the Burger Court outlawed domestic "national security" wiretaps without judicial permission and prohibited states from interfering with most abortions, it generally followed Nixonian lines of social conservatism. Court decisions limited the immunity of witnesses from prosecution, allowed non-unanimous jury verdicts in state criminal cases, and compelled news reporters to testify before grand juries. The Burger Court also facilitated enforcement of the death penalty by ruling that state capital punishment was constitutional if the appropriate statutes were worded carefully and applied without discrimination. The Court further pleased Nixon conservatives by opening the door to "local option" on obscenity and pornography censorship in 1975.

DÉTENTE AND ESCALATION

Despite his rhetoric over domestic discipline and order, Nixon believed that the presidency was concerned primarily with foreign affairs. The most innovative aspect of his administration was the movement toward relaxation of tensions with both China and the Soviet Union. Ever since the Communist Revolution of 1949, the People's Republic of China had remained unrecognized by the United States. Cold Warriors, including Nixon himself, continually warned that recognition would entail abandoning the Nationalist government on Taiwan (Formosa) and would legitimize Communist subversion against established regimes. Beginning with Harry Truman, each Cold War president backed away from conciliatory steps toward China, fearful of appearing "soft" on communism. But when the Chinese made diplomatic overtures in 1969, Nixon reasoned that he could win concessions from both China and the Soviet Union if he took advantage of the deepening rift between the two rivals. Accordingly, the president began to establish communication with the Chinese and eased restrictions on American travel to the mainland. By 1971 Nixon no longer referred to "Red China" and he encouraged an American table tennis team to go to Peking. When the athletes were received warmly, the United States announced the end of a twenty-one-year embargo on Chinese trade and accepted Peking's seating in the United Nations several months later.

The China détente was formalized when the president toured the Communist nation early in 1972. Although the visit was largely nonsubstantive, millions of Americans witnessed the highly publicized event through satellite television. Nixon and Chinese Premier Chou En-lai released a joint communiqué that pledged the two nations to "peaceful mutuality," but the most important part of the negotiations involved an American promise to withdraw military forces from Taiwan and accept Peking's contention that the island historically belonged to China. Three months after Nixon had achieved détente with the People's Republic,

he traveled to Moscow. President Johnson had met amicably in 1967 with Premier Alexei Kosygin, but that meeting was not substantive. This time, Nixon and Communist party leader Leonid Brezhnev signed a Strategic Arms Limitation Treaty (SALT), limiting construction of antiballistic missile sites and nuclear delivery systems. Although the treaty did not rule out the development of new weapons, the Nixon-Brezhnev talks produced agreements on Berlin and trade. In July 1972 the United States agreed to sell the Soviets $750 million worth of grain, about one-fourth of the entire American crop. When Brezhnev visited Washington the following year, the two leaders signed additional pacts covering nuclear arms, cultural exchanges, and peaceful uses of atomic energy.

Like Johnson, Nixon held out the promise of peace in Southeast Asia. But détente with China and the Soviet Union only heightened the president's desire to maintain credibility — the image of national strength and determination in global affairs. "Precipitate withdrawal" from Vietnam would be a "popular and easy course," Nixon told the American people in 1969, but he warned that defeat and humiliation would bring the "collapse of confidence in American leadership." Although the president believed in both the rightness of the war and the need to end it, his fear of surrender brought the United States four more years of destruction in Southeast Asia.

Once Nixon indicated willingness to resume the bombing of North Vietnam in early 1969, the North Vietnamese responded with a fresh offensive, and the president ordered a new "pacification" program in the Mekong Delta. As the nation's chief executive sought "peace with honor," bombing of villages, destruction of crops, and removal of peasants once again characterized the bloody conflict. By mid-1973, the Nixon administration had unleashed four million tons of bombs on Indochina; twice the tonnage ordered by Johnson and one and one-half times the total dropped on Europe and Asia in both World War Two and the Korean War.

Despite Nixon's refusal to accept a Communist victory in Vietnam, he understood how massive commitments of fighting men had destroyed the Johnson presidency. Accordingly, as disaffection mounted among soldiers and the domestic public, the president announced a Nixon Doctrine by which ground troops would be withdrawn while the United States escalated the air war and provided economic and military aid to the South Vietnamese. Amid massive antiwar demonstrations in the fall of 1969, Nixon told a television audience that "we are Vietnamizing the search for peace," and began to move toward an all-volunteer army. By the spring of 1970 the president had withdrawn 110,000 troops and announced a "Vietnamization" program to train the South Vietnamese Army to assume the burden of the fighting.

As Nixon stepped up troop withdrawals, however, he continued to expand the war. Fearful of public opinion at home, the president ordered the secret bombing of insurgent forces in Cambodia during March 1969. To prevent disclosure of the covert air war, conducted even without the knowledge of the secretary of the air force, military officers established a bombing command system outside ordinary channels and falsified or destroyed all records of sorties. But in 1970 Nixon went public when he told a stunned nation that twenty-five thousand American and South Vietnamese ground forces had entered Cambodia in an "incursion" designed to "shorten the war." The object of the invasion, the commander-in-chief explained, was "cleaning out major North Vietnamese and Vietcong occupied territories," and destroying

the "main headquarters for the entire Communist military operation in South Vietnam." The president also hoped to bolster the anti-Communist military regime that recently had taken control of the Cambodian capital.

For Nixon, Cambodia was a test crisis whose importance lay in the manner in which Americans revealed themselves to the world. The president proclaimed that the United States could not act "like a pitiful, helpless giant" and confided that he would rather be a one-term president than see the nation become a "second-rate power" and be defeated for the first time "in its proud 190-year history." Referring to an "age of anarchy both abroad and at home," Nixon emphasized American will and determination by resuming the bombing of North Vietnam.

Failing to find Communist insurgents, American ground troops withdrew from Cambodia two months later, pulling out on the very day that Congress passed a prohibition against their continued presence. But in February 1971 the president revealed that the South Vietnamese Army had invaded Laos with American air support. American bombing in Laos had not abated since the early sixties, but the invasion represented a new tactic, and the administration placed a news blackout on the inept attack. American planes also continued daily bombings in North Vietnam in what the Pentagon described as "protective-reaction air strikes" to cover withdrawing American forces. By the spring of 1972, however, South Vietnamese troops were in chaotic retreat from the northern provinces, and the Communists were moving into the central highlands. Angered and faced with the failure of Vietnamization, Nixon announced the mining of North Vietnamese ports. Three months after his triumphant visit to the People's Republic, the president labeled the

North Vietnamese "international outlaws" and ordered the bombing of railroad lines leading to China. He also instructed the air force to hit industrial targets in populated areas of North Vietnam and sent American B-52s to attack the Vietnamese dike system. Nevertheless, polls showed that 60 percent of the American public believed that the president was doing everything he could to end the war.

One month before the 1972 presidential election, National Security Adviser Henry Kissinger and North Vietnamese negotiators secretly agreed to a military cease-fire. Under Soviet influence, North Vietnam had decided to postpone a political settlement but won the right to keep its military units in the South. As the Nixon administration stopped the bombing of the North, Kissinger confidently proclaimed that peace was at hand. But when South Vietnamese leaders rejected the truce, Kissinger abruptly announced the suspension of negotiations and resumption of the air war. In the "Christmas Bombing" of 1972, B-52s attacked populated areas and wiped out a children's hospital at Bach Mai resulting in hundreds of casualties. Despite private and official criticism from world leaders of all ideologies, the Nixon administration offered little explanation for the most intensive bombing in military history. But it was clear that the United States supported Saigon's reluctance to relinquish South Vietnamese territory held by the Communists and that Nixon and Kissinger hoped to build up fears of American retaliation should North Vietnam overwhelm the South.

Nixon finally announced a Vietnam peace agreement that would "end the war and bring peace with honor" in January 1973. But there was little in the accord that could not have been negotiated when Nixon assumed office four years before. During that time, twenty thousand Americans lost their lives and fifty thousand more were wounded in Vietnam, while South Vietnam suffered even more casualties than it had in the Johnson years. The formal peace settlement provided for the withdrawal of the twenty-five thousand remaining American troops in exchange for American prisoners of war. But the peace treaty also provided official recognition of the National Liberation Front by the United States and resolved the nineteen-year controversy over the two Vietnams by declaring the 17th parallel a provisional boundary instead of a political or territorial dividing line.

Although the truce did not affect American bombing in Cambodia, military involvement in Vietnam ended with withdrawal of the last troops and return of the remaining POWs in March 1973. The administration arranged a televised homecoming for the released pilots, but nothing could erase the fact of American capitulation in the most unpopular war in the history of the United States. Altogether, the Vietnam War left over 56,000 Americans dead, more than 300,000 wounded, over one million Vietnamese slaughtered, and ten million homeless. But the injury to national cohesion went far beyond the awesome destruction and the $140 billion in war costs.

THE FAILURE OF NATIONAL UNITY

Continuation of the Vietnam War proved fatal to the Nixon administration and to social peace at home. When the "twelve wise men" of the corporate elite had informed President Johnson that the war was unwinnable in 1968, they anticipated a reversal in American policy. Like-

Protesters gather at the Moratorium against the War, Washington, D.C., 1970. (Charles Gatewood)

wise, most Americans assumed that Johnson's abdication signified an imminent end to hostilities. But the slow pace of Nixon's withdrawal broadened the base of antiwar sentiment. By the fall of 1969, 57 percent of the country favored a specified deadline for complete disengagement. On October 15, Vietnam Moratorium Day, 40,000 demonstrators marched in Washington, 65,000 rallied in New York City, and 100,000 gathered on the Boston Common to hear Senator Edward Kennedy propose total withdrawal within the year. A second moratorium in November brought out the largest political gathering in American history.

While peace rallies and marches occurred across the nation, more than 250,000 demonstrators gathered at the Washington Monument. When ten thousand protesters were teargassed in front of the Justice Department, Attorney General Mitchell remarked that "it looked like the Russian Revolution." But one million Americans had demonstrated peaceably against the war in the fall campaign.

College campuses were relatively quiet until Nixon announced the invasion of Cambodia in April 1970. But escalation of the war literally set the nation's universities on fire. At Kent State in Ohio, Governor James Rhodes called in the National Guard to prevent further demonstrations after students burned the campus Reserve Officers' Training Corps building. Just a few days before, Vice President Agnew had denounced student unrest and urged Americans to "act accordingly." Rhodes blamed the Kent violence on agitators "worse than the Brown Shirts, the Communist element and also the night riders and the vigilantes." On May 4, Kent State students failed to respond to a dispersal order at a noon rally and threw rocks and bottles at guardsmen firing tear gas. Finding themselves surrounded, several of the tense guardsmen wheeled around and fired rifle shots into the crowd, wounding nine and killing four.

The Kent State deaths electrified a nation already shocked by news of the Cambodian invasion. University presidents had warned Nixon that there was no hope of restoring peace on American campuses without ending the Vietnam War. Following Kent State, Interior Secretary Walter Hickel wrote Nixon that "youth in its protest must be heard." But Agnew responded to the killings by blaming "elitist" permissiveness toward "psychotic and criminal elements" for the "traitors and thieves and perverts... in our midst." The president appeared more uncertain. He assured the nation that the Cambodian invasion would not exceed a twenty-one-mile limit and would be over in three to seven weeks; he also told reporters that he knew "how deeply" antiwar protesters felt and that "everything that I stand for is what they want." On edge and unable to sleep one evening, the president made fifty-one late-night telephone calls and spoke to Kissinger eight times. Finally he left the White House to engage several antiwar demonstrators in small talk beneath the Lincoln Memorial at 5 A.M.

Never before in American history had white students been fired upon by forces of the state. Within days, student strikes closed 350 universities and colleges, while hundreds more suspended classes. As ROTC bombings, window smashing, and building occupations broke out across the nation's schools, the American system of higher education ceased to function. At Jackson State in Mississippi, two black students were killed when police inexplicably fired on a college dormitory. But at most institutions, moderates channeled activism into letter campaigns, antiwar petitions, and doorbell ringing. Under a plan devised at Princeton, some colleges gave released time for students who wished to campaign for antiwar candidates in the fall elections.

The student strikes of 1970 made it clear that social peace and continuation of the war were incompatible, but the massive disruptions marked the last cry of campus protest. The Kent State shootings intimidated further demonstrations in a period in which draft calls were falling off and students increasingly were concerned with a declining job market. Yet thirty thousand demonstrators arrived in Washington during May 1971 to protest the invasion of Laos by blocking traffic and employing civil

disobedience to disrupt the functioning of the capital. Monitored by a joint command of the CIA and local police, twelve thousand people were swept off the streets in the largest mass arrest in American history. But the arbitrary arrests involved widespread suspension of legal procedures in the first assignment for the administration's Intelligence Evaluation Committee. Four years later a federal court awarded $12 million in damages to those who had been improperly detained.

Like Johnson and his Cold War predecessors, Nixon believed that the fight against world communism was a test of the president's personal character. But the Vietnam War politicized all aspects of American life, and the federal government lay in the front lines of the attack on institutional leaders and traditional sanctions of authority. Starting with the Johnson administration, the government acted to stem the tide toward anarchy and political disrespect, fearing the very existence of the nation to be at stake. Johnson's Department of Justice prosecuted baby doctor Benjamin Spock, Yale chaplain William Sloane Coffin, and two others for aiding draft evasion in 1968. Through the Internal Security Division of the Justice Department, the Nixon administration continued to use the courts and unauthorized wiretaps to suppress dissenters. In 1969 a federal grand jury indicted eight leaders of the 1968 Chicago demonstrations, accusing them of conspiracy and violation of the antiriot provisions of the Civil Rights Act of 1968. The explosive trial of the Chicago Eight became a showplace for radical protest and revolutionary culture. Insisting that the government was using the case to discourage dissent, Yippies Jerry Rubin and Abbie Hoffman wore long hair, talked back to the judge, introduced songs as evidence, and displayed NLF flags. When Black Panther

Bobby Seale would not proceed without his bedridden attorney, Judge Julius Hoffman ordered Seale gagged and chained. Judge Hoffman cited defendants and their lawyers for 175 acts of contempt during the five-month trial. The jury verdict in 1970 erased the conspiracy charges but found five of the defendants guilty of individual intent to incite riot. Four of the

contempt citations were upheld in another trial in 1973, but charges against Seale, who won a separate trial, were dropped.

Although federal grand juries collected information on radicals and antiwar groups, prosecution frequently faltered in court. A grand jury indicted the imprisoned Berrigan brothers and five others in 1970 for conspiracy to kidnap

MAP 17.1   THE THRUST INTO CAMBODIA

Reprinted by permission from TIME, *The Weekly Newsmagazine; Copyright Time Inc. 1970*

National Security Adviser Kissinger. But another jury failed to convict them two years later when the prime evidence turned out to be a whimsical letter delivered to Philip Berrigan through an FBI informer. Thirteen Black Panthers also were acquitted of conspiracy to bomb New York City department stores in 1971, while a New Haven jury failed to agree on a verdict in a case that charged Seale and other Panthers with conspiracy to murder an alleged police informant.

Not satisfied with court proceedings, the Nixon administration mounted an intense public relations campaign against antiwar activism and radical violence. Assistant Attorney General Richard Kleindienst called for the repression of "ideological criminals" in 1969 and described the antiwar movement as "national subversive activity." Meanwhile, the president told a South Dakota college audience that "fundamental values" were "under bitter and even violent attack in America" and that "We have the power to strike back if need be, and to prevail." Stung by massive antiwar activity in November 1969, the president called demonstrators a "vocal minority" and appealed for support from the nation's "silent majority."

But it was Vice President Agnew who assumed the burden of the administration's attack on the moratoriums of 1969, referring to antiwar activists as an "effete corps of impudent snobs who characterized themselves as intellectuals." Within its first year of office, the Nixon White House had become convinced that liberal-dominated institutions such as the Supreme Court, mass media, and universities were preventing the president from reaching the silent majority. Agnew complained to a Des Moines audience that a "tiny enclosed fraternity of privileged men" in TV journalism distorted presidential addresses through the "instant analysis" that followed televised speeches. He contended that "a small band of network commentators and self-appointed analysts" had tried to obstruct the president's effort to bring peace to Vietnam. The implications of the vice president's criticism were crystalized when the newly confirmed chairman of the Federal Communications Commission requested transcripts of the network commentaries on Nixon's Vietnamization speech. And White House communications director Herbert Klein threatened that if the networks and press did not correct their bias against the president, "you do invite the government to come in."

Agnew also had criticized the print media for concentrating on bad news instead of good. But the day following the November moratorium, newspapers published the first reports on the recently uncovered My Lai massacre. The highly publicized case resulted in a military trial and the 1971 murder conviction of Lieutenant William Calley. While the army brought minor coverup charges against a brigade commander, Calley was the only career officer to be convicted. The case brought an emotional burst of support for the defendant from Americans who insisted that Calley had only performed his military duty. Another segment of opinion held that he had been made a scapegoat for American brutality in Vietnam. Intervening in the volatile case, Nixon promised to review the final sentence and permitted Calley to live in his own quarters at a military base. A military review court later reduced the lieutenant's sentence to twenty years.

Nixon's intervention in the Calley case indicated his desire to win support from patriotic blue-collar ethnics and the lower middle class. His encouragement of working-class patriotism was part of an administration effort to construct an image of national war enthusiasm. To counteract protests over Cambodia and Kent State, White House aides also created bogus citizen groups such as the Tell It To Hanoi Committee, while the Republican National Committee signed hundreds of names to form letters endorsing administration policy.

The climax to the Nixon campaign came during the congressional elections of 1970. In order to defeat candidates it described as "radical-liberals," the White House created its own Committee for a Responsible Congress. Nixon visited ten states in four days during the campaign, making his own prestige and student demonstrations the central issues. In San Jose the president jumped on top of a car and made the peace sign, deliberately provoking a crowd of protesters into angry response. "As long as I am president," Nixon declared, "no band of violent thugs is going to keep me from going out and speaking with the American people." Meanwhile, Agnew referred to domestic rebels as "misfits" and "garbage." By the 1970 elections, however, much of the American public had tired of the administration's abrasiveness and desired social peace. Speaking for the Democratic candidates on election eve, Maine's Senator Edmund Muskie castigated the administration for a "politics of fear." The next day, Republicans gained two seats in the Senate but lost nine congressional seats and eleven governorships.

WATERGATE AND POLITICAL REPRESSION

The public relations campaign and court action against radicals proved insufficient for an administration that continually found itself beset by threats to social order. When the liberal

New York Times publicized the secret bombing of Cambodia in 1969, the White House ordered the FBI to install "national security" wiretaps on the telephones of four newsmen and thirteen administration aides. To stop further leaks, White House assistants hired two former police agents as private investigators, but their tasks included surveillance of Senator Edward Kennedy, a potential candidate for the 1972 presidential campaign. Kennedy had driven his car off a bridge during a late-night accident at Chappaquiddick, Massachusetts, drowning a woman who was a former campaign aide. Questions concerning the senator's relationship with his companion, in addition to his delay in reporting the accident, made Kennedy a logical choice for White House undercover investigations.

By 1970 Nixon pressed for a coordinated program of domestic intelligence to counter the threat of internal dissent. Following the Cambodian invasion, presidential aide Tom Huston drafted a proposal for an interagency intelligence unit composed of the FBI, CIA, National Security Agency, and the Pentagon intelligence agencies. The illegal Huston Plan called for burglary, wiretapping, mail openings, campus informants, and monitoring of international communications, but the presidentially approved program was implemented for only five days before FBI Director Hoover squelched it. Hoover feared disclosure of the unlawful procedures and hoped to maintain FBI control of domestic security. Despite the demise of the Huston Plan, however, the FBI continued its counterintelligence program against radicals, the CIA carried on illegal domestic spying, and the NSA maintained electronic surveillance of international messages. In late 1970 the White House settled for an Intelligence Evaluation Committee to coordinate surveillance of radicals.

The crisis atmosphere of 1970 produced another administrative offensive when Marxist candidate Salvador Allende was about to be confirmed as president by Chile's national assembly. Kissinger privately warned that Allende would pose "massive problems" for the United States in Latin America and told the president's national security advisers that they could not "stand by and watch a country go communist due to the irresponsibility of its own people." Nixon quickly ordered the CIA to organize a Chilean military coup. When that did not materialize, government and private lending agencies refused credit to Chile, creating unbearable pressures on that nation's economy, while the CIA continued to provide funds to opposing politicians, friendly media, and anti-Communist unions. Between 1970 and 1973 the United States spent $8 million in the covert effort to turn Chile against its elected president. Finally, Allende was assassinated in a bloody coup in 1973, and a military regime abolished Chilean democracy.

When the *New York Times* began to publish the secret Pentagon Papers in 1971, the Nixon White House faced still another self-created crisis. McNamara's study of the Vietnam War focused on the continuity of government duplicity during the Kennedy and Johnson administrations. But National Security Adviser Kissinger feared that future leaks might threaten Soviet and Chinese confidence in the American ability to conduct secret negotiations. Shortly after federal courts refused to permit the government to stop publication of the Pentagon study, Nixon authorized creation of a Special Investigations Unit (the "Plumbers") to prevent administration leaks. When Daniel Ellsberg, a former Defense Department planner, confessed that he had released the papers to expose government lying and help end the war,

the Plumbers burglarized the office of Ellsberg's psychiatrist to gain information that could be used to discredit the former Pentagon aide. Ellsberg and Anthony Russo were indicted for espionage and conspiracy in 1971, but the government dropped the charges when it refused to produce wiretap logs that contained conversations involving the defendants. Presidential assistants John Ehrlichman, Charles Colson, and others subsequently were convicted of various charges related to the smear campaign against Ellsberg, and in 1974 a federal court ruled that a president had no constitutional right to authorize a break-in, even when national security and foreign intelligence were involved.

As the 1972 presidential election approached, the Nixon administration turned its intelligence capacity to more partisan matters. Since 1970, the Internal Revenue Service had been using tax audits to harass individuals and organizations with "extremist views and philosophies" and had provided confidential information about these targets to intelligence and law-enforcement agencies. But in 1971 the White House prepared an "enemies list" of 280 individuals whom it perceived to be allies of the Democratic party. The list of those to be audited included liberal congressmen, labor leaders, prominent media and show business personalities, and Democratic fund raisers and contributors from the corporate world. But the IRS declined to pursue these partisan demands. Nevertheless, Nixon operatives began undercover investigations of Republican antiwar presidential candidate Paul McCloskey, Democratic candidate Edmund Muskie, Democratic Party Chairman Lawrence O'Brien, and syndicated columnist Jack Anderson. In February 1972 Anderson reported on a memo from a lobbyist for International Telephone and Telegraph. The memo referred to an arrangement by which the Department of Justice had approved an ITT merger in return for a $400,000 contribution to the Republican National Convention. When John Mitchell resigned as attorney general in March to become the president's campaign manager, his successor, Richard Kleindienst, faced hostile confirmation hearings in the Senate. Although Kleindienst finally was confirmed, he pleaded guilty in 1974 to false Senate testimony about the ITT affair.

During the 1970 elections, the White House had channeled $400,000 in secret funds into the Alabama gubernatorial primary in a futile effort to defeat George Wallace, a possible presidential candidate for 1972. Desiring to place Nixon above the battle of the re-election drive, Chief of Staff H. R. Haldeman organized a Committee to Re-Elect the President (CRP) in 1971. With the assistance of Commerce Secretary Maurice Stans and the president's personal attorney, four hundred "dummy" corporations directed secret corporation campaign funds to CRP. Although oil companies, airlines, and defense contractors contributed substantially in an effort to win preferential government treatment, the leading donor was the Associated Milk Producers, which hoped to assure administration continuance of price supports with a $422,000 stipend. While Republicans stalled passage of a campaign disclosure law early in 1972, financier Robert Vesco contributed another $200,000 to Nixon's campaign. Vesco was under investigation by the Securities and Exchange Commission for an alleged $250 million looting of mutual funds. A subsequent trial acquitted Maurice Stans and John Mitchell of influence peddling in the case, although Vesco had fled to Costa Rica with the president's nephew.

CRP made extensive use of the unprecedented $55 million collected by its fund raisers. The committee directed intelligence operations against the strongest Democratic contenders for the presidential nomination and worked covertly to support the weakest. A "dirty tricks" operation issued false and misleading literature "signed" by Democratic candidates and engaged in other pranks designed to embarrass the Democrats. A particularly effective ploy involved a letter planted in a conservative New Hampshire newspaper that accused front runner Muskie of making a derogatory reference to New Englanders of French-Canadian descent. Furious and exhausted from campaigning, Muskie appeared in the snow outside the newspaper office and wept as he vehemently denied the contrived charge. The emotional outburst signaled the decline of the candidate's fortunes.

As George McGovern became the most likely candidate for the Democratic nomination, CRP began to focus on the Democratic National Committee and Chairman O'Brien. Accordingly, CRP Director Mitchell approved a covert entry into Democratic headquarters at Washington's Watergate building complex. When a wiretap on O'Brien's telephone malfunctioned, however, the CRP team returned for a second entry. On June 17, 1972, five CRP operatives were arrested for burglary inside the Watergate office of the Democratic party.

Although presidential press secretary Ron Ziegler dismissed the entry as a "third-rate burglary," CRP and White House aides began an immediate coverup. Americans would not discover the fact for two years, but Nixon personally conducted preliminary steps in the Watergate coverup. Acting on an idea suggested by Mitchell, the president ordered aides to request the CIA to stop an FBI inquiry into the source of Watergate funds. To protect Nixon, frantic aides improvised a day-to-day conspiracy. Wiretap records were destroyed at CRP headquarters, campaign officials lied to the FBI and grand jury, incriminating evidence was removed from a White House safe, and law-enforcement agencies were subjected to pressures for "cooperation." When those measures proved insufficient, Haldeman and Ehrlichman devised an elaborate scheme to provide "hush money" to the Watergate defendants. Yet at an August press conference, Nixon pretended that his counsel, John Dean, had completed a Watergate investigation for the White House. "I can state categorically," the president declared, "that no one in the White House staff, no one in this administration, presently employed, was involved in this very bizarre incident."

NIXON'S RE-ELECTION

Campaigning as an outright opponent of the Vietnam War, Democrat George McGovern brought an evangelical message of peace and social concern to newly enfranchised young voters, middle-class reformers, and racial and cultural minorities. The Twenty-sixth Amendment to the Constitution, ratified in 1971, awarded the vote to eighteen-year-olds, bolstering the South Dakotan's hopes for a new Democratic coalition. Winning the largest number of delegates in the 1972 primaries, McGovern broadened his emotional antiwar stance by denouncing inflation, unemployment, and administration connections to big business, while promising tax reform and a shift of spending from defense to social needs. George Wallace had used the busing issue to take the largest popular vote in the primaries. But Wallace was

shot in May 1972 by an assailant with no apparent political motive, and the resulting paralysis left him unable to continue the campaign. With the failure of mainstream candidates such as Muskie and Hubert Humphrey, McGovern had little competition at the Democratic Convention in Miami. Following the McGovern Committee reforms of 1968, party delegates had been chosen in primaries, caucuses, and other elections during the convention year. As a result, four-fifths of the 1972 delegates were attending their first national convention. The new rules also required equitable representation for certain social groups. Consequently, women constituted 38 percent of the Democratic delegates, blacks 14 percent, and those under twenty-five 13 percent. In addition, over one hundred delegates publicly acknowledged themselves as homosexuals.

The climate for the McGovern candidacy had been prepared by New Left critiques of the war, black and radical demands for social justice, and the counterculture of middle-class youth. McGovern enthusiasts believed that the Democrats finally had rejected both party bosses and the Vietnam War. Even Mayor Daley of Chicago was unseated when the Illinois delegation was cited for violating party reform rules. But as the McGovern revolution attempted to replace the New Deal coalition with a "politics of conscience," working-class ethnics felt deserted. Even though 1972 polls showed that a greater percentage of blue-collar workers were critical of Nixon war policies than the general sample, working-class Americans associated the McGovern candidacy with draft card burning, campus destruction, street riots, and disrespect for national values. These fears were crystalized when the convention defied McGovern staffers and openly debated culturally abrasive issues such as abortion, gay rights, and the le-

Frank Rizzo

1920-

Frank Rizzo, an Italian-American, a high school dropout, and a career police officer, won national headlines when he was elected "law-and-order" mayor of Philadelphia in 1971. As police commissioner, Rizzo was known as a "tough cop." Called from a formal dinner in 1969, he confronted an angry disturbance at a black housing project with a nightstick jammed into his tuxedo. When four policemen were shot in West Philadelphia the following summer, Rizzo proclaimed that the black neighborhood was no longer "civilized" and warned that the "only other thing we can do now is buy tanks and start mounting machine guns." Blaming the attacks on Black Panthers, whom he described as "imbeciles," the commissioner personally supervised a raid on a Panther house during which suspects were stripped naked on the street.

Rizzo won the 1971 election because he understood the fears and resentments of Philadelphia's working-class ethnics. As street crime skyrocketed in the early seventies, inner-city Americans became increasingly impatient with "liberal" judges and permissive schools. Large numbers of Italians, Irish, Poles, and Jews also believed that public agencies were spending hard-earned tax dollars on "handouts" to blacks and racial minorities. Rizzo promised law and order without tax increases and talked about preserving neighborhoods, decent families, and public morality. "I'm a man of action who gets things done," he told Philadelphians in 1971. "Nobody owns Frank Rizzo."

But once in office, Rizzo did nothing to stop the increase of inner-city crime. In a city in which two-fifths of the population was black and in which 90 percent of black crimes of violence were directed against other blacks, Rizzo's rhetoric only heightened racial antagonism.

Unlike ethnic leaders such as Barbara Mikulski of Baltimore and Steve Adubato of Newark, Rizzo never addressed the substantive problems of urban working people, black or white. Rizzo closed the public hospital, permitted schools and public housing to deteriorate, raised wage and real estate taxes by 30 percent, and tried to hide an $80 million budget deficit. While claiming that social welfare costs were exorbitant, Rizzo padded city payrolls with personal favorites and accepted $130,000 in private funds to refurbish his own office. As hundreds of city jobs were exempted from the civil service merit system, Rizzo assumed control of a $65-million-a-year patronage system. Charged with awarding city contracts in exchange for loyalty to his machine, the mayor became the first public official in history to take a lie detector test and fail. When a newspaper ridiculed the fiasco with an offensive satire, union allies surrounded the daily's headquarters and physically prevented its distribution.

Frank Rizzo was a product of seventies disillusion with governments that could no longer produce what they promised. But unlike Governor Jerry Brown of California, who initiated state policies based on ecological and fiscal limitations, Rizzo had no program whatsoever. Like Richard Nixon, he concentrated on destroying his enemies by building his own power base. Proclaiming that "Rizzo Means Business," the mayor of Philadelphia won re-election in 1975 with the support of the loyal ethnics and downtown business interests. The following year Jimmy Carter campaigned against Rizzo bossism in the Pennsylvania presidential primary. But in the November election, the Rizzo machine provided Carter with the Democratic victory margin in the state. Moments after the network announcement of Carter's triumph, the president-elect telephoned Frank Rizzo. "You really knew what you were talking about," Carter said in thanks. The ethnic political machine, refurbished by the social tensions of seventies urbanism, still was alive and well in American politics.

galization of marijuana. Although McGovern tried to communicate his vision of a just society in ordinary language, a carelessly presented plan for a guaranteed income conveyed confusion about economics. The fatal blow to the campaign came, however, when newspaper reports indicated that vice presidential candidate Thomas Eagleton had been hospitalized several times for emotional depression. McGovern first gave Senator Eagleton a "1,000 percent" public endorsement, then asked for his resignation, thereby creating an image of indecisiveness and hypocrisy. R. Sargent Shriver carried the Kennedy mantle onto the 1972 ticket, but McGovern's strength as a trustworthy candidate had been irreparably damaged.

The Republican Convention provided a stark contrast to the openness of the Democratic conclave. Security was so tight at convention headquarters that delegates could not leave their hotels without a badge. Three thousand "Young Voters for Nixon," organized and paid by White House advance men, paraded through convention festivities reciting "Four more years, four more years!" Surpassing Johnson's 1968 efforts at Chicago, the Nixon White House scripted the entire convention proceedings and platform, deriding capture of the Democratic party by a radical clique and repeatedly depicting the chaos of the McGovern convention. "Let us reject," Nixon stated in his acceptance speech, "the policies of those who whine and whimper about our frustrations and call on us to turn inward. Let us not turn away from our greatness."

Nixon's campaign followed the strategy outlined in Kevin Phillips's *The Emergent Republican Majority* (1969), which sought a new coalition of Wallace voters, white southerners, urban supporters in the Southwest, working-class Catholics, suburbanites, and rural Americans. These voters had not benefited from costly welfare programs erected after World War Two, and many depended on military defense spending for their livelihood. While McGovern charged that the administration was "the most corrupt in history," the president placed himself above politics and pointed to Kissinger's negotiations with the North Vietnamese. The results of the Nixon strategy were spectacularly successful. The president received 61 percent of the popular vote, nearly equaling Johnson's landslide of 1964, and carried every state in the electoral college except for Massachusetts and the District of Columbia. While McGovern took only 29 percent of the southern vote, Nixon reversed Democratic domination of the white ethnics by winning a majority of Catholics, Irish-Americans, and Italian-Americans. But in a show of widespread political apathy, less than 55 percent of eligible voters cast ballots in the 1972 election, and 39 million qualified Americans did not even register to vote.

Following the balloting, Nixon consolidated his hold on the federal bureaucracy and cabinet by appointing White House loyalists. To reduce "big government," the president also vowed to cut back domestic spending. In October 1972 the Senate had killed a Nixon request for a $250 billion limit on congressional spending. Three months later the president impounded $12 billion already appropriated by Congress, including a water pollution bill that Congress had overridden a Nixon veto to pass. Continuing his austerity program, the president appointed an acting director of OEO and instructed him to liquidate the antipoverty agency. Program reductions followed in the Job Corps, Model Cities, slum rehabilitation, and aid for education, science, and health. Critics argued that Nixon had converted a financial management technique into an instrument for thwarting congressional will and asserting the president's own priorities.

Ever since the Cambodian invasion of 1970, Congress had been debating the enactment of a time limit for the entire American presence in Southeast Asia. Shortly after Kent State, two congressmen broke away from an official Vietnam tour to visit Con Son penal island, where they discovered tiny concrete cells set in the ground and covered with bars. The shackled inmates of the "tiger cages" turned out to be political prisoners of the South Vietnamese government. The following year, two thousand Vietnam Veterans Against the War shocked the nation by throwing their battle medals on the steps of the Capitol and pleading with senators to end the "mistake" in Vietnam. Stung by the deteriorating military situation, demoralization at home, and prohibitive war costs, the Senate voted to end the entire foreign aid program in 1972 if the administration did not bring the disruptive war to a close. Five months after the Vietnam truce of early 1973, Nixon finally accepted a congressional deadline on funding for the continued bombing of Cambodia. To assure no repetition of presidential wars, Congress also overrode a Nixon veto to pass the War Powers Act in November 1973. The law provided a sixty-day limit on the commitment of troops abroad without congressional consent and stipulated that CIA activities were to be reported to Congress "in a timely fashion." Despite Nixon's strong objections, Congress was beginning to repair the erosion of its foreign policy powers, reversing a trend that had characterized national politics since World War Two.

THE WATERGATE COVERUP AND NIXON'S FALL

While McGovern attempted to connect the Watergate break-in to the White House in the 1972 campaign, the early stages of the coverup succeeded in confining prosecution to the original seven defendants. But by the time the Watergate trial opened in January 1973, two of the men, E. Howard Hunt and James McCord, had received promises of executive clemency from presidential assistants in return for continued silence. At the close of the trial, federal judge John Sirica read a letter from McCord that charged that the other defendants had committed perjury and that "higher-ups" were involved in the Watergate break-in and coverup. A former CIA employee, McCord resented what he believed to be a White House attempt to place blame for Watergate on the agency. But Hunt, another CIA veteran, continued to press for executive clemency and $130,000 for the four Cuban-American burglars and himself. Hunt had participated in the break-in at the office of Ellsberg's psychiatrist and warned that he might have to review his decision to remain silent. On March 21 counselor Dean brought the Hunt demands to the president's attention at an Oval Office meeting, outlining a "cancer on the presidency" and estimating that eventual hush-money payments could reach $1 million. Instead of backing away from the coverup, Nixon ordered an immediate $75,000 payment to Hunt. The next day the president told Mitchell: "I don't give a shit what happens. I want you all to stonewall it, let them plead the fifth amendment, cover-up or anything else, if it'll save it — save the plan."

By April 1973, however, McCord's revelations had triggered an outpouring of evidence that implicated top White House and campaign aides in the Watergate break-in and coverup. In an apology to journalists, press secretary Ziegler declared all previous White House statements on Watergate "inoperable." Nixon then announced the dismissal of Dean and the resignation of Attorney General Kleindienst and the president's two key assistants, H. R. Haldeman and John Ehrlichman. But Nixon denied personal involvement in the Watergate coverup. To satisfy critics, the president nominated liberal Republican Elliot Richardson to be the new attorney general and stated that Richardson could appoint a Watergate special prosecutor. When the Senate insisted on the appointment before confirming the new attorney general, Richardson named Harvard's Archibald Cox, a former solicitor general in the Kennedy administration.

The Watergate crisis escalated in May 1973 when a special Senate committee, chaired by Democrat Sam Ervin, began a televised investigation of the scandal. Nixon responded to charges of his personal involvement in Watergate by admitting that he had ordered aides to restrict early stages of the Watergate probe on grounds of "national security." But former presidential counsel Dean testified about Nixon's continuing knowledge of the coverup and provided evidence of the administration's illegal manipulation of the IRS and the intelligence agencies. Dean's staggering allegations, however, were surpassed by the committee's discovery that the president had installed secret tape-recording devices in his own offices in the White House.

Once the existence of the White House tapes was disclosed, Nixon was forced to battle both the Ervin Committee and Special Prosecutor Cox in an attempt to withhold the evidence that could implicate him in Watergate crimes. The president's attorneys claimed that executive privilege gave Nixon the right to preserve the confidentiality of conversations with advisers. But in October 1973 the Circuit Court of Appeals upheld Judge Sirica's decision to review personally nine subpoenaed tapes. In response, the White House proposed that Senator John Stennis, an elderly Mississippi conservative, review the tapes and provide summaries to Sirica and the Ervin Committee. Nixon's counsel also requested that the special prosecutor relinquish the right to further subpoenas. When Cox rejected the offer, the president stunned the nation by firing him and abolishing the special prosecutor's office. Attorney General Richardson and his deputy, William Ruckleshaus, both resigned rather than carry out the Cox firing.

The "Saturday Night Massacre" brought what the White House described as a firestorm of protest, including 250,000 genuine telegrams to the president's office. Nixon's popularity, registered by Gallup at 68 percent following the Vietnam cease-fire in early 1973, plummeted to 27 percent, and pro-Nixon newspapers deserted the president in droves. The White House had not anticipated the massive response to the Saturday Night Massacre, and relinquished the disputed tapes to Sirica a few days later. Nixon also appointed Leon Jaworski, a Houston lawyer, as special prosecutor. But to Jaworski's chagrin, the White House now claimed that three of the nine tapes did not exist, while the others contained gaping blank spots, including one that lasted eighteen and one-half minutes. A technical panel appointed by both the White House and the special prosecutor later reported that the eighteen-and-one-half-minute gap was caused by five separate manual erasures.

By the end of 1973 the president was on the defensive. Fifteen officials and key aides, including Vice President Agnew, already had resigned from the administration. Agnew had pleaded "no contest" to charges of income tax evasion in early October. The vice president also had been under investigation for conspiracy, extortion, and bribery, all part of a "kickback" scheme in which he had received bribes from Maryland contractors for nearly ten years. Adhering to the succession provisions of the Twenty-fifth Amendment, ratified in 1967, Nixon nominated House Republican leader Gerald Ford for the vice presidency, and Congress quickly confirmed him. But Nixon had his own financial problems as well. Shortly after the Cox firing, the IRS announced that it was re-examining the president's back taxes. In response to questions concerning his personal finances, Nixon told a televised meeting of newspaper editors that "People have got to know whether or not their president is a crook. Well, I'm not a crook." The president released a sweeping personal financial report, but questions remained concerning the back-dating of a gift of vice presidential papers, large tax deductions, financing of personal properties, and home improvements at public expense. Several months later the IRS reported that the president of the United States owed over $450,000 in back taxes and interest penalties. Concerned over possible criminal activities in the White House, the House of Representatives voted 406–4 in February 1974 to authorize the Judiciary Committee to initiate impeachment proceedings against Nixon.

The rest of the president's term involved a futile effort to release as little evidence as pos-

sible to the Judiciary Committee and the special prosecutor. With great fanfare, Nixon publicized a carefully edited version of some subpoenaed tapes in April 1974, but the cynical and manipulative quality of White House conversations prompted even Republican Senate leader Hugh Scott to describe them as "deplorable, shabby, disgusting, and immoral...." The turning point of the Watergate drama came in July when the Supreme Court decided unanimously that the president had to surrender the subpoenaed tapes. A claim of presidential privilege based on confidentiality, the Court ruled, "cannot prevail over the fundamental demands of due process of law."

As Nixon prepared to turn over the tapes, the Judiciary Committee voted three bills of impeachment against the president. They charged Nixon with obstruction of justice, abuse of power, and unconstitutional defiance of committee subpoenas. Judiciary supporters of the president had insisted that available evidence was not solid enough to produce a "smoking gun." But in August the "smoking gun" emerged when the president's attorneys forced the White House to release transcripts of Nixon's conversations with Haldeman six days after the Watergate break-in. The president had clearly directed his aide to order the CIA to call the FBI off aspects of the Watergate inquiry. Now Nixon admitted that he "was aware of the advantages this course of action would have with respect to limiting possible public exposure of involvement by persons connected with the re-election committee." Nixon also confessed that he had kept the crucial evidence from his own lawyers and Nixon supporters on the Judiciary Committee, and that portions of the newly released tapes were "at variance with certain of my previous statements." The president admitted that impeachment by the full House was a foregone conclusion, but hoped that the charges were not sufficiently serious to merit conviction in a Senate trial.

Despite Nixon's hopes, however, public opinion had turned against him and no more than fifteen Senators out of one hundred still supported the president. On August 8, 1974, the thirty-seventh president of the United States announced an unprecedented resignation. The following day at noon, as Nixon flew to San Clemente, Gerald Ford took the oath of office. "Our long national nightmare is over," the new president told the nation. "Our constitution works. Our great republic is a government of laws and not of men."

FORD AND CARTER

President Ford faced a nation shaken by the traumas of Vietnam and Watergate. But government credibility suffered another blow when the president announced one month later that he was pardoning Richard Nixon "for all offenses against the United States which he . . . has committed or may have committed" during his presidency. The Judiciary Committee quickly initiated hearings to discover whether Ford had made assurances to Nixon before the resignation. But the new president insisted "There was no deal, period," and explained that the pardon was designed to remove the disruptive Watergate issue from the national spotlight and move on to the future. Yet the majority of Americans believed that Nixon should go to jail for his crimes, and Ford never recovered his initial popularity. In the reaction against the former president, Congress angrily

reduced Nixon's transition funds and nullified an arrangement by which the General Services Administration had provided Nixon with custody of White House documents and tapes. White House tapes in possession of the special prosecutor and John Dean's testimony proved crucial in the coverup convictions of Nixon aides H. R. Haldeman, John Ehrlichman, and John Mitchell in January 1975.

Ford nominated former New York Governor Nelson Rockefeller to fill the vice presidential vacancy. But Rockefeller, whose family fortune exceeded $1 billion, faced hostile questions about extensive loans and gifts to state officials and family financing of a vicious biography of a former political opponent. In the post-Watergate atmosphere, such ethical issues received careful congressional scrutiny. When the vice president finally took the oath of office in December 1974, the United States had the first nonelected presidential and vice presidential team in history.

Despite Nixon's vetoes, Congress had acted vigorously during the 1974 economic recession. It passed the first housing bill since 1968, added $25 billion to public school assistance, revived OEO, and provided nearly $12 billion for a six-year program of mass transit. To counteract joblessness, which climbed over 7 percent by late 1974, Congress also created an emergency work program and extended unemployment benefits and coverage. Other reforms included new federal standards for private pension plans and a presidential campaign finance bill. The campaign reform law, another legacy of Watergate, provided the first use of public money to finance presidential campaigns and primaries and limited private contributions and campaign spending. Proponents argued that the law separated presidential politics from the power of money, but significantly, Congress refused to extend coverage to its own election campaigns.

When Congress ignored Ford's key anti-inflation proposal — a 5 percent tax surcharge on corporations and the middle and upper class — and easily overrode a veto to extend veterans' education benefits to Vietnam servicemen, the president took his antispending crusade to the voters. But Watergate and the Nixon pardon worked against Ford in the congressional elections of 1974. Democrats gained forty-three seats in the House to give them more than a two-thirds majority and captured another four seats in the heavily Democratic Senate. Despite their overwhelming numbers, however, the Democrats were not able to erect an independent program. Congress scaled down a Ford tax cut, ended depletion allowances for large oil corporations, and curbed investment tax shelters. But congressional leaders had to compromise with the president on a temporary energy package. To reduce energy use and stimulate fuel production, Ford had pushed for increased oil prices and the deregulation of natural gas. But under great pressure from constituents, congressional Democrats found price increases unacceptable. The Energy Policy and Conservation Act of 1975 provided oil price controls for forty months by scheduling a temporary rollback to be followed by gradual increases. Congress and Ford came to another compromise when the president reluctantly agreed to sign over a $2.3 billion loan to New York City. Burdened by the urban dilemma of rising welfare costs and a decreasing tax base, New York had come close to defaulting city bonds in 1975.

With Henry Kissinger implanted as secretary of state, Ford attempted to continue Nixon's emphasis on balance of power in foreign affairs. The United States and the Soviet Union signed an arms agreement in late 1974 that limited the number of offensive strategic nuclear weapons and delivery vehicles. Kissinger also continued his peace mission in the Middle East, where American energy needs dictated the stabilization of hostilities in the oil-rich area. Through his efforts, Egypt and Israel concluded an interim peace agreement in October 1975 that brought the withdrawal of Israeli troops from Sinai passes and oil fields and furthered negotiations toward a final political settlement. Nevertheless, the American Jewish community began to be concerned with the administration's tilt toward the Arabs.

Awakened by Watergate and Vietnam excesses of presidential prerogative, Congress resisted administration efforts to conduct an independent foreign policy. When the agreement between Egypt and Israel called for stationing of American technical observers, for example, Kissinger was closely questioned about secret commitments to Israel. Congress also forced a partial embargo on arms deliveries to Turkey, which had invaded the Greek island of Cyprus, and undercut Kissinger by denying the Soviet Union most-favored-nation status in trade until it relaxed restrictions on emigration, particularly for Soviet Jews and other dissenters. Furthermore, Congress defeated administration requests for increased military aid to South Vietnam. Without American air support, the strategic retreat of South Vietnamese forces from the central highlands turned into a rout, and Communist divisions easily swept south. On April 30, 1974, an emergency helicopter evacuation completed the removal of one thousand Americans and fifty-five thousand Vietnamese dependents from Saigon. A few hours later General "Big" Minh surrendered South Vietnam to the parading soldiers of the Provisional Revolutionary Government, Saigon was renamed Ho Chi Minh City, and the war was over. "This closes a chapter in the American experience," Ford announced laconically.

Like no other event in American history, the Vietnam War showed the limits of American power, and Ford indicated that the lessons of the debacle had been learned. Yet one month later the president sent troops to recapture an American merchant ship taken by an over-zealous outpost of Cambodian Communists. The *Mayaguez* incident was quickly resolved at the cost of several American casualties, but it indicated a presidential reluctance to accept both the American loss of pride in Southeast Asia and the tarnished image of the United States as a guarantor of world order.

Congress also rebelled against further administration moves in mineral-rich Africa. Press accounts had revealed that the CIA was covertly aiding an anti-Soviet faction in a civil war in the former Portuguese colony of Angola. Backing away from the possibility of another Vietnam entanglement, Congress ignored Kissinger's pleas and prohibited further military aid in a rider to the defense appropriation bill. Ford bitterly condemned Congress members who had "lost their guts" and derided an "abdication of responsibility," but he promptly acceded to their demands. Never before had Congress exerted such control over foreign policy conducted by the CIA.

The determination to supervise the CIA stemmed from revelations publicized in 1975 by the Senate Select Committee on Intelligence Activities. Public hearings sustained newspaper accounts of illegal surveillance, LSD experiments on unsuspecting subjects, political spying and mail openings at home, and covert attempts to overthrow other governments and murder their leaders. A system of "plausible denial" shielded presidents from specific knowledge of unsavory details. Testimony also indicated that the CIA and other intelligence agencies spent $7 billion to $17 billion each year.

Public bitterness over Watergate made personal trust a key issue in the presidential campaign of 1976. Former Georgia Governor Jimmy Carter emerged as the Democratic front runner after defeating a host of party contenders in a series of early primaries. Espousing a combination of southern populism and economic conservatism, Carter spoke quietly, talked of replacing the professionals in Washington, and promised to restore ethical moralism to foreign policy. At the most harmonious Democratic Convention in memory, a unified party rallied behind Carter and liberal vice presidential nominee Walter Mondale. It was the Republicans who were divisive in 1976, however, as California's Ronald Reagan attacked Ford from a conservative perspective and criticized the Nixon pardon. But Reagan's effort faltered in the closing weeks of the campaign, and Ford won the nomination in a close convention vote. The president chose another midwesterner, Kansas Senator Robert Dole, as his running mate.

Carter emerged from the Democratic Convention with a thirty-three-point lead in national polls. Intent on winning the presidency in his own right, Ford campaigned strenuously on the need to curb spending, but fell short by two percentage points and two million votes. In the electoral college, the tally was a close 291 to 241. Although the president carried the entire West except for Hawaii, Carter rode the strength of Mexican-American votes in Texas and strong black support to sweep the entire South. Moved by regional pride and an affinity with Carter's roots in evangelical Protestantism, black and white southerners provided the can-

THE DEMOCRATIC WHISTLESTOP

DEMOCRATIC WHISTLE

a train for a change

Jimmy Carter campaigned in 1976 to restore trust to presidential government. (Peter Southwick/Stock, Boston)

didate with 90 percent of his national plurality. As a result, Ford joined Republicans William Howard Taft and Herbert Hoover as the only twentieth-century presidents to be denied second terms by voters.

As the United States celebrated its 1976 bicentennial, Americans seemed to have lost confidence about the course of social events. Inflation, Vietnam, and Watergate acted to diminish faith in strong presidents and their global aspirations. But dependence on overseas raw materials and sources of energy, as well as a changing world balance of power, introduced

elements of complexity in the nation's foreign policy that Americans found frustrating.

Carter continued to request increases in the defense budget and criticized Soviet treatment of dissidents as a violation of international standards of human rights. But to the dismay of conservatives, the administration also laid the groundwork for a less militant foreign policy. After a lengthy Senate debate, the president signed a new Panama Canal Treaty in 1978. The agreement provided for full Panamanian control of the canal by the year 2000, although the United States reserved the right to intervene to preserve the neutrality of the Canal Zone. The treaty also required payment of nearly $1 billion in compensation to Panama. Andrew Young, Carter's black ambassador to the United Nations, worked to refashion the American image in the Third World by denouncing apartheid in South Africa. Young also defended the administration's refusal to recognize the government of Zimbabwe Rhodesia until the dominant whites permitted political participation by black revolutionary organizations. While Carter continued to denounce both Cuban and Soviet involvement in central and eastern Africa, the United States confined itself to supplying airlifts and verbal denunciations when secessionist guerrillas violently overran several towns in pro-American Zaire during 1978.

Following the foundations laid by Nixon and Kissinger, Carter moved to stabilize relations with China and the Soviet Union. The United States formally exchanged ambassadors with the People's Republic on New Year's Day, 1979. But the president received criticism even from liberal Democrats such as Senator Edward Kennedy for severing diplomatic ties with Taiwan at the insistence of the Chinese. The administration appeared willing to suffer this political discomfort because it hoped for stabilization in Southeast Asia and increased trade with China. But promises of peaceful order in Asia seemed uncertain when the Chinese briefly invaded Vietnam in response to armed Vietnamese interference in Cambodia. Despite a Chinese warning that an aggressive Soviet Union stood behind Vietnam's expansionism, Carter moved toward another arms agreement with Moscow. SALT II, signed by the president in May 1979, proposed to establish further areas of equity between the two superpowers in certain nuclear missile systems. But congressional

conservatives, whose number moderately increased in the 1978 elections, hesitated to push détente because of growing Soviet influence in Africa, Cuba, and the Middle East.

American energy needs directed much of Carter's attention to the oil-rich Middle East. As revolution and armed conflict rocked Afghanistan, North and South Yemen, and Iran, the president hoped to promote Mideast stability by arranging a peace agreement between Egypt and Israel. Following a dramatic visit to Jerusalem by Egypt's Anwar Sadat in late 1977, Carter brought Sadat and Israeli Premier Menachem Begin to Camp David for a personal summit. When further negotiations stalled early in 1979, the president flew to the Middle East to continue his low-key diplomacy. Egypt and Israel finally signed the historic peace treaty in Washington in April 1979. The treaty provided for Israeli withdrawal of military forces and civilian settlers from the Sinai Peninsula. In return, Egypt agreed to open the Suez Canal to Israeli ships and end its economic boycott against Israel. Full diplomatic relations between the two nations were scheduled for 1980. Separate provisions of the treaty also committed the United States to military and economic assistance to both countries. The most controversial stumbling block to Mideast stability, however, continued to be the fate of Palestinians living in Israeli-occupied territories. To the dismay of Arab critics, the 1979 treaty provided for a five-year transition period in which the final status of the Palestinians would be negotiated.

Just as Carter was succeeding in attaining peace between Egypt and Israel, a massive social revolution was overturning American interests in Iran. But for the first time since the advent of the Cold War, American leaders were faced with a hostile revolution that had no ties to Soviet or Chinese communism. Led by the Moslem cleric Ayatollah Ruhollah Khomeini, hundreds of thousands of Iranian nationalists overthrew the pro-American Shah Mohammed Reza Pahlavi in early 1979. Khomeini's followers demanded a Moslem state that would withdraw from military cooperation with the United States and limit sales of oil to the West. Underestimating the fervor of the revolutionary movement, Carter first indicated support for the shah and then watched helplessly as most of the dictator's military and political supporters deserted to the Khomeini forces.

Following the Iranian revolution, corporate and government leaders in the United States feared the spread of Moslem nationalism to Saudi Arabia and other sources of Mideast oil. Accordingly, American corporations began to store crude oil in case of future import problems. By the spring of 1979, the nation faced another gasoline shortage and increased prices at the pump. Carter continued to press Congress for a comprehensive energy program that would include deregulation of oil and natural gas prices and a contingency plan for rationing automobile fuel. But Congress had difficulty in determining how heavily the oil corporations should be taxed and placed strict limits on the president's power to implement rationing. The prospects for energy production appeared even more grim when a nuclear power plant near Harrisburg, Pennsylvania, leaked radioactive steam and gas into the atmosphere for several days in April 1979. The worst accident in the history of the nuclear industry brought cries of protest from antinuclear power activists, who argued that utility corporations had not yet devised safe means of controlling radioactive waste and that nuclear plants were inefficient producers of energy.

The energy impasse typified the administra-

tion's difficulties in solving domestic problems in the late 1970s. Rampant inflation, unhindered by a presidential request for a 7 percent limit on wage increases, seemed to aggravate the normal competition of pressure groups and organized lobbies in Congress. As a result, the administration retreated from earlier endorsements of comprehensive tax reform and national health insurance. Inflation and loss of faith in government also stimulated a national taxpayers' revolt. Led by Governor Edmund G. Brown, Jr. of California, whose constituents had placed a ceiling on property taxes through a voters' initiative, some Americans began to call for a constitutional convention to compel a balanced federal budget. Brown also talked of the need to preserve the ecological balance of the planet while seeking possibilities for the development of outer space. Despite Brown's planetary concerns, and despite Senator Edward Kennedy's entry into presidential politics late in 1979, most Americans closed the decade in sour confrontation with the realities of rising prices and economic stagnation. For the people of the United States, a century that began with the opening of overseas frontiers reached its closing stage with a retreat from military adventurism and troubled concern over the question of national and economic limits.

SUGGESTED READINGS

The Nixon years are outlined with brilliant insight by Jonathan Schell, *The Time of Illusion: An Historical and Reflective Account of the Nixon Era* (1975). The relevant chapters in Alexander Kendrick, *The Wound Within: America in the Vietnam Years, 1945–1974* (1974), describe the interplay between the Vietnam War and political ferment at home.

See also Weldon Brown, *The Last Chopper: The Denouement of the American Role in Vietnam, 1963–1975* (1976).

For portraits of the Nixon administration, see Rowland Evans and Robert Novak, *Nixon in the White House* (1971), and William Safire, *Before the Fall* (1975). Battles over law enforcement and the Supreme Court are described by Richard Harris, *Justice* (1970) and *Decision* (1971). The appropriate section of Otis L. Graham, Jr., *Toward a Planned Society: From Roosevelt to Nixon* (1976), presents a detailed account of Nixonian social management and administrative innovation. Gary Wills, *Nixon Agonistes: The Crisis of the Self-Made Man* (1971), offers a critical psychological study of the thirty-seventh president.

Overseas investment and the weakening of the seventies economy are summarized in the concluding sections of Gabriel Kolko, *Main Currents in Modern American History* (1976), which may be supplemented by appropriate segments of Arthur S. Miller, *The Modern Corporate State: Private Governments and the American Constitution* (1976). A provocative assessment of seventies economic and political trends is Kirkpatrick Sale, *Power Shift: The Rise of the Southern Rim and Its Challenge to the Eastern Establishment* (1975). The relevant chapters of Stanley Aronowitz, *False Promises: The Shaping of American Working Class Consciousness* (1974), dramatize seventies labor discontent.

Explorations of the dissatisfaction of ethnic Americans include Richard Krickus, *Pursuing the American Dream: White Ethnics and the New Populism* (1976), and Michael Novak, *The Rise of the Unmeltable Ethnics: Politics and Culture in the Seventies* (1972). For a specific illustration, see Joseph R. Daughen and Peter Binzen, *The Cop Who Would Be King:* *The Honorable Frank Rizzo* (1977). The conservative response to the counterculture and radical protest is described in Richard Scammon and Ben J. Wattenberg, *The Real Majority* (1970).

For Watergate, see *The Senate Watergate Report: The Final Report of the Senate Select Committee on Presidential Campaign Activities* (1974) and House Judiciary Committee, *Impeachment of Richard M. Nixon, President of the United States* (1974). Two informative Watergate memoirs are H. R. Haldeman with Joseph DiMona, *The Ends of Power* (1978), and John Dean, *Blind Ambition: The White House Years* (1976), while the road to disclosure is chronicled by Carl Bernstein and Bob Woodward, *All the President's Men* (1974). The vice presidential scandal is presented by Richard M. Cohen and Jules Witcover, *A Heartbeat Away: The Investigation and Resignation of Vice-President Spiro T. Agnew* (1974).

The most comprehensive treatment of foreign affairs in the early seventies is Tad Szulc, *The Illusion of Peace: Foreign Policy in the Nixon Years* (1978). National security management is brilliantly analyzed in Richard J. Barnet, *Roots of War: The Men and Institutions Behind U.S. Foreign Policy* (1972). For CIA activities in Chile and elsewhere, see Victor Marchetti and John D. Marks, *The CIA and the Cult of Intelligence* (1974). Illegal agency activities at home are chronicled by the *Report to the President by the Commission on CIA Activities Within the United States* (1975). For a critical assessment of Carter, see Robert Shogan, *Promises to Keep: Carter's First 100 Days* (1977). A sobering essay on loss of faith and ecological and economic challenge in the seventies is Robert L. Heilbroner, *An Inquiry into the Human Prospect* (1974).

Spotlight: The Meaning of Watergate

The expansion of twentieth-century presidential power began with the New Deal. Franklin D. Roosevelt presided over the permanent presence of executive agencies in the economy and an ongoing mobilization in global politics. Following World War Two, full employment and material benefits derived from large corporations at home, positive direction from executive government, and domination in the world economy. But continued economic expansion depended on open access to the rest of the world. As the Soviet Union began to consolidate its sphere of influence, American global interests could not be sustained without huge government expenditures.

Two developments coincided with the evolution of the Cold War. First, the government encouraged Americans to see national aims as individual goals, articulating foreign policy as a messianic crusade against global communism. Second, the tools of management, bureaucracy, and military technology merged in a massive national security establishment. The expanded office of the presidency presided over both developments. The chief executive assumed personal responsibility for defining and implementing the national security. Presidential elections in the Cold War period hinged on the perceived ability of candidates to manage a gigantic military-industrial complex under the pressure of global conflict.

Roosevelt and Truman had set precedents for unlimited presidential action in the national interest during World War Two. Secrecy, deception of the public, and mobilization of all resources for uncontained violence emerged as accepted methods of total warfare. Nuclear technology furthered the need for government secrecy. The Cold War widened definitions of vital national security, causing security managers to believe that policy making was too complex for people to understand. The Central Intelligence Agency conducted covert foreign policy, accountable only to the National Security Council and the president. Presidential and military advisers remained responsible only to the Oval Office. By the sixties, presidential managers from the corporations, military officers, and national security bureaucracy constituted a powerful elite unaccountable to the American people.

Administrative consolidation depended on the passivity of those Americans not included in the ruling hierarchy. But after 1945, members of various outgroups began to challenge the managerial consensus. Urbanization brought minority groups together so that each could mount organized pressure and protest. Expanded media and education raised expectations and permitted people with common problems to find each other. By the sixties, the nation confronted a civil rights revolution among minorities and a cultural revolution within the middle class that seriously threatened the established administrative authority.

Social and political consensus collapsed entirely as the Vietnam War dominated public attention. To the national security establishment, Vietnam symbolized American will to prevail in world affairs. To the dissidents, however, the war symbolized government malignity and hypocrisy. Believing that control was necessary to limit turmoil and preserve social institutions, military and intelligence agencies turned their attention to "national security" enemies at home. To do so they imported "dirty tricks" and espionage techniques customarily employed overseas. But the major threat of the Vietnam years was to national political consensus, not internal security. Both Presidents Johnson and Nixon rejected CIA reports that insisted that domestic radicals were not supported by foreign governments.

Nixon's first wiretaps were necessary only because the president refused to reveal administration war policy to Congress and the American people. Even some of the president's own national security aides disagreed with him.

As intelligence gathering increased in the sixties and seventies, the line between national security management and partisan politics disappeared. In 1962 President Kennedy moved jurisdiction of internal security from the National Security Council to the attorney general's office headed by his brother. A year later Attorney General Robert Kennedy ordered FBI wiretaps on Martin Luther King to clear associates of King before the administration endorsed his leadership of the civil rights movement. During the campaign of 1964, President Johnson's press secretary requested FBI reports on all persons employed in Goldwater's campaign office. CIA and army surveillance during the Johnson years provided data on antiwar members of Congress, and the FBI passed purely political information about United States senators to the president. During the closing days of the 1968 election campaign, Johnson ordered FBI surveillance of a woman close to the South Vietnamese government to determine whether the Nixon camp intended to sabotage the Vietnam peace negotiations.

The Nixon administration attempted to consolidate the cumbersome national security bureaucracy by hiring its own operatives. But Nixon's undercover agents quickly systematized the gatherings of political intelligence. Other aides attempted to harass political opponents through the IRS. By distorting the statutory purpose of the regulatory agencies, Nixon's people moved toward a permanent perpetuation of their own power. The use of "dirty tricks" in the 1972 campaign was another effort to deprive those without power of equal competition with those who held power. CIA techniques of forgery, false advertising, disinformation, espionage, and finally burglary invaded the two-party system.

But it was the Watergate coverup, not the break-in, that brought down the Nixon administration. Through overconfidence in the ability to manipulate public opinion with the prestige of the presidency, Nixon nearly destroyed the office. Instead of burning the lethal White House tapes, he tried to withhold evidence through incantations of executive privilege, national security, and the integrity of the presidency. But the case continued to surround him, as a vigilant judiciary, a revitalized press and Congress, and an uneasy public cooperated to preserve the nation's institutions. The Saturday Night Massacre of October 1973 informed the country that a president who had agreed to a set of rules wished to change them when he seemed to be losing. The Nixon transcripts conveyed an image of White House amorality and cynicism. Fully a third of the taped conversations were devoted to rehearsals for public lies.

Johnson had seriously eroded the credibility of the presidency with lack of candor about Vietnam. Nixon seemed to leave little hope that any integrity remained. In 1975 Americans also learned that Presidents Eisenhower and Kennedy had indirectly sanctioned CIA assassination plots against foreign leaders. Ford's pardon of his predecessor added to these doubts.

Triggered by the disruptive war in Southeast Asia, Watergate arose from an attempt to repair fault lines in a thirty-year Cold War consensus. The imperial presidency was its immediate victim. But the national intelligence establishment, from which Nixon operatives borrowed their techniques, remained intact. Though more accountable to congressional oversight and less prone to covert activism abroad, policy-making elites remained shrouded in secrecy. By the time President Carter assumed office in 1977, Watergate, the Vietnam War, and domestic dissent were distant memories. But while the excesses of presidential power had been temporarily curbed, Americans had yet to come to terms with the true meaning of national security.

Index

Index

Student Evaluation of
TWENTIETH CENTURY LIMITED
(Noble/Horowitz/Carroll)

Your comments on this book will help us in developing other new textbooks and future editions of this book. Please answer the following questions and mail this page to:

College Marketing Services
Houghton Mifflin Company
One Beacon Street
Boston, MA 02107

1. What was your overall impression of the text? _____

_____

2. Did you find the book easy to read and understand?　☐ Yes　☐ No

If not, what problems did you have? _____

3. Did the illustrations clarify the text in a useful way? _____

_____

4. How would you rate the following features of the text?

	Excellent	*Very good*	*Good*	*Fair*	*Poor*
Biographical sketches	☐	☐	☐	☐	☐
Spotlights	☐	☐	☐	☐	☐
Photographs	☐	☐	☐	☐	☐
Writing style	☐	☐	☐	☐	☐
Interest level	☐	☐	☐	☐	☐
Treatment of minority groups	☐	☐	☐	☐	☐
Descriptions of historical events	☐	☐	☐	☐	☐
Completeness of coverage	☐	☐	☐	☐	☐

Feel free to comment on any of the above items. _____

_____

5. Which chapters were required reading for your class? _____

_____

6. Did you read any chapters on your own that were not required reading?

_____

7. Did your instructor assign any additional books for this course?

☐ Yes   ☐ No   If so, what were they? _____

_____

8. Did you find the book stimulating? Did you find yourself strongly agreeing or disagreeing with what you read?

_____

9. Did you feel that the book gave you a good grasp of American history in this century?

_____

10. Did you find the bibliographies useful for further reading and research?

_____

11. Do you have any suggestions that might help make this a better textbook?

_____

Name of your school: _____

Prerequisites for this course: _____

Number of students in the class: _____

Your age: _____

Your major: _____